The ART of CREATING STORY

The ART of CREATING STORY

by William H. Coles

Story in Literary Fiction

© 2020 William H. Coles. All rights reserved.

First edition

No part of this book may be reproduced, stored in a retrieval system, or transmitted by any means without the written permission of the author.

Published February 2020

Story in Literary Fiction
99 West South Temple #1802
Salt Lake City, Utah 84101

www.storyinliteraryfiction.com

Cover art by Anna Sokolova
Interior design by Susanne Howard

ISBN: 978-0-9984376-6-8 (softcover)
ISBN: 978-0-9984376-7-5 (hardcover)
ISBN: 978-0-9984376-8-2 (ebook)

Library of Congress Control Number: 2020901835

Publisher's Cataloging-In-Publication Data
(Prepared by The Donohue Group, Inc.)

Names: Coles, William H., author.
Title: The art of creating story / by William H. Coles.
Description: First edition. | Salt Lake City, Utah : Story in Literary Fiction, 2020.
Identifiers: ISBN 9780998437668 (softcover) | ISBN 9780998437675 (hardcover) | ISBN 9780998437682 (ebook)
Subjects: LCSH: Fiction--Authorship. | Fiction--Technique. | Creative writing.
Classification: LCC PN3355 .C55 2020 (print) | LCC PN3355 (ebook) | DDC 808.3--dc23

TABLE OF CONTENT

ESSAYS 1

STORY 3
- Literary Fictional Story 5
- Character in Literary Fictional Story 7
- Narration of Literary Stories 11
- Drama in Literary Fiction 21
- Desire and Motivation in Literary Fiction 25
- Credibility in Literary Fiction 29
- Dialogue 31
- Improving Dialogue 37
- Characterization Improves Dialogue, Motivates Plot, and Enhances Theme 39
- Techniques for Excellence in Creating Character in Literary Fiction: Action, Conflict, Character-based Plots, Change, Dialogue, Setting 45

CRAFT 55
- Momentum in Literary Fiction 57
- First-Person Point of View in the Literary Story 65
- Top Story / Bottom Story 77
- Strong Voice and Attention to Time 81
- Humor and Fiction 87
- Emotional Complexity in Literary Fiction 91
- Conflict in Literary Fiction 95
- What Exactly Is a Character-Based Plot? 101
- Writing in Scene: A Staple for Reader Engagement in Fiction 105
- Creating Story World (Setting) in Literary Fiction 113
- Perception in Literary Fiction: A Challenge for Better Narration 119
  - Creating Quality Characters in Literary Fiction 125
  - Mastering the Power of a Literary Fictional Story 133

THOUGHTS AND ADVICE 137
- The Anatomy of a Wannabe Literary Fiction Writer 139
- Author's Attitudes 147
- How Literary Stories Go Wrong 149
- Preparing to Write the Great Literary Story 153
- Victims as Characters in Literary Fiction 159

INTERVIEWS 163
   Lee K. Abbott Interview..167
   Steve Almond Interview..181
   John Biguenet Interview..193
   Robert Olen Butler Interview..201
   Ron Carlson Interview 221
   Lan Samantha Chang Interview 235
   Charles D'Ambrosio Interview 245
   Peter Ho Davies Interview 255
   Jonathan Dee Interview..265
   Tom Jenks Interview...281
   Fred Leebron Interview..291
   David Lynn Interview 303
   Michael Malone Interview...315
   Lee Martin Interview 341
   Rebecca McClanahan Interview..355
   Josh Neufeld and Sari Wilson Interview 369
   Richard North Patterson Interview 385
   Michael Ray Interview 403
   Jim Shepard Interview 419
   Rob Spillman Interview..437
   Kirby Wilkins Interview 447
   Susan Yeagley and Kevin Nealon Interview..............................463

Appendix A, BLOG POSTS 489
   How do unsuccessful novel writers build houses?...................491
   Ferreting out MacGuffins in a literary fiction story...............493
   Lasting literary story characters mature and blossom
   like sturdy oaks. How do you do that? 495
   What would you do if you had a chance to,
   right now, start your life again? 497
   What do you do to make scenes come alive in literary fiction?...............499
   If you're a writer and no one reads your stuff,
   be sure to make your openings irresistible................................501
   Mastering the power of a literary fictional story......................505
   When is a fiction story a literary art form?...............................507
   How writers "murder their darlings" (and stay out of prison) 509
   Character-based plot: not easy but so effective 511
   Want to write literary stories that last?......................................515
   Errant simile and erosion of literary style.................................517

To be … and when not to be … in developing literary style 519
A prescription for creating great literary fiction 521
Rate and logic in revealing story information in literary fiction 523
Creating great scenes in literary fiction without
excessive, ineffective, detail! 525
Mastering the power of literary story 527
How funny are you? 529
Fictional dream, literary style, and storytelling 531
Keep readers involved when writing literary fiction stories 533
What EM Forster taught us about flat and
round characters and how to use it 535
Are you a storyteller? 537
Action and imagery 539
When to use backstory in literary fiction 541
Why select stories succeed best as literary fiction 543
A fiction-writer changes style with image-words 545
What to do for writer's block 547
Improve storytelling by flexiblity in writing style 549
Career planning for aspiring, literary-fiction-story writers 551
A secret of great literary fiction stories as art 553
Is it, or is it not, irony? 555
Meaning in the literary fictional story 557
The quest for greatness in literary fiction
and the failure of authorial self 559
The seven fundamentals for writing fiction stories 563
What do you do to make scenes come alive in literary fiction? 565

Appendix B, SHORT STORIES 567
The Gift 569
The Amish Girl 583
Speaking of the Dead 601
The Miracle of Madame Villard 613
The Stonecutter 635
Homunculus 645
The Necklace 657
Suchin's Escape 669
Clouds 685

Short Stories by William H. Coles 691
Other Books by William H. Coles 691

ESSAYS

STORY

Literary Fictional Story 5
    What defines a literary story? What should an author strive for?

Character in Literary Fiction 7
    Starting ideas to help the imagination form richly presented characters that contribute to plot and story momentum.

Narration of Literary Stories 11
    Narration of any story is a complex process that involves POV, voice, respect for a narrator, and authorial skill. And there are few resources for learning. This essay presents principles and guidelines for the narration of effective literary stories.

Drama in Literary Fiction 21
    Drama is conflict and action, elements best presented in scene. The writer of a literary fictional story is often trained in the craft of beautiful prose for telling a story, a skill that may work against reader involvement in a dramatic presentation of the material. This essay considers the role of drama in fiction.

Desire and Motivation in Literary Fiction 25
    Desire and motivation provide the quality, power, and credibility of why characters do what they do. This essay provides ideas and examples for writers aspiring to improve characterization and plot by expanding ideas about desire and motivation.

Credibility in Literary Fiction..29
   Thoughts about how authors must make credible decisions about how to build characterization and advance plot.

Dialogue 31
   Great dialogue in literary fiction serves multiple functions but never detracts from story progress or purpose.

Improving Dialogue 37
   Dialogue doesn't come naturally to writers; learn techniques to succeed.

Characterization Improves Dialogue, Motivates Plot,
and Enhances Theme...39
   Characterization in literary fiction should be created for effectiveness, not just described.

Techniques for Excellence in Creating Character in Literary Fiction: Action,
Conflict, Character-based Plots, Change, Dialogue, Setting......................45
   Essential techniques for building memorable, effective characters in literary fictional stories.

Literary Fictional Story
by *William H. Coles*

Definitions
- **story:** an account of an event or a series of events
- **fictional:** describing imaginary people or events
- **literary:** writing that is important and memorable, with lasting artistic value

Imagination
The literary story is imagined; it is not a memoir that recounts real events that the narrator knows occurred or has experienced. Although a real happening can stimulate the imagination for the basis of a literary story, to present a memoir as fiction ignores the potential of imagination-based creative elements. Imagination allows growth of characterization, motivation, and setting, and provides a special memorable experience for the reader.

Structure and Theme
The author of literary fiction explores the imagination for just the right story elements to describe an event via a series of scenes. The author then structures the story and establishes a thematic goal that will influence character and plot development.

Characterization
Characters in the literary story must be interesting, complex, and developed, and contribute to the story with author-controlled prioritization. The author creates each character's emotional story arc to fit in with motivations and actions of the other characters, and to contribute to plot momentum. The characters in a literary story are unique, yet they cannot be bizarre. They can have heroic characteristics, but they cannot be superheroes with powers beyond expected human limits. In good stories, the reader has thorough knowledge of who the characters are and why they do what they do. The story follows a progressive, focused unity, and character development is always consistent with conflict resolution in the story. In essence, story resolution must be in accord with everything the characters have done in the story. That is the essence of storytelling.

Plot

A literary story has a character-driven plot with carefully developed and sequenced motivations; which is presented through scenes structured with conflict, action, and resolution; and results in sufficient emotional involvement to provoke enlightenment or reversal of thinking in the reader. Successful storytelling depends on the author's personal traits, beliefs, and opinions, but the author is not part of the literary fictional story; rather, the story demands the author's willingness to imagine the most effective characterization and plot motivations to assure story momentum and achieve reader delight.

Character in Literary Fictional Story
by William H. Coles

Characterization in literary fiction has special importance, and authors need to develop their own sense of responsibility for full and effective character development.

Development

Character is everything in literary fiction. It does not replace plot and setting, or theme and meaning, but it intimately relates to all of these. Although characters are sometimes categorized as round or flat, every character in fiction must have complexities and uniqueness that may or may not be written on the page. A character that does not need to be fully presented for the story may appear two-dimensional, but there should be three dimensions in the creator's mind. Full character development assures that the author has thought about the story as a unit. Depth of understanding of all characters ensures that underlying motivations are reasonable, dialogue is believable, and logic of action is clear.

Complexity

Creating a unique character—one that is not stereotypical—is the essence of great fictional stories. The character will be adopted by the reader, and the characters will drive the momentum of the plot. At the start of character development, there are no restrictions; a character emerges unencumbered. Then that character must be perfected for the plot. The character must be unique but remain believable and within the boundaries set by the suspension of disbelief all fiction requires. The character must not be stereotypical yet must feel comfortable to the reader in a familiar way. As a memorable character develops, the reader becomes attached and admires the character in the same way they would begin to like a new acquaintance as a friend. This reader attachment is often associated with liking the character, but affinity is not absolutely necessary. Respect and/or admiration are also strong attachments for a reader to a character. As the author creates an emerging character, subtle choices and imaginative attributes given to the character must keep within the overall story guidelines set in the contract between author and reader. Subsequently, in revision, scenes, thoughts, actions, conflicts, and motivations that do not contribute maximally to the character engaging the reader and driving the plot forward are eliminated, or at least changed.

Maximizing Opportunities
To create a character for a reader in a literary story, there are a limited number of things the character can think or do. In a short story, even for the protagonist, there may be only ten to twenty key characterization opportunities. Often there are fewer. In a novel, with its longer timeline and wider range of development from the direct story line, there are more opportunities for a character to show his or her true colors, but ultimately even these openings are limited. How do authors make the most of these opportunities? First, character development must be reasonable for the story and for the sensibilities of the reader. The actions and thoughts of the character must also be unique, with elements of surprise, so that the actions and traits embed in reader memory. In-scene showing of a character's actions, thoughts, and opinions has better impact than narrative telling. And character development leaves more impression on the reader when in-scene story time predominates over backstory or narrator comments on past character action.

Misconceptions
Inheritance play or no role in an author achieving the memorable characters required for great stories. Study, hard work, practice and imagination are the keys to success. And focus on story as art places responsibility for excellence on the author. when authors believe their writing trances allow characters to emerge to tell the story as creators, the result is less than should be epected. Characters are imagined and created—not discovered and described—for maximum story effectiveness.

Significance
Stories, to be great, should be significant and meaningful. A major way for an author to instill these qualities in storytelling is through effective characterization and dependence on structured story elements.

Stereotypes
A stereotypical (oversimplified or standardized) character is to be avoided in literary stories, but stereotypes, in fact, abound in many stories, and are often essential. Comic superheroes, for instance Spider-Man, are so rigid that cartoonists must adhere strictly to the visual and story history that is familiar to the reader. In detective fiction, Hercule Poirot, Agatha Christie's detective, is

consistent, crime after crime. He has a role that defines him and is required for the storytelling as she created it.

In literary fiction, every character is, by nature of the creative process, born stereotypical and then developed to some non-stereotypical threshold. This improves reader interest and augments story quality. But in stories with multiple characters, they cannot all be unique, vibrant, and memorable; some stereotypes are unavoidable. This is not bad. Over-development of too many characters may create unbelievable and/or ineffective fiction. As in all fiction, the proper balance is uniquely individual for each writer's style and sensibilities.

Character in Different Types of Writing

Although many would reflexively disagree, it is true that memoir, creative nonfiction, and biography do not allow the potential character development available to the fiction writer. Yet many, if not the vast majority of, fiction stories today are simply authors telling something that happened to them or to someone they know with little departure from reality and calling the result fiction. When a character and his or her traits are merely described, the result does not have the imaginative structure of fiction and relies on narrative telling rather than in-scene engagement. Lyrical writers—the poets of prose—find it easier to experiment with language through nonfiction. This is not all bad and is very enjoyable to many readers, but it does not address how to create great fictional stories. In fiction, characters emerge, plot progresses, meaning arises, and the structure supports a story that is created in the imagination and then skillfully crafted to provide entertainment for the reader. Fiction demands that the reader know more than the characters, and often more than the narrator. Fiction is less reliant on the discovery of something already known than on the awareness of how and why something happens based on character and plot. In memoir, biography, and autobiography, the character is formed before the writing starts. The author chooses accurate descriptions of happenings. There are few decisions allowing change for the betterment of the story.

Character and Plot

In literary fiction, character moves the plot. Consider some brief plot descriptions:

1. The plane crashed.
2. The drunk pilot crashed a stolen plane.
3. The grief-stricken pilot, rejected by his second wife, fails to listen to a transmission from the tower and is injured in a midair collision.
4. The plane was shot down by enemy fire.

5. The nearly bankrupt airline failed to pay maintenance man Joe Hubbard for two months and Joe refused to perform a routine maintenance check, yet Max Fine, the supervisor, allowed the plane to fly. The plane crashed.

These scenarios demonstrate how plot can be circumstantial (1, 4) or character motivated (2, 3, 5). (These scenarios are not suggested as worthy of development.)

Authors must characterize well to create great stories. Time and multiple tries are required, and a healthy dissatisfaction with all early opportunities is essential. In fact, during the creative process, authors continuously seek improved characterization, never being satisfied with mediocrity.

Narration of Literary Stories
by William H. Coles

Definitions
To learn the skill of narrating a story in fiction, authors, teachers, and students must know what words mean and not confuse terms or use them interchangeably. Note in particular the difference in meanings of "narrative" the noun and "narrative" the adjective, as well as "narrator" versus "character," and literary fiction and memoir:

- narrate (v): to give an account of something in detail
- narrator (n): somebody who tells a story or gives an account of something
- character (n): one of the people portrayed in a story
- narration (n): the act of telling a story or giving an account of something
- narrative (n): 1) an account of a sequence of events in the order in which they happened; 2) a discussion or speech about the policies, opinions, or proposals of a political party (e.g., "The senator's narrative . . .")
- narrative (adj): having the aim or purpose of telling a story, or involving the art of story telling
- author (n): the creator or originator of something
- fiction: stories that describe imaginary people and events
- literary fiction: serious, character-based fiction, as opposed to genre or popular fiction that is plot based
- story: an account of a series of events
- memoir: an account of events written from personal knowledge
- autobiography: an account of someone's life written by that person
- biography: an account of someone's life written by another person
- creative nonfiction: literary or narrative journalism using literary skills in writing nonfiction

In-scene vs. narrative telling
Authors must clarify their own thinking about how to provide story information: 1) story advanced by telling a sequence of events; 2) in-scene reader involvement by showing character action; 3) descriptive narrative; 4) dialogue; 5) images and

setting. Show-don't-tell has been the imperative in literary fiction for centuries, but fewer and fewer authors comply. The result is fewer good stories created as an art form.

Point of view

Character "points of view" are often used by a narrator to tell a story. First person and third person are most commonly used. (Second person is trendy but rarely provides lasting reader satisfaction necessary for great storytelling.) The narrator has a point of view that may be used for improving time management of story progression or for information that is not within the reasonable range of the character's senses, memory (life experiences), education, or intelligence. Point of view has many definitions. Most commonly writers think of point of view as (1) a position in space, time, or development from which something is considered. But point of view can also be (2) a manner of evaluating something, or (3) a reasoned opinion about something. In essence, a character point of view is not simply a position for considering physical action in a story; it is a character-revealing way for the narrator to present story information to the reader. And there are complexities of point of view that, if not appreciated (or if mismanaged) will cause the reader to question unnecessarily the character's reliability and credibility.

It is not helpful to think of a point of view in storytelling as a camera, as is often taught, because evaluating story action and opinions are beyond the scope of a camera. This broad, all-definitions approach to point of view is especially useful when considering use of narrator and character points of view together. An example:

> I despised Amy. She was beautiful, I'll give her that, but she thought the world revolved around her—that God made other people admire her. Never once did she think of me, or anyone, as a human with feelings.

The structure of this paragraph in first-person point of view is common, acceptable, and useful. But first-person point of view is tricky. Consider that we, as readers, don't know the story truths. Did the point-of-view character really despise Amy, or was he (or she) madly in love but unwilling to reveal their feelings? And then, he (or she) makes a judgmental statement that she is "beautiful." Is that true? And by whose standards? Then he (or she) states Amy's thoughts about God, motivations, and refusal to think of others. Is it true that Amy thought this?

The ART of CREATING STORY

When we don't know what is true about the speculations of the first-person narrator, we don't have reliable information to build character, become attached, or form opinions. First person prevents the reader from knowing facts, and the result is a lack of reliable information. It builds character and promotes understanding of motivation, yet it has a complexity that requires a reader to suspend disbelief in the character's capabilities. In essence, telling what Amy thought and wanted is not within reasonable boundaries of the first-person point of view. Of course, it is acceptable as speculation, but fact is stated as truth (what she thought). Yet it is necessary information that is best thought of as "narrator-information" since a narrator usually knows all about the story world and has the reader-acceptable gift of knowing what all characters think. Consider this:

> I was so in love with Amy that I had come to despise her. She was sitting at her dressing table in front of a mirror, admiring her vibrant youthful skin, her full head of coal-black hair, and dark brown eyes. I moved to her side to look at her. She shifted her gaze to avoid me.
> "Did you ever love me?" I asked. "You let me think that you cared."
> She turned her back to me.
> "Witch. No one loves you," I said, angry now that I was with her and she was thinking only of herself.
> "Just go. Jason is coming," she said in a soft, emotionless whisper that hurt me to the core.

This passage, a little overwritten for emphasis, reveals story-world truths about both characters: the man is in love and dealing with his rejection, the beauty and the vanity of the woman, and her lack of empathy. By moving in scene and creating dialogue conflict and emotional depth, we bring probable story truth to the reader and strengthen characterization and story impact.

Third-person narration in-scene is an alternative to avoid the awkwardness of first-person narration and the unreliability of truth that deadens characterization and story. 1) In scene. 2) In descriptive-narrative.

In-scene third person narration

> Amy refused to look at Bobby, whose abrupt entry into her bedroom frightened her. She laid her hairbrush down and with both hands gathered her shoulder-length black hair behind her head, fastening it with a silver clip. Her face had lines of apprehension, and she had a brief moment of anxiety. She could see him in the mirror as he shut the door and moved to her.
> "I've had it," he said.

> "Please," she said, avoiding his angry stare at her in the mirror.
> "I'll kill him."
> He had no right to threaten. She'd never led him on. He was nobody.

Descriptive-narrative. Now the information—pride in beauty, lack of empathy, religiosity delivered in narrative:

> Amy sat at her dresser in her bedroom. She saw Bobby enter uninvited and approach her from behind. She refused to turn around. She would ignore him. He had threatened to kill her fiancé. Her heart raced. She looked in the mirror and struggled to control any hint of fear. That would only inflame him. He told her to listen up; he was serious. She prayed silently but he refused to leave.

Again, information imparted; there is no question of the characterization, even though the in-scene presentation is probably more effective than the straight narrative. Information provided through a character—first or third person—that is not reasonable makes that character unreliable, whether intentionally or unintentionally.

In essence, it is perfectly reasonable, and often necessary, to use a first-person character as the more story-wise narrator, but it must not be accidental, it should not be obvious, and it must be consistent for the story being written.

In general, resist thinking that unraveling complexities of point of view is unnecessary—the "if it works and I wrote it, it must be good" approach to creating fictional stories. Authors must be aware of the subtle and complex layers of point of view to use point of view effectively. It is inescapable. Well-reasoned opinions about point of view are essential for all authors who want to be in control of the storytelling process and what they provide for a reader.

Voice

Voice and point of view, although related, are not the same. Voice is everything a character does and says that helps identify that character. Point of view is the microscopic (close) or telescopic (distant) way a character delivers story information. And while characters deliver story information in their own voice, a narrator is telling the story—even in the first person. Multiple voices are often used but should be consistent.

Principles of narration

Great stories are told by a narrator, not a character. A narrator uses a point of view to deliver the story. When done seamlessly, the reader becomes engrossed and does not register *how* the narrator is delivering story information, either directly or through a character. It is most effective if a narrator is present in both first-person or third-person points of view, although the narrator may be more submerged in first-person point of view. A narrator is created by an author, but should be thought of as a distinct intellect who is telling the story.

Thinking of oral story tradition when writing

In academic discussions and workshops, terms are frequently used without common understanding as to their meaning. In this way entire careers have been riddled with confusion about the basics of storytelling and the unique problems of the written story. It is often helpful, in discussions of point of view and narrators, to recall an oral storytelling tradition. The storyteller is always telling the story. And the teller, who is often not the original author, is in control of narrative passages, action, dialogue, and internal reflection.

At times the storyteller relies on suspension of disbelief—the idea that the storyteller could possibly know the information presented—to build tension and drama. And listeners can have transcendence as if they immerse themselves in the character's living self. Imagine Ornesto, a storyteller, recounting Henry James's story "The Turn of the Screw" to a high school literature class in 2007. James published "The Turn of the Screw" in 1898. Ornesto, to be effective in his dramatization, will make the material as familiar to his contemporary audience as possible. He is telling a story already open to decades of interpretations. He might dip into Flora or Mile's minds, choosing the most relevant facts for his purpose, or characterize Mrs. Grose with room left for the 2007 listeners to fill in their own details. Ornesto may make Peter Quint as evil as he can, choosing his words (mostly if not all from James) for best effect.

Ornesto is the narrator—knowing all about the story world and choosing story facts from a limited story-world perspective. (James is considered the creator of the story world, with knowledge outside the story world.) Note that as narrator, Ornesto will make the best choices about story information for his audience. Fiction writers often ignore this separation advantage of author from narrator from character(s). Now Ornesto, to keep his story moving effectively, will narrate, and may well use points of view other than what author Henry James would. Here is a useful rule: although the fiction author writes the story, the author should not tell the story. The narrator tells the story (that is created by the author) and moves within the limits of the story world. And the narrator uses the narrator's voice for certain story information, and uses character point(s) of view to deliver other story content. This prevents stray authorial ideas from entering the story. By clear conceptualization of author-narrator-character delivered information, authors add ease to reader understanding but when contemporary writers choose a single character's point of view exclusively, as if it were a selective filter, they often limit the potential of the story.

Terms
Narrator intrusion. Narrators contribute to the story presentation and direct decisions about character contribution. A narrator's contribution is an intrusion to be excised if it creates a diversion to excuse the author's inability to write effective prose. But good judgment is necessary. If narrator information does not fit into the continuous fictional dream of the story provided for the reader at that moment, it is an intrusion and should not be included. Authors must use narrative techniques while remaining true to quality storytelling.

Authorial intrusion. Any thought, opinion, or emotion of the author is detrimental to creating a story as an art form. Most common are political ideas or comments on real-world social change. (The story may deal with these issues, but through action-enlightenment, not narrative emotional descriptions.) Author intrusion often borders on essay and propaganda and is not compatible with great fiction stories. (Although this does not mean that themes and meaning important to the author are not integral to great stories; they are, but they are expressed through careful story structure and skillful, craft-savvy presentation.)

It is also important that authorial morality is understood and consistent. All good literary stories are constructed on a moral framework that is easily perceived by the reader. Moral fiction is the cardiovascular system of a literary fictional story, and is provided by the author as a matrix in which the characters and narrator act. Of course, the morals of characters and narrator may differ—this provides conflict, suspense, and change in characterization and story. Yet presence of authorial morality provides the mirror surface off which different moralities reflect.

First-person point of view is the same as the narrator. When the narrator collapses into the first-person character, although it seems logical and acceptable, it sets up often-unaddressed (but perceived) questions in the reader's mind as to who is telling the story, the credibility of the narrator, and whether suspension of disbelief should be continued. Many contemporary stories don't differentiate between information sources, or indicate whether the information delivered from a particular source is credible.

For example, in first-person in-scene construction of a story passage, to be accurate, the first person can only tell and comment on what is happening in the story within the range of their five senses at that moment in story time. Along the same lines, if the first person comments on the past, it has to be within their intellectual capabilities and memory for story events, and when speculating, within the characters' capabilities and established sensitivities. But narrators are different. Every narrator tells about something that happened from a period where time has progressed, knowledge has increased, history expanded, understanding explored. For a reader to accept information outside the logical thoughts and perceptions of the first-person character, the reader must believe the first-person character is older and looking back on the story, now wiser and acting as a narrator, or accept a narrator's contribution to the story as created by the author to help the reader understand the story. This takes considerable authorial skill; most authors, with little concern for logic, don't consider a sliding scale of reliability for credible information delivery. Perhaps few readers care about details. But many readers stop reading when they think the writing is bad, and bad fiction can come from the lack of clarity in storytelling due to confusion over first-person/narrator relationships.

Close (or tight) vs. distant character points of view. The reader's sense of how close the character is to the story action is created by syntax, word choice, and ideation. This is true in all choices for story, including presentation, dialogue, narration, description, internal reflection, and even exposition. As a character seems more distant from the action, they function more and more as a narrator.

The author who recognizes character and narrator information in close and distant terms is able to present more consistent voicings, in-depth character reliability, and easily grasped imagery, and will be in better control of the writing process. In essence, flexible use of narrator information (that is, information not filtered through a character's point of view) provides essential story information that is outside the character senses, knowledge, and/or intellectual capabilities. This is useful technique in nearly all stories.

Narrator point of view. The narrator point of view is not a silo in a field of character-point-of-view silos. Narrators *tell* stories and it is not useful to consider a narrator point of view as similar to, or equivalent to, a character's point of view. Narrators float above the story in a hot-air balloon with useful overviews that characters cannot achieve from their restricted silos.

Omniscient narrator (i.e., knowing everything). Narrators know only about their story worlds. They know more than is told by a character, but they do not know all that the author knows, and they should not tell what the author knows and believes outside the story world. This is an important distinction for an author who wants to tell stories clearly, logically, and effectively.

Omniscient author. This implies that the author knows all truths. Impossible! Authors know only what they perceive of their world and think in their insular minds, and they are never omniscient. Omniscience is reserved for deities. To apply "omniscient" knowledge to a story becomes distracting and ineffective; the restrictions of being a unique human direct and intensify the storytelling in ways that being universal and "omniscient" as an author will not achieve. The term "omniscient point of view" applied to use of multiple points of view of characters and narrator is not useful. Use of multiple points of view provides different information about stories that should not be considered collectively as "omniscient."

Multiple third-person points of view does not equal an "omniscient point of view." Points of view in a story are not spices in a stew that give a blended effect. Points of view are pears, figs, cashews, marshmallows, all in a bowl and consumed separately (even if simultaneously) with sometimes memorable and always distinct individual effects that contribute to the whole experience of eating. "Omniscient point of view" does not mean multiple points of view, despite as often implied in discussions of the craft of writing.

Story world. Story world is restricted, selective, purposeful, intense, directed, and never random. It is where the characters act, and it is what the narrator delivers to the reader. In good fiction, its boundaries are sacrosanct.

Narrator epiphany. In general, narrators tell stories and may or may not change. Usually characters change from revelations or change the way they think about something thanks to story action. To avoid confusion about who the story is about, narrators tell a story and usually do not change significantly. But there are exceptions. Many stories have very effective narrators blessed with revelations and reversals in thinking that may or may not be similar to a character's. Note too that when the author is considered equal to the narrator, a narrator enlightenment is awkward, if not impossible. Strong ironic meaning is also often lost when there is loss of distinction with respect to character versus narrator. As a useful rule, how characters and sometimes narrators change in a story needs to be under the author's control and thoroughly considered before and during writing, and in revision.

Timeline and point of view. A character's point of view changes with the advancement of the story time (as does every human in real time). Here are the three elements of point of view, all of which form part of our understanding of what point of view can be: position in space or time; mental attitude or opinion; or manner of evaluating.

Drama in Literary Fiction
by William H. Coles

Great fiction is surprise, delight, and mastery.
Conflict-action-resolution is the writer's most essential tool.
Dramatic writing is more than just revealing prose.
Drama in literary fiction is mainly created through:
- a core story premise,
- unique and fully-realized characterization,
- and logical and acceptable motivation.

Drama in literary fiction is choosing well what information is best for the story and then providing that information predominantly in action scenes.

Suspense

Suspense is a feeling of uncertainty, excitement, or worry over how something will turn out. Suspense contributes to drama, but it is not the sole element of drama in literary fiction. Suspense in literary fiction can involve the fear of something happening to a character we like or respect, where the character's personality affects the outcome of plot elements. For example:

> Jane books a flight to New York. The pilot arrives late and ignores the usual preflight checklist. The fuel tanks are less than a quarter full.

If we fear something happening to a character we like or respect, the suspense is heightened. Yet there is something lacking in this plot construction of the character-driven element of literary fiction:

> Jane calls her clandestine lover to fly her to New York in his small plane to meet with her estranged husband. Her lover is distraught over her refusal to give up her efforts to patch up her marriage. The lover arrives hung over from drowning his sorrows and fails to complete the preflight checklist. The plane's fuel tanks have not been refueled.

Character-driven plots differ from circumstantial plots. Note how the second scenario also allows for complexities in the resolution that may reveal more about the characters and contribute to the meaning of the story—say, love is the root of disaster. The lover might sacrifice his life for Jane, or vice versa. Again, character generation of plot creates literary fiction. In popular fiction, the resolution may be simply a plane crash or an emergency landing and the arrest of the pilot.

Withheld information

All stories have withheld information. As an author, you can only tell so much. But *why* an author withholds information contributes to the quality of the story. And *when* an author chooses to reveal story information is critical to story success; the expectations here are different in genre fiction than in literary fiction.

In melodrama (involving stereotypical characters, exaggerated descriptions of emotions, and simplistic conflicts and morality) crucial information is withheld to create suspense. This is reader manipulation that the reader must accept; the reader knows the teller of the story knows who killed the rector but the reader accepts, for suspense, not knowing until the end . But in literary fiction, all information crucial for the story (this is an author being true to the story and not using the story) is presented for the sole purpose of engaging the reader. Then the reader becomes involved in (and with) the characters resolving their conflicts—not only in being told what is withheld—and the result is a change in the reader, a realization that nothing in their world will ever be the same because of their involvement in the story.

How story information is used—whether delivered or withheld—is the skeleton of how different authors create their own unique stories. Authors of literary stories must not exploit a reader's interest and involvement through false handling of story facts. Instead, the reader must become involved in the story action and accept character change—and experience change in themselves.

Literary stories are harder to write and require more intense reading than nonliterary stories. A casual reader, not caring about involvement in the story, will prefer stories based on withheld facts—who murdered whom, for example. This reader (and all readers will have this mindset at times) does not want to expend effort to become involved in a literary story. In fact, this is how most stories are told and enjoyed today. And it is an admirable skill for an author to write for this reader effectively. But literary fiction is an alternative choice for readers in the mood to be involved.

Let's say you write a story about a pregnant teenage girl traveling alone cross-country for an abortion. For many authors, the story may be about the revelation of who fathered the child, and the discovery of this withheld information will delight many readers. But you could reveal all the circumstances of the pregnancy. What if it were incest and her father raped her, or what if the gym coach at school had seduced her on the trip to the finals in field hockey? Everything is up front. Now you set forth the structure to bring the reader into how the girl will solve her conflict—an unwanted pregnancy by someone she hates. You will reveal her nature and her capabilities. You will find a premise: forced love destroys a normal life, for example. And you will engender understanding in the reader that enlightens or changes existing thought.

Drama Is Action

Most beginning writers do not have the instincts to write stories by creating conflict, action, and resolution in a series of scenes that involve the reader. Beginners simply tell story happenings, often with complicated and inflated (or static and boring) prose.

Narrative description (telling)
   Paul was jealous that Helen could sing with so much passion that others couldn't take their eyes away from her as she performed.

In scene (showing)
   Helen held the floor-stand microphone with both hands. The piano player began the introduction, hunched over the keyboard. Helen took a deep breath and sang with a soft breathy voice, her eyes closed until the refrain, when her gaze swept the audience of strangers, all watching her. She sang three verses and smiled at the end without a bow. The crowd applauded. Paul approached her as she climbed down off the stage.
   "I wish I could sing like that," he said. "I don't have your ear for perfection."

In-scene action and showing should be the major portion of a literary story. But true narrative telling, when condensed—and not as a vehicle for asides and recall and reflection—can be useful to advance the story.

Narrative telling (quick, effective)
   The ship sank.

In-scene showing (more story time, more engaging)
   The ocean liner listed, taking on water through the portside torpedo hole.

The bridge shuddered from two explosions in the engine room, and the crew struggled to release the lifeboats. The bow disappeared beneath the surface first, soon followed by the hull.

The feeling of momentum must not be lost in a story. The key is learning how to write with action (see also **Momentum**).

Examples from *A Story in Literary Fiction: A Manual for Writers*.

Desire and Motivation in Literary Fiction
by William H. Coles

Desire: wanting to have something or wanting something to happen.
Motivation (or motive): the reason someone acts or behaves in a certain way.

Desire and motivation are essential to good storytelling and are among the most defining features of literary fiction. They are integral and dependent on all the other elements of fiction. With story development the desires and motivations of characters may change or expand. As we look at what desire and motivation can do in a story, we should keep in mind these principles:

- In creating scenes, author knowledge of valid character desires allows writing that is maximally effective.
- For storytelling, core character desires that drive all action are more effective than superficial or poorly considered desires that are questioned, either consciously or subconsciously by the reader, as significant for motivation.
- Core desires of characters (and people) are not easily determined.
- Motivations interact and must be logical for story and character, and a change in a motivation expressed in scene, thought, or even backstory will change the effects of other motivations.

At times, identification and incorporation of desires and motivations in early story drafts is difficult, but as characters develop and action in the plot progresses, incorporation in later drafts and revision becomes more practical, if not essential. Therefore, discovery of desire and motivations late in story creation often requires significant revision and restructuring. In creating motivations, remember significance (all-consuming with serious consequences), credibility (would this character, as developed, really do this?), and emotion (action from specific feelings from the character rather than mere whimsy).

In essence, stories are about people, and to create great stories requires in-depth consideration of characters' desires and motivations. A character is not a few planks nailed together floating down a river to a calm sea; a character is a carefully crafted one-person sailboat that must tack against the current, catching the right winds, struggling to move upstream to the river's gushing source. What makes the little sailboat struggle and why? It would be so easy to let the river dictate direction and destination. It is sad for modern literature that many contemporary stories are simply descriptions of real or imagined events of characters floating through life. Great fictional stories have logical desires and motivations embedded in the drama.

In memoir or biography, an author describes events that happened and interprets the perceived desires and motivations of the character from the actions in the story. But in the fictional stories, the author can imagine the best desires and motivations of a character, and these desires and motivations must be strong; drive the plot; be logical and credible with improvement by multiple revisions; and heighten the impact of the characters' reversal of existing thinking or enlightenment (i.e., theme and meaning). To be successful, the author must understand desires and motivations, build on desires and motivations with characterization, be open to discovery of more effective desires and motivations as writing progresses, and be willing to revise for most significant desires and motivations. Finally, the desires and motivations must relate directly to character change in thinking or enlightenment that creates meaning in a story.

How Desire and Motivation Are Used in Literary Fiction

First, consider a common misconception: that great authors create characters by either describing an interesting character from life with fictional tools, or imagining an interesting character and then describing them. The truth is, great characters are built layer by layer through character actions and discoveries, not just by describing features and traits or feelings. Characters grow from every action made, every thought considered, every word of dialogue spoken. Each molecule of character development must have some relationship to the matter it creates, and much of the cumulative, synergistic interaction of the elements of character development are created by the overriding effect of a strong desire, recognizable to the reader, and logical motivations as they relate to story and other character elements. Yet paradoxically most authors still describe characters from life, or imagine them.

Describing characters, rather than creating them, loses the advantage of building a dynamic character who will act with desires and motives clear to the reader, propel the plot forward, and compel some significant change in thinking.

A second misconception is that a story that fails to provide the desired effect can be corrected by intensifying and expanding the prose. In fact, failed stories are often overwritten because authors seek to give significance through word choice, syntax, clever metaphors, and sentimentality when actually story structure and character desire and motivations need to be fixed. A significant story is created through actions woven into a beautiful fabric using threads of desire and motivation.

Characters need unified and dominant desires and motives. This may not occur in life, where we find people driven by many desires and motivations, often with random application to life's challenges. But characters in a structured story require significant and focused reasons for action. This allows intensity in character development scene after scene, chapter after chapter, that is cumulative and synergistic.

Core desires are fewer than might be expected and act as a premise underlying all character motivations in a story. Examples of good core desires are not easy—every character is unique—but to get the idea, consider that fear of eternal damnation is a better desire for an author to work with than guilt over a clandestine sexual experience. An unsatisfiable need for adoration provides broader application than an inability to pass by a mirror without looking.

As character motivations are developed scene by scene, always seek the core desire that motivates. Then develop and revise accordingly, always seeking continuity from scene to scene.

Desire and motivation in literary fiction must be significant, but need not lead to violence or horror. Significant desire and motivation does not equate to murder, rape, or abuse of a child: significant motivations can result in beautiful interactions among characters. The literary fiction writer has the opportunity to create stories of lasting impact in dramatic and meaningful ways without violence-related suspense/action scenes. Literary fiction does not depend for excellence on the louder bang, the brighter flash, or the hotter fire. For the author, that is often the joy and the challenge.

Credibility in Literary Fiction
by William H. Coles

Credibility—willingness to accept something as true in the characters and in their story world—must be meticulously nurtured in the literary story as an art form. Often credibility slips with illogical progression of plot ideas, or with poorly integrated character thoughts, actions, and words. Readers will fail to connect to a story where there is erosion of credibility, and the writing will not succeed. Even if the story requires suspension of disbelief (as all stories do to some degree) there is always a dependency on the absolutely logical association and progression of ideas for good writing.

Credibility in plot logic is the easiest to identify and discuss. As characters move through the story, choices are made for their action in the plot. Lazy or untalented choices will sink the story. For example, a prodigal son arrives at the bedside of his dying father whom he has not seen since childhood. What happens next? He falls on his knees and weeps. He smothers his father to death with a pillow. He asks his sister to bring him a drink. He remains motionless, unable to feel emotion. And so forth. There are so many choices, but there is only one right choice for any one great story. An author finds that best choice after seeking alternative after alternative. Most of these choices are made in the mind. But often an outline helps for timing and positioning, especially with critical story actions. Never take your first thought as your best—it rarely will be.

In characterization the credibility issue constantly lurks. It is a common author error that makes the reader reject and dislike the story, to varying degrees. Credibility issues operate on two levels. First, the immediate: Is immediate story action, thought, reflection, or words of a character logical for that moment, and for what the reader knows about that character at that moment? Second, overall: Is the character developing in the story logically and along lines closely related to the story's theme? Characters are chosen for a story by authors for the capabilities of either having significant enlightenment about something or for their potential of have significant change in their thinking and beliefs about something. As characters are developed, details and actions must be logical for how the characters will be irreversibly changed.

Credible emotional in-scene content must match exactly what is needed for the story at that moment. It iis not sufficient to crank up the language with four-letter expletives, two-word sentences, brightest and loudest descriptions or abstract language (e.g., "he was flooded with fear and love"), but with terse, clear, concrete language and structure. And surprise must be credible, too.

It may seem odd, but credibility need not relate to the reality of the reader's world. Credibility is judged by the story world created by the author and told by the narrator. In other words, a plot shift or character decision in a story set in 1929 needs only be credible for the story, never mind the reader's time in existence. As the story is introduced, a contract of details is established between author and reader—unstated, of course—that continues to develop throughout the story and will establish what is and is not credible.
Authors cannot afford to risk rejection of a story by a reader because of failure to address credibility issues.

In summary: for credibility, the final story product, whether a novel or a short story, must have reasonable thoughts and actions built on logical associations and progressions, total reader acceptance of timing and progression of story elements, and total believability that the emotional content of the writing matches the need for story development.

Dialogue
by William H. Coles

Great dialogue in literary fiction serves multiple functions, but never detracts from story progress or purpose. Writers who write dialogue well have a special gift that they've continually nourished. We can all learn to improve. Consider this example from classic literature:

> "If I were in heaven, Nelly, I should be extremely miserable."
> "Because you are not fit to go there," I answered. "All sinners would be miserable in heaven."
> "But it is not for that. I dreamt once that I was there."
> "I tell you I won't harken to your dreams, Miss Catherine! I'll go to bed," I interrupted again.
> She laughed, and held me down; for I made a motion to leave my chair.
> "This is nothing," cried she: "I was only going to say that heaven did not seem to be my home; and I broke my heart with weeping to come back to earth."
>
> Emily Brontë's *Wuthering Heights*

This dialogue example has action, conflict, revelation, and voice. It serves multiple purposes.

Basic Rules of Dialogue

In fiction, successful dialogue serves at least one, and usually more, of these purposes:

- advances story
- develops character
- moves plot
- illuminates theme or meaning
- provides time transition, usually subtle
- changes direction of plot, usually through conflict
- creates voice and tone, either for story or character
- provides understanding of enlightenment for characters
- illuminates desire and motivation

- supports attribution with consistent syntax and ideation
- meets rhythmic necessity of human speech compatible with story dialogue
- adds drama (through conflict and resultant action)
- provides movement for story ideas and plot

In fiction, successful dialogue (almost) **NEVER**:

- is used only to break up a narrative passage
- tells what was really said in an author's experience
- provides exposition in any way that questions credibility
- is static prose
- provides prose context for author-clever simile (or metaphor)
- slows down story-plot movement
- inappropriately provides setting that is better in narrative
- addresses author opinion
- mimics what a character might say in the real world
- is a conversation in quotes without story purpose

In great fiction, dialogue is not intuitive—it does not come naturally to writers. Most importantly, for effective dialogue in fiction, authors cannot simply describe a dialogue from real experience or from an imagined scene. Basically, dialogue is always created for the purpose of story development, and therefore it cannot function as a tape recording of reality, and it must be stripped of nuances that may not be true to the story or confuse the reader. In revision of dialogue, these questions are useful: Is dialogue logical? Does it fit character desire and motivation? Does it support theme and meaning? Does it move?

Ideas for Improvement

Character
Think of dialogue from the character's story "reality." When revising a specific dialogue segment, ask if the dialogue is logical for the character's educations it true to story time and the character's age? Does it match the character's emotion of the moment? Does it fit the character's credible thinking and perceptions of the moment?

No *authorial thinking in dialogue*
Literary fiction is objective. Author ideas and opinions should not drive dialogue; only those ideas and opinions that are consistent with characters and serve the purpose for the story.

Avoid direct answers (kills movement)
    "Is that a Gila monster?"
    "Yes, I think it is."

This is not a usable dialogue. This fills time and page space, but it does nothing for drama or story. What about, "Stay back, they bite!" But this has no realism. When nothing is working, look for a greater problem. Should the idea be expressed in dialogue at all? Let's think about this for a minute. "Is that a Gila monster?" may not be direct character dialogue that is useful in any story. The dialogue is being used to inform the reader of the presence of a potentially dangerous creature. For dramatic fiction, a scene must have a purpose, and it must have action. "Is that a Gila monster?" has no effect in fiction. It sounds contrived when we really need drama and conflict between the character(s) and the forces of nature (monster). Realistically, the dialogue speaker must be afraid, or planning escape, or figuring out a way to kill the beast, or admiring its unusually threatening size. If nothing works, a key revision might be to remove this information from dialogue.

Avoid "talking heads" (two-character ping-pong dialogue)
Although frequently necessary, dialogue limited to two characters (or talking to oneself in an internal monologue) can quickly become dreadfully boring. Conflict is essential, as in every dialogue passage, to maintain the necessary energy. Creating dialogue takes practice. Some examples:

Agreement:
    "That bull is a pussycat."
    "I don't know why they put it in the draw."

Conflict inserted (with exposition that may not be reasonable for some readers):
    "That bull is a pussycat."
    "You don't know nothin'. He damn near killed Prettyboy. Knocked him out for two days."

More characters (four here) leads to more information conveyed:
    "That bull is a pussycat."
    "Knocked out Prettyboy."
    "Shouldn't be in the draw, anyway. No reason to get mangled by some crazy man killer."
    "Comes from a family of good bulls. Wish I had more like him."

Avoid simile and metaphor
Never use rules to guide your dialogue creation, but do carry a caution about simile and metaphor. It is often impossible to find the right simile that fits the context and is credible for the character's intelligence and experience. An extreme example:

"Ignore her," she said. "She looks like Marie Antoinette with a sex change."

This author is trying to be clever and failing because the simile has no meaning or valid imagery.

"She looks like shit."

Even if the author argues that this is in the vernacular of the character and helps define him or her, the simile is cliché and adds nothing to the writing. Any metaphor that calls attention to itself in dialogue should be deleted.

What exactly happens?
Desire and motivation? Movement? Exposition? Logic? Conflict? Some examples:

Draft 1.
"Don't do it."
"I won't."
"It's one of the most difficult maneuvers we have in skydiving."
"I've never wanted to take the risk."

No conflict, even when there is opportunity for conflict. Static, and not credible. The pacing is wrong for the content. And it contains exposition (about skydiving).

Draft 2.
"Don't do it."
"It's why I came."
"Think of Janie and Sally."
"No time to think of my children."

Exposition about children is inappropriate for this story scenario. If children's names are already in story, this is redundant, and even if not previously introduced, mention of children is not logical if someone is about to jump out of an airplane; that is, it is not a useful response to a fictional situation. Note that for the experienced skydiver, jumping out of a plane might be an everyday experience that *would* allow discussion about children, but rarely, and it would take careful construction. In fiction dialogue, the emotion at the time of jump must be strong and felt by the reader through the dialogue. No sense of emotion comes through in this dialogue, making the discussion of children unlikely.

Draft 3.
"The ripcord won't work."
"You're saying that to scare me."
"It's defective."
"You packed it."

This has some conflict, which is an improvement. But this is still not usable dialogue. Purpose must relate to story, and purpose must be the right choice for a dialogue segment. Clearly the author in creating this dialogue has confused purposes in mind. Is this segment about defective equipment? Desire to direct someone, blame someone? Learn about one or both characters? And if so, learn what? A good writer demands dialogue work for the story and has a clearly identifiable purpose related to the story and story moment in time. If this really is about defective equipment, maybe it shouldn't be in dialogue. Probably better in a narrative passage.

Draft 4.
"You've less than ten seconds."
"What about you?"
"Count. Pull the cord. You've got to be clear."
"Where is your chute?"
"Five, four . . ."
"Where is the pin?"

"You've got to be clear" probably means clear of flying objects, including the plane. This is information no one would utter—it's too obvious. This problem usually indicates a need for a narrative passage or information delivered in another way, possibly via internalization. Also, is "You've less than ten seconds" credible? Wouldn't a character say, "Hurry!" Same revision logic for "Count. Pull the cord. You've got to be clear." "Pull the cord!" is more efficient and appropriate.

Draft 5.
"Jump."
"Not without you."

Assuming it's already established that the two experienced skydivers are in an in-flight emergency with one parachute, there is an opportunity for learning about characters—a moment of grace.

About sound

Beginning writers often spend years seeking the right sound for their dialogue. Sound is important, but only when the dialogue fulfills a primary purpose of doing something important for the story. There are many ways to make the dialogue sound good. To be aware of the sound it may help to read out loud, and if you're serious, record yourself and listen to the playback. Always remember, dialogue in fiction is not the way people speak, yet paradoxically it has to *seem* to be the way people speak. How to do that? First, there has to be a natural rhythm to the context in which the speech is given. If dialogue is related to an audience with the Pope, speech patterns will differ from those in a bar conversation with Jelly Roll Morton. When writing, notice how the same content can have incredibly different rhythmic presentations. Create alternatives, and select the best ones for your writing and story. Musicality is more important in some styles than others; it is always present, but it must not dominate when story purpose of dialogue might be lost.

Final thought

The challenge of creating your own effective dialogue will not come from copying some writer you love to read. Of course, read and learn. And then practice. But in the long run, you will need to make many decisions about dialogue in your stories. These decisions—essential for voice, movement, clarity, purpose, and credibility—are based on how you think about and create fictional stories and can only be solved by you. You are the creator, and when you succeed, your writing will be well received and you will have found your own unique style.

Improving Dialogue
by William H. Coles

Contemporary writers fail to make the most effective use of dialogue, which for many writing genre and memoir—and first-person-fiction authors—probably doesn't impact their career goals. But for the serious literary writer building characters that are integral in plot development and provide theme and meaning to a work of well-crafted fiction, the search for new ways of thinking about and creating effective dialogue are crucial to great characters and great writing.

A good fictional character is built by a combination of story actions and, usually to a lesser extent, descriptive narrative. Technically, dialogue can be the most useful way a character expresses emotions, emotions that often give special impact to a reader because the character is often unaware of what they are revealing—the pulse of dramatic irony at work. In dialogue sections, there are a number of thoughts and skills an author can use to create consistent characters with plausible emotions said in realistic, yet necessarily surprising, ways. Here are a few guidelines.

No exposition. In some writing, skillful exposition is possible and necessary. But when building characters who will engage the reader and evoke sympathy, exposition through dialogue pushes the reader away. It reminds the reader that the character is only the writer's tool to tell a story, rather than a unique (albeit fictional) individual worthy of caring and involvement.

No author presence. In fictional dialogue the character is speaking for him- or herself. The character is not a marionette for the writer. Nothing can hint of an author's idea or presence. (The writer can effectively use the narrator as storyteller and incorporate ideas there.) Writers must honor the character they build and not use the character's personality for their own (the writer's) needs and aggrandizement. Let the dialogue build the character. In genre and memoir, the author may write characters using their own (the author's) ideation, experiences, and syntax. The result weakens character credibility and development.

Don't insert character-antithetical cleverness. Unless you're Noel Coward or Oscar Wilde, serious fiction calls for few if any jokes and never clever sayings. Don't seek admiration for your wit. Let humor come from the inherent thinking between the characters, and irony in the plot. Irony, sarcasm, and metaphorical, layered contrasts are the humor tools for the writer of serious fiction. Slapstick can detract from credibility and erode dramatic momentum.

Make dialogue believable. Absolute adherence to characters saying what the readers think they would say if perceiving themselves as the character is essential. A writer must know and target the reader. This builds trust and bonding with character that results in memorability and uniqueness.

Let characters react to other characters. Sophisticated, seamless description of characters reacting to other characters, or reaction through the dialogue, strengthens the emotional, often subliminal, impact on the reader. Rather than describing a character's emotion, let another character see it and react.

Consider dialogue among characters. This is a valuable way to answer questions in the minds of the reader about plot, characters, and what the story is about. It advances the story and integrates character into story momentum.

No soliloquies. Honor the character. Expounding on extraneous topics, or even a hint thereof, is not credible or useful for character development.

Gauge dialogue to character intelligence (not some other standard). Don't make the dialogue smarter or dumber than the character uttering it.

Character-based fiction is a gift from a fiction author to the characters created. Let the characters be themselves and never let them default as tools for the author to tell his or her story. Well-fashioned characters begin to grow, embed themselves in a reader's memory, and evoke emotions in ways no other prose, or visual or auditory storytelling, is capable of. To master effective dialogue is not easy and not attainable by all, but to try is well worth the effort.

Characterization Improves Dialogue, Motivates Plot, and Enhances Theme

by William H. Coles

Learning effective characterization for literary fiction is essential for great stories. Imagined characters reveal theme and meaning and drive the plot action in some way; they are not simply bystanders to fatalism. Character traits in fiction are infinite: confident, conceited, domineering, outspoken, shy, short tempered, violent, passive, et cetera. The traits that spring most readily to mind often tend to be descriptive of appearance (e.g., overweight), or of personality (e.g., garrulous). But for the serious, character-based fiction writer, other characteristics are essential for creating character-specific voice and dialogue, assuring synthesis of logical desires and emotions in characters, and displaying levels of intellect and imagination of the character. Consider these ideas for in-depth thinking about characterization in fiction.

Humor. A sense of humor is essential for human bonding and social existence. What makes the character laugh, and what triggers that response, reveals the core, inner self. Irony is a complex form of humor that should often be part of character development. In general, how is a specific character humorous, and how does that character respond to story humor?

Civility. Being polite and courteous to others springs from caring about others' feelings. Does your character have a touch of civility, or is the character unable to display civility? This can be important in plotting and to maintain credible yet surprising plot progression and character interaction and conflict. Good dialogue can use character civility for identification and consistency of characterization and for understandable motivation. A lack of civility can likewise motivate characters and drive plot.

Morality. Every human's concept of virtue and evil, good and bad, differs. Morality contributes strongly to how a character acts in a story, and is often a source of inner conflict. What is the morality of a character? How would it be expressed in in-scene development (most effective) and narrative description?

Every story is a moral cobweb, and individual character morality may differ for ironic and dramatic effects.

Metaphor. Avoid inaccurate or degrading metaphors (e.g., "she looked like a decaying walrus"). Effective character-compatible metaphors are difficult to create, but ineffective ones damage the quality of writing and storytelling and are not useful.

Religion. Does your character believe in a superior being? Does that superior being direct their lives? Is a divine presence vengeful, benevolent, just? Does the character pray? Does the character believe in human will, or predestination? When present, it is often important to carry religious belief of the character into dialogue, and often into theme as well.

Voice. Voice is everything a character or narrator does, thinks, says, feels. Most great fiction maintains distinct character and narrator voices, but in contemporary fiction, the authorial voice often dominates, suppressing differentiation of characters' and narrators' voices. How does voice manifest in your fiction? Can a character voice be easily identified?

Creating characters with distinct voices is a skill. An all-pervasive authorial voice created by authors intent on describing events (usually personally experienced) rather than through imagined action, reflection, and conflict must be avoided. For the most part, this trend has produced energy-deficient fiction and meaningless storytelling.

Characterization has diminished to physical description and avoids character action; logical, credible, unique character motivation; and desire. In successful fictional works—works that are remembered, reread, and passed to future generations—characters are humans separate from the writer. Successful characterization drives action, creates ironies, and embeds humor. Effective dialogue—with action, reaction, and internalization—is ideally expressed with the thoughts, feelings, and ideas of the character.

Speech. Speech reveals how characters think, and after a time, who they really are. Dialogue is an effective way to build character, but it must be crafted for a purpose, not just written as a description from life, or an imagined scene, to fill space. And of course dialogue is a major way to reveal character in scene without hearing details from a narrator or author; character speech allows a reader to develop a sense of the individuality of the character, a phenomenon that occurs when the author has created characters with distinct voices and personalities.

Winning. What does the character need to win—in the moment or in life? This is an essence of fictional story. The character must desire something, must want to win something. Is it admiration, content, domination, superiority, revenge, love? Real life is often a constant adjustment to get along—to survive and procreate—without pain or threat of death. But the fictional character, living in the story world of conflict and imbalance, must have a need to win something that will help make them unique, and, for most literary storytelling, this winning is most effectively presented through action and dialogue.

Fear. What does your character fear—failure, drowning, humiliation, death?—and how does that fear affect his or her life?

Hurt. How do your characters hurt others—physically, psychologically, verbally? Do they humiliate, condescend, disagree, lie, exaggerate, ridicule?

Emotions. What makes your character laugh and cry on both a daily level and throughout life? Are emotional responses mainly positive (e.g., love) or negative (e.g., anger)? Is your character (ideally) displaying a range of emotions, and what emotion predominates? Even though angry, passionate, focused, and dedicated characters help drive plots, characters described from life are frequently depressed, loveless, and noncreative, and seriously erode story and characterization. Find predominant emotions and be sure that the majority of character emotions expressed in the story result in positive action—that is, contribute to strong characterization and plot movement, not inaction that slows story momentum and makes characterization flat and uninteresting.

Victimization. Strong, effective characters often see themselves as victims of circumstance or birth, and are most effectively created through an objective narrator who can present the victimization without the self-pity, self-absorption, and negativity that might be expressed through the character. Victimization is often a tragic flaw in a character and can precipitate nemesis, so it is useful, yet it can also turn readers away from engaging with and caring about the character. If your character is controlled by victimization (e.g., not being given or taught the skills to succeed, feeling the unjustly ignored, being from a minority ethnic background), work to present the victimization objectively, although the character's view is almost always subjective, so the reader can identify and sympathize with the character's burden.

Response to criticism. How does your character respond to criticism? With open ears? With anger? With cynicism? Criticism can insert conflict in fiction, and your character's responses will need to be logical and credible while simultaneously as unique and interesting as possible.

Memory. How does a character remember things? Does he or she always try to be accurate, using qualifying speech when they're uncertain? Or do they inflate or minimize for their own advantage? What do they tend to forget, and why?

Gender. Is the gender of the protagonist right for the story? Would a change in gender be more engaging, provide better support for meaning, or allow more accurate establishment of enjoyable voice?

Truth. What is truth (in accordance with fact or reality) to the character? How does he or she perceive truth in his or her world, and how does it relate to the real world and the worlds of other characters? (Potential for conflicts.)
Conformity. Is the character concerned with social acceptance, rebellious against accepted norms, or just apathetic? Does he or she conform to local, national, or world societal standards? How does this desire to conform or not conform relate to the story being created?

Beauty. Beauty is in the eye of the beholder, and what a character finds beautiful—as revealed through dialogue and the internal thoughts of characters—can reveal their inner self. Humans find pleasure in what they think is beautiful: music, art, motion, nature, proportion, symmetry or asymmetry. How might your character react to these contrasts of beauty?

Characters' choices about what is beautiful or not can add dimension, establishing them as dynamic, fascinating individuals. These choices about beauty may never be expressed directly in the prose, yet still reveal characters' attitudes through action, dialogue, internalization.

Characters in great, lasting, stories are sculpted by every word chosen; the construction of every prose element; the rhythmic pacing; the character-specific accuracy of metaphors related to character development; and the actions and reaction to the plot, be it fatalistic or character-based, or (usually) both. To achieve this in fiction, an author creates from a broad knowledge of the world and humanity. In almost every instance, character development is more effective when an author imagines what the character (not the author) feels, thinks, and does in the story setting.

Great literary fictional characters are created for a story purpose that will please a reader, and, to be most effective, are not described in exact detail from reality or imagined reality. To create effective characters, an author must build the character word by word, idea by idea, action by action. To be good storytellers, authors must be able to live as the character would speak, think, and empathize with the character's choices. Few writers attain this skill, but all should try.

Examples of character development in literature:
Heathcliff and Catherine (*Wuthering Heights*); Anna Karenina and Levin; Homer's Odysseus; Jane Eyre; Elizabeth Bennet, Mr. Darcy, and Mr Collins (*Pride and Prejudice*);
Helen and Mr. Wilcox (*Howard's End*); Freddy and Fredericka; Emma (*Madame Bovary*); Randall Patrick McMurphy (*One Flew Over the Cuckoo's Nest*); Rodion Raskolinikov (*Crime and Punishment*); Charles Marlow (*The Heart of Darkness*); "The Stone Boy"; "Miss Harriet"; Felicite in A Simple Heart (*Flaubert*).

Techniques for Excellence in Creating Character in Literary Fiction: Action, Conflict, Character-based Plots, Change, Dialogue, Setting

by William H. Coles

How do the most well-received literary fiction writers create memorable characters? In essence, literature is a written work of lasting art, fiction is imagined story and characters, and characterizing is creatively forming a character rather than describing from memory (memoir, biography). Here are techniques and principles in storytelling provide literary-quality characterization: action, conflict, character-based plots, change, dialogue, setting.

Action
Showing story and character in action scenes with concrete imagery, supportive narration, and dynamic prose enriches display of character emotion, morality, desire, history, and worldview—all with pleasurable, enlightening, and lasting effects on readers. Of course, narrative telling is important. It can be more figurative, abstract, and metaphorical. But for intensity and impact, in-scene action is often the better choice to develop character with story. In-scene storytelling can engage and involve readers more than telling narration. This first example tells of a happening. There is no action or significant characterization:

> Harry flew a kite at the beach to entertain his invalid son, but the kite got away, and Harry seethed with anger.

Here is the same event with in-scene action that helps develop character:

> A wind gust elevated the dragon kite and the string ran through Harry's hand fast enough to hurt.
> "Let me do it, Daddy," his son Raymond said, as he limped to Harry's side. The boy held out his hand that trembled nonstop from a congenital palsy. Could he hold the string? Fly the kite? He wanted to so badly.
> "Hold tight," Harry urged, placing the string in the boy's hand. The kite dipped then suddenly soared, the string taut again.

The boy cried out. "I dropped it." Harry reached out but the kite had ascended too far to grab the trailing string. The untethered kite disappeared, driven out to the sea by a gusty offshore wind.

"I didn't mean to," the boy said, "Please don't hit me."

Conflict

Dramatization in plotting is accomplished by presenting characters with conflicting desires, emotions, actions, and thoughts, and by inserting conflict in dialogue of verbal exchanges. An example of dialogue without conflict:

> Jane says to her father: "I'd like to hike to the top."
> Her father says: "A smashing idea."

Now two examples with character-revealing conflict embedded:

> Jane: "Let's climb to the top."
> Father: "I'm too weak. And you know I hate heights."
> Jane: "Stay here, then. I knew I shouldn't have brought you."

Or (different character revelation, more muted and kinder):

> Jane: "I want to climb to the top."
> Father: "I can't. You know what the doctor said."
> Jane: "We can stop for a coffee, then."

Character-Based Plots

In successful literature, characters' strengths, weaknesses, fears, lack of experience, failures of intuition, etc., frequently drive plots. Character-based plotting in narrative telling may augment opportunities for characterization. Compare these examples:

> The night was dark and stormy, the plane's instruments were not functioning after a lightning strike, and the plane crashed, killing all aboard.

Now the same event but with character-based plotting; the character's hubris causes the accident and fulfills an opportunity for character development:

> Aaron, a wealthy businessman excessively proud of his invincibility and with inflated belief in himself and his abilities, chooses to fly his private airplane at

night with limited experience in bad weather and crashes, killing himself and his passengers.

A character's thoughts, feelings, and actions should be integral to logical plot progression rather than reactions to fatalistic or serendipitous plot events.

Plot Concepts
Fatalism:
> Pablo spotted the meteorite as it plunged through the atmosphere and unsuccessfully ran for his life.

Serendipity:
> Harry was starved, walking the streets for a handout, when he came across a ham and cheese sandwich wrapped in cellophane lying on the sidewalk.

Character-motivated plot progression:
> Mary, fed up with her lying abusive husband, drove with her children to live with her mother in Canada. When she came to the mile-long suspension bridge, her lifelong fear of heights made her ignore a "road closed" sign and she detoured onto a wintery road in an attempt to reach the ferry. The car skidded on black ice, plunging over a cliff killing all.

In essence, a meteorite kills the man (fatalistic), a hungry man finds food (serendipity), a mother's fears and distress kill her and her family (character-based plot).

In-Scene Character-Based Plotting
Flaubert (in *Madame Bovary*) has a character-based scene development that reveals attributes of both Emma and her husband Charles that add to their individuality and complexity. The basic plot of the scene is: Emma Bovary, as a ruse to meet her lover in town, convinces her husband, Charles, that she needs piano lessons. After a few weeks, everyone thinks her piano playing improves (text abbreviated):

> One evening when Charles was listening to [Emma], she began the same piece four times over, each time with much vexation, while he, not noticing any difference, cried—"Bravo! Very good! You are wrong to stop. Go on!"
> "Oh, no; it is execrable! My fingers are quite rusty."
> The next day he begged her to play him something again.
> "Very well; to please you!"

And Charles confessed she had gone off a little. She played wrong notes and blundered; then, stopping short—

"Ah! it is no use. I ought to take some lessons; but–" She bit her lips and added, "Twenty francs a lesson, that's too dear!"

"Yes, so it is rather," said Charles, giggling stupidly. "But it seems to me that one might be able to do it for less; for there are artists of no reputation, and who are often better than the celebrities."

"Find them!" said Emma.

The next day when he came home he looked at her shyly.

"Madame Liegard assured me that her three young ladies who are at La Misericorde have lessons at fifty sous apiece!"

[Emma] shrugged her shoulders and did not open her piano again. But when she passed by it (if Bovary were there), she sighed– "Ah! my poor piano!"

And when anyone came to see her, she did not fail to inform them she had given up music, and could not begin again now for important reasons. Then people commiserated her– "What a pity! she had so much talent!" They even spoke to Bovary about it. They put him to shame, and especially the chemist.

"You are wrong [. . .] my good friend [. . .] by inducing madame (Emma) to study; you [would be] economizing on the subsequent musical education of your child," [the chemist said.]

So Charles returned once more to this question of the piano. Emma replied bitterly that it would be better to sell it. This poor piano that had given her vanity so much satisfaction–to see it go was to Bovary like the indefinable suicide of a part of herself.

"If you liked," he said, "a lesson from time to time, that wouldn't after all be very ruinous."

"But lessons," she replied, "are only of use when followed up."

And thus it was she set about obtaining her husband's permission to go to town once a week to see her lover. At the end of a month she was even considered to have made considerable progress.

The plot progresses, revealing Emma's deceitful clever, selfish, unscrupulous behavior and Charles's doting, clueless, naive, yet caring nature. The writing adds to the composition of unique, lasting, memorable characters.

Change

Great characters in literature change in some significant way—enlightenment, an epiphany, a recognition of responsibility, caring, a gracious gesture from a mean soul, a commitment, accepted responsibility for a failure, a change in perception, acceptance of a truth, realization of consequences from an action, a change in morality, a coming of age, a new way of thinking. Characterization is also enhanced when a character faces but fails an opportunity for change. For example:

> A young girl goes to court with her brother, younger sister, and aunt to attend the indictment of her father for the murder of her mother and discovers a truth that forces her to take on maternal caring for her siblings.
> *Dr. Greiner's Day in Court* (free)

> The son, long embarrassed by his father—an illiterate stonecutter of funerary statuary—falls in love with a woman client of his father. The woman, who is twice the boy's age, wants a tributary statue of a famous man she worked for. The tributary statue by his father is so revealing of the dead man's true complex but not totally malevolent nature that it helps the woman forgive the man's sins against her, and the boy discovers repressed pride and love for the father.
> *The Stonecutter* (free)

> An older man lives with a divorced woman he is unwilling to marry. Although he finds her interesting and companionable, he is not sure a commitment to marriage would satisfy her need for a surrogate of her former husband. While the couple are touring India, the theft of a valuable necklace results in the death of a fellow traveler and the circumstances brings the man to realize his partner's love and need and he makes a commitment to marry by giving her a necklace symbolic of his love.
> *The Necklace* (free)

> The husband attending a funeral to give a eulogy for his dead, estranged wife meets a young college student also present to deliver a eulogy who helps him forgive his dead wife's transgressions so he can deliver a remarkable tribute to the flawed woman.
> *Speaking of the Dead* (free)

Character-Specific Dialogue

Effective fiction requires dialogue specific to the character speaking. It is a common trap for an author to write same-sounding dialogue for all characters (and narrator), mimicking how the author would engage in conversation. A character's dialogue should be consistent with the experiences, worldview, intellect, morality, memory, imagination, and education of that character. This requires authors to write dialogue imagined from, and specific to, the brain and soul of each of their characters. In the following example from the short story "Reddog," two of the characters are a criminal charged as an accomplice to a hate-crime murder and a young woman researcher in graduate school pretending to be studying the wants and motivations of murderous criminals (but also secretly seeking facts that would help abolish capital punishment). The prisoner, the researcher, and the assistant warden each speak with identifiable, specific characteristics. An example of interaction between assistant warden and prisoner:

>On Christmas Day my second year in prison for murder, my mother stopped coming to visit. She doesn't call and I can't get in touch with her. In August, she missed my twenty-fifth birthday. A couple months later, my sister came and said, "Mother doesn't want to think about it anymore. Try to understand." I did try.
>Eventually my sister quit coming; she had a lot on her mind with her van full of kids—and no husband. So I go a year with no visitors, and when I get dragged to administration to face an assistant to the warden, I'm half-crazy.
>"A graduate student working in criminal justice wants to include you in her experiments," he said. "Your choice. Two or three times a month. Goes on your record as good behavior."
>Sessions would be out of maximum security . . . like a mini vacation.
>"Hey. What's with the experiments," I said. "She stick you with drugs, stuff like that?"
>"Just talk."
>"Hey, Captain. She a looker?"
>"Don't get your fantasies revved up. She's a pro."
>"You be there?"
>"Just you and her. And high security."
>"Maybe I get out of max sooner?" I asked. You get a cell in the main building and you could talk to guys, set things up.
>"Can't promise." He walked around the table, stuck a ballpoint pen in my cuffed hand, and showed me where to sign. "Consent papers," he said.
>You need a magnifying glass to read the print on the last two pages. "I don't know about signing anything," I said.
>"It's permission to talk, record, use information," he said.
>"I thought this was research," I said. I hated do-gooders and I didn't need rehabilitation. I needed parole, miraculous DNA evidence, a new trial.
>"I don't give a shit what you do. I'm here because the warden says to cover our ass legally. It's routine. No one's trying to screw you. No one cares."
>"She ain't a lawyer, is she? She ain't trying to retry the case or something."
>"She's a student. We checked. She was a paralegal before she went back to grad school. She's demonstrated against the death penalty. Arrested once

but never charged. She won't violate your rights, if that's what you're thinking. You don't have rights."

I signed her papers with a bump-and-a-line so no one could ever read my name.

A later interaction of the prisoner with the graduate student:

She wrote on her pad for a while.
"You a real doc?" I asked her.
"Does it make a difference?" She still stared at her pad. Her voice was a little squeaky.
"You ain't one, or you would have said so."
She shifted in her chair. "Please try to keep to the subject."
"You my subject, sweetie pie."
"Ms. Pearlstein," she said angrily.
"You got a first name. Like Virginity?"
"Where were you when you first saw Sean McGarity?"
"Maybe you called Chastity. Chastity Pearlstein!"
"Answer my question!"
"I love the way your lips wiggle," I said.
She slammed her folder on the table. "I don't like smartasses," she said. "I've got too much to do." She nodded to the guard and she picked up her papers and her tape recorder. She'd spent less than five minutes with me. That was no session!
"Up yours," I said, but she was already out the door. The guard pointed at me, his first finger straight out like the barrel of a gun. The bastard. The guard closed the door and called for transfer. In a few seconds, I'd be on my way back to maximum.

Here's another example from "The Activist." Eleven-year-old Ether Mae is with her mother and her older sister, Pearl Anne, in a double-wide trailer immediately after Pearl Anne delivers an aborted dead fetus:

"I ain't going to stand for it," Mama said. She said this often.
She held a small dead human about as long as an ear of corn. Even though the head was too big, the hands too small, you could tell it might have been somebody.
"Push down," Mama said.
My sister moaned. With a gush of blood the afterbirth slid onto the bed. Her skin was white as wood ash. "I don't feel good," she said.

"Shut up, Pearl Anne," Mama said. "Shut up and grow up."

"I'm seventeen."

"You're acting like a two-year-old."

"I'm going to throw up," Pearl Anne said.

I wasn't feeling so hot either.

"Go get some towels, Ether Mae. Help get Pearl Anne cleaned up."

I didn't move. Pearl Anne got herself into this fix, not me. I'd never had a boy put his thing into me. Pearl Anne said it felt funny but not so good that she couldn't do without it. So she'd decided to quit. She wanted more respect. She quit too late.

Now Mama moaned and held this dead thing. "My grandchild," she said. "Didn't I tell you to get some towels?"

"Don't want to." I backed away a little.

"You'll get the stick. You're too old to have me telling you what to do." I was eleven.

I found some rags and two towels and got them wet under the faucet in the sink, then squeezed the water out.

"Goddamn it. Wring them out. You're dripping all over the floor," Mama screamed. "What's that doctor's name wouldn't treat you, Pearl Anne?" she asked.

Note: character specific dialogue is dependent on word choice, syntax, ideation, but as important is the dialogue segment, when it's delivered, is it logically and credibly related to the character's worldview, experience, education, intellect at the moment in story time. Dialect and speech impediments should be used sparingly.

Perspective
Character-focused imaging

The perspective of a scene can be close or distant. Variations of use depend on authorial style and purpose of the scene (and story). Close perspective, bringing the reader into the scene, reveals character traits. By contrast, distant perspective is essential for delivering broad perspective of setting, and contributes to imaging but not so much to characterization. See these two examples:

Close perspective. From the short story "Dilemma":

After the explosion they were quickly inside the room. The gun had fallen to the floor. His son had fallen to one side; his face gone: the lower jaw blown away, a few upper teeth haphazardly clinging to flesh. Nose and lower lids gone, the deflated eyeballs wrinkled like a fallen soufflé. His son's legs, then his arms, went into spasms; he was alive but without air.

I'm a surgeon, he thought. Focus. Think like a doctor and not a father.

His wife had crumpled to the floor, her hands over her eyes, wailing.

He held his son's head with both hands; straightened the torso. "Get up," he said to his wife. "You've got to do this." She stood. "Slide the pillow under his shoulders."

He let the head fall back hoping to find the glistening end of the trachea. There were no landmarks, only flesh and blood, and bits and slivers of bone.

Distant perspective. From Herman Melville's *Moby-Dick*:

> There now is your insular city of Manhattoes, belted round wharves as Indian Isles of coral reefs—commerce surrounds it with her surf. Right and left, the streets take you waterward. Its extreme downtown is the battery, where that noble mole is washed by waves, and cooled by breezes, which a few hours previous were out of sight of land. Look at the crowds of water-gazers there.
>
> Circumambulate the city of a dreamy Sabbath afternoon. Go from Corlears Hpok to Coenties Slip, and from thence, by Whitehall, northward. What do you see?—Posted like silent sentinels all around the town, stand thousands upon thousands of mortal men fixed in ocean reveries. Some leaning against the spiles; some seated on the pier-heads; some looking over the bulwarks of ships from China; some high aloft in the rigging, as if striving to get still a better seaward peep. But these are all landsmen; of week days pent up in lath and plaster—tied to counters, nailed to benches, clinched to desks. How then is this. Are the green fields gone? What do they do here?

Characters in fiction are often stimulated by real-life persons and events but are most effectively rendered not by remembering and describing alone but through authorial skill in creating characters. Imaginative, accurate, objective prose storytelling is written with the objective of reader engagement, entertainment, and enlightenment. For best results, authors of literary stories should have altruistic motivations in telling their stories—absent authorial ego, catharsis, or a need for attention or guilt relief—and seek for the story and the characters to stimulate new or renewed reader thinking about the human condition.

CRAFT

Momentum in Literary Fiction *57*
    Ways to create movement and action-key elements in great fictional stories.

First person Point of View in Literary Story *65*
    Expert use of 1st person can help make a story great. And it is more than using a pronoun.

Top Story/Bottom Story *77*
    Top story/Bottom story can help authors structure their writing to write the best literary stories.

Strong Voice and Attention to Time *81*
    A literary fictional story is a magical perception–an engaging illusion–that is an unbroken continuum.

Humor and Fiction *87*
    To create great literary stories, prose fiction must be vibrant and interesting, and never trivial. Every writer has a better chance for excellence with the accomplished use of the right elements of humor; how, then, do humor elements work in fiction?

Emotional Complexity in Literary Fiction *91*
    In some ways, emotional complexity, beautifully rendered, clearly defines literary fiction from genre fiction.

Conflict in Literary Fiction 95
    Conflict is the engine of literary fiction and the bait for reader engagement.

What Exactly Is a Character-Based Plot? 101
    For literary stories, stories about people coping with being human, characters actions, motivations and desires affect plot action and plot outcomes. What is a character-based plot and how do you construct it?

Writing in Scene: A Staple for Reader Engagement in Fiction 105
    In conjunction with narrative description, writing in scene is the heart of reader engagement and pleasure and is the core for significant meaning in literary story.

Creating Story World (setting) in Literary Fiction 113
    Be effective and don't be boring. Hone your techniques for imagery and action.

Perception in Literary Fiction: A Challenge for Better Narration 119
    How characters and narrator perceive the story world from their unique personas and worldviews can help writers with imagery and momentum in their fiction writing.

Creating Quality Characters in Literary Fiction 125
    Learn the techniques to make your characters special in literary fiction.

Mastering the Power of a Literary Fictional Story 133
    How to create your literary story for impact, memorability, significance, longevity, and meritorious praise.

Momentum in Literary Fiction
by William H. Coles

By tradition, literary fiction tends to be serious—and static. A valuable alternative for literary fiction writers is making their writing vibrant with motion—full of energy that is transferred from page to reader. Action! And all of this action in writing comes from word choice, well-constructed sentences and paragraphs, and from clear transfer of ideas that avoid obscurity. Then, a story has action in the majority of its elements and momentum that transfers enlightenment and meaning with quality of storytelling rather than just narrative ideas unrooted in images, action, and events.

Overall, to engage, entertain, and enlighten receptive readers, story information should move a story forward. Most memorable and admired fiction stories are tidal waves that carry water fowl, trees and plants, and man-made elements, broken and mangled; and when the wave encounters obstacles it engulfs them and then dislodges them inexorably. Stories should not be stagnant puddles waiting for an occasional shower to maintain their existence. It is the author's challenge, if not duty to most readers, to create a tidal wave. This is a quest not accomplished in a few sittings before a computer screen. Learning to write with story momentum is a lifelong dedication, better learned by some than others.

Words can have action or be inert, often with aspects of both. Authors, for the sake of the reader, must seek action words, but only when the new word improves meaning and effectiveness of the writing.

Verbs
Look for different degrees of action in the following (note how action is related to specificity):

> ate / swallowed
> moved / walked
> understood / discovered
> told / described
> told / elaborated
> went / drove

lay / reclined
cooked / fried
cooked / poached
killed / bludgeoned to death
began / ignited

Certain verbs may convey a degree or type of action that does not suit the scene or the narration. For instance, "His humor ignited her admiration" is not an improvement on "She smiled at his joke."

Nouns
In description of settings—or any story narrative, for that matter—nouns need energy. When possible, image nouns should be concrete (e.g., "hawk") rather than abstract (e.g., "object"). At times, no choice may be available, but when it is, choose so as to contribute to story imagery and momentum. Here are nouns with different energies:

rock / hawk
telephone pole / computer
road / river
shadow / glitter

What story would you want to read: one about rocks, telephone poles, and a road in shadow, or one about hawks, computers, and a river that glitters? The right word associations make good writing better.

Adjectives
Adjectives restrict a noun or a verb form, and this can be desirable or undesirable. Compare adjectival effectiveness for lively writing:

motionless steamroller
waiting steamroller
tilted steamroller
rusted steamroller
dead acrobat
breathless acrobat
plunging acrobat
immortalized acrobat
revered acrobat
decaying acrobat
perspiring acrobat

Adjectives are not interchangeable; each has a different energy relationship to its noun in that specific context. Authors must make the right adjective choices or their writing dies. Sometimes no adjective is best: "hear the crow," may be better than "hear the cawing crow," for example, because cawing is not useful—it is what a crow does if we hear it. On the other hand, certain adjectives are an absolutely necessity for clarity. "White whale" means more than "whale."

Adverbs
Consider these examples:

>   talked incessantly
>   talked often
>   talked irritatingly
>   talked lovingly
>   talked uncontrollably
>   talked loudly
>   talked softly

Note that every one of these adverbs could be replaced by a construction that shows rather than tells. Instead of "loudly," an author might use, "He shouted and little Jennie winced and covered her ears." (Probably too many words for too little effect. In this instance, maybe the adverb is better: "Jake spoke loudly to her.")

Adverbs can be valuable, brief sources of information. Still, authors must control selection and usage. Adverbs too often flag an author's unwillingness to seek the right verb. "Yelled loudly" could be "screamed." "Moved rapidly" could be "jumped" or "ran" or "scurried." These are specific, concrete words rather than nonspecific, indefinite words. Adverbs also often confuse point of view (and narration) in storytelling. In "He saw the enemy soldier unwillingly aim his rifle," the "unwillingly aim" briefly shifts the point of view from the soldier to a narrator. Remove "unwillingly" and there is no point-of-view shift.

Concrete vs. Abstract Words
Concrete and abstract words have different effects. For action writing, the former are almost always better:

>   tuberculosis / disease
>   Joe / population
>   Atlantic / ocean

> March 22 / future
> tarragon / spice
> violin / instrument
> G note / sound
> triplet / rhythm

In revision, replace abstract, indefinite, theoretical words with words that engage rather than simply tell. Are there better, more concrete, alternatives? "Violin" is better than "instrument" or "musical instrument." Too many abstractions cumulatively destroy good creative writing, while carefully chosen, concrete words build momentum and pleasure in reading. Beware, however, that fiddling with words cannot make writing great. Too often writers spend time in revision at the granular level when the entire structure needs change.

Avoid Obscurity

When a reader reads an author with muddled thinking, the reading slows, the reader's interest wanes, and the story is not successful. Action with concrete imagery is necessary and is directly proportional to clear, logical, and credible thinking. Nothing stagnates a story more than obscurity. Paradoxically, some authors believe obscure writing is clever and stimulating—but those are pseudointellectual ideas. In general, obscurity and vibrant storytelling do not mix in fictional literary prose.

A writer has an idea. It could be concept or image. The writer uses words and their arrangement to transmit an idea to a reader. It's not simple. Every human is different, with a unique way of thinking, past experience, memory capacity, and education. We assume we think as most others do, and they assume the same of us, but there is wide variability. Authors must think clearly and logically to improve the written communication of their ideas. Do not cling to mediocre ideas and then obscure them in writing, hoping that the obscurity will make them seem more interesting or more significant than they are.

Authors transmit clear thinking through accurate word association; careful attention to modifiers and antecedents; concrete ideas; and for many, a mental image clarified before it is described. Fine-tune your thinking to make your writing effective in conveying your ideas. The reward is improved stories that are significant and last.

Use Proper Constructions

Avoid muddled constructions and unclear associations that make reading difficult. Choose best sentence types and constructions for the prose of the story-moment. For instance, don't use a pronoun where the antecedent is not clear, and don't present subordinate ideas whose the relationship to the main idea is not clear. Here is an example of a *periodic sentence* (subject and verb at end of compound sentence):

> Body trembling, air trapped in his lungs as he'd forgotten to breathe, he jumped from the plane, pulling the ripcord.

Following is a *loose sentence* (subject and verb at the beginning of compound sentence):

> He jumped from the plane, pulling the ripcord, as his body trembled, air trapped in his lungs as he'd forgotten to breathe.

The emphasis and effects are different. Both are fine when used in an appropriate writing context. Sentence length and sound, as well as structure, should also be varied with attention to rhythms and tension of the story moment.

Avoid Inappropriate Poetics

Resist oxymorons, especially overwritten ones that are not related to story purpose. An oxymoron is a figure of speech with contradictory terms, for example "falsely true," and it can be an effective poetic technique but is rarely, if ever, useful in fiction. Oxymoron, by definition, is opaque, if not obscure. It is often effective language in love with itself and in literary fiction prose it can stop the action.

Alliteration refers to repetitive sounds at the beginnings of words ("tiny tinsel-like tots teetering together") and also bogs down a reader of prose fiction. Although it may be useful in some poetic contexts, it will seem amateurish in fiction.

Metaphor is the muscle that enlivens the skeleton of fiction and illuminates new understanding. Fiction needs clear metaphors, but don't keep the reader guessing with overly obscure ones. Likewise, with the simile. In fiction, it is essential that one's similes have perfect logic to be accepted by the reader. "A is like B" helps the reader understand A (and usually B) better. The effect of the comparison depends on differences between the two. If there is no difference, there is no effect. "A rose is like a rose" produces no effect. The rose here is not clarified for us. And if there is too much difference between A and B—"A rose is like a locomotive"—the comparison is unbelievable, and there is also no effect. "A rose in spring is like an exploding star at the beginning of time." Not great, but at least it stimulates thought.

Avoid constructions such as, "He would never use that to do this again." Even if the context provides some clues as to meaning, vague pronouns frustrate a reader. Better: "John would never use a spoon to dig a grave again."

Dynamic Imagery
Many authors don't think about momentum in imager but images in writing can provide story momentum, unlike a photograph, which is frozen and static. Strange that many authors write descriptive scenes as if re-creating a photograph. Movement in images is a privilege that fiction allows authors. In writing, the reader's mind is active in creating and forming images. Basically, authors don't paint still-life images even if motion is implied (such as a coffee cup falling off the edge of a table). They paint portraits that intrigue and engage the reader with scenes that live on the page. "There was a bird on a limb" is static. "The flying bird settled on the limb" is improved with some action. "The olive branch quivered when the claws of the sparrow grasped the sturdy twig" has lot of action. (Overdone, but you see the principle.) Consider:

> The locomotive with colorful cars behind followed the track that snaked through the valley.

Any motion perceived is really implied. Now with action:

> The steam of the locomotive reddened the face of the engineer as he leaned out the window. The track curved many times ahead. He wondered, as the clouds gathered, if the printed banners with the czar's name flapping above the red, green, and white decorations so carefully applied on the cars behind by the birthday celebrants would be dampened, maybe even destroyed, by rain. He gripped the waist-high metal lever jutting up through a slit in the floor and shoved it forward. The locomotive strained ahead, tilting to the left when it reached the first turn.

Consider the following narrative statement, which is static, no action:

> Janie adored animals. She went to the shelter and adopted a dog named Firefly that she loved at first sight.

Now the same information developed in-scene with action:

> Janie opened the steel door to the animal shelter on First Street. No one was behind the wooden table that served as a reception barrier. She walked back thorough a doorless opening into the converted two-car garage. She stopped. Stacked cages lined each side of the passage. She held her breath at the foul smell. Barks and meows filled the air and she squeezed her eyes shut for a moment. She walked forward until she saw a white dog on its haunches, quiet except for a tail slowly moving back and forth stirring up the sawdust on the cage floor. Its eyes looked unfalteringly at her. On the cage door was a tag that read "Firefly. 6/14."
> In the back driveway an attendant was hosing down cages.
> "That dog, Firefly. I want to adopt him."
> "Sorry, I think he's spoken for."

In-scene action requires more reader time than narrative telling. And because it takes up precious storytelling time, it must have a legitimate purpose, must energize the story. Does it develop the character? Does it enhance motivation? Does it contribute to physical movement through story time that is directly plot related? Does it allow imagery and setting to be established subtly, without cumbersome self-importance? Does it contribute to voice? Is it related to theme and meaning? If action doesn't do a lot, then a short narrative bridge may be better.

Avoid Backstory

Backstory (anything that happened before story's ostensible start) necessarily affects, and often halts, story-present momentum. The basic rule? Backstory must advance front story. Ask yourself: Does this backstory provide needed characterization, add necessary exposition, explain motivation, help move the plot, clarify motive for plot action? There is almost always a more effective way to inform the reader than backstory.

Another problem with backstory is the awkwardness of in-scene development at a time other than story present. Most backstory involves narrative description of the past, excessive amounts of which kill the overall movement in an otherwise well-written literary story.

Make Dialogue Active

Dialogue needs action. This is accomplished primarily by word-choice and ideation. Avoid directly answering questions in dialogue. Consider the following:

"Is that a bear?" Joe asked.
"Where?" Sam said.
"Over there."
"Damn. I think it is a bear."
"What are we going to do?"
"I don't know."

Versus:

The bear reared back on its hind legs, roaring.
"Don't move!" exclaimed Joe.
"I'm going to throw up." Sam moaned.
"He's seen us."
"I dropped my rifle."
"Start making noise. Maybe we can scare him."

First-Person Point of View in the Literary Story
by William H. Coles

Purpose: to explore character development when using 1st person point of view in literary storytelling.

Most fiction writers are successful without exploring the intricacies of 1st person point of view. But to achieve high-character development for the great story that has character-based plot, authors improve their writing by understanding how characters affect readers, and then employ the effects through controlled story writing.

Terminology
point of view = point of view.
1st person refers to "I" pronoun usage in a prose story, but the "I" character may not be the protagonist or even a major character.

I. Mastering 1st person point of view

For great stories, authors must choose points of view for the right reasons. In 1st person point of view unique advantages and disadvantages that will vary in importance according to story structure and content. Of course, abilities of the author are always in play.

Advantages
* In narrative telling of the story to the reader, 1st person point of view allows the sense of having been there (or being there in the present tense), and a memoir quality of telling my story as the straight-scoop to you the reader. There is a psychic and physical closeness to the action that provokes an intimacy.

* 1st person point of view gives the reader constant characterization -- that is the thoughts and actions of the "I" character. All other characters, even if the protagonist is not the "I" character, are secondary because of limited access to their thoughts and actions. This consistent access to one character's opinions

and attitudes often strengthens voice and allows easier access to sarcasm, cynicism, and injection of surprise-humor.

* The 1st person point of view flows more easily into an intuitive writing style, giving an author a certain freedom from the necessity of structure.

Disadvantages
* In 1st person, the acceptance of a character's dialog changes. In 1st person point-of-view dialog, the reader knows that all characters' dialogs other than the 1st person are actually being presented, and might be altered in tone and credibility, by the 1st person. Some themes and meanings require reliability on the integrity of character dialog to reach meaningful impact on the reader. A 1st person character who is unreliable tends to confuse the reader as to what and who to believe in a story. In character-based fiction, this may work against significance and the perfection of the story.

Example.
We were standing at the edge of the thousand-foot drop on Mount Hood. Carol shivered and looked away from me.
"I'd like to shove your ass into eternity," she said. I smiled.
"I'm not joking," she said.

In the 1st person point of view presentation, we do not know what Carol really said, or meant, in the story world; we know only what the 1st person point of view told us she said. But in third person presentation, through a narrator or a character, the reader may interpret Carol's words differently, and with an interpretation specific to each reader that will affect the story differently.

At the precipice, Paul looked down the thousand-foot drop to the snow-covered rocks below.
Carol stared at the side of his head, her fists clenched.
"I'd like to shove your ass into eternity," she said. He expected warmth, but her gaze made him unsure what to think.
He smiled.
"I'm not joking," she said. The arrogant bastard. She knew exactly what she had to do.

There are many ways to structure this mini-scene, but the examples show how Carol's words can be interpreted and accepted differently in different points of view. At times, a scene can be given more impact by not filtering all information through the single conduit of the "I" character.

* The 1st-person point of view limits knowing what other characters feel and think -- characters who may have a more informed view of the story world and may be better sources of significant conflict, emotion, and action.
* Because of limitation mainly to the mind of the "I" character, the reader has no comparative gauge to test credibility of the "I" character's view of the world, accuracy of story presentation, or validity of opinions and conclusions. Credibility in storytelling is a fragile, at times abstract, phenomenon that, when highly developed, may allow significant impact of story meaning. But when lack of credibility in character, plot, and/or story world perceptions is present in excess, the chances for a significant effect of great story purpose are often lost.
* In "I" character, when the character is in-scene and distant from the action, easy access to credible and accurate information is lost.

II. Using 1st person point of view

How comfy the use of a single character in the 1st person point of view (or first person point of view with narrator function) is for an author. How easy the telling is.

> "I was sitting at this gay bar studded with full-sized Michelangelo statues of David at each end, and this girl couple walks in, one ugly, but the other so gorgeous she made my heart throb. In a split second, I was falling in love with a dyke, and I hadn't even thrown back a gulp of my straight up Port Ellen."

The mood is chatty with attitude, a story that will be interpreted entirely through a character who provides the reader with only his/her opinions, thoughts and abilities to observe and articulate the story. The character is inherently unreliable by the nature of the 1st person POINT OF VIEW -- can any individual really know and interpret the real truths that exist around him or her? And this story type will often rely on the ironies created by the differences the "I" persona perceives in his/her world.

There are many flexible approaches to the use of "I" character. This story could be altered to more in-scene, less subjective (ugly, gorgeous, love are each subjective opinions) delivery, which will result in seemingly more objective story information and often a change of attitude.

> "My heart pounded when I saw a five-foot-two blond with her girlfriend. She walked with a confident stride, her short shorts creasing the flesh of her thigh with every step. She smiled and looked away. I gulped my scotch and wondered if she could switch-hit the way I was imagining."

Moving into the objective scene telling, rather than relying on subjective narrative telling, sets a little different tone and is more action oriented.

Now compare a delivery from 3rd person point of view (multicharacter plus narrator but not "omniscient").

"Jared sat on a red Naugahyde barstool with his foot on a brass rail, close enough to touch the life-sized statue of Michelangelo's David that stood at bar's end as decoration. He'd wanted Johnny Walker Black, but the bartender had quotas to meet by serving the most expensive drink possible, and Jared had wound up with Port Ellen scotch that didn't do much for his sour mood. When Doris entered with Camille, their arms linked to express their attachment, Jared's gaze turned to her, and she smiled, not sure if he realized that the obvious desire he couldn't hide would never be satisfied."

Note how information is presented with possible consciousness of multiple characters and the narrator.

narrator or protagonist providing information (point of view)

protagonist (character) information (point of view)

minor narrator information (? point of view)

Doris's, and possibly Camille's too, information (point of view)

> "Jared sat on a red Naugahyde barstool with his foot on a brass rail, close enough to touch the life-sized replica of Michelangelo's David that stood at bar's end as decoration. *He'd wanted Johnny Walker Black, but the* bartender had quotas to meet by serving the most expensive drink possible, **and Jared had wound up with Port Ellen scotch** *that didn't do much for his sour mood.* When Doris entered with Camille, their arms linked *to express their attachment,* Jared's gaze turned to her, and she smiled, *not sure if he realized that the obvious desire he couldn't hide would never be satisfied.*"

Skeptics can reasonably argue that these complexities of point of view are artificially created with various interpretations and that authors should do what feels right and is effective for their purpose in their writing. That is the essence of style, one might point out. Yet, in literary fiction, an author is trying to intensely engage the reader and provide lasting and significant insight for the reader with ideas never before considered. For success, expert characterization and a character-driven plot are necessary, and the more control the author has of the writing, and the storytelling, the better chance for creating a lasting, enjoyable, significant story. Understanding point of view clearly and knowing the potential of efficient point of view usage, helps authors write their best stories.

III. Distance in 1st person point of view: psychic and physical

1) Psychic distance vaguely means how important the character's emotions are in driving plot progression. 1st-person character limited psychic distance in a scene restricts emotional developments in a scene. When action is character-based, in third person, multiple emotional-based actions of different characters may enhance scene effect. When story presentation allows multiple-character psychic-distance with varying action involvement, aspects of reasonable and objective information about characters, plot, and meaning may be more significant. As a result, the core purpose of a scene is often better achieved by varying psychic distance with multiple characters.

2) Physical distance is the distance the character is from the action. It is external for the character. Physical distance allows more expansive imagery and broader interpretations. Different possibilities exist between a 1st person point of view plunging to almost certain death in seat number 24C in an airplane while telling or in-scene showing the predeath moment and a narrator who describes (even in-scene) after the fact the same disaster by telling or showing the character from a later point in time than depicted in the story, and being able to imagine, and feel, from yards, or miles, or eons away from the action. More objectivity becomes possible, albeit with a loss of immediacy.

IV. Awkward Constructions in 1st person--a summary.

The effects of 1st person point of view in storytelling are distinctly different and somewhat more restrictive than other narrative techniques, and 1st person point of view is often chosen by beginning writers because the style is intuitively easier to write. Also, as previously mentioned, there is an immediacy and intensity effect, a sort of whisper-in-our-ear phenomenon that provides an intimacy between narrator and reader. Problems do exist, however. The 1st person point of view has difficulty expressing the feelings of others and relating action that is necessary for story when the 1st person cannot be interpreted as reasonably privy to the information or is not present at the event. These problems may make for awkward prose.

Examples: awkward constructions in 1st person.
   1) From the fire in her eyes, I knew exactly how she felt—enraged and hurt, and probably a little embarrassed, too.

Comment: Is there a different effect of the same information presented in 3rd point of view? *She felt engaged and hurt and the fire in her eyes* disturbed *me*.

   2) In the dressing room, I knew the Hardrocks were tuning-up on stage, their grimy hands turning the geared pegs, the strings whining with tension.

Comment: The first person imagines a scene outside his or her physical in-story perceptive possibilities. They might hear the strings whining but can't see grimy hands turning pegs. Here are possibilities for credibility acceptance, the first in 1st person, the second in 3rd person. a) *I opened the dressing-room door a crack and there were the Hardrocks tuning up on stage, grimy hands turning geared pegs, strings whining with tension.* b) *The* Hardrocks *tuned up on stage, grimy hands turned geared pegs, the dysfunctional whine of too-tight strings drifting into the dressing room.*

V. Feelings
Great stories enlighten or reverse thinking about something and have theme and purpose. To reach maximum potential, great stories must be structured for purposeful delivery through dramatic events and have clear understanding about how the story is narrated -- with elements of narrator reliability, clear moral thermometer-readings, and logical motivation reasonably tied to all other action and motivations in the story -- and, probably most important, dedication to story purpose rather than author-performance.

Writing in 1st person point of view makes delivery of story easier—there are certain shared attitudes with the reader that can easily bring a sympathetic response -- and it is easier to tell feelings of love and hate and jealousy than to show them through action that never uses an abstract word such as "love" or "anger" to describe the emotion. In general, action with conflict and resolution usually in-scene objectively presented is more effective for creating memorable emotions in the reader than 1st person describing events and personal feelings where feelings of other characters cannot be credibly be delivered by the limited 1st person point of view.

A 1st person character *telling* feelings does not have the same impact on readers as *showing* how feelings are experienced and how in-scene action with multiple points of view reveals credible story-related feelings to a reader.

1st person may seduce an author into making intuitive decisions about the story structure and narration that may not be the most appropriate choices for the best story and the management of emotional responses.

VI. Narrator and "I" character

Most writers just do a 1st person point of view conceptualization of 1st person. But "I" delivery of story information needs more thought than just doing. Consideration of a narrator function should be considered. One problem is all pervasive in "I" delivery -- point of view is often imagined by the writer as knowing something, with all its limitations, as one of the five senses. Thoughts and feelings are restricted in the 1st person and take on added subjectivity, possible unreliability, and may elucidate character more than propel story.

In storytelling, an author creates, a narrator tells, and a character acts. It is usually more prudent not to alter this in 1st person by collapsing the author into the character to narrate the story. All stories have narrative information that may be awkward or unbelievable when delivered by a 1st person character. And for great stories, the narrator also has to be more knowledgeable about the story world than the character, even in 1st person point of view. This is one essential ingredient for useful ironies. Narrators provide crucial and, for best effect, truthful information and are necessary in almost every story. Many 1st person stories simply use the 1st point of view to surreptitiously provide narrator information, but this can lead to disbelief and mistrust of the character that in turn leads to a feeling of artificiality in the storytelling.

Authors can't resist, at times, interjection of opinions and attitudes from the author's sensitivities from her-or-his real world into the story world. It can be as subtle as a single disruptive adverb or adjective or the use of disjointed phrases, clauses and sentences.

Examples.
> She was killing him. He would have no water, and he would die of thirst. The idea pleased her. She held a glass before him and tipped it so water flowed onto the floor, ignoring the drought that had raged in the city from effects of global warning.

Note how extraneous thoughts, no matter how important to the real world, can push the reader away from the story.

> Numb with cold, I watched the insecure skier start into the turn, his mental fear freezing his responses to create disaster.

The adjectives "insecure" and "mental fear" are questionably knowable by a first-person narrator in scene, and for an instant, change the point of view to the skier. Different construction needed if the skier's insecurity and fear are to be addressed and are essential to scene interpretation and character building (through images, speculation, or action are possibilities).

In general, narrators should be more objective and reliable than characters, so in 1st-person a "narrator-presence" to provide information the first-person cannot know may be needed to establish objectivity and reliability that is important for clarity and story purpose.

When an author becomes narrator, there tends to be a blurring, or confusion, of the telling time. In storytelling, the real-time creation and the narrator time of telling can effectively be different, and these may be different from story-action time. This may allow irony and justify cynicism. An author writing in March of 2008 may do well having a narrator, even in 1st person, tell the story from the time of 1875 about a character acting the story out as a 1st person point of view in 1862. The differences, however, need not be years, but may be weeks, or days, or fractions of an hour.

Examples of a 1st person scene with different aspects of points of view

1. The first-person telling as narrator and first-person point of view.

> There was no doubt the ship was sinking. The captain sat alone, stone-faced in his cabin, an illustrious career turned infamous in minutes. In the radio room, the operator had twisted the knob off the now silent radio and laid his head on his arms. Below deck, the engineer failed to seal a compartment door, and a rush of water banged his head on a girder causing him to lose consciousness before he drowned. (narrator information)
>
> I watched as the lifeboat hit the water and rocked violently for a few seconds. Someone pushed me from behind. "Dear, God," I said. I jumped and felt my lower leg crack as I hit one of the wooden seats that broke my fall. "Move out of the way," someone said kicking me in the ribs. (back to 1st person information)

Many readers (and writing instructors) would not accept this construction as allowable in 1st person. A narrator provides information that the 1st person point of view character cannot know at the time although he, or she, delivers this specific information. For many readers who find pleasure in serving as point of view police, any deviation from a 1st person point of view is an error, or at least a slippage in writing skills. Engaging a reader in a scene may be hindered when using narrator-function in first person when the "I" person is in scene and couldn't know the information delivered.

Here is what might be suggested, or required, in revision.

2. In this example, dialogue is used to deliver story information that can still preserve the 1st person point of view.

    We were crowded near the railing on the port side, the deck slanting twenty degrees.
    "The Captain's taken to his cabin. He ain't seeing no visitors," a man said.
    "Career ruined," a sailor said.
    "A dead man," said another.
    "The radio's out."
    "Engine room flooded a few minutes ago. I saw the engineer floating face down with my own eyes."
    Someone pushed me from behind. I looked down to the lifeboat as it hit the water and rocked. A deck officer shoved me. Three of us fell at the same time. My leg cracked as I hit the edge of a wooden seat. Pain seared upward. Someone kicked me in the ribs.
    "Get out of the way," he said.

For many, this attempt to provide, through dialogue, the story information wanted is awkward. It rings with a lack of credibility and artificiality and therefore makes the scene seem less real and harder to accept and enjoy. A major distraction is that the dialogue is delivered as the speakers are facing death, and it has a barroom chatty tone (due to exposition mistakenly filtered through dialogue).

3. The information might be provided through internal reflection.

    I imagined the Captain alone in his cabin, a man with a stellar career ruined. I doubted the distress signals were going out anymore. In fact, the bridge had become silent and eerie among the yells and shouts on the deck. A man said the forward compartment had flooded, he thought he heard the cries of the engineer who suddenly became silent. The lifeboat dropped, the winch handle spinning to a blur. Someone pushed me and I fell, hitting the gunnels. My leg cracked and a searing pain shot upward in me. Someone kicked me in the ribs to move me out of the way to clear space for others to fall.

But this seems awkward, too.

4. This is another try with a much more internal approach.
With the deck slanting, I could not stand without gripping a rope or a metal ring fixed to flooring. My fall had broken my leg above the knee; pain seared through me with every movement. But I held on, waiting for the cries to signal when a rescue boat might be below. I was close enough to the rail to be in the crowd who would jump to the twenty feet or so below the slanting deck.

"I can't jump," a woman whispered to me, sobbing, clutching my leg to keep from slipping violently into the rail. I yelled out in pain. Was she an evil woman? Did she deserve to die? There was no time to lower her into a boat securely and safely. She'd have to jump. She'd have to be forced. Was there someone to do it? Even with my leg whole, I could never shove a woman, or any human, to possible death. She had to make that decision, not me.

"Do you have family?" I asked. That brought more sobs and she did not answer. The ship's horn blasted. The passengers panicked and began to jump. A few hit the boat, but most went into the water, looking for something to cling to--a deck chair, an oar, some piece of ocean debris. They'd all be unconscious in two to three minutes, motionless with the cold, clumped with broken ice. I began to pray.

There is no right way. And when solutions don't readily come up in 1st person, 3rd person or narrator presentations might be considered. But to change a point of view is a drastic undertaking, and an even more crucial question might be asked: Are the information and the scene necessary? Is it time to delete this scene?

Most authors don't consider alternatives for delivering narrator-based information, in a first-person point-of-view delivered story. They go with the gut feeling of what works and that usually results in the author and character being inseparable. And many of these authors are successful and accepted by readers and have no need to change if they are satisfied with their work. But ignoring narrator function is not the right attitude for creating the great story. *Don't let the ease of writing* fictional *memoir in 1st person--without narrator function considered--hamper the potential of a story.*

Present tense and 1st person point of view
In any presentation (point of view), a story is told from a time point related to the existence of the author and the reader. This can be thought of the period in which the story is set. Many writers create the "I" story as if it is occurring in the time of the writing. But "I" stories often have two "I's," the older "I" who is telling the story as a time-distant narrator, and the younger in-story-time "I". The two can be significantly different in looks, experience, attitudes and beliefs, and authors using the first-person should be clear as to which "I" is telling the story; both "Is" are really speaking from world views and separate times of existence in reality. The author needs to be sure the reader will understand which "I" is telling the story in any specific story time for clarity and credibility, the older or the younger.

In truth, all stories have happened. Even futuristic stories have happened in the creator's mind and are being told as if having occurred. No one reading a story actually lives the story, of course, either at the time the story is created or the time the story is supposed to happen. At times, present tense is used to create a sense that the story is happening now. This is a deception—an often acceptable and effective deception--but still not a reality. Verbs indicating present action require suspension of disbelief that the story is happening now. Again, all stories have happened. This deception, and the need to accept the deception, can complicate effective in-depth characterization and confuse backstory and front story.

The pleasing effects of 1st person immediacy and strong voice may become tiresome at times and adding the inherent deception of present tense may work against reader enjoyment. Still, both present tense and 1st person serve important roles in every writer's choices for best story presentation.

Top Story / Bottom Story
by William H. Coles

Story, by a more traditional and limited definition, is a series of imagined related scenes with conflict and action while developing meaning and enlightenment for characters and unique enjoyment for readers. Writers can improve their writing of stories by thinking of two (or more) stories—top story / bottom story—interacting to provide action and meaning that blend with synergy into one. Most effective stories have the action and plot in top story and the lyrical prose with emotional and intellectual enlightenment in bottom stories.

The traditional story has become less common as the array of prose forms published as fiction story is increasing: tone-based lyrical prose, memoir-based descriptions of enjoyable events and experienced emotions, character sketches, and a boxed version of loosely related, overly clever ideas. Many of these non-story forms do not provide the pleasure for readers who seek the traditional story. Regrettably, writers have few resources to learn effective storytelling with imaginative prose that results in literary stories.

Two essentials of a good story are imaginative structure and dramatic prose. Effective drama in the written story requires an overall plan as to the form so that what is written on the page supports the drama and theme. Great stories are not simply disseminations of previously withheld information. Good storytelling is not scratching a lottery ticket to discover the winning number, or digging deep in the dry earth to find a dinosaur femur, or progressively filling in the boxes of a crossword puzzle. Drama is humans in conflict acting to resolve their problems in meaningful and enlightening ways. Literary stories supply information as the plot requires. They avoid suspenseful manipulation of the reader, and as a result maintain credibility that intensifies meaning. (In contrast, genre stories follow a familiar plot structure, with deliberate suspense followed by relief: murder, investigation, discovery of murderer.) Literary stories are harder to construct, have dramatic action and character desires and motives feeding an escalating momentum, and require careful conceptualization before writing. One way to create a story is to conceive it as two stories that are seemingly one, a top story and a bottom story.

As an example, consider a possible top story:

> John loves his fiancée. John's brother seduces the fiancée. John kills his brother. John is convicted and jailed. The fiancée marries someone else.

Developing a bottom story will give nuance to the top story:

> The fiancée really loves John but has a personality that can't turn anyone down because she can't stand the thought that someone might not like her. John loves her unconditionally and can't face the reality of her vacuous personality. Jealousy consumes John's brother takes advantage of her weakness. John's anger turns to hate; John is shocked at his own lack of remorse after he kills his brother; the murder was intense and felt like vengeance for childhood wrongs the brother inflicted. His brother's lust and his wife's infidelity don't seem to justify murder. He laments his action and grieves the loss of his brother.

The diagram below helps visualize the action of top versus bottom story. The top story (solid line) reaches a climactic plot point and the action declines. At the same time, bottom story (dotted line) becomes more intense and rises, crossing the declining top story and now becoming the top story, revealing theme and meaning (or epiphany) based on character enlightenment.

The possibilities are endless, of course, but a successful top story tends to be an active presentation of a series of conflicting events that resolve in interesting and satisfactory ways. It is plot oriented, and often in-scene. The prose tends to be succinct, action oriented, void of passivity, and strongly attached to conflict and action. The prose advances plot and supports logic, and depends on suspense regarding what will happen as circumstances dictate.

Prose action without bottom story may lose reader engagement in character, decrease caring about character outcome and erase theme and meaning. Bottom story tends to deal with conflicting emotions, and poses thoughts about who we are and why we are here, so that theme and meaning take on significance for the reader seeking knowledge about the human condition. Bottom stories tend to be character based. They are more emotional, emphasizing core desires and justifying feelings. The prose may be lyrical (even with elements of poetry) with in-scene action relating more to emotional conflicts and reversals of thinking (enlightenment). The prose clarifies and justifies character change. It may be internal reflection. And it tends to present plot information when needed, creating suspense not through information manipulation but by dramatic irony and concern for characters' problem solving and action that results in change. Authors should remain alert for moments when the bottom story becomes static and boring, or dissolves into narrative description (telling). Authors love to write in bottom story and tend to express in it personal, rather than story-oriented, thoughts and feelings, which may take over with baroque intensity, hurting the story.

Thinking about top and bottom story enables focus on different modes of reader engagement early in the story. Top story lends itself to objective ways of engaging the reader: hero, trickster, imminent danger, and barely surmountable obstacles are all characteristics that are plot oriented. Bottom story allows more subjective engagement of readers in character, for instance through injustice, false accusation, shared (or at least accepted) motivations with character, and common morality. As a story develops, there is a plot-oriented, action-motivated series of events that embody conflict, action, and resolution, structured for reader engagement with the characters and their concerns.

The actual elements of top story and bottom story may be mixed in the final story product. The advantages of thinking with two different stories that are nevertheless incorporated in the unified final achievement ensures action and meaning, and builds significance while suppressing the tendency for trivial writing.

The origin of "top/bottom story" is not definitively known. Reviews use the terminology, often to criticize literary fiction lacking sufficient plot, as in, "This has no top story." Top and bottom story, although they might not be explicitly labeled as such, also come up in the context of converting a fiction story into a screenplay, for instance when the bottom story in the written version is sacrificed for the sake of focus on the top story, even when the bottom story is strong and gives nuance to the whole.

Even authors who concede that top story and bottom story thinking has some value may reject the concept as too structured or too contrived—a siphon for creativity: "I love to put my character in action and see where the character goes." These authors believe in making creative decisions moment to moment and happily line up random details like mismatched pearls on a strand. But attention to structure may allow for a more expanded, intricate, and effective deployment of creativity.

Decide on a structure (even though it frequently will change) and make your creative decisions before you start writing. With a little practice, anyone can begin to discern top and bottom story at work in many great stories. Knowing what makes a story work increases story understanding and significance.

Strong Voice and Attention to Time
by William H. Coles

A literary fictional story is: *a magical perception—an engaging illusion—that is an unbroken continuum delivered through prose that—by a meaningful, interesting series of events involving characters that a reader comes to know and care about—creates emotion and enlightenment or permanent change in the reader's thinking.*

No other storytelling medium comes even close to what prose fiction can accomplish for a select group of readers, and no other medium of expression is as hard to master and as hard to use successfully as prose.

For a writer, an essential skill is control of the story timeline that allows clarity of writing, consistency of voice, and logic and credibility of the story illusion.

Real Time versus Story Time
Real time is what every human lives. It is a human invention, not necessarily a divine truth. Humans live and die. Living takes so many minutes and is defined by humanity's perception of the physical world. Who knows if outside human meaning, collective consciousness, and experience, time has any meaning? Writers, who create in real time, must adjust story conceptualization to create a credible story in illusion, where time is compressed. Real time is how we orient our existence. Story time is constricted time, structured and paced to make the read story seem real.

Story time
Story time is also the time a reader spends with the story from beginning to end (interruptions in the actual reading not included). Story time can be a few minutes, many hours, or days. It requires well-executed transitions, careful attention to narration, and exclusion of opinions, facts, and language not true to the story world. Lack of attention to time differences between real time and story time can cause reader confusion, even rejection of the story.

It is not easy for authors to write about real time in constricted story time. Stories take place in the past, and by necessity they are condensed so we can read them in a minute fraction of the (fictional) time described. Writers have various techniques at hand to orient the reader: transitions, flashbacks for backstory, writing in-scene, moving characters in seconds of story time through action that would take hours or days of real time, and careful adjustment of pacing (of both action and the prose itself).

Importance of adhering to timeline
All this has meaning when it comes to storytelling with the written word. When we write, we must construct a story, then recreate the story through the abstraction of prose. A story with an accurate story timeline (being sure to avoid discrepancies such as a character aging twenty years but the prose plot indicating it happens in six months); feels credible and engaging; provides an in-depth immersion in the story, which is denser and more rewarding for the reader; and heightens discovery of significant facts about how a human life can be better lived. Laudable story presentation in prose is most often associated with clear management of time and unbroken story illusions. Pacing, transitions, and consistency in condensation of different story time segments are all dependent on the writer/creator's skillful timeline transference to a reader.

Story writers create an imagined world and a series of events in the mind of a reader without direct visual or auditory sensations. Readers must convey, from abstract letters on a page images, feelings and complex thoughts. A writer's skill is dependent entirely on the interpretation of language delivered. Literary fiction prose stories succeed if the they convey intact and credible (for the story world) illusion and if they are meaningful, progress smoothly, and seem to be lived (or that they could have been lived). The reader must understand and accept the illusion as it is presented (and the story takes on special impact); and the reader must subconsciously follow a progressive time line that is delivered in a minute fraction of real time, but gives the illusion that characters living the story would do in real time.

Transfer of an illusion of a story being lived is dependent on many techniques:
- Story told mainly in action scenes.
- Author always objective, accurate, and true to the story.
- Author maintains distinction between characters who live in the story present and narrators who tell stories from a world view different from story world.
- Author creates on the premise that every element of a story has story purpose.

Presentism

"Presentism" refers generally to ideas and perspectives from the present introduced into writing about or descriptions of the past; the concern here is about a distortion of truth about the reality of the past. Presentism is a subtler issue for the fiction writer than for, say, a professional historian, but it still can contribute to loss of effective story illusion and credibility.

All stories are written about the past—by anywhere from a few hours to the edge of eternity. As time progresses, the physical world changes, and a writer's interpretation of the world changes in perception, opinion, cultural characteristics, and linguistics. Writers—and the narrators they create—operate in a potentially very different world from the story world, and the story weakens when the present world of the writer (or narrator) seeps into the story world.

Time has a considerable effect on the voice in fiction. Voice is everything a character does, thinks (unique to prose), and says in a story. In any story, many voices may be present: characters, narrator, or (rarely) an author. Each voice is limited to characteristics consistent with the story world; in other words, a voice in a story cannot include features from what would be in the future of the story world. Presentism in this context is the insertion or assumption of information from outside the story's timeline into the story's timeline where it doesn't belong.

Presentism for the writer can result in loss of credibility and authenticity in voice and confuse the timeline of the story. Lest you think this is only important in historical fiction, it is also a crucial consideration for great literary fiction. Readers inherently know when voice errors disrupt a story, and will not like the writing. The reader may perceive the issue as stylistic when actually it stems from faulty conceptualization, construction, and adherence to the timeline.

The future does not yet exist, and the present becomes the past as soon as we live it. Therefore, the reader is always reading from a point which is the writer's future, of which the writer cannot know everything. This time that the reader has lived since the time of story creation is filled with change: people, the world, and the reader all have changed in perceptions, opinions, morality, linguistics, and perception of truth. Even though the reader's interpretation of a story inevitably will be subject to some presentism, the presentism should be minimized with story-time valid information on the story's timeline.

For a lasting story, one that will remain meaningful to future generations, effects of presentism must not decrease enjoyment or change the interpretation significantly. But can a writer possibly adjust for it by changing their writing habits? Probably not. All they can do is write with the greatest possible clarity of presentation and meaning, create strong, believable characters, honor the timeline of the story, seek effective transitions, minimize ineffective backstory, and most of all create effective time-consistent voices for the characters and narrator. The pitfalls of writing for a future reader generally relate to credibility, logic, appropriate morality interpretation, and acceptance and enjoyment of fictional voices.

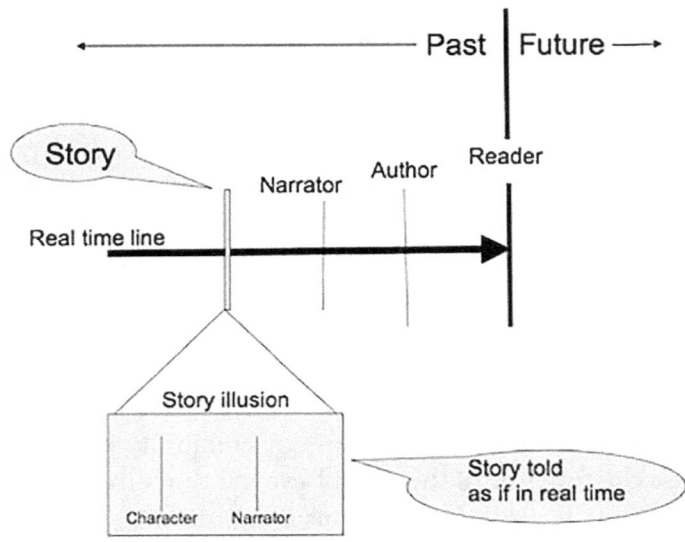

Presentism and Point of View
Think of a real-time timeline as a horizontal line. To the right place a vertical line, the reader line: all to the right is future, all to the left is what a reader knows and thinks from his or her past experience. To the left of the reader line, place another vertical line, which is the author line. The space between reader line and author line represents passage of time that is past for the reader and future for the author. The reader brings information to the story from this time, but the author can know nothing about it. This is the source of reader presentism.

Now next to the author line draw another vertical line, the narrator line. All the lived time to the right of the narrator line is not available to the narrator—only what is to the left. The narrator tells the story using only information important to the story that can be known from his or her position on the timeline. Note that the narrator (and the story) are imagined but represented on a real timeline. This can be the source of inappropriate real-time information being inserted into imagined story time.

Now, to the left of the narrator, draw a vertical line that represents the story. This may be so thin as to be invisible, because story time on a real timeline can be very short.

Note that characters give story information only within story, and speak with a unique voice from a time that precedes the position of the story on the real timeline. See how when narrators are chosen to be characters, the presentation requires skillful manipulation of time. If the narrator has been imagined to deliver the story from a different moment on the real time line from the author, and not within the story time, careful attention to information sources and voice is necessary.

In third-person point of view, these relationships among author, narrator, and characters should be established and consistent. This is essential for strong voice and effective character development, and for clear reader understanding regarding who is thinking what and when. In first-person point of view, a writer may intuitively collapse the narrator into the author. This can weaken the characterization and the credibility of the story. An author who maintains a concept of a narrator telling the story in first person often creates a stronger voice that filters out useful information for characterization and story momentum.

Not infrequently, writers make author, narrator, and character indistinguishable in the story. This is easier to write, and at first seems to have the advantage of dispensing with worries about time, because now the author is telling the story as a character in story time. But there are awkward complications. For instance, restriction of what information can be credibly presented from outside story time; difficulty in creating valuable ironies capable with fiction; reduced opportunities to vary a voice that may become boring; limitation of thought to primarily one character with danger of repetitive and boring writing style; tendency for subjective description from inside out, rather than objective revelation of motivations and desires of all characters; and in attention to character reliability, which is always in question in first-person point of view.

The story time line is an illusion. It is always condensed when compared to real time; otherwise the reader would perceive it as insufferably slow. Dialogue is likewise condensed. Dialogue should not be a transcription from life at the pace of life; it is best created for effect on the reader. (This is a large part of the reason why disguised memoir is never effective fiction. Many readers who enjoy the illusion of a great fiction story are soon discouraged by seemingly static, boring story lines described from reality.)

Voice must be consistent. Any hint of exposition, mainly by the narrative or the narrator, has no place. Dialogue should also have unique traits that support the voice being delivered—essential for credibility and voice strength. And probably most importantly, its pace must fit the story illusion of real time. Writers write from a real-world, real-time presence, whereas characters act in story time. All stories are illusions created by a writer through the written word. No story is perceived by a reader as it would play out in real time.

So every writer faces a significant dilemma. How, when all authors know is real-time existence, do they create stories that are condensed, compact, squeezed, compressed with respect to your own real time? Writers can only create from their perception of a changing reality. Opinions change, how they see objects changes, how they feel about things changes, ideation of imagery and persuasion changes, and language is constantly evolving. Relentlessly, the present becomes history.

When creation of a story illusion on a timeline uses different time-related thoughts to create the illusion of story that is always in the past, by either a few minutes or millennia, misrepresentation occurs. The story is like an illusory soap bubble, vulnerable to the slightest assault to its perfection—the smallest bump can destroy it. For the writer, errors in time, voice, logic, and credibility all destroy the illusory bubble that is a great fiction literary story.

Humor and Fiction
by William H. Coles

Humor, in the main, is pleasing, and thus it can contribute something beneficial to a literary fictional story. But definitions and generalizations about humor are hard to come by. What specifically amuses us? Who finds what funny? How exactly can literary fiction be enhanced in this respect? Whatever we might identify as humor is always dependent on various inciting conditions and receptive states that are likely constantly changing.

Consider humor on a spectrum, with one end presenting buffoonery, ridicule, slip-on-a-banana-peel sort of humor, whether visual or auditory, and on the other end humor based on ideas—perhaps incongruous ones, or involving a new awareness, or mutually understood and agreed-upon disparities. Irony operates on this more intellectual end of the spectrum, which represents arguably the most useful humor concept for writers of literary fiction.

A dominant characteristic of humor is surprise, which is entwined in expectations and misdirection. Closely related are comparisons—a subject of extensive academic literary analysis—that create incongruities and disparity from norms, and that are therefore unexpected and pleasurable to encounter.

Timing is a crucial element and authors must work with feeling of the right time for disparity and misdirection will produce the desired humor effect.

There are dangers of humor in fiction. Genre fiction writers can be comedic, but literary fiction using humor can seem forced and artificial if not done well. Humor that is not well thought out or reasonably incorporated can offend readers, even. Misconceived humor may ridicule and demean crucial characters, which in turn spoils a story's effect. In spite of the pitfalls, literary writers can learn to incorporate humor for better character development and enjoyment, without loss of credibility or strong sympathetic reader involvement. It takes practice, skill, talent, and much thought about story and story purpose.

Humor is a rich resource for writers. One's sense of humor changes as life progresses, and although any serious dissection of contemporary humor will soon enough be outdated, new humor elements constantly increase resources for a contemporary writer. Compare humor possibilities available to Mark Twain to those in the tool kit of the twenty-first century writer.

Story and character
In well-crafted fiction, a series of actions or events engage the reader and stimulate meaningful change in the characters, and this character enlightenment translates to enlightenment in the reader. Less effective fiction is done through telling or description of events via narration, which hobbles the creative imagination. But stories presented through action, and narrated with sophistication, lend themselves well to the intricacies of humor.

Humor defines us in more ways than we might think, and reveals more about us than we might realize, making it a useful author's tool. This is true with fictional characters, too. Important characters must be unique, credible, possess at least a touch of hero, and be capable of changing people and events—and capable of inner change. Characters cannot be cut off or inaccessibly boxed in the writing to the possibility of change. They must possess and effectively express emotion, action, thought. In literary fiction, the characters carry the story, and if they fail to engage the reader, the story fails. Three unavoidable elements in developing memorable characters are core desire, a morality weathervane whose position is always known by the reader, and humor.

Using humor elements
Successful humor in prose fiction can be embedded in the author's creative style, but this does not mean that others to whom it comes less naturally can't gain a thorough understanding of what humor can do for their writing. For instance, descriptive narration of a humorous event is almost always doomed to be less humorous than the experience of the event itself. We've all tried to describe to others a past event that made us laugh, failed, thrown up our hands in exasperation, and said, "You had to be there." As writers, we have to put our readers "there." Successful humor in prose comes when readers experience through the characters' actions.

A joke or a funny after-dinner story is rarely useful for the literary writer. Instead, understand the possibilities of humor and then incorporate them into your overall approach:

- surprise (something unexpected, often involving a shift in perspective)
- misdirection
- incongruous juxtaposition
- exact timing of inciting and responding
- ridicule (perhaps involving social nonconformities)
- a cognitive shift created by a discovery, or a solution to a puzzle or problem

Not everyone has the same sense of humor or capacity for humor. Humor is specific to each individual and depends on a host of variables: location, culture, maturity, education, intelligence, and other elements of context.

Irony

For the literary fiction writer, irony is the expression of meaning by saying the opposite, or some other incongruity, and can create a humorous effect. Literary analysis has developed various terms for the subtypes. *Verbal irony* is saying the opposite of what is meant. ("What a wonderful play!" when half the audience left before the end of the first act.) *Situational irony* is an outcome very different from what was expected. (A contractor builds a church that looks like a cow barn.) In *dramatic irony*, the reader or the narrator realizes implications of words or acts that the characters do not perceive. (Oedipus is unaware that he has killed his blood father and committed incest with his blood mother. So, when Oedipus tells his brother-in-law that only a fool can commit grave sins against family and expect mercy from the gods, both a reader—or audience—understand the implications of his words better than Oedipus does. Dramatic irony.)

Irony usually evolves as the story structure is formed, as the writer creates. Rarely if ever do preformed specific ironies structure the overall story, nor are they injected into a finished story like drugs into a vein. However, the kinds of ironies that drive *parody* and *satire* are often concretely formed before, or early in, the writing process. Satire, broadly, is the use of humor to characterize human stupidity or vices. Parody is an imitation of a writer's style with deliberate exaggeration for comic effect.

Summary

Humor pleases readers of literary fiction and develops characters into more memorable and useful entities. It offers specific advantages to writers learning to write prose fiction. It arouses interest in the story, sustains attention, helps the reader connect with the characters, emphasizes and relates ideas, creates images in reader's mind, makes the story more memorable, and makes readers feel good.

Emotional Complexity in Literary Fiction
by William H. Coles

Emotional complexity, beautifully rendered, demarcates literary fiction from most genre fiction. Of course, both forms employ characters, dramatic plots, tension, and even mystery. But a literary story's emotional tangles and reversals do more to elicit reader emotions. But emotional complexity must be earned. It must be credible to the reader, and logical for the character's complexities and for the story plot, and there must be elements of surprise without being unfaithful to the character's established mores, sensitivities, and beliefs.

Every character has some essential desire that drives his or her actions in a story. And once a character's desire is established, an oppositional force or character is introduced. The ensuing conflict leads to the character achieving satisfaction, accomplishing their desire. For example, if a character wants to believe God is love, the opposite might be, God is uncaring. If an essential desire for a character is self-adoration for his or her talent, the opposite might be fear of losing or not having the talent, or crippling shyness. These opposites develop an inner conflict that propels the character into action, and the emotions involved will be identifiable to the reader and establish strong character sympathy.

Emotional complexity
A character's desire stems from basic needs or wants. Needs come from inner turmoil with two or more competing sides: bad /good, hate/love, true/false, and so on. A character may act with overly friendly behavior, or sullen inaction from a painful sense of abandonment. If a character feels unjustly accused, it may be opposed by anger, or timidity, or spite. Seeking these emotional conflicts and interactions helps in developing characterization, story momentum, and reader interest.

Delivery of emotions in a story must be appropriately paced and have appropriate intensity. Much of this is instinctive for some authors, but when a story is not working, it may be helpful to analyze the rate of delivery of the emotional information.

Hyper-intense emotions narrow an author's options for characterization and plot development. A character in a murderous rage experiences narrowed thinking that may limit effective story and/or character development. Likewise, erotic intensity limits emotional and dramatic options for the writer. A character in a sexual situation is focused in all-consuming way, which limits authorial use of the other interesting and potentially essential conflicting actions that enhance characterization.

Emotion delivered through action
Emotions, as noted above, are most effective when presented through action, even though action takes more story time to express and is harder to write than narrative. It evades sentimentality, is more credible and significant, and more deeply engages the reader. Consider this small sentence:

> He loved Peggy.

"Love" is a general and abstract (as opposed to specific and concrete) term. We haven't learned anything specific from this about the man's love for Peggy. The narrator is telling, whereas the information would be more credibly established by showing in a longer, more concrete, in-scene passage:

> In the night, eyes closed but not yet sleeping, he conjured an image of Peggy. She haunted him with her mysterious smile and magnetic blue eyes, misty yet so distant. He knew to touch her would be impossible, but she would not fade away.

The practice of transferring emotions to the reader, as opposed to telling the reader about a character's emotions, is not so easy to explain. Compare "She was so sad," to "She wept, her body trembling." One is telling, one is showing. Or: "'Go jump in the lake,' he said angrily," to "He grabbed her by the ankles and held her over the cliff while she pleaded for mercy." Note how the second example uses action to indicate emotion rather than simply telling the reader how a character feels.

Internal reflection and backstory delivery
Love, hate, jealousy, and so on are abstractions—nonspecific words with multiple interpretations. For greatest impact, the writer must imagine concrete action scenes that convey emotion to the reader. Weaving emotions into one's characters is difficult, and in narrative prose, story can be disrupted by extraneous, non-story-related emotions:

> Jake put the 707 on autopilot and studied the radar screen. He would have to decide whether to bypass the storm or fly through it. He asked the copilot for further updates from ground control and looked into the night, remembering a storm at his aunt Bertha's house when he was twelve. A startling bolt of lightning had hit a tree that burned for hours and while the thunder pounded, Bertha held him close. He remembered the lavender scent of her perfume, the feel of her beating heart.
>
> Ground control reported two additional cells with high winds and advised diversion. But he couldn't be late on this leg again. He pressed on, instructing the passengers to prepare for a bumpy ride.

Here, moving into a character's consciousness (either in third person or first person) and the expository information or backstory is antithetical to good prose. In revision, ask yourself: What is the purpose of the passage? Are the emotions essential to this story, and, if so, is the intensity level appropriate? Can I more seamlessly insert information into dramatic action without backstory or internal musings?

Characters in literary fiction must experience complex change as they progress through the story arc. They can express sentiment but should not be sentimental, and they must operate logically given the story's plot and characterizations. Every great literary story depends on unique, emotional complexities.

Conflict in Literary Fiction
by William H. Coles

Conflict is the essence of drama, which all literary fiction requires. It provides the momentum of happening and change and is crucial on all levels for delivering information and building characterization. Conflict produces the changes in characters that engage a reader, and conflict and action do what description and telling of feelings and situations cannot.

The best storytellers have a knack for engaging the reader, for bringing them inside the skin of the story. They carry readers through via a succession of interrelated action scenes. But many contemporary authors seem to lack the ability or desire to do this. Their storytelling is fundamentally about "me"—my thoughts, my life, my accomplishments—sold under the guise of fiction. But for lasting success—a story that will persist into the future of great literature as an art form—authors should strive not for personal catharsis, but for an expression of story ideas with drama and conflict that they create for their characters.

In life, everything seems to move toward inertia. Throw a rock into the air and it falls to the ground, motionless. Pour water into a glass and it settles and becomes still. We are born, we live, but things tend always toward solitude and inaction, and of course we are all eventually motionless in death. Even fiction writers often succumb to this natural tendency and write stories that seemingly seek a state of inertia. This is especially the case when a story relies on narrative description of past events in place of dramatic action scenes. Inertia is avoided by in-scene, in-the-moment action. Writers must learn to instill conflict in in all aspects of their prose—conflict that presses on toward resolution . . . or perhaps no resolution after a struggle.

Write lively dialogue
Conflict in dialogue is essential. Even snippets of dialogue should have conflictual elements to interest a reader. Almost never is this type of interchange useful:

> "Do you plan to join the church?"
> "Yes, I think I will."

This is flat and uninteresting, and will disrupt the flow. , it must be revised or omitted. The information, if necessary, can be provided in a few words of narrative:

I decided to join the church.

In the examples below (overwritten for emphasis), note how conflict helps establish the emotion of the dramatic present and enhance characterization. It also allows, when appropriate to situation and character, a subtle layering of backstory information:

"Do you plan to join the church?" / "It's none of your damn business"

"Do you plan to join the church?" / "The church never did anything for me; why should I?"

"Do you plan to join the church?" / "Your piety irritates me."

"Do you plan to join the church?" / "Will you join too?"

Drama in storytelling.
In fiction, dramatic elements are necessary to move the reader sentence by sentence, idea by idea. And drama provides tension—conflict is established, and readers, especially if they sympathize with the characters (regardless of whether they *like* them, which can be a completely separate matter), become tense about what will happen. Withholding information to incite tension is not a useful strategy in literary fiction. In *genre* fiction, when the author and the narrator know who killed the parson, tension lies in the discovery process with respect to the murderer. It's mechanical, rote, and can easily come off as contrived for some readers. In *literary* fiction, characters and their decisions and foibles, not contrivance, drive the plot. All plot information essential to the story is delivered when needed, not withheld purely for tension. Now readers feel actually involved in what happens to a character they care about. And they will discover tension via a series of logically structured and logically interrelated scenes filled with conflict among the characters in language and syntax.

The beauty of language is enhanced when motion and conflict are incorporated in the prose to maintain a reader's interest, word by word. The reader's mind should be constantly active in creating and forming images. Authors who effectively create still-life images, one by one, are missing opportunities; they should

The ART of CREATING STORY

be intriguing and engaging the reader with scenes that live on the page. *There was a bird on a limb.* Static. *The flying bird settled on the limb.* Improved with some action. *The olive branch quivered when the claws of the sparrow grasped the sturdy twig.* A lot of energy.

Word Choice

Some nouns have life and motion; some not so much: Sparrow. Nail. *Butterfly. Comet. Ocean. Atom.* Building. Pebble. *Tadpole.* Vacuum. *Hurricane.* Skeleton. *Flame.* Puddle. Learn to discern between the animate or inanimate, the moving or motionless. Maintain awareness of the quality of the word in regard to movement. Drama is movement and change—and the conflict it implies. Description of animate things, rather than inanimate, is always better for story in literary fiction. Emphasize action over description and/or exposition.

Modifiers

Inanimate things on the page can lend themselves to burned-out effects. Ask yourself: With modification, could they now imply motion (and impending conflict)?

    hand / trembling hand
    knife / serrated knife
    car / race car
    gun / Gatling gun

Changing general terms to specific ones can likewise enhance action:

    soil / muck
    meteor / shooting star
    spice / cilantro
    horse / thoroughbred
    painting / hunting scene

Strive for motion when the story's pacing allows. "He sat in the chair," might be improved, if space permits, to "He put his hands back for support, bent his knees, and painfully lowered himself into the wheelchair," which conveys action, imagery, and information.

Syntax and conflict

Syntax (how ideas are delivered) can change the energy of a sentence, often by clarifying the conflict. How to deliver the basic message that Grandpa killed Granny?

> At the funeral, and for years after, grandfather never mentioned the day he hammered Granny into her grave.

The construction—past, distance, telling—conveys a fait accompli tone that might not be ideal.

> Grandfather killed our Granny.

A telling, rather than action. Consider:

> No one was witness to the deed. We had to imagine Grandfather standing over the bed and smashing our sleeping Granny's skull with a hammer.

Action is filtered through the character's imagination, but action and conflict are still present because of in-the-moment construction.

> Grandpa stared at the hammer as Granny's blood began to congeal into her hair and fragments of skull bone.

In-scene action with tension present (what happened? is she dead?).

> After he killed Granny with a hammer, Grandfather washed imagined blood off his hands every hour of the day until the skin was raw.

In-scene action, plus implied emotion of guilt; movement; and internal conflict revealed.

> We thought Grandfather an intelligent man, well educated, respected in the town, but we discovered his true self the night we discovered Granny murdered in her bed and Grandfather laughing hysterically a few feet away.

A telling, albeit with much information conveyed. The only action here is description of the past: Grandfather laughing. It is an unsuccessful sentence, its potential energy dissipated in great part by the complicated construction. Note also how rearranging the terms and phrases of a sentence changes its emphasis. In general, whatever noun-verb structure comes last in the sentence will have the strongest, most lasting effect. Note too that the more general the wording (as opposed to specific) and the more complicated the phrasing, the less the effect. Complex constructions lack the energy and impact of simple, terse ones, although all stories need a story-specific balance of both types.

An interesting story avoids over-matching of emotions. In a love story, the love interests are always unequal. One party is never sure if their feelings are reciprocated; or one is loaded with guilt from a previous affair. Out-of-sync emotions add dramatic energy to the writing, because of course conflict is drama. Keep emotions changing and flowing in nature and intensity, and always relate the emotion to the character's core need or desire. Consider these examples of internal conflict:

love / hate
sympathy / blame
fear / sentimentality
pliant / resistant
understanding / unyielding

Humor as source of change and conflict
All humor requires disparity, surprise, a change in perception that activates a humorous response. Humor can express conflict. Ridicule, a type of humor, is one example. Say, a woman sports commentator jokes on-air to an older colleague: "What was it like, Cliffy, when you played tennis . . . you know . . . in the age of the dinosaurs, when the technology couldn't give us the speed of the ball on serve?" Here the attempt at humor by ridiculing the age difference implies competitive conflict in the relationship. We infer that the woman commentator may be insecure, or actually mean-spirited.

Conflict and action are essential to literary fiction, and there are unlimited ways to discover the use of conflict and action to please readers through character development and reader engagement in the story. Persistent practice in writing dramatic prose is necessary throughout a writer's career.

What Exactly Is a Character-Based Plot?
by William H. Coles

Stories with significance have theme and meaning. A character-based story, where coincidental happenings and fatalistic plot progression is secondary to character strengths and weaknesses, is one way, if not the best way, to achieve this. Most writers are somewhat vague on the meaning of a character-based story. A genre writer, dependent as they are on plot twists and surprises that characters react to rather than effect, would readily believe a mystery, suspense, or thriller story, even a superhero story, qualifies as "character-based." Batman saved Gotham City. What can be more character-based than that, right? But "character-based" means something different in the context of a literary story's meaning, theme, and enlightenment. Here, the plot actions are driven, or at least affected, by the characters' human characteristics—their foibles, flaws, or special gifts. Of course, Batman is a good guy with special (superhuman) gifts. But his humanity has little to do with saving the city. It's more the case that evil threatens the city and he happens to be in the right place at the right time with the right skills to avert disaster. He is a creature of the plot rather than the plot's heartbeat.

Here is a story that has lasted for hundreds of years. It serves as an example of character-based story.

> Once upon a time, in a village near the deep dark woods, Little Red Riding Hood wishes to take Grandma, who is ill, a basket of goodies. Red will have to walk through the woods to get to Grandma's house, which is in another village. "Be careful," her mother says. "Go straight on the path and do not talk to strangers." Red enters the woods and on her journey leaves the path to chase butterflies, pick bluebells, and dip her toe in a cold, refreshing stream, ignoring her mother's warnings. She meets a wolf who wants to gobble her up but can't because there is a woodsman nearby. The wolf asks where she's going and whom she will visit. Red tells all. The wolf runs off to Grandma's house, imitates Red's voice to gain entrance, and devours Grandma. When Red gets to Grandma's house, the wolf has dressed in Grandma's nightclothes. He tells Red to enter. The wolf exposes himself little by little and climbs into

Grandma's bed. Red listens to his smooth talk and asks him about his big eyes, hairy arms, and big teeth. But still unsuspecting, she climbs into the bed and the wolf devours her.

What has held this story in the collective consciousness for centuries? Certainly it carries three significant messages: listen to and obey your parents; innocence and naïveté can lead to terrible harm; and don't trust a wolf in grandma's clothing. There is also the effective metaphor of the wolf for a child predator. But the story's staying power also has much to do with its structure. In this character-based story, the plot moves forward thanks to Red's human characteristics, especially her foibles: she holds onto her childhood innocence, and she disobeys her mother.

The same story could be framed as genre fiction and it would still be interesting, but likely not as timeless:

> Little Red Riding Hood is kidnapped from the woods near her house. A few hours later some bones and scraps of skin are found at her grandmother's house a mile away. The police are called and discover from the gray hairs trapped in grandma's hand-woven throw rug that the wolf did it. The wolf escapes (or not). Red's mother grieves.

This version is a statement of happenings. Red is part of the plot, but she is not driving the plot by disobeying her mother and wallowing in her innocence. The wolf metaphor is less effective when the story changes from fantasy to a more reality-based police procedural. Here is another genre framework, this time action-adventure:

> Red decides to go to Grandma's house for a visit. In the deep dark forest, she meets a woodsman, who is tracking a wolf that has eaten two children in recent weeks. Red wants to help find the culprit. The woodsman agrees and sends her out as a decoy. The wolf tries to attack Red, but she stabs him with a knife the woodsman gave her. The wolf runs away, but the woodsman follows the trail of blood and finds the wolf near Grandma's house. After a life-threatening duel, the wolf is killed. Red and the woodsman fall in love.

In this story, again, most of what happens in the plot is circumstantial. Red's character is not nearly such a motivator of the plot. What she says, thinks, or wants is largely irrelevant—the same story could be written with Pinocchio's sister as the major character.

Restructuring the story allows Red's decisions to drive the plot.

> Little Red Riding Hood's Grandma, who lives in another village, is very rich and plans to gift her a new dress, a box of Swiss chocolates, and bath oil at Red's birthday party the following week. But Red wants her presents now, even though her mother tells her to wait until her father can accompany her through the woods, which can be very dangerous. Red is impatient and goes anyway, meets the wolf in the forest, and is devoured.

Red is driving the plot again, this time with significant human motivations and a more meaningful moral takeaway: greed and impatience can be disastrous. There are two important points here for a writer seeking to create great literary fiction: structure the story to feature human motivations and failings through character-based plot and make the story significant. In Red's case, the significance is partially related to the dire consequences of getting eaten by a wolf after her seemingly almost innocuous actions.

Writing in Scene: A Staple for Reader Engagement in Fiction
by William H. Coles

The art of *in-scene writing* in fiction is critical for allowing a reader to enter the fictional story and vicariously participate in the story to discover meaning and pleasure. It is one on the main skills in creating great fiction, as opposed to memoir and creative nonfiction. *In-scene writing* is illusory and created by a process difficult to dissect. To start, *in-scene writing* is not narrative descriptive writing, although certainly scenes with timelines, beginnings, middles, and ends are often created in narrative description to great effect. But narrative description tends to static and tends to increase psychic and physical distance from the action in the scene. Not so in scene where the writer brings the reader in close to the action leaving space in the writing for the reader to imagine and participate.

FIFTEEN COMPETENCIES FOR CREATING IN-SCENE WRITING.

1. Direct viewing with feeling of action as if it is occurring "now" in story time.

Note differences in these two scenes.

> The apple fell from the lowest branch, landing in a muddy puddle too shallow to allow a splash.
> (A narrator, from a distance, relating happening.)

> The skin on his right hand blanched where he gripped the cold steel of the pistol, and his left hand, bloody from the knife cut, supported his right wrist but only slightly decreased the trembling.
> (A narrator through third person, bringing immediacy, action, and intimacy through the use of the senses of the character and "close up" imagery.)

2. Switching to present tense.

Switching tense has to be carefully considered; switching tenses can be disruptive and break a well-crafted fictional dream of the reader. However, in some circumstances, a switch to present tense from past tense can add immediacy and intimacy with the action in certain scenes and styles of writing–but not always!

Past tense.
He wiped the scalpel blade on a square piece of sterile gauze. Then he cut her open, the blade engulfed in skin and fat until the blood oozed.

Compare–

Present tense.
He wipes the scalpel blade on a square piece of sterile gauze. Then the blade cuts the skin to disappear into muscle and fat until the blood oozes.
[Note need for verb change, which demonstrates different construction sometimes needed for past and present tenses.]

The advantages of present tense over past, as is often true, are based on taste and context. Don't switch tenses when the there is minor or no improvement in the storytelling, or when the tense switch calls attention to itself. If it must used, it must be seamless.

Example of inappropriate use of a tense switch. Too abrupt and disrupts sequence.

He was called to the OR, the patient had a distended belly, and he scrubbed quickly. He wipes the scalpel blade on a square piece of sterile gauze. Then the blade cuts the skin to disappear into muscle and fat until the blood oozes.

3. Incorporating sensual detail and attributing to the specific character when appropriate, not to the narrator.

Narrator POV
She felt the touch of his fingers on her breast as he leaned over to kiss her ear.

Character POV
Her ear knew the abrasive feel of his dry cracked lips and her skin the exploration of her breast by his fingers seeking her always sensitive nipple waiting to be excited.
OR
My ear knew the abrasive feel of his dry cracked lips and his exploration of my breast by his fingers seeking my always sensitive nipple waiting to be excited.

The ART of CREATING STORY

4. **Use strong verb forms.**

    A) Avoid participles (often weakens effectiveness of action verb).

    He *believed* in her. (Stronger)

    He was always working at *believing* in her.

    B) Avoid past perfect constructions (except when needed for orientation on the story timeline). He traveled. NOT He had gone. OR He had traveled.

    C) Avoid passive constructions whenever possible EXCEPT where progressive tense can be used to advantage. *He was perfecting his technique by practice.* USUALLY PREFERABLE. *He perfected his technique by practice.*

5. **Use perfectly crafted dialogue appropriate for in scene.**

Example from classic literature
   "If I were in heaven, Nelly, I should be extremely miserable."
   "Because you are not fit to go there," I answered. "All sinners would be miserable in heaven."
   "But it is not for that. I dreamt once that I was there."
   "I tell you I won't harken to your dreams, Miss Catherine! I'll go to bed," I interrupted again.
   She laughed, and held me down; for I made a motion to leave my chair.
   "This is nothing," cried she: "I was only going to say that heaven did not seem to be my home; and I broke my heart with weeping to come back to earth; . . ."

Wuthering Heights
Emily Bronte

6. **Use pinpoint imagery.**

Pinpoint imagery expressed succinctly and with room for reader to create their own unique images is usually better that lengthy descriptions of a setting. It may be useful to think of pieces of a jigsaw puzzle. What are the fewest number of pieces that would suggest the whole of a puzzle? Each piece has to pinpoint the most revealing aspects of the whole. The feather of a bird, the foam and mist at the foot of a cascading waterfall, the windshield wiper of a car, etc., examples where a revealing bit may be better than a descriptive whole. This concept engages the reader whose imagination fills in the whole mentally with unique personalized imagery.

7. As an author, pay attention to the story timeline.

Backstory does not lend itself to in-scene writing. Backstory is in the past, before the story (or sometimes scene in a novel) timeline starts, and essentially loses any sense of immediacy. Write on the timeline in the logical position of story progression in the story present (not necessarily present tense). (Don't forget or confuse the timeline of the story, which in-scene writing must adhere to logically while satisfactorily sequencing story information for the reader.)

8. Consider judicious use of past and present <u>progressive tenses</u> for reader engagement.

Using present progressive.
He drives the car off the cliff. COMPARE He is driving the car off the cliff.

Using past progressive.
He ate his pancakes. COMPARE He was eating his pancakes before tasting the coffee.

9. Action and prose with momentum are essential to good in-scene writing.

Word choice

Look for different degrees of specific action in the following.

> ate–swallowed
> moved–walked
> understood–discovered
> told–described
> told–elaborated
> went–drove
> lay–reclined
> cooked–fried
> cooked–poached
> killed–bludgeoned to death
> began–ignited

Look for nouns that have energy. EXAMPLES: *low–high energy*

> rock–hawk
> telephone pole–computer
> road–river
> shadow–glitter

Concrete and abstract words have different effects on a reader. For action in-scene writing, concrete is almost always better. EXAMPLES: *concrete–abstract*

> tuberculosis–disease
> Joe–population
> Atlantic–sea
> March 22–future
> tarragon–spice
> violin–instrument
> G note–sound
> triplet–rhythm

10. Use proper constructions to make in-scene writing effective.

Authors write to be read; authors must avoid constructions or unclear associations that cause reading to be difficult, especially in in-scene writing.

Sentences. Chose best sentence types for the prose of the story-moment. Tight subject-verb, subject-verb-object sentences are concise and often serve well in in-scene writing.

Examples of compound sentences that are often needed for clarity and variation, but with caution in in-scene writing so as not to slow momentum in the writing:

Periodic sentence (subject and verb at end of compound sentence). "With his body trembling, his breath trapped in his lungs when he failed to breath, he jumped from the plane pulling the ripcord."

Loose sentence (subject and verb at the beginning of compound sentence). "He jumped from the plane pulling the ripcord with his body trembling, his breath trapped in his lungs when he forgot to breath."

The emphasis and effect are different in these sentences. Both are valuable when used in an appropriate, receptive, creative-writing context. Sentence length and sound, as well as structure, should also be varied with attention to rhythms and tensions of the story-moment.

11. Manage ideas effectively.

1. Don't present subordinate ideas when the relationship to the main idea is not clear. *He feared Jason, always believing that honesty is the best policy.*

2. Movement in images is a privilege fiction gives to authors. In writing, images are created in a reader's mind, which is active in forming the image. Basically, great authors don't create still lifes, they paint portraits that intrigue and engage the reader in scenes that live on the page.

—*There was a bird on a limb.* Static. *The flying bird settled on the limb.*

Improved with some action. *The olive branch quivered when the claws of the sparrow grasped the sturdy twig.* Lots of action.

3. Prose with momentum. Consider your preference in the following:

The locomotive with colorful cars behind followed the track that snaked through the valley.

Any motion perceived is really implied. Now with action:

—*The steam of the locomotive reddened the face of the engineer as he leaned out the window. The track curved many times ahead. He wondered, as the clouds gathered, if the printed banners with the czar's name flapping above the red, green and white decorations so carefully applied on the cars behind by the birthday celebrants, would be dampened, maybe even destroyed, by rain. He gripped the waist-high metal lever jutting up through a slit in the floor and shoved it forward. The locomotive strained ahead tilting to the left when it banked into the first turn.*

12. In fiction, and especially when writing in-scene, make antecedents clear.

Avoid constructions such as:

He would never use **that** to do **this** again.

Even if the context provides some clues as to meaning, these vague pronouns frustrate a reader. Here is a possible improvement:

John would never use a **spoon** to **dig a grave** again.

IN-SCENE WRITING REQUIRES CLARITY AND AUTHORIAL SKILL TO TRANSMIT IDEAS WITHOUT OBSCURE IMAGERY AND QUESTION-INDUCING SYNTAX.

13. Minimize narrator stage direction; let action set the stage, for best in-scene results.

EXAMPLES:

He went to the door and twisted the door handle.

COMPARE

The noise from his opening the door alerted the fugitive.

14. Balancing fictional style elements.

Consider carefully the length of in-scene writing to narrative description. Both techniques are usually necessary for a successful story, and the relative use of each will vary from story to story. In-scene cannot deliver all narrative can, and vice versa. Choose wisely for best development of your effective style. Think: what will it do for the reader you want to please?

15. Parting thought.

Genre writers depend on in-scene writing. Their readers expect to be engaged in the plot and characters' story world. In contrast, contemporary literary writers, especially academic fiction writers seem unwilling to master in-scene writing, or willfully ignore it. Could it be a sense of superiority in the belief that writing lyrical narrative description as fiction is more intellectual? Regardless of cause, readers deserve to be served the best writing and storytelling, whether genre or literary. And every story needs a carefully considered balance of fictional elements, in scene and narrative description being among the most important in any style of storytelling.

Creating Story World (Setting) in Literary Fiction
by William H. Coles

A literary fiction writer orients a reader as to where and when the action takes place by the setting (story world). Well-constructed purposeful settings evoke images, establish mood, and can supplement characters' motivations and feelings in the moment.

In essence, with the start of every new scene (if not carried over from previous scenes), the author establishes where, when, who, what, even in stream-of-consciousness or backstory reflection.

In great literary stories, something happens. Life is a progression of thoughts, heartbeats, and physical movement; stories progress through time and often move through locations. Characters pop in and out. In contrast, essays are static and memoir is life lived with no opportunities for an author to imaginatively create characters and what happens to those characters that live in stories. Imaginative creation of setting promotes story purpose, theme, meaning, and stimulates images, a sense of continuous action, and thought . . . and enhances storytelling.

TECHNIQUES
Attribution of dialogue to characters can provide well-paced and effective setting particulars:

DIALOGUE ATTRIBUTION EXAMPLES

1. "I won't do it," she said signaling the waiter for a check. (This attribution provides details in addition to who's speaking, both direct and subconscious information: in a restaurant, finished eating, speaker able to see (waiter), able to signal (not impaired), able to speak.)

2. "Let us all rise to the occasion," he said gripping the edges of the podium and sweeping his gaze deliberately over the audience. (Here images are stimulated in attribution—podium, gripping edges, sweep of gaze, the intensity of gaze—but also there is a sense of urgency added to the words actually spoken. But be cautious. Depending on the context before and after, this attribution might have too many redundant or unnecessary words. Attributions can be overdone so always weigh effectiveness, pace, and consistency with the prose style established.)

Settings differ with a point of view change of character or narrator. So, to be effective, in any scene in any story, a reader should be aware of the point of view and how that specific character perceives the story world from that point of view and, in addition, know a change in distance of the point of view or a passage of time.

EXAMPLE: time passage in narrative. "The ice cream melted." Using imagery and action can often be more effective than: "Three minutes passed." The idea is to signal passage of time and momentum with the stroke of a small detail.

In literature, story environment is transferred through language, not vision or hearing. Authors are not illustrators or actors; they create images with well-chosen words and imaginative diction. Imagine a scene as scattered pieces of a jigsaw puzzle. The writer stimulates an image with selected effective puzzle pieces. And many readers, from their own worldview and experience, fill in mentally with missing pieces to complete the scene. Fewer details are needed if individual pieces of the puzzle are maximally effective in stimulating reader to create the whole image. The "puzzle piece" is best when concrete (paper clip), not abstract (fastener). The word choice should be image-generating (cracked porcelain teacup, or, the blue and yellow scattered pieces of the shattered decorated Easter egg). Modifiers are usually more effective in setting when not judgmental (e.g. rather than huge, which is a judgement, better to say six feet tall for accuracy—but only if it fits). Avoid clichés. Use nouns and adjectives that evoke images in a few words—fifty-story skyscraper, not tall building. Once you instinctively incorporate the right pieces of the puzzle in mind, you can then deliver them seamlessly.

Brevity in-scene building is best. Long descriptive passages are for past generations. Find clever ways to use your puzzle pieces in dialogue attribution, internal reflections, narrative, back story. Be sure to use fresh and exciting image fragments, especially in narrative.

Principle 1 (occasional exceptions)
Keep your settings alive with momentum: whenever possible change

1) abstract to concrete images,
2) passive (and past perfect) to active constructions.

EXAMPLES:

Abstract
Passive/past constructions
The weather *was* unpleasant. It *was raining*. The gray sky reflected from the wet street surface. The side street *was rarely used* by automobiles and ice would soon form on the sidewalk and the metal lampposts with gas burners that *had to be lit* each evening by a bent old man who *had never failed* in his duty for decades.

REWRITTEN

Concrete
Active
The old lamplighter painfully climbed his step stool to hold his quivering flame to the cast-iron gas streetlamp. The light rain would turn to ice. Pedestrians might fall. Cars skid. But in forty-eight years of evening service to the City of Charleston, he never failed his daily duty to protect.

Principle 2
Avoid excessive description; it is almost always static.

Example A is static.
The small black bird with the brilliant red wings and inquisitive yellow eyes perched on the white picket fence just out of reach of the tabby colored cat with a scar on his leg and his one eye half-closed and scarred from some long-ago fight.

Example B is active.
The red winged blackbird glided in for a landing, and the battle-tested tabby cat leaped up, claws out, and caught only the edge of one of the bird's wings to scratch a brilliant red feather loose that floated down to the garden path as the bird safely landed on the fence a few feet away.

Bland adjectives and adverbs, or extended, vague metaphorical comparisons deaden desired effect; use action verbs and nouns that provoke images.

The predominate modes of writing literary fiction–diction, character, narration (point of view), plot, image–change with each specific story and writer. The predominant mode for a story may require adjustment of setting detail for best effect and an author will need to prioritize specific detail appropriately.

Here are EXAMPLES of setting with detail embedded in scene action.

> First, with ineffective subjective abstractions: The <u>place</u> was a <u>mess</u> and she was <u>cleaning up</u> with little enthusiasm and carelessly waved <u>things</u> around frustrated she had to do the <u>work</u>.

> Second, with more concrete, objective writing: A clutter of clothes on the floor and dirty dishes in the sink had to be cleaned up with her boyfriend Baylor coming to visit. She hated cleaning; she kicked scattered trash into a pile with little enthusiasm, frustrated by a forced sense to impress when she really thought Baylor was not worthy of her effort.

EXAMPLES OF SENSORY AND CONCRETE DETAIL IN DIFFERENT points of view.

Note (1) how details are used in the three different scenes below and (2) the use of sensory detail (hot, nude, stove, sink, blotch, etc.).

1. Dialogue predominating with enhanced setting.

> "You're pissing me off," I said looking at my watch. We couldn't make the movie if we'd left fifteen minutes ago.
> "I'm trying," she whined.
> I softened a little. She did try all the time. She was just slow and stupid.
> "I wish you loved me," she said picking up a saucepan with coffee she'd reheated for me and moving toward the dishwasher. I reached to help but she jerked pan away, not in the mood to be pampered. Hot liquid spattered on her bare legs. She screamed with pain.
> "Goddamn it," she said. Red blotches blossomed on her thigh.
> "It wasn't my fault," I said not moving, refusing to help.
> "I wish you were dead."

2. Narrative first person description with setting details.

> I was in the kitchen of my girlfriend Ellie's house watching her load the

The ART of CREATING STORY

dishwasher between the four-burner stove and the porcelain sink. We were already late for the movie. She'd picked up a saucepan she'd used to heat instant coffee and spilled hot water on her.

"Damn it," she screamed. She wasn't wearing any clothes and a red splotch developed on her leg.

3. Narrator writing in scene with a narrator.

Ellie heated left over coffee to boiling in a saucepan. Jake stood behind her fidgeting.

"I don't want coffee now," Jake said. "We'll never make the movie."

"I can't ever please you," she said. She grabbed the handle to empty the pan in the sink.

"Leave it," Luke said. He reached to take it from her but she turned away unwilling to be pushed. His hand hit her arm and hot liquid spilled on her naked belly, ran down her exposed thigh; the skin turned red, ready to blister.

"I hate you," she screamed.

"I'll go by myself," he said ignoring her moan as she slumped to the linoleum floor.

Two FAMOUS EXAMPLES

Here are two famous story openings that set the stage for the reader effectively.

1. First, "Barn Burning" by William Faulkner. Note Faulkner's provision of setting is in scene with sensory detail and more than one point of view (narrator and boy).

"The store in which the justice of the Peace's court was sitting smelled of cheese. The boy, crouched on his nail keg at the back of the crowded room, knew he smelled cheese, and more: from where he sat he could see the ranked shelves close-packed with the solid, squat, dynamic shapes of tin cans whose labels his stomach read, not from the lettering which meant nothing to his mind but from the scarlet devils and the silver curve of fish – this, the cheese which he knew he smelled and the hermetic meat which his intestines believed he smelled coming in intermittent gusts momentary and brief between the other constant one, the smell and sense just a little of fear because mostly of despair and grief, the old fierce pull of blood. He could not see the table where the Justice sat and before which his father and his father's enemy (our enemy he thought in that despair; ourn! mine and hisn both! He's my father!) stood, but he could hear them, the two of them that is, because his father had said no word yet."

2. Second, *Moby Dick* by Herman Melville. In the novel opening, the narrator describes at a distance with an imperative, 2nd person tone, the use of poetic language (image provoking words and tight effective metaphors at their best), and detail incorporated in expression of emotions and mood (with lots of energy in the language). The style may seem archaic but don't miss the value of the writing technique.

> "There now is your insular city of the Manhattoes, belted round by wharves as Indian isles by coral reefs—commerce surrounds it with her surf. Right and left, the streets take you waterward. Its extreme downtown is the battery, where that noble mole is washed by waves, and cooled by breezes, which a few hours previous were out of sight of land. Look at the crowds of water-gazers there.
>
> Circumambulate the city of a dreamy Sabbath afternoon. Go from Corlears Hook to Coenties Slip, and from thence, by Whitehall, northward. What do you see?—Posted like silent sentinels all around the town, stand thousands upon thousands of mortal men fixed in ocean reveries. Some leaning against the spiles; some seated upon the pier-heads; some looking over the bulwarks of ships from China; some high aloft in the rigging, as if striving to get a still better seaward peep. But these are all landsmen; of week days pent up in lath and plaster—tied to counters, nailed to benches, clinched to desks. How then is this? Are the green fields gone? What do they here?

Perception in Literary Fiction: A Challenge for Better Narration

by William H. Coles

Story: account of people and events told for entertainment.
Fiction: literature in prose that describes imaginary people and events.
Literature: written works of lasting artistic merit.

Fiction is imagined and created storytelling. It's not just description of reality. And literature is an art form with lasting merit. To fashion story as art in fiction, authors create illusions of characters and story worlds and they structure story and shape characters to engage, entertain, and then enlighten, usually about new or renewed thinking about the human condition. The challenge is to maintain a quality illusion that forms and lasts in the reader's memory. It is directly related to a writer's skill in creating unique characters and images and expressing motives and emotions through imagination dedicated to story enjoyment and meaning.

One way of achieving mastery of created fiction is excellence in narration (telling). All writers know point of view and consider third person versus first-person narration. Second person narration is rarely effective and not recommended to achieve artistic merit. The structure of narration in fiction is: characters act, narrators tell, authors create. Narrators are always telling the story, even when those narrators use character point of view. And it is the quality of the narrator's skill that measures story success. Authors describing their reality from their worldview is the contemporary style, the literature-of-self, but this rarely contributes to excellence in storytelling as art.

Of course, the author is creating the narrator. But authors seeking to create fiction as art, must step outside their limited worldviews into the expanded understanding provided by imagined worldviews of narrators and characters. Authors creating fictional stories must learn about the real world outside their experiences and understand human nature in the real world through the eyes and ideas of others to be able to create significance in-character development and plot construction and realization; authors must learn, experience, consider, and perfect technique and then create from outside what would be the default for average writers who restrict themselves to their own unperfected personas and worldviews; and authors should create a narrator as a distinct entity, a skill that forces the author to create for excellence, to make choices that are best for story, and ignore the average author's goal of becoming a writer through personal aggrandizement using inferior prose or trying to impress with ill-conceived pseudo-intellectual displays of thinking and writing.

When creating stories, action, desire, motivation, credibility, reliability, accuracy of prose are all essentials of process. The writer stays true to these fundamentals. Creation of art is not just ostentatious hyperbolic-prose or dependence on bizarre plot twists or shocking disregard for societal norms, it is great characterization and story purpose and meaning all presented with clarity, credibility (for the story world) and reliability (or lack of reliability) of characters created by author for best support of story meaning and significance.

When narrating a fictional story, the narrator speaks from their unique point of view and perspective or a character point of view and perspective. Perspective is important to orient the reader and when carelessly or rarely considered, results in defect in storytelling. Perception is related to insight and understanding. How people with unique experiences, intellects, memories, and worldviews receive and interpret stimuli. It is different for each character and the narrator (if narrator is created as separate entity by the author.) In a story for example, one character might perceive the killing of an endangered grey wolf as an illegal act that should be punished, another perceive it as just end to an annoying predator of domestic animals, another as extermination as just revenge for rumored injury to a human, and another as an assault on a noble and ecologically valuable species. These perceptions change the prose and the storytelling when in the point of view of a character (or narrator).

Perception is also valuable when in a narrator (and, on occasion, a character) point of view and another character share a scene in the story. How the "stage" character perceives the story world embedded in the narrator's point of view enhances character development, provides variety in the prose imagery, and helps elucidate motivations and actions in the plot.

Perception in Narration

In this story, set in France during the revolution, a boy's father is killed and his mother suffers from a lethal neck tumor. The boy seeks a miracle for his mother and takes her from Paris to a coastal town where a saint-of-healing's bone is preserved in the vault of a cathedral. On the way, he meets an out-of-work musician whose benefactor was beheaded, and a teenage orphan girl seeking a family and love. His mother, at first a sulking victim of her condition, becomes an enabling mother intent on providing a future for her son.

Example 1.

A. Narrator point of view **without regard to character perception.**

> Jean-Luc went near the northwest corner of the Place. A girl his age walked along in front of two boys and a girl. She came from the rich part of town by the quality of her dress. Must have cost two thousand sous.

B. Narrator point of view but writing with **worldview perception of the aristocratic girl**—dresses, fashion, class, privilege slippers, pink, delicate, cheekbones, porcelain. (These details would be natural and important to the aristocrat, but not necessarily the first choices of a narrator).

> Jean-Luc went near the northwest corner. An aristocratic girl his age paraded stately along the path followed by two boys and a girl, all fashionably dressed. The girl's full-length, white silk dress floated around her and the points of pink slippers peeked out from under the hem with each step. How delicate she was. Her high cheekbones spoke class and privilege. Her brown eyes brooded in the frame of her light, straw-colored hair. Her slender hands were as if fashioned in porcelain.

Example 2.

A. Narrator point of view without thinking of perception of on-stage character.

> Emile sang of a new song and played his lute. Charlotte and Jean-Luc rested. Sapphire repaired the tear in her dress. She tied the fabric to conceal the hole.
> Charlotte faced away from the others pulled up her dress exposing her legs. From her waist, she untied a string that held a small cloth sack. She removed a cloth pouch, knelt next to Sapphire, and unfolded the layered linen to expose five gleaming needles."

B. Narrator (same) point of view but with *perception* of a seamstress mother dying from a throat tumor: cooking fire, shawl, tear in dress, fabric, conceal hole, loose skin, buttocks, cloth sac, skirts, fine linen, folded, needles, gleam, reflections.

Emile played the lute, mouthed the line of a new song, and picked a melody on two of the few remaining strings on his lute. Charlotte and Jean-Luc rested. Sapphire, wrapped in a shawl, worked to repair the tear in her dress. She had tied the fabric into a crude knot to conceal the hole.

Charlotte stood, turning so she faced away from the others. Charlotte shamelessly pulled up her dress exposing her loose-skinned, wrinkled buttocks. From her waist, she untied a string that held a small cloth sack. She let her skirts down and opened the sack, removing a piece of fine linen, folded over twice and four inches long. She knelt next to Sapphire and unfolded the linen to expose five needles.

Example 3.

A. Narrator point of view **without regard to character** *perceptions*.

"Emile turned to Charlotte. "I can help," he said. From the cart, he retrieved candle stubs he melted and carried to Charlotte.

B. Narrator (same) point of view but now utilizing *perceptions* **the out-of-work court musician**—goat cart, candles, pot, fire embers, wax consistency, testing temperature with finger.

Emile turned to Charlotte. "I can help," he said. He went to the goat cart and returned with candle stubs in an iron skillet that he placed on a few embers at the edge of the fire. The wax melted. He carried the skillet to Charlotte, testing the wax temperature with his finger. He carefully covered her swollen red knuckles. She smiled at the relief from her pain and flexed her hands able now to help Sapphire with her sewing.

The narrator is telling story in each segment, but as each character is on stage, the narrator- telling shifts and is filtered through character perception. This provides dominant details from the character's person and worldview, (not the narrator's or other character's). Doesn't that seem an advantage for the best effect of prose-fiction storytelling? The idea: perception and point of view (perspective) are different but both enhance storytelling when used with precision.

This use of narrative *perception* is left to instinct by most writers, many successful, and the purpose for analysis here is to provide alternatives for those writers seeking better storytelling and better prose.
Examples from the short story *"The Miracle of Madame Villard"*

Dialogue and Perception

Perception considerations in dialogue responses.

Possible responses from different characters each with their unique perceptions of the story world that (1) reveals something about them and (2) when credible, specifically builds characterization:

> Accusation: "You're a freaking misogynist."
>
> "That's not true!"
> "Screw you."
> "You're misguided in so many ways."
> "You're mistaken."
> "You don't know what you talking about."
> "I'll kill you if you ever say that again."
> "You're crazy."
> "You're one stupid son of a bitch."
> "Bless you."
> "Moron."
> "You might want to reconsider."
> "God forgives you. I will too."
> "It takes one to know one."
> "Shut up."
> "Degenerate."
> "You're psychologically disturbed."
> "You've got a corncob up your ass."
> "I've never been so insulted."
> "Who exactly do you think you are?"
> "You lack knowledge of what a misogynist is."
> "You ought to buy a dictionary."

For every character a writer creates, the *perception* expressed in dialogue, which should not be confused with perspective, should be unique. After all, a specific point of view is already established; the character is speaking. It's the *perception* that must relate to character (as created by the author) and the dialogue using speaker perception must be credible for the character in the story world and consistent with character as perfected for story.
Dialogue created effectively builds characterization.

Scene. A very wealthy, materialistic older man is in his art-filled living room. His young wife enters carrying their six-month-old baby girl. She trips on a Tufenkian carpet crashing into a Ming dynasty waist-high vase that falls from its black-lacquered stand and slinters. As the woman braces for a face-front fall, the baby is thrust from the woman's arms onto the stone hearth.

Here are possible characterizing responses from the rich man.

1. "How could you?" he yelled at the wife. (Blame. Lack of respect. Not treated as equal.)
2. "She's bleeding," he said picking up the baby. (Love and caring. Concern.)
3. "My God, it's irreplaceable," he said picking up a jagged-edged piece of porcelain. (Loveless. Materialistic. Thoughtless.)

Choosing to use perceptions in action.

Note how action, using the man's perceptions of the world, can also characterize with the same scenario as the dialogue:

1. He rushes to the vase. (cold materialism without love)
2. He picks up the baby, desperately looking for signs of life. (love, caring)
3. He hits his wife with a closed fist. (blame with no love or respect).

1st person, literature-of-self, and perceptive limitations

When authors using 1st person narration and choose not to create a narrator as a distinct entity, authors usually default to their own perceptions of their worlds and what the story world should be. This is when authors concede to using description of world memories and experiences, description limited to their perceptions, and ignore need for imagination and creativity that enhances characterization and setting and invigorates plot. The result is dull prose and storytelling with missed potential for engaging, entertaining, and enlightening readers. Yet, sadly, memoir-based "fiction" storytelling as "literature-of-self" is prevalent in the output of contemporary "fiction" writers.

Creating Quality Characters in Literary Fiction
by William H. Coles

How do the most well-received literary fiction writers create memorable characters? In essence, literature is a written work of lasting art; fiction is imagined story and characters. When an author uses imagination for creating characters who compliment the storytelling, a character can become the dominant feature of the story, can contribute to plot development, and with consistent emotional and intellectual arcs often is the source of a reader's discovery of significant theme and meaning. Here are techniques and principles in storytelling that provide literary-quality characterization: Action, Conflict, Character-Based Plots, Change, Dialogue, Imaging.

ACTION
Showing story and character in imagistic action-scenes conveys characteristics, emotion, morality, and worldview whenever possible. Of course narrative telling is important, but in-scene storytelling can engage and involve the reader often with more intensity and impact.

This example tells of a happening. There is no action or significant characterization:

> Harry flew a kite at the beach to entertain his invalid son. But the kite got away, and Harry seethed with anger.

Here is the event told in scene and with action that develops character:

> A wind gust elevated the dragon kite and the string ran through Harry's hand fast enough to hurt.
> "Let me do it, Daddy," his son Raymond said as he limped to Harry's side. The boy held out his hand that trembled without stop from a congenital palsy. Could he hold the string? Fly the kite? He wanted to so badly.
> "Hold it tight," Harry said placing the string in the boy's hand. The kite dipped then suddenly soared, the string taught again.
> "I dropped it," the boy said crying. Harry reached out but the kite had

ascended too far to reach the string.

Harry cursed as the kite disappeared untethered, driven out to the sea by the off-shore wind.

"I didn't mean too," the boy said, "Don't hit me."

CONFLICT

Dramatize by keeping characters in conflict (reveals character). When plotting, this is accomplished by (1) presenting characters with conflicting desires, emotions, actions, thoughts, and (2) inserting conflict in dialogue of verbal exchanges.

For example of conflict in dialogue:

Jane says to her father: "I'd like to hike to the top."
Her father says: "A smashing idea."

There is no conflict in this exchange. But there is potential.

Now with character-revealing conflict embedded;

Jane: "Let's climb to the top."
Father. "I'm too weak to do that. And you know I don't like heights.".
Jane: "Stay here then. I don't care."

This conflictual exchange conveys something about characters and plot. And there are always many ways to reveal different character traits. What if father said:.

"I don't want you to go. You know what the doctor said."?.

A caring response in a clash of wills about the climb.

CHARACTER-BASED PLOTS

Character-based plotting in narrative telling often augments opportunities for characterization. Compare these examples: straight-forward narrative telling and then character-based plotting:

"The night was dark and stormy and the plane's instruments were not functioning after a lighting strike; the plane crashed killing all aboard."

The ART of CREATING STORY

Now the same event but with *character-based plotting*; the character's hubris *causes* the accident. An opportunity for character development.

> "A wealthy business man excessively proud of his invincibility chooses to fly his private airplane at night with limited experience in bad weather and causes a crash due to his poor decisions based on his inflated belief in himself and his abilities, he kills himself and his passengers."

In essence, plots can reveal essential character traits. In successful literature, characters' strengths, weaknesses, fears, lack of experience, failures of intuition, etc., frequently drive plots.

CHANGE

Great characters in literature change in some significant way: an enlightenment; an epiphany; a recognition of responsibility; a caring; a gracious gesture from a mean soul; a commitment; accepted responsibility for a failure; a change in character's perception, acceptance, realization of consequences from an action; a change in morality; a coming of age; a new way of thinking, etc. But characterization is also enhanced when a character fails the opportunity for change.

EXAMPLES

A young girl goes to court with her brother, younger sister and aunt to attend the indictment of her father for the murder of the children's mother and discovers truth about the father that forces a coming of age to take on maternal caring for her distraught siblings and stressed aunt.
From *"Dr. Greiner's Day in Court"*

The son of an illiterate stonecutter of funerary statuary falls in love with a client twice his age. He helps her to forgive the abusive dead man whose statue of tribute crafted by his father is so revealing to all of the good rather than the evil of his past. The boy discovers pride and love for the father who had so long embarrassed him.
From *"The Stonecutter"*

An older man is living with a divorced woman unwilling to commit to marry when the two go on a tour of India where the theft of a valuable necklace results in the death of a woman and the circumstances bring the man to realize the value of the woman he loves and then expresses to her a long delayed commitment to marry.
From *"The Necklace"*

The husband attending a funeral to give a eulogy for his dead estranged wife meets a young college student also attending to delivery a eulogy who helps him to understand forgiveness of his dead wife and allows him to conquer his fear of a failed eulogy and deliver a remarkable tribute to the dead woman. From *"Speaking of the Dead"*

UNIQUENESS (AVOID STEREOTYPES)
For a major character, actions, thoughts and descriptions must seem as unique and fresh to a reader as possible. Avoid stereotypical rendering.

Madame Bovary by Gustave Flaubert, Chapter 1, an excellent example of ironic, humorous storytelling producing unique, memorable characters.

> It was about this time, that is to say, the beginning of winter, that she seemed seized with great musical fervour.
> One evening when Charles was listening to her, she began the same piece four times over, each time with much vexation, while he, not noticing any difference, cried—
> "Bravo! Very good! You are wrong to stop. Go on!"
> "Oh, no; it is execrable! My fingers are quite rusty."
> The next day he begged her to play him something again.
> "Very well; to please you!"
> And Charles confessed she had gone off a little. She played wrong notes and blundered; then, stopping short—
> "Ah! it is no use. I ought to take some lessons; but—" She bit her lips and added, "Twenty francs a lesson, that's too dear!"
> "Yes, so it is—rather," said Charles, giggling stupidly. "But it seems to me that one might be able to do it for less; for there are artists of no reputation, and who are often better than the celebrities."
> "Find them!" said Emma.
> The next day when he came home he looked at her shyly, and at last could no longer keep back the words.
> "How obstinate you are sometimes! I went to Barfucheres today. Well, Madame Liegard assured me that her three young ladies who are at La Misericorde have lessons at fifty sous apiece, and that from an excellent mistress!"
> She shrugged her shoulders and did not open her piano again. But when she passed by it (if Bovary were there), she sighed—
> "Ah! my poor piano!"
> And when anyone came to see her, she did not fail to inform them she had given up music, and could not begin again now for important reasons. Then

people commiserated her—

"What a pity! she had so much talent!"

They even spoke to Bovary about it. They put him to shame, and especially the chemist.

"You are wrong. One should never let any of the faculties of nature lie fallow. Besides, just think, my good friend, that by inducing madame to study; you are economising on the subsequent musical education of your child. For my own part, I think that mothers ought themselves to instruct their children. That is an idea of Rousseau's, still rather new perhaps, but that will end by triumphing, I am certain of it, like mothers nursing their own children and vaccination."

So Charles returned once more to this question of the piano. Emma replied bitterly that it would be better to sell it. This poor piano that had given her vanity so much satisfaction—to see it go was to Bovary like the indefinable suicide of a part of herself.

"If you liked," he said, "a lesson from time to time, that wouldn't after all be very ruinous."

"But lessons," she replied, "are only of use when followed up."

And thus it was she set about obtaining her husband's permission to go to town once a week to see her lover. At the end of a month she was even considered to have made considerable progress.

CHARACTER-SPECIFIC DIALOGUE

Dialogue should always be specific to the character speaking. Note that character-specific dialogue is dependent on word choice, syntax, ideation, but as important is the dialogue segment in revision is determined to be logical and credible and directly related to the character's worldview, experience, education, intellect and the moment in story time when the dialogue is delivered.

Example One.

On Christmas Day my second year in prison for murder, my mother stopped coming to visit. She doesn't call and I can't get in touch with her. In August, she missed my twenty-fifth birthday. A couple months later, my sister came and said, "Mother doesn't want to think about it anymore. Try to understand." I did try.

Eventually my sister quit coming; she had a lot on her mind with her van full of kids – and no husband. So I go a year with no visitors, and when I get dragged to administration to face an assistant to the warden, I'm half-crazy.

"A graduate student working in criminal justice wants to include you in her experiments," he said. "Your choice. Two or three times a month. Goes on your record as good behavior."

Sessions would be out of maximum security . . . like a mini-vacation.

"Hey. What's with the experiments," I said. "She stick you with drugs, stuff like that?"

"Just talk."

"Hey, Captain. She a looker?"

"Don't get your fantasies revved up. She's a pro."

"You be there?"

"Just you and her. And high security."

"Maybe I get out of max sooner?" I asked. You get a cell in the main building and you could talk to guys, set things up.

"Can't promise.". He walked around the table, stuck a ballpoint pen in my cuffed hand, and showed me where to sign. "Consent papers."

You need a magnifying glass to read the print on the last two pages. "I don't know about signing anything," I said.

"It's permission to talk, record, use information," he said.

"I thought this was research," I said. I hated do-gooders and I didn't need rehabilitation. I needed parole, miraculous DNA evidence, a new trial.

"I don't give a shit what you do. I'm here because the warden says to cover our ass legally. It's routine. No one's trying to screw you. No one cares."

"She ain't a lawyer, is she?. She ain't trying to retry the case or something."

"She's a student. We checked. She was a paralegal before she went back to grad school. She's demonstrated against the death penalty. Arrested once, but never charged. She won't violate your rights, if that's what you're thinking. You don't have rights."

I signed her papers with a bump-and-a-line so no one could ever read my name.

From the short story "Reddog"

Example Two

"I ain't going to stand for it," Mama said. She said this often.

She held a small dead human about as long as an ear of corn. Even though the head was too big, the hands too small, you could tell it might have been somebody.

"Push down," Mama said.

My sister moaned. With a gush of blood the afterbirth slid onto the bed. Her skin was white as wood ash.

"I don't feel good," she said.

"Shut up, Pearl Anne," Mama said. "Shut up and grow up."
"I'm seventeen."
"You're acting like a two-year-old."
"I'm going to throw up," Pearl Anne said.
I wasn't feeling so hot either.
"Go get some towels, Ether Mae. Help get Pearl Anne cleaned up."
I didn't move. Pearl Anne got herself into this fix, not me. I'd never had a boy put his thing into me. Pearl Anne said it felt funny but not so good that she couldn't do without it. So she'd decided to quit. She wanted more respect. She quit too late.

Now Mama moaned and held this dead thing. "My grandchild," she said. "Didn't I tell you get some towels?"
"Don't want to.". I backed away a little.
"You'll get the stick. You're too old to have me telling you what to do.". I was eleven.
I found some rags and two towels and got them wet under the faucet in the sink, then squeezed the water out.
"Goddamn it. Wring them out. You're dripping all over the floor," Mama screamed.
"What's that doctor's name wouldn't treat you, Pearl Anne?"

From the short story "The Activist"

CHARACTER-FOCUSED IMAGING

The perspective of a scene can be close or distant for a reader. Variations of use depend on authorial style and purpose of the scene. The use of close perspective is often valuable for characterization; by allowing the reader into the scene, character traits are revealed. In distant perspective, so essential for delivering broad perspective of story and setting, characters contribute to image but not so much to characterization. See these two examples:

Perspective

1) Close perspective.

After the explosion they were quickly inside the room. The gun had fallen to the floor. His son had fallen to one side; his face gone: the lower jaw blown away, a few upper teeth haphazardly clinging to flesh. Nose and lower lids gone, the deflated eyeballs wrinkled like a fallen soufflé. His son's legs, then his arms, went into spasms; he was alive but without air.

I'm a surgeon, he thought. Focus. Think like a doctor and not a father.

His wife had crumpled to the floor, her hands over her eyes, wailing.

He held his son's head with both hands; straightened the torso. "Get up," he said to his wife. "You've got to do this." She stood. "Slide the pillow under his shoulders."

He let the head fall back hoping to find the glistening end of the trachea. There were no landmarks, only flesh and blood, and bits and slivers of bone.

From the short story "Dilemma"

2) Distant perspective.

Heinrick eased the family car onto the railroad tracks with Agnes sitting bound and gagged inside in the back. Heinrick killed the engine. Billie Bob parked his car on the road. Even when they untied her, Agnes did not struggle or speak. Billie Bob put her gently into the driver's seat. Agnes remained still and Billie Bob put the can of chloroform he'd used to knock her out back in his pocket. "Good," Heinrick said. Billie Bob secured the doors from the outside. Heinrick stood behind him breathing hard and fast. Agnes had regained her senses and stared straight at Billie Bob, nonjudgmental, without a hint of fear, and a faint smile that disturbed Billie Bob but inflamed Heinrick all over again.

In minutes, the Amtrack engine whistled around the bend; both Billie Bob and Heinrick were sure the train would not slow for the remote crossing. The headlight pierced the darkness. The barriers descended, The warnings lights flashed. Heinrick stood near a tree by the roadside and watched the express bear down on Agnes, the definitive object of vengeance. Billie Bob stayed down near the barrier to the last minute to be sure Agnes didn't get free from the car somehow.

From the short story "The Wreck of Amtrack's Silver Service"

Final thought.
Characters in fiction are often stimulated by real life persons and events but are most effectively rendered when engagement, entertainment, and enlightenment of the reader are the prime considerations and achieved through authorial skill in creating characters through imaginative, accurate, prose-storytelling. Literary stories have altruistic reasons—usually void of authorial ego, catharsis, need for attention, or relief of guilt—to tell their stories and seek to stimulate new or renewed thinking about facing the human condition in our lives.

Mastering the Power of a Literary Fictional Story
by William H. Coles

A writer's imagination in fiction opens the gates to creating great literary stories. Authors must master skillful characterization for today, but they have the benefit of access to centuries-proven story structures from creative writers of the past—Tolstoy, Chekhov, Dostoevsky, Flaubert, the Brontës, Sophocles, Hemingway, Faulkner, and so many others.

Most writers today seek admiration, fame, and fortune through their work. Nothing is wrong with that; for many it's a tried and true path to happy and successful careers. But some authors write because they want to create meaningful stories that contribute to our greater understanding of constantly evolving humanity, and desire their stories to be read, reread, and passed onto future generations. Homer, Austen, Conrad, Melville, Forster, and Woolf deeply affected their own generations and those that have followed by uniquely portraying thoughts and emotions, core human desires and moralities, with drama, imagery, and action.

How can a writer today achieve memorable meritorious stories? Study the techniques of the storytellers of the past that are indelibly etched in the collective human consciousness. Discover elements of powerful lasting literary stories that work for you as an author and incorporate those elements into your writing and storytelling.

Stories are about events and people. In great literature, story frequently reveals not only what happens but how humans live and how life changes them. There are no secret formulas, but there are commonalities that generate power for stories to move and evolve with humankind into future generations.

Write with purpose.
As you write your story, know what drives you to do so. An author who has a purpose—to show effects of victimization, for example—seeks to clarify their prose, scenes, characters, narration, point of view, and plot to make it all more focused and unified, especially in revision.

Theme and meaning.
"Theme" refers to recurrent ideas; "meaning" to significant ideas. What can a reader learn that is new and significant from reading your work? For example, what has made the story of Little Red Riding Hood persist over centuries? Its key themes include innocence and vulnerability. Its key meanings including obeying your elders, not talking to strangers, and the possibility of predators in disguise. There are many versions of the story and most of them exhibit robust story structure and imagery.

Change.
Characters change as stories progress, as do their readers if the story is truly great. Both may experience enlightenment (discovery or experience a new way of thinking), a shift in morality, a reversal, or a coming of age. Examples of stories with clearly evident character change (all available for free online) include:

> *"The Necklace":* Through tragedy, discover the value of another human being.
> *"Reddog":* A rare truth is not an effective motivator when delivered by a chronic liar.
> *"The Activist":* Coming of age by making a decision to defy an abusive mother.
> *"Homunculus":* A circus dwarf loves a full-size apathetic trapeze artist and loses the valuable love of her coworker.
> *"Speaking of the Dead":* Discovering the healing value of forgiveness.

Drama.
Whenever possible, show in-scene dramatic conflict and action. Abstract and static descriptions of character and scene (telling) are necessary but often less effective in developing characterization than in-scene action. "She was a kind, gentle, woman" is brief and concise, but not too engaging, in part because it involves abstractions that may be subjective on the part of the narrator. The following involves less telling, more showing:

> Elizabeth stopped before a scraggly, wheelchair-bound beggar with dry, blotched skin and unkempt hair.
> "What are you doing?" John asked, with iritation. Elizabeth slipped a ten-dollar bill from her shoulder bag.
> "Don't do that?" John stripped the bill from her hand. "He's a faker, fully capable of work, and more money stashed away than we have.
> Elizabeth found a twenty in her bag and handed it to the man, who took it without speaking or looking up to Elizabeth.

"Damn it." John grabbed Elizabeth's arm and pulled her away. "The ungrateful son of a bitch."

"He's needy for a few seconds of attention. Confirmation he exists."

The preceding possesses in-scene action, imagery, and character-specific dialogue, and indicates that Elizabeth is kind.

Unique and fascinating characters.
Attend to your characters' core desires, abilities, imagination, motivations, sense of morality, and worldview. Make them vivid and believable. Consider as part of your study how imagination brought past characters to immortality: Felicity (Gustave Flaubert, *A Simple Heart*); Flem Snopes (William Faulkner, *The Hamlet*); Anna Karenina (Leo Tolstoy, *Anna Karenina*); Margaret and Helen Schlegel (E. M. Forster, *Howards End*); Jane Eyre (Charlotte Brontë, *Jane Eyre*); Elizabeth, Jane, Mary, Lydia, and Catherine Bennet (Jane Austen, *Pride and Prejudice*); Captain Ahab (Herman Melville, *Moby-Dick*); Emma and Charles Bovary (Gustave Flaubert, *Madame Bovary*); Clarissa Dalloway (Virginia Woolf, *Mrs. Dalloway*).

Compare these to such famous characters as Jay Gatsby (F. Scott Fitzgerald, *The Great Gatsby*), Luke Skywalker (*Star Wars*), Hercule Poirot (Agatha Christie), Clark Kent (alter ego of Superman), or Mike Hammer (Mickey Spillane). For the most part, the character development is not character based; instead the plot determines who they are.

Structure.
   A) *Beginning, middle, end.* Seems simple but essential when storytelling with emotional, intellectual, visual changes that need to be fortified in time progression.
   B) A carefully considered *timeline*, essential to avoid common errors in credibility and logic.
   C) *Character-based plots.* Useful when plot progression depends at least partially on the nature of a character(s) strength and/or weakness and relies less on fatalism and serendipity for plot change.
   D) Logical and credible *emotional arcs.* Awareness of character's emotional progress makes credible and logical sequencing of scenes.

THOUGHTS AND ADVICE

The Anatomy of a Wannabe Literary Fiction Writer.................................... 139
    Some writers will never write the great literary story. What is it that holds them back from their potential?

Author's Attitudes: Fine-Tuning.. 147
    Writing for wealth and fame are not motives that create great stories. Here are ideas on how to adjust your thinking for writing your best work (that might just bring you wealth and fame).

How Literary Stories Go Wrong... 149
    Authors often tend to try to improve their stories with poor choices. What happens?

Preparing to Write the Great Literary Story.. 153
    Best stories form, are prioritized, and revised before the first words are written. And there are skills to be honed. How is it accomplished?

Victims as Characters in Literary Fiction.. 159
    Objectivity paradoxically can engage reader and evoke sympathy.

The Anatomy of a Wannabe Literary Fiction Writer
by William H. Coles

When readers and publishers fail to recognize and appreciate their work, most literary writers respond by compulsively writing more and revising what they've already written. The real failure is not in prose manipulation, but is concealed in who the writers really are, how knowledgeable and intelligent they are, and what fiction-writing deficiencies they carry in storytelling skills. These failed writers believe, mostly erroneously, that simple repetitive changes in wording and syntax, grammar correction, and reformatting are significant improvements. But the real improvement lies in writers (1) finding, as truthfully as they can, who they are, why they write, and what it is about their inner selves that will make their writing valued by readers; (2) developing their mental and emotional resources; and (3) learning and perfecting how to tell significant stories in the prose medium.

To find one's true self as a writer is not easy. We, as writers, can judge only from our own levels of incompetency. For valid self-assessment, we must mainly rely on the objective microscopy that is provided through honest assessment of us by those we trust. But, we do have self-reliant ways for improvement available: We can examine how our own motivations and desires affect the creation of characters, and then carefully construct characters with their own motivations and desires that relate to the story purpose. In effect, our own motivations and desires rarely, if ever, are right for the story we are creating. It is these characters, embodied with their own worthy personalities, that will effectively drive a plot line and promote experienced enlightenment about being human in the great literary story.

One major barrier to improvement is a writer's self-absorption. For fiction writers who prefer writing from life experiences and the subjective soup of me-thoughts and me-ideas, advancement in writing great literary fiction with vibrant, unique, story-oriented characters will not come until those authors can dissever themselves from their characters' actions and emotional arcs. In fiction, subjectivity limits the number and quality of the decisions necessary to create great dramatic fictional stories based on conflict and enlightenment. Therefore, writers must learn to write about what might happen in their fictional worlds, and not what happened to them in their real past (usually altered in some way to qualify, they think, as fiction). It is not easy, and for some it is impossible.

The backbone of writer failure may well be the inability to learn and/or the lack of opportunities for beneficial study. This may not be the fault of the writer. There are few resources to learn fictional prose storytelling that are memorable and significant. Consider these learning sources:

1) Learning in writing groups is the blind leading the blind through a maze of bear traps and landmines. No one would believe a group of briefly educated humans who wanted to be neurosurgeons would get together weekly to discuss the experimental surgery they have been practicing in their garages and basements. Yet, both surgery and writing require study with experts—as well as knowledge learned from many intellectual and skilled disciplines over many years. Writing groups, plump with inexperience and discordant ideas, are almost never of any useful value to the serious writer.

2) Learning in organized workshops is the carpenter teaching musicians with hammers and saws to play Beethoven's Archduke piano trio. Even in high profile traditional workshops, teachers are rarely capable of developing the special talents of an individual writer to achieve creation of an art form (a fictional literary story). Fundamentally, there is no right way that is applicable to all. As a result, many teachers use the wrong tools for the wrong job, and their teaching is little more than useless for the dedicated fiction writer. At worst, the incompetent teacher can, and does, inappropriately humiliate and discourage a talented writer in the workshop setting. And these incompetents often descend into dogmatic pronouncements that stifle understanding and creativity.

3) Learning in MFA programs is not of guaranteed quality, and may not just be mediocre, but detrimental to a writer's improvement. MFA programs, many hastily formed by universities, colleges, and organizations to maintain relevance and solvency, often hire teachers untrained as educators, and untalented as writers, to teach creative writing. This practice results in suppressing understanding of the complexities of the art of fiction and the vibrant essence of great storytelling. More than a few traditional programs are so inbred by tired, untalented teachers choosing and supporting unimaginative writers like themselves that the writing from these programs takes on a clone-like mediocrity that brands its origin. By default, these educators promote teaching of scholarly nonfiction and pop-culture memoir as fiction, without the quality of story writing equal to that of imaginative fiction.

Creative writing programs labeled as "academic" emphasize lyricism over drama, often prefer obscure to clear prose, and mistakenly believe that a lack of understanding by a reader is the desired result of their own "writer-intellectual" superiority. They teach revision as grammar and syntax, metaphor and oxymoron-excessive prose, rather than the dynamic and suspenseful expression of the desires and conflicts of characters about whom the reader has come to care, like, or at least respect through the story. Some academic workshops digress in education by having students sit around a table holding hands with eyes closed for long silent periods in the hope that images and words will float up from the unconscious, like images sought in a Victorian séance to communicate with the dead. Some highly acclaimed academic workshops spend a week policing manuscripts for point of view inconsistencies, while the needs that should be addressed are imagining effective story structure and learning how to build memorable characters through meticulously crafted, interrelated, character actions in dramatic scenes. In some workshops, a teacher presents a personal memoir story, and then details how to turn it into fiction by shifting the timeline and changing the prose emphasis of certain events. This practice might well derail a student's progress in learning to write their own great fiction.

Academic workshops and courses also fail to demand a writer have a thoroughly understood purpose for writing a story as well as, on a construction level, all the prose elements of that story. This results in picking at prose when the writer hasn't decided what he or she is really writing about, and how he or she will achieve a story purpose. It is almost unarguable: Failure to find and build purpose in storytelling makes coherency of a prose fictional story with effective characters, plots, or emotional arcs unlikely. And, it is not uncommon that the poorly educated, poorly trained teachers who are allowed the privilege to teach creative writing are guilty of:

(1) Ignoring emotional character development for the ease of plotting from life experience.

(2) Accentuating the cute, the bizarre, and the shocking (which have only temporary effects on value in story telling).

(3) Failing to develop author understanding of the human soul, its flaws, and what really is responsible for its strengths.

(4) Ignoring the value of sophisticated narration.

(5) Thinking that lyricism alone can sustain great story effectiveness.

(6) Learning from popular textbooks on fiction writing, which—with a few significant exceptions—are often writing efforts of poor writers with teaching appointments or responsibilities who write the learning of fiction as Lego instruction, with rigid rules and inflexible actions; like assembling a bicycle from parts while reading a fold-over slip of paper with fine print instructions and a diagram on Christmas morning. Some of these authors write texts composed of famous authors' stories with personal, short, subjective-value comments, but with little to no insight into a writer's process.

Quality fiction as an art form has especially suffered from the high profile, traditional MFA programs where graduation almost guarantees publication of the work generated in the program. The published work is rarely quality writing or storytelling. Once published, eager, unaware readers perceive literary fiction as obtuse in meaning, boring, and with pseudo-intellectual ideation. Many dedicated readers have turned away from reading literary fiction for enjoyment (and agents refuse to try to sell it), while the authors from these programs read to fellow graduates or a small group of readers who admire writing credentials and rationalize that the quality is better than it is. The detriment to fiction as an art form has been significant, and for the writer seeking to achieve their personal best, MFA programs can permanently derail that possibility.

With so few valuable or easily accessed resources for learning available to the fiction writer, only one reliable way to learn emerges. Each writer must discover from those authors who have gone before, what it is about the writing of a successful literary art form that will be useful for their own careers as contemporary writers. It's not just copying a favorite author's style, either. It's mastering understanding of knowledge, intellect, the environment and opinions (and attitudes) of the author's times; the emotional complexities of the author that affected the writing; the associations with other writers (examples: Bloomsbury group, Shelley's Swiss mountain writing buddies), and the effects of societies mores (Examples: Austen, James, Charlotte and Emily Bronte, Forester, Chekhov, Flaubert).

Authors need to be curious. How did they do it? Then, what can I learn from them so I can do it? How can I, based on what I've learned from others, create fiction that engages, entertains and stimulates thoughtful responses about human existence? One key question has to be addressed repeatedly with each work studied: What were these authors' purposes in writing? One dominant purpose persistently stands out for all: to tell a story where something happens that is meaningful and entertaining to the reader. And without exception, successful fiction writers write to please a reader—, not all readers, but specific readers seeking enjoyment through reading. Now, the beginning writer must learn, not only how to construct sentences and paragraphs, but how stories and the creation of stories in the prose medium can be best created to please a reader. It's the way they imaginatively form and narrate a story. The craft of prose, although vitally important, is secondary.

Many unsuccessful writers fall into the trap of first person point of view, the path of least resistance that leads to mediocrity in many stories from a failure of the author to form a story in the most pleasurable and significant way. This is often disguised memoir writing, even when authors believe they are imagining a story, because writers insert themselves into the story to become the first person storytellers.

> The night our baby died, I'd been watching Survivor, turned off the TV, and tiptoed back to the baby's room. The door was open. The moonlight filtered in through the window near the crib, and I could see from the way her feet were caught in the twisted blanket that she was motionless. I ripped off the blanket. Her skin was pale. Her eyes opaque and unblinking. She was dead.

Look at a different narrator approach to the same scene (also overwritten for contrast).

> The moon was almost full in a cloudless sky, and all but the brightest of the infinite stars were dimmed by the cold pewter light that filtered through the window into the nursery, creating weak lifeless shadows of the newly decorated, painted chest of drawers on the white shag carpet. Karen opened the door noiselessly. Cindy was asleep; there had been no sounds over the electronic monitor from the nursery to their bedroom. The blanket in the crib was wadded and covered the small lump of a child. She placed both hands on the edge of the crib and looked down. She stripped off the blanket. Cindy was motionless, face up with one leg caught at the ankle in the space between two crib slats.

Or another.

> "Check Cindy," Karen said sleepily, her head buried in her pillow.
> "You go," Henry said, the blanket pulled up to his eyes, his back to his wife. Karen turned away from him. "I always go."
> Henry put his feet on the floor and felt for his slippers. "Goddamn it," he said.
> Karen was acting a little too prima donna-ish for him. Okay. She'd had the

baby. She said it often enough. She was bitter and depressed, and she thought it was his time to suffer. But it was not right to aim her frustrations at him. She'd slipped into a victim mentality placing blame on him, as if he were a stranger who had raped her.

At the end of the hall, he listened at the half open door to see if Cindy were awake. There was no sound, and he entered softly, his heart now beginning to feel the joy he always felt when he was near his daughter. She had recognized him on sight for the past few months, a smile lighting up her face. Last Saturday she'd said "Da Da," for the first time, before she even said "Ma Ma." He shuffled to the crib. Cindy lay face up, her mouth parted, her lips still.

These examples show how alternatives need to be tried to be true to the story. But none of the above could be used for a story; they are not quality writing. The characters have not been developed in the mind of the author. Reader identification with well-developed characters is an essential perquisite for: dialogue that shimmers with the appropriate thoughts and attitudes of the character for the moment, setting that supports plot and characterization, and accurate prose choices that support the story as a whole. These elements need to have formed characters and meaningful plot in place, followed by revisions that are purposeful and directed.

These examples represent a necessary process of trial and error that is limited by first person narration alone because of restrictions in the narration. First person narration produces tethered imagination—, limitations of distance, dominant internalization, limited point of view, and troublesome credibility problems for a reader. It requires extension of suspension of disbelief, and often contributes to inferior storytelling and poor quality fiction. Yet, it is amazing that more than almost three quarters of all contemporary "fiction" stories are written in first person. Admittedly, it is, after all, the easiest and most natural way for a human to tell a story, but for a large number of stories, it is not the most effective path to great, memorable fiction as an art form.

In general, great writing is less doing and more thinking, and the study of great fictional prose stories that need to be dissected not only for technique, but also to comprehend the thinking and planning used by those who have created lasting stories in different ways. A writer must learn how prose can effectively transfer ideas and emotions and enlightenment to the modern reader. Each great writer is different. Every reader is different. Every individual student's learning will be different (exciting potential).

A great writer's success is specific to each work, so learning to write by copying the prose of a great writer, which is advocated by some teachers, is not helpful. Instead, learn what are the opportunities of great fiction for memorable and significant story telling: the accuracy of word choice; mechanics of humor in prose; writing with drama and conflict; the elements of mystery, and how those elements differ in literary fiction and drama. Learn the strengths and weaknesses of stage drama and film for effective storytelling, and what about prose can make it superior; how to write in scene and in the moment; understand the complex development of narration of story in prose and how to overcome the almost constant difficulties in story presentation; how syntax affects story result; how to create imagery that is more than a still life; and understand sentimentality and sentiment, objective and subjective prose.

There are few academic or private teachers who are teaching the complexities of fiction at levels that will make a talented writer emerge. However, self-analysis and self-learning from successful fiction writers develops a writer's skills to the maximum.

Writers also need the time and opportunity to live and fail, and to fail often. Few writers working full time without freedom to think will ever write great fiction. Fiction writing is a serious, time-consuming art form. Busy people don't have the time to develop the skills, and their energy is drained by the consistent, monotonous requirements of their work. And it is rare for hobbyists who write occasionally to create great literary fiction. Writers must have time and the will to develop soul, to think about metaphysical questions that plague us throughout life, and why we are cursed with no answers. Many great writers are tragic figures (Wolff, Faulkner, Hemmingway). Some are insane (Poe), alcoholics (Cheever), victims of inexplicable injustice (Shelley), or invalids (Chekhov [TB], O'Connor [Lupus]). For many of these, their flaws and their worries seem to have driven their intellect to search for explanations, a process that would then benefit generations of readers through their prose.

Of course, drinking a lot or planning suicide are not sure ways to great writing. But it emphasizes the need for living one's life so that in imagining literary fiction of merit, there is something to stimulate the imagination. Great blues musicians have said, you can't play the blues unless you suffer: lose your woman or man, lose your job, go to the electric chair, get trouble in the mind, find out your love is cheating on you, pop your guitar string. Maybe it's true of writers, too. What are the experiences writers have that stimulate great fiction worthy of study by any student of the art form?

The ability to write great literary fiction is not a genetic gift given to anyone who can learn to read and write. The talent for great writing is, however, probably inherently in some and not others. And for those who have the gift of creating great stories, they will be able to create those stories only with extensive learning, tireless practice, persistent self-assessment, and a career-long desire to improve.

Author's Attitudes
by William H. Coles

To reach maximum potential, fiction authors must discover who they are and why they write. In many ways, telling fictional stories is a performance that can be compromised or destroyed by ill-conceived attitudes about writing.

CORE QUESTIONS

Do I write to master the skills and concepts of writing as an art form, or do I write stories to explain experienced emotions?
Great stories are dramatically constructed art forms—sculptures in words—that produce enlightened change in characters and readers. Stories are not beautiful descriptions of abstractions lived such as love, hate, revenge, jealousy. And great, memorable, significant stories are not created to purge the author of an emotional or intellectual crisis.

Do I strive to tell a creative fictional story based on imagination, or am I writing a memoir or biography?
The memoir is a popular and legitimate form of writing, but writing requires skills that often conflict with imaginative fiction. Adherence to the truth of what happened, or the belief that a story based on a true story is equal or superior to the created fictional story, are destructive attitudes for the fiction writer. Most great stories are not just told from life; great stories may be *stimulated* by life but are often more successfully expressed through a dramatic, significant series of fictional events.

Do I write for creative excellence, or for fame?
All authors want recognition for their work. But that recognition should be for writing stories that entertain and enlighten. Desire for fame as an author can result in energy expended in marketing and self-promotion, restricting time available to create a great story. Writing a story is a selfless process, and poor writing should not be promoted to the uninformed as worthyor solely for profit.

Do I write to provide meaning through entertainment and enlightenment, or to persuade to some presumption?
To persuade a reader to a preset opinion does not support the creation of great stories. Fiction authors enlighten about human nature; essayists, editorialists, and columnists persuade readers to agree with their opinions. Fiction authors who insert unrelated opinion into their stories risk propagandizing (spreading deceptive or distorted information about policy, ideas, doctrines, or causes).

Do I rewrite to improve my creative story skills, or do I revise to transform my prose into obscure text with an intellectually intense meaning?
Great stories fail because of ineffective characterization or incredible conflicts and actions. Stories rarely fail because the prose is not fancy enough. Yet most authors revise through prose adjustment in style and craft when valuable revision really comes from structural adjustment, clarity of intent, and idea change.

Do I believe stories are dramatic events for a reader to experience, or written words for the reader to interpret?
Fictional stories entertain and enlighten through drama—conflict, action, resolution. Readers become involved in a great story; they do not simply observe it. The writer's challenge is to engage the reader from beginning to end, not just describe events. Successful writers actually provide only enough information on the page to stimulate the story in the reader's mind. It is one of the wonders of reading great fictional stories that for each reader the story interpretation is unique based on the reader's intelligence, experience, and creativity.

Do I believe stories are structures whose unity is discovered as the reading progresses, or that they are meandering observations described step by step?
Authors limit their creative potential when thry start a character on a plot line to see what they will do. Stories should be carefully constructed, presenting details actively chosen to create images and ideas in readers' minds. Details are not chosen just to record them. Stories are like jigsaw puzzles, where the author supplies essential, clearly detailed pieces that are complete, accurate, interesting, and dramatic, and the reader fills in the rest. Authors who insist that an unstructured mode is best—and then proceed to write rather than structure-and-write—miss potential reader enjoyment that is only possible with a well-constructed fictional story. Write a story as a unit, not as loosely associated ideas discovered moment by moment.

How Literary Stories Go Wrong
by William H. Coles

In literary fiction, the author creates, through imagination, a story that causes some enlightenment or change in thinking about the human condition. If the author is successful, the story is unforgettable. The reader's enjoyment comes from sympathizing with the characters (which can happen even when they are not likable) and finding satisfaction in realizing how character traits drive the plot.

In today's publishing environment, genre and commercial fiction survive and flourish while literary fiction barely hangs on. But for many readers, literary fiction is still the most enjoyable reading, providing satisfaction that commercial fiction cannot. For the serious writer, literary fiction is not memoir, nor creative nonfiction, nor dependent on autobiographical material. These techniques are commonly used and accepted in what is now published as primarily "nongenre," or mainstream fiction, but they erode the imaginative decision-making process behind the best action and details for characterization, and the most effective and credible motivation for plot energy. Devoted writers find literary fiction difficult to craft but a worthy goal. But when the characterization and plot depend more on the reality of what has happened than the imagination, the writer loses an artistic edge of excellence. Such writers tend to depend on prose manipulation and fail to grasp the advantage of characters well imagined and plots motivated with innovative desires and frustrations.

SYMPTOMS OF UNSUCCESSFUL LITERARY STORIES

Failure to engage the reader.
The success of a literary story requires reader engagement not just with the story action but with the protagonist. The reader wants to experience what the character experiences and must sympathize and relate to the character as early as possible in story development.

Overly clever prose.
Great literary stories relate series of events with conflict and action that result in meaningful resolution through enlightenment or change in existing thought. The author achieves this through careful word choice; logical thought progression; concrete, fresh images; and perfectly chosen metaphors and enlightenments. The story is never improved when the author favors cleverness (lyricism, abstraction, neologisms, unclear phrases) over accuracy, logic, freshness, or right metaphors—when the prose is treated as more important than the story. Of course, some readers seek and enjoy expansive prose. And lyrical prose can be beautiful when it is clear, image-filled, and significant. But too-clever prose is inflated, expanded, baroque, and not conducive to succinct, purposeful story writing. Great literary stories are not showcases for an author in love with his or her skills in manipulating language. Rather, the words are like notes whose pitch and positioning produce a melody that evokes a human effect, and the quality and value of the effect is consistent whether presented by a symphony, a rapper, a jazz combo, or a monastic modal organ. Great writing has that core melodic value, unencumbered by a tendency to overdo, or sublimate, the presentation. Cleverness is prose is, of course, mostly a subjective evaluation, but when clever prose becomes irritating, most readers will agree on the feeling and stop reading, or at least lose concentration.

Excessive and static details.
Setting is essential for story. Excessive description of setting is not. And when description is excessive, it is almost always static. Compare the examples below:

> A small black bird with brilliant red wings and inquisitive yellow eyes perched on the white picket fence just out of reach of the tabby-colored cat with a scar on his leg and one eye half-closed and scarred from some long-ago fight.

> The red-winged blackbird glided in for a landing. The battle-tested tabby cat leaped up, claws out, but caught only the edge of one wing. A loosened feather floated down to the garden path as the bird safely landed on the fence a few feet away.

Too many adjectives, adverbs, or extended, vague metaphorical comparisons can deaden the desired effect, while action verbs and nouns provoke images.

In-your-face attitude.
When characterization and plot motivation begin to fail to produce effective and meaningful stories, there is often a dependence on voice and a character's attitude to try to make the story stand out. The writing filters character thinking

and speech through an in-your-face, often counter to existing convention and authority, and confrontational—usually descriptive—narrative. Even when done well, the effect is limited. In literary fictional stories, characterization develops when deeper character traits are dependent on action, response to events, and in-scene development for credibility. In-your-face narrative can be useful in a character sketch, but rarely for characters who behave with strong, credible motivations to drive the plot in significant ways—ways that are the skeleton of literary stories.

Fatalism.
Fatalism means plot predictability. In genre fiction, the reader expects murder, investigation, justice. Man woos reluctant woman, they fall in love. Terrorist threatens the White House, is thwarted. Plots in literary fiction are character driven—that is, the action results from free-will decisions undertaken by the major characters. Rather than ferreting out a murderer, a reader learns motivations and desires (the how and why), which must be understandable and credible (the hard part). Life as lived may sometimes seem predestined and fatalistic. Fiction, however, moves ahead on the foundation of human foibles, and is exciting and unpredictable—never predestined.

Shock value.
Too many failed stories were written to fulfill—often a realistic need for some readers—an expectation of shock. Horror films delight those who enjoy shock. But in literary fiction, a shocking action, or the revelation of a visually uncomfortable detail, detracts from effective character development and character-driven plot. Shock may have its (limited) place in a literary story, but it cannot be a major element. Innovation, surprise, and uniqueness are all elements of good writing, but in literary fiction, stretching for shock—for instance via a detailed description of an alien-like animal devouring a human small intestine—is not the sort of technique that will lead to anything more than a temporary value that detracts from the creation of a great literary story.

Insignificance.
Great literary stories were written for a purpose. They say something, and they say it effectively. Fiction allows for story development unhindered by descriptions of real life, and provides unlimited choices in character motivations and actions that support the story's purpose and momentum. Significant fiction is never loosely conceived.

The author's conscious will must control the story creation. The story cannot simply be an accumulation of ideas that bubble up from the unconscious;

nor should it be a description of a real-life experience whose significance is tagged on later, like a stamp on a letter. Significance comes from planned story progression, shifts to a new way of thinking and understanding on the part of the characters (enlightenment about the human condition), and enlightenment of readers themselves, which when different from the character's enlightenment produces meaningful ironies.

Significance directly relates to the reader's emotional experience. Reader emotions vary in intensity and type from story to story (joy, fear, sympathy, love, anger, et cetera). Emotions are best evoked by total engagement in the fictional dream that requires inclusion of the reader in the story rather than simply treating them as a listener. This means showing why and how in scene or dramatic narrative, and not simply describing real or imagined events or thoughts.

In essence, a story will never be significant when a reader finishes and has no idea why it was written, and/or can't remember characters or what the story was about. Writers must master not only the craft of interesting dramatic prose, but the entangled process of purposeful storytelling.

Preparing to Write the Great Literary Story
by William H. Coles

Literary fiction is not an easy road to either fame or fortune. Two reasons play an important role: authors who write literary stories have fewer readers than authors of commercial fiction and nonfiction, and editorial and publishing decisions to accept genre and memoir writing instead of literary fiction. Still, there is a reader need (and market) for literary story as an art form that requires time and skill to create. In this difficult publishing environment, creative achievement alone seems to reward those serious authors who are dedicated, obsessed, and who see literary fiction as a valuable achievement. These authors serve those readers who find enjoyment in the literary story.

Core goals to create a significant literary story.

1. Achieve excellence in craft of writing.
2. Identify elements—including drama and structure–of all great stories.
3. Write to involve the reader through story action, not to tell an imagined or real story with fictional embellishments.

A. INTRODUCTION

An author of literary fiction must absorb:

(1) Craft (skill in doing things). The craft of writing must emphasize clarity and readability in the product. Learning craft is a continuous process that makes the quality of the writing progress throughout a writer's career. Although mastery of craft is essential to great stories, too many writers work hard on craft and ignore other as important elements in their development as storytellers.

(2) Storytelling. Storytelling is: an accomplishment more dependent of thought and judgment, and therefore less well defined than the more technical aspects of craft; harder to learn and teach than craft; and has fewer resources for writers to learn to improve.

(3) Drama. Drama through the written word is the foundation for successful literary fiction as an art form. To create drama, character and plot are the foundations generated by a vivid and unique imagination that establish a writer's control of his or her process of creating fiction.

(4) Characterization. Every major character should be created as if that character will be unique, memorable, and a lasting presence in the collective consciousness of educated readers.

B. ELEMENTS TO MASTER

1. Drama in storytelling.

Drama is conflict, action and resolution. For intense drama, the desires of the characters must be significant and based logically on the foundation of character development. In literary fiction, dramatic conflict is more effective among believable and respected characters, rather than super heroes or abstract inanimate threats like asteroids on a collision path with earth. The concept of dramatic writing that is engaging is not easily conceived or easily engrained in the writing process. Although complex, the most important skills for dramatic development are related to character development and creating scenes that contribute to the story in interesting ways. Most failure in creating drama occurs when authors strive for emotions in the characters—and the reader—with description, rather than creating the emotions through actions and conflicting desires. Description is an easy trap for a writer. And too much description is often a sinkhole for a reader. Description is dependent on language manipulation, not logical character action. Instead of description, authors must learn to frequently involve the reader in the story action by showing the action through a character or narrator rather than having a character or narrator describing action or environment.

Literary examples can point the way, but only practice and discovery can affect learning. Poets can be great storytellers, but storytellers are not primarily poets, and the belief that lyrical prose creates a great story is the antithesis to reality. Writing effective literary stories does not depend on how lyric the descriptive prose, or how erudite, or how difficult ideas are to access. Great fiction is primarily in scene action with clear logical thinking. Of course lyrical prose can be clear and logical and support a story, but it cannot compete with a reader's enjoyment of the story by stagnating the dramatic action. The key for writers is understanding the difference between describing a feeling—love, anger, jealousy, etc.—and creating these feelings that will dominate, not emote, in characters and subsequently readers. Few authors master this idea, even many who are widely successful. As a serious fiction writer, using dramatic action to engage a reader to a point where emotions are stirred in the reader should be the primary accomplishment.

2. Narrative description.

Effective narrative description is necessary for great fiction. But excessive narrative description is tempered—but not eliminated—in great writing. Narrative allows condensation of time that will increase the reader's feeling of movement through story time primarily because it allows the freedom of story pacing that is more restricted in scene action. Narrative description also allows extended continuous action to be summarized allowing capture of reader interest. But probably most important, when lyrical passages (including summary, stream of consciousness, and internal reflection) are needed in the presentation for enjoyment in the reading, narrative description is often the best way to create the desired effect. But for most authors, narrative description is easier to write—more intuitive—and it tends to be overdone. As a general rule, the process on narrative description should have purpose, that is it should develop character or move plot, and not be a vehicle for inflated prose.

3. Desire.

Think of the desire that motivates in conflict, action and resolution rather than image and setting. How does a character respond to major and minor events? Many teachers of creative writing believe that authors should strive in their writing for a moment where the character creates the story on the page. The teachers imply some mystical intracranial invasion of the author by the character, almost supernatural, that frees the writer to let the character do the work.

But character takeover is often a harmful goal. In terms of the literary story, where success of creating an art form requires control of story structure and meaning, letting the character create story, thrusts the story into uncontrolled zones of purposeless writing and random unconnected ideas. For reader satisfaction, everything that happens in a story to a character needs to have a purpose in full control of the author.

Authors need in-depth thinking, with choices made, about characters' motivations before sitting down to write. Motivations must be significant, logical, and appropriate for the conflict, action, and resolution of the story and motivations must be right for the scene, for the logical and synergistic actions with motivations in all other scenes, and consistent with the development and progressive understanding of the motivation at any time in the story. This demands consideration of the structure and interactions of all the characters in a story.

Character motivation in a story is never static; it is always changing, like hundreds of vipers in a pit where each snake, at any instant, has a unique relationship to every other, and that relationship will change in the next instant, wiggling, advancing, regressing until it's over. In great stories, theme and meaning are often more effectively transmitted by emotional discovery rather than intellectual explanation. Essentially, this means showing, not telling; in scene, not narrative description and summary; concrete not abstract thinking and writing, creative process not descriptive process; structure of responses, not random reflection.

4. Backstory.

Backstory should only be employed in a story when it is necessary to advance the front story. In most great stories, backstory is avoided by structuring the story form so the front story is advancing without interruption. In addition, when writing backstory, the timeline of the story is shifted to a time before story beginning. This often deadens the effectiveness of a front-story passage. Compare these two examples—awkward and overwritten to make a point—where there seems to be a definite shift in momentum when backstory is used to provide essentially the same information in the passage that does not rely on backstory.

Example 1. No backstory

> The curtain parted just far enough for Maria to step forward into the spotlight and then closed. She bowed to the audience applause and cupped one hand in the other in a gesture of formality to lead to the opening note of the aria. She nodded to the piano player who, after a pause, started playing. The first notes expanded out over the audience. He was playing introductory chords now. Maria listened for the cue to pinpoint her starting note, that always difficult major seventh so peculiar and unique to this composer. My God. The pianist had skipped the refrain with her critical cue note. She must have the cue. He was new but no mistakes could be tolerated. He was headed for her beginning. How could he do that? Maybe he would still return, do it right. She glared, tried to make eye contact. He plodded on. The audience turned into a thousand

hostile critics instead of an adoring group of friends she liked to imagine. He was seven bars from her entrance. Here it comes. God! She took a deep breath, searching her memory for some clue to the starting pitch.

Example 2. Backstory

The curtain parted just far enough for Maria to step forward into the spotlight and then closed. She bowed to the audience applause and cupped one hand in the other in a gesture of formality to lead to opening note of the aria. She nodded to the piano player. He started the intro. She had met with him briefly yesterday. A dull sullen young man, but attractive with dark brown eyes and an inerasable black shadow of a shaved dark beard. She had carefully explained how she needed the refrain in the intro before the aria. She could only start when she heard the fifth to orient her to the nonchordal tone the composer insisted on using. She thought he had understood. And they had practiced, in the short time available, only the passages themselves. Now he'd forgotten the refrain. He finished the intro and went directly to the verse. She felt the panic rise in her. There was no way she could hit the crucial major seventh. And there was no way she could not go forward. She felt the audience's expectant stares. She heard their breathing. When she sang the note, the pianist's head jerked toward her. He knew what he had done.

In the backstory, there is a slowing down of front story action without backstory contributing to front story in any special way. For most writing, backstory is more detrimental than additive when it is not necessary to advance front story.

5. Irony.

Humor, in its many forms, is different for every human. Authors need to be aware of the mysteries of irony and humor in general. Irony is a form of humor where what happens is not what might be expected. To incorporate irony in prose, in depth exploration of human needs and expectations as well as a clear understanding of social interactions of the story time are needed. The study of irony is time well spent for the writer of literary fiction.

6. Meaning.

Meaning—and theme—in literary fiction is essentially a change or reversal in the existing way of thinking about something. Characters change during storytelling in meaningful ways . It is part of successful dramatic structure that includes expert character development. But it is the reader's awareness of meaning, at times not articulated or even formed as a complete concept, that represents the success of the author of literary stories.

7. Morality.

All writing is strengthened by a concept of what is moral (issues of right and wrong). In essence, character actions and thinking exist in a moral cobweb. This morality need not be spiritually or legally correct, but it must be consistent for the story, and the moral cobweb established must control logical actions in the story. Morality is formative, not controlling. Authors who feel strongly about a moral view, usually their view, may impose on the reader an almost threatening challenge to accept their attitudes. This is not useful in storytelling where concepts of morality are used for desires and motivations of characters rather than saving the reader from damnation.

Victims as Characters in Literary Fiction
by William H. Coles

Creating a fictional character needs to serve the story being told, and in some way needs to attract and hold the reader's interest , a connection that may not be likeable or sympathetic but must be strong enough to engage the reader to produce at least some satisfaction in having read and acquainted oneself with the character.

Great characters of classic literature almost always have a touch of hero in them. In the story world, they exude qualities such as persistence, morality, perseverance, determination, strength, confidence, intellect, and/or unfailing expectations that things are going to turn out all right, qualities that rise to above average. These characters, in fiction, show resistance to the status quo, often in the face of insurmountable odds that involve conflicts in which the character must use skills, and often develop additional skills, in order to succeed. Success and failure, of course, will vary from story to story but it's the struggle, the quality, and the authorial delivery that grab the reader. Readers generally want to root for a character who succeeds by using imagination and hard work. If the author of fiction writes to evoke reader sympathy without significant reader engagement, there can be unwanted consequences. Sympathy comes from empathy for the plight of others. When a static character is in a dire, and often unjustly deserved, state and narrative description is used to tell of past events and feelings, empathy is harder to attain. For the inexperienced author in this context, the danger of failure to create for desired reader response is sentimentality rather than empathy–and even bathos–by the reader for the character and the situation.

The difference between a static character described to evoke a sympathetic reader response and a character in a struggle with desires and motivation aimed at solving a problem enmeshed in intellectual, emotional, or physical conflict that evokes reader empathy results in two opposites that, by being aware of them during story construction, can improve a writer. Basically, the writer's choice is inaction told versus action shown. (The comparison is like the difference in viewing a tableau vivant of Manet's nude in the park or attending a theatrical production of Richard the Third, the "My kingdom for a horse." guy.) And for the success of most fictional stories, these differences are not just points on a sliding scale; instead the choice is either or, and for good fiction and good stories to reach greatness, a choice must be made, or at least considered, to where the story creation is effectively under authorial control.

In most effective stories about victims, the character rails against the circumstances to improve his or her lot. Authors often fail to reach story potential of acceptance, enjoyment, and memorability by allowing the character to wallow during excessive authorial narrative descriptions of the injustices, and by forcing the reader to make judgments about the credibility of injustice in the circumstances and accepting the character's response to the person or event that caused his or her (the character's) present state of existence. Consider two situations with different character responses.

A fourteen-year-old girl taken hostage and isolated by a religious fanatic and raped daily for six months returns to society and does not devote herself totally to anger induced revenge and punishment, but allows the law to make judgments against the mentally deranged man who tried to destroy her, and sets up a foundation to prevent such events and to help those who are victims, return to a normal productive life. A reader's response to this situation will most often be intense sympathy mixed with admiration (and often wondering if he or she, the reader, would be capable of the same response).

Consider now a forty-year-old woman, beaten and raped in a death-threatening attack by an ex-husband she hadn't seen for many years. She recovers from serious injuries in hospital and then in a shelter for abused women. She suffers severe depression, and for years is unable to return to her former job; is unable to relate to people or make friends; and spends almost every waking hour watching television and eating fast food brought to her by a neighbor. She's on welfare and she feels victimized by a government who will not provide her what she thinks she deserves. Finally, she kills herself by swallowing one hundred and fifty aspirin tablets.

A reader may have sympathy for this second character, but little admiration. And if a writer chooses this type of story scenario, the reader may be forced to make judgments about the character that may not be effective for good storytelling and characterization. What if the woman is a prostitute, and the reader sees willful and unacceptable, maybe immoral, decisions and actions by the character as faults deserving of punishment. What if the ex-husband abused her from rage induced by his own victimization—from an unfair treatment in his job as a crane operator—and the abuse to his ex-wife was one time, never before inflicted or repeated. The woman as victim might not be easily accepted, and valid sympathetic reader responses lost. What if the woman lied to authorities and her caregivers about her lifestyle and the nature of her once loving husband, to gain sympathetic financial and emotional support from the caregivers. Some readers may not relate, others may, but the manipulation of emotions for gain might squelch acceptance of victimization. These characterization effects can be used to effect or avoided, depending on the writer's intent. The writer can often, by story construction and characterization, better control positive, enjoyable, memorable reader response by always striving to create a specific response in the reader and not defaulting to using clichéd self-victimization as the sole source of an expected reader's sympathetic (without admiration or respect) response.

In essence, when an author takes the static choice of self-serving obsession with the injustice of the "victimizing" as a mode to write about victims, the emotions most often expected from the reader are sympathy for the character, outrage, or anger at something other than the character's consumption of the problem producing tension and caring about what will happen. The reader is asked to respond to the cause of the injustice rather than the character's response to the injustice. As readers, we have been moved for decades and even centuries with classic characters striving for change and not succumbing to victimization as an excuse for inaction: Jane Eyre, Elizabeth Bennett, Anna Karenina, Heathcliff, Milly Theale (The Wings of the Dove), Emma Bovary, Captain Ahab, Charles Marlow (Heart of Darkness), Scrooge, Cinderella, even Flaubert's Félicité.

In contrast, when reader empathy for the character's plight and admiration for the character's response are a writer's desire, the creation of a victim-character who allows victimization to stifle their will and then dwell on the injustice of their plight, eager to blame and expose causes (rather than eliminate causes so others will not be affected), the ability to elicit true reader empathy is, to say the least, tricky. Here are the reasons why.

A described victim is: a sufferer, the injured party, the prey. Born victims are: losers, patsies, suckers, and often fools. But these traits are subjective, as well as the idea of who is a victim and who is not.

A reader judging a person as a victim requires agreement that the victim has been injured or wronged unjustly, and that the judgment is beyond reasonable argument. In most story creations, the average author cannot predict a specific reader's response to the described victim—, a response that may be crucial for story acceptance. But authors in control of their storytelling do write to create specific responses in their targeted readers. Knowing the character and controlling the story for the reader's response can accomplish this.

When creating victim-as-character in fiction, the victim's self-perception is important. When negative self-perception is a result of unjust (and often inexplicable) harm from a person or event, the character is easily absorbed by the injustice, causing inaction. This inaction prohibits the character from redefining themselves and their life situation, and creates negative emotions of self-sympathy and pity, feelings often that expect selfless, all-consuming physical, emotional, and intellectual aid from others. The greater the expectations of the victim, the less likely those in contact with the victim will be able to fulfill the need for untethered pity, and a reader will have a less empathetic response. So, attention to how the victim perceives their misfortune directs (1) an active response to improve one's state, or (2) a passive submission to life's challenges.

But, characters created to regain their self respect or productivity, not expecting or requiring responses based on the sympathetic feelings of others, of which the character maneuvers and manipulates those sympathies by trying to become a more intently pitied victim, will appreciate sympathy, but not require it, and focus their daily feelings and actions on rejecting self pity, and reaching out beyond their present situation to the benefit of others. Writers who have control of their story creation can, with attention to victimization and a character's responses, create great fiction if they write well and embody in their character some trait beyond the ordinary, some thoughts that are unique without a trace of cliché, and a touch of the hero that most exceptional literary characters possess.

Consider, as a writer, these goals: (1) stay objective; (2) don't succumb to converting a reader to your assessment of injustice in victimization; 3) make your characters unique, incapable of clichéd thinking and response in regards to victimization; (4) avoid predetermination of the validity of the injustice—let the reader determine her or his opinion from the storytelling.

There are no absolutes in writing great fictional stories, but there is awareness and avoidance of mediocrity.

INTERVIEWS

INTERVIEWS

Lee K. Abbott Interview 167
Steve Almond Interview 181
John Biguenet Interview.. 193
Robert Olen Butler Interview...201
Ron Carlson Interview 221
Lan Samantha Chang Interview 235
Charles D'Ambrosio Interview 245
Peter Ho Davies Interview 255
Jonathan Dee Interview.. 265
Tom Jenks Interview 281
Fred Leebron Interview 291
David Lynn Interview 303
Michael Malone Interview.. 315
Lee Martin Interview 341
Rebecca McClanahan Interview... 355
Josh Neufeld and Sari Wilson Interview............................ 369
Richard North Patterson Interview...................................... 385
Michael Ray Interview 403
Jim Shepard Interview 419
Rob Spillman Interview.. 437
Kirby Wilkins Interview 447
Susan Yeagley and Kevin Nealon Interview 463

Lee K. Abbott Interview

22 June, 2011
William H. Coles

Lee K. Abbott was born in 1947 in the Panama Canal Zone and grew up in Las Cruces, New Mexico. He received bachelor's and master's degrees from New Mexico State University. After studying at Columbia College, he earned a master of fine arts from the University of Arkansas in 1977. He has taught at Colorado College, Washington University, Rice University, and Case Western Reserve University. He is currently a humanities distinguished professor in English at Ohio State University at Columbus.

William H. Coles
I'd like to start with your conceptualization of story. What is the essence of story? What features are important to you?

Lee K. Abbott
At the heart of story, for me, is character. Any longer, I don't remember what has happened in a story as much as I remember who it happened to. I get my thrills by being obliged to inhabit the life of someone different from me, though they might be struggling with the same things that I, away from the page, have been struggling with. The whole notion that Ahab is the reason we have *Moby-Dick*—the notion that writers are busy committing to each other those people who galvanize their imaginations.

William H. Coles
Does a story have to have a beginning, middle, and end?

Lee K. Abbott
Yes. I'm old-fashioned in that regard. I'm convinced that the stories I respond to best do have beginnings, middles, and ends.

William H. Coles
In the traditional concept of a short story, what are the key differences between essay and memoir?

Lee K. Abbott
I've actually written a short story that I call an essay, because I imagined the writer thinking of it as an essay. It is also a cheap trick to persuade the reader that the stakes are really higher because it actually happened. Of course, it's an act of the imagination. But I don't like to otherwise confuse or inflate the different genres. I like to sit down to a personal essay with the belief it actually happened as the writer says it did. That it is actually true. Now, memoir, we all understand the personal essay and the memoir are constructed. It's not possible to remember conversations that took place thirty years ago or more, but I trust the writer to reproduce a faithful simulacrum of the events. They are true insofar as they address the heart of the moment. And they do so without contrivance, without duplicity, without anything else that lies within the fiction writer's tool kit.

William H. Coles
How important is short story in our contemporary lives?

Lee K. Abbott
Well, if you talk to the commercial sorts, they tell you it's not very important at all. And it is true, I'm guessing, that most of us who write short stories know—and beginning short story writers quickly learn _that there is no market for short stories. Yet, I persisted in writing short stories because it's the thing, it turns out, that I can do. I don't have the patience, or the intelligence, or the discipline, or the knowledge to write a novel.

William H. Coles
So, the short story has decreased in popularity, and it seems TV and film have become the primary media for delivery of the short story. Why has prose as an important source of short story decreased?

Lee K. Abbott
Reading is work in the way watching TV isn't. And remember, the good short story writer is taking advantage of all those tools, as I call them, that the TV, film, or stage writer doesn't have to deal with. For me, a story is a whole lot more than the actions that happen in the dialogue. For me, much of the importance lies in the feelings and thoughts that would otherwise go unrecorded were I in a different genre. Picking up a story is just work. You've got to know those words, you've got to have a memory, you've got to give it enough time. You know the story is not going to be over, as a TV program is, after twenty-three minutes. It might take shorter; it might take longer.

William H. Coles
Do you have any feeling about the type and quality of short story that is now being selected and published being different than the traditional stories of HenryJames or Flannery O'Connor or Anton Chekhov?

Lee K. Abbott
I think there is a lot more variety now. It's not bad. I'm not here to say it's bad. As Don Bartholomew used to say, he found it difficult to find a point of view kinky enough to call his own. Culturally speaking that might be the case, but I think when it comes to imagining the real world, we've got a dizzying variety of writing styles, writing approaches, writing aesthetics, writing material. It's fun. It's one of the fun things about going to a bookstore. If you're not surprised by what you find there, you're not paying much attention.

William H. Coles
You've expressed the importance of voice that seems important in contemporary short stories. I don't mean to be flippant, but what is voice?

Lee K. Abbott
Glad you asked. I actually have a definition.

William H. Coles
Good!

Lee K. Abbott
I think it's the last thing that comes to a writer, and I think it's a function of material. My notion is we're put on Earth to write about something. And I was put on Earth to write about six hundred miles of southwest desert where all the things that happened to me first occurred, where I found a language unique to that place. Can you imagine John Updike, who wrote florid prose, without his being a preacher's kid, a schoolteacher's kid, in rural suburban Pennsylvania? Can you imagine William Faulkner without Oxford, Mississippi? Can you imagine Cormac McCarthy absent El Paso or Santa Fe? I think we find our material, and once we acknowledge our material, embrace our material, along with it comes a way of talking about it. That's voice.

William H. Coles
Those examples relate to setting. Is voice dependent on setting completely?

Lee K. Abbott
Setting is one feature. I've been asked what kind of stories I write. I have a kind of stock answer, nonetheless a true answer: I write about things that interest me. The things that interest me on the page are relationships between men and women, between father and son, between men as friends. I've got this whole category that I call trash compactor story, which is Walt Whitman meets the ayatollah of rock and roll . . . postapocalyptic stuff where I get an opportunity to use those great lives that belong to someone else. So, for me, material is coupled with a kind of language I find myself speaking whenever I sit down to do a story. I turn into a somewhat different guy, with a much different tone, as it were.

William H. Coles
Would you agree that voice could be everything that a character does, thinks, says in a story?

Lee K. Abbott
I guess it would be true that part of the way I say things depends on the way I see things, or hear things, or experience things. My job usually is to follow one person through a series of events, noting for the reader how those events register. I suppose that's a function of the way I am away from the page.

William H. Coles
I ask because beginning writers have difficulty digesting what voice is. To create it, they fall into a hyperextension of personalities, salacious material, overwrought prose. How can the beginning writer find voice other than looking to setting and following the character through events?

Lee K. Abbott
I don't want to sound too mystical, but I think voice finds the writer and not the other way around. I published a lot of stories that you would not believe I'd written because I don't sound in those stories the way I sound in the stories that I'm best known for. I published a lot of stories were very "craft smart"—smartly put together, polished to a high shine—but they were ultimately empty. There was nothing invested in them other than the desire to make—well, a story. My mantra is that getting on the page ought to cost you something. That is the kind of thing I tell myself when I find myself two pages into a story that is only a puzzle or a scarf joint.

William H. Coles
S-c-a-r-f? [A scarf joint bevels two pieces of wood (or metal) so that they fit over or into each other.]

Lee K. Abbott
Yeah. It's one of those things I know how to do.

William H. Coles
You brought up an interesting concept the other day and that was, when working in the first person you used a double . . .

Lee K. Abbott
"Double I" is what I call it.

William H. Coles
H. Coles
"Double I." Thank you. I'd like to come back to this, but first, I'd like to know what the advantages and disadvantages of the first person?

Lee K. Abbott
Earlier in my career, I thought the chief advantage of the first-person point of view was that it was nearly impossible to violate. You were either there to witness the events, or you heard about them from somebody else. I, as a writer, couldn't tell anything about the "I" as a character when the character didn't know it. And then I reread *Moby-Dick* and discovered that Ishmael relays a lot of conversations that he is not around to witness, which is to say Melville wasn't paying a lot of attention to the veracity of the point of view he had chosen. But nowadays I think there are no limitations on the first person, as I understand how complex it can be. I'm thinking of *A Book of Common Prayer* by Joan Didion, which is a first-person book, but at the same time the narrator reports conversations and events that she wasn't around to witness, about a character who is dead before the book begins. So it seems to me every bit as rich in possibility as third person, even third-person omniscient. That was fun to discover, but I only did so when I discovered the exploitation of what I call the "double I".

William H. Coles
The "double I" is able to create a narrator . . . almost an objective narrator through the first person. So, you've got your "I" and you're separating this "I." You can do that with time—say, an older narrator and a younger narrator—the same person but at different times in his or her life. Can you do that with other features? Changes in attitude, for example, or changes in political parties, or religious beliefs, to establish a sense of the "double I"?

Lee K. Abbott
You can tell a first-person story that's about a discrete sequence of events, but you can bring to that events that lie outside the story. As I always say, in theory there are two first persons in a story. There is the one who experiences it and the one who tells about it. The one who tells about it is privy to all the events before the first word is written. Naturally, the second "I" brings a different understanding to what's happening in the dramatic present than the "I." And sometimes great hay can be made between the tension of what I once was and what I am now. The importance is what "I am now" can bring to shine on "what I was then."

William H. Coles
Is this also an opportunity for irony?

Lee K. Abbott
Oh, indeed.

William H. Coles
How does that mechanically work?

Lee K. Abbott
I like irony of a special kind, namely, narrators, who have irony about their former selves. I don't like the sort of irony that some writers indulge in as an opportunity to lampoon their characters or trivialize them. I don't want to be in that category.

William H. Coles
Or ridicule?

Lee K. Abbott
Yes. I don't want to be in that business. I see this as one of the benefits of adopting the "double I."

William H. Coles
When you go to the third person, narration becomes more complicated in different ways. When you're thinking of the narration of the story, do you think in terms of the character acting out the story, the narrator delivering the story, and the author creating the story? In that scenario, the narration falls to the narrator. The narrator, of course, can be collapsed into the character. Academics always teach a set of rules, for instance, you have to stay within this character's POV that cannot be violated. Yet Virginia Woolf's *The Common Reader*, or Henry James's *The Complete Notebooks of Henry James*, or James Wood's *How*

Fiction Works contain writings about their authors' views. How, as an author, do you approach these inconsistencies and difficulties in narration? How do you use them effectively to develop the characterization that's so important to you as a writer?

Lee K. Abbott
Let's not underestimate the importance of white space as a device to signal to the reader that change is afoot. I can use white space to change place; I can use white space to change time; I can use white space to change the point of view. I think of white space as the great escape. You can write a story in a series of limited third-person POVs. The first one is James's, the next one is John's, the next Jeff's, then Judy's. And you can tip the reader off with white space.

With respect to violations, there is the long-honored tradition: one hallmark of your ability as a writer is your ability to cling to a single point of view. I have this thing I call the contract with the reader. I used to have a teacher named Jim Whitehead, who said that by the end of the first sentence of a story, you've been taught not only how to read it but how the writer will write it. Which is to say, if I write the first sentence in a limited third, but by the third page I find myself in somebody else's mind, then I violated the contract I developed with the reader in the first line. I deceived him. I promised in the first line this would be third-person limited, but no, it turned out to be third-person omniscient. In that case, let's go back to the reader and make it clear that it is omniscient. Establish the tone, the language, get the POV right, announce the focal character, plant the stout stake, as Henry James says. That's why we spend so much class time on the first two paragraphs of a story.

William H. Coles
You can conceptualize a story world for each character as a sphere that contains all their experiences and thoughts, and then you think of the narrator (not always, of course, but) as a distinct narrator with a distinct sphere from the characters. This narrator, if you're going to use a separate point of view, has his or her own world with distinct experiences, views, thought, opinions, memories. All stories have happened, and quite often the narrator's sphere comes later, often much later, than the character's sphere. Does a writer need to pay attention to the narrator's sphere as compared to the character's sphere?

Lee K. Abbott
I'm a big admirer of Henry James. He invented a variation on third-person limited called "central consciousness" that you discover by playing the following game. The story is told in the language of the focal character, if the focal character

can tell his own story. But of course the character can't, so that falls to the narrator. I like to think . . . in my stories, you cannot discover a narrator. You can only discover more of the character—in the third person in particular—because I'm drawn to the language you leave to Jeff on the page.

William H. Coles
I'd like to consider an author sphere. We've got the character sphere, the narrator sphere—sometimes those are one thing—and then the author sphere. The author sphere is everything about the world that the author knows about the real world and the story world, and contains a variety of information depending on whether the author has a narrow or broad knowledge of the real world. But author-sphere knowledge often seems distracting, if not negative, for story development and quality. Should the characters' and narrator's spheres be consistently distinct from the author's sphere? Do you see what I mean? Do you agree? The author's "second self."

Lee K. Abbott
I do know what is called the author's second self. When I sit down to put my fingers on the keyboard to tell a story, I'm no longer Lee K. Abbott who raises children or married his wife or was once upon a time an Episcopalian. I am the Lee K. Abbott who writes stories. I'm an author who has been taking his measure for a long time, and I know that the Lee K. Abbott who tells stories has blind spots, weaknesses, predilections, tics even, so the Lee K. Abbott who pays his taxes is smart enough to recognize that the Lee K. Abbott who writes stories might be a three-trick pony and it's time to learn new tricks, et cetera. I do believe I become somebody else with the same name who has told all these stories in the past, who has got a way of telling a story. That's it for me. That's where I am.

William H. Coles
What we're talking about, it seems, is authorial intrusions, and this sounds like a legitimate way to decrease the possibility of unproductive authorial intrusions. However, I sense that for most contemporary writers, author involvement in the story is a given.

Lee K. Abbott
For those writers who are more experimental, more postmodern than I am, the whole point of the story is to draw attention to how smart the writer is. This is not something I believe. But these are things that form the aesthetic of someone

who is in the business of playing author. And I'm not. The form has meaning, too. I try to use form in story to say something else about character.

William H. Coles
Do you find that your liking of a story, even when you're critiquing it, relates to attitudes of the writer toward writing, toward how and why a writer writes as well as toward the conceptualization of the theme and meaning of the story? Particularly, do you see writers who want to be writers? "I'm going to get published and therefore I'm going to sit down for three hours every day and write," as opposed to the writer who wants to create a story that has an impact on a reader, and tells them something about what it means to be human, that entertains them. Is that a fair question?

Lee K. Abbott
It is a fair question. All questions about the writer's art are fair. I'm not much interested in philosophy for myself. I've got nothing to tell anybody. I have imagined experiences to share, but I've got no lessons to be learned. We have a form for that; it is called expository essay, where there are points to be made. I'm not here to make points. I am here to try to connect a reader to something made out of words and oblige them to share that world for its duration. My sole criterion for an effective piece of fiction is: if it moves me. If the writer has done the work and I have forgotten about myself, I've been moved. I left my world and entered that world, had that complete experience and ravished it.

William H. Coles
Is that related to the idea that as a reader, you never see the world again exactly the way you saw it before you read the story?

Lee K. Abbott
Yes, it is. I can name dozens and dozens and dozens of stories and novels that have made me, for better or worse, me. And they still have an enormous effect. I think, as a citizen and a human being, I'm far better off having spent so much time with Robert Stone or Eudora Welty's works.

William H. Coles
You recently mentioned feeling sad that humor is leaving the contemporary story. You gave an example of a story with a zinger at the end. Quite often you hear, now, in readings, humorous pieces utilizing surprise and reversal. As you work for that kind of humor, is it antithetical to story theme and meaning? In other words, can you, when you're working on humorous stories, negatively affect the ability to create significant meaning in the characters?

Lee K. Abbott
I don't think so. No. I think it is a perfectly legitimate way to tell about the species. I worry about a culture that won't take its comics seriously.

William H. Coles
Because that's laughing at self?

Lee K. Abbott
Maybe a lot of people think comedy is a cheap art. And yet we take such pleasure from it. We love to laugh.

William H. Coles
Well, we have to. It's part of living.

Lee K. Abbott
And I don't mind making comedy part of the world on my pages, because it exists in my life.

William H. Coles
Do you include irony in that conceptualization? Why write a story if you know how it's going to turn out?

Lee K. Abbott
Oh, yes.

William H. Coles
It's not just guffaw?

Lee K. Abbott
No, no. It's a spectrum, like anything else.

William H. Coles
In writing stories, do you advocate outlining and blocking?

Lee K. Abbott
I've never done that. I always see that as curious. Why write the story if you know how it's going to turn out? Yet, lots of writers I respect do that, so my advice always—to anyone who is interested in my advice—is to do whatever. Go about it any way that results in a story. If you need to outline, do so.

William H. Coles
If you're wedded to emotion and emotional arcs in stories, would you think it's helpful to outline—not necessarily on the page, but in the mind—the progression of that emotion through the story so that when you're writing a scene, and the character's actions in that scene are consistent with what's going to happen and what's happened before?

Lee K. Abbott
I think if you're looking for continuity, or unity as it were, that's easy to do in a short story. I would think it much more difficult to do in a novel. I can see the wisdom in making notes about the progression in a really long piece of work, but in a short story you're thinking about four or five, six moments at most. You can keep those moments between the ears. One thing I like about stories is that they always take a turn. In the middle. After the opening move. At the end. They go someplace you haven't anticipated. And if you're really smart about your work, you'll ask yourself, "Why am I going there?" I think the answer, then, lies in the stories.

William H. Coles
And that's a process of discovery, rather than determining ahead of time the switch or change?

Lee K. Abbott
I'm like an architect who doesn't design the whole building. Just the front door.

William H. Coles
What is drama? How is drama in prose different than drama in film?

Lee K. Abbott
It's all about conflict. About X wanting something and being denied it, or getting it and being dissatisfied with it. [*laughs*] It's what Faulkner calls the human heart in conflict with itself.

William H. Coles
So conflict can be internal as well as external.

Lee K. Abbott
Indeed.

William H. Coles
It doesn't have to be plot related?

Lee K. Abbott
No, no, no. Many of the stories in James Joyce's *Dubliners*, including "The Dead," take place between somebody's ears.

William H. Coles
And that results in change in character and reader?

Lee K. Abbott
It can. But as we talked about in class the other day, I don't believe character has to change for you to have a story. Character *may* change, but I don't think it's a requirement.

William H. Coles
Could you give us advice on the revision process? What are the goals? What are the techniques you find effective?

Lee K. Abbott
I'll quote the former director of the Iowa Writers' Workshop, Paul Engle: "Writing is rewriting what you've already rewritten." And he's right. Never mind how poetic that sounds. I think God gives you maybe one story that comes out of your head whole and doesn't need a blue mark on it, but for the most part writing involves discovering your mistakes and fixing them. Discovering the artistic infelicities that we all want to make. Finding the inconsistencies. Getting rid of the self-indulgence. Getting rid of the superfluous. It's heightening the stuff you gave short shrift to earlier on. These things you can only learn by doing. I know now, because I've written and published a zillion stories, that for me it takes seven, eight, nine drafts before I'm fairly confident I've discovered everything wrong. No matter how tickled I was by it before.

William H. Coles
Does this relate to a very helpful approach, which you demonstrated in class, to ask certain essential questions: How could that have happened? Why did she do that? Looking for motivations, looking for veracity of facts—being a fact checker, and being sure the timeline is correct. Those details?

Lee K. Abbott
Oh, yes. I give everything to my wife. She's no literary critic and she has no desire to be, she's just a reader. But when I give her the story, I give her the story with a bunch of questions in my mind. Like: "Pam, did you understand why he did what he did on page three?" And if she says, "No," then I say, "Okay, then I didn't account for motivation in sufficient detail." Those kinds of things. "Do

you know how many hours passed between this and that?" You have to learn to become your own best critic. You have to learn what questions to ask, especially the questions that might reveal how idiotic you are. How dumb or blind you've been.

William H. Coles
I'd like to thank you very much for his interview; I learned a great deal. My admiration for you as a teacher and a writer continues to soar.

Lee K. Abbott
My pleasure. Thank you very much.

Steve Almond Interview

8 June, 2012
William H. Coles

Steve Almond is a former adjunct professor at Boston College who now teaches at Grubb Street, Annabel Island, Writers@Work, and Tin House. His most recent collection of short stories is *God Bless America* (Lookout Books, 2011), and his latest novel is *Rock and Roll Will Save Your Life* (Random House, 2010). He reviews books for the *Boston Globe* and the *Los Angeles Times*.

William H. Coles
What is your concept of story as it has developed throughout history? How is story important to culture, and to individuals? And how is it being used today as an educational resource, a learning resource?

Steve Almond
Let's start big: I think stories are how people do different things. How they make sense of their experiences. How they give their experiences shape. How they get things off their chests. How they put their wishes and fears into the world so they're understandable—and hopefully beautiful—to another person. Certainly they could be educational, but I don't think the kinds of stories I'm interested in are directed toward any specific goal beyond the reader feeling more human than they did before. There might be lots of other things that stories are doing: teaching a lesson, making us excited, whiling away a few minutes while we're bored and in need of a world to escape into. The best stories do all of those things, but centrally they awaken people to their internal lives, allow people to experience sometimes uncontrollable unbearable difficult dangers, exalted feelings. The story gives the characters faces, puts them in danger, emotional or otherwise, and sees what happens.

William H. Coles
It enlightens the reader to the human condition. Is that fair?

Steve Almond
"Enlighten" is okay, but I think of stories as implicating the reader. You don't just feel entertained or enlightened; you the reader feel implicated. When we read about Holden Caulfield, hopefully, almost inevitably, we're experiencing the part

of ourselves that is heartbroken, confused, mourning, outraged, adolescent. That part of us doesn't go away. If you read a great book, even if it's about a character like Humbert Humbert, who would be considered depraved, dangerous, and criminal in real life, reading about his internal life and his uncontrollable desire for Lolita—how does it make us feel? My attitude is that this is a creepy guy who got what he deserved; and I too have felt desires that are dangerous and wrong and I can't control them; and how nice it is, how liberating it is, how scary it is, how human it is, that someone has written a story that speaks to that in such a sustained and beautiful way.

William H. Coles
You seemed a little uncomfortable there with the word "entertained" as related to a story. Shouldn't a story entertain?

Steve Almond
Absolutely. I'm not uncomfortable with that at all. I'm saying that a good story does lots of different things. It doesn't do any one thing; you can't reduce it. Human beings have needed stories and have been using stories to do many different jobs in their lives. I'm interested in stories that entertain the reader, of course. In class I say no amount of fancy language will take the place of weak action. And to have action, you have to place characters in danger, push them into dangerous situations. You need to stick with them when it's coming down all around them, and inside them. To me that's the hallmark of exciting stuff. But I'm really interested in stories where I feel implicated, involved in a necessary way—emotionally, psychologically, even morally involved by what I'm reading. I realize I've made the same mistakes, had the same desires, suffered the same fears as the characters.

William H. Coles
You mention reader engagement, and you say you maintain that engagement with action. Is it valuable for new writers to maintain that engagement by considering the Aristotelian basics of storytelling? Beginning, middle, end, et cetera. The progression. Are those important?

Steve Almond
I'm not going to argue with Aristotle. Yes, of course, people understandably try to describe story, its forms. And if you hear any reluctance, it's likely because it feels like such an instinctual part of our consciousness, it's serving so many different functions, and it can happen in so many different ways that to say, "Okay, here's what storytelling is and should do, and what form it should take," necessarily feels reductive. Because I could say, well, what about stories where

the narrative jumps around? Do those have a beginning, a middle, and an end? Does that mean that stories in song, or stories in Symbolist poetry, don't have beginnings, middles, and ends like narrative? Now, I'm a great fan of beginnings, middles, and ends, and not manipulating your chronology to confuse your reader unnecessarily. So I'm not an advocate of just going out and doing your thing, and there, that's a story. A story has to take the reader somewhere emotionally, intellectually, and psychologically. You have to be a willing accomplice; your consciousness has to be willingly kidnapped by the story. But beyond that I don't have a whole lot of rules. There are rules that hold true in most cases, such as beginning, middle, end, but aside from that, let it rip.

William H. Coles
Fiction seems to present opportunities for storytelling when other forms do not. Fiction allows you to develop characters as needed to enhance story and meaning. Plot is developed in ways that are useful for the story's meaning and enlightenment.

Steve Almond
Yes.

William H. Coles
But you teach a course in which you combine fiction, memoir, and essay simultaneously. Teaching writing in a number of different forms seems competitive to teaching the specifics of fiction that develop special stories. How in your mind do you separate essay, memoir, creative nonfiction, fiction? And is it necessary to do so?

Steve Almond
They're not all the same thing. Creative nonfiction (or whatever they call it) is a radically subjective version of events that objectively took place. Anytime the author consciously represents an event that has taken place, asserting that it took place ("nonfiction" it says, there on the spine), they've made a contract with the reader that this is a work of nonfiction. If you assert that something took place and you know it did not, then you're making a different sort of work. It's fiction. It's a wonderful kind of work to do because you can design your own world for maximum impact. Implicate the reader in the deepest way. But you can't say—or at least I feel it is wrong to make a false contract with the reader when you say—"in this work of nonfiction I tell you only things that happened" and then knowingly mix things up because it's more dramatic and exciting.

In my nonfiction books I put at the beginning a proviso: "Look, all of this happened many years ago; I do my best to try to recollect it." If I changed some names, or if I'm actually constructing characters, I would concede to that. Or I'd say, if this was the case, "The events I'm describing are altered." In other words, why not just take a minute at the outset to tell the reader, for instance, it's a work of nonfiction but there are a few aspects changed. I feel strongly about memoirs where people make stuff up because it improves the story and don't admit it to the reader. My solution for that in my writing is to say, "Well, gee, I wish this had happened," and I'll go off on a reverie. The reason Oprah picked the James Frey book *A Million Little Pieces*, and the reason it got published, is because it's a searing story that involves prison and all these people—who turned out to be made-up characters. They came out of James Frey's imagination. On the one hand, I don't want to put Frey down for writing a book that people found compelling, but I do think it was dishonorable to make things up and call it nonfiction. It's a radically subjective version of events that objectively took place. When I was a kid, I remember hitting my older brother on a backswing with a baseball bat, hitting his lip, and his lip exploded with blood. I have a particular memory of that episode. When I later asked my brother, "Hey, do you remember that time?" he had a completely different memory. Who's right? I don't know. We don't have a film. We don't have evidence. Probably it's a mixture of our two memories. One thing we both agree on is that it took place. And I can see the scar on his mouth. You understand what I'm saying?

William H. Coles
Sure. You often say: tell the truth about things that matter to you most deeply.

Steve Almond
The reason I'm comfortable teaching cross-genre is that the essential thing I'm trying to put across is so basic: tell the truth about things that matter to you most deeply. You want to find a fictional disguise? Do it. You want to deal it straight-out as a memoir? Do it. If you want to tell it in a postmodern essay, do that. But the fundamental ingredient is a sort of radical candor and disclosure, and a kind of courage, I guess. And there are other things: avoiding nonessential words, not wasting the reader's time. Basic rules that I feel apply no matter what kind of writing you do.

William H. Coles
There is an overall author attitude that seems to relate to this—namely, the position of the author in the telling. Objective storytelling and writing versus subjective storytelling and writing. That would seem to cleave memoir from nonfiction—that in fiction, the quality seems to improve the more the author

divorces him- or herself from the writing and moves to a broader view of the world, and a broader view of experiences to create plot and characters, rather than focusing on their own experiences totally. Not that personal experiences can't stimulate fiction. Is it valuable for authors to recognize objective prose writing in fiction as opposed to subjective?

Steve Almond
It's tough. Again I'm bristling at the idea that there are absolutes. Anything you write is subjective because you're choosing what gets included in the story or not. Right? Even if it *sounds* objective, like verifiable truth, you're choosing to include certain facts and exclude other ones. That's a big decision. History texts are pretty subjective affairs. What are you going to call history? What matters?

William H. Coles
Isn't the concept of the author creating stories and the narrator telling stories valuable in fiction? Can't the narrator become the entity that generates the emotions in a reader, telling the stories from his or her world with unique perceptions, opinions, and observations? I think the actions in the story generate emotions in the reader, not the author's narrative descriptive telling. Tell them a good story in a lucid way.

Steve Almond
Yes. But that has less to do so with the distinction between fiction and nonfiction and more with the fundamentals. Whichever voice is speaking to us readers in fiction or nonfiction, a close, very close, intimate point of view versus a distant third that hovers above like in Kurt Vonnegut, or Leo Tolstoy—those distinctions seem less important to me and to the reader than the quality of the voice the reader gets intuitively. The voice that's talking to them is a truth-telling voice, and a voice that shouldn't waste their time. As you say, tell them a good story in a lucid way. Bring them the action, the emotional, psychological, and moral action-drama they want. That's the big distinction I make between stuff that works and stuff that doesn't. If they could find, I think, texts where you can say, this is a memoir but it's written like a scientific treatise, and it's also objective. It's also true on the fictional side. Everything that is written is deeply autobiographical. Holden Caulfield came into the world out of J. D. Salinger's imagination, his deepest preoccupations. There isn't some separate protocol from the deepest recesses of your mind and your heart called the imagination; it's the heart of who you are. Anything you dream up, if it's any good, is coming from your deepest preoccupations, obsessions, fears, regrets. It's a fictional disguise for that. But it's always coming from deep inside you if it's any good. I don't think it's possible to write in a way that isn't subjective.

William H. Coles
That's true. But isn't there in classic fiction a certain dedication to the consistency of voice, be it the voice the narrator (a very important aspect of classical fiction) or the character voice? The authorial voice, quite often dominant in contemporary literature, both in fiction and in memoir, is always present on the page. Whereas if you look at classical fiction—Jane Austen, the Brontës, C. S. Forester, Tolstoy, Anton Chekhov, Fyodor Dostoyevsky—the author doesn't intrude. Jane Austen doesn't come in with her personality.

Steve Almond
Because she has the narrator to do that.

William H. Coles
My point exactly. Austen is always there. The reader knows she's there. But she's objective in her creation in the sense that she's consistent in her dedication to the purity of the narrative voice, and the character voices. Is this valuable thinking for a writer who wishes create more effective, more profound fictional stories? The author creates the narrator to guide the reader through the fictional world.

Steve Almond
One characteristic of people's earlier careers, including my writing, is that I didn't think about creating a narrator—an independent entity known as the narrator. I'm the author. I'm telling the story. Maybe it's third person, maybe some character is telling it, and me, the author. But no, there is actually a narrator! Jane Austen wrote those novels, but the voice that tells those novels is Jane Austen's narrator. That voice is created to guide the reader through the fictional world. The author creates the narrator. There has been a tendency in recent years to jettison the narrator.

When you encounter a text where the author and the narrator converge, it is usually a confusing text to read, because there isn't a narrator recognizing that the reader needs to be kept oriented, that the reader needs to know X, Y, and Z in order for the scene to be gratifying, emotionally satisfying, dramatically satisfying. I think there has been a tendency in recent years to jettison the narrator because we're surrounded by art, movies, and TV shows where there isn't any narrator. It's just you seeing what you're seeing. Maybe there's a voice-over, but most of the time you are flying without a narrator, encountering what you encounter. That's why it's so difficult to do movies from books.

In books there is this entity of the narrator. We're used to being instinctively in tune with storytelling, but visual stories in movies and TV, the dominant media of our age, won't work by the same rules, which results in a tendency to consciously or unconsciously ape the movies and TV and jettison the narrator, which results in a lot of people plunging into scenes without us really knowing where we are. We don't have a camera to show us the room we're in, the building we're in; we can't pull back to see the larger neighborhood. We just have the words on the page. So if you, the author, know where we are, that's not enough. You need to create a narrator who tells everything you know. Not just, "'Hey, what are you doing there?' The boy had fallen down the well." Versus, "The officer walked up and looked down the well and said 'Hey, what are you doing down there?'" See what I mean? The narrator has been jettisoned.

William H. Coles
Is the application of this discussion different in narrative description versus in-scene dramatic story development?

Steve Almond
A lot of people are reluctant to have their narrator set the scene. They've been told in workshops, "Show don't tell, get to the action, stay in scene," and they overlook or mistrust, or are scornful of, the pleasures of direct exposition. The most famous example I can think of is John Williams's novel *Stoner*, which we looked at in class, where the first three paragraphs tell the story of that guy's life. As you might read in an obit. John Williams is saying, "Hey, reader, you're just going to have to go with me, this is not a guy who had a big consequential life, he wasn't a hero, he wasn't a soldier, he wasn't a famous politician, he wasn't a lover, an athlete, a musician, a star. He was one of the uncounted. There was nothing sensational about him. But he was still a human being, and here's his story." Pretty gutsy thing to do, and there is a lot of pleasure in having an author who will tell us who we're going to be reading about and what the circumstances of his life were in a matter-of-fact way. Young writers are very mistrustful other than "Action! We're in scene. It's happening." There's these vivid details and observations, but those don't mean anything unless they're located within a particular consciousness, and that consciousness is located in the larger world. That's what Jane Austen, Tolstoy, and the writers of the nineteenth century were so good at—strong, independent narrators.

William H. Coles
Let me ask you about voice. You seem to respond strongly to interesting, innovative voices. Whether in essays, memoirs, and fiction, voice seems to be a pleasure for you when it's well done. But to me, when a strong voice is authorial,

as it often is in contemporary writing, there seems to be a danger of slipping into sentimentality—into the telling of emotions rather than allowing emotions to emerge through actions. In your sensibilities, when it comes to storytelling, do you think a dominant authorial voice degrades the quality?

Steve Almond
I don't know about it degrading the quality of the storytelling.

William H. Coles
My opinion, obviously.

Steve Almond
It seems to me there are many people writing wonderfully and many others still trying to figure it out. As for the question about voice, I think everybody responds to strong, vibrant voice—voices that appear to be radically subjective, fearless in their honesty, transgressive, daring, willing to tell ugly unpleasant hidden truths. We love it when language surprises us, sounds euphonious. In other words, I think most people respond to the same pleasures in voice, in the sense that the person telling the story is not going to waste their time. Tell them a story that has an emotional, psychological, moral payoff. And doesn't confuse them. That's the basics of what I'm reading for. And if the voice satisfies those criteria, I don't *decide* to listen; I'm already listening.

William H. Coles
If you look at story, especially fictional story, as truly dependent on characterization (I assume you agree that there is such a thing as a character-driven plot), what would you suggest to a writer trying to develop that? How do we bring innovative, effective characterization to our writing? How do we make the thoughts and emotions of the characters drive the plot?

Steve Almond
First, you simply have to pay attention. The author has to give the narrator power to notice the right details. And the author must force the narrator to push the characters into situations we avoid in real life. Art is in part about pushing characters into precarious situations and then slowing down when the character is in the midst of it, overrun by the system. In James Joyce's story "The Dead," there's this wrenching moment when he discovers his wife loves somebody else, and he changes. He's paying attention. He's trying to cope with that. He looks out the window and the world intensifies, kind of electrifies. So that's what you're trying to do. You're trying to find a character who's alive enough to get into some sort of trouble and see him through it, or at least not

fail. That's the central thing for short stories. For memoir, you have to do the job of memory or recollection of your own experiences; and for essays, those of historical figures who are compelling to you. In my case, thinking about candy [for *CandyFreak*], but not just candy as a pleasure, but also the function it served as an antidepressant. In other words, your obsessions should lead you into as much trouble as your character's would.

William H. Coles
Let me ask you a little about conflict.

Steve Almond
NO!

William H. Coles
Well, *DAMN YOU!* [laughs] My question is that conflict seems so essential to develop a character and engage a reader, and yet to introduce conflict in a story on all levels, not just the plot level, seems impossible at times. Can you give us hints as to how to get conflict into writing?

Steve Almond
I myself don't always do it effectively. Most people, including writers, avoid conflict off the page. So they avoid it on the page. The best example on my mind right now is Matthew Clam's *Sam the Cat*, where you've got a character deeply invested in being a ladies' man. So you put them in danger—or worse, in conflict with themselves, which is the ultimate form of conflict. You can have an antagonist come in; there's Iago, he gets Othello all jealous and enraged. Anybody can introduce a villain and make conflict happen, and they should, I exhort them to. A good villain is priceless, more precious than rubies. But I find fascinating conflict that is not just external. Conflict of the self. In that Klam story, you have this ladies' man whose whole identity is predicated on super masculinity. What do you do to this character to force him into conflict with himself? You give him a homosexual urge that will not go away. You destabilize the character. Of course people don't like to be destabilized in their real life, so they resist doing it in their fiction. But that's where the good stuff is: when the characters are knocked off balance and forced up against a version of themselves that's terrifying.

William H. Coles
You said something today about humor that I thought was very valuable. You said that one can develop a humorous writing style.

Steve Almond
Let me amend that a little. What I was trying to say was that everyone has developed a sense of humor in order to cope with unhappiness, awkwardness, embarrassment, whatever. It's less a matter of developing a humorous writing style and much more a matter of realizing that the way we deal with tragedy and awkward feelings off the page, which sometimes is to use humor, also works on the page. It's instinctive within the writer rather than a tool to be pulled out of the writer's toolbox.

William H. Coles
Thanks for that. I've had humorists say in interviews that you can't dissect humor. As soon as you try, the humor is lost. That seems right. Yet when writing in revisions, aren't there potential opportunities to insert it that the writer can identify? Humor has a setup, some sort of reversal that stimulates a response. You yourself do that naturally. And you're an excellent speaker because you've got that sense of what will be funny. Do you think writers should seek these opportunities, or just let them come? Or at least, what do you find true in your writing?

Steve Almond
I'm aware. For instance, if something lousy or embarrassing happens to me, I'm ashamed and embarrassed about it right now, but I know that down the road I'll write about it. I'm not trying to be funny. I am trying to be honest, and my sense of humor will naturally arise to tell the story. I'm not interested in the jokes that help me avoid pain. I'm interested in jokes that allow me to experience the experience within. Few people set out to be funny; I think people who are funny set out to be less unhappy. And the way they do it is with little bursts of forgiveness that take the form of jokes.

William H. Coles
If any of our readers would like to study with you, are there opportunities they can take advantage of?

Steve Almond
In the Boston area, I teach at Grubb Street all the time. Three-hour seminars once a month. I do a lot of conferences. I teach down at Annabel Island, often at Tin House—a wonderful conference. I try to keep a list on the website. If they don't find something, they are welcome to email me and ask, "Are you coming to this part of the world?"

William H. Coles
Do you have reading recommendations?

Steve Almond
I just read Jess Walter's new novel, *TKtitle*. He's a wonderful writer, and this novel is a perfect combination of page-turning action and deep psychological interiority. And my book *This Won't Take But a Minute, Honey* has a list of books I recommend.

William H. Coles
Terrific. Thank you very much for talking with storyinliteraryfiction.com. It's been a pleasure and I've learned a lot. Congratulations on the excellence of your teaching and the excellence of your writing. It's inspirational.

Steve Almond
I'm glad. Thank you.

John Biguenet Interview

21 November, 2009
William H. Coles

An O. Henry Award winner, John Biguenet is the Robert Hunter Distinguished University Professor at Loyola University in New Orleans, where he teaches creative writing. Among his six books are an acclaimed volume of short stories, *The Torturer's Apprentice* (Ecco, 2002), and a novel set in Louisiana, *Oyster* (Ecco, 2003). He also is an award-winning playwright and served as a guest columnist for the *New York Times* after Hurricane Katrina and the collapse of levees in New Orleans in 2005.

William H. Coles
I was fascinated by your lecture yesterday, in particular your implication that the literary story is in decline. Why is this, do you think?

John Biguenet
I'm not sure there has been a decline. It's just the opposite: our society is so immersed in stories that a kind of narrative exhaustion has set in. Every viewer of television and film can almost always predict where a plot is headed. The same is true of the other kinds of stories to which we are introduced every day in advertising, the news, and literary fiction. I think writers are facing a real predicament in terms of what it is that fiction should do when there are so many sources of storytelling and such experienced consumers of narratives.

William H. Coles
Has the quality of the fictional story changed in your mind? I ask because there is the sense that memoir and nonfiction have been replacing the fictional prose story.

John Biguenet
Because there is something potentially unexpected in the way real life works out, nonfiction doesn't face quite the same problem of outcome prediction on the part of the audience. I think it's one reason that reality television has become so popular—the possibility that something unpredictable will force the story in an unexpected direction. This element of the unpredictable is one reason why sports are so popular. We know the game's rules and boundaries, which is to

say we know the structure of the story, but the unexpected element of an injury, for example, or a bad call by the referee, can affect the ending of that particular tale. Those kinds of narratives have attracted larger and larger audiences in part because traditional narratives suffer from more predictable conclusions.

William H. Coles
Have you seen a change in how writers narrate stories?

John Biguenet
Not necessarily. I think short stories have increasingly imitated the novel, and often have taken as their subject relationships between people. But I'm not sure six or seven thousand words are enough to develop two characters and the arc of their relationship fully—and I don't think that is what the short story was designed to do, actually. The novel is better suited to that type of tale.

William H. Coles
You've noted that today, nonfiction content is one of the ways to attract new readers to the novel, and that the quality and the choice of this nonfiction content is important. Could you expand on that? Specifically, I'm thinking of how you've used Louisiana to find the often-unknown aspects of the oyster industry, the human conflicts in that specific arena. How can writers seek their own valuable nonfiction for their fiction?

John Biguenet
The novel has traditionally had a great deal of nonfiction material in it. From the beginning of the Western novel, particularly, readers learned something of how the world worked. But by World War II that type of information was being conveyed by many different media, and so today the novel has lost one of its central reasons for existence, which is the conveyance of information unknown to the reader. I think that's one reason for the success of writers who are talking about immigrant experiences, like Jhumpa Lahiri, for example, or in another way Nathan Englander in *For the Relief of Unbearable Urges*, who talks about a Jewish community that is not well known to most readers. Those writers have attracted an audience, at least in part, because their books provide previously unknown information about the world. At the same time, of course, the books are very well written.

William H. Coles
Is there a wealth of potential in stories exploring the integration of various immigrants into US society?

John Biguenet
Since the United States is becoming increasingly diverse, I think there is a great deal of curiosity about the many communities that make up the country now. And the writers from those communities who have arrived recently in the United States bring greater insight into the daily lives of those immigrants. Those communities have not had so many voices before in our national conversation. Writers from those communities can find wide readership, at least in part, because their narratives continue to do what the Western novel has done since its founding in the mid-eighteenth century: bring us news of something we don't fully know.

William H. Coles
As you look at the importance of the nonfiction content of a novel, is there any danger of decreasing the importance of characterization?

John Biguenet
Oh, no. Just the opposite. When we talk about nonfiction content, we're talking about the setting in which a character becomes eloquent. In *Huckleberry Finn*, for example, the character of Jim and the character of Huck become fully eloquent in the context of the journey they're taking. It is impossible for us to think of ourselves as human beings outside the place in which we find ourselves. But places where characters have found themselves often have been places that are unknown or only vaguely known to the reader.

William H. Coles
What elements are necessary for a writer to develop an effective work of fiction?

John Biguenet
A writer becomes an author by demonstrating authority in two ways: over the craft of writing, and over the subject matter.

William H. Coles
How important is imagination now in literary fiction, as opposed to writing from experience?

John Biguenet
American fiction tends to follow the conventions of realism, and those stories that pay attention to realism will follow experience. In the rest of the world, fiction is often fantastic, and places as much emphasis on the imagined as on observed experience.

William H. Coles
As you begin to develop your novels' character-driven plots, what does that mean to you? In other words, how do you conceptualize character-driven plots as opposed to plotting in a genre sense?

John Biguenet
If a story depends on things being out of balance, that absence of balance will be evident in a character who is capable of change, and so a story that begins with such a character will seek to discover how that person can achieve a sustainable balance. The setting of such a story also will reflect that imbalance. But it begins with ambition, lust, greed—some imbalance in a person that can be depicted in a plot.

William H. Coles
Does that relate to a core desire that is out of balance, or a foible?

John Biguenet
Not just a foible but something essential to the person. Think of it as a crack running through the character—which we all have, of course—but one that is capable of remedy as the character chooses one alternative rather than another to restore him- or herself to equilibrium.

William H. Coles
You're a student of story and have valuable historical and cultural perspectives. What is valuable for writers to study about the development of story over the ages? I'm particularly thinking of how the oral tradition contributed to the written story and how drama was inserted.

John Biguenet
To balance on the one hand what the Greeks, for example, were doing in their drama and epics and what Anton Chekhov was doing in the nineteenth century with the short story is quite a leap. The forms that emerged out of the issues that each of their communities faced shaped the structure, and in a certain sense directed them toward a certain medium. The short story, as we practice it, is basically a nineteenth-century invention, and it responds in some sense to the Industrial Revolution and urbanization. But it's difficult to trace a linear path of stories vis-à-vis cultures.

William H. Coles
Are there stories that you recommend for study? For instance in Chekhov?

The ART of CREATING STORY

John Biguenet
I admire enormously "The Lady with a Dog." There are many stories by Chekhov, by Nathaniel Hawthorne, some by Edgar Allan Poe, certainly by Henry James.

William H. Coles
What Henry James stories might you recommend?

John Biguenet
I think "The Real Thing" is very interesting. It looks at the ways in which imagination can be bound by reality, and the necessity for imagination to remake what it observes.

William H. Coles
Do you think "The Turn of the Screw" is important?

John Biguenet
It's about ghosts, so in some ways it's at odds with most American literature, which has followed a realist tradition. But I think that everything James writes, because of his focus on the sentence, is something from which we can learn.

William H. Coles
How about earlier? Hawthorne?

John Biguenet
In Hawthorne you can see the invention of the form. In a sense he's inventing the genre of short stories as he writes them, though with a high level of artistry. It's fairly unusual to see someone both inventing and mastering a form simultaneously.

William H. Coles
What is the contribution in terms of structure?

John Biguenet
Structurally, to focus the short story on a single moment of crisis. When you compare one of Hawthorne's tales to *The Scarlet Letter*, you see two very different things happening. He's employed the novel for a complex unwinding of character, and the short story for a crisis that leads to a kind of decision through which the character could put his or her life back in balance.

William H. Coles
I sense that dramatization has been lost somewhat in contemporary writing. Is it possible to trace dramatization through the development of both the short story and the novel?

John Biguenet
I'm not sure about the term "dramatization." But I can say that the character has to embody the conflict. My story "The Vulgar Soul," for example, has to do with what exactly religion says about human experience if one strips away belief in the supernatural. Unless it's addressing something entirely imaginary, religion must describe something observable. If one has no belief in God or the soul, is that to dismiss five thousand years of human thought in this area? Or does religion, even without belief, have something useful to say about human experience? To try to get at that question, I used a character devoid of religious faith who is afflicted with the stigmata and followed how his embodiment of this apparently religious experience works upon him. Although it doesn't engender any religious feelings, it does bring him insights about himself and what it means to be a human being.

William H. Coles
Do you prefer writing in the first person or the third person? I know you'll say it depends on the story and how it develops, but when do you choose, why do you choose, and what are the advantages?

John Biguenet
The first person is somewhat immediate, and the third person is somewhat distanced. It depends on how much space you want between the action and the reader. If you want the reader jammed up against the action, first person is more likely to accomplish that. If you want the reader to lean back a bit and be in a better position to make judgments about the choices the character is making, the third person better accommodates that.

William H. Coles
Is it fair to say that if drama is conflict, as you suggested—that is, conflict, action, resolution—it's important to do that in scene rather than in interiorization or narrative description?

John Biguenet
Yes. I think readers grow weary of philosophical monologues relatively quickly. Series of scenes unfold very much as life seems to unfold, and so scenic development is easier for the reader to grasp with sustained concentration, I think.

William H. Coles
What is the role of meaning in your short stories and novels?

John Biguenet
I don't know about meaning, but there is a difference between the elements of fiction—like plot, characterization, setting—and the subject. In the end, the story is about its subject, which is not the same thing as its plot.

William H. Coles
Is there morality in fiction?

John Biguenet
I don't know about morality in the religious sense, but if you think of stories as mainly about things being in balance or out of balance, then if someone is out of balance, it may feel to that person a moment of moral crisis. How do I bring my life into balance? It may have no religious implications, but more a question of taking too large a portion for myself or distorting reality through a lie, for example, and therefore throwing things out of balance. How do I bring myself back into balance? That's the question of fiction.

William H. Coles
What's the responsibility of the writer in endings, particularly in the great short story that will be remembered and persist into future generations?

John Biguenet
A great short story frames a choice that may be unexpected and will bring us to a new way of understanding the particular imbalance the story has depicted. We come to understand greed or deceit or infidelity in a new way, perhaps a more complex way. It's in the conclusion where the writer, through the character, reveals a new way of thinking about the problem—probably not providing an answer, but reframing the way we think about the question.

William H. Coles
Do you have thoughts about James Joyce's epiphany and how that relates to imbalance?

John Biguenet
Joyce was employing a particular form that expressed its climax as an insight that might be accepted or rejected.

William H. Coles
Maybe on the religious side?

John Biguenet
Perhaps. However, I don't think he is suggesting a religious solution to the problems his characters face. But he was raised within a religious culture, and it provides a form for him to think about the problems a human being confronts. The epiphany is simply the structural manifestation of the reframing of the human problem that Joyce offers.

William H. Coles
What are the major reasons that stories do not succeed today, in terms of being great stories but also in terms of getting published?

John Biguenet
I'm not sure about publishing, but a story fails because it has nothing to say, or perhaps because what it has to say is badly said. It does come back again and again to the craft of the story and its subject. Does the author have the authority to write about this matter and the authority of craft to depict it effectively?

William H. Coles
What about beginnings, and how stories are shaped?

John Biguenet
Because modern readers know so much about narrative, we certainly cannot begin with a great deal of exposition. The story must usually begin with rising action and go from there to integrate the character and the setting as the action continues to rise.

William H. Coles
John, thank you very much for participating. It's been very enlightening.

John Biguenet
Thank you, Bill. It's been a pleasure.

Robert Olen Butler Interview

January, 2011
William H. Coles

Robert Olen Butler won the Pulitzer Prize in 1993 for his collection of short stories *Good Scent from a Strange Mountain* (Groove Press, 2001). He has published sixteen novels and six volumes of short stories. He is a Francis Eppes Distinguished Professor holding the Michael Shaara Chair in Creative Writing at Florida State University.

William H. Coles
You teach at Florida State University. Are you a native Floridian?

Robert Olen Butler
No, I've only been at FSU for ten years. I'm originally from the St. Louis area—just across the river in Granite City, Illinois.

William H. Coles
Where did you go to school?

Robert Olen Butler
Undergraduate at Northwestern, and I took the master's at the University of Iowa. But as a playwright, not in the fiction workshop.

William H. Coles
Did you have mentors at Iowa who were important for your career?

Robert Olen Butler
No. [*laughs*] I was studying playwriting, and I studied with a couple of very good playwrights and they were helpful in that realm. But my mentorship came later. I studied with Anatole Broyard at the New School in the mid-1970s. If I call anyone a mentor, it would be him. He was, for many years, the primary daily book critic for the *New York Times*.

William H. Coles
When you switched from playwriting to prose, was it deliberate?

Robert Olen Butler
I had gone to Northwestern thinking I would be an actor, and I studied theater. But at some point I decided I wanted to write instead of interpret in my art form. I assumed, because I was interested in the theater, that I wanted to write plays, but as it turned out I was a terrible playwright. My most impassioned writing was going into the stage directions, which is a bad sign for a playwright. And what that implied was that I was a fiction writer. I was gobbled up in the pre-lottery-day draft after getting my master's degree. I ended up in Vietnam, and one thing and another led to the realization that I'm primarily a fiction writer. Ultimately you do not choose your medium, it chooses you.

William H. Coles
People who are not "writers" often choose the wrong thing to write about.

Robert Olen Butler
Sure. But natural writers will often try to force themselves into a form—novel, story, screenplay, poem—that is not necessarily the appropriate form for the way they see the world. If they are writing not from ideas and the will, if they are not creating work in a fundamentally crafty way in order to produce an object of entertainment, if, in fact, they are writing from the artist's impulse, which is a deep, inchoate vision of some sort of order behind the apparent chaos of life on planet Earth, they'll be driven then to express that vision in the creation of the object—the art object. If they are that kind of writer, they may well end up trying to write in forms that are not best to articulate that vision of the world. They have the impulse to express their notion of the human condition, but perhaps—I'm talking about myself—I had not yet given myself over to that vision sufficiently for it to dictate its own form, which might turn out to be fiction, and indeed initially was strictly the novel, and then graduated to short stories, and then began expressing itself in even shorter forms for a while, until now. Most recently I've returned to the novel. When the muse knocks on our door, you have to let her in, let her slip off her diaphanous gown and take you where she wants you to go.

William H. Coles
In terms of the writer focusing on the idea of view of the world, where does the entertainment value of prose come in? Does that work against the entertainment value?

Robert Olen Butler
It certainly could. You know, I'm not sure that many people, in the pure sense, are entertained by many of the great works of literature. The entertainment

value of literature is an aftereffect. To create a work of literature, if you have an entertainment intention, it will destroy the work of art. You have to let the vision of the world dictate the work . . . and I'm talking about art now. There are plenty of other perfectly splendid fictional forms—genre and entertainment works—where their authors' a priori intentions are to entertain. The kinds of work I'm talking about are created because the author has a deep intuition about the world and an insistence, even an obsession, about expressing that vision but does not know what the vision actually is until she creates the object. Her creation is as much an act of exploration as it is of expression. If you're saying, "I've also got to entertain as I do this," then that puts you in a different place within yourself. It cuts you off from the deep initial impulse to write. You start writing things in order to entertain, so the decisions about the created object are no longer being driven by how the writer deeply sees the world.

Some of my books are very funny, but I have never sat down to be funny. The humor comes only from the way I'm seeing the world. If my intention was to be funny I would not be serving the expression of the complex vision of the world that is really my most important goal.

William H. Coles
Let me ask you about entertainment. It seems to me that entertainment for a writer (and the intention and vision of the world) are not competing, even on the artistic level, and that for the writer, entertainment is necessary to hold the reader's interest. You've got to entertain a reader throughout the story in order to deliver what you've learned about yourself or your vision of the world. What can a writer do to entertain that person and engage them?

Robert Olen Butler
Anyone who is writing from the impulses I'm talking about, anyone who is creating a work of art, if they do what you said, would destroy the work of art. If Marcel Proust had done what you're suggesting, that million words of *Time Remembered* [*À La Recherche des Temps Perdu*] would never have come out that way. And for it to come out some other way for the sake of entertaining his readers would then destroy, in fact, the heart and soul of that book's vision of the world.

William H. Coles
In *Anna Karenina*, Tolstoy entertains chapter by chapter.

Robert Olen Butler
What you're confusing here, Bill, is intention and effect. Tolstoy did not write with the intention of entertaining. He did not write in the trance state in which he put himself to pull out the deep story of Anna Karenina and her world, and what that implies. He was not even thinking about the human condition. But that's what's working at the heart of it. Yet, in the process of creation, if he is also thinking how to make this book entertaining, and if he makes decisions of plot and character and tone and voice in order to accommodate that, then the art of the work is destroyed.

William H. Coles
I understand your point.

Robert Olen Butler
But this is very important. Great books do also entertain. A great writer with both an artistic vision and a gift for storytelling who then expresses that complex vision of the world, but in the way that stories fundamentally, inevitably, organically structure themselves, then the object that's created will not only be a work of art but will also, intrinsically, have entertainment value.

William H. Coles
Yes.

Robert Olen Butler
A crucial distinction. I'm talking from the artist's point of view.

William H. Coles
What if I say not "entertainment" but "engagement"?

Robert Olen Butler
I will still argue with you about the artist being conscious of the need to engage. It cannot be. It cannot be.

William H. Coles
I think you've convinced me.

Robert Olen Butler
But you raise an important question. Let's think about literary fiction as simply another genre. If you say you're writing a mystery story and I have to make readers laugh, or whatever, you're confusing genres. And then I have to make sure the protagonist falls in love with the beautiful woman . . .

William H. Coles
Right.

Robert Olen Butler
If I feel in my mystery I have to work in laughter and romance, then there is something wrong. Now, some mysteries have humor. And some have romance. But if you feel that from the conception you have to work them in, the mystery will suffer. The genre of literature requires it be built fundamentally on the illumination of the human condition. And if you've got to make people hang on every chapter ending, you're mixing genres.

William H. Coles
Let's move on. You brought up humor. Your new book is humorous. How does humor work in prose? What about humor makes prose more exciting? Here again you might answer me in terms of intention, and I know you don't have the intent to be funny. But you must have an inner sense of what will make people laugh.

Robert Olen Butler
I don't think about it until afterward, and then only when people ask me the question. But for me, the humor of my work—there's a lot of laugh-out-loud stuff in *Hell*, for instance, and this even confuses some readers. If you're going to see the humor as intentional and an end in itself, you're going to see the book on a shallow level. All the humor there, even the stand-up-comedy one-liners, is fitting into some larger, organic whole. And for me, in my work, there is a better word to understand those humorous parts: irony. The irony is not an intentional effect, I would hasten to add. It is, ironically, the disparity between human intentions and their actual effects. The ironic humor comes from the distance between what we understand about ourselves and what is truly going on in ourselves.

William H. Coles
You're talking about the characters.

Robert Olen Butler
Exactly. Irony is behind almost all of the humor in the book. Even the gaggy one-liners, in the larger organic wholeness of the book, are operating not in isolation as "is this a funny joke" or "is this not a funny joke," does it make you laugh or does it not make you laugh, or does it make you groan, or does it make you ask, "What the hell was that?" That's not the point. The humor reflects on the function of humor in the larger view of the human condition. *Hell* takes on

the zeitgeist in its wholeness, and how this present world, in fact, is a paradigm for how human beings have lived forever, the ways we have always lived, the ways we yearn to succeed, yearn for great things and fail miserably, or yearn for terrible things. There is a certain grace in seeing those things for what they are, which is possible only by the ongoing interaction of all the tiniest elements in the book. Most of the laughter is absolutely rooted in that. One effect is that the tears and the laughter are never really separated. The comedy and the tragedy are intimately entwined.

William H. Coles
You didn't write to the ironies, did you?

Robert Olen Butler
Exactly. Everything I've been saying tells you that. It has to do with the ways in which characters are yearning to define themselves. And really, that's at the heart of all narrative. Fiction is the art form of human yearning. What we are striving for. And plots in books are simply yearning challenged and thwarted. And so that's the way the irony and the humor come out in the book, by my being focused entirely on each character who passes before me, each character that yields him- or herself up from my unconscious in the ongoing organic context of the book. The thing that my creative intuition goes to instantly is: What is the character after? What does the character want at the deepest level?

William H. Coles
A core desire.

Robert Olen Butler
At the deepest level. And if there is a unified field theory of yearning in fiction it is: I yearn for self, I yearn for an identity, I yearn for a place in the universe.

William H. Coles
And recognition.

Robert Olen Butler
Not recognition. Not at the core. Because recognition is the kind of surface response that may or may not lead you to your true self. In fact, the desire for recognition may indeed be the kind of surface goal that leads that character astray. That may be one of the challenges of yearning for self.

William H. Coles
I see.

Robert Olen Butler
So, in my line-to-line creation of the book, I'm following, being guided by, the yearnings of each character who's in front of me. And it's only from that that these other effects occur—the humor, the irony that we're talking about. It's not on my mind. It's not an intention. It just happens to be a natural part of the objects I've been creating from this desire to explore how I see the world.

William H. Coles
This is sort of a minuscule thought, I suppose, but do you ever think about dramatic irony as a part of the structure of a story, particularly in short stories?

Robert Olen Butler
Forgive me for quibbling with every question you ask, because you ask it as if that's the way I create the story. I don't think of it! No. But dramatic irony is almost always present in my writing, especially since I work so often in first-person narrative. All first-person narrative—since it is from the subjective point of view of a specific person who inevitably sees things through a complex scrim of memory and perceptions—has to come to terms with dramatic irony. And most of the stories and novels that I write embrace and use dramatic irony. The reader often knows more about the character's circumstances and responses than the character knows about himself. That sort of dramatic irony is almost always at work in modern fiction, most fiction that's being written.

William H. Coles
That's valuable.

Robert Olen Butler
Yes. In my genre of literary fiction, dramatic irony is at the heart of most really good work.

William H. Coles
You're here in New Orleans to research for your new novel. I'm interested in your process. What are you looking for? What do you write down in your notebooks? Part of the reason I'm asking is because you say you don't have intentions when you start, but you must, as you research, begin to develop intentions about what you want to do with the story, or novel, in terms of humor or plot or structure. Characterization, too.

[*silence*]

Am I wrong?

Robert Olen Butler
You're wrong. [*laughs*] In the terms of how you put it, I would not endorse those terms. "Now that you're researching, you've got intentions." No! I don't have the kind of intentions you're talking about. The characters are coming up out of my unconscious. My intuition is focusing on what they deeply yearn for. The world in which I place them and the circumstances that are beginning to present themselves—those things challenge the characters' yearnings in certain ways. And in my research here and what I'm absorbing, I'm open to those kinds of inspirations.

William H. Coles
But not in a directed way.

Robert Olen Butler
Not in a directed, intentional way. And anything that comes to me in terms of turn of plot, or what a character might do or say, it's always in those terms. It's by concrete action and sensual moments that inspiration comes. But even that has been noted in the background and is open to transformation in the line-to-line creation as I write. What I'm really researching are the sensual details. Because in my genre, everything is told in the moment through the senses. A work of literary art is like a symphony or a ballet or a painting or a movie. All of those are entirely moment-to-moment sensual experiences. I look from the balcony of the room in which one of the main characters checks in at the beginning of my novel with the intention of killing herself, and I'm trying to find out what the trees are around the pool, what the smells are in the morning in the French Quarter.

William H. Coles
Right here, for example.

Robert Olen Butler
The way the sun comes in my balcony door in the afternoon.

William H. Coles
And you're striving not to be disruptive, but to be emotive, how you react to these stimuli.

Robert Olen Butler
Exactly. Because every sense detail that goes in the book is not there just to paint a picture or create a scene. In my genre . . .

William H. Coles
Which is literary fiction as an art form . . .

Robert Olen Butler
Exactly. Every sense detail is there with an organic function in the larger piece. I do not stop and give, no matter how beautifully written, sensual portraits of the landscape or the room independent of the character's point of view or her intentions. That the smell that comes in through the open French doors here is a mixture of coffee and somebody making roux, but with an undercurrent of rotten fish and piss against the wall, the description of that moment, the sensual description, is moving toward something about being alive, but with an undercurrent of death. What I will finally end up with, if I get it right, is the organic, resonant, correct description to fit a woman who has just checked into the hotel with the intention of killing herself. So it's not a set piece where we do the slate roofs and gumbo, and the pigeons sitting on the roof.

William H. Coles
That would be description of setting.

Robert Olen Butler
And it could be a beautiful description of setting, but Henry James said landscape is character and in the work of literary fiction, every tiny detail has to organically resonate into everything else. So I was gathering all the organic sense details that were also authentic to the place in which this work is set. But which details will end up in the book will happen only in the act of creation, where everything has been drawn through the governing principle, which is the yearning of the central characters.

William H. Coles
And you're gathering this for in the moment. You're not gathering this for narrative distance—a description of Oak Alley, for example. You're gathering details that are unique to the French Quarter. But it's not a description of a specific place.

Robert Olen Butler
Exactly. And that's the great thing about narrative. And this is why narrative can be entertaining as well. There's ongoing interaction, the tension between the character's inner life and the outer life around her. It's why fiction exists. There is no other art form that can do that.

William H. Coles
Amen.

Robert Olen Butler
That can capture the central fact of all of our existence. Which is that we are utterly subjective entities reacting to an external world around us.

William H. Coles
And we're alone, too.

Robert Olen Butler
Exactly right. That's true. And in that sense, we are utterly alone. Even though there are other critters floating around here with the same subjectivities, there's this insuperable barrier, which is why literature exists. And this is probably the ultimate in entertainment value. A work of literary fiction will ultimately allow the reader, if my genre is done correctly, to leave herself and enter into the other in a way that we don't otherwise get a chance to do. And that's engagement! And that's entertainment! Of a high order. And the irony is that if you are consciously trying to entertain, you lose the ability to do that.

The artist lets go of the entertainment intention in order to entertain in the most profound way. I will draw you out of yourself and into this other entity. And in a way that you don't have to project into it. When we read romance novels, for instance, and weep real tears, it's not because there is this other living, breathing character on the page. It's a flat character, but the flatness allows the reader to project into it. It's self-referential. I always say the difference between literature and non-literature is the difference between making love and masturbating. There may be certain similarities to the physical effect, but one is a closed loop. It's self-referential. The other . . . when you make love truly, you leave yourself and enter into the other. And so that's what literature does, which is supremely entertaining, it seems to me.

William H. Coles
You write frequently in the first person. I'm interested in your narrative concept and approach. How do you think about the relationship between author as creator of story, the narrator as teller of the story, and the character that acts in the story? When you get into a first-person story . . .

Robert Olen Butler
. . . you take out that middleman . . .

William H. Coles
...you can take out the narrator or collapse the author into the narrator. Is there a way to author a first-person story and still present story through a narrator? That would be a more objective narration. Is that possible? How do you think about it?

Robert Olen Butler
Hell is the first book I've written in third person since *Wabash*, which was published in 1987, so it's been twenty-two years. But you'll notice that the third-person narrator has a distinct personality and often allows the character to speak in first person.

William H. Coles
This is Hatcher McCord?

Robert Olen Butler
Yes. Well, no. The third-person narrator is not Hatcher McCord. There is a third-person narrator. That third-person narrator is sometimes omniscient with Hatcher and sometimes slides into the inner consciousness of other characters. And also, sometimes the third-person narrator lets Hatcher speak in his own inner voice. There are always italics in those outbursts of first person. And then characters pass by, everyone from Jezebel to Richard Nixon, who speaks in the first person as well, that the third-person narrator allows to happen. That's the way I've gotten around third person and first person in the same book.

But for the previous twenty-two years, first persons are first persons. And the voice on the page remains unremittingly the speaker of the character. My approach, I think, goes back to my actor training, because I was trained as an actor at Northwestern University. In method acting you work from the inside out; you make your own internal sensory mechanism come into alignment with the internal sensory mechanism of the character. This is somewhat similar to earlier when I was describing the woman responding to the smells in her room. And then, your external performance comes from that. When I write first-person voices, I think I'm getting into that same method-acting groove. I let my own sensory mechanism and my own unconscious come into alignment with the unconscious of the character. When I'm writing well, I feel as if, by going deeply enough into my own personal unconscious, I begin to tap into what Jung calls the collective unconscious, and I feel as if I'm able to draw my insights into the characters from there. So, if you can as a writer tap into that deeply shared humanity, that collective unconscious, you can embody those insights in characters that may not be very similar to yourself, and yet are deeply connected to you by our shared humanity. And the voices flow from there.

William H. Coles
The problem that writers run into when they think about first person in that way is the timeline. In the sense that the author is writing from sensibilities, historical knowledge, attitudes, and morality of his or her present, so the narrator is in story time. The problem is, if there is too much of the author in the narrator, the story may lose credibility. The author's knowledge brings illogical and non-credible information into the story that then weakens the story; it becomes unreliable. Do you understand what I mean?

Robert Olen Butler
I do. And this is the danger of intention that we've been talking about. It's a type of recurring theme. Because if your intentions are coming from your modern intentions, your philosophy, your attitudes, your conscious ideas, they are coming from your twenty-first-century self, and then you take on this narrator from some other period, or even some other gender, some other whatever—if you're writing from your head, if you're writing from intentions, you're thinking your way into the work, then that's going to be an almost insuperable problem because what you're trying to put into your character is of you and your time. But the literary writer does not write with intentions or preconceived effects or attitudes or ideas. Art does not come from the mind, it does not come from rational analytical thought, it does not come from ideas; it comes from the unconscious, from the place where you dream. So, you internalize the character that you're writing through and you understand the external world of that character. And by the way, you conduct historical research the same way you come to this hotel to research a novel, looking for smells and shapes of doorknobs and the ways in which that character moves through the physical world.

William H. Coles
Compatible with the story.

Robert Olen Butler
Exactly. And I have to say there's a kind of mystical element to all this. If you tap into your art and the collective unconscious, and if you are really channeling authenticity from there, these characters fill themselves out. You let go of your own intentions. You just focus on the inner life of this other entity, this other soul, which is living in this other sensual world, which, by research, you absorb and understand and fully imagine, and you focus on what that character profoundly wants, the yearning. Then you let that voice speak. That's the only way to deal

with the problem you describe. Which is a real one. It's not something you can train for; it is something that happens for you.

William H. Coles
That's very helpful, because this is at the essence of problems beginning writers run into all the time. And they don't know how to deal with it, or even recognize that it can be a problem.

Robert Olen Butler
Beginning writers need to understand, if they aspire to this particular genre, literary fiction, when they're ready to try to write works that will eventually achieve literary quality, they have to stay within the range of their own authenticity, within their own unconscious. They have to write very close to people, the characters, who are like themselves in many surface ways. Now, this is from a guy whose voices have come from parrots and furniture—I wrote a story from the perspective of a waterbed in a story called "Titanic Victim Speaks through Waterbed"—but it was all still about human beings. Kafka's cockroach was still about a human being. But my first five published novels have central characters very close to who I was. But I must hasten to add—and this is not a digression, a secondary point, or parallel point, but crucial to process—neither can you consciously write, if you're going to do this genre, from literal memory, from the specific, overtly remembered events of your life.

Graham Greene, the great British novelist, once said, "All good novelists have bad memories. What you remember comes out as journalism, what you forget goes into the compost of the imagination." And his compost of the imagination is the same as the unconscious I've been talking about. The beginning writers need to stay close to themselves, their most intense, white-hot center, but only the stuff of their inner selves that they have forgotten, that they have composted. They need to stay within the range of their own authenticity, but for an artist the "authentic" is the assimilated, the stuff of what is functioning now as self-rooted imagination. Eventually, if they do that book after book, story after story, year after year, they'll have the ability to break through to the collective unconscious. In the meantime, they have to stick close to their own core.

William H. Coles
But in the writing, don't they have to back away from closeness? To look at the story objectively.

Robert Olen Butler
No!

William H. Coles
To provide objectivity to the character rendering. You don't believe that?

Robert Olen Butler
No, I don't. On the contrary. When you say you have to back away and look at it objectively, the inevitable implication is that it's from the rational mind, that it's analytical. In the genre of literary fiction, it's exactly the wrong thing to do. No, it stays subjective. Even all the craft and technique they've learned, all of that has been learned in writing workshops and literature classes in objective, thoughtful, analytical ways. And the danger with those ways of learning is that the nascent writers of literature have gotten the impression that this is how works of art are created—that you learn craft and technique and then when you write, in order to edit, you back away from work to be objective, and you analyze the problems and consciously apply craft and technique to fix them.

William H. Coles
You lose something?

Robert Olen Butler
You lose everything. Let's go back to the Graham Greene quote. He was obviously talking about life experience, but it's also true about craft and technique. The only craft and technique you have legitimate access to is the craft and technique you forgot, that has dissolved into the unconscious. So, when I say "stay subjective," it doesn't mean just wild ramblings. First of all, the character's yearning will be the center of gravity and shape every choice. Secondly, the craft and technique you've learned is now operating at that subjective level. Because you have learned it so well, you have forgotten it. It has become second nature to your unconscious. It has become part of the compost.

William H. Coles
So there is a sort of objective application of the subjectivity.

Robert Olen Butler
No. There is no objectivity. You may have to learn it all objectively to start with, but you do not have legitimate access at that point. You apply it intuitively.

William H. Coles
Yes. I can see where that might be valuable.

The ART of CREATING STORY

Robert Olen Butler
It has to dissolve into the subjective self in order for you to have full access to it. I mean, how did Michael Phelps swim when he first started? The first time in the pool, he had to objectively adjust his stroke, he had to learn things in an objective way. At that point, when he was first learning technique, his body was doing things partly at the behest of his mind. But he could not become an Olympic champion until all of those things had been turned into muscle memory. Not an understanding of technique. The coach will tell you, "Look, your hand has to come onto the water this way; you need to keep your head so; you're splaying your feet when you kick, they need to be kept closer," and for a while he hears the technique objectively and applies it consciously, but he never breaks a world record in that state. It has to turn into muscle memory. Same for the writer with craft and technique.

William H. Coles
Got it.

Robert Olen Butler
So, you do not back off and think. What you do is dissolve everything you've learned and must know into the subjective, into your unconscious. so it functions there.

William H. Coles
How does revision fit into all this?

Robert Olen Butler
The corollary for a reader of everything I'm saying is this: in the primary and only necessary encounter with a work of fiction, you are not meant to understand it in a rational, analytical way. You are meant, as you read a work in this genre, literary fiction, to thrum to the work. Thrum. Like a string on a stringed instrument.

William H. Coles
For a long time after the primary encounter. Forever?

Robert Olen Butler
Yes. But in terms of this essential encounter with a specific work, it's the aesthetic response I'm trying to describe. You are responding in a sensual, emotional, visceral way. And not with analytical ideas. So how does the artist revise? You use your good Graham Greene bad memory, and you forget your own work such that you can go back to it and read it without filling in the blanks with

what you thought was happening on the page when you wrote it. You encounter your own work afresh and you thrum to it. You go: thrum, thrum, thrum, twang. Ah, the twang. When you get to the twang, contrary to what you learn in all writing workshops, you do not step back and objectively analyze the problem and then consciously and willfully apply your craft and technique to fix the problem. For one thing, the problem with the twang to begin with probably originated in your falling out of your unconscious and starting to will something into the work. But even if the problem occurred while you were in the proper trance, you're not going to be able to revise properly by turning the revision into conscious, rational thought. What you do is you return to the part that twangs, you go back into your unconscious, and you redream it. Rewriting in redreaming. You revisit your unconscious.

William H. Coles
Not restructuring?

Robert Olen Butler
Not restructuring. Redreaming! But if you have properly assimilated your craft and technique, and you're focusing on the essence of narrative, which is the yearning of the character, then redreaming will be restructuring.

William H. Coles
Let me carry this into the interesting series of videos you did for Florida State University, in which you took a photograph—it was a photograph of a biplane where the wing was falling off—and then your story started with the imagining of people on the ground who saw it happen.

Robert Olen Butler
One man's perception.

William H. Coles
Wasn't his son there too?

Robert Olen Butler
Yes, his son was there. But it was in the father's voice.

William H. Coles
Then you walked through that with a very methodical progression that doesn't exactly fit into the process you've been talking about. How, in the development of that story, do you see what we've been talking about?

Robert Olen Butler
Did you see all thirty-four hours of that project?

William H. Coles
No. It's been some years.

Robert Olen Butler
How much did you see?

William H. Coles
I saw maybe seven hours.

Robert Olen Butler
I don't see how you would think that's a different process. It wasn't. It's exactly what I was preaching.

William H. Coles
Okay. I'll go back and look.

Robert Olen Butler
Now that we've talked, you should go back and look, because you may have been interpreting what I was doing in a way that you've been continuing to ask your questions.

William H. Coles
I see. [*laughs*] And irritatingly, too.

Robert Olen Butler
No. Not at all. Not in the least. I hope I'm not irritating you by taking issue with you. Because you're asking really good questions, and you're asking them, Bill, in exactly the way every student who has come to me for twenty-five years is thinking about them. You are giving articulate voice to the fundamental misimpressions of all those craft and technique classes that all the aspiring artists of the world are taking. So I'm glad you're asking them this way, because it's is exactly how they're approaching this. But now that you've heard what I said, you should go back to that video . . .

William H. Coles
Is it still up?

Robert Olen Butler
Yes. It's up forever. Reexamine it, because I think you'll find it's embodying what I've said.

William H. Coles
Could we tell the readers how they can access the videos?

Robert Olen Butler
All seventeen sessions are available for free download at iTunesU. Just go to the iTunes store and search for "Inside Creative Writing."

William H. Coles
Terrific. What can we expect from you in the future? We know of the new novel.

Robert Olen Butler
All I can tell you, given my answers here today, [is that] I'm in the novel of the moment. I don't know what the future is. But right now, I'm writing a novel called *A Small Hotel*, which is set in this very place, the Olivier House in New Orleans, and also at Oak Alley.

William H. Coles
A lovely place.

Robert Olen Butler
Along the River Road.

William H. Coles
I love that place. The oaks.

Robert Olen Butler
And as I mentioned, there is a woman who checks in who is intending perhaps to kill herself while her husband—well, her ex-husband . . . well, he's not her ex because this very morning she has skipped the court appearance that would finalize the divorce—he's checking into Oak Alley with a woman friend. And all the assumptions you would probably make from that are wrong. There's a lot of complexity here.

William H. Coles
It's tantalizing.

Robert Olen Butler
Yes. And I'm staying with the third person with this novel.

William H. Coles
Where can people learn more about writing from you?

Robert Olen Butler
I recommend people follow my website, which is robertolenbutler.com, and I'd recommend my book *From Where You Dream*.

William H. Coles
Thank you very much for this interview. It's been exactly what I wanted and will be valuable for our readers in terms of finding new ways of thinking about writing, about how to create story, how to get a vibrant art form on the page.

Robert Olen Butler
It's been a delight, Bill. A pleasure to talk to you.

Ron Carlson Interview

10 July, 2010
William H. Coles

Ron Carlson is Director of Creative Writing at the University of California, Irvine. He received a Masters degree in English from the University of Utah. He has published widely both novels, his most recent *The Signal* (Penguin, 2009), and short stories. He wrote *Ron Carlson Writes a Story* (Graywolf Press, 2007), a nonfiction book for writers. His stories have appeared in many anthologies, including The O'Henry Prize Series and The Pushcart Prize Anthology. He is a popular lecturer and teaches in workshops throughout the country.
Ron Carlson Writes a Story (Graywolf Press, 2007).

William H. Coles
I'd like to start with basic definition. How do you define "short story?"

Ron Carlson
Well, wouldn't it be great if we could just get a definition? But it's elusive. Of course, a short story is not a single thing done a single way. It is constantly being invented. One of the conventional ways we can talk about it is that something happens in time to someone. People go through an event that reveals something about them, what kind of characters they are. Event reveals character.

William H. Coles
Is there a difference in your mind, as a fiction writer, between essay, character sketch, memoir, and fiction? Does the use of the imagination or a specific structure set the fictional short story apart from other genres?

Ron Carlson
There is a great deal of talk about this now. We have two instruments: memory and imagination. We think of imagination as wild and free, and memory as responsible. In fact, neither is totally objective. More to your question: stories have a rise and a fall. They take place in-scene. Although there are scenes and commentary in memoir, its purpose is to deliver information more than it is to ask a question dramatically.

William H. Coles
What is the importance of story to humans? Why do humans seek out stories? What is it about stories that makes our lives better?

Ron Carlson
I don't think they are separate. People live by the evidence around them, and that evidence is stories. We learn in family, groups of friends, and society and culture. There are stories we share, stories we are drawn to, and stories we reject. Stories that are offensive, arresting. I don't think of stories as secondary, as frosting on the cake of culture. I think of stories as the center of culture. Sometimes we confuse them with literary studies that may be arcane or off to the side, but in fact a father and a son, a mother or a daughter, are constantly sharing stories. It's the way we learn to live.

William H. Coles
Do you find that readers experience different stories of yours in different ways? And if so, what creates the difference in the interpretations? I ask because a fiction writer may wonder if he or she shouldn't write for a certain reader who reads in a certain way.

Ron Carlson
There are a lot of answers to that. My answer is that the reader's not going to come along unless I write the story. The only reason I write the story is because I want to read it. So, I'm the reader. Many things about my stories are provocative for me, but I'm not sure I can offer the best explanation of any of my stories. People come up to me and they respond to different parts of a story. I sometimes think they got something different than I intended. But I'm writing with everything I've got. I only have one speed. When I'm writing I don't think about the reader. I'm trying to make the best story, the story I want to read. Many times I'm writing to find out what the heck is going to happen. So I'm not surprised that people come back and remember a specific image or another moment. It almost seems secondary to my process.

William H. Coles
Do you think that differences in interpretation, when they are multiple, are a result of the strength of your story?

Ron Carlson
I don't know. It all depends. As I said, I'm not good with this side of it. I get into my stories. So many of my stories I don't understand; I'm trying to figure

them out. I write them as well as I can. As a teacher, I figure what should be done to someone else's story, but it's not something I would like to do to my own. If I were working with a table of writers, I would almost never mention the reader. Clarity is important, and we all know the importance of establishing the narrative side. But to tailor something for a reader . . . I mean, when you write, no one else can be in the room. Not your priest, your rabbit, your brother, your sister, your children, and if they are, you're working for market, in a way. People who write for television write for market. And it's fraught with a kind of compromise. I think of myself as a sort of benevolent writer, and in writing you can't compromise. As soon as you start cutting corners, the word gets around. A lot of that writing gets published. It's all right. When I read someone's story, I want to read his or her story. I don't want to read their culture's story, their family's story. I'm very interested in what that person's thinking.

William H. Coles
What is voice in fiction?

Ron Carlson
It's not clear. It's spoken about a lot. Everyone talks about voice. It's related to point of view. Really, what it is, at its finest, is prose that's occupied with a sensibility. We understand that when certain writers are describing changing a tire, there is something more going on.

William H. Coles
It has purpose . . . or meaning?

Ron Carlson
No. We could call it attitude; we could call it sensibility. The prose is charged with a person. People are always talking about liking the voice. We think about it in the first person, or someone with a dialect. It's not that. It's the angle of prose and the way it fits. Sometimes it's authorial, third person, or it's first person. So it's talked about a great deal but it is still ambiguous.

William H. Coles
In addition to the character voices, first and third person, and the authorial voice, is there always a narrator voice also?

Ron Carlson
Yes. If you look in the big book of technical terms, there are nine, but the truth is there are probably more than nine. There's a voice you use to tell a story to

a child: "Once upon a time . . ." There are others that start in the first-person vernacular. People want a fiction checklist: dialogue, imagery craft, point of view, and voice. If you look at John Updike writing the Rabbit stories, the novels, it evolves and it becomes his senses and his sensibility. It's that little bit of humanity in the prose. That's as close as I can come.

William H. Coles
When you're in scene as a writer, is it important to keep the voice—not the point-of-view voice but your sensibility voice—clear for the reader so that scene has a more significant impact?

Ron Carlson
Clarity is the goal. But clarity has a lot of different faces. Sometimes you have somebody who writes in staccato fragments, and we understand the pressure of the prose. Other times someone writes in five-line, elegant, complex sentences, and we understand that. Consistency and clarity are always the goal. A writer develops her voice over the course of five, six, eight, ten stories. Not that there is the same voice in each story, but there is a confidence that begins to come into the prose where you understand these language elements are not just being laid together like bricks. There is more force than that.

William H. Coles
So there is the authorial voice—you said "her voice"—always there in the fiction, in the stories.

Ron Carlson
Well, there is a lot of flat-footed writing. Where someone—obviously the juice goes off—gets her books, leaves the library, gets in her car, and goes home and has a drink. It sort of becomes bricks without mortar. I'm not exactly sure about that. I know that sometimes you can write an entire story where you get a certain type of voice. I'm writing a detective story now and I like the guy very, very much. I have no idea what's going to happen to him. But he's very self-deprecating. He's trying to attempt precision in the way he talks that is right at the edge of being comic, and I like it.

William H. Coles
Do all characters need to be likable?

Ron Carlson
No. There is a lot of talk about this. A character needs to be effective. By effective,

I mean there is a contact point between the character and the writer. For some reason the character's engaging. Bundren in *As I Lay Dying* is not a likable character, but you can't look away. Again and again it's like that. We have a mix. Characters should be some type of mix. Even Iago from *Othello,* who comes as close as any famous literary character. Nobody is all bad. But he's engaging. There's contact.

William H. Coles
Is there a need for respect?

Ron Carlson
It depends on the reader. I think no. Readers read. If the story is engaging on a certain level, we take the characters seriously and understand there is moral authority. If the story is not well made, we can see through the costumes of the actors and see who is holding the light. Then we wonder. It's like in *Huckleberry Finn*, where he can see the one guy acting, and Huck loves the actors who are so histrionic you could see it, and he thought that was acting, as opposed to an actor who acts in such a way as it disappears and you are sort of threatened by what the characters do.

William H. Coles
Is there a need for a touch of hero in every fiction character?

Ron Carlson
I don't know about that. I'm much more interested in a touch of credibility. "Hero" is a big word. Full of charge. People do their best. And sometimes it's not very good, I think.

William H. Coles
What do you think of credibility in first person? Because when all story information comes through the consciousness of a single narrator, there is always the question of credibility and reliability. If that's true, how do you handle it? Is there a way to use credibility or lack of credibility to best purpose in your story?

Ron Carlson
When you tell a story in the first person there are always two stories. There is no such thing as an objective narrator. Even if you write a letter to your friend about your trip to Russia, it's always going to be tilted, there are going to be elisions. When the first person is used, we understand that there is going to be: first, the story of the events; and second, the effect of the events on the narrator, implied

or stated. So that allows us to begin to understand. I'm acknowledging that I have my proclivities, and my vulnerabilities, and my liabilities. As a narrator, I'm going to tell the story anyway. There is no greater first sentence than: "There is no way I can tell this story without getting in trouble, getting some on you." So we have in the first person the worst possible narrator—one pretending to be (or the author would believe to be) fair-minded, evenhanded, levelheaded. A window instead of a prism. First person is always a prismatic lens. Never a clear lens. Once you acknowledge that, you can really go. So a baseball player who is telling the story of the game is fabulous, but a baseball player who is telling a story because of his error is a better narrator.

William H. Coles
Is the distance between narrator and narrator as character useful in terms of credibility and reliability? Do you understand what I mean?

Ron Carlson
Yes. The narrative distance, the distance between when I'm telling the story and when the story happened. The factor of time and point of view is never talked about. If I'm looking back and telling a story about what happened to me in sixth grade, that's different than if I'm looking back and telling something that happened to me this morning. One of the things about telling a story in the sixth grade, I might have polished those lies so well you can see them as a sort of enamel. The story of this morning would have other features. Being unreliable doesn't mean not being unforceful. It can have power and be unreliable. Unreliability takes a lot of forms. The minimizing, the maximizing, the euphemisms, et cetera.

William H. Coles
You teach the advantages of, after starting a story, providing exposition for the reader to build character as soon as possible. Are there ways to provide exposition without stopping the story action?

Ron Carlson
Exposition is not necessarily the story. Some stories have zero exposition. When there was no exposition in a lot of stories—that came along in the 1980s—we called it minimalism. It was minimal because there was a minimal amount of story information. In Raymond Carver's stories, and those of other successful minimalists (so-called, a word that didn't last very long, which is sort of good) the exposition is implied. So, a person tapping his lip at a window... we'd understand that he was under pressure and having trouble not drinking. Minimalism

came along because it was a reaction to the turgid and deadening exposition we'd seen in the conventional stories of the 1940s and 1950s. When you get something going like a man and woman out to dinner and then you flashback to how they met and how they were in college it just became burdensome. Like I said, turgid. Now in a story we want to know who the characters are. Many times the value of a story is established in exposition of scenes, which have their own energy. Narrative evidence—that is to say, short stories embedded in the story itself—don't necessarily create drag. I never have to worry about pacing in most of the student stories I see.

William H. Coles
Do you have suggestions for framing scenes in terms of pacing?

Ron Carlson
I talk about scene. What you're offering is scene. I'm not exactly sure what you mean by framing a scene. You have things that take place. That's the framing. So you have people in a moment or a room or a situation, and you remember they are in bodies and there is kind of a dance going on and you see what they're saying, honoring the fact that people may not be able to say what's on their minds, or capable of their own distress in that regard, or articulate. When you ask somebody how they are, you rarely get the story. Scenes are about real people and real places . . . and the complexities. You can't explain it. You're setting it out. Then you have to pay attention and see what they do.

William H. Coles
In relation to long descriptive narrative passages, I've heard you use the term "energize." Are there specific ways to energize narrative? Is it word choice? Is it syntax? How do you do it?

Ron Carlson
I don't know about it. Your story is alive. The writer is interested in surviving the draft. What most stories need is coherence, more specificity, and more drama and bodies, like putting people on stage. If you put two people on a stage, they don't announce their ideas to each other; they have to talk to each other about what they are doing. Put them together, see what they do and how they do it. A good scene, for example, would be between two people putting together lawn furniture, and one of them wants to explain to the other where the gold is hidden. But it's hard to do, so they say, "Hand me that wrench." There is always an in and an out. There is the thing going on in the current moment between two people in the world, and then there is what they're thinking. And most

often, what deadens a scene for me is when the ideas start to creep out and the author starts to use characters as announcers for those ideas.

William H. Coles
You have many ways for finding a stimulus for a story. In fact, you recommend keeping a writer's notebook for ideas. Once you have found stimuli for stories, how do you determine which are the best to develop into good stories?

Ron Carlson
You gather what you can, and I think indiscriminately. You gather things that stick to you. We're all magnets. A story you think is worthy I might not think is worthy. One of the things you can't teach is what a person chooses to write. Nor *should* you. When you choose to write your story, I want to read the story you chose. I don't want to choose it for you. Write a story about diabetes. If it matters to you, then it has a legitimate claim on your time. When I look at my list of story ideas, certain ones want to claim me. There are certain ones I know. Usually it is a matter of image, and I do not know the sort, but I do know they're going to drag me in such a way that I'll have to swim the length of the pool before I touch bottom again.

William H. Coles
This is a slippery question, but what is the effect of TV on the fiction writer's approach to stories? Has it changed what writers write? Is it influencing them?

Ron Carlson
I don't know what media does to readers. I think TV is TV. It's a little bit like what E. L. Doctorow said when they asked what he thought making a movie did to his book. He said, "They didn't do anything to my book; it's right over there." I think reality TV is comical and sad. It's not very satisfying. I think *Bounty Hunter* is magnificent. I'm smiling about that. I think much more to the point is the internet and the addiction to email and online, this constant input. Young people in this country have an ongoing stream of media input. When I was fifteen, I had no media input. I had a television and a bicycle. I got a little television every day, but not much. And I had a radio, but not much. When the phone rang, it was not for me. I did not have a telephone. So I had a lot of empty time. I had ideas. I was alone. I daydreamed. I generated things. I talked to myself. I goofed off. I doodled. You put a phone in every fourteen-year-old's pocket, and all of a sudden they're connected all the time to everyone. I think the alone time, the focus, and the intensity to write a book is being diminished, but we won't know that for thirty or forty years. So I don't know. I'm sorry that

people don't have a little more time alone. I want more writers to be honest about the fact that if you're using the internet, that is not right. That is some type of community yahoo. It is not a useful activity for writers.

William H. Coles
You're referring to Facebook and Twitter and things like that?

Ron Carlson
All of it. Email. As soon as you open the window on the world and let everybody else in. I'm very interested in what other people are thinking from time to time. So, I wouldn't read the paper all day long. Nor would I want something blowing in my ears all day long. I think we'll learn to be more discretionary in use of media. I was just down at dinner and someone said the longest tennis match in the history of Wimbledon is underway. I said, "Really." She pulled out her phone and read me the article. It has just ended. It's dark there. These guys had been playing for two days. A hundred games of tennis.

William H. Coles
This excessive social networking is peeking into individual lives. I wonder if some writers don't see that as a resource. I'm thinking of film credits and book jackets that declare, "Based on a true story." It brings up the question whether truth needs to be in fiction. Does it? After all, fiction is made up. Should fiction writers be thinking about truth to be effective?

Ron Carlson
No. Not at all. If *Hamlet* is based on a true story, is it better? The truth is that most films are badly made. Only 10 percent of films are designed well because there is so much committee work and so many people have their hands on it that the original talent gets muted and insulated by all the commercial instincts, and committees, and focus groups. Fiction is an art because readers wonder, "Did that happen?" And I would say, "No." And they say, "Is it true?" And I say, "Yes." It's like painting. Where it reaches us. "Based on a true story" is a very popular phrase because people think it's a marketing term. And if you think of it as a marketing term, you're sort of talking down to the masses. You're saying, oh, they need information. Not only is this an interesting story, but the bear really did eat the guy.

It's sort of goofy. The movies are goofy. But come on. It's got to be scary as hell. The people I've known who made movies spent a lot of money, and they were all out there. But if I spent a lot of money, if I spent six million dollars, I would do everything that I could to contact everyone I could. I'd tell 'em, yeah, it's about a little girl with pigtails loose in the mountains. No, it's about a talking cow that drives a helicopter. Yeah, and it's got some mice who cook. They're fabulous, actually rats. And I would market the hell out of it. When you write a book, you don't have to spend six million dollars. You can write a novel for about sixty dollars. I have a table. It leaves me free. I can bring in the elephants when I want to. And then, when I consult my committee, it's just me. That committee changes and I don't think I'm right all the time. I'm stubborn, and I'm passionate, and I'm intense about my view given the day I'm having it. I'm very interested in readers saying, "Oh, I read your story; I wasn't sure. Were they in the warehouse in the last scene?" And I say, "Oh, that's not clear?" So, yeah. That's great. Thank you. But I do not want them to say, "That was terrible, what happened to the women, there should be more music at the end of the story." And I'm thinking, well, I love music too, but no, not in my story. If it was a film, I'd be stuck with it. You'd have to bring in music.

William H. Coles
Are there films you recommend that fiction writers see to get a sense of progression and dramatization?

Ron Carlson
No. I don't know any that would help a writer except taking a bath in the great films: *King Kong*, 1933; *Frankenstein*, James Whale, 1931; *The Lost Weekend*; *Harper*; Paul Newman's film *The Hustler*, which is like a novel, it's a beautiful film. These are just movies that I've seen recently. It's interesting about *No Country for Old Men*, Cormac McCarthy's novel, because if you read the novel and then see the movie, the fidelity to the novel is remarkable. I can't remember having seen a movie follow a book so closely in twenty-five years. I track popular culture. I watch television. I don't watch reality television. Sometimes I watch a little junk TV. I just saw *Splendor in the Grass* with Warren Beatty, that fifty-year-old movie. So, I believe in seeing what other people do with movies. I was astonished that when I was in my thirties, I was enjoying movies that I would not have written. I was allowing people who had made decisions I considered generic to have their way with me. It was a liberating thought. I thought, "Wow, I would never have made that choice." Yet they made that choice and it sort of got me. That's the difference between being a writer versus a reader, or a writer versus a viewer. You look at it all. I mentioned Alfred Hitchcock earlier this week. One thing about Hitchcock: there is always stuff in his movies. Even *The Birds*, which is sort of silly, has some birds in it. I don't want to offend any *Birds* fans, but that movie left me flat.

William H. Coles
I agree. Are there instructive works of fiction, either short stories or novels, that you feel are iconic for instruction of writers in fiction?

Ron Carlson
A writer reads all the time. And a writer reads everything. You don't put down a book until you know why you're putting it down. It's not necessary to read everything. I just read *Tobacco Road*, and I thought it was an awful book. That book sold a hundred and ten million copies. It was on Broadway eleven years. But I think the classics we read all the time. I love to read the old stories by Edgar Allan Poe and Nathaniel Hawthorne and then going forward in American literature. Mark Twain is a great writer, all of his stories and essays. *Huckleberry Finn*.

William H. Coles
Herman Melville?

Ron Carlson
I taught and read *Moby-Dick* for years. Ernest Hemingway is hard to beat. I think he is a very, very powerful influence, the ratio of things to words is nice and tight. He screwed it down tight for the first time. After Hemingway, the twentieth century opens up. There are lots of good writers. Raymond Carver, Ann Beattie. I like Richard Ford's stories. I love John Cheever. John Updike's novels, and his stories too. Flannery O'Connor. D. H. Lawrence. But they're all so different. I'll be reading something and there are choices I wouldn't have made. And I like Cormac McCarthy.

William H. Coles
Would you recommend V. S. Pritchett?

Ron Carlson
Sure. I don't know his work very well. Writers are all under the influence of what they think a story is. Many times in undergraduate classrooms, that comes from film. So, there's a problem in the rise and the fall. And there is television. Half of my work is dismantling their understanding of a story and opening their tolerance for complexity so they can deal with it. That honest-to-Pete darkened shadow that people have. The idea of reading is so valuable. If you were trying to explain baseball to someone who had never played it . . . in literature, how wide is the ballfield? I have writers who come to stories and think it's only between first and second. They haven't read. It's a big ballfield. I remember

reading Virginia Woolf and all of a sudden the playing field kept getting wider and wider. Oh, you can do that? We find and seek influences. Emulate, emulate, emulate. Imitate, listen, listen, and we find ourselves in the middle.

William H. Coles
You're an excellent presenter and reader. How do you choose the right story to read aloud, and how do you prepare?

Ron Carlson
Well, you've read your work aloud in the study. Nothing leaves my room without being read aloud. Reading aloud is better than a focus group for me because I can find and hear the metrics and the lyrics that fit my mouth. The other thing is, I've been doing it for a thousand years. I try to slow myself down. I try to be very considerate of the audience because they're out of their houses at seven-thirty at night, it's God awful, they're looking at me and I'd better deliver this thing with the kind of confidence that doesn't embarrass anybody or make them squirm. And then I pick things I like, that I want to hear. I try to pick new work that is not published in a book, because if people want to see my books, they can buy them and read them. I've never read from a book in order to sell the book that night, but I know writers who do it. And that's fine. It's just not what I do. I always travel with one or two new drafts, things I've done in the last six to eight months, and that's a great joy for me. This has been my custom now for thirty years. And I've had some really good readers tell me that I'm a good reader. Tim O'Brien said that once to me. It meant a lot to me. I'm not an actor. When actors read your works, you hear a whole other thing. And bless them. Actors have another strand of DNA that I don't know about. I'm a teacher. So I want my work to stand up. I want it to be clear. In an evening of entertainment, I don't particularly want to make a lesson, but I want to deliver the manuscript, the story, in a way that's coherent to the group.

William H. Coles
What consideration do you give to the length of presentation?

Ron Carlson
If you're reading alone, you can read for forty minutes if they've invited you. If it's a hall, you can take questions and answers, and the evening can go an hour. It cannot go an hour and one minute. If you're reading with other people, you always want to be the person who reads last. And I always want to be the person who reads the shortest. If I go last, then I can make it fit. I have material. I have four-page material and I have twelve-page material. If you read alone for over

forty-seven minutes you are not going to go to heaven. If reading with another person and you read over twenty-five minutes, you're putting your chances in jeopardy.

William H. Coles
It's been a pleasure speaking with you. Thank you very much for participating in this interview.

Ron Carlson
Absolutely, Bill.

Lan Samantha Chang Interview

July 26, 2012
William H. Coles

Lan Samantha Chang is an American novelist and short-story writer who has studied and taught creative writing at Stanford University, Harvard University, Warren Wilson College, and the University of Iowa, where she is currently the director of the Iowa Writers' Workshop. She has received numerous fellowships and awards, including the PEN Open Book Award for *Inheritance* (Norton, 2005) in 2005.

William H. Coles
Story is so important to humanity in general. When you write, what is your concept of story? What is the essence of story for you?

Lan Samantha Chang
For me, a story is connected to the human experience as lived through time. I'm particularly interested in the passage of time and all of its attendants such as memory, desire, prophecy, and fate. Time, for me, is inextricably linked to my understanding and rendering of human experience through narrative.

William H. Coles
How do you choose the narrator?

Lan Samantha Chang
You know, I don't have a brilliant piece of advice about that. I have found in my work that this is one of the most challenging aspects of a book's conception. In one novel, for example, it was two years before I figured out who the narrator would be. That was my first novel, *Inheritance*, which spans several generations of a Chinese American family. When I was learning to write, cutting my teeth on stories as a graduate student, I noticed that I would often be able to tell a story quickly and fluidly if I knew who was telling it, and yet sometimes it would take me three-quarters of the time it took to draft the story just to figure out who the narrator was. Sometimes I'm able to reach for the narrator instinctively. Other times, such as when I was writing my novella, *Hunger*, I reached for the narrator and resisted her many times before I eventually decided to write from her point of view. I tried two other perspectives before I finally admitted to

myself that it was indeed the mother's perspective that I needed to write from. And then once I did, having gone through the others unsuccessfully, I was able to write the novella pretty quickly.

William H. Coles
Do you think of the narrator as separate from the author, or do you think of them as fused? Or is the relationship different for different works?

Lan Samantha Chang
Clearly the narrator is of the author, comes through the author, is rendered by the author. But I tend to think of my narrator as separate from me, as much as any of my characters is separate from me.

William H. Coles
So the narrator can change throughout the work as you develop it?

Lan Samantha Chang
Oh, absolutely.

William H. Coles
You don't have to have the same perception of the narrator throughout?

Lan Samantha Chang
No, not at all. Like many beginning writers, I began by writing in the first person, and I wrote work from the point of view of a narrator who was fairly similar to me. And then—it's pretty traceable, actually—as I kept writing, my narrator grew further and further away from that sort of categorical definition of me. So for example in *Hunger*, the majority of the pieces (almost all of them except one) were written from the first-person perspective of an Asian or Asian American woman. And many of the narrators were adolescents. At the time I wrote *Hunger*, I was in my late twenties and suffering through a protracted adolescence myself. In my next book, I insisted on a first-person female Asian narrator, and yet I found it impossible to stay in her perspective. The story was too large for her to experience herself. So I created a point of view that allowed her to imagine the points of views of others, including men. And then in my most recent book, I broke out of the first person altogether and wrote in the third person, and the protagonist was a white male. The point of view came pretty close to his head at times, and at times backed off. I now feel that I could write from many perspectives. I have an understanding that's been developed over time, and I understand the costs and benefits of writing from first or third.

William H. Coles
What is your conceptualization of voice in literary fiction? As a beginning writer, it's hard to grasp voice. Yet it's a term we use so frequently.

Lan Samantha Chang
I have two ways of thinking about voice. One is purely instinctive, and it's the way I respond to voice as a reader. I instinctively know if a piece is written in a voice that I will believe, that I'm interested in following. I feel it instinctively if the voice has authority. My other idea of voice is, of course, related to teaching. I think of narration, choice of narrator, voice, diction, diction of the narrator, language. I think about humor, tone, attitude. I think of consistency and flexibility of the tone and of the other elements. And all of that is encapsulated into a larger sense that a voice must be strong and believable. I break it down when I'm teaching. I try to break down the ways that voice works, and I talk in class about which aspects of a voice are working and not working.

William H. Coles
Is there an advantage to having a distinctive voice for a character or characters, or for a narrator, from an authorial voice?

Lan Samantha Chang
Sure. It depends on the kind of writer you want to be. But great writers, even the ones who try to make their prose as transparent as possible, leave an authorial imprint on their work.

William H. Coles
How does point of view relate to voice?

Lan Samantha Chang
Point of view is one of the most, if not the most, important element in the creation of voice. The narrator is going to have an angle toward the material that determines the tone of the entire piece.

William H. Coles
What engages a reader in a story? I'm sure it depends upon the reader, but . . .

Lan Samantha Chang
This is so interesting. It does depend upon the reader. That's becoming more and more clear to me as I get older. When I first started writing fiction, I had a clear idea that a reader would become engaged with a character who has something at stake. The character, it's often said, must want something and want it intensely,

and the writer must create obstacles to their desire. I assumed that if all of this was well done, the reader would follow. I still think that's true. But I have read extraordinary work that is less dedicated to this approach. My example would be *The Rings of Saturn* by W. G. Sebald. It is the most mesmerizing, hypnotic work, yet the narrator's day-to-day personal needs are not often mentioned in the novel. It starts off by saying, "I decided to take a walk along the coast of England." By the end of this walk, he's emotionally devastated. All the book does is describe the places he goes and what he's thinking about at each place. And the novel is this extraordinary catalogue of the effects of colonialism over hundreds of years.

William H. Coles
Interesting.

Lan Samantha Chang
He visits the most desolate, ruined places, and there's a sense of both great sadness and great horror. It's an amazing book. I never had a feeling that the book was plotted in the traditional sense of the word. So, my ideas about this have evolved over time. The kind of fiction I write, the kind of fiction I'm interested in writing, has to do with characters who desire something very much.

William H. Coles
Yes.

Lan Samantha Chang
And now I can't remember the original question!

William H. Coles
You've actually answered it very well. The elements for having a reader move on in a story often relate to information and information release. I'm particularly thinking in terms of genre fiction, where the key information is *not* released, and the function of the story is to deliver that information after creating some suspense around that non-delivery. But in literary fiction, suspense is more about worrying about something that will happen to a character that you really like.

Lan Samantha Chang
Oh, that's interesting.

William H. Coles
So you have to develop the character in a way that the reader cares about and

then develop the situation so there's interest in what's going to happen to that character.

Which allows you to load the information of the story up front. Does that make sense?

Lan Samantha Chang
I don't know what you mean by loading the story information up front. But the first thing that occurs to me from what you just said is that it's an interesting point, if I understand correctly, that in literary fiction things happen to the characters. That could be true, and it also could be a sad commentary on the state of literary fiction now. We're so attached to our characters that we don't want them to do bad things. We don't want to think ill of them. We don't want them to be the agents of their fate, so to speak. I find that interesting. I'm not sure I agree with it, so I'm not sure how to answer your question.

William H. Coles
Is literary fiction actually character-based fiction as opposed to plot-based?

Lan Samantha Chang
I think it depends on the author.

William H. Coles
Is the concept of a character-based work of value in the sense that that what happens in the story actually evolves from the character's personality, morality, thoughts and rather than a fait accompli.

Lan Samantha Chang
I don't want to simplify or define what literary fiction or commercial fiction is. We want to keep all of our readers in this broader world of possibilities. But I do understand what you're saying about the relationship between plot and character for the novelist. I'm thinking about E. M. Forster's awareness in *Aspects of the Novel* that it's very difficult to develop the plot, focus on the plot, think about the plot, make the plot do what it needs to do without sacrificing in some way the character. And conversely, the writer who focuses the most energy on character development will end up, on some level, letting the plot drop away a bit. So there is that tension for the novelist. I'm just not persuaded that all literary fiction is character based and that all commercial fiction is plot based.

William H. Coles
Forster seems to do character-based writing in *Howards End* in the sense that almost everything that happens is really from characterization that drives the

plot, which without vibrant, three-dimensional characterization would be very contrived in many ways.

Lan Samantha Chang
He does have lovely plotting in his books, though. I really love *A Room with a View*, which strikes a very delicate and sort of pleasurable balance of character and plot. I think his example of the person who was thinking of character over plot was Henry James. And I would put Henry James further to the left on that continuum of Forster.

William H. Coles
The reason I ask these questions, of course, is not only to explore the need to identify and learn from the differences among books, but to think about approaching writing as a new author.

Lan Samantha Chang
For a new author, the smartest thing is not to think about what it is you're writing, not to try to put it into a preexisting category, but look into yourself and find what you think is most powerful to you, most important to you. And then write from there. All of that other stuff will come in time. Establishing the connection—establishing, discovering, and developing one's own preoccupation—seems more important to me than looking outside of self.

William H. Coles
And what's important to you in terms of how to live?

Lan Samantha Chang
I suppose it's about how to live. But also it relates to emerging writers and developing writers. I think about it all the time.

William H. Coles
How do you approach handling backstory?

Lan Samantha Chang
My attitude toward backstory has changed over time. When I first wrote fiction, I was enamored of authors such as Alice Munro, who often worked three or four or five levels of time simultaneously into one story, creating a fluid sense of time. And so I began my work with a very flexible idea about how to use time. And then over the years, as I studied, I became aware of the power of linear narrative. Then because there's such a cultural insistence on linear narrative in so many ways, my obsession became about how and where to work in movements

outside of linearity, and then also how the linear experience through life tracks or ambushes our sense of what we know and who we've been. In my most recent novel, *All Is Forgotten, Nothing Is Lost*, I was most interested in portraying the movement from youth to experience and age because it seemed to me that in the revisiting of youth with age, youth becomes so much clearer. I decided to portray that in a very linear way. There's one huge flashback in the middle of the book. It's necessary, and I just sort of took a deep breath and thought, okay, this is a huge flashback you're throwing in here. Just do it.

William H. Coles
And you're pleased with it?

Lan Samantha Chang
Actually, it's my favorite book that I've written.

William H. Coles
Because of the flashback?

Lan Samantha Chang
No. Because the novel came out of me in a piece. I understood it, and yet felt a pleasurable sense of discovery at the same time as I was writing it. And I feel certain about it in a way that I did not feel certain about some other things I've written.

William H. Coles
That's very valuable, because you're looking at backstory as it relates to the front story or the story present. How about backstory with expository information in which there's need to get certain facts into the narrative? Do you consciously *not* do that in a flashback?

Lan Samantha Chang
Backstory as factual exposition? Any movement in time in fiction should be done for five or six reasons. It shouldn't simply be expositional because that's wasting space and time, and it waters things down.

William H. Coles
So, your exposition is in front story.

Lan Samantha Chang
Yes, whenever possible in a linear narrative. Backstory should be, I think, reserved for significant scenes.

William H. Coles
And character development through . . . ?

Lan Samantha Chang
Scenes.

William H. Coles
But often in backstory you're into reflection, either character or narrator. Does that compete with scene development?

Lan Samantha Chang
Sure. I mean, if any scene contains some reflection, and most scenes do, a flashback would . . . I guess I can't figure out why you're asking me that question.

William H. Coles
Backstory often stops momentum, stops character development in ways that are sometimes negative.

Lan Samantha Chang
That's what some people believe. It's not always true.

William H. Coles
But it does occur. Don't you think?

Lan Samantha Chang
It does. What I often see in student stories, and in my own drafts, is that the drafting reaches a point where the writer is not sure about something about the characters. In my own writing I want to know about something that happened before the story started, and so I write it, flesh it out. I write a scene from the past. But often I need to cut those scenes in revision. This is part of my process. But I don't think we should develop a draconian rule that flashbacks are bad. Some of the most beautiful books have extended passages set in the past.

William H. Coles
The goal would be to utilize flashback to the best advantage for your story, the characters, and the plot. I ask the question because it's so hard sometimes to structure these things when you're writing. All of a sudden, you're in backstory for four or five pages. How do you recognize its contribution and how do you do it right? I presume it is not only from inherent talent, but also from experience, education, comprehension of the process.

Lan Samantha Chang
I don't think it's something to be worried about. In a draft, writing about anything is okay. At some point, though, the writer has to look at the draft and ask, What of the story do I want to keep? Where is the story in this? What is this about?

William H. Coles
How do we become good revisers?

Lan Samantha Chang
I don't have a boilerplate answer. I am thinking of something that happens in student stories that I see frequently, and in my own work, which is that writers protect their characters. They don't want to let them get into trouble, or see them acting in an unattractive way. And so the characters sometime float through the stories where very little happens. On the other hand, stories are generally about situations in which trouble occurs. Ultimately, we have to let our characters get into trouble.

William H. Coles
In life, humans try to avoid conflict. But conflict is essential for a story. As writers, we need to allow our characters to be in conflicting situations, both in story structure as well as emotionally. Do you consider epiphany and enlightenment? Particularly in short stories?

Lan Samantha Chang
I had a professor, John L'Heureux, whose definition of a short story I thought useful: a short story is about a moment after which nothing will ever be the same again. This moment does not have to be insightful.

William H. Coles
Insightful for the character or insightful for the reader?

Lan Samantha Chang
Either. I think that the recent mulling over epiphanies and whether or not they should be used is coming from a concern that there might be fads in storytelling, and following fads doesn't lead to the creation of the most vivid or original stories. So many people get into writing because they have something unique that they want to express in themselves, and yet when they begin to write stories, they turn to templates such as *Dubliners* and try to copy them. Sometimes that can actually lead to beautiful work. But it's not always useful. The most important thing an emerging writer must do is develop their own voice and aesthetic.

William H. Coles
Yes. I think that attitude makes you a very valuable teacher.

Lan Samantha Chang
There's a kind of obsession with the idea that if writing is going to be taught in the classroom, there must be a correct way to teach it and there must be a correct way to write. And I've seen many teachers with very strong ideas about what they think fiction should be who impose those ideas on their students. To a certain extent, this is valuable. A strong student comes into contact with a strong teacher who has a clear aesthetic and he or she sharpens him or herself against that aesthetic, either adopts it wholesale for a period of time and then moves away from it . . . or challenges it. I've seen a lot of that challenging taking place in the classrooms where I teach. I think it's appropriate. A developing voice or aesthetic is sometimes well sharpened against the voice and aesthetic of authority figures. And yet other students, in the presence of a teacher with a very strongly developed and imposing aesthetic, will cave and adopt it, bow to authority and think that they should write exactly as the teacher says. That's a problem.

William H. Coles
Particularly in creative writing workshops, where there is often little value to the set rules that you're talking about.

Lan Samantha Chang
Well, there are things even the most rebellious and original, generative writer needs to hear about his or her work. This is where the flip side of the problem comes into the picture. A writer can be deeply original and strong minded, and still there are times when they need a teacher to say to them, "This isn't working." If they can't hear that, then they'll never be able to write work that appeals to readers. In my case, since I admire many aesthetics, I try to look at each story in class on its own terms. This is the basis of the way I run a workshop. However, as I said, there's a great value in the kind of teacher who has a strong aesthetic. It seems to me best if a student is exposed to more than one teacher.

William H. Coles
That's very valuable. Thank you so much for this enlightening interview.

Lan Samantha Chang
You're welcome. It's been a pleasure.

Charles D'Ambrosio Interview

July 19, 2008
William H. Coles

Charles D'Ambrosio grew up in Seattle and now lives in Portland, Oregon. He attended Oberlin College and the Iowa Writers' Workshop. He has published two collections of short stories, *The Point* (Little Brown, 1995) and *The Dead Fish Museum* (The Dead Fish Museum, 2007). His writings have appeared in the *New Yorker*, *Paris Review*, *Zoetrope All-Story*, and *A Public Space*. He received the Whiting Award and is a Rasmuson Fellow.

William H. Coles
I'd like to start with a basic question. What do you feel are the most important story elements a student of writing must learn?

Charles D'Ambrosio
First there are the small parts. For instance how dialogue works, particularly on a functional level. Description, and writing setting. Good, solid sentences of prose. I would say character, action, conflict, but none of those can happen unless you can construct scene. Scene is the element that pressurizes the rest.

William H. Coles
What are the elements of a scene? Does every scene have a beginning, middle, and end?

Charles D'Ambrosio
Let's say that in the traditional model every story's going to have a beginning, middle, and end. You can monkey around with that, jazz around with it, maybe begin in the middle and refuse an ending. But if we're looking at that kind of traditional situation with beginning, middle, and end, a scene is not going to work quite the same way. It can't end. Certainly it can't have an ending the way that a story has an ending, because it's got to come to some sort of close; it has shape, but it can't close down, because the story can't end. Not only that, but it wants to add energy to the story. It has to transfer. So there is going to be an internal shape that ends the scene but takes you into the next one or takes you further into the story.

William H. Coles
But there is action in every scene, isn't there?

Charles D'Ambrosio
Well, scene is, I suppose, it's a . . . yes, because it happens right in front of you. Generally you're going to be in the present of the story, although it can be set in the past, I suppose.

William H. Coles
But you can have narrative description?

Charles D'Ambrosio
Right. But let me talk about scene in opposition to summary. Summary is a way to move general time, to cover lots of information to fill in background. Scene is where time is; time shows up in its detailed form. Time slows down. We're not covering, "Then for the next five years, she'd wandered the globe, blah blah blah, then she took you into this hotel and her ex-husband showed up and something happened." That's time in its detailed form. A scene, in general, is going to contain that.

William H. Coles
Is it essential for a writer to have an idea as to what they're going to be writing about and how the story is going to be structured?

Charles D'Ambrosio
I don't think so. Everybody's going to discover their own process. Some will work from an outline. I don't know many short story writers who do that. But if that's your process, then why not? Katherine M. Porter said in an interview, "I never start a story without knowing the ending." For me, I do not like to know the ending. I like to remain uncertain for as long as I possibly can. That said, when I start a story, I have a general feel. I can feel the whole thing. I'll take little notes on the side but I don't elaborate too much because I want a little of that tension of not knowing where I'm going, being surprised, being in the dark.

William H. Coles
But you do have an idea?

Charles D'Ambrosio
A general idea. But you know, they're really not ideas in the conceptual sense. More like an image—I can see it floating out there on the horizon. I don't know what it means but I'm going there. What will actually happen? I don't know.

William H. Coles
Let me come at it from a different angle. Why do good readers of literary fiction read stories, and what do you do as an author to make them happy?

Charles D'Ambrosio
Why do literary readers read short stories?

William H. Coles
Some people will read anything—the phone book. But why do readers come for a story? What brings them back to stories, and what brings them back to the same story over and over?

Charles D'Ambrosio
I know why *I* read some stories over and over. To me it's some mix of the harmony. I hear music of the creation. The stories I've read over and over again, I can feel the whole thing in any one of the sentences, you know. I love that aspect of the short story; it's almost like reading a poem. I think some people read short stories to get a glimpse of other lives.

William H. Coles
Is it ever to experience an emotion created by the action itself . . . and the reader involvement in the story that creates an emotion?

Charles D'Ambrosio
What's the question?

William H. Coles
I'm still trying to work on why readers read. What do we do, as beginning authors, to create some emotion for a reader? People get emotional after a story, don't they?

Charles D'Ambrosio
I think so. I do. The emotions are all over the place. From dark to sad to humor. The funny stuff. Humor is the easiest one to register—not the easiest one to write, the easiest to register. The laugh is pretty much involuntary. I like funny stories. I like funny writers. Everybody has a different idea of funny, though.

William H. Coles
Most of the humor deflects off something serious, doesn't it?

Charles D'Ambrosio
I would say so. Lorrie Moore, for example, is a very funny writer, but there is a quotient of sadness sewn through. The sadness and the humor come out of the same place. That's what I love about her work, the mixture of those things.

William H. Coles
A story is not just an idea, not just an event, not just an emotion that an author has had that is significant and that he or she wants carried to the page. But still, aren't these the sources, these experiences, that generate stories?

Charles D'Ambrosio
To me there seems to be a danger when as a writer you take these sources, these experiences, and set them into descriptive narrative because you've lived them. A lack of distance from the story and a lack of action. How do you teach the action of a story, how to make it live? I don't know that you teach that thing. That's the art of it. That's a little dependent on the individual student, too. And it's the elusive thing that threads through what you can teach, whether you're teaching about scene or dialogue. Whatever that drive is. But I know exactly what you're talking about because of my own maturation, my ability to write sentences. That was there from the beginning. I could always write good sentences. I could always assemble them into paragraphs. But I had a hard time generating story logic as opposed to reality logic. I could kind of follow the plotting in the reality of a situation, but not heighten it. A lot of that is art—increased skill with dialogue and scene but also understanding the efficiency, so that as you compress things, the moments carry more tone, weight, and energy.

William H. Coles
And you're getting more specific and you're slowing down a little.

Charles D'Ambrosio
And you're following the logic that is necessary to the art.

William H. Coles
And the reality you're bringing to the story.

Charles D'Ambrosio
How does a beginning writer keep away from the static? How do you get momentum in the writing?

Charles D'Ambrosio
Again, I don't know that it can be named, but it's like developing an unrelenting

drive that will not allow that static. But if you read twenty pages, they're not all going to be static. I think of a story as a field of energy, for instance, and there are some high points and some low points. The high points are where the writing turns on, the sentences get better. That's what you keep. The low points, you go back and rewrite until they rise, they begin to have that energy.

William H. Coles
And all that has passage of time. You've got to start someplace; you've got to end someplace.

Charles D'Ambrosio
Yes. You go back at it. You're unrelenting in your drive for that and develop a feel for it. But it does happen over time.

William H. Coles
In actual time, but also with the writer's time invested in creating the story.

Charles D'Ambrosio
Yes. You can't ask the time to cough up the whole story at once.

William H. Coles
Okay. I'm going to ask a question that probably does not have an answer. It's one of those things that no one can get a firm grasp on but everybody refers to it with familiarity. And when they do refer to it, they assume everyone is talking about the same thing. You're particularly good at this—that's voice. And something about tone. What is voice, and how do we learn to create it as beginning writers? How do we go back and look for right and wrong in the voices we create?

Charles D'Ambrosio
To me voice is the musical side of the sentences, so it's partly about having an ear. If you can do dialogue, chances are you can probably do voice. You can bring a voice to a third-person narration, and certainly to a first-person narration, but it's the musical nature of sentences, where you actually hear the sound in a meaningful way, and those sounds have meaning and nuance as important as any of the content. You develop a musical idea, for example a long sentence, an open vowel sound, or how to make things happen quickly, or the ear for developing ironies inside people's mistaken ways of speaking. When someone is a bully, you don't have to say so; you make the sound of a bully.

William H. Coles
Part of this is syntax. And there is a lyrical aspect, too. But what about content?

Charles D'Ambrosio
Content is important. Single gestures, it should be seamless . . . content and voice. But if I was going to lead with one, I'd go with the sound, and then expect the content to come along with it.

William H. Coles
Is it reasonable to say that an isolated bit of dialogue in a story should be identifiable with a character without attribution?

Charles D'Ambrosio
Yes, very definitely. But it's the same type of thing. If you have somebody who's angry, you know, their dialogue should sound angry. They shouldn't just say, "I'm angry with you." They should *sound* angry. People say mean things they don't mean, and you don't have to say that it's angry, and I think you should be able to write in a voice, for instance, an angry person, and create the sound of anger, the feel of anger, right on the page.

William H. Coles
Recently in class you said you didn't think theme was important until later.

Charles D'Ambrosio
I don't.

William H. Coles
But theme is important to meaning?

Charles D'Ambrosio
Theme is important on the reading end. But I don't think it's that important for writing—at the outset. I think there is a tendency to get thematic, and when you're thinking about theme, things line up with things when really what you're trying to do is capture something much more energetic and elusive than the themes. Themes are what happens when the story cools down. Write at first to be hot, and follow more elemental aspects of the story before you organize themes.

William H. Coles
You've stated that you exhaust the usual of a story and then you come to language, which I assume is more lyrical and narrative. When you come to language, doesn't that bring you more to theme?

Charles D'Ambrosio
I think theme might help guide you at the tail end of writing. You might decide on some primal or primitive level that things belong or don't belong based on thematic decisions. The whole idea of exhaustion comes out of Flannery O'Connor, who says that a story's meaning does not begin until the adequate has been exhausted.

William H. Coles
And that connects to your thoughts on language, too.

Charles D'Ambrosio
Yes, yes. We're sitting here being civilized, and that's not where the story begins. I have bad manners. I'm exhausted.

William H. Coles
I've been meaning to talk to you about that. [*laughing*]

Charles D'Ambrosio
And things are going to break down after the adequate is exhausted.

William H. Coles
I heard an interesting lecture today on researching facts for stories. But isn't it also important for a writer to research their own attitudes about morality, the meaning of life, who we are, why we're here? Is such self-learning legitimate research for writing stories?

Charles D'Ambrosio
Oh, sure. Our thoughts and experiences can't help but feed in. Just like anything else. Our religious interests, or passions, or spirituality . . . those are experiences. You know, writing resists abstractions, so you can't stick a philosophical work in the middle, but you might have a philosophical interest, or a character who is philosophical.

William H. Coles
But it's not an essay.

Charles D'Ambrosio
But on the other hand fiction, particularly the short story, is a very flexible form, so you can have a story in the form of a philosophical essay if you gesture toward the form.

William H. Coles
What is the role of truth in literary fiction? I mean not reality truth, although there must be some borders established for reality truth. What is the role of story truth? How is truth important to credibility?

Charles D'Ambrosio
The only truth is the art. It's cold, it's harsh. To me the reality of fiction is richness, complexity.

William H. Coles
Then the right/wrong issues are not important. Even on the character level?

Charles D'Ambrosio
No. There is nothing inherently right or wrong. To me the sad truth of fiction is that a rock is just as important as your mother dying of cancer. In fact, I'd go even further: if you can't write about the rock, you're not going to be able to write about the mother dying of cancer.

William H. Coles
Why?

Charles D'Ambrosio
Because creatively they are equal. I completely believe that. You have to care about both equally. Don't choose. That's my sense of the morality. I think most people would say it's an amorality, or lack of it. You want that kind of clarity. And all people do . . . the good and the bad. That's the only way to get down into that complexity where you see—as I read in that Vivian Gornick essay—the loneliness of the monster, and the cunningness of the innocent. Where you see the complexity inside the conflicted nature of the individual.

William H. Coles
You were on a panel recently about conflict. To expand, how do beginning authors relate to conflicts? Beginners often reach for swords and pistols to find the conflict. But characters can be in conflict with something more abstract. How do you identify the energies that come from conflicts?

Charles D'Ambrosio
There are so many different ways. Part of it is vision. You see conflict all the time. Those oppositions exist within the world. I don't think it's a matter of generating them with guns. Look for sadness inside a happy moment, or our ability to experience pleasure because we've understood pain. Those are conflicts,

but on a visionary level. We see how things are connected such that one person's success may be intimately tied to someone else's missed opportunity or failure and the writer is not making choices. The successful person is not more valuable than the failed person. And the writer appreciates both. And those are set in proximity. There are so many ways to get at it. You don't have to start with the guns. I mean, what's Hamlet's problem when the ghost shows up? What's the deal? We're haunted by ghosts. You can't put your ghost away. There's a conflict. All that stuff.

William H. Coles
That's so expansive for the beginning writer. We have the opportunity to look for conflict everywhere on all levels—energy levels, and intellectual levels too.

Charles D'Ambrosio
Yes, right.

William H. Coles
Well, this has been terrific. A great opportunity and value for the website www.storyinliteraryfiction.com.

Charles D'Ambrosio
Pleasure for me. Glad to be part of it.

Peter Ho Davies Interview

31 July, 2013
William H. Coles

Peter Ho Davies is a contemporary British writer of Welsh and Chinese descent. He was born and raised in Coventry, England, and moved to the United States in 1992. He was a physicist before studying English at Cambridge University. He is a recipient of fellowships from the Guggenheim Foundation and the National Endowment for the Arts, and has taught at the University of Oregon, Emory University, and the University of Michigan (as director of MFA program), where he now teaches creative writing.

William H. Coles
Let's start with a general question. What is story to you? What about it do you convey to your students, but also what does it mean for humanity and culture?

Peter Ho Davies
It's funny and coincidental that we were talking this morning in class about E. M. Forster's distinction between story and plot. Story in his view is a sequence of events—the king died, the queen died—whereas plot imposes causality and motivation—the king died and then the queen died of grief. I guess that's the way I tend to think about the function of fiction in our community, in our civilization, in our humanity. It performs in Foresterian terms the role of plot. By thinking about causality and the motivations that underlie events, we better understand the lives we have lived or that others have lived around us. So one could regard plot—causality, motivation—as the place where we find meaning in event, why one thing happened after another, how one thing relates to another. I think for writers and for readers, and even listeners in oral storytelling, what we're searching for in life is what it means. There are lots of ways to think about that. From larger scale to smaller scale, some obviously religious, some philosophical, but also more simply on a level of character motivation and emotion. That's what drives me. I think about my life, the lives of people around me, the contemporary world and the historical world that predate me—I think, what did it mean, why did it happen that way, what caused these things to take place? That's what drives me in my fiction.

William H. Coles
So a story enlightens in some way, expresses a meaning about how to live based on how fictional characters and real "characters" live?

Peter Ho Davies
I think so, but I'm not necessarily saying this is *the* way to do it, this is *the* way to live, or this is *the* meaning of life. I think stories are offered as thought experiments. This is not *the* way to live but *a* way to live. We, as writers and readers, get to explore those decisions. What does it mean if I were that person? What if I walked in that person's shoes? That doesn't mean that was a definitive version. It's an exploration. I'd like my stories to contain meaning . . . it just doesn't have to be the definitive meaning. The effort here is to find in randomness some sense of meaning and shape, some sense of direction.

William H. Coles
There is movement and there is change, in both the characters and the readers?

Peter Ho Davies
I think that's right, although there can be a separation in that regard. We can talk about stories in which we want to see a character change, but it's also incredibly powerful to see a character fail to change.

William H. Coles
So the potential for change has to be there, potential that may provide meaning.

Peter Ho Davies
Precisely.

William H. Coles
Are most successful stories, particularly in prose, flirting with metaphysical questions that we don't know the answers to? Why are we here? Is there a God? What is beauty? What is justice?

Peter Ho Davies
I'm reminded of the lecture yesterday where mystery was talked about . . . as Flannery O'Connor talks about it in various ways. And that might begin to bump up against the metaphysical in the ways you're talking about. I'm interested in stories that are successful to me, stories that I would aspire to write, stories I'm intrigued by. There is at the heart of them some human mystery, also some characterological mystery. We have been talking in workshop about informational mystery, which is often contrived by the author by holding back (from

the reader) information that the characters already know to make the reader read on, looking for the crumbs and the clues, even if that feels manipulative to the reader. But I'm interested in mysteries that, in part, can't be solved.

It's hard to talk about this without speaking of my work—out of laziness or not being well read, I always revert to my own work in these contexts, but it's the work that I know best. I think of a story of mine called "The Ugliest House in the World," in which a child has died and one of the protagonists feels guilty. The struggle in that story is that the character is not legally guilty—an accident has occurred—but because it has occurred on his property, he feels emotionally guilty. And other people have ascribed guilt to him. It feels as if there is a tension to this character being guilty and not guilty. Of course I'm no lawyer, but I feel the character is not guilty. And my sympathy for him is actuated by the fact that he feels guilty. And so what intrigues me about that character is that he is simultaneously guilty and not guilty. And that's a mystery. How do we address something where two mutually exclusive opposites are enshrined in the same human being? It remains fascinating to me, an impenetrable mystery. Human beings are capable of embodying opposite ideas simultaneously. That reminds me of my background as a physicist many years ago when I was particularly captivated by wave particle duality, where two mutually exclusive concepts can be used to describe the same phenomenon of light or matter.

William H. Coles
How do you work on delivering emotion such as guilt on the page, in the story, without demeaning the intensity of the emotion or the character? How especially do you deliver it through action?

Peter Ho Davies
We're inclined to deny guilt, but the denial itself often points toward guilt. I'm intrigued by what I feel is a misdirection in character. The denial of it doesn't mean it doesn't exist. Denial is the signal that the guilt is felt.

William H. Coles
One stimulation that came from your discussions was the overall concept of narration. I find it difficult to conceive a sophisticated understanding of narration of prose stories because it's so different than developing a story in film, or orally. As writers, we have so many more things we can do with narration as opposed to other forms of storytelling, but with that come many techniques we can abuse. You mentioned the differences between classical narration and contemporary narration for the modern academic writer. In the old narrative techniques, a writer worked in a structured environment—beginning, middle,

and end, conflict and resolution. There were emotional displays through action. There you have the opportunity to use a narrator. The term "omniscient" always bothers me a little because it means all-knowing, godlike, and in fiction writing "all-knowing" omniscient seems best applied to multiple points of view with omniscience only in the worldviews of the characters the writer has created and chooses for the delivery of story.

Peter Ho Davies
Right. An omniscient narrator who has the ability not just to be all-knowing but to enter the consciousness of many characters.

William H. Coles
That's pretty well defined. But in contemporary times, the author becomes the narrator and actually dictates what goes into the story. In classical times the narrator could be objective.

Peter Ho Davies
Actually, I would argue the reverse of that in some ways. In the classical sense, we associate Charles Dickens's narrators, Jane Austen's narrators, with Dickens and Austen. They are all-knowing, all-seeing, as by definition the author of a work is. But they are also out to offer us judgment. Or, more gently, guidance as to how we see and interpret their characters.

William H. Coles
Okay.

Peter Ho Davies
But it also is explicit how to feel about these people. They'll show it, but they'll often tell it. To me that's a mode of narration, the classic mode, which is enjoyable to sink into as a reader, and which also speaks to a time and a period when narrators were godlike, authors were godlike. I certainly don't feel godlike, and I think a lot of contemporary writers likewise don't feel godlike. I don't think we draw unto ourselves the right to be omniscient, but also we are hesitant in our judgment. That's a reflection perhaps of the way cultural movements, scientific discoveries, and the entire history of our entire civilization over the last couple of hundred years has chipped away at traditional visions of faith and our position in the universe and our relationship to God. Now we see omniscience in the context of a modernist like Virginia Woolf—a roving omniscience capable of dipping in and out of various characters. But Woolf does not step back in between those moments as often as in previous incarnations and offer an explicit authorial judgment of those characters.

William H. Coles
Which Leo Tolstoy was very happy to do. But Woolf also describes the authorial narration, especially in the nineteenth century, as almost incandescent. The authorial presence as incandescent. Meaning, the author is not directly present in the story description but everything that is said, every action taken, every judgment made, stamps the author as the creator. I think that's especially true of Austen, too. Austen isn't *in* the drawing rooms, but she's always there. Also true of Emily Brontë's *Wuthering Heights*.

Peter Ho Davies
I don't know that quote of Woolf's, but it is lovely phrasing. It's been a while since I read her, but I agree that her authorial presence illuminates the characters.

William H. Coles
Hers is an intellectually generated presence, don't you think? She was smart. That helps. But it does put her directly in the book. She's objective, not necessarily needing to make the story her personal story.

Peter Ho Davies
Objectivity is interesting and may reflect a weakening of faith in some ways, but also the ascendancy of scientific method. Again this all leads to the sense of the nineteenth-century author as a chatty narrator presence receding in a lot of contemporary work. We stand in the wings, rather than as an impresario at center stage.

William H. Coles
Memoir has become so dominant in contemporary writing and seems to have almost drowned out classic fiction. But with time, memoir has slipped into the narrative techniques of fiction. Many writers seem to approach story as a confessional, or cathartic, a tool for revealing events or emotions they've had in their life. And without hesitancy to alter facts in memoir, or use life for description in fiction. Isn't this degrading the quality of both memoir and fiction? As a teacher directing writers to write with meaning and the possibility of contributing to the literature of our generation, do you see an erosion of quality with this trend, and are you concerned?

Peter Ho Davies
I don't see that a lot in my own teaching experience because my students are supposedly all working on fiction, and I engage with the work as fiction. As I said in class, my supposition is that any fiction has to be built from autobiographical experiences in *some* way, but we will approach it as fiction. If I were

teaching memoir classes, I might deal more directly with these questions. There are dangers in that movement, but I don't want to decry it entirely. There has been a small shift, but not massive, in marketing strategy. What we call memoirs today, particularly those written with fictional techniques, in an earlier generation we would have described as autobiographical novels. Something I do, and that most fiction writers do in some form or other. The question is, how far is that fiction disguised, how far it is projected away from the self. The danger in memoir ultimately is that it accentuates the authority of "this really happened," which can sometimes be a blunt force and supersede the authority of persuasion, plausibility, which I think of as fiction's traits. The elevation of memoir can sometimes make fictional persuasion pallid by comparison. Outrageous things can happen, and if I tell you it was outrageous and it really happened, you are obliged to believe it. If an outrageous thing happens in my fiction, I have to work a little harder to make you believe it. Things are less believable in fiction than they are sometimes in a piece that purports to be nonfiction.

William H. Coles
That goes to the very first thing you asked in class. You asked people to describe why they write. This would seem to say that for quality stories, the focus should be on reader response. There are dramatists who say success in plays is not so much the emotional and intellectual transference on the stage, but what happens to the audience. Margaret Atwood's *Negotiating with the Dead* mentions a number of authorial motivations for writing, including a few focused on entertaining and enlightening another human being.*

Peter Ho Davies
In that list of reasons Atwood compiled for why writers write, there are, very loosely, a couple of categories. I would describe them as high and low motives. Some of the lower ones are very human, very individual, but I think we might recognize them or own them. I write for revenge, I write for money, I write so my children can have shoes, that sort of thing. But set against that are goals like to justify the words of God to humanity, to tell stories that will be forgotten if they are not told, to right wrongs. These are motives that are directed toward the reader. And I guess what I like about that list is that you don't have to pick one of the reasons. We are all of us made up of many of these reasons. And again, speaking of characters and contradictory ideas, I think we write for ourselves *and* we write for others. I don't think it's a choice; I think it's those two things simultaneously. It's about an act of communication. The communication is self-communicating to you. You can never quite separate those two figures.

William H. Coles
If you want to be a writer, and you enjoy writing, whatever your motivation is, go ahead and do it. But if you look at writing as your desire to see the quality of fiction reach a certain threshold, how do you create great fiction to engage a larger number of people, to attract agents and publishers who are looking for quality, even in a market that may not see big-money potential? It seems to me that if an author is going to write fiction that reaches a certain quality, it can attract those now averse to fiction, so it is important for that writer to identify in themselves reasons to write that are not monetary. Otherwise monetary goals will dominate and dictate their writing so they never reach standards of creative excellence. Admittedly as defined by me.

Peter Ho Davies
Interesting. One of the reasons we write is to know ourselves. We can't communicate ourselves, and our visions, and our sense of character, until we know ourselves. The kind of recursive writing in revision is an effort at that understanding. We write it, so we think we know what we mean by it. But one of the things we discover in revision is what we *really* mean by it. We deepen the meaning in the process—change the meaning in various ways.

William H. Coles
I'd like to think about the fictional dream. Should stories, and should authors, try to engage the reader—because it seems like the fictional dream is a thermometer on whether you've engaged a reader—and should stories entertain?

Peter Ho Davies
Oh, sure.

William H. Coles
I've had a number of academic teachers say that if your purpose as a writer is to entertain a reader, you lose the ability to create literature as an art form. Some authors write to please themselves, ignoring a reader.

Peter Ho Davies
That's interesting. A dichotomy is being suggested that you cannot do it all—that you can entertain *or* do something serious and artful. I would say it's quite clear that examples of great literature that we have from the past are with us today because we are entertained. They not only entertain, they entertain in rich ways. There are academics who read whatever they might read, however esoteric it might be, because in some sense it entertains them. If we think about this in the large sense of entertainment, intellectual stimulation is entertainment.

Michael Chabon, in his essay "Trickster in a Suit of Light," pointed out that we suspiciously view entertainment as a sort of gaudy pleasure. But there are many ways in which deep reading, scholarly reading, is also about a satisfying engagement with another. We all in some way aspire to entertain. We just don't *only* aspire to entertain.

William H. Coles
Struggling fiction writers may go to a highly poetic style of writing: metaphors, flowery adjectives and adverbs, alliteration and onomatopoeia. How does that affect the development of story as structure? To me it takes away, especially for the beginning writer of fiction, the ability to instill conflict, drama, theme, and meaning in story. Excessive poetics seem to hinder development of effective emotional arcs, theme-useful plots, depth of characterization that drives plot events (rather than just responding to plot events). This seems to be happening to a significant degree in contemporary fiction, where a story is overwhelmed by an abundance of attention to language complexity that results in obscurity and inaccuracy for story development.

Peter Ho Davies
It's hard to generalize, and I hesitate to in some ways. Some of these things are affected by taste. Probably many of us, if not all of us, come to writing with a fascination for language. We are drawn by language. And as young writers especially, we may enjoy the fun house of language, enjoy language to excess. That's part of the joy, part of the play. But it probably indulges us more than it does our readers. Sometimes it can get in the way of narrative. It's also sometimes true that younger writers (although older writers are also prone to this) think they need to sound "like a writer." Out of our own anxiety, we think: What does a writer sound like? I'll just sound like that. And sometimes that does result in florid language, excessive language.

William H. Coles
The default for storytelling is narrative description about feelings, about events, about characters. It's what we go to without much thought. Can you teach a creator of imaginative fiction about story development in-scene, in-the-moment development, internalization, effective dialogue, accurate metaphor, and characterization? Are those teachable, or inherent?

Peter Ho Davies
Some people have a greater or lesser aptitude for them. But I think we can help everybody toward them. Sometimes it's about listening to your story, listening to the language. Certain word choices that might have been subconscious might

provoke the questions: Why did you choose that word? Why did that character use that word? Does that provoke a way of thinking about the character that hasn't previously been considered? Does that provoke a potential query for plot that hasn't previously been explored? So, I do think these things are not always separable. The language is how we tell the story. Our analytic mindset, the way we apprehend the world, the way we teach creative writing—we like to chop it up. And I'd like to think that fiction puts it back together. These are not either-or; they are both. We have to tear them apart to do the analysis to begin with. Then we have to engage with the issue of synthesis and put them back together again.

William H. Coles
Thanks. That helps a lot. We've been talking about how beginning writers set ourselves up. How do we think about writing, how do we think about story, and what do we need to study? Copying a successful writer is great to a certain extent, but it's not so useful if you want to develop as an individual, your own style. You've allowed us to see alternatives in ways of thinking that can help us develop self as a writer while creating effective, entertaining stories. It's been a valuable discussion. Thank you for participating.

Peter Ho Davies
I'm very happy to do it.

*A few examples of why writers write, from Margaret Atwood's *Negotiating with the Dead*:

Revenge
Fear and fascination with mortality
Enduring fame
Leaving a name
Fear of obscurity
Tell a story
For knowledge
Chance to battle an evil monster
To remember the loved and the lost
To bring back the dead to the living
To learn from our ancestors

Jonathan Dee Interview

July 12, 2012
William H. Coles

Jonathan Dee is a professor and novelist who teaches at Columbia University, the New School, and Queens College in Charlotte, North Carolina. He was formerly an associate editor of the *Paris Review* and a personal assistant to George Plimpton. His most recent novel, *The Privileges* (Random House, 2010), won the 2011 Prix Fitzgerald prize and was a finalist for the 2011 Pulitzer Prize for fiction.

William H. Coles
What are the essences of story that you conceptualize as you write?

Johnathan Dee
I begin with a premise that I can't necessarily work too quickly. One of my favorite anecdotes is from William Maxwell, who used to say that when he had an idea for a story or a novel, he would sit at his desk and put his feet up and think about it for the morning. And if, in the course of that morning, he could think of the ending, he wouldn't write the story. He would take that as a sign that the idea was not a fruitful one because there was nothing in it that wasn't easily discovered. So, when I think about a story, I think about a credible psychological character arc over the long term, and I think about the principles of drama, of conflict, and tension between opposites. I wish that I could boast that I could see everything entirely when I begin a book, but I never can. It works itself out.

William H. Coles
There was an interesting idea about form and content that came from one of your students when he joined you leading a seminar the other day. He made the point that there's always a controversy about form and content, and he implied that there really is no difference between them. Do you agree? Or do you think in terms of form time when you're sitting back with your feet on the desk, even though you may not think of an end, and do you think in terms of emotional arcs and beginnings, middles, and ends? Would you ever create form from content?

Johnathan Dee
As a writer, I wouldn't say that form and content are indistinguishable, but I will say that I can't go forward past a certain point until I feel like I've solved the story's formal problem . . . until I've come up with a kind of idiosyncratic form that meets the needs of the story. And it's not because I tend not to write very heavily plotted novels. I never have a sense of one size fits all or of having a template that any story will adapt to. It's the other way around. I need to find the shape of the story, and until I find that, which involves obviously a lot of trial and error, I tend to get up to the, you know, the thirty- or forty- or fifty-page mark and then just go back and start again and again and again until the answer presents itself.

William H. Coles
How do you deal with timelines in stories? Do you think of timelines at the beginning? Or do they just sort of come to you as you go along? And if that's true, at what point do you usually begin to think in terms of story . . . something that happens over a time period?

Johnathan Dee
When you say timeline, do you mean the span of time that the story will cover?

William H. Coles
Well, yes, all of that in fact. But if indeed a story is a number of sequential interrelated scenes, do you think of those scenes in terms of the relation to the timeline? For scene length, scene interactions, scene positions in the story, and for dramatic effects—that sort of thing?

Johnathan Dee
I do, yes. Particularly if you're writing a novel that contains multiple perspectives or points of view, you have to be keenly aware of the clock running at all times. In my case of not going backward any more than absolutely necessary, it's a constant balancing act, and it definitely determines things like length of scene. When you know that you have, along the same timeline, to switch to another perspective, you don't want to go past the point where you're going to pick up that perspective.

William H. Coles
The other day, you said that people are no longer reading novels. Why not?

Johnathan Dee
Did I say that? I sure hope people are still reading novels.

William H. Coles
I'm quoting you exactly. [*laughs*]

Johnathan Dee
People are reading fewer novels that are printed on paper, that's for sure. I know that the number of men reading novels, for whatever reason, is going down.

William H. Coles
Most male college graduates don't read a novel after school.

Johnathan Dee
Yes. I'm reminded constantly by my publisher that women buy most of the novels. And I think that novels themselves are getting shorter, and that's probably more than anything in response to technology. But if I said that, perhaps I was just getting carried away because it's overstating the case to say people don't read them anymore.

William H. Coles
But do you think that there's a gender influence on both the selection of novels that are published as well as the type of the novel written? Just to carry the thought a little further, is gender bias affecting the popularity or the enjoyment traditionally gleaned from novel reading?

Johnathan Dee
I'm sure it's true. I mean, I only see the inner workings of the publishing industry in regard to my own books. But my impression is that of course publishers respond, like any business, to the market. And in this case, it's a market that . . . if it isn't contracting, it's not greatly expanding. I do know that they would never tell me what to do. They would never advise me to create a novel along a certain line because it would be more commercial. However, you can see the excitement level uptick when, for instance as in my forthcoming book, the protagonist is a woman in her forties. You can see their eyes light up over that.

William H. Coles
What's the title of that book?

Johnathan Dee
It's called *A Thousand Pardons*.

William H. Coles
From your days of reading for the *Paris Review,* and your multiple readings of

contemporary literature, is the state of literary fiction changing? I want to say degrading or degenerating, but that's not quite fair. Has literary fiction changed over the years?

Johnathan Dee
The artistic state of fiction you mean?

William H. Coles
Yes, exactly. And the purpose for writing.

Johnathan Dee
I think there are still just as many essential writers now as there used to be. I think any literature is generational, and writers are always acting in response to changes. I think right now, there's a bit of a reaction to the big fat American novel, the idea of the ambitious, socially panoramic novel as practiced by Johnathan Franzen, or earlier by Tom Wolfe, or more traditionally by Norman Mailer. That's less in vogue than it used to be. I've lived and written long enough to know that if something goes away, it will come back again. The important part is to have something to rebel against when you define yourself as a writer.

William H. Coles
What do you see as the differences between literary fiction, memoir, essay, and creative nonfiction?

Johnathan Dee
I tend to be more dogmatic about that than most writers, even of my generation. I think that the line is pretty bright, and I like it when writers try to keep the line as bright as possible in terms of what is acceptable to fudge or correct, and what is not.

William H. Coles
You mean in terms of credibility and truth and veracity?

Johnathan Dee
Yes. I'm incensed, for instance, when people try to defend something like, let's say, a little piece of the James Frey book, and say, well, the response to the revelation that what was purported to be truth is in fact made up. Truth, fiction. What's the difference? There's a kind of faux sophistication to that that I really find enraging. My very valued and great former teacher, John Hersey, wrote a great essay, a beautiful essay, I think in the 1970s, called "The Legend on the License." He was writing in that case mostly about Truman Capote. But

it's amazing how much he saw coming in that respect, and how much he was already trying to put a sort of conservative stop to notions that he could see taking hold that early, even though *In Cold Blood* and books like that are, in most respects, wonderful books.

William H. Coles
Do you see a difference in the readers among those different disciplines, and the effects on those readers?

Johnathan Dee
I doubt if I can answer in terms of the effects on readers. I'd be interested to know if the contemporary readership of novels skews more toward women, and if there's a similar tilt in terms of nonfiction. Maybe there is. My own experience with my own students is pretty uniform. I don't get the sense that men like memoir better or anything like that.

William H. Coles
I've come to believe that well-written fiction, in the classical sense, has an interesting potential for a certain reader, a reader who likes character-based plots, meaning, and enjoys thinking about metaphysical questions as opposed to the reader who really enjoys the sort of voyeuristic sensibilities of memoir and creative nonfiction. The rewards are different and techniques of developing those rewards are different.

Johnathan Dee
The participation is different, too. We've talked about this in class, that when you're in a novel, the sense that you're trying to create in the reader is a sort of experimental self, a blended identity. And this is particularly true when the main character in a novel happens to be not a wonderful person, or even just someone whose experience is very far removed from yours. You want to make the reader share that self for a while. Raymond Carver once said that good fiction is always a bringing of the news from one culture to another. And in memoir, you don't get that because you never lose the sense that what you're reading about is not even hypothetical. Your own experience is the experience of a genuine other.

William H. Coles
Has there been a tendency, in your experience as a teacher, for students to conceptualize fiction as embellished memoir? In the sense you must reach deep into yourself, bring yourself to the writing, bring your family, bring your experiences in the world, and then when it gets finally into the grist mill, it comes out

creative nonfiction and loses the creativity and the inventiveness of creating a fictional story? Do you see that trend at all?

Johnathan Dee
I would say it a little differently, in that that's always been the default option, or at least the common option, for young would-be novelists—to draw at first on their own experience because that's all they have to draw on. The autobiographical first novel is not a recent invention. But one thing that is different nowadays is that more young writers will consider writing their first book as a memoir. The first time I can think of that being done was Frank Conroy's book *Stop-Time*, which I think was in the late 1960s. A beautiful book. At the time it was completely unprecedented for a young writer to make his first book-length publication nonfiction in that way. It used to be the presumption that you would turn it into a novel somehow.

William H. Coles
Is the concept of character-based fiction something that you teach specifically?

Johnathan Dee
As a writing teacher, I try very hard—and it is very hard, because I believe in certain things passionately—to do things the way I do them for a reason. However, I don't think you're doing anyone a lot of favors as a teacher if you try to move them away from their own expression and write more like you. Unfortunately, I know a number of teachers who do that. I do my best to be as completely empathetic as possible in the classroom. Even if someone is writing the sort of book that I personally would never write or perhaps would never even read, I don't feel it's my job to pass judgment in that way.

William H. Coles
You had an interesting comment in class about morality in fiction. In good fiction, is morality suspended?

Johnathan Dee
Yes, moral judgment.

William H. Coles
There is always some moral cobweb in good fiction . . .

Johnathan Dee
Absolutely.

William H. Coles
. . . that is defined by the author, and the characters work under it, this moral umbrella with defined moral thinking and actions. That's where the judgment comes in, but the judgment is on the reader's side, judging the characters. I wanted to be sure that I had it right from your point of view.

Johnathan Dee
Yes. When I'm writing a novel, the primary objective is just to write a good novel. I think that novels that are too explicit about the judgment to which they want to lead you are not interesting to read, even if you agree with the judgment. You see what I mean?

William H. Coles
Sure.

Johnathan Dee
An author's moral point or moral stance may be completely unimpeachable, but if the characters turn into essentially moral archetypes or figures in a parable so that you can see developments coming before they happen, then that to me is not a novel worth reading, no matter how correct it is. So, a moral judgment is not banished, or considered invalid or irrelevant, but it's suspended. It's held aloft. It's delayed at least until the book is closed. At that point, you can make up your mind about it. But if you feel that your mind is definitely made up about the characters and about the proceedings in the middle of the book, then the rest of the book is really just like watching a sentence carried out. And a sentence carried out against fictional figures of your own invention seems to me like shooting fish in a barrel.

William H. Coles
We write novels and critique them in class, and there seem to be two things that fight against each other: plot progression and character development. Is there a difference in your mind between genre fiction as related to plot—how it's written, and how it's received and how it's enjoyed—and how literary fiction is perceived, enjoyed, and related to character development and character change? When you read words in a novel for the first time, do you sense if they are plot oriented or character oriented?

Johnathan Dee
Well, yes, I do, of course. And I think a writer who's very good on this subject is E. M. Forster in *Aspects of the Novel*, where he talks specifically and a little surprisingly, really, about plot and character, not only as different forces, but

sometimes as opposing forces. This is from the point of view of the writer. That they have their very different imperatives that need to be juggled and constantly reconciled and constantly compromised because the strict attention to long-term character development can be critical in terms of plot and vice versa. Different books have had a different imperative for me in terms of plot. I guess I can say that they all contain an element of long-term psychological character development. Only some of them are really plot heavy. Some are much plot heavier than others, and the most recent one, I think, I was very conscious of wanting the whole thing to be constructed and of the characters being in service to that construction.

William H. Coles
Characters have flaws and strengths that contribute to the plot, to change the action of the plot. As we writers work to help the reader enjoy a change in thinking about the characters and the story world, is it helpful to construct stories more as literary writers, not as genre fiction writers? Do you find the union between the strength and flaw helpful in teaching to emphasize the character aspects for literary fiction?

Johnathan Dee
Yes. And I think from a writer's perspective, the essential thing about what you call a character flaw, and I do see this a lot in student work sometimes, is that a character will be drawn to such an extreme that the problem is not credibility; the problem is that there's only one direction in which that character can develop. Either way, if somebody is too villainous or too virtuous, it only gives you one direction in which the book can go, and the reader picks that up very quickly.

William H. Coles
Literary fiction always seems to me to shine a little bit more if it deals in some way with a metaphysical question. What is beauty? What is love? Who are we? Why are we here? Do you feel that too?

Johnathan Dee
It's a good question. In my case the answer is yes, I do think about those things. But when I think about them, I try very hard to forget them. Because I feel like if you let any answer or commentary to a question like that into your own work, it has to be generated by the work and you have to keep your focus very narrow. You have to keep your nose close to the ground, by which I mean you have to attend to the characters and their story and let thematic or symbolic concerns emerge from that.

Another answer to the question is to say that there's a tension. I think probably every good writer is aware of the difference between discussing the questions you're talking about, like what William Faulkner used to call the eternal verities, and also addressing the question of whether or not writing a novel is a matter of leaving a record of what life was like in your own time. What the answers to these questions were in your own time. So, there's a balance between wanting the book to connect to something eternal, so that at least in theory someone could pick it up in another culture, in another society, in another century, and still find something to connect to, and wanting it to speak to your contemporary audience and to address the way things are now, and thus differentiate it from novels that are about the way things used to be.

William H. Coles
In some ways this seems like an attitude adjustment for authors. You've got to go out and kill a whale, or work in a diamond mine. But I'm wondering also, would you recommend thinking about these metaphysical questions, and humanity, in a way that it prepares you in your writing to begin to deal with depth of characterization in different ways?

Johnathan Dee
I'm not sure. I'm not sure I'm grasping the question.

William H. Coles
The whole idea is about people who might dwell on these questions. I mean, some of these metaphysical questions are religious in a way. Some are philosophical. Some are political. When students are advised to go out to climb a mountain or work on a cruise liner and think about their experiences in an objective way, not so much a subjective way, it helps them prepare for writing literature. And what about existence? I mean, are we here just to survive and procreate? Or is there something else? What did the ancient Greeks feel about that existential part of existence? Is there something about the mysteries of life that can help a writer develop an attitude about how to create characters, and how we develop stories with meaning?

Johnathan Dee
It definitely helps to think about humanity. It's one of your duties as a fiction writer to read about those questions and what other thinkers have said about them . . . and to think about your own answers as well. It's also true, though—it's in the nature of every writer I've ever known, and I'm sure it's true for you too—that you don't really know what you think until you write it. You know what I mean? I know many writers, including myself, have had the sensation of

thinking of a story idea and then writing it, even if that takes place over several years. The writing itself is a kind of answer to the question of why you found it interesting in the first place. You can begin with questions about broader philosophical matters, or questions about existence, but I feel like often the story itself is the answer. It's the coming up with a way of thinking. Writing a novel is itself a way of thinking; it's not just a way of expressing thoughts you've already had.

William H. Coles
In class, as manuscripts are critiqued, it seems often that students are looking for credibility of actions, ideation, opinions, and there's a resistance to suspension of disbelief—you know, "I don't believe that's going to be true." It's a search for veracity, really, in the story itself. And yet suspension of disbelief has been a necessary tool for writers. Do students who critique want to find truth and erase suspension of disbelief to discover the overall moral or meaning of the story? Does credibility make for better literary stories? That's the most complicated question I've ever asked.

Johnathan Dee
Well, we're all in here in a workshop setting, and we're obviously at something of a disadvantage in that we're not reading whole books. We're reading small excerpts from books. Any good book will establish the terms of its relation to the real. And any good book (obviously I'm far from the first to say this) teaches you how to read it as you read it. And since we don't get that experience, since we're sometimes reading nothing but chapter 15, our default setting as readers is the real. That's where we begin.

So yes, you're right, we hear that question a lot in class. But students are not given enough to work with on the page in order to start thinking about things in a different way. That's just the nature of workshops. One of my all-time favorite examples of that idea of a book teaching you how to read it, or at least showing you right away that you are on some plane other than the real, is the novel *Waiting for the Barbarians* by J. M. Coetzee, a great South African, Nobel Prize–winning novelist. *Waiting for the Barbarians* is a kind of extended parable about racism and colonialism, but you know instantly, even though the language is very familiar, that he wrote it before the end of apartheid. The settings are generalized but familiar. The very first thing that happens in the book, in fact in the very first sentence, is, "I have never seen anything like it." And then there's a long, elaborate description of a visiting government official at this colonial outpost who is wearing something on his face. The description is clearly of a pair of sunglasses. In that first paragraph, that one detail, you realize that you are in a world where no one has seen sunglasses before; it lets you know that other assumptions you might have are not assumptions that these characters have. You are in a very recognizable but explicitly fictional and different world . . . and I love that.

William H. Coles
Right, and a valuable technique used, probably not consciously. It demonstrates the need to see the novel in its entirety. I didn't mean to imply that reading portions of a novel was unique to your class. It's a widespread practice. I was looking for ways to avoid crimping the overall critiquing setting. And you've answered it. The most accurate, and fair, critique probably comes only after reading a whole novel.

Johnathan Dee
Yes, ideally that's what we would say. The class I teach normally at Columbia now is an all-novel workshop, and there are a small number of students who submit repeatedly, and you actually can, if they're productive enough over the course of a semester, read the whole novel. That makes a big difference in understanding and critiquing.

William H. Coles
I'm not surprised. In workshops, what do student critiquers do that is most valuable to you as a teacher?

Johnathan Dee
It's people who internalize the idea. It's very easy for me now because I've been doing this for decades. But for people who are new to this setting, it's hard to realize that you have to learn to read a different way. Normally, when we read, we read reactively, as I do when I go home and pick up a book. I'm not engaged in reading that book in such a way that I would be thinking about different ways to write it. I would just be reacting to the way in which it has been done. But the ideal student or critiquer in a classroom is someone who is constructive and always operating from the presumption that what's in front of him or her is not fixed, it's temporary. They should read it not in terms of their own goals as a writer, but in terms of—insofar as you can pick them up—the author's goals and try to figure out alternative strategies, alternative techniques, for getting closer to the author's goals.

William H. Coles
You talk of suspense and drama often in your classes. To achieve suspense in genre fiction, information is withheld or manipulated, then finally revealed.

Whereas in suspense for literary fiction, a character is created for the reader so that the reader is invested in that character and then the story makes the reader worry that something is going to happen to that character they care about. All information essential for the story is presented up front, or at least when needed for the story, without withholding it or manipulating it. I've heard you discuss this in different ways, and I wonder if you could expand on it now.

Johnathan Dee
As you know, the word "suspense" unfortunately has a sort of genre connotation itself. I mean, sometimes it's something much simpler, more on the order of uncertainty. But to try to answer the question, I'll offer an anecdote from Alfred Hitchcock. Maybe you've heard this before, Alfred Hitchcock's classic definition of suspense versus surprise. Imagine that you're filming two men sitting at a table having a cup of coffee, and after five minutes a bomb goes off underneath the table and they're both killed. That's shocking. Now imagine that same scenario, but in addition to the two men sitting at the table drinking coffee, you also show the bomb. Then those same five minutes, which are filled with the most banal conversation, people asking for more sugar or whatever, become unbearable because you're in possession of more information than the characters have. Suspense via withholding information, I think, is so simple that ultimately a good writer will decide that it's not worth doing. There's suspense generated that way, and then there's suspense that's generated by a profusion of information, by your having everything that you need to make sense of the scenario, and especially if the characters are in possession of some of that. I'm always in favor of profusion of detail rather than the kind of artificial withholding of detail as a way of generating uncertainty, of generating a sense of irresolution or waiting for something to happen.

William H. Coles
It's difficult, and it varies with every story, doesn't it?

Johnathan Dee
Definitely. I do feel I have a stronger sense now of how hard it is to be original.

William H. Coles
I was surprised in one of the seminars you said that you never think about readers when you're writing.

Johnathan Dee
I don't; it's just a fact. It's not a conscious decision, and as I said, that's not to say that I don't care about readers. I mean, from the moment something is done,

if I print it out and hand it to you, then I'm in agony over what you think of it. But when I'm actually engaged with the page, I'm engaged with the sentence. I'm only thinking about how to make it good enough for me. I don't know why that's true, but it's true.

William H. Coles
What are the things you want a reader to get from reading your work?

Johnathan Dee
I'd like a book of mine to be morally provocative in a way that other forms of entertainment or other forms of information aren't. But that's a really good question. I think the reason I became a writer, the same reason probably most writers become writers, is that there was just nothing else, even as a young person, in the world that gave me a particular pleasure than reading a good story. And so I guess the primary answer would be that I want what I do to be good enough and well-crafted enough and ingenious enough to give others that same pleasure. Beyond that, as I get older, my goals get a little loftier, and I do feel I have a stronger sense now of how hard it is to be original. I would like readers to think, when they finish a book of mine, that it's not like anything they've read before. And I'd like it to be morally provocative in a way that other forms of entertainment, or other forms of information, aren't. A record of what it's like to be alive and conscious now.

William H. Coles
You'd like them to remember it. You'd like them to be engaged in it so that they can get involved in the action as well as the characterization.

Johnathan Dee
Definitely.

William H. Coles
You would like them to have some changed perception of the world and humanity, or is that going too far?

Johnathan Dee
I'm thinking of the classic definition of poetry—that it makes the strange familiar and the familiar strange. Yes, ideally, if you do all those other jobs effectively and correctly, then when the book is closed it will make the reader see at least some aspects of the world around him or her in a fresh way. That's one reason why I don't write historical novels. It's not that I hold it against other people when they do it, but I don't understand what would draw readers to it when there

are already a lot of good novels about, say, the eighteenth century. I don't see why you'd go back and write another one. A novel should be a kind of artistic, moral, and philosophical engagement with what's around you. But that's just me. Other writers will have a different way of looking at things.

William H. Coles
This is a touchy one, and I say that because in other interviews I've had a lot of different reactions to this. But do you want readers to be entertained?

Johnathan Dee
Yes, I do. Obviously there are different scales of entertainment. You know, seeing a thirty-second cat video on YouTube is entertaining. It's a different grade of entertainment than the entertainment I feel when I'm reading Leo Tolstoy. Yet Tolstoy is hugely entertaining. Entertainment is not the *only* thing I want to do, but yes. I can keenly remember the disappointment of reading certain books that you know are good, and you have been told are good, and you know, in some sense, they're good for you. But they just aren't entertaining when you're reading them. They feel like medicine. I felt that way about Gertrude Stein, just for one example.

William H. Coles
I agree. I've had people say that if your purpose as an author is to entertain, you cannot write literary fiction as an art form. Does that ring true to you?

Johnathan Dee
I would insert the word "only" there. If your *only* purpose is to entertain, then that might make more sense. But even that's still a pretty broad generalization. I'm sure Jonathan Franzen wants to entertain the bejesus out of his audience.

William H. Coles
The last thing I wanted to talk to you about in this very interesting and stimulating discussion is authorial presence in fiction. When you analyze classical fiction, the greats rarely have an authorial presence in the narrative, although the author might directly address the reader at times. I mean the authors were obviously there, but their authorial presence wasn't directly in the voice or the narrative telling. Examples might be the Brontës, Jane Austen, Gustave Flaubert, and even Anton Chekhov. The author is present as the creator, but there is not an authorial presence in voice or point of view. Whereas today, in contemporary fiction, the author is almost always there. The author is really giving his or her identity through the characters, with the characterization, through the dialogue, through almost every voice within that story setting. Would you agree?

Johnathan Dee
I see what you mean. I think that the movement would be more from the idea of authorial omissions to the idea of authorial subjectivity. That's an idea that's sixty or seventy years old, but the notion that what makes the only validity in fiction is to see as one person sees . . . and that there is something presumptuous, and godlike. And by virtue of being godlike, outdated in terms of writing, even if you don't have the presence in the prose that you're talking about of writing from a position of divine authority. You know, I mentioned in class the other day, this quote from Flaubert: "An author in his book must be like God in the universe, present everywhere and visible nowhere." That was a great idea then. You don't see it much in practice now. Now, there's one sensibility that's front and center: that there should be a more divine sensibility than there is in the prose. That is, I think, now considered presumptuous.

William H. Coles
To regain the enjoyment of reading classical literature, should we bring back the concept of a narrator telling stories, characters acting out in the stories, and authors creating stories—but that the author does not become the narrator in a fusion sense? Do you think we could create as authors today that really objective sense of wonder plus subjectivity that the classic people created?

Johnathan Dee
Sure. I'd love to see it. I mean, it's a little bit different than the problem I was talking about before, of generations reacting against each other and trends going away and coming back. Because this is really, I think, the whole question of point of view in fiction that is related to a more oceanic, philosophical change in the way we live and think. And even in the role of religion in our lives. But that said, I'd love to see it, and there's no reason why it couldn't be done. Who knows, maybe that's the next frontier.

William H. Coles
This has been great. You're a great person, and great to talk to about literature. It's been very enjoyable. I appreciate your willingness to talk to www.storyinliteraryfiction.com

Johnathan Dee
My pleasure. Thank you for asking.

Tom Jenks Interview

January, 2012
William H. Coles

Tom Jenks is the cofounder and coeditor of the online literary magazine *Narrative*. He is a former fiction editor of *Esquire*, literary editor of *Gentleman's Quarterly*, advisory editor of *Paris Review*, and senior editor at Scribner's, where he edited Ernest Hemingway's posthumously published novel *The Garden of Eden*. With Raymond Carver he coedited the collection *American Short Story Masterpieces* (Dell, 1989). Jenks's stories and articles have appeared in *Vanity Fair*, *Esquire*, the *Los Angeles Times*, *Ploughshares*, *Story*, and elsewhere.

William H. Coles
What is your concept of story? What does it mean to society?

Tom Jenks
Storytellers are mythmakers. Stories explain the things that cannot otherwise be explained. Part of storytelling is the experience of life, and another part is the meaning that the storyteller brings to the story.

William H. Coles
Has storytelling and its effect on readers changed with society and its progress? Specifically, is it harder for a writer today to put meaning and theme into prose?

Tom Jenks
The present always tends to seem like a difficult, complex time. The past can seem simpler, but that of course is an illusion. Stories move along a line of human emotion, the truthfulness of human emotion. Emotions don't grow old, emotions don't change. We may tend to be distracted by current phenomena such as social media or information technology, or the ebb and flow of economics, the haves and the have-nots, or whatever else you want to point to in terms of contemporary problems. But what we always look to in story is human nature. Great stories always center on that.

William H. Coles
The demographics of readers who look to story for what you just described are changing dramatically. A significant majority of readers are women, often in

midlife; something like 80-plus percent of men don't read a novel after they graduate from college; fewer literary books are being published; and agents don't seek out literary fiction. As the readership changes, is the receptive base for prose stories dying?

Tom Jenks
I don't think so. Vogues change, fashion changes, and for a short time one thing may be more popular than another. Memoirs may be more popular than novels, or nonfiction may be more popular at sometimes than others. Finding support for poetry is like finding Fabergé eggs. Literary work in terms of pop culture is always a subset. Mass culture is less interested in literature per se than in entertainment. Good literature entertains, but it doesn't *purely* entertain. If you look at Hollywood and the movies that are being made, if we take Hollywood as a representation of pop culture, we could observe that many of the stories that come out of Hollywood originate in books. Movies, television shows, online and mobile media: at the root of much of it is story. Good newspaper articles have a basis in narrative. They do! This is human nature. I don't think it's ever going away. But at its highest level of performance, there is a smaller audience for that than there was for Barnum & Bailey. That's just how it is.

William H. Coles
Do you perceive a growing tendency for authorial involvement in story, in the sense of memoir? I get the sense that you feel that good writing is ubiquitous in both memoir and fiction. In memoir the author is in the story. But great literary stories seem less author based. As you teach fiction, the authorial presence is filtered in complex ways. You express the roles of narrator and character and the relationship of the author. But when the author is openly present in fiction, the readers are attracted by the need for prurient voyeurism, or confessional. Doesn't the authorial presence in fiction work against the potential of great writing by negating imagined characters and plot outside the author's experience? Doesn't the influx of memoir into fiction writing alter the traditional success of fiction as an art form, because the choices available for great dramatic storytelling are more limited?

Tom Jenks
Well, that was a long question! [*laughing*] Whoa!

William H. Coles
I'm asking if, as an editor and a publisher, you are seeing more authorial involvement in fiction, to the point of it becoming "me-fiction."

Tom Jenks
I don't know that I have an absolute answer to that. An awful lot of people are writing today. One of the good effects of modern education is that there are vastly more people now who can write at a level of relative proficiency than there were in the nineteenth century, for instance. And there are a lot of writing schools and degreed writers coming out of these schools, so there is a culture of writing that didn't exist previously. Along with that, there's been a trend in mass culture toward an iconography of the self. Leo Tolstoy, in his essay "What is Art?" noted that among a hundred works one will be a diamond and the rest will be paste. That's the perennial circumstance. The real article has always been very rare. And there are degrees from indifferent to wonderful.

It would be easy to say things are deteriorating. There was a point in the technological revolution when there was definitely a falling off of reading, and it was a big concern to everybody who cares about literature, but now that the technology has progressed to the point that its intersection with literature is becoming clearer, as with devices such as the Kindle and the iPad, there's been a reversal toward more reading rather than less. Prior cycles have seen the publishing business more conducive or less so for various kinds of material. Whenever the fashion shifts, concern arises. Bookstores are dying. Amazon is bad. Google is bad. But really it's all just change, metamorphosis.

My belief is in the human imagination, the human spirit. It's not a given that everything turns out well, but with care, attention, and persistence, things do tend to turn out well. People who are interested in reading, writing, and storytelling are usually interested for the right reasons: a desire to communicate, connect, understand, share. It's a basic human need. Storytelling is a vehicle for it.

William H. Coles
The reason I asked the question was not so much about the deterioration of story, but rather the insertion of self into fiction among writers trying to learn the art of fiction. I think that authors who insert themselves produce a different result than authors who do not limit themselves to their own world and experiences. Is it useful for beginning fiction authors to resist the insertion of self if they wish to write at a higher level?

Tom Jenks
I think everybody writes out of some desire for self-expression. That's part of it. But then, ideally, it moves from the personal to the impersonal. The material is set free from the individual self and becomes available in its entirety, in its trans-

parency, to anyone. The work invites connection and participation, as opposed to "look at me."

William H. Coles
One of the concepts I always admire in your teaching is the idea that characters act out stories, narrators tell stories, and authors create stories. Could you articulate how the narrator's perception is always present in the story, as distinct from the characters' view?

Tom Jenks
It's hard to do better than Virginia Woolf's *The Common Reader* in terms of writing and thinking about writing. In her discussion of incandescence, the idea is that in the best work the author's personality is completely dissolved in the work. The author is omnipresent but nowhere visible in his or her personality. Woolf uses the example of William Shakespeare.

William H. Coles
And *Wuthering Heights*.

Tom Jenks
Well, she uses the example of *Wuthering Heights* as a situation in which incandescence is not entirely achieved. The personality of the writer evinces itself in a way that causes an eruption or a break. The author's individual emotive expressiveness creates a disruptive ripple in the story.

William H. Coles
But Shakespeare?

Tom Jenks
In Shakespeare we're reading Shakespeare, but he has completely deployed his personality by giving over the characters. He's orchestrating it all without our observing his presence as such. Tolstoy is another great example. There are three great characters in *Anna Karenina*: Anna, Levin, and Tolstoy. We experience Tolstoy's nature only via his gifts in the storytelling and not by literal autobiographical acquaintance with him. And in the best memoir, something similar happens. We know the author by what the author has to say about life, about events, and about characters other than the self. Constant, steady self-involvement tends to create a closed loop that holds a reader outside the experience of the story.

William H. Coles
When we go to the movies and are engaged and react—for instance in *Howards End*, the Merchant Ivory's film—and then we read the novel, we might have a different sense of engagement, and a slightly or totally different reaction. It has to do with the differences allowed in storytelling with film versus fictional prose. In film, everything is images, action, dialogue. How do we, as beginning writers, use internalization, internal reflection, and access to memory in our written stories to best advantage?

Tom Jenks
I don't watch films the way I read literature, which is to say, with a few exceptions, I don't take film as seriously as I might. It is an art form, but it's been said that the good films made from books are best made from not-very-good books. There are exceptions. You mentioned *Howards End*. John Huston's *The Dead*, a film version of the famous James Joyce story, is another example. Novels can do a lot of things that films can't do. And often novels do things that don't lend themselves well to film. The depth and nuance of characterization don't translate easily to film, especially if the characterizations are interior. In film, what carries a story are the images. *Jaws* is a perfect film—it doesn't need any dialogue. You can just watch the images. The whole story is there.

A holy grail of a certain kind of filmmaking is to let the images do the work. The point of view is provided by the camera. Novelists and storywriters do another kind of work: they put it on the page. Film initially took inspiration from the page and imported literary techniques into moviemaking. A line space became a jump cut. But a writer trying to learn to write by watching films or TV may fall into a fallacy of trying to import the techniques of film straight into literature. Most of the time this is a mistake because there is distortion or exaggeration in the translation, or so much is left out in film that needs articulation on the page. A film audience understands the story from the images, but in written storytelling the language itself does the work.

William H. Coles
Is the translation easier for a genre writer than for a literary writer, since genre is not usually based on a character-driven plot?

Tom Jenks
I don't know enough about genre work. When I watch film, I'm just passing the time. I don't enjoy many films. Few worthwhile ones are being made. The film business sometimes posits the audience as the chumps out there eating popcorn in the theater.

William H. Coles
In literary fiction a writer focuses on character-based emotional arcs, engaging a reader's interest and sympathy. Is that kind of work a good place for beginning writers to look for inspiration?

Tom Jenks
Yes, look to the best authors, the best stories, for inspiration.

William H. Coles
In an imitative way?

Tom Jenks
Imitating things you love is a great way to learn. Many writers start out that way. Look at the influence of Homer on Virgil, Virgil on Joyce, Joyce on William Faulkner, and Faulkner on Gabriel García Márquez. You take inspiration from what came before, and then you go beyond.

William H. Coles
You've known a lot of writers. Who has astonished you in particular? Your associates have included George Plimpton, Raymond Carver, and Peter Taylor, to name only a few.

Tom Jenks
I was lucky. I went to New York for grad school, and to help pay the bills I worked in publishing.

William H. Coles
Did you major in English?

Tom Jenks
Literature was my undergraduate major. English literature, American literature. But when I went to work in publishing, I found that academic knowledge was almost useless. Discussion and analysis of completed works by dead authors, often from a theoretical perspective, is quite different from trying to be of use to a living author with a work in progress. I was lucky to land in New York at a time when there were a lot of interesting people around. Fiction and the short story were experiencing a great vogue. There was a lot of excitement and interest in it. Right away I got to meet everybody I wanted to meet, and I got to work with a lot of them.

William H. Coles
And did you watch writers working creatively? Can you explain the process?

Tom Jenks
Somebody once said that creativity involves putting together two or more things that don't seem to go together. Today we hear a lot about creativity. It has become a pop cult idea that everyone is creative. Knowledge, resourcefulness, spontaneity, habituated mastery, strength, sensitivity, perceptiveness, accuracy of touch, and nimbleness are all elements that lend themselves to the creative impulse. Jazz is an improvisational art form, but the artist's ability to improvise is based on habituated ability with the music, with the instrument.

William H. Coles
That's a good analogy.

Tom Jenks
Once I was working with Robert Stone on a piece. I had made an excerpt from one of his novels for *Esquire*—this was in the 1980s—and in making the excerpt I made a couple of cuts and the remaining material needed to be stitched back together. Bob came into the office, sat down at a desk, and in a matter of minutes wrote a few sentences. I looked at them and said, "That's great. That does it." And he said, "That's what you do. You bring 'em down and you take 'em up again." The cuts had needed some transitional material with dramatic force. Bob saw right away what was needed and performed it. He takes great pride in his discipline. Some of it is natural talent, and some of it is accomplishment.

William H. Coles
Can beginning writers learn how to create conflict and drama if it doesn't come to them naturally?

Tom Jenks
Have you read Graham Greene's *Our Man in Havana*?

William H. Coles
No.

Tom Jenks
I'm reading it now for the first time. It's extraordinary. The premise is that there's a vacuum cleaner salesman in Havana in 1958 just before Fidel Castro's revolution. The salesman is enlisted by a British intelligence operative to be "our man" in Havana. The salesman doesn't really want to be a spy, but he needs the money—he's a single father with a daughter who wants a horse. The

British operative wants our man not only to collect intelligence but also to form a network of intelligence operators. So the salesman just makes it all up. He invents agents, he invents information, and his imagination just runs riot. He needs an agent. So, here's a name, here's a story. Oh, wait! Oh, no! There's a complication, and he has to get rid of an agent who doesn't really exist, so how to do it plausibly? We watch the salesman create fictions, and we're also watching Greene's imagination at work. It's satirical, of course, and hilarious. In daily life most of us go out of our way to avoid conflict, if we can. We think, "Don't say that!" Or, "Oh my God, let's don't have that happen." But the story writer is going in the opposite direction. Let's make as much trouble as we can. Let's really stir it up.

William H. Coles
I think it was Greene who said the duty of a novelist is to forget, while the duty of a journalist is to remember. The idea is that what you forgot would be internalized to emerge as creativity.

Tom Jenks
Greene looked at what was going on in Cuba at the time and wrote *Our Man in Havana* quickly. It's short and was timely when he published it, and it holds up very well today. Not many writers can sit down and say, in effect, I see something happening in the world right now, and not only am I going to write a story out of it, but the story is going to be a satire that's connected to Joseph Conrad's *The Secret Agent* and exists prominently in a long line of literature of this type. But Greene's novel is also a genre unto itself because it has so many different modes. It's a wonderfully dense piece of work that reads like a horse race.

William H. Coles
Thanks for the recommendation. I look forward to reading it.

Tom Jenks
Creative activity is a basic human need, but not everyone has the kind of creative ability that goes into writing a great story or novel.

William H. Coles
What's the difference between ordinary creativity and exceptional creativity?

Tom Jenks
When my middle daughter was in preschool, the kids were painting pictures and one of the teachers would say "that's good," or "that's bad." But kids don't want or need that sort of valuation. Instead they want, "Wow!" Or they want

some specific, practical, helpful information that includes some note of encouragement. They want to paint. But of course, the results are not all equal. In our time, there's a sense in the adult world that everybody is creative and everybody can be creative. Everybody is equal. The internet helps reinforce this sense of creative equality—whatever anyone writes is equal to what anyone else writes, and anyone's opinion of what anyone writes is equal to whatever else anyone has to say on the subject. Look at the reader comments on Amazon—most are contentious and negative, a flourishing of uninformed opinion and spleen. Information technology is democratic by virtue of access. Art is not democratic. Reading is democratic. Viewing is democratic. It's meant to be, and should be, accessible to all. But the creation of art is not really democratic.

William H. Coles
How does intelligence relate to this?

Tom Jenks
Well, it depends on what kind of intelligence you're talking about.

William H. Coles
Augh. [*laughs*] That's slippery.

Tom Jenks
The intelligence quotient, or IQ, has been an accepted indicator of degrees of intelligence. There's a scale, 160, 145. God help you, you could have 90. The numbers are meaningful to some extent. But another mark of intelligence is how well a life is lived. There are many kinds of intelligence other than raw IQ. There's emotional intelligence, intuitive knowing, common sense, and specific gifts for music or math or horse trading. Having a high IQ is not necessarily predictive of success.

William H. Coles
Or of creativity?

Tom Jenks
Individuals with a very high IQ can fail at life and sometimes fail ultimately at the very things they're best at. Bobby Fischer comes to mind.

William H. Coles
Anyone setting out to be a writer might wonder, Am I capable of doing this? Am I capable of creating art at the level I want? Can I assess my abilities? Am I smart enough, with enough background, enough life experiences?

Tom Jenks
You never know what you can do until you do it. And if you've done it once, maybe you can do it again.

William H. Coles
I wish we could go on with this conversation forever. Thanks so much for contributing to storyinliteraryfiction.com.

Tom Jenks
Thank you.

Fred Leebron Interview

June 15, 2012
William H. Coles

Fred Leebron is professor at Gettysburg College, where he teaches fiction. He is the director of the Pan-European MFA program at Cedar Crest College in Pennsylvania, the director of the MFA program at Queens College in Charlotte, North Carolina, and the director of the summer program at Hollins College at Tinker Mountain, Virginia.

William H. Coles
How do you define the classic literary story?

Fred Leebron
Well, I think that's part of the problem. If you start trying to define the elements of a classic literary story, then you're looking at some kind of literary straitjacket. There is more than one way of looking at classic literary fiction. You can say the classic elements are conflict, crisis, resolution, or you can broaden that and say the classic story allows for the illusion of progression, the suspension of disbelief, the sense that the story lingers in the reader's mind long after he or she has finished reading it, and that the characters go on beyond the last page. So, it depends on how narrowly you want to define it.

William H. Coles
In class you mentioned that an author hoped her work would endure, and you pointed out that no author can really tell whether their work is going to endure. Could you look at a few literary works from the past—for instance *Howards End*, *Pride and Prejudice*, *Moby-Dick*, *Wuthering Heights*, or *Madame Bovary*— and try to articulate the elements that contributed to their endurance?

Fred Leebron
Enduring novels are bigger than their own times. That's the definition of endurance, but it's a twofold definition. The first is, it's bigger than its own time, thus it endures; the second is that something is going on in the work that you can see makes it greater than its own time. It transcends the temporal limitations that the author brings to the page. By definition it extends beyond, and it extends before. *White Noise* would have meaning to someone in the 1990s, but I

think *White Noise* will endure and have meaning thirty years after it's published, and probably would have had meaning thirty years before it was published.

William H. Coles
But is there a way we can learn from what was specifically done in those novels that we can apply to our own writing? I'm thinking of your nine essential stakes of storytelling: birth, sex, death, friendship, family, money, identity, spirituality, and liberty.

Fred Leebron
I think it begins with universality. That the work has a greater meaning to more people than the people it might have been written for in the first place. You can break apart any work of fiction and go to those nine essential stakes. Those are the paradigmatic stakes in fiction writing. Everything comes from that. The character is at risk in some way such that someone else reading it from another time and another culture can still see that struggle and identify with it. That's what universality offers: identification. Beyond that, it's not only to be willing to have that quality of risk; the characters must seem human, real, complex, and motivated by multiple and complex reasons rather than by singular or simple reasons.

William H. Coles
You've discussed suspension of disbelief in class. You see that as a conscious tool used by writers. But as a writer deals with suspension of disbelief, there is the danger of losing credibility. As you lose credibility, you move into fantasy as opposed to reality. When you lose credibility, do you begin to alter effective characterization in literary fiction, and thereby lose the meaning you're trying to develop through characterization?

Fred Leebron
It seems to me that you are saying—although I'm not sure I fully understand the question—that suspension of disbelief implies you have to do a lot of evocation. You have to make the work real to the reader to leave his or her world behind. And in doing all that evocation, and scenic writing, you might be focusing too much on setting and not on characterization? Is that sort of it?

William H. Coles
More in the thrust that if you require a reader to suspend disbelief, then you're moving them away from the reality of characterization and the solidity of what reality can bring to characterization and meaning.

Fred Leebron
I'm not so sure about that, because what you're requesting them to do is leave their own world and enter your world. Now, your world might be the same as their world, for this type of reader it might be 2012 in the United States. But then you're hopefully going to have readers in Asia, Africa, South America, and that's going to become a different feeling for them. So what you're saying is that they will naturally resist, and in resisting, they might turn away from character because they don't believe the world the character lives in. Suspension of disbelief means making the character's world believable, and somehow accessible to the reader, so the reader can enter into and experience that world with the character and remain outside the world.

William H. Coles
With equal effect.

Fred Leebron
With equal effect. Yes.

William H. Coles
Consider a movie such as *Avatar*, where you have to suspend all sorts of disbelief, and the film does try to express some morality and awareness of injustice and environmental threats, and compare it to something like E. M. Forster's *Howards End*. Doesn't the book have greater story impact than the movie?

Fred Leebron
Because of the realism?

William H. Coles
Yes.

Fred Leebron
You're not really arguing about suspension of disbelief. You're arguing that in the school of fantasy, romance, and sci-fi it's harder to suspend disbelief than in the school of realism. That makes sense to me. And what's funny, it all still comes down to character, whatever entity it is, and how real the emotions are, and the reader's identification with the emotions.

William H. Coles
It seems to me, for a writer, one of the most difficult challenges is effectively developing character on the page. There are techniques you teach very well—of description, of interaction, of internalization and emotional progression. Are

there special advantages to moving the character into action to aid in development and demonstrate characteristics? Especially as opposed to narrative description. Are there advantages of working in-scene, and do you recommend the use of action in prose?

Fred Leebron
Action generally results in character development as opposed to characterization.

William H. Coles
Is there a difference?

Fred Leebron
Well, characterization is who the character is before the story starts.

William H. Coles
Ah. I see.

Fred Leebron
And character development is how the character changes over the course of the story. So action is generally going to change an event. You know there are three levels of action in any narrative: event, interaction, evocation (to bring or recall to the conscious mind). Action will often result in character change, so that's character development. So, yes, if we're talking character development, if nothing happens, it's hard to argue why or how the character changes. Now it's also true that the world is complex, and any minor movement can lead to revelation in the way that anything can serve as a mnemonic device. We can recall something we thought we understood, and understand it in a new way. So it doesn't have to be some huge event or interaction that precipitates character development, as long as it teaches us to experience something that we thought we knew in a different light.

William H. Coles
That's an important differentiation. What are the most important concepts of narration for beginning writers to grasp, and to study? I ask because it seems that narration is so complex and produces widely different effects.

Fred Leebron
I think the biggest thing for beginning writers to learn is the difference between anecdote and story. In anecdote it's the situation that matters; in story it's the characters. The story affirms the value of individuals in the way it unfolds and becomes different from what it was. So, if an anecdote is just: "A and B go out

to dinner, the waiter serves a bad steak, someone throws it against the wall, and A is arrested," it doesn't matter who the character is. In story, it's the character that makes the story transcend itself.

William H. Coles
As writers develop stories, they look at points of view, they're making decisions regarding first person or third person, issues of distance. But in every story there is a basic idea that the author is creating a story, a narrator is telling the story (even in first-person narration), and a character is acting in the story. In each of those narrative silos, should the voice be consistent when delivering the story through character or narrator or author?

Fred Leebron
It's a very interesting question. It goes against monotony and predictability and reader comfort. I like making my readers uncomfortable, feeding their expectations rather than meeting them. I do like a story where there are more levels of voice in play and where you do get that inconsistency. But most people would say they prefer consistency. Most editors would say, "I don't know why you've got that second level of voice in here, and I don't know how to take that, whether it's ironic, or prejudicial, or instructive." What I'm trying to do is have a secondary effect as well as a primary effect. I like the distinction between narrator, authorial, and character voice, and I think it's a very useful distinction to hold once you've got the reader settled.

William H. Coles
The extension of that would seem to be, if you look to classical literature, the distinction between narrator and character. There is rarely an authorial voice. In contemporary writing and teaching, the authorial voice seems always present, usually predominant. Authorial predominance seems to give the freedom to offer authorial thoughts, opinion, and perceptions (even feelings of setting), that seems to move the classic concept of fiction, authorless-voice construction into memoir. If, as an author, you're trying to sort out the advantage between memoir and fiction, it would seem that separation of authorial voice from the story-telling would be worthwhile. The idea is to remove the subjectivity of the author to make the story live through the objective delivery of voice in narrator and character worlds. Does that make sense? And doesn't the persistent presence of authorial voice collapse the advantages of classic fiction techniques with distinct voices?

Fred Leebron
If it is a consistent authorial presence, it does diminish the useful distinction

among the three because then it's always there. But the authorial voice doesn't always have to be there. That's like the distinction between Nick in *The Great Gatsby* as judge and Nick as actor. He's not always capable of standing there and pronouncing judgment and offering wisdom. He's so caught up in the action, he can't. So if you're going to have authorial voice, it's better to have it with ebb and flow rather than an undercurrent.

William H. Coles
What is voice? We use it all the time, but I can never come up with a useful definition.

Fred Leebron
Voice is the marriage of style and point of view and the sound that it makes in the reader's ear. So you have word choice, tone, mood, and the influence characters have over it as well. Literally, voice is the sound of the story in the reader's ear, as if it were spoken aloud. But it's much more complicated than that, and it has many more symphonic qualities; there are many more instruments available than that. It's the element that everyone likes to talk about, but few want to define it because if you define it you break it up into various components, and various subdivisions as well.

William H. Coles
Voices are created because of what you just described in certain time periods.

Fred Leebron
Yes.

William H. Coles
There are only certain ideas and thoughts and words that can come from a specific voice because the voice has its own individual world—experiences, thoughts, ideas, and opinions specific to the time the voice speaks in. You can't discuss the World Series in 2012 in a voice of the moment in a story happening earlier. Is it valuable to keep the narrator, character, and authorial voice true to the world and the time from which the voices are spoken? Do you see what I'm getting at in terms of paying attention to the story timeline?

Fred Leebron
The voice that knows more than the reader diminishes the reader. I'm a big fan of the bend in the river, where all time is accessible and you can go forward and backward, even if you're at a fixed point. So I don't mind the infection of voice on earlier events as long as the reader can share it with the author, so to speak.

They're co-creators of that voice, and they each understand where that voice is coming from. And that's where the hard part is, because what you're describing is the voice that knows more than the reader and that is where a problem lies, because the voice that knows more than the reader diminishes the reader and makes the reader understand that the story has already been told. And that becomes an issue because it diminishes the natural surprise of narrative.

William H. Coles
You talk a lot about risk taking as an author. What are the various levels of writing where risk can be applied? It's more than just releasing yourself in prose, isn't it?

Fred Leebron
Right. There are three types of people who can be at risk: the writer, the reader, the characters. What the writer is risking is a bit different than what the reader risks. The reader risks being taken in or out of his or her comfort zone and feeling as if this is something I don't want to be in but I'm still in it. And I'm still risking going forward, and why am I doing that? The writer's risks are more complex. You can risk yourself in terms of not knowing where you're going and having to back from there to some place of control (the risk of loss of control). There's the risk of not knowing what you're doing and trying techniques that are antithetical to your usual tried-and-true approach. And sometimes the reader will sense that, and sometimes they won't, but you know yourself when you're stretching and trying to transcend your limitations as an artist. Like if you've never written something in the second person and you're going to try. So, there's risk in technique. There's also risk in content when you're writing too close to a real truth and exposing something that's uncomfortable or even hurtful—and also risking offending the reader. Do you really want to do that? There's risk in meaning if you write meaning that you know everyone will disagree with. A story that would show the good side of Adolf Hitler, for example. Or a story you yourself disagree with. Why are you writing that? Why are you participating in that? And the characters are obviously at risk in their various ways as to what's at stake. But the risk for the writer is always the gravest. If you can get the reader to believe they risk as much as the writer, you've really achieved something.

William H. Coles
With respect to a writer risking revealing emotions, were you talking about the writer's emotions or the characters'? Or is that all the same?

Fred Leebron
I don't think it's all the same. I think they're separate. And there are two different

risks. If you're going to flay open a character and lay the character's emotions bare on the table, that's one thing. But if you do it to ostensibly to yourself, where you're ripping up yourself as opposed to character, that's a whole different level of risk.

William H. Coles
It seems the delivering of emotions can be done subjectively or objectively. In contemporary writing, emotions are mostly delivered subjectively, and often through an authorial point of view. Are there situations where objective presentation of emotions, by which I mean through the story structure and action rather than narrative description of how either the author feels or the character feels, has an advantage?

Fred Leebron
Where you know how the author feels?

William H. Coles
Where the emotion delivered to the reader is an objective rendering—meaning, story-based, character-based, character or narrator voice, without authorial feelings.

Fred Leebron
The advantage of objective rendering is that it allows other emotions to exist. If it's really objective, then everyone can get their own emotion out of it.

William H. Coles
Yes.

Fred Leebron
And that becomes very interesting. Which is sort of like saying Flannery O'Connor intended that the grandmother was trying to save herself when the reader reads the grandmother is trying to save *The Misfit*. It's the same thing. It's objectively rendered so everyone can potentially get something different from it. The issue is that you want that as a writer, you mean to be something that the reader gets.

William H. Coles
Or what you feel?

Fred Leebron
What you feel. What you mean. You want the reader to get it. And you

understand that if they don't get it, the intent doesn't marry the effect and it's a different story than you intended, and you can live with that.

William H. Coles
I see. So in general we ought to lean toward objective rendering?

Fred Leebron
It's a strategy. Subjective rendering has tons of judgment and it's fun to read, as in *The Great Gatsby*. Objective rendering is always going to have a multiplicity of meaning.

William H. Coles
How do you work on a timeline? You like the . . . how do you call it? The flexibility?

Fred Leebron
The elasticity.

William H. Coles
Yes, elasticity of timelines. Yet you're very conscious of how long a story takes.

Fred Leebron
How much narrative time the story takes on.

William H. Coles
But you're also aware of how much reader time it takes to read a story. That is how reading time relates to the time that passes. There seems an advantage for an author to be aware of where they are creating on the story timeline. How do you structure your timeline as you're writing? It must be important to keep a mental timeline because it helps judge how long scenes and ideas take, as well as where things should go. But do you also do it physically?

Fred Leebron
Yes, I do it physically. When I'm done, or when I'm stuck, I'll do a literal timeline as to how much time the story is taking on, both in the narrative present and in the narrative past (backstory), and potentially in the narrative future. That gives me a sense of all the time I'm missing, and what opportunities there might be in that time.

William H. Coles
Does it also help you with the rate of revelation of story information?

Fred Leebron
Definitely, because a lot of the information you need is in the past. So you have to have an awareness of the past as you go forward. And also, if you want to give a sense of the world beyond the story, you have to have a sense of the story in the future as well.

William H. Coles
If your backstory begins to bludgeon your story, overwhelms it, is that a moment to look at the timeline and see if the information delivered in the backstory can't be delivered in story present?

Fred Leebron
Sometimes it means you have to reorder events. You have to move them on the timeline to make it work. It depends on the nature of the work. Some authors are perfectly happy to have a heavy presentation of the past in their stories or books. But if your intent is this forward-moving narrative present and you find the past coming in and overwhelming the present, then you have to make adjustments.

William H. Coles
In terms of information and the rate of revelation, do you think about the information that's crucial to the story? I ask because one difference between genre fiction and literary fiction is the former creates suspense via withheld information—what's going to happen or be revealed?—whereas in literary fiction you basically deliver all story information as needed for story progression, and then show how everything works out. Suspense comes from the reader's curiosity about what is going to happen to a character they care about. I know you've suggested outlining in terms of plot. How do you bring story information in dramatic ways, and how do you determine the rate of revelation?

Fred Leebron
It would be nice to have something revelatory in every sentence. Sentence by sentence revelation. But you're talking more about the bigger revelations. The epiphanies. The realizations of the things you don't know. You want to have a sense of the higher-stakes revelation.

William H. Coles
Yes.

The ART of CREATING STORY

Fred Leebron
Higher-stakes revelations need to occur in a novel more frequently than you'd think to keep the reader engaged.

William H. Coles
And earlier?

Fred Leebron
And probably earlier, too. To me, revelation is about loss of control, and finding your way back from moments of loss of control. So I'm always looking at the various pivots that get me where I don't know where I'm headed and how I'm going to get back. That can be a character's interior thoughts that go on too long, or it can be an obstacle that arises that we didn't anticipate. In terms of revelation, I like to think in terms of surprise. When the material surprises me when I write it, as opposed to I knew it was there all along. I'm looking to surprise myself as often as possible.

William H. Coles
How does surprise relate to suspense?

Fred Leebron
As you said, suspense in genre fiction is withholding information, withholding development, that the writer knows. Whereas surprise is something both the writer and the reader don't know.

William H. Coles
Suspense is augmented, maybe, by the reader wondering what will happen to a character they care about?

Fred Leebron
Yes. The "shot index" in revision.

William H. Coles
You've talked about that in class. What is a shot?

Fred Leebron
It's a Hollywood term referring to the camera shots you need to get through the movie. Exterior. House. Porch. Ron and Mabel talking. That's the shot. Right? So, how many shots do you have in your book? You've got the camera, you've got the setting, and you don't really have to move it a lot. When do you need the new angle and the new setting, versus the same setting but a different camera angle? You're trying to look for all your scenes in your work, and those scenes are

just found where you have to change the camera angle and thus changing the shot. Literally, the camera eye.

William H. Coles
Is it useful to think also in terms of how an artist might approach it? As in a storyboard?

Fred Leebron
Yes. It's very much like a storyboard. Except I don't think the storyboard concept can contain a whole novel. The purpose of the shot index is to contain the whole novel on an eleven-by-fourteen piece of paper.

William H. Coles
But the storyboard concept gives you more depth, implies action, and may suggest more emotion than just a camera shot. Maybe useful in chapters?

Fred Leebron
Yes, I can see the storyboard concept working very well in chapters.

William H. Coles
You do shot indexing in the latter part of the revision process. Is that correct? How exactly, and when, do you utilize it?

Fred Leebron
It's a way of looking for repetitive material figuratively and literally, and looking for material that moves by dramatic fracture inch by inch, step by step. Trying to see where the bold leaps occur and where the omissions occur. Sometimes omissions are good, and sometimes you need to address them. So you're looking for gaps, you're looking for speed, you're looking for opportunities, and you're looking for waste. That's how the shot index helps me.

William H. Coles
Fred, thank you very much for contributing to www.storyinliterryfiction.com. It's been a great pleasure and I've learned a lot.

Fred Leebron
So have I. Thank you very much.

David Lynn Interview

25 June, 2009
William H. Coles

David Lynn is editor of the *Kenyon Review*, a distinguished journal of literature, culture, and the arts. He received his BA from Kenyon College, where he now teaches, and his MA and PhD at the University of Virginia, where he studied with Peter Taylor. He is on the board of directors of the Council of Literary Magazines and Presses. In 1995–96 he was a senior Fulbright scholar in India. He lives in Gambier, Ohio.

William H. Coles
John Crowe Ransom founded the *Kenyon Review* seventy years ago. What was Ransom's original concept for it? Was he trying to re-create the Fugitives in Nashville?

David Lynn
The Fugitives was a group he was a tangential part of. In a lot of ways he'd already outgrown them, and they never really had a single organ as such, they were just a group of people who had a program about agrarian writing in the South in the 1920s and 1930s. Ransom was brought here by the new president of Kenyon College, a young man named Gordon Keith Chalmers, who was very ambitious and dynamic. He had great hopes to turn Kenyon into a national and international presence, and he and his wife, the poet Roberta Teale Swartz, had all along envisioned starting an important literary journal. There were relatively few of them in those days, unlike today when there are hundreds and hundreds. Then there were only a handful of significant literary journals in the country. They came here with that ambition, and that was part of how Chalmers lured Ransom from Vanderbilt to Kenyon in 1938.

William H. Coles
There was a *Fugitive* magazine briefly in Nashville. Was Ransom involved with that?

David Lynn
I don't know. I know he was associated with the group, but I don't think he had any editorial responsibilities.

William H. Coles
What was the mix in the beginning days of the *Kenyon Review* in terms of fiction, essays, and nonfiction?

David Lynn
Very few stories, fiction pieces. Ransom wasn't much interested in them. It was mostly scholarly essays, reviews, and some poetry.

William H. Coles
Has your concept of that mix changed since you've been here?

David Lynn
Well, I think all literary reviews are a product of their historical moment. When in the eighteenth century you had the *Edinburgh Review* or the *London Review*, they were very much reflections of that period and so were almost entirely reviews of current books, ideas, and affairs. The idea of adding original creative writing came later. When Ransom started the *Kenyon Review*, there were very few scholarly journals per se. Ransom had a journal that spoke to a scholarly community that was involved with literary criticism, as well as other writers and people interested in creative writing. What happened in the 1960s and 1970s was greater specialization: more and more journals aimed at a particular audience of the scholar and not the general reader. In the 1980s, the heyday of so-called literary theory, that was especially true. And in the meantime, journals such as the *Kenyon Review* became more oriented toward creative writing per se.

What I've been looking for is a mix of creative stories, poems, and essays as well as interesting intellectual engagements that are aimed at a well-educated general reader rather than a scholarly specialist. So, for example today I accepted an article by Paul Goldberger, the great architecture critic, called "Why Architecture Matters." It's a brilliant discussion of architecture and art. And the challenge is there, too. But it is very much for a general reader—you know, the intellectually curious reader, not a specialist. That is what I see as our role today.

William H. Coles
Is there a conception of the "Kenyon story" in fiction?

David Lynn
Absolutely not! There are so many journals in the country and the world, and more and more of them are electronic; some of them very much have a predilection. For a long time there was a journal called *The Formalist* [ceased

publication in 2004], which only published formal poetry, which is fine. We don't do that. I'm looking for the best, most innovative, most eclectic writing out there. I look for variety as much as possible. I wouldn't want there to be too much similarity in any given issue among the poems or stories or essays.

William H. Coles
I don't mean to dig at this too much, but are there common elements of the fictional story that you look for?

David Lynn
Well, you know, it's really what the old Supreme Court justice said about pornography: "I know it when I see it." I do have a philosophy that all successful art contains two particular elements, though they're very general; one is surprise and the other is delight. That's actually on the T-shirts for this summer's writers' workshop: "Surprise and delight." All successful art has to surprise you in some way. You have to have a little bit of a gasp, a "gee, that's unexpected." Otherwise it's boring, otherwise it's predictable. Likewise, the word "delight" is deliberately capacious. It suggests an involvement not just of the intellect, but of the emotions. To a poem, a story, a creative essay, you have an emotional response that might be anything from tears to laughter. Both tears and laughter are a kind of delight as we engage with those things.

And lastly, there is a third category that's of a different order, and that is mastery. I'm not going to put anything in the *Kenyon Review* that doesn't reveal real mastery over the craft, the strategy, the skills of the particular work. That doesn't mean that a young person can't possess a certain type of mastery. But it means an absolute confidence in the way language is used.

About a year and a half ago we launched Kenyon Review Online, which is at our website, KenyonReview.org, and it does not reproduce what's in the journal. It is a complement to the print journal. And whereas the *Kenyon Review* seeks to be timeless—look at our back issues, I think a lot of them remain as moving, as fresh, as powerful as when they were first published—KenyonReview.org seeks to be more timely, more experimental, a little more out there, a little wilder. It has a different flavor to it than the print journal. I think, given where we are today as a culture and an international community, that is a good thing.

William H. Coles
Would you recommend that new writers, or developing writers, write to effect an emotion in the reader?

David Lynn
I think all creative writing involves emotion. To me that's one of the defining aspects of literature as opposed to other kinds of writing—political writing, philosophical writing, anthropological writing, which can be very well executed and smart and engaging. But one of the things, not the only thing, that characterizes literature is an emotional engagement.

William H. Coles
Sometimes it's hard for writers to determine what their value is, whether they have talent or not. Are there talents that great writers possess that cannot be learned?

David Lynn
I do believe there is such a thing as talent. I do believe there is such a thing as inspiration. And this goes to the heart of whether creative writing can be taught. I think it can be, to a certain degree. Good teachers can teach new ways of thinking about literature. They can teach strategies and techniques; they can help authors read in a new way and think about their work in a new way. Ultimately it's up to the individual writer to make that little, but essential, stretch to the next dimension of surprise and delight. I remember after I'd been writing on my own for a couple of years and went to the University of Virginia, I was working with my friend and mentor, Peter Taylor, one of the great story writers in American history. After a few years, I went up to see him one day (I'll always remember this) and said, "Peter, you've been very kind and supportive to me and I appreciate that; I've learned a great deal from you. But if the time comes when you feel that I've gone about as far as I can go and I'm not going to be the kind of writer that I want to be or you think I should be, will you tell me?" Peter roared and leaned back, this great leonine Tennessee head and deep drawl and laugh, and said, "I can't tell you that. Only you can decide when that moment comes." And I think he was very right.

William H. Coles
I've heard that Peter Taylor was a minimalist as a teacher, that he said very little. You were lucky to have him say that much.

David Lynn
[*chuckle*] That's right. Most of what you learned from Peter was in private or with a drink in hand. Not in the classroom.

William H. Coles
Going along with teaching in a tangential way, you've created your workshops

here at Kenyon with the idea of developing and working on segments of writing created here rather than the singular review of manuscripts, or didactic lectures. You've often stated that this is working very well for you. Why is that a better teaching tool than the traditional workshop?

David Lynn
Well, I don't think it's necessarily better. It's different. You know, every workshop, or college or university, wants to differentiate itself. So in one way that's how we separate ourselves from Bread Loaf or Sewanee or other great writing programs. But also, it's my program, and it suits my temperament. Much as I like to sit around and socialize, I think adults who pay the money, and most of all take the time—the big thing is time, not money—if you take the time to come to a writers' workshop, you want it to be as productive as it can be. What I try to do is exhaust them during the week, but also, ironically, energize them—give them a kind of momentum not just in terms of ideas and things to think about, but that will carry on in their busy lives. That's what we're all about.

William H. Coles
In the classroom setting, the technique seems to develop a great deal of camaraderie and synergistic interaction among the students. Would you agree?

David Lynn
Absolutely. That is one of the great things of modern times. There is a large and growing community of people in the United States who are involved in literary pursuits. They form a great community. Yes, it's most intense within the individual workshops. With great teachers, there is a special bond that carries on after people go out into the world.

William H. Coles
I'd like to discuss the MFA programs, whether full time or limited residency, and what they are teaching and how. It is distinct from what the Kenyon workshop teaches, and different from the goals of the Kenyon workshop. How does a talented, energetic young writer approach an MFA program for their individual development? I think that the MFA programs at times put a lid put on a student's potential depending on the instructor and/or the quality of the program.

David Lynn
There are hundreds of programs out there now, and of course there is a range in quality, as there would be in any pursuit. One of the most important things is that young people don't immediately go to MFA programs after college. Writers

need something to write about; they need lived experience. And immediately after college, most of their experience in the world is academic. If they've only been undergraduates, that really limits them. I tell students all the time: "Go live; go teach English as a second language in Japan; go work in a salmon cannery in Alaska." I don't care what it is. Go where your only responsibility is to put food in your mouth and get a roof over your head. Use the rest of your time to read and write. I think young writers need to write. And they need to read voraciously . . . and not just contemporary stuff. Fashions change, and it's important if you're going to be a serious writer to read voraciously to learn the history of the craft.

With MFA programs, one has to be very clear about why one goes. What are you going there to do? For example, there is this idea that if you get an MFA, you jump through all the hoops, you do everything that is required, you come out the other side with a parchment in your hand and that means you're a writer and employable as a teacher of writing. Neither of those is true. There is no guarantee. As opposed to when you come out with a medical degree, or an engineering degree, or a law degree: you put in the time, you passed the test, and you can get a job in those professions, hopefully.

In creative writing, publishing has very little to do with what your degree is. It really has to do with who you are as a writer. And in terms of teaching, there are very few jobs and many, many candidates . . . and it's hard. So you have to be very clear that you're not going for those reasons. The reason you get an MFA is to spend a couple of years engaged in writing and thinking and reading with other talented and committed people, both students and faculty, for the pursuit itself. That's noble! That's worthwhile. There is nothing wrong with that. But that is very different from going there as a career path. A career path is great but you can't count on it.

William H. Coles
You suggest that young fiction writers go out and live to find things to write about. How do you take life experiences and filter them into great fiction as opposed to, say, memoir?

David Lynn
That's a good question and I'm going to give an answer that pisses off a lot of people. Memoirs are fiction. Memoirs, in some ways, are no less fiction than nonfiction. Anytime you take the raw experience of human life and transfer it first to memory, and then to language, you're changing it. And as you change it, as you shape it, as you choose this perspective or that incident to recount, you're

changing whatever the original experience was into artifact. Some memoirs have different strategies and trajectories than fiction, but not always—sometimes it's very hard to tell them apart. I'll give you an example. There is a wonderful man named Don Zacharia, who is the proprietor of Zachys wines in New York, a very successful wine business. As a young man he was an excellent writer, and in the 1980s he sent a story to the *Kenyon Review* that was published and received a Pushcart Award and the editors of the *Kenyon Review* labeled it memoir. I found out later, because Don became a wonderful member of the board of trustees, that it was entirely made up. It was fiction. But because of its tone and shape, others thought it was memoir. So it's a very slippery slope. I'm not going to say there is not a distinction between memoir and fiction, but I'm actually very interested in works right now that deal with that boundary between the real and the made-up, between the fictional and the so-called truth.

William H. Coles
But for the writer seeking to write quality fiction, the tendency to write memoir through narrative description, through first-person point of view, through trying to hold decision-making processes to the truth rather than choosing the right decision to make the fiction great, seems a potential problem.

David Lynn
I'm not sure that's true. You know Marcel Proust wrote *Remembrance of Things Past* largely out of autobiography and memoir, but no one questions that it is fiction. He plays with that distinction and paradox all the time within the work. I don't have a lot of patience with young people writing memoir, I have to say. I think much of the time, not always, it's a mistake. The reason is that memoir, like much fiction, depends on distance. The narrator and/or the author need some distance from the story they're telling in order to make sense of it. Most of the time, not always, you're telling a memoir in order to understand it, not simply for the pleasure of the reader. Unless you've got some distance in time and space and thought and maturity from the experience you're recounting, it's not likely to be a successful memoir.

William H. Coles
What is the role of drama in fiction?

David Lynn
That's a great question, and something I talk to my students about all the time. It's a very hard thing to get them to see. The essence of fiction is drama. And the essence of drama is tension. Unless there is tension, some type of dramatic conflict leading to some kind of explosion, there is no reason to tell the story.

This is something writers often forget to ask themselves: Is this story worth telling? It may be beautifully written, it may be innovative in all kinds of ways, but is it worth telling? And usually that question has to do with the drama in it, and the stakes of the drama. The stakes have to be significant. Something significant has to be at risk. And the drama has to matter; otherwise the story is not worth telling. And if that's the case, no one is going to care.

William H. Coles
How do you apply the same thinking to characterization? That you want the characters to be alive and dramatic, not flat. Is tension a clue for us in characterization? Is there something we need to look for in motivation and desire?

David Lynn
That's one of those areas where we get down from the more general to the more specific. Yes, you have to have some sort of characterization. You have to have character. Especially in realistic fiction, which is 90 percent of what we read and write. But there is no one way to do it. There is almost an infinite variety of strategies and techniques to make characters appear real. When I say we deal most of the time with realism, realism is an illusion. The typical thought is that realism mirrors reality, but that's not true at all. Realism creates the illusion of reality, a reality that a reader will believe in.

William H. Coles
It's a credibility issue?

David Lynn
It's not at all what the real world looks like. For example, you'd never write dialogue the way people actually speak.

William H. Coles
When hiring teachers of creative writing at the college, what qualifications do you look for?

David Lynn
We have an entire procedure, as we do with regular members of the academic faculty. We watch them in sample classes. We want to hear and see them teach, and then we have interviews with them about how they teach and why they teach and the strategies they use. In creative writing, obviously, I'll be looking at their work as well to see if it's up to standards, sophistication, and the innovation that we would hope for. That's different than the summer programs. In the

workshops, I hire writers whose work I know, whom I've met and like, and who I think will be successful members of the faculty.

William H. Coles
Can someone be a good creative writing teacher without being a good writer?

David Lynn
Certainly. The two don't necessarily go together. I think on the other hand being a successful writer, to a certain degree, increases your credibility as a writing teacher. In some ways that's unfortunate because I do think you can understand how something works and teach it when you may not be able to do it yourself. It's rather like athletics. Ted Williams could hit a baseball, but he was a lousy coach. And it works the other way as well: some great coaches were second- or third-class players. That's true in creative writing as well.

William H. Coles
Is a key element imagination?

David Lynn
That's a little too general for me. I don't know. Teaching certainly involves imagination. It involves thoughtfulness about how to express things. It also involves intuition and empathy. There is a lot going on that is both an art and a science.

William H. Coles
As a publisher and an editor—and now I'm not referring specifically to the *Kenyon Review*—are you pleased with what is being sought and published in the realm of literary fiction?

David Lynn
Well, you've got all the troubles of the commercial publishing industry in New York, which is falling apart for a variety of reasons, and then the nonprofit market, where most literary magazines are, is struggling in the present economic crisis. And yet there is an enormous amount of really great stuff being written and published. I would venture probably more than ever before. Far more than any of us can read. I can't even begin to scratch the surface, though I try. One result of all the writing programs is that there are thousands of really talented, dedicated people out there writing, and an enormous variety of work being done. And a lot of international work coming into the United States in one way or another, which is incredibly exciting. So I may have quibbles with this publisher or that publisher, or the trends in publishing, but the fact remains that there is great, great stuff out there.

William H. Coles
As an amateur, it seems to me the publishing industry is going more to memoir and nonfiction—I know you don't separate those—than fiction.

David Lynn
For me, literary nonfiction is just about the most interesting category out there. I don't want to get too philosophical about it, but the problem with fiction is that most of the conventions that we follow go back three or four hundred years—literally. Although there is great fiction being written using those connections, there are times when it feels a little bit tired. Whereas literary nonfiction, although it's had many different versions over the years as well, has very few conventions per se. You can enjoy lots of unexpected things with nonfiction as long as there is some kind of shape to it. I'm excited and interested in it. A lot of what I myself prefer to read is nonfiction.

William H. Coles
How important is the story and the integrity of the story in literary nonfiction, both in your enjoyment and in the choices you make?

David Lynn
As I say, it depends on the piece. They don't have to have much story per se. They can be wonderfully interesting and impressive. I happen to live and breathe for story. Stories are the essence of being. I love them. But there are lots of other ways of communicating effectively.

William H. Coles
What's the role of the internet and electronic publishing? Are you interested in Amazon as an outlet for the *Kenyon Review*? Do you think the online magazine will be growing in the future?

David Lynn
I do. I think that electronic readers are going to play a greater and greater role. I don't think they're ever going to totally displace the printed book, at least for a while. But especially for things like travel. When you're traveling, it's really nice to have an e-book with you, to have multiple books and be able to read wherever you are. It is affecting bookstores tremendously, and I think it will affect commercial publishing a lot and how it's structured. But I'm a fan. I have no problem with the e-books at all. I think people who care about literature are going to become more and more a niche in a largely already fragmented society. I think there are always going to be people who read literature with a passion.

And within that niche will be people who read printed books and people who read e-books. I have no problem with that.

William H. Coles
Thank you very much for participating in this session.

David Lynn
My pleasure, Bill. Great questions. I really enjoyed it.

Michael Malone Interview

26 February, 2009
William H. Coles

Michael Malone is a native of North Carolina and lives in Hillsborough, North Carolina. He is a highly successful author of mystery and comedic novels, many set in his home state, including *First Lady* (Sourcebooks Landmark,, 2001), *Uncivil Seasons* (Sourcebooks Landmark,, 2001), and *Time's Witness* (Sourcebooks Landmark,, 2002). His novel *The Killing Club* (Kingswell, 2005) reached number 11 on the *New York Times* best-seller list. His mystery story "Red Clay" received the Edgar Award for Best Short Story in 1997. He is also an award-winning head writer of television drama, having written for *One Life to Live* (1991–96, 2006–7) and *Another World* (2003–4). He is a visiting professor at Duke University, where he teaches American film studies.

William H. Coles
Let's start with a basic question. What does "story" mean to you?

Michael Malone
I think it's at the heart of what it is to be human to tell stories, narratives of our lives, of the lives of people we know, of our country. Humans want to tell a story. If you listen to people talk, which you absolutely must do if you want to write fiction, you'll notice that they talk by telling stories to each other and they do so primarily through dialogue. I go, "I can't meet you at five o'clock." And he goes, "Then it's all off between us." And I go, "How can you say that to me?" When conversing with you, people will tell you a story, a narrative, with a beginning, middle, and end.

William H. Coles
Is this a regional characteristic? Is it more common in the South to use dialogue to tell stories?

Michael Malone
In the South they certainly will talk more. [*smiles*] It will be a longer story. I'm a native North Carolinian, and when we first moved down here from the North (as I call it) my wife, Maureen Quilligan, said, "I knew you were crazy, but now I find out everybody is like this down here." And secondly, she had to learn how

to talk. As if you had gone to France and you had to learn how to speak in their style, with their certain social codes. In the South, you can't say, "I want to buy a ham." You've got to say, "What wonderful weather, what a wonderful sky, it's blue as my cousin's eyes, well his one eye 'cause one eye got shot out when he went hunting . . ." Then this story stuff starts.

William H. Coles
Does this story in conversation, which is so essential to human interaction, contain the elements of beginning, middle, and end?

Michael Malone
I spent a part of my writing life writing serial drama, which very famously has no end. A soap opera is designed never to end.

William H. Coles
But it has some sort of end before the last commercial?

Michael Malone
It has arcs within arcs. I had spent years writing "high art"—literary fiction—and in the groves of academe, teaching literary fiction, and everything in me said, "Beginning, middle, end." So one of the first things I had to learn was not to end things: When I was first talking to Agnes Nixon, who created *One Life to Live* and *All My Children* and so forth—a marvelous Southern woman—she said, "Michael! What are you doing? Everything in your stories is building to a climax. All together everyone falls in love or dies. No! It has to come in waves. One wave crests, another is behind it, another behind that." She would say, "Turn the diamond slowly. Each facet will sparkle in a different way." That postponement of the "end" was the source of her famous motto: "Make 'em laugh, make 'em cry, make 'em wait." But for me, having spent most of my creative life writing short stories and novels, I liked returning to closed narratives, building an arc into an overarching structure. It might take a week, or like *The Great Gatsby*, a summer. It might take a day, *Ulysses*. Or it might take a year. One novel of mine, *Dingley Falls*, a creation novel, takes place over a week. Another novel, *The Last Noel*, takes place over forty years, but only at certain Christmases (every chapter is at a Christmas meeting between the two characters).

William H. Coles
I hear you thinking about a timeline that starts the action of a larger arc, and then you have small ends to smaller arcs at the end of each specific TV drama.

The ART of CREATING STORY

Michael Malone
I came at writing for daytime television from studying Charles Dickens's way of serializing his novels. That they were serialized made a huge difference in how he wrote: just one chapter at a time. Chapter 1 is already out and published when you are writing chapter 2. I have a novel coming out in May that I spent many years working on, *The Four Corners of the Sky*. It took ten years before I felt I had that novel right. I go back again and again, revising. In serial you can't do that.

William H. Coles
So your story is a broad story with many subliminal and subordinate stories within. When you write a novel, that novel is part of the broader story that is told in your life's work.

Michael Malone
Critics have always said about my work that it is various, more various than the novels of others might be. At times I write in what are called genres. Some people write only detective stories, or only science fiction stories, or only historical novels. My Hillston novels are detective novels, but I have also written in the picaresque genre a Henry Fielding-like large canvas, *Handling Sin*. But while I work in different ways, there is going to be a core meaning to all my novels. Whatever I am in my moral beliefs, in my style, in my political beliefs, it will be in all my fiction. One of the things that draws me to the detective form is its public arena. Crime fiction takes you into the world. For example, the plot of *Time's Witness* involves the death penalty. Once you have crime, you have a courthouse, you have lawyers, you have the police. You have a public world of economics and history.

William H. Coles
Expanding rather than constricting.

Michael Malone
Whatever I am as a writer will be in all the fiction, whatever "the story." Speaking story, people often ask me, "Do you write the plot out? Do you outline a sketch of each chapter?" Do I know exactly where I'm going when I start? No, I don't. It's Ralph Waldo Emerson's stairway of surprise: "How can these stairs be climbed save through the process of Reincarnation?" And it is a surprise. You start ice skating, as Emerson also said: "In skating over thin ice, our safety is in our speed," and you don't exactly know where you're going. But what I do, and every writer has a different way of doing it, I have a substructure coming out of a formal construct, an imitation in the old Renaissance sense of what that means.

So, if in *Dingley Falls* I am writing a novel about a town, I know George Eliot's *Middlemarch* is underneath it and other novels like *Middlemarch*. *Handling Sin*, the picaresque novel, came out of my saying to my wife jokingly, "Hey, I'd like to write the funniest novel ever written." And she said. "Too bad for you, it's already written. Don Quixote." She's a Renaissance scholar. So I went back and read *Don Quixote* and said, "Okay, that's the structure!" What I'm talking about is a blueprint. The structure is going to be a journey. With *Handling Sin*, I drew a map, literally; the characters go from North Carolina to New Orleans. And because it's a novel of a spiritual journey in a particular faith, they're going to start on the Ides of March, they're going to be here on Monday, there on Thursday, home on Easter Sunday. As for the characters that Raleigh Hayes, the insurance agent who is the main character, was going to meet . . . I did know that Raleigh didn't want to meet anybody, and therefore he was going to need to meet a lot of people, and involve himself in life, in handling the clutter of life.

William H. Coles
People liked that novel's multiple, rich characters.

Michael Malone
The Last Noel had a very different structure: the civil rights movement. In this particular place, these two people meet—an African American boy and a Caucasian girl. He's the grandson of her family's maid. The minute they meet, the reader is resting on other fictional childhood encounters such as the meeting of Pip and Estella in *Great Expectations*, Heathcliff and Cathy in *Wuthering Heights*. That heritage. No novel is ever written that isn't on the shoulders of every novel that went before.

William H. Coles
How do you maintain drama, in the sense of stage drama with conflict, and the changes needed for dramatic conflict, on the page versus for film and TV? And how do you translate story conflict to prose? The transition seems to be a tough one. In the end, what is drama? How important is conflict? And how do you maintain that conflict in prose?

Michael Malone
You could have a modernist novel where two people stare out the window for two hundred pages. But I am an absolute fervent believer that something needs to happen. That storytelling is about creating an interest in what happens next, about making the reader or the viewer want to know what happens next to people they care about. Now if you take out the part about "people they care

about," you're left with circumstantial suspense fiction that is just focused on plot. Or if you leave out plot and just focus on character development.

William H. Coles
Becoming more character sketch, essay oriented?

Michael Malone
Yes. I think character and plot have to go together. I am always telling students when I'm teaching writing—which can't be taught but can be learned—that if a character just stands here, there's no story. But all I have to do is nervously look at my watch, then look over here, and then look over there, start pacing, and suddenly the viewer is saying, "What's the matter? Who is he waiting for? Why didn't that person show up? Is he in danger?" And then you have your reader wanting to know what happens next.

William H. Coles
That's a conflict of ideation?

Michael Malone
There is contemporary fiction that makes us ask what's happening now, that wants to play with sequence and time frame—may for example go backward in time, or may have multiple voices. But good fiction, old or new, will have solved the same narrative problems. At the heart there are five core tools to writing fiction: you have to find a voice; you have to have a sense of place; you have to have believable characters; you have to put the character in action (I mean, Aristotle said it long ago: drama is character in action); and then you bring your unique style to the narrative. For me, often what comes first is not the plot, not the story, but the voice. That voice can be first person: "Call me Ishmael." It can be third-person omniscient: "It is a truth universally acknowledged . . ." as Jane Austen begins *Pride and Prejudice*. But you must find that voice. And you can search for it for a long time.

For example, take the narrator of *Time's Witness*. I wanted to write a novel set in the South, the subject matter of which I wanted to be race and the death penalty. Who and how shall I tell that story? I started three or four different ways—using different characters, different voices. Finally, I said, "Wait a minute. The character I want to use to tell that story is already in the story. It's the partner of the narrator of that earlier novel, Cuddy Mangum. I've got to let him talk."

William H. Coles
There's the voice of the character, but there's also the voice of the narrator, possibly the author. When you emphasize importance of voice, is there any danger of decreasing the action (objective writing) that develops logical motivation and lessening the impact of the core desire the character is built on? In other words, does focus on the cleverness and uniqueness of the voice detract from the essential driving aspects of character expressed in action, rather than told?

Michael Malone
You gain, with first person, immediacy and intimacy; you lose the larger point of view. The individual character can't know all things. One way writers get in trouble is by trying to get too much general information into first-person voices.

William H. Coles
You could call it narrator knowledge, basically.

Michael Malone
Yes. It's awkward. There's an alternative: Jane Austen uses it in *Emma*. It is a limited third-person voice; you as the reader are constrained by being focused on Emma. One of the brilliant revelations of that novel is that the reader suddenly realizes they've made the same mistake as Emma: "Wait a minute! I'm actually wrong about everything!" That's wonderful. Comedy reminds human beings that they are in this together.

William H. Coles
And that is the issue of credibility?

Michael Malone
Yes.

William H. Coles
As the author backs off the character from the action in the novel, the reader questions the credibility of the storyteller (and story) in the first person.

Michael Malone
As for credibility, first, fact is no excuse for fiction. It doesn't matter that it didn't really happen. Franz Kafka tells us somebody woke up and found they were a cockroach. But what *does* matter is that once you accept that narrator, once you create that fiction world, it has to be credible. It doesn't have to be factually true, but it has to be real to the reader.

William H. Coles
Or they have to believe it could really have happened even though they know it's not real.

Michael Malone
Yes. That's willing suspension of disbelief. And anything that violates that is not successful, which is why in a novel such as *Time's Witness*, I had lawyers going over the trial scenes for me so there wouldn't be technical errors in how a trial is conducted. So that that reader doesn't think, "Ooohh, that's not right." We've all had those experiences as readers caused by everything from poor copy editing to plain old inaccuracies. My new novel, *The Four Corners of the Sky*, is about a young woman who is a Navy pilot, so I had pilots go over the factual details.

William H. Coles
You don't dive when you're about to stall at a hundred feet from the ground sort of thing.

Michael Malone
Exactly. One little example was a moment when I had a character holding a helmet by a strap. A pilot I consulted said, "Absolutely not! We don't have straps anymore. We could have a strap to a headset. But you're thinking of some old John Wayne movie." Those things pull you out.

William H. Coles
Because you're breaking the fictional plane . . .

Michael Malone
. . . and the reader's belief in the story. As you're saying, the incredible stories are dangerous for that reason. They break our belief. Otherwise you can make up any world at all—a world where everybody is miniscule, or everybody is big.

William H. Coles
When we look at essential need for conflict in prose—you seem to do that so well in your Justin-Cuddy novels, a scene never goes by where conflict isn't occurring. You always have some conflict—moral, social, and so forth. Is that something we, as struggling writers, need to look for in revising our scenes? Do we need to have conflict on the dialogue level, the moral level, even on the ironic level?

Michael Malone
I would say yes. The conflict can be on an internal level, too. For example, a

character brooding about whether to get a divorce. Or whether to quit their job as a corporate banker and go to Tahiti like Paul Gauguin.

William H. Coles
That's a fundamental environmental structural conflict?

Michael Malone
Yes. It doesn't have to be an adventure in the wilderness. It can be whether to have the courage to acquire the things you think you lack. To stand for your conscience. They can be quiet acts, as Henry David Thoreau said, quiet acts of desperation: "The mass of men lead lives of quiet desperation. What is called resignation is confirmed desperation." The acts don't have to be charging armies in *War and Peace*. But there has to be something that makes us want to keep reading, listening. I recall once driving across the country with my daughter, who was in her twenties at the time, and I was playing an audiobook of Leo Tolstoy's *War and Peace*. She said, "I don't want to listen to this, Dad. This is some old nineteenth-century thing." But we listened. One disc ended where Natasha has left the letter saying that she's running off with Boris. Will Pierre find the letter before it goes off to Prince Andre so Natasha's life won't be ruined? Can he stop this elopement? And Maggie, my daughter, said, "Where's the next disc?" She was on the floor of the car searching.

There are many valid reasons to suspend narrative drive. In my novel *Dingley Falls*, each section ends with a visit to a world outside the town, a satiric world about how the government has built a secret base manufacturing anthrax—this was long before it really happened—and these set pieces purposely stopped the movement of the characters in the main plot. The novel goes back in time to the hero's childhood at the end of every section. So it tells you something about the character that you need to know. But it stops the action. When you do this, you take a risk. I've had editors say, "Can't we take these things out?" No. Not if they're crucial. In another novel of mine, I'm reading it now—because I'm going to a reading club at Duke University next week and the members want to read *Foolscap* because it's about a Southern university, not unlike Duke in many ways—and if you don't read a novel for twenty years, you don't remember it, even if you wrote it.

William H. Coles
Two weeks, sometimes.

Michael Malone
Yes. I probably remember *Huckleberry Finn* better than I remember *Foolscap*.

I'm enjoying it. *Foolscap* has a five-act structure (it's about plays) and has this university setting. But an intermission New York setting, and then a London theatrical setting where the story goes as the hero leaves the page for the stage. As a result, we meet new characters and bring them into the canvas. I tend to work on a larger canvas than a lot of my contemporaries. I like a large canvas because I'm interested in the communal connection among diverse people, which is why music occurs in my novels, because the collaborative process of performing music is the incarnation of our human impulse to connect. The canvas may be, for some readers, more people than they can care about. But what I'm saying is: care about these people. That's my request of the reader.

William H. Coles
I'd like to ask you about character-driven plots as the essence of literary fiction as it developed through Austen, Charlotte Brontë, and others. The modern trend is for more circumstantially driven plots. What is a character-driven plot? What is its value for the modern writer?

Michael Malone
I don't think you have to give up one to have the other. That may seem obvious, but there is a way that plot and character have split apart in valuing contemporary fiction. And that's a shame. Because, yes, you should have both. Great fiction is driven by great characters, themes, styles. But great fiction tells a story narrative, too. And when it's great, the more you read it, the more you hear and see. Maureen, my wife, has spent her whole life reading Edmund Spenser's 1590 epic poem *The Faerie Queene* over and over, and John Milton's *Paradise Lost* (1667).

William H. Coles
Makes me shiver—my lack of knowing and understanding. Books go into the world and do work.

Michael Malone
But epic poems are stories, too. I remember Maureen reading aloud to me *The Odyssey* in the new translation from 1961, by Robert Stuart Fitzgerald, a critic, poet, and translator of Greek and Latin classics. The story was so mesmerizing! Those characters! The light had faded in the room and she was still reading. I think you can have a page-turner with strong characterization; you just have to turn the pages more slowly. People don't buy a record album they like and play it only one time. Why do they think that if they buy a good book, they should read it only once? There is always more to know about characters in good novels. You mentioned Brontë as writing character-driven stories. Yes! When we think

of *Wuthering Heights*, we feel we know Heathcliff, we know Cathy. The depth of their characters is at the heart of the book. However! In *Wuthering Heights*, a great deal of plot happens.

William H. Coles
Yes. Even though it may be wandering on the moors. It's one of my favorite novels.

Michael Malone
Is he going to make it back in time to stop her marriage? What is he going to do when he learns she has married? What's she going to do when she realizes she's ruined her life?

William H. Coles
But all of those obstacles are character oriented.

Michael Malone
God knows, you can't get more dramatic than his digging up a grave. However, if we didn't care about Heathcliff and Cathy, those actions would not be as meaningful or dramatic. By developing great characters, you develop great drama. Now the stage is different because of actors. One of the first things I learned going into television writing, where you write a play a day—an hour-long drama a day—I was writing excessive dialogue for the actors, because they can do so much. A course I teach at Duke is called "American Dreams, American Movies." Why does America love the movies it loves, and what does it tell you about those movies? The students always ask, "Why don't you include *Citizen Kane*?" I say, "It's not a movie America loved in the same way it loved *Gone with the Wind, Casablanca, Singing in the Rain*, and so forth." Just thinking of the films I mentioned, what flashed through my mind is the camera coming down Rhett Butler's face as Scarlett O'Hara sees him; in *Casablanca* when Ingrid Bergman looks at Humphrey Bogart and is saying goodbye and walks away—those scenes don't have any dialogue. Notice that I slipped to "Bogie" and "Bergman." Those are the names of the actors, not Rick Blaine and Ilsa Lund.

So, the page and the stage, as you asked me—they are very different, yet the same techniques are employed in both. And one of them, dramatic irony, works just like it works in *Oedipus Rex*. We have heard from Tiresias, the blind prophet, that this guy has murdered his father and married his mother, and then he comes on and says: "I gotta find out who murdered this guy and caused all these problems." And we know who did it: Oedipus himself. And that works wonderfully for storytelling. In my comedy *Handling Sin*, for example, Raleigh Hayes thinks he knows everything, and we know that he is wrong.

William H. Coles
And that's dramatic irony. As you bring your talents to TV and film and you write more and more dialogue, as you begin to depend upon dialogue for the transmission of emotions, isn't there the danger of sentimentality?

Michael Malone
One of the dangers of dialogue is talking too much. When writers get into trying to convey description or plot information through dialogue, it just sounds awful. Another danger is writing dialogue rather than hearing dialogue. When young writers say to me, "I want to write—how do I start?" I say, start by writing down what you hear. A lot of people want to be writers but they don't want to write. You have to write. And to write, you have to read. That's what I mean by every novel is riding on the shoulders of those that came before. But fundamentally, to write characters, you have to listen to them. Dialogue is not written, it is heard. Too often writers do dialogue in the formal way they would write a letter. Instead, hear that voice. I have a chapter in *Handling Sin*, for example, toward the end—writers sometimes do things for pleasure without knowing if the reader's going to notice—a chapter in which a lot of people are talking, and the reader is never told by the third-person narrator who's speaking. You're never given the name, because by then, you've been on this six-hundred-page comic journey with these characters and you know who they are. Every one of them speaks differently. Each has a voice.

Back to story: whether on a page or on a stage, something must happen to the characters. Take for example *The Cherry Orchard*, where it seems nothing is happening, yet in fact something is happening. The fact that the family declined to do anything to solve their problem has just destroyed their whole world, and that's what Anton Chekhov meant when he said, if you open your play with a rifle on a mantelpiece, it's got to be fired before the curtain goes down. Any object introduced in a story must be used later on, or else it should not be introduced in the first place.

William H. Coles
I didn't know that was Chekhov's quote.

Michael Malone
The Cherry Orchard has a very strong plot. And a comic plot. You asked about sentiment. Constantin Stanislavsky directed *The Cherry Orchard*, and Chekhov

was incensed that Stanislavsky was directing as if the play was a sentimental tragedy. People can't see around the borders of their own lives, so they look with a periscope through fiction.

William H. Coles
When you talk about wanting to be a writer, would you agree that what you want to do is create feeling and ideas and thoughts in the reader through action—showing—as opposed to expressing inner feelings and ideas?

Michael Malone
As I keep saying, I don't think strong plot and strong characters are necessarily different.

William H. Coles
You equate the two?

Michael Malone
I think they can be put together. That faith that both are as possible today as they were a hundred years ago is at the core of what I'm trying to hold onto as a writer. A work can reach a great variety of readers who read in different ways for different reasons. There doesn't have to be a choice between a plot and what I used to call the Knopf book of white borders and very little but very artful prose. A novel can be as beautiful as a poem in its prose style, and nevertheless have strong characters—and a broad canvas—and be in the world. I was in school in the 1960s, and that period's political public involvement is very much a part of my sense that fiction has a moral duty, a public duty. When we write, like Walt Whitman, we're writing for the nation, we are telling what truth we know about the human condition, about the political history of the world we live in. When I say to young writers, "Okay, you've got your plot, you've got your characters, you've got your place (and we haven't talked much yet about place). Now! What's your purpose in writing? Is it simply to explore your own psyche? Who's your reader? Is it to get a girl or boy to fall in love with you?" My first novel was a love poem to Maureen. It was a valentine, as lyric poetry often is: "Come . . . be my love."

William H. Coles
Isn't the great advantage of writing prose the ability to capture the attention of the reader (if you're good), and engage them so they become emotionally involved in your story? To incite a memorable, lasting, emotional experience in relation to characters in ways that no other medium really allows. Maybe it's not the intensity exactly, but there is something special about *Wuthering*

Heights, something special about Heathcliff. My wife and I still discuss who and what Heathcliff was. And that seems to relate to an attitude about writing that writers don't pick up, the idea of special potential of fiction. We don't focus on writing to engage the reader, to change the reader.

Michael Malone
So, ask yourself, why are you writing, for whom are you writing? Imagine your ideal reader. Coming out of the rhetoric of narrative poetry, early novelists were very aware of addressing an audience—poets are always addressing the muse—and audience became "the reader." "And so dear reader, I married him." That's from *Jane Eyre*. The writer's relation to the reader is very, very self-conscious. Mark Twain is extremely aware that Huck Finn is talking to a reader, and the irony of having that naive narrator is functioning on all sorts of levels. But what do you as a writer want? Do you want to change how the reader thinks or feels? Do you want to have the reader carry the book into his or her own life? [*Long pause*] Yes, you do! Yes, we can!

William H. Coles
I was hoping you weren't going to say no!

Michael Malone
And some *would* say no. I'm always deeply upset when I go into a bookstore and they've got the Hillston novels *Time's Witness*, *Uncivil Seasons*, and *First Lady* among the mystery books, and they've got my other novels in literature—or fiction. No! William Faulkner's *Intruder in the Dust* is a mystery novel. *Crime and Punishment* is a mystery novel. There are good mystery novels and there are not-so-good mystery novels. In the same way, comedy is traditionally considered lower than tragedy. No. Comedy is doing—very specifically—the work of reminding human beings when it is right to say yes, to connect, just as tragedy tells them when to say no, to separate. I have been deeply touched when readers finish *Handling Sin* and say, "I gave this book to my sister. I hadn't spoken to her in ten years, but I gave her *Handling Sin*, and she calls me up laughing, and now we're back together." Or, "My friend was dying and I brought the novel to him in the hospital. It brought him comfort." I believe that books go into the world and do work.

William H. Coles
And that's the value of writing.

Michael Malone
One value. Let me go back to *Wuthering Heights*. There are some books we come

upon during our youth that help us (for good or ill) with the ways in which we fall in and out of love. At that young age, I used to listen to Gustav Mahler and Sergei Rachmaninoff. I couldn't bear the intensity of it any more today. But when you're first encountering romantic music and novels, you are alive with a responsiveness that is a part of youth. I remember a friend in graduate school who was sobbing one day because she had just finished *Anna Karenina*. She said, "My own life is so pale and gray in relation to the vividness of the fictional world." I agree with your point that fiction, as in extended prose narrative, can do something that lyric poetry doesn't do. That nonfiction, no matter how wonderful it is, doesn't do.

William H. Coles
I would even include creative nonfiction.

Michael Malone
Yes. There is magic about the fall into fiction—I think of it as a fall, as if into a lake, and swimming underwater.

William H. Coles
It's thicker than water, it can hold you more.

Michael Malone
That's one reason I'm very concerned about the Kindle. It's physically different from the feel of a book. But I know people who have Kindles who say, "Don't worry, it's like a book." According to them, Kindle is working for people who love books because they don't have to lug fifteen heavy objects off on vacation. They say, "I'm still reading the fifteen books!" I don't know. I think there is something perfect in the construction of a book.

William H. Coles
I agree.

Michael Malone
Turning those pages is just magic.

William H. Coles
I did a little survey at the AWP about the Kindle. A lot of people didn't know what it was. Most people had never used one. Some people remembered after prompting that they'd heard about it. But I wasn't impressed that Kindle was so successful overall.

Michael Malone
I remember I resisted the computer. I wrote by hand, with a pencil. All the way through the first six or seven novels. Because I'm listening to the voices of the characters, I don't want any noise when I'm listening. When the laptop came in, and it was completely silent, and you could move your hands over the keys just like a pencil and hold it on your lap just like a notepad, I shifted to the laptop.

William H. Coles
And you were happy?

Michael Malone
It's very hard to go back once you've done that. But sometimes I wonder, "Why not? You've got an eraser on a pencil. You can write and you can delete." I do worry that there is a kind of gratuitous revision produced by the ease of the computer.

William H. Coles
Cut and paste.

Michael Malone
But I'm not sure. I worry. I'm also frustrated that I can't see out to the edges. In a way, seeing around the edges is a sort of metaphor for what I want for my fiction. In *Dingley Falls*, there's an optical instrument factory in the town, and the narrator says that fiction makes periscopes like that factory. People can't see around the borders of their own lives, so they look with a periscope of fiction.

William H. Coles
Interesting thought.

Michael Malone
Through fiction, they are testing their hearts. For instance, perhaps the reader never liked the kind of person who's a neighbor who borrows things and breaks them, but once he or she meets this kind of person in *Handling Sin*, Mingo Sheffield, they're asked to see his gifts. But the laptop won't let you see the edges, and that bothers me. On the other hand, perhaps it's like reading old Egyptian scrolls.

William H. Coles
Do you think the future of the story is in the written word, really? The editor Michael Ray recently pointed out the importance of the novel to story in the nineteenth century, and the importance of film to story in the twentieth century.

He wondered if, in the next century, interactive storytelling, as in contemporary computer video games, would be the next venue. Could that be the preferred conveyance of story of the future?

Michael Malone
I don't know. I know they tried that, where you could choose your plot—for children. I don't know how it went. But look at the success of graphic novels. I know that newer generations are more visually attuned than mine. I know that colleagues who teach their Victorian novels have had to change their courses because some of these younger readers can't process huge, fat, triple-decker novels. So instead of teaching Charles Dickens's *Our Mutual Friend*, they're teaching the shorter *Great Expectations*, and so forth. Does that mean that younger readers are not narratively just as sensitive and sophisticated? No, it doesn't.

I remember making a prediction long ago that the short story was going to make a comeback. Children's shows like *Sesame Street* accustomed children to shorter narratives. Another thing I've noticed happening is a preference for a protected distance from narrative, a play with meta-narrative. The author is very consciously showing us narrative as narrative, playing with sequence, with allusion, with parody, satire, mixing film with written texts. Much of the narrative heritage of these younger artists comes from film and television. Seventy-five years ago, film was grabbing up everything and using everything it could find from the stage and the novel. Now the stage and the novel are grabbing story and style up from film. From a larger perspective, and at the core of your question about the written word—for a long, long time people got their story orally, not from print, because not everybody could read. The latter has been a pretty brief phenomenon, and a pretty bourgeois phenomenon. Will we go back to oral storytelling?

William H. Coles
Oral storytelling and prose seem related. Both use the mechanism of the receiver's creativity. Something is suggested, and the reader's mind creates its special interpretation. Whereas in film you're throwing everything at them and telling them to accept and remember it because it's important to understanding the story, without the receiver creative element. If you go back to oral story, it may take away the word, but it still requires imaginative input from the listener (like reading) in contrast to simply ingesting film.

Michael Malone
You can hear *The Odyssey*. You weren't supposed to read it. You were supposed to

hear it. I find it fascinating, the public's interest in hearing readings by writers. People will go to readings, or listen to a recording of a novel—one they've read, or one they wouldn't read. Maybe it's true that young people actually go to Barnes and Noble to pick up other people, but at least they're there. There are books all around them, and maybe they're going to take one down that they like. The Harry Potter phenomenon taught us, if nothing else, that people who haven't read will read if you give them a good story and compelling, relatable characters. Now, what is Harry Potter? It is good old Dickens plus the C. S. Lewis kind of magic. It is something all children feel—being an outsider and special at the same time. The little orphan who has great gifts but needs to connect to others.

William H. Coles
Potter, for me, seems pretty sloppy story writing. I think there are better, more meaningful ways to resolve conflict than have an owl fly in with a message-resolution.

Michael Malone
But readers love it. I asked a librarian last night, has young people reading Harry Potter led to other books being read? Yes. The kids say, "You don't have any more Harry Potter? Okay, what else have you got?"

William H. Coles
I admire your teaching film in academics. If you love story, the history of how film developed in telling stories is really fascinating. I have four films I want to talk to you about. Frankly, I don't understand why these film stories—they're disparate in many ways—held on. Is it the novels they're related to? Is it the story itself? Is it the presentation? Is it Vivien Leigh?

Michael Malone
Gone with the Wind?

William H. Coles
Yes. The four films are *Gone with the Wind*, *A Tree Grows in Brooklyn*, *The Great Gatsby* (I've heard you mention you did not like the point-of-view choices in the film), and *WALL-E*. The reason I bring up an animated film is because I have an emotional reaction to the romance. How can that be possible in an animated story? What makes these films successful?

Michael Malone
Let's take *Gone with the Wind* first. It is in some ways very different from the

novel on which it's based. People are far more likely to know the film than the novel. The film clarified and simplified the narrative. For example, in the book she has a number of children, and in the film she only has Bonnie. *Gone with the Wind*, if you go with the box office figures and adjust for inflation, is still the top-grossing film of all time. Why? In the same way that Jane Austen is the hottest screen property there is? Because both Scarlett's story and Elizabeth Bennet's story are Cinderella stories. That's the classic core.

William H. Coles
You mean *Pride and Prejudice*?

Michael Malone
All Austen: *Pride and Prejudice, Sense and Sensibility, Mansfield Park, Persuasion*—they're all on TV and made into movies because her narratives tell a core story about female desire, and desire fulfilled. In every one of Jane Austen's novels the heroine ends up with a big, nice house. And that move of the narrative is toward that home. "When did you know you loved me?" Darcy asks. "I think it was the first moment I saw your house." Daisy: "Oh, my God, what a beautiful house." Gatsby says, "I built this house for you." Scarlett: Tara, Tara, Tara. Rhett tells her, "I'm going to give you back Tara." So, it's about female desire that is rooted in . . .

William H. Coles
. . .a fundamental desire.

Michael Malone
Gone with the Wind also speaks to the nation, as all classic films do. Our heritage. This movie came out in the 1930s, in the Depression, people were starving, they wanted a heroine who is saying, We can pull it together and I'm not going to starve! Nor are any of my kin.

William H. Coles
And pull down those drapes. I'm going to have a dress!

Michael Malone
She's saying, I can make this work. I will build this house. I will get all the food. I will get out of these hard times. This is a war epic without any battle. All we see of soldiers is retreats. The only person who shoots a Yankee in the movie is Scarlett. She's the warrior, the epic hero. Also, *Gone with the Wind* has a classic romance plot: two very different men are in love with her: elegant, poetic Ashley, and the dashing and successful one who honestly sees her for what

she is, Rhett. See here Heathcliff and Edgar Linton from *Wuthering Heights.* Movies like *Gone with the Wind* succeed because they have a classic narrative structure that is embodied by stars with chemistry. If you don't have either the structure or the stars, you don't have a classic movie. You can have one and not the other—story but not chemistry, or chemistry without story—but it takes both to create a *Gone with the Wind* or a *Casablanca.* Usually a romance story. *Titanic.* Same story as *Shakespeare in Love*. It's interesting to me that all the film adaptations of possibly the most perfect American novel, *The Great Gatsby*, have failed. There is a way in which, try as you might, the embodiment of the dream needs to stay far off, dreamed, that green light. Movies let us down. That's not Daisy, that's not Gatsby.

William H. Coles
But it's Nick's story.

Michael Malone
But how do you deal with the narrative whole? Yes, Nick tells the story and the hero dies. Unlike *Sunset Boulevard,* for instance, where the hero tells the story after he dies. That movie opens with the narrator lying dead in the pool, saying, "You may wonder how I got this way, but let me tell you. . ." *The Great Gatsby* stepped away from the narrative, and that's one reason why it is a deeply flawed film. Often the best films aren't the best novels. The movie *Gone with the Wind* is better than its source.

William H. Coles
Did you like *WALL-E*?

Michael Malone
I loved it. Again, it is fundamentally a love story, although it is a story about our human community in relation to the whole world and what we've done to destroy it. It's a remarkable film, without dialogue for the opening half hour or more. But why do you cry in *WALL-E*? Because of the heroic romantic hero. WALL-E grabs hold of that rocket ship and he goes up in space because of Eva.

William H. Coles
Like Heathcliff, except he's successful.

Michael Malone
WALL-E is a profoundly socially responsible story about our shared human condition. I think it's a brilliant movie. WALL-E ends up saving the world. Actually, Eva's rather like Scarlett. *A Tree Grows in Brooklyn*—I don't remember

the film as well, although I remember loving it in the way I loved *Meet Me in St. Louis*, another nostalgic film capturing a family.

William H. Coles
The reason I brought it up is sentimentality. It's very sentimental when viewed from today's perspective.

Michael Malone
"Sentimental" is the word we've been dancing around this whole time, and I find myself in a position, in regard to my own work, of defending myself. I say, "What does this mean?" Sentiment means to think, to be, to feel.

William H. Coles
To emote.

Michael Malone
And now the word "sentimentality" is synonymous with "maudlin." For an eighteenth- or nineteenth-century writer, saying something was sentimental, or that a man had sentiment, would not be negative. It would be descriptive. How did this happen? Because increasingly we value detachment from feeling, and therefore we love art that maintains distance for us: parodies, satire, alienation from story. Anything that stops that alienation makes you "sentimental." In fact, what "sentiment" does is create, intensify empathy.

William H. Coles
Isn't that an interesting observation!

Michael Malone
We step back from anything that makes us cry. We respond to our news now, which *should* make us cry, with laughter. Jon Stewart's *Daily Show*—that's a news show presented as a comedy. Tina Fey brilliantly shows us Sarah Palin in a way people can laugh at—and recognize her as a figure of comedy. It is what Jonathan Swift brilliantly did: make the reader see the absurdity. It's a marvelous gift. But the human heart will never stop feeling. The more they feel for the other, the more sympathy, the more tolerance. The movie *Slumdog Millionaire* for example. It doesn't start like a romantic comedy; it starts with a torture scene. But it is in fact a classic romantic comedy. Its plot is like Charlie Chaplin's *The Gold Rush*. It could be Frank Capra's *It Happened One Night*. The boy gets the girl . . . and the money, because he doesn't care about the money, only the girl.

I've given you two sentimental examples. Chaplin? He wants to make you cry while you're laughing. A Frank Capra film is almost a synonym for cinematic sentimentality. I think that's ridiculous. All Capra's movies bring you to the edge of darkness and then pull you back, reclaim you. His hero says, "I'm going to jump off this building, I'm going to jump off this bridge. I can't stand my life." Then they learn theirs is a wonderful life. It's life.

William H. Coles
Would you recommend *Mr. Smith Goes to Washington* or *Mr. Deeds Goes to Town*?

Michael Malone
I love Capra. You know who hated *Mr. Smith Goes to Washington*? The US Congress. The US Congress was outraged by it because they rightly saw it as a scathing attack on their good-old-boy corruption. That movie was played over and over in Paris during the occupation because of Mr. Smith's refusal to be defeated by powerful dark forces. He filibustered for something that might today be thought sentimental: that in a democracy the government belongs to the people. "I'm going to keep fighting for this lost cause." So when I'm told that a novel of mine is sentimental, and I have heard that often, I say, fine. "Sentimental" is not a dirty word. Easy sentiment, or hypocritical sentiment, yes, they're cheap. But we've thrown human emotion out with Victorian tears. *The Last Noel* ends with the death of the heroine. Some readers said, "How can you do that? You made me cry." And I say "Good. You should also have known from page one that she was going to die. Just like Cathy in *Wuthering Heights*, she is going to die." But somehow we can't let ourselves feel. As I said, *Slumdog Millionaire*, which did win Best Picture at the Academy Awards, is very sentimental. He gets the girl because he's only on the quiz show to find her.

William H. Coles
She sees him on TV.

Michael Malone
And he gets the money, too. Charlie Chaplin in *The Gold Rush*.

William H. Coles
And it's a comedy because it comes out so well. The end scene—all the dancing between the trains—is wonderful.

Michael Malone
It *is* wonderful. And just like in *Cinderella* and *Pride and Prejudice*, the girl finds true love. And he's a prince! The triumph of comedy.

William H. Coles
I think, over the past hour, we've captured your sense of humor, which is one of the reasons I was eager to interview you.

Michael Malone
I want to make the reader laugh out loud. I love it when a reader says he or she was told, "Get out of the bedroom," by a spouse because they were laughing so loudly. But I also want the reader to feel our shared human sorrow and to think our shared human cruelties and injustices. To think, while reading *Time's Witness*, "Maybe it is unfair that African Americans are disproportionately executed in this country. I should think more about that." I would love it if a reader said, "I've changed my mind about the death penalty because I read about it."

William H. Coles
That's the enlightenment that prose can deliver.

Michael Malone
That's the epiphany that narrative can give you. Now a poem can give it to you as well. A memoir can certainly give it to you. I do think you're quite right that there is a way in which memoir is replacing fiction. Memoirs are being written today that would have been constructed as fiction at some point. Thomas Wolfe, for example, if he were writing today, might have chosen to write *Look Homeward, Angel* as a memoir. Certainly in the novel he didn't even change some of the real names. And you know those things "really" happened in that dining hall, in that house, just the way he described them. I think something is lost by writing memoir instead of fiction. There is a way in which readers want the story to be true, to have happened. And that is used as a selling point. Comedy is the art of who we are, who we want to be.

William H. Coles
"Taken from a true story!"

Michael Malone
"Based on . . ."

William H. Coles
". . . real events!" That's an interesting idea. It seems when you're writing from experience you're not making a lot of creative choices, and that begins to blunt the dramatic possibilities, it begins to blunt the characterization enhancement—or, I don't know, augmentation. But most of all it begins to blunt the meaning,

because the meaning is already set. The set enlightenment lacks the advantage of creative choices that intensify meaning.

Michael Malone
I used to teach a fiction course at Yale with someone teaching a simultaneous nonfiction course. We had public readings at term's end, and we said to the students, don't say if what you're reading is fiction or nonfiction. And no one could tell. There's always a slide between the two, life and art. The fiction writers will say it really was a true story, and the nonfiction people will say, well, the true story was boring, so I changed it. We certainly have seen instances where people admitted to having made up their memoirs, or conversely have admitted their fictions were true.

William H. Coles
The key is being effective for the reader.

Michael Malone
I think, here's my memoir at age twenty-two, then here's my memoir at age thirty-two . . . well? You know, in his twenties William Wordsworth wrote a memoir, but he did it in iambic pentameter. And he kept working on it until he died forty-five years later.

William H. Coles
He had an interesting intellect. But there are too many memoirs today.

Michael Malone
I agree. If something sad happens to you in your life, you want to write a memoir about it. You can't see it yourself unless you do. I remember a group of people at the edge of the Grand Canyon; they had taken a Polaroid picture of a little map marker of the Grand Canyon, and they were looking at the picture. So, they were three times removed from the Grand Canyon; it was as if they couldn't see it unless they could reduce it to a picture.

William H. Coles
It's such a pleasure to be talking with you about fiction and prose. It's such a special storytelling medium to be working in. So much potential.

Michael Malone
I do think what you said about limits, endings in narrative art, is crucial. A point I'll end with: if you follow the characters where they want to go, and if you listen to them, they will take you places you don't expect. You have to trust in that

process. It's magic, the absolute trust in the imagination. If you try to control it from the outside and put shackles on it, preconditions, or say, "I have to have X happen by page ten," or "I have to have the book end by a certain page count," you will miss hearing things and seeing things. I've gone back and looked at some of my notebooks and found that always there might be six different adjectives for a dreary day, but there would be no changes in the dialogue because I'm hearing the characters speak. I let go of thought. I suspect a sports analogy would be that it's like a pole vault. While you're vaulting you're not thinking it's too fast or too slow, although you are adjusting to those possibilities.

William H. Coles
I would submit, though, that your story is already created inside you, and you do have direction, and what you are discovering is what you think is the right direction of the story. Because it does seem that a writer can create an effective scene if they don't know what is going to happen at the end of their story. It is so easy to create in an unstructured scene events that go against the character and the plot.

Michael Malone
Then you go back. And revise. And revise. Over and over, like you pole vault over and over. That's what I mean. There are hundreds of faults from page one on revisions of my books. Every day you go back and redo what you did before because every day you know the story better, you know the characters better. You go, "Wait a minute," and revise. In the novel *Uncivil Seasons*, this wonderfully outrageous character, Briggs Cadmean, says about two-thirds through, "How dare you think that I murdered a woman. I would never do that." Well, I *was* wrong. I thought he was the murderer. But if you just listen, everything's going to be there in the text, from the opening page onward. The end is going to be in the beginning.

From the first moment, you know that Nick Carraway (in *The Great Gatsby*) is going to make a moral decision about people we're going to meet, a decision that is based in his character. It is going to cause him to take an action in the end, and that action is going to be to stand with Gatsby. To say to Gatsby, "You're worth the whole rotten bunch." And then to leave the East because he didn't want any part of those rich careless people who caused Gatsby's death. So that first moment when Nick talks to us, what you see in that moment you will see in the rest of the novel.

William H. Coles
I hear you. Yet in flipping the flapjack, many people let themselves wander

through the story because don't have the inner, concrete feeling about the story in general.

Michael Malone
Yes.

William H. Coles
I mean, you know the story is there.

Michael Malone
And one has a gift for storytelling or one does not. There's a curious difference between people's assumptions about the art of writing versus other arts. Everyone can talk; everyone who is literate can write; we all tell stories. And therefore there's a way in which everyone assumes "I can write; I want to write; so I can write." And in a sense they can. But not everyone has the gift. No one would say, "I think I'll be a great ballet dancer. I'll be Mikhail Baryshnikov," or "I'll be Luciano Pavarotti," or "I'll be Babe Ruth." If I tried to sing like Pavarotti, I'd run out of this room. Some people have gifts. Writing fiction is both a gift and a craft. That's what I mean when I say you can't teach it but you can learn it. If you have a gift, you can learn how to hone that craft so you don't make mistakes that you might otherwise.

William H. Coles
This brings us to my last question, and it's a tough one. I have found, as a writer, that there are very few learning resources out there. Workshops tend to be ineffective. Academics are not teaching fiction well, especially the intricacies of fiction as we've been talking about today. There are very few how-to books that elucidate issues such as the credibility problems in the first person, for example. Where can I go? Where would you suggest, as a person with limited time in this world, I go for learning?

Michael Malone
You've got to read. But not a manual. Then write about characters you love. What are they doing? Get yourself into a writing group because you have to be heard. You have to have someone who is listening, saying, "I don't know what you mean by that," or "I've got to tell you, I love you, but I got bored reading that manuscript." You need a group. Writing groups—most I've heard of are primarily women—go off together and have a wonderful week, working each morning and then reading each other's work. One of the purposes of a writer's workshop, like Iowa, is that you get that audience, that moment of sharing material. Writing is a very lonely, isolated life. Also, these groups provide contacts. There's no use

in pretending that writing well is the same as finding agents and publishers. Authors need contacts in a world where publishing resources are shrinking. We all need all the help we can get.

William H. Coles
So, get in groups with people you can trust, people you can get to know and can give you feedback.

Michael Malone
Best of all is being around writers who are doing what you are doing. And being around great readers. I have been quite fortunate in my life to be married to a professional literary critic; that's what she does, and she's very good at it. I used to argue with her, but now if she just says, "Hmm," I take a deep breath and go back and change it. Sometimes the things you don't want to let go of are the things you should.

William H. Coles
This has been such a great pleasure.

Michael Malone
Wonderful. I've enjoyed it.

William H. Coles
I'd like to come back every day!

Michael Malone
Neither of us would get any writing done.

Lee Martin Interview

25 June, 2009
William H. Coles

Lee Martin is the author of *The Bright Forever* (Broadway Books, 2005), a finalist for the Pulitzer Prize, and the memoir *From Our House* (Bison books, 2009). He was born in Illinois and received his MFA from the University of Arkansas. He has received numerous awards, including the Mary McCarthy Prize, the Nancy Dasher Award, the Glenna Luschei Prize for Literary Distinction, the Lawrence Foundation Award, and fellowships from the NEA and the Ohio Arts Council. Currently he is a professor and director of the MFA Program in Creative Writing at Ohio State University.

William H. Coles
Let's begin with a general question about the importance of story. As a writer, you have dedicated your life to story. How important is story for human development and for human pleasure in our society today?

Lee Martin
Story is the way we interrogate, explore, and come to understand our lives. I think it's a human necessity, in a certain sense of the word, that we tell stories in order to document, interrogate, understand a little bit better than we would without the stories. If you go far, far back into history, people have always told stories, not only for entertaining but to come to understand the human being a little better.

William H. Coles
What is the uniqueness of fiction in prose storytelling as it differs from cinema? What elements do storytellers in prose need to address differently than in, say, a screenplay?

Lee Martin
I have to admit that I don't know a lot about screenplays, and I've never had an interest in learning about screenplays, but it seems to me the thing that a novel or a short story can do that a screenplay has a harder time doing is entering into the consciousness and interiority of a character. When we write stories and novels, even though our attention might be on what happens next, we also

have to pay attention to the inner lives of the characters. That interiority is often stripped away when a book is adapted for the screen. I know of books that never got made into movies for that very reason. It's not easy to get the interiority on the screen without sacrificing some of the narrative tension of this scene coming after that scene.

William H. Coles
And that's what makes you enjoy teaching and writing story? The interiority, as you say, that is possible in prose fiction?

Lee Martin
Yes. I'm really excited, with fiction, about how language operates when we start to talk about things like interiority. There's a music to language that I value as a fiction writer, and so much of that comes through in the entering into a consciousness. That's what I sometimes miss in a cinematic form. The nature of the medium is such that our attention is on what's happening, rather than on what someone is making of what's happening. I understand that even in cinema there is a way to create a consciousness, there is a way to give a point of view to a particular scene or a sequence of scenes, et cetera, but I always miss the music of the language, which is the language of musing, thinking, synthesizing.

William H. Coles
That process must be there in memoir and creative nonfiction, but it is certainly not the same, and certainly the rewards are not received the same way. And yet I sense much of what is published today is just memoir that is not true in some areas. In other words, an author is looking at exactly what happened in the past and describes what moved him or her, trusting the reader will be moved, too. Fiction seems to offer so many different choices to develop the story; you've got choices about plot and character. Would you agree?

Lee Martin
First of all, let's talk about nonfiction. It's unfortunate that we've had a slew of memoirs recently that have turned out to be false. I've published a couple of memoirs. I write both fiction and nonfiction, and I really value the things that good memoir writing can do. So it's unfortunate that the whole form has been cast with some suspicion because of some examples of malfeasance lately. Your question suggests, where is there more freedom: in writing memoir, or in inventing, as we do when we write fiction? I've always contended that it is easier to write memorable fiction than to write memorable memoir. Here's my reasoning (and some people won't agree with this, and that's fine). If I'm writing a memoir and I'm ethical about it, then I am bound to literally tell

what happened and I cannot create something that didn't happen. I can't have a character do something that she didn't actually do. I can't even dramatize an aspect of a person's character if it is not true to what the person is or was. But when I'm writing fiction, I can do all of that. I can make something serve the story I want to tell by creating another aspect of a character, by having that character perform a certain action or say a certain line of dialogue. One would think that that would mean there's much more freedom in fiction. And that is true, I think there is. With freedom comes selection.

William H. Coles
And imagination?

Lee Martin
And imagination, exactly. Because as soon as I start to imagine something for a character, I have a larger realm of possibility than I do if I'm working with a real person in a memoir. Because I have a larger realm of possibility, the thing that I choose becomes much more important and significant. In other words, how do I know I'm choosing the right thing? That choice is literally made for me in nonfiction. In nonfiction, I simply have to pay close attention in my memory, in my recollection, and in my interpretation, to make sure I'm getting, in advance, characters accurately portrayed as they were or are in the real world. In fiction, I'm choosing from a wide variety of possibilities, and I think the onus for making the proper choice is greater. And that's why I think . . . I don't even know now what I said to start with. I guess I'm starting to contradict myself now. Is it easier to write fiction or nonfiction . . . what did I say first?

William H. Coles
You said it was easier to write fiction than nonfiction. That memoir was harder to write. I think your point was that you don't have the freedom in memoir.

Lee Martin
Right. In nonfiction you're bound to the facts.

William H. Coles
This is delicate, and I don't know exactly how to express it—it may be related to personal aesthetics that we've talked about before. But it seems to me that writers go into memoir with a different attitude than writers who write fiction. I'll say this in a confrontational way, I'm afraid, but the memoir writer assumes that his or her life is important to the reader, important enough for a reader to enjoy and find it entertaining—which can be true but often it's not—and I sense there's more than a little arrogance behind that. The whole idea that this is how my life

made me feel and I'm sure that I can describe for you the intensity of my feeling though my memoir writing. Whereas the fiction writer says, my main goal is to entertain my reader so they have an enjoyable experience and at the same time come away with something new. There's a dedication to the reader's response. A fiction writer says I'm willing to do anything with my imagination and my freedom to make that happen. In the memoir, you always have that background attitude that it's my life and experience that's important, and you, the reader, should enjoy it. That seems a huge difference in attitude. I care because what is often published as fiction now is really memoir. That worries me as someone who loves the great fiction of the past.

Lee Martin
I think what you say is sometimes true, but I would consider a memoir that carries that tone of arrogance, that assumption that "here is my story to tell and everyone will be interested in hearing it," an inferior form of memoir. Because to me, the impulse that brings me to fiction is the impulse that brings me to nonfiction. It's to try to explore something, to try to understand something.

William H. Coles
With the reader.

Lee Martin
Yes. When I tell my story of my father and the loss of his hands in a farming accident in *From Our House*, I don't know when I start that story what I think about that whole experience. So I can't make the assumption that the reader is interested in my father's or my life experience. I can only make the assumption that I would like the reader to eavesdrop with me as I discover and explore.

William H. Coles
Good point. That's really illuminating for me.

Lee Martin
The same impulse carries me into a novel like *The Bright Forever*. What can I find out about a community's experience of the disappearance of a nine-year-old girl? And what can I find out about the lonely life of a mathematics tutor in that town who may have some culpability in the matter?

William H. Coles
I'd like to explore timeline with you. Is a timeline important, and, if so, what attitude should we have regarding it when we write short stories or novels?

Lee Martin
It's particularly important, at least to my way of thinking, in the short story, as the form relies so much on time compression. We could go back to Edgar Allan Poe and his belief that a story should be capable of being read in one sitting. We could talk about unity of effect and how a specific timeline contributes to the unity of a short story. I've always noticed that if the circumstances of a story have a particular time limitation applied to them—for example, if some problem has to be resolved within the day, or the month, or whatever the time period is, then the stakes go up immediately because we understand these characters have a limited amount of time to deal with this problem and come to some sort of resolution. I also think it's important, just structurally for a story, that there be a timeline anchor. That no matter how far out we might spiral into the past or into the future, we're always coming back to this baseline, which is a timeline. There is something happening in the dramatic present that requires our presence in the story. I think we're money ahead if the writer keeps coming back to that . . . no matter if the writer is layering backstory or flashing ahead into the future or whatever.

William H. Coles
When you layer in backstory, you are avoiding chunks of backstory that break the continuity of the timeline, which is continually moving forward, providing the momentum.

Lee Martin
Right. And I think "momentum" is an excellent word to use because you've got to keep the story moving ahead, keep the narrative moving ahead, and one way to do that is to pay attention to the timeline.

William H. Coles
Let me bring in the problem of backstory as it relates to the timeline and the problems of voice. When a character speaks in backstory, that character doesn't have access to the story-present timeline. The character doesn't have access to the history, the sensitivities, to the social mores within the time of the backstory (outside the timeline). Is it important for credibility to be certain the voice is consistent with what knowledge is reasonably available?

Lee Martin
It's a tough question to answer because it relies on point of view. For example, I can answer the question differently if we are talking about a third-person narrative versus a first-person narrative. Do we expect different things, different sounds, different voices from the first-person narrator when the person enters

some expository section that's giving backstory? I guess we do expect something a little different. We expect a more reflective voice, right?

William H. Coles
Yes.

Lee Martin
And in the first-person present of a story, we expect the narrator to tell us what happens in sequence, keeping that story stretched tight as it moves along the narrative line. In the third-person story, we expect that type of storyteller's narration . . . once upon a time there were three little pigs (to go to an old children's story), and then one day the big bad wolf came and started to huff and puff and blow the house down . . . well, when we shift into backstory in the third person, then do we also expect a certain alteration in the register of voice or sound at that point? I think we do.

William H. Coles
I think so too.

Lee Martin
We signal with a shift in register that we've entered a different mode of discourse. It's not a mode of narration at this point, it's a mode of gathering.

William H. Coles
I'd like to carry that a little bit further and stay with the third-person point of view for the moment and think of author presence, and a narrator voice that is specific for the narrator's and characters' voices. The character is limited to the timeline and story time, so that everything you develop in dialogue and internal reflection is restricted to the story time. But the narrator has lived longer, is further away (in terms of psychological and physical distance) from the story, and does not have the exact same responsibilities as the character who is acting out the story. The character and the narrator have different voices. And of course, the author has his or her world to call from with vastly more information, which should not enter most stories. In thinking about this as we write, if a writer is choosing metaphors, if he or she is making decisions about ridicule, or about society, or looking for certain ironies to develop, all these language skills influence a story, especially ironies, and will develop differently in the narrator's view, the character's view, and the author's view. In thinking about this, is it important when the author is creating a story and the narrator is telling the story at that moment that you're always in the narrator's world,

which is different than the character? When you move to character, should you be careful not to carry the narrator's voice?

Lee Martin
I actually think that there is a successful blending of the central consciousness of a third-person story—say, the consciousness of a character named Bobby with what I like to call . . . I sometimes call it the narrative voice, or sometimes the effaced narrator. I don't think of that storyteller's voice, that "once upon a time" voice, as the author's voice at all. I never think of it in those terms. I think of it more in terms of the narrator of the story. And then, through the skillful management of point of view, that voice can blend nicely with the consciousness of the central character.

William H. Coles
As long as it's credible for the timeline.

Lee Martin
Right.

William H. Coles
All stories are told in the past, and the narrator is telling from a different time than the character in the timeline.

Lee Martin
As long as it's organic for all the elements of the story. For example, just on the language level, let's say we have a story set in the South in 1963 . . . I'm just grabbing something out of the air . . . and you have a third-person narrative through the perspective of a character who lives in Jackson, Mississippi, who's involved in a certain set of circumstances. If that story shifts into the storyteller's voice, and if it starts grabbing at metaphors and any kind of figures of speech, those metaphors have to come from that world of 1963. And so this conversation we're having about this point, Bill, is actually part and parcel of how all elements of a story contribute to an organic whole.

William H. Coles
Yes. In first person, is it ever of value to separate the narrator from the first person, and without letting the narrator be the author, so the conceptualization of this type of voice integrity can be maintained as you develop a first-person story?

Lee Martin
In first person in a piece of fiction—and this is something I've been curious about for a long, long time—I think there a difference between first-person narration in fiction and first-person narration in memoir. We know that there are going to be two "I's" in a piece of memoir. There is the "I" who lived the experience, and the "I" who looks back on the experience and tells us about it. Now, within that, there are probably going to be a number of other "I's" because the self is made up of so many distinct parts. I think in fiction it's pretty much the same. Anytime someone speaks in the first-person point of view, you have someone who is looking back on him- or herself in a particular time in his or her life. And that first-person point of view is sometimes the participant, sometimes the spectator. A good writer distinguishes the voices of those two entities.

William H. Coles
In essence, then, one of the two "I's" acts with a narrator function. The "I" who is looking back is like a narrator. That's helpful. I am interested in elements of writing in-scene and in the moment. Often we'll tell a story with narrative discourse, but it has distance from the action. What are the elements of getting into the scene, and into the moment?

Lee Martin
This may be too simplistic, but I always advise my students who are starting to write stories to open with a specific person in a specific place engaged in a specific action. So, for example, a story could open with a simple line: "One day at noon, Bob reached into his back pocket and the handkerchief he had placed there in the morning was gone." Specific person, specific place, specific time, specific action. A skilled storywriter will make that initial action reverberate through the entire story. A sequence of events will proceed from the fact that Bob couldn't find his handkerchief one morning.

William H. Coles
You mean the mystery reverberates, or the action itself?

Lee Martin
It could be both. In that case there is sort of a mystery, a trivial mystery that I outlined, although it could have great consequence if I build the story right. Yeah, the mystery of what happened to the handkerchief, that's one thing that reverberates, but also, what will Bob have to do now that he doesn't have the handkerchief? What will his next course of action be? Will he retrace his steps? Will he try to find it someplace he's been during the day? Will he decide to buy a new handkerchief? While he's buying a new handkerchief, will he step on a

young lady's toe? Will that young lady accuse him of being forward with her? There are a number of things that can happen from this very simple opening of person, place, and action.

William H. Coles
I perceive a slight trap there: as you begin to develop character or try to advance the plot, you as an author may try to use internal reflection and bring in backstory, observations of the world and life, and other opinions. That seems to slow down stories, yet it's necessary to keep the action significant and moving in-scene. Is there a way to solve that?

Lee Martin
I like to think about what a character carries with him onto the page. What has happened in that character's life before the events of the story start to unfold, and that "grand story" of the case of the missing handkerchief that we're spinning here? If for example that handkerchief was the last handkerchief that Bob's father used before he passed away, then it has some sort of value to Bob, right? That's the little piece of backstory that will make the sequence of events have more significance. It's not that he just has to find a handkerchief; it's that he has to find a handkerchief that has some sentimental value. So, there is a way to get the story started with person, place, time, space, action, and then to layer in the little piece of information that this is what the handkerchief was. And then we go back to the story.

William H. Coles
This is where it's crucial for what you've often said is the right choice at the right moment for the story. Because if the character decides he wants to discuss polyester fibers as opposed to cotton in handkerchiefs, that this or that type doesn't absorb snot as well, or something like that. To not stop the front story, the right choice has to be made, not about fiber or snot.

Lee Martin
You're right. If the writer decides at that point to talk about the difference between cotton and polyester fibers, then they have put our attention on something with no consequence to the unfolding sequence of events.

William H. Coles
You've quoted Eudora Welty, something like, "Place is everything."

Lee Martin
Welty talks about how "place is fiction." That certain stories proceed from certain

settings, and the specific setting lends itself to a certain realm of possibilities for stories.

William H. Coles
I don't mean this to be a confrontational question, but that seems to be really limiting in a sense, because of the emotional complexities that you teach. Isn't there a trap in terms of thinking of setting in fiction? I know the answer will be that the setting will set up the emotional development, but shouldn't a story be able to exist as readily in Jackson, Mississippi, as in Chicago?

Lee Martin
Short answer: no! [*laughs*]

William H. Coles
Why?

Lee Martin
Here's the way I look at it. And this is not my original observation. If a story has no specific setting, if it's not attached to place in some way, then it seems not to be happening at all. Now, I'm going to offer up two different ways that stories can be attached to place. Stories can proceed from specific places because of the character's sense of attachment to the customs, habits, mores, culture of the place, but they can also proceed from a character's resistance to the mores, culture, values, et cetera. Should a story set in Yazoo City, Mississippi, be the same story when it's set in Chicago? In a sense, stories are universal. They're about the mysteries of being human, and they're about love, and death, and spiritual faith. In that sense, yes, things that happen to people in Yazoo City can have the same reverberations through love, et cetera, if they're set in Chicago. But my contention is that as soon as we change the setting of the story, we change the cultural backdrop. The cultural backdrop allows different things in one place versus somewhere else.

William H. Coles
In writing opinions about cultural settings, isn't there a danger of ridicule and then moving into satire? I have the bias that too much satire in prose fiction begins to ruin the story itself.

Lee Martin
There's absolutely a danger of only seeing the stereotypical in a particular culture and place, and this connects to an important issue in story writing. A storywriter's task is to present characters and their situations and their places as fully

as they can see them. And often that means seeing the aspects that transcend the stereotypical. We do not want to read a story set in one particular locale, coming from one particular culture, that only perpetuates the stereotypes that have been attached to said culture. The writer needs to look carefully at the human beings instead of the culture.

William H. Coles
What talent, or talents, do great writers have that cannot be learned? What elements of a great writer are instinctive?

Lee Martin
This is a tough question. You know I'm in the business of teaching people how to write fiction and nonfiction, and I've always said I can teach craft, and I can take almost anyone—I think I can, anyway—and give them a sense of what story is. But can I teach them that extra something that makes the stories they write memorable and lasting? There you have to start thinking about imagination, freshness of vision, the ability to see that any one thing contains its opposite. I don't know that I can teach that. I think I can teach people to look for the surprises we wouldn't expect, but I'm not sure I can teach the sort of flair, the pizzazz, that makes something make an impression on the reader.

William H. Coles
But you can teach the reversals, and the alternatives for the reversals, and the identification of that sort of thing.

Lee Martin
Right.

William H. Coles
I have a question about workshops, but what you've just said pretty much sums up what you do for students to help them improve.

Lee Martin
Yes. The two things I learned as I was going along—and this is the order in which I learned them—are the techniques of storytelling, and then to make those techniques pay off. For me that involved looking into the mysterious aspects of human behavior.

William H. Coles
So for you that's the key of it all. Human behavior. For a student of creative writing, what would you recommend as an investigation into the important

historical development of story? Going all the way back to ancient times. How can students get a sense of how stories developed and how they are still developing today?

Lee Martin
I think people have to keep reading the masters. I get a little concerned that most of the reading being done today is contemporary in nature. If you want to be a really good short-story writer, how can you do that if you haven't read Anton Chekhov? You should try to figure out exactly how something gets made on the page. But I don't think you should be too concerned about tracing the development of storytelling. You should be concerned with exposing yourself to the various ways to tell stories, so you can start to define your own aesthetic of storytelling.

William H. Coles
What if you looked at Cain and Abel, or *Ulysses*? Those stories have lasted forever. Or Shakespeare, who has some obscure plots at times, yet the stories just last forever. How did they do that, and how do we re-create that in a contemporary setting?

Lee Martin
If you look at any of those examples, you'll find that the lasting value resides in the complex interaction of characters. An interesting exercise is to look at, say, the Cain and Abel story and try to write a contemporary story that borrows from it.

William H. Coles
What are five past books that you would recommend to students wishing to learn techniques of fiction? For example, *Wuthering Heights* is one of my favorites.

Lee Martin
I think there is a lot to be learned from Henry James. *The Ambassadors* is a book that I resisted all through my college years, and then finally got old enough to understand why it was important. *The Great Gatsby* is instructive for first-person point of view. Ernest Hemingway is instructive for the restraint of language and paring down of narrative, also demonstrating the expansiveness of character. I had one more . . . Oh! Virginia Woolf's *Mrs. Dalloway* is a wonderful book to read to see what can be done with stream of consciousness. It's just a matter of finding those books that illustrate various techniques for us.

William H. Coles
I'd like to thank you very much for participating in this interview. It's been a great pleasure talking with you.

Lee Martin
Great pleasure. Thank you very much.

Rebecca McClanahan Interview

October, 2008
William H. Coles

Rebecca McClanahan is a successful author of poetry, fiction, and creative nonfiction. She won the Glasgow Prize in nonfiction for *The Riddle Song and Other Rememberings* (Walking Stick Press, 2006). Among numerous other publications, she has written two books on writing: *Word Painting: A Guide to Writing More Descriptively* (Writer's Digest Books, 2014) and *Write Your Heart Out* (Walking Stick Press, 2001). She teaches frequently in workshops (Kenyon Review, Gettysburg Review, Hudson Valley Writers Center, to name only a few) and two MFA programs (Queens University of Charlotte and Pacific Lutheran University in Tacoma, Washington). She has been honored extensively with national prizes and awards.

William H. Coles
To start, what do you see as the differences between memoir and fiction?

Rebecca McClanahan
For me, memoir is the more challenging of the two genres. I feel that fiction is circumscribed only by what the reader will believe, so my impulse while writing it is to entertain any number of possibilities as to what could happen to this character, any number of what-ifs. That is a very different approach from what I use in memoir and other forms of nonfiction. Memoir in particular requires a great deal of destruction on the part of the writer—that is, destruction of the text that is already there. When I'm writing a story, I don't feel I have to destroy or dismantle anything . . . I'm building it from the ground up.

In memoir, however, so much depends on selection. Memoir is not a record of one's life—not at all. Memoir is a selected and shaped text that attempts to find what I call the weave or the texture underneath the life, that thing that folds the life together. It might be an idea that has surfaced over and over, or an event you keep returning to. In writing memoir, you're trying to make meaning or shape out of the raw material of your life. You're definitely not trying to re-create your life. That's impossible. My students get very upset when they feel they have failed to *re-create* their grandmother on the page; or they've not *captured* the essence of their hometown. Writing is not about capturing something; it is about making a text, and because writing is made of words it will never re-create or capture a human being, a place. All writing, I suppose, is a failure when you hold it up against the light of reality. Yet you can suggest the event, the passions, the obsessions of one's life, try to find out what pattern of meaning they make, and hope that there will be something there that the reader will connect with.

William H. Coles
How do you deal with the elements of truth?

Rebecca McClanahan
Truth and fact and accuracy?

William H. Coles
Yes.

Rebecca McClanahan
I have to tell you, Bill, I am not so fond of that question. Questions of fact and truth have gotten a lot of press lately, while other important aspects of nonfiction have been overlooked. It's why I don't like the term "creative nonfiction." I prefer "literary nonfiction" because when people hear "creative" attached to "nonfiction" they immediately go to the fact/truth/accuracy element and overlook the hundreds of ways in which nonfiction can be done in a creative way.

But to answer your question, there are a number of ways to strive for both accuracy and truth. A lot depends on what kind of text you're making. When you're looking back in time in memoir, you're using memory as your main access. So, of course, there will be huge loops of experience that will be missing—that's a given—and there may be loops of misunderstanding and inaccuracy. You weren't wired when you were four, so for instance you will have to re-create to the best of your ability a sense of the conversation you remember your grandparents having one night. No one expects the conversation to be an accurate transcription. However, when an event is in the more recent past, like last week or your surgery two years ago, you can do some fact checking. Actually, you can even fact check long-gone memories by asking other people who were there what their recollections are. You can check the weather of the day. You can look at old photographs, and check to see if—oh, indeed, that wasn't the way the car was at all. We didn't even have the station wagon yet. Those sorts of things.

William H. Coles
How about the timeline? When you look for patterns in memoir story, do you change the chronology?

Rebecca McClanahan
The only time I have knowingly done that was in the essay "Aunt" in *Riddle Song and Other Rememberings*. Well, I didn't actually change the chronology; what I did was collapse several similar events into one to make it easier for the reader to imagine the moment. There is a pivotal scene in the essay in which I describe my great-aunt (she was seventy years my senior) massaging my aching legs. I was eleven at the time, and I had what we used to call "growing pains" in my calves. I remember very strongly that this physical act represented a moment of change in my relationship to her, my recognition that I did need her, that I did love her, that she wasn't just an old woman my mother had brought to live with us to take up space in our already-crowded life. So even though she had indeed massaged my calves several times, I chose not to re-create every single occurrence. Instead, I made it one event—for the reader's sake.

William H. Coles
How do you perceive voice? In all writing it seems that voice and tone are important. Do you find difficulties between genres in what you want to create for the reader?

Rebecca McClanahan
Voice and tone. Yes, so important. And sometimes so difficult to get right. One of the great joys for me is discovering the right key in which to sing the particular piece I'm working on. I think voice is extremely important. Judith Kitchen talks about this element a lot, the importance of the distinctive voiceprint or the sense of a guiding consciousness. It's set in motion from the first sentence on. Or it isn't. I was trained in music, and I feel I have a pretty good ear for voice and rhythms, but sometimes I'm so far off from my material—I just don't get the right match. So I let go and let the voice lead the material, take the lead. I enjoy voice-propelled pieces, and I have written some, mostly the briefer essays.

William H. Coles
Do you check voice by revision and hearing the sounds, or are there craft elements you use as you are creating the voice?

Rebecca McClanahan
I don't know that I'm conscious of it. I do know, when I'm rereading, if something doesn't fit. For instance, in the middle of a piece like "Loving Bald Men," if I were to come out with an overly serious statement or a pompous pronouncement, I would know that did not fit with the voice of the speaker. I like to try out various voices in my writing. And a lot of the voiceprint is found in the rhythm of the sentence. For example in "Signs and Wonders," the New

York piece, which is very voice oriented, the sentences are ratta da da da dup . . . dit dit dit dit . . . It starts out with jackhammers opening the sidewalk—"you know the drill"—and the sentences are very fast and furious. On the other hand, the essay "Interstellar" uses sentences in a totally different way. "When you're the sister of a sad and beautiful woman," it begins, which is a whole different lay of the land, so unlike the New York piece. So you play out different voices depending on the personality of the piece. Is this a reverie? Is this a meditation? Is this an in-your-face-slap the way New York feels to me sometimes? You need to produce the emotional landscape of whatever you're writing about, and you do that partly—no, not partly, always!—with the rhythm of your sentences, where you pause . . .

William H. Coles
Word choice?

Rebecca McClanahan
Word choice, of course. Even the sounds of individual words. Do you want something soothing to the ear or do you need an ugly word, jagged prose? Everything is subservient to the task, you know, and you just have to bow before the work at hand and say, "Okay, what do you want to be when you grow up?" That is what I ask every piece I write.

William H. Coles
Many writers, when they are writing prose, have difficulty grasping the concept of musicality. You've described many things that contribute to musicality, and there is the essence of hearing the music. Does a musical background help?

Rebecca McClanahan
I don't think it hurts.

William H. Coles
And does reading out loud help?

Rebecca McClanahan
Yes. Any exercise that helps you see and hear the work in a new way. I do lots of craft exercises, and I have my students do them, too. For instance, I totally believe in imitation as a way to practice the language, and I frequently have my students do things like grammatical rhymes and other Rebecca McClanahans of modeling. Listen to the sentence at the opening of "The Fall of the House of Usher." Isn't it beautiful? "During the whole of a dull dark and soundless day

in the autumn of the year . . ." I memorized that whole passage, among many others. It's one of my hobbies, memorizing poems and short prose passages.

William H. Coles
The New York editor Rob Spillman has suggested that students of writing sit down and type out passages to see how other writers have created those rhythms.

Rebecca McClanahan
I've done that. One terribly bleak summer when nothing was working out, when my writing was totally flat, I decided to type out a chapter from *War and Peace*.

William H. Coles
That took you four years.

Rebecca McClanahan
I'm a fast typer! Actually, sometimes I copy the passages out by hand, just to get inside the syntax and see how different it is from author to author. It's like doing finger exercises on the piano. When I was a child learning to play those exercises—I hated them, I just wanted to play "Moon River" or whatever corny thing I was learning. But the fact is, the finger exercises helped. They came to my aid later on. Most writers don't practice enough; they think everything they write has to be a Rebecca McClanahan performance, everything they write has to work. I gave up on that a long time ago. Mostly, I practice.

William H. Coles
In one of your interviews you talked about story in poetry, and no story in poetry. I wondered what your conceptualization of story is. What is it you place in a poem to make it narrative? What are the elements of story, particularly for the nonfiction writer? Are those nonfiction elements different than fiction elements?

Rebecca McClanahan
It's a huge question. I'm pretty traditional in the way I think and teach fiction. I don't know that I'm traditional in the way I practice it. But I think of story as generally character driven. The character wants something; the story has . . .

William H. Coles
. . . a beginning, middle, and end.

Rebecca McClanahan
Yes. And somewhere along the way, forces intervene. He or she doesn't get what

he or she wants; then there is a scene in which things turn. So, I think that way about fiction, but in fact many of my stories don't seem to have that trajectory. Nor does my nonfiction. But I want stories that show how we are alike in all the important ways, no matter how different we all seem. I want stories that break my heart and heal it all at the same time. That's what I look for as a reader. I also very much respect humor in writing because I think it is very difficult to achieve. I think we tend to forget how important humor is, even in serious fiction and serious nonfiction. I love the play of words; I love when characters say strange or funny things. Well, I'm getting off the subject, I'm sorry. What makes a story? I do know that something has to change . . .

William H. Coles
In the character?

Rebecca McClanahan
In the character, and even in a poem. There must be a turn. In other words, the reader must end up with the writer in a different place from where they began. It can be a movement through time, or a movement of meaning. The essay might be elegant, beautiful, maybe even more so than a poem. A truly well-crafted essay is the self talking to itself. It's an attempt to put a thought on trial, or an idea or an experience, to see it in as many ways as possible. It's like a snake eating its own tail. A really wonderful essay never answers anything; it just opens up more questions. But so does the best fiction, the best poems.

William H. Coles
Would you agree that everyone needs stories in the same way they need food and sleep? If that is true, is there something that we, as authors, need to satisfy when telling a story, something that teaches a person to live more effectively? Do authors need to have goals for reader enlightenment when they're telling stories?

Rebecca McClanahan
You're talking about a moral imperative.

William H. Coles
Yes. But maybe not that strong. More in the sense that everything should have meaning.

Rebecca McClanahan
Definitely. For instance, I'm not much of a language poetry fan. Sure, I enjoy playing with words and seeing where that leads, but finally I want to be moved

to a different place as a reader and as a writer. If I begin in despair, I don't want to end there. Yes, I have written some very dark things, but I think literature is a way to shine a light through the darkness. I don't say that in a reductive way. I don't believe you can expect that light to happen, and you can never force it to happen, but I think it happens naturally when you really get to the truth of human experience. That is why I love nonfiction; I love interviewing people; I love reading their letters. For four years now I've been reading other people's letters and listening to their stories, and if you just listen, the light cracks through, it breaks through. The act of story making itself is shouting to the darkness, "I exist!" and "I want to leave something!" even if it is just for one person. It's an act of faith that something continues, whatever that something is.

William H. Coles
Narrator is a difficult concept for prose writers. How do you think about narrators? Does it vary in your different genres?

Rebecca McClanahan
Yes. Very much.

William H. Coles
How do you perceive author involvement, narrator involvement, and character involvement in what goes on the page? How do those interact, and how do you make them effective?

Rebecca McClanahan
I thought about this a lot for a talk I did at AWP. I recall the image I used was of Russian nesting dolls. First you have the flesh-and-blood person sitting at her desk, that's the writer.

William H. Coles
That's outside? The outer doll?

Rebecca McClanahan
Yes. That's the over voice. Then locked inside, the next doll, or whatever you want to call the next figure, would be the author of this particular text. (Not the flesh-and-blood person. The flesh-and-blood person is larger than that—you could be a doctor, father, grieving wife, whatever.) Locked inside the author is the next figure, the narrator, and depending on the piece that you're writing, there may be a whole lot of little narrators locked within the main one. For example, if you're writing a long memoir piece in which you shift back in time to a child's perception, the child's voice might be more—what we call unreliable

than the main narrator. The narrator in memoir is extremely complex. When I'm writing poetry or fiction, I feel I have a great deal more leeway in the kinds of narrators I employ. But in nonfiction, I feel more limited. The narrator is closer to myself, my deepest self.

William H. Coles
There is a collapse of the inner and outer figures in the nest?

Rebecca McClanahan
Right. In nonfiction, the two figures are closer. Because you're using words, of course, you're still creating a narrator that isn't totally you. Still, there are limits. For instance, I don't think the unreliable narrator exists.

William H. Coles
You mean in nonfiction?

Rebecca McClanahan
Yes.

William H. Coles
But you do believe there is an unreliable narrator in fiction?

Rebecca McClanahan
Yes. Of course.

William H. Coles
Because that's a useful tool in fiction?

Rebecca McClanahan
Right. That's why it bothers me a great deal when I open a literary journal and the table of contents doesn't distinguish between nonfiction and fiction, but just says "prose." Because as a reader, I have a whole different expectation when I know the life is directly connected to the story. And I keep thinking, what if I open one of these journals one day, one of these journals that doesn't distinguish between fiction and nonfiction, and the first sentence is, "The night I murdered my four daughters, the moon outside . . ." I would think, "Wait a minute! I want to know that this is fiction." It's very important to me in nonfiction and essay to remain as close to the actual truth, the authentic happenings, as possible. I know, for instance, that to readers of my essay "Back" in *Gettysburg Review*, it is important that I did not invent my cancer diagnosis and surgery. It's an

important responsibility for nonfiction writers to know and to acknowledge that readers enter a text differently when they believe the facts of the life represented. Joe Mackall talks about this in the introduction to the very first issue of *River Teeth*, which is one of the finest magazines of nonfiction.

William H. Coles
The impact on the reader is different?

Rebecca McClanahan
It is.

William H. Coles
Is the entertainment value different between fiction and nonfiction?

Rebecca McClanahan
Oh, Lord.

William H. Coles
Either the quality or the intensity of the entertainment for you?

Rebecca McClanahan
You know, I've never thought of literature as entertainment. Maybe it is. Well, of course it is, but I've never thought about that. You mean am I more *engaged* if I know there is a life behind it?

William H. Coles
It would seem so. From what you say.

Rebecca McClanahan
Not always. Actually, I'm really tired of memoir right now, and I have been for about five years. "Me-moirs" I call some of them. There are so few that are done well. So, no, I don't think it's the life standing behind the writing that makes it engaging. It's all in how it's told.

William H. Coles
Now, in fiction, the engagement of the reader is, at least, dependent on the choice of the narrator, don't you believe?

Rebecca McClanahan
Oh, yes.

William H. Coles
There's a way to think of fiction as author creates, narrator tells, and character acts, and you can develop conflict, movement, irony, and emotional involvement among these effectively. But it seems from our discussion that a reader tends to be more moved by nonfiction than fiction.

Rebecca McClanahan
No, I don't think just because it's nonfiction that it's more moving or life engaging. I'm just saying we have different expectations when we read different genres. And what really bothers me is when I feel that a memoirist is not being as authentic as possible. Then I begin to question their motives. It makes me sad when people feel they need to invent an important life and call it theirs. Rainer Maria Rilke talks about this problem in *Letters to a Young Poet*. I'm paraphrasing here, but he tells the poet, "Don't blame your life, blame your paucity of imagination, blame your own lack of attention." I guess I love nonfiction because I love the smell of real oranges, real people, the special spot on the back of babies' necks. An incredibly interesting world is in front of our noses, but most people do not value their own experience, don't really feel that there are deep wells of meaning to be found in their own lives. What's important is the level of attention that you give to the smallest things.

William H. Coles
Writers have descriptive skills to describe the concrete—you've written about description—but how do writers effectively write about abstractions? Those abstractions that are so important to us but so unfocused that when a writer tries to deal with them, things get boring and the pages don't get turned.

Rebecca McClanahan
I think it was Eudora Welty who said that you can't create emotion with emotion, it must be embodied. No, it was Flannery O'Connor. But I think embodiment is the way to create emotion.

William H. Coles
So, we don't talk about anger. We show anger.

Rebecca McClanahan
Well, of course. You could show it by a character's action. Or you could hook it to an image or a metaphor to make someone feel what the anger is like. I'm not a believer in placing metaphor or simile; I think true metaphor arises naturally in the scene and in the experience of the emotion that comes to you. I'm not against using abstractions; they just have to be grounded. Unless, of course,

you're writing a text that wants only to engage what I call the SAT brain. But if you really want to make the reader's blood boil—or to break the reader's heart—it has to be with a little gesture. An embodied emotion. It's the small things that break our hearts.

William H. Coles
In some ways, it is almost a prison for the writing. If you want to deal with abstractions like infinity, gravity, morality, divinity, you've got to be able to express those with concrete, not abstract writing. Do you agree?

Rebecca McClanahan
Right.

William H. Coles
The simile and the metaphor seem to be an area where inexperienced and untalented writers become clever and cute when dealing with abstractions, and the quality of the metaphors seems to be lost more easily.

Rebecca McClanahan
Again! I believe that metaphor lives and breathes very naturally in every life, every culture. Our language is filled with metaphor.

William H. Coles
We make decisions based on metaphor.

Rebecca McClanahan
Yes. Politicians use metaphor, usually poorly. Ministers and teachers use it. A lot of metaphors are embedded in verbs.

William H. Coles
You do a lot of teaching. You teach in an MFA program.

Rebecca McClanahan
Two of them.

William H. Coles
And you teach in workshops. Based on your experience, are there ways for new writers to avoid the traditional submit-a-manuscript/critique-the-manuscript style of teaching? This, for many, results in nonexperts making possibly unhelpful suggestions. Students come away with manuscript adjustments but not really tools for how to write. There must another way.

Rebecca McClanahan
Well, I can talk about what I think makes a good workshop—or ways that writers can learn to feed themselves and their writing. First of all, as you already know: read, read, read, read, read. We are what we read. I'm astounded at how many people take writing workshops yet never read. I'll say, "What are the last three nonfiction books you've read?" "I don't really like to be influenced," they'll reply. But reading is freeing, liberating. It frees you to see all the multiple structures writers employ. In workshops that I lead, I'm not interested in fixing. Workshops can be dangerous, even when they are very positive, because what we are trying to do quite often is fix something. Even if everyone loves your work, your readers in workshops are trying to come to a consensus, or a committee agreement, for the story.

William H. Coles
Whether it's good or bad?

Rebecca McClanahan
That's right. So, following that model, the best way to help is to boil something down to its least interesting, least troublesome component. But usually the trouble spots are the doors into the better story, the more interesting story. Workshops traditionally want to pare down and fix where the trouble spot is, remove the apparent problem.

William H. Coles
They are fixing symptoms, when what's actually called for are structural changes. Would that be fair?

Rebecca McClanahan
What you're looking for in your respondents is description. You want people to describe to you what happened to them when they read your piece. Where did they get lost? What does the work remind them of? What is the next place it might go? Not "You misspelled buses," or "This just didn't do it for me." How is that supposed to help the writer?

William H. Coles
Are there how-to books that you recommend?

Rebecca McClanahan
Yes. I have several book lists on my website. There are PDFs that people can download.

William H. Coles
Tell me about the website. Why should you have a website? What are the goals? How do you do it? What are your expectations?

Rebecca McClanahan
I didn't have one for a long, long time. But I also didn't have email for years. So I may be the wrong person to ask. But I do think that it can be a good communication tool—for my students and for others who might want to sample my work or the work of other writers. It just makes it easier for people to contact you. Recently we added audio to my site. There are many people out there in communities where I might never do a reading, so this is a way they can hear the voice of the author. Which is important in poetry, at least.

William H. Coles
Do you recommend professional design for your websites?

Rebecca McClanahan
I don't know.

William H. Coles
Did you do your own?

Rebecca McClanahan
No. My husband's a webmaster.

William H. Coles
So, you do recommend someone.

Rebecca McClanahan
I'm sleeping with my web designer. [*laughs*] I'm lucky that way.

William H. Coles
As a serious, accomplished writer in so many genres, how has the influence of commercialism affected you? How do you maintain a quest for quality in a market that demands the predictable? How do you keep to writing art rather than what will sell?

Rebecca McClanahan
Which circle of hell do you want to talk about? I've been through all of them. If you go on my website, you'll see the article I posted about fear, rejection, and persistence in the writer's life. It's the page with the broken pencil! I've been

writing seriously for more than thirty years and every several years I want to pull the plug on it. I'll be an interior designer; I'm going to work in a bakery; I'm going to go back to teaching children. And then something happens. There will be a little note from a lady out in Nebraska who read something I wrote and made fourteen copies for all her grandchildren. Breaking copyright laws, of course, but who cares? Little things like that keep you hanging on. But yes, the market is extremely difficult. And it isn't just difficult for us as writers; it's difficult for the agents, and for the editors, most of whom got into their job for their love of literary work.

William H. Coles
For quality.

Rebecca McClanahan
Yes. Right now, on my desk I have a stack of letters praising a particular manuscript and in the same breath saying sorry we can't publish it. There is no market. It's just the way it is. But I think good work does get out there, eventually. And when it does, we writers need to read it, to support it. We are part of the literary community. Of course, you can't subscribe to every magazine where you hope your work might appear, but you can do your best.

William H. Coles
When I was traveling recently, I picked up a copy of *Wuthering Heights* to enjoy. I realized that if Emily Brontë were alive today, she would have no chance of publishing this piece of quality writing.

Rebecca McClanahan
We should all aspire to be posthumous writers.

William H. Coles
I'd like to thank you very much for this interview for www.storyinliteraryfiction.com. It's been a great pleasure and I've learned a lot.

Rebecca McClanahan
Thank you.

Josh Neufeld and Sari Wilson Interview

August, 2012
William H. Coles

Sari Wilson is an author and editor. She attended Oberlin College and was a Patricia Rowe Willrich fellow in Stanford University's Wallace Stegner Creative Writing Program. Her fiction has appeared in *Slice, Agni, Third Coast, Shankpainter*, and others. She is married to Josh Neufeld.

Josh Neufeld is an alternative cartoonist, author of the widely acclaimed *A.D.: New Orleans after the Deluge* (Panthean, 2010), and illustrator of *The Influencing Machine: Brooke Gladstone on the Media* (Norton, 2012). He was a longtime artist for Harvey Pekar's series of autobiographical comic books *American Splendor*. He is a graduate of Oberlin College and recipient of the Knight-Wallace Fellowship 2012–13 at the University of Michigan. He is married to Sari Wilson.

William H. Coles
I'd like to start by asking each of you about your basic concept of a story. As writers and as artists, how do you define story in your respective disciplines?

Sari Wilson
:It's a great question, and I don't know that I have a great answer. It's a conversation I've been having with myself as a writer. You know, in the Aristotelian method a story is a very formulaic concept, with a three-act structure and a protagonist, an antagonist. Those are all useful ways of thinking about story. But I'm not rigid in my own conception of what a story is. I have tried in my prose to be as minimal as possible, to create a story with as few of those elements as I can, so for example just an image and a character. And I've come to the conclusion that you do need more of those traditional elements than I would have hoped or even thought. For a while I tried to adhere to the Joycean concept of a story—one that is character-based and culminates in an epiphanic moment. I still find it one of the most powerful forms. My own attempts with it have been largely frustrating; it's harder to pull off than it looks.

All of this means I personally have turned more and more to traditional elements of storytelling that have been with us throughout the world's cultural development—you know, a climax, conflict, an antagonist, a protagonist. Not to say that I adopt all of those, but I refer more and more to them. I think there's something very primal about a story, deeply embedded in our unconscious, its elements handed down to us from our forebears.

William H. Coles
So you see story as a structured thing that progresses, things happen, and purpose matters?

Sari Wilson
And the purpose, it's truly cathartic. I think storytelling provides both personal and cultural catharsis.

William H. Coles
It's therapeutic . . . and the receiver of the catharsis is the author? Or do you think in a fictional way, an author is creating a cathartic response that is not particularly his or her own?

Sari Wilson
I do.

William H. Coles
Josh, is that the way an artist thinks about story?

Josh Neufeld
I'm a cartoonist, so I'm not an artist solely, but a storyteller who uses art in similar ways—a narrator as opposed to a single image that you draw inferences from and have an emotional response to. I know that's not necessarily a story, but it may be cathartic or educational. But that's what I love about this woman, Sari. She's thought so much more deeply what it is that we do. I've been lucky to have her by my side and have learned through osmosis over the years. So much of what we're speaking of, she's spent a lot of time studying. And I've gotten the easy bits from her and simplistically kind of put them together.

Sari Wilson
Maybe you don't articulate things in a theoretical way, but you've worked very hard to explore how a story works in visuals and narrative.

William H. Coles
Something you said in class, which I thought was fascinating, was about the Marvel comics in the 1960s when everything was starting out. Those comics

were such simplistic stories. The art was applied, and then the writer would come fill in the story with the script. The stories were simplistic in that there would be, say, a disaster coming—a meteor headed toward Earth—and Superman takes the Eiffel Tower and jabs the meteor and everything is okay, the threat obliterated. They were illustrated in a pleasing way. But what audience did those stories appeal to, and is that audience still available? If so, do they still respond to that basic story element? I'm interested in how basic stories illustrated in graphics have evolved.

Josh Neufeld
I'm not a reader of those superhero comics anymore, but I don't want to sell them too short because I understand what Stan Lee and Jack Kirby were doing back in the 1960s, what made the work so fresh and such instantaneous hits and a whole new way of doing superhero comics compared to other comics, particularly DC. Those had become incredibly formulaic and were seen as just for kids. Those early Marvel comics combined the intimate experiences of everyday people, real people living in the real world, with cosmic, cataclysmic, melodramatic events of superhero worlds. Peter Parker as Spider-Man is not like Superman who lives in this made-up city and has a middle-class job, and we never even think about his job much. Spider-Man's a working-class kid in Queens who struggles with getting dates. After an event he becomes a superhero, but he still has all these troubles and anxieties and a lot of emotional conflicts. There was a complexity and a connection with people's own experiences as teenagers, and maybe even kids in college, that was much deeper than in DC's work, which was made for eight- to ten-year-old kids.

William H. Coles
There was an element of soap opera, too, wasn't there? In which the reader would wonder what's going to happen in the next episode?

Josh Neufeld
Very much so.

William H. Coles
But that venue seems to be going away or getting lost in a sense. I mean, you don't have people waiting weekly for superheroes anymore.

Josh Neufeld
People are still making lots of comics and people are still buying them avidly. As you know, the delivery system is changing. Because of the crisis of print and publishing, the superhero publishers are trying to find ways to use digital

delivery—iPad comics and stuff. But there's still a lot of interest in those magazine-style, cliffhanger-oriented, superhero fantasy comics. And look at all the movies that come out every summer based on superhero comic characters. So clearly those stories with that kind of escapism still have an audience.

I went through a period where I started seeing those stories as fascist fantasies or power fantasies of powerless children. This identification with characters who can do anything, break any bond, resist anybody telling them what to do, and act out simplistically . . . just make these decisions about good and evil. That was when I started to lose interest in that form of storytelling, in terms of the kinds of stories that I wanted to tell. I got much more connected to telling stories about real life.

William H. Coles
You are now delivering stories in the areas of journalism and creative nonfiction. Your work on New Orleans, *A.D.: New Orleans after the Deluge*, is admirable. I've lived in New Orleans for a number of years. Your graphic novel was very moving for me. How do you make it so moving when everybody knows what happened with Katrina?

Josh Neufeld
It's funny, but it took readers telling me what was working for me to be able to articulate it. I couldn't have told you when I was making it, "Oh, I'm doing this because I think through comics I'll be able to connect you on a more intimate level to these people's experiences and somehow it will ring truer or have more resonance than any other way that you've seen that same story." I just did it because I'm a storyteller who works in comics. And I had a personal reaction to Katrina. I volunteered at the Red Cross and was very connected to that experience, and then got the opportunity to tell the story with selected group of New Orleanians who lived through the storm. It was exactly the right project for me. I knew it and didn't even analyze it for a second. It was obviously a thing to be done. Once the publication was online and the responses started to come in, I began to understand that there is something about this form that connects us all on an intimate level.

William H. Coles
Does it have to do with the pacing? I've learned from you that comics require different pacing than prose. And also compared to film, in the way that you have to slow down. Does that slower pacing allow you to get across certain points that have a little more depth in terms of characterization and meaning?

Josh Neufeld
Maybe. When I thought about giving the story structure, I chose the moments that resonated the most with me when I talked to the subjects and heard each person's story. I started thinking, what were the parts that I was going to make into comics? I knew which ones were going to work in that form the best, that would be most powerful.

And yes, I mean, if you look at *A.D.*, it's a lot of short scenes and then edits to other short scenes with a lot of inferred things that happen. In between those, you fill it in yourself. And that keeps the reader engaged and at the same time gives you a lot of information, visually and character-wise, that you maybe aren't even realizing you're getting until the whole thing is over.

William H. Coles
What is a graphic novel? What's the definition?

Sari Wilson
Long-form narrative sequential art.

William H. Coles
Is there such a thing as a graphic memoir? Or graphic creative nonfiction?

Sari Wilson
There should be. The publishing world doesn't have those terms yet because the graphic novel is still a new form for them. So they just lump all the forms under one term to separate it from comics. That term "comics" has certain connotations that the book publishing industry wants to get away from. So, "graphic novel," for whatever reason, has kind of stuck. If the form continues to grow, it hopefully will acquire more subgenres because not everything is a graphic novel. As you say, there is graphic creative nonfiction, graphic memoir.

William H. Coles
I'm particularly impressed with Alison Bechdel, a graphic artist who creates work about her life with a father who is a pedophile and an undertaker and she's a lesbian. Much of her work seems to be pure memoir . . . but it seems to me in the comic form it tends to slide toward sentimentality. However, in your journalistic approach, sentimentality is not a major problem. You're pretty close to reality, objectively told, the whole way.

Josh Neufeld
What's your definition of sentimentality?

William H. Coles
Essentially, the an author or creator asking a reader for emotions that are not earned on the page.

Josh Neufeld
Right. But there are ways to undercut that. I think you're right that it's a risk, you know, anytime. It can be so intimate and so easy to tell all those subjective stories so close to the protagonist that it's easy to slide into some sentimentality. Well, I think that my work with Harvey Pekar and *American Splendor*, which I really recommend, is that it taught me so much about *not* doing that. Pekar is an expert at telling stories from his point of view that continuously undercut any movement toward sentimentalism. It's hard to figure out how he does it because he structures his stories so differently than most people. They don't follow a three-act structure most of the time.

Also, like I said, I've gleaned so much from being around Sari and her writing, her drawings, her short stories, her novels, and her avoidance of sentimentality. So I try hard to avoid it as well. But there are still moments where you can't be afraid of sentiment. There's a big distinction between sentimentality and sentiment.

William H. Coles
A huge distinction, yes. Sentiment is so valuable for any artist to cultivate.

Josh Neufeld
In a project I did recently about Bahrain, there's a character who was at a political demonstration that suddenly turned violent and the police cracked down and killed a bunch of people, including one of his best friends. When I got to the point where that was revealed to the reader, they saw the character crying. I hoped I had earned that moment, and I wasn't going to shy away from it.

William H. Coles
Sari, let's talk about your concept of narration in stories. As a novelist and short-story writer, you have a certain limitation in narration—first person or third person—that is not as critical as in the comics. For example, in a short story or a novel told in first person, you've got limited distance and you can tell only what is in the perception of the first person. It's true, in third person you can bring in such a wider story view and provide a breadth of information. But, it seems, this is restricted when compared to comics.

Sari Wilson
Are you asking about the graphic form?

William H. Coles
Not specifically. I'm asking how a writer's concept of narration in the first-person and the third-person point of view are related to graphic illustration with prose. As we were working on our graphic novels this week, some issues emerged regarding how the narrator was going to speak about this or that, and if first person or a narrator should be used. It leads me to wonder how you conceive, from your writer's view, narration, point of view, and voice in the graphic novel as opposed to prose.

Sari Wilson
A couple things. The limitation of the story format of comics compared to the prose perspective is that you need to be very strict with yourself as a writer about what absolutely needs to be there and what can't be shown visually. If there's something that can be shown rather than told, and we talked about this a little bit, it's taking the show-versus-tell maxim to another level; it's extending it if you're using caption boxes to accompany an image.

As an example let's take the *Playboy* comic we did, which is actually first person, so maybe in some ways it's a good example. It's a limited point of view. We never get outside the point of view of that character. If we have a woman walking through the lobby of *Playboy* magazine, do we say, "I walked through the lobby of Playboy magazine?" You could, and maybe there would be a reason for that, but I can't think of one right now. Generally you wouldn't—you're going to use that small amount of caption-box real estate for something that will add to the reader's experience of that moment.

So: so far we've got the visual information, a woman walking through the lobby of *Playboy* magazine, we have a Playboy bunny, we have the images on the wall, we have a kind of streamlined shiny magazine. What can I, as a writer, add to this moment? Because in this case I'm writing in the first person, and I'm also filtering it through the point of view of this narrator, which is a very limited point of view. I'm trying to get into the head of that woman in her mid-twenties and convey that experience of what young feminists think, so there's that layer. The next image is her walking by a bulletin board with a breast cancer awareness poster. In that case, I thought okay, it was surprising from her perspective.

So, I'm in her perspective and to the extent that the story works—and I'm not sure it does, it was an experiment—we're in her head and we're experiencing this world or this environment through a young feminist's eyes. We're sympathetic to her, but I guess I didn't want it to just be that. To go off on a tangent for a moment, there is a problem with the form in that writers and comics tend to think, okay, if you're in a point of view you have to stay there, and that doesn't make for interesting comics. I wanted, and this is something that is done better in prose, to have a kind of omniscience as well as a point-of-view character.

Anton Chekhov does this beautifully, right? You're in a character's point of view, but you also have the space to allow the reader in. You don't see it done that often in comics. Maybe that's the literary quality I do feel in Alison Bechdel's *Fun Home*, which is first person at times. Does this make sense?

William H. Coles
Absolutely, and it's exactly what I was looking for in the sense that there do seem to be different problems. The prose writer can learn from the graphic arts in the sense that the graphic artist always has to have the scene in mind. I mean, there's a panel that has to have the appropriate point of view. If we have to be looking through that "I" person at the right door, at the right painting on the wall, and so forth. And it has to be consistent, of course, if you're going to stay in that point of view from panel to panel. But you have a lot of flexibility in prose writing because the visualization is not quite as stringent.

Sari Wilson
Which can be a problem, right? Because as a prose writer, you can get lost. You have so many choices, especially with point of view and moving in and out to view, that it's hard to limit yourself. It feels constricting yet also ultimately necessary for a successful story.

William H. Coles
And if you're not successful, then you begin to lose credibility. You lose a meaningful impact on readers who are now thinking, "Well, that couldn't happen." I'd like to talk about the techniques that you teach in your graphic novel course. I think they're almost more important from the prose writer's standpoint than from the graphic artist's in the sense that there's so much to be learned about how you bring the prose into visualization. Prose writers should spend so much more time on visualization than they do; they need to have a mental, visual process going to maintain credibility, to maintain point of view, to ensure they don't say something that could not possibly happen. I worry that fiction writers don't care much anymore about those sort of details.

Take for instance *Little Red Riding Hood*, a common story. Red is going to Grandma's house and her mother says, "Don't talk to anyone. Go straight to Grandma's house. Don't dilly dally, the woods are dangerous." Red goes running off and soon comes upon a wolf. She says, "Hi, Mr. Wolf." Mr. Wolf says, "Oh,

The ART of CREATING STORY

you're such a cute little girl. Where are you going?" And she says, "Okay, I'm not supposed to tell but you're so friendly. I'm going to Grandma's house." The wolf says, "Ha, ha," and runs off to devour Grandma and disguise himself so when Red arrives he sweet-talks her into grandma's bed and devours her too. This story has basic themes: Don't talk to strangers. Don't disobey your mother. Don't be naive about the world. How would you two, working in collaboration, begin to work through this story? I suspect the first thing would be to write the story as I've sort of outlined it. What's next?

Josh Neufeld
Actually, our first step would be to talk about it in the way you just did—meaning, characterize, articulate the themes, outline the morality underlying the events. The last thing I'd do would be to draw a little girl and a wolf because it's been done a million times and it just wouldn't be interesting to me to do it yet again, whether in comic form or any other form. I would want to find what the key exegesis of the story is, and the characters and their counterpoint to each other, and then try to find some interesting, layered way to bring it to life in comics.

William H. Coles
As you look for these themes, is that how you underline or outline where the "beats" are, as you put it?

Sari Wilson
Yes, Josh is getting at the a brainstorming part of our process.

Josh Neufeld
Before we even start with a script or anything, we figure out what the actual story is. Is it compelling enough for us to spend the time to make the comic?

Sari Wilson
Then I'd go and write out the story in prose form. Then we would look at the prose and break it down into beats. Beats are visually potent moments of action or significance.

William H. Coles
Are they always action moments?

Sari Wilson
No, and that's a new thought I took away from our workshop. I usually think of them as action moments and traditionally, like in superhero comics, they would be action moments. But I think your story is a perfect example of sectioning

out beats that could be moments of silence. Ultimately you're looking for the narrative through-line. Another way of getting at that could be visual beats. If you were to break down this story in its most elemental way, what moments will you need to show?

Josh Neufeld
So, Sari, if we started with a shot of the cottage that the girl and her mother live in, we'd come into the cottage and have a two-shot of the mother and the daughter together, setting up the scene, and then maybe a shot of the mother telling Red, "Don't do this, don't do that." The daughter's reaction is a reaction shot. Then we'd have a shot of Red leaving the house—either walking out the front door or we'd see the house in a distance.

Sari Wilson
A couple shots of it.

Josh Neufeld
Okay, and then there'd be probably a shot of this scary-looking forest with the path going into it. She continues on and then maybe there's some choices of whether to go on and off the path or not. She sees a beautiful little glen off the path filled with butterflies and flowers.

Sari Wilson
Could we do the wolf's point of view?

Josh Neufeld
I was thinking that we would get her to that glen . . .

Sari Wilson
. . . now outside her point of view . . .

Josh Neufeld
. . . and then, once she's there we'd have some shots of her playing and beautiful moments of a butterfly, or clouds . . .

Sari Wilson
She gets distracted. That's a key moment.

William H. Coles
That's an advantage of drama in comics. In prose you can't just jump to the wolf entrance without setting the scene.

The ART of CREATING STORY

Sari Wilson
No, but you could get more distance. You could come out of a close third into a more distant third.

William H. Coles
Or you could use a narrator. But going to the wolf's point of view would be easy in a comic; nobody would even blink twice. I mean, it would be great. So that's an advantage of graphic novel presentation. Give us a couple more.

Josh Neufeld
So, then from the wolf's point of view we see the girl in that glen, but it's framed by dark grass and leaves all the way around, so we know that he's hidden in the depth of the forest. Then maybe another few shots of her gleefully playing and then . . . looking up . . . we see the wolf actually enter . . .

Sari Wilson
. . . she senses something before we even see it.

Josh Neufeld
Yeah, but maybe she doesn't look scared . . .

Sari Wilson
Right.

Josh Neufeld
. . . even though we know she *should* be scared.

Sari Wilson
Well, that's one of the themes. Innocence. And then you have the dialogue. With the dialogue, you'd switch points of view. Or you'd have both of them in one shot and then you'd have the wolf's face, Red's face, wolf's face, Red's face.

Josh Neufeld
I would want to think about when to introduce the Grandmother as a character.

Sari Wilson
Sooner?

Josh Neufeld
Do we reveal the horror of her being killed by the wolf, or do we keep it more secret and don't let the audience see the wolf actually kill the Grandmother?

William H. Coles
Comics can use flashback, right? Could you go back to pre-story present and have an interaction between Red and the grandmother then come back?

Sari Wilson
. . . anticipating . . .

William H. Coles
. . . therefore, you've established the Grandmother Red loves and I'm so sorry that she got killed.

Josh Neufeld
Yes.

Sari Wilson
I just feel like flashback is a little cheesy in comics. It has to be truly earned. It's such a frequently used approach that it's almost a cliché. I mean, as in prose, flashbacks can be easily misused.

William H. Coles
I think they're way overused in all genres.

Sari Wilson
So you need to be strict with yourself about whether there's honestly no other way to get the information in.

William H. Coles
We've at least got her through the forest, and assuming that we continue this process all the way to the final gory end. What's the next step?

Sari Wilson
When I do beats, I usually do them quickly. I might give myself ten minutes. That's the virtue of the beat process for me and I do use this beats thing for prose now. In fact, when I sit down to work on a scene, I'll say, "Okay, where are the key elements, like visual moments, that I want to depict?" I'm giving myself five minutes because I don't want to think too much. If you start thinking, then you're off somewhere. And then, I list them: Ch, ch, ch, ch, ch. Five things. I

The ART of CREATING STORY

mean, we're really breaking it down. It could be: Red with her mother, Red walking the forest, Red meeting the wolf, Red in the Grandmother's cottage.

That is the artful craft of writing in the comics format for me, which is similar to writing a screenplay. And that is using the script format, which we've talked about. So, a panel each page, okay, thinking about what is a page. I would start with the description of the panel, in prose format but visualized. And then, whether there's dialogue or captioned sound effects. All the way through the script. That takes a lot of time. Maybe a week.

William H. Coles
Do you do that together or alone?

Sari Wilson
If I'm writing and he's illustrating, I do it, and then he will read the draft and give feedback. Then I'll go back and revise, through four or five drafts. Then he begins to draft out.

William H. Coles
I noticed that you were thinking in terms of where you were placing people in scenes visually, and you're placing them in the prose-process theme sense, too. It would seem the combination of that is valuable. Prose writers work in isolation and they never seem to talk or think about visualizing what's going to happen in their story and what the reader's going to think about it.

So, the script comes together and you begin working on sketching the characters—you try to achieve consistency in how Red's going to look, how Grandma's going to look, that sort of thing. And you begin to finalize visualization of the environment. Yet so often, just one detail enables the reader to imagine the rest.

Sari Wilson
My scripts are pretty detailed. Josh likes detailed scripts. And when I've done work for hire, they likewise ask for as much detail as possible. The artist may use it or has the freedom to go off on his or her own. But the artists appreciate a lot of detail.

Josh Neufeld
Especially if it isn't a story you made up yourself, the writer's details help fill in that picture for you, the artist. Sometimes my process is that I end up drawing the most obvious choice of something, or at least the most obvious to me, but

it doesn't have some essential thing that makes it feel real, unique, and fully imagined. Sari's scripts often have some little detail that I never would've thought of that really sells what we're trying to do with the story. Other times, something about her suggestion might strike me as wrong, so I ignore it and go with my own impulse. I love that part of the collaborative process.

The other trick is seeing if the way Sari imagined breaking the story down into pages, and how many panels are on a page, works with the way I'm seeing it. Even when I write my own scripts, when I'm writing with my "writer hat" on, I'm imagining these images but not thinking too carefully about the way the panels work together and fit on a page. And when I put on my "artist hat" and I start to draw the script, I'll see that a certain panel needs to be very large, or even fit all the way across the page, or go from the top of the page to the bottom. If that doesn't jibe with the way it was paneled out in the script, then I need to rethink things. Maybe blow a page up from one to two pages, combine two panels, or add a third panel—a beat of silence or a reaction or something. That's a fun part because it's intuitive, rather than the laborious, craft-oriented part of the work.

William H. Coles
So at this point, you're thinking about what's going to be said in prose?

Josh Neufeld
She's already written it in the script.

William H. Coles
But when you go to put the words in, do you ever edit that prose?

Sari Wilson
He's very faithful to the script.

Josh Neufeld
Actually, I do sometimes change the words. I sometimes find when translating the script to the final art that a dialogue balloon is too long, or is redundant because the words are already expressed in the art. Captions often get cut. The descriptive, narrative, omniscient narration stuff—you find you can cut it as you get to the final stage. But dialogue balloons and speech between characters is so important in some stories. Sometimes you realize, wow, we really need a line of dialogue here. Or maybe you see an opportunity to give a little more humanity, a little more idiosyncrasy.

Sari Wilson
I didn't know that.

Josh Neufeld
I'm working on a story right now with a journalist where a lot of the scenes had to be imagined, re-created in a sense, to tell the story because the action wasn't clear enough or you didn't get to sit long enough with each thing to comprehend what was happening. We needed dialogue to slow the reading experience down and hit some of the points hard enough. And to help create character. Sari actually came in and has been working with the writer, who's a good friend of ours, to fill some of these scenes up a little more with dialogue. The woman who wrote the story, it's her first time writing a comic. She was surprised. She said, "Oh, I thought that when you write comics you're always taking away writing." But not necessarily.

Sari Wilson
That's true, and in that way, it's like a . . .

Josh Neufeld
. . . a silent movie.

Sari Wilson
A play, it's like a play.

William H. Coles
But the neat thing about the dialogue in comics is that you don't always need exposition. You know writers who try to slip exposition into their dialogue. It usually doesn't work. But as a cartoonist, you don't need that. You've got everything you need on the page, even feelings and internal thoughts.

Josh Neufeld
Exactly.

William H. Coles
This has been great. Thank you both for talking about creating comics and your process. This is of great value to the prose writer/storyteller who seeks expanded ways to think about story. It's been a pleasure talking to you.

Josh Neufeld
Thank you.

Richard North Patterson Interview

8 June, 2014
William H. Coles

Richard North Patterson graduated college from Ohio Wesleyan University and law school from Case Western Reserve University. He studied fiction with Jesse Hill Ford at the University of Alabama Birmingham. He's received the Edgar Award for Best First Novel and the Grand Prix de Littérature Policière. Sixteen of his novels have been *New York Times* best-sellers. He was assistant attorney general for the state of Ohio, a trial attorney for the Securities and Exchange Commission, and the SEC's liaison to the Watergate special prosecutor. He retired from the law in 1993 and turned to writing fiction full time.

William H. Coles
You changed careers from lawyer to author. Who were the authors you admired? I know Leo Tolstoy is one of your favorites.

Richard North Patterson
Yes. But one doesn't claim to be influenced by Tolstoy unless they have delusions of grandeur.

William H. Coles
[*laughing*] I see.

Richard North Patterson
I was inspired by Tolstoy. Allen Drury, who wrote *Advise and Consent*, the Pulitzer Prize–winning political novel, was an inspiration to me. He wrote, at least in that book, credible authentic fiction with convincing characters in a very complicated, treacherous, fascinating world—a world of presidential politics surrounding the confirmation of a secretary of state. As I got on in writing, I took that as a model for some of the things I wanted to achieve. I wrote a book about social problems that portrayed broad social and political contexts like the death penalty, or the Supreme Court, but I also tried to give the characters an intimacy that engaged the reader in a reality. I did a lot of research to be sure it was authentic.

In terms of how I got started writing, for an example that perhaps made me feel I could do it, I have to go back to Ross Macdonald, who wrote something like eighteen Lew Archer detective novels. McDonald was a very erudite man. The novels are psychologically sophisticated. As I looked at the Archer novels—I read more than a dozen in a row without yet thinking I was going to write—I realized I assimilated some of what Macdonald did. He wrote a very clean sentence. He had a psychological interest in his characters. But there were two things that were really a help to an aspiring writer who had never written a novel before. He wrote in the first person. That simplifies the narrative considerably. You're always in the same person in the same voice and moving forward in time. It's very linear. And that's the other thing: a mystery novel by its nature has a plot. It has a beginning, middle, and end. It's wonderful to surprise your readers but it's a sin to surprise yourself. From Macdonald I learned the ending resonates back to the beginning, not only in coherence of narrative, but also in psychological consistency of characters. So you don't have a character behaving randomly; you end up the novel so the reader can figure it out. That was really the jungle gym that gave me a purchase on the messy business of writing novels.

Obviously, I soon quit writing mysteries and by now I've written novels with all sorts of points of view, in all sorts of different settings, and all sorts of different characters. But without the example of Macdonald and his novels, I don't know that I ever would have written.

William H. Coles
You're admired for your research, and I'm interested in that process. You're dedicated to that process. Yet you write such imaginative fiction. How do you bring together the points of knowledge that you want to use, and how do you use them? In fiction, imagination allows you to create certain ideas to support the story and characterization; you're carrying in realism.

Richard North Patterson
First of all, I think writing is like method acting. In order to do it well you have to believe in your characters and the world you're inhabiting. The way to do that, if you don't know about a world, is to find out about it until you really feel comfortable with it. The second thing is that I believe readers are sophisticated people, and whether or not they know about the world you're writing about, they know intuitively whether *you* do or don't. The third thing is that if you're writing about something like the death penalty, it's not just for kicks; you have a serious obligation to get it right and inform the reader. I don't mean to compare myself to Upton Sinclair or Émile Zola, but the idea of presenting a socially significant context realistically and responsibly was always important to me.

One of my favorite examples of this—and there are all sorts—is my novel *Protect and Defend*, which in a way was my homage to *Advise and Consent*. *Protect and Defend* involves a newly elected young president who nominates the first woman chief justice of the Supreme Court, whose nomination is quickly ensnared by a very difficult abortion rights case that she can't duck, one that involves issues of parental consent and so-called partial-birth abortion, which is, of course, a misnomer. I had to do a number of things for that book. I interviewed women who had late-term abortions; I talked to people who were experts in parental consent laws; I talked to pro-choice people and pro-life people.

William H. Coles
And physicians?

Richard North Patterson
Yes. But one of the trickier parts is writing about a president. Fortunately at that time I had a friend who was one—George Bush senior, with whom I spoke. One of my favorite research days was when I went to Washington, it was 1998 or 1999, and sat down with Bob Dole, who was the majority leader. In my research process, I'll send the interviewee a list of questions that occur to me and an outline of the plot so we're not wasting time and they can think in advance about the context. My interview with Bob Dole was complex, but it boiled down to this: If you're the majority leader, and a Democratic president has nominated this pro-choice judge, and you determine the path of right reason is to defeat her, how would you do it? He told me. And it was brilliant. He's a nice guy.

William H. Coles
Funny guy?

Richard North Patterson
Very funny guy. Master of the senate. Among the things he told me was he'd consider filibustering this nomination. (Since he told me that, the filibuster had become routinely used in judicial appointments.) So I'm back in my hotel room in DC dictating notes from my interview with Senator Dole and the phone rings. A woman comes on and says, "This is the White House, the president can see you this evening. Do you have time to come over?" I said, "I imagine I have time for President Clinton." So I did. And I said to him, "Well, Mr. President, if you were going to save this nomination, how would you do it?" Clinton's a genius. We're off to the races. We were designing ads, we were picking out the issues to focus on, we were trading seats on commissions for senatorial votes. He brought out the Ruth Bader Ginsburg file and looked at that nomination. And it was brilliant. I walked out of the White House that evening and figured I

had the coolest job on the planet. That kind of research is necessary for someone who is curious about all sorts of things, and I distilled all that was said and it's all in the book. It's at a level I could never have achieved without the interviews. It's a striking example of discovery.

William H. Coles
A couple of more questions about background. I saw a speech you gave to a group of lawyers where you talked about how being a lawyer helped prepare you for a writing career. You listed a number of skills in litigation (investigation research, narrative, characterization and psychology, writing clear compelling prose) and characteristics of lawyers (curiosity, openness to arguments and new information, intellectual honesty, devotion to decency and the rule of law, protecting rights and the interests of society) that helped you prepare to be an author. A lot of people are changing careers now, especially since as a population we are living longer. Can you extrapolate from all that to speak more generally to aspiring writers with backgrounds not necessarily in the law?

Richard North Patterson
Anyone who is successful is disciplined, and they've figured out how to do their work well. And they take it seriously. They may not feel like doing the work on a particular day, but they do it because that's what you do. That's a habit of mine that translates to writing. To me, one of the worst mistakes is thinking of writing as a mysterious process that awaits inspiration: when the moonlight is right, you'll write something brilliant. To me, writing is work and requires showing up and respecting it. And realizing you have things to learn is important. Second sight is also important; I'm sure as a doctor you thought back to your experiences and tried to think of something better than what you did. I've known authors who wrote 80 percent good enough first drafts and didn't take them any further because they couldn't accept criticism and sit down and do the work. So, any of us who have done the work in one profession in order to succeed have the work ethic if we choose to apply it to writing.

The other thing, of course, is that we all have stories. If you think about the things we've learned about the people in our lives or pressure situations, while you may not be writing about those things exactly, the emotions, the lessons, do translate. So I think there are ways in which any profession can serve the art of writing. The thing about being a lawyer, as I pointed out, was that I wrote a lot for America's most tired and cynical audience: the judges and their law partners. I learned to write clearly and well, and not waste words. I realized my first word was not necessarily my best word. I learned about brevity. I learned that writing was a craft that required work. I also had to arrange a bunch of messy facts into coherent narratives, which is the art of plotting narrative in fiction. I had to know something about the psychology of my client, perhaps the jury, and even the judge. That's the characterization part. People will tell you the damnedest things. And the courtroom is also the focus of some of our great social problems and there is always surprise lurking at hand. It is a very rich venue for fiction writing. I don't know that being a dentist would have been quite as good.

William H. Coles
That may be unfair!

Richard North Patterson
I daresay that some dentists would write great fiction. But I happened to come along at a time when people had a lot of interest in the law.

William H. Coles
You know, when we're talking about the influence of professions, is there something beyond technique and perspective that authors need to identify with? I'm speaking particularly about morality, about attitudes, about metaphysical questions—who are we, why are we here, what makes us human. Is it helpful for authors to consider these mysteries?

Richard North Patterson
Those things are absolutely important to your point of view. They're important to enrich the writing and the characters. Who are your characters, what do your characters want? What do they care about? What code, what expectations of themselves? What drives them? All of those things are very important. I write a lot about family. And I think a great deal about family. In some ways we're always children for all our lives, and we're the product of those things that change us. For good or ill, I'm a parent. I've been a stepparent. You think a lot about how your actions affect other human beings in that context. So yes, I think questions about behavior, duty, morals, and cause and effect are all important. I would not hold myself out to be the moral-majority poster boy by any stretch, but I do consider these things.

William H. Coles
Not to be sentimental, but is the ability to love selflessly as a way of life also important?

Richard North Patterson
I think that's a major element in being a parent. I think about that when I portray relationships in fiction. The thing I've always thought about as a parent

is that my kids are not about me. They're not here to realize my ambitions or reflect my version of glory on me. They're people who are given to me in trust, kind of, by fate. The question is: How can I help them be the best versions of themselves, the best and happiest versions? That necessarily involves loving them independently of your own needs. And parents who fail to do that, fail as parents. That's an important aspect of love, and I portray its presence and its absence, and the effect of that.

William H. Coles
I know you were born in San Francisco, but you have spent a good deal of time in Ohio. How do fiction authors take the settings and societies of their youth and make use of their experiences in specific cultures to write better, or to prevent mistakes in storytelling?

Richard North Patterson
I'll give you a for-instance. I grew up in Bay Village, Ohio, which is a fairly provincial suburb of Cleveland, and there was one big thing that resonated there: whether Sam Sheppard did or did not kill his wife. The way that resonated in that small town struck me and basically became the basis for my novel *Silent Witness*. So very definitely our environment affects what we express as fiction writing. I'm fortunate enough to have lived in all sections of the country at one time or another, and that was very helpful. When I wrote *The Spire* it was an affectionate, fun (although the plot was a bit grim) evocation of Ohio Wesleyan brought forward to a time when I was writing hopefully for a younger demographic than I am now. It made me think back on those days a lot. Fondly, I would say, for the most part. I came back to Ohio Wesleyan to serve on the board for a number of years, gave the commencement speech there. So I have chosen to live other places—in part because I am a great sufferer from seasonal affective disorder so I'm always in pursuit of good weather—but I could say Ohio gave me such things as a legal education, and a better undergraduate education than I deserved at the time, that I have taken profitably into my career.

William H. Coles
How do you see your fan base? Do you perceive a difference in the way men and women interpret your novels? And finally, how do you handle reviews? Do you read them, or do you ignore them? And if you do read them, how do you gain information about how and why you want to write?

Richard North Patterson
I think there are more women than men that read fiction.

William H. Coles
Or read in general.

Richard North Patterson
I would guess the majority of my fans are women, although I can't prove that. I like to think I'm writing for an intelligent audience. A reader once told me that I made her think too much; I somehow couldn't work up the feeling that I should apologize for that. I am disappointed sometimes because of the way I've been marketed, which strikes me as a bit of a reduction of what I actually do, and that people who read me because they know me are actually surprised by how much they like me because the description put forth in marketing the books is more generic and narrow than what I actually do. That's a frustration. In terms of reviews, I read every one I can get my hands on. I have generally been well treated, but not uniformly so . . . no writer is. I am pleased by the good ones, I'm fatalistic about the bad ones.

William H. Coles
That's a good attitude.

Richard North Patterson
I don't know that I learn much that I don't already know from reviews. I learn what people like, I learn what people don't like sometimes. I can say "that's interesting" or I can say "screw you, I wasn't setting out in the first place to write the kind of book you wanted me to write." I've won some awards, which is nice. I remember I was writing a novel and went down to lunch and picked up the mail and there was *Time* magazine with a pretty nasty review of *The Final Judgment* by someone who had given me a pretty good review before. It doesn't make you feel great to read that your protagonist is a stick figure in drag.

William H. Coles
That would destroy me.

Richard North Patterson
I'd had better moments. But you know what? I ate my sandwich; I closed *Time* magazine; and I went back upstairs and just kept on writing. That's what you do about the business of being reviewed. Writing is a public act; hopefully people are reading and noticing what you do. And if you write to be read and noticed, you can't complain when someone reads your work and doesn't like it.

William H. Coles
That's pragmatic. You're often praised for your characterization, and in your works it is easy to see your emphasis on human nature. And in the thriller genre, and mystery.

Richard North Patterson
I really resist "thriller suspense." To me, I'm a novelist. There may be elements of suspense or whatever, I may write fiction with a narrative and a plot, but I try to infuse in my work the sense of any good novel, which is to say a sense of psychological realism, of character, of well-rendered setting, of a narrative that makes sense, of subjects who are important in readers' individual lives, but also of social importance. Frankly, it drives me crazy when people try to put me in a genre. Truth is, I've written all sorts of things. I've written geopolitical novels about the Israeli-Palestinian problems, about transnational terrorism by non-state actors, about the abuse of human rights in Africa. I've written political novels at the presidential level. I've written about the death penalty. I've written courtroom dramas. I've written psychological novels.

The one thing I haven't tried to do is be funny. Although I think there is some humor in my novels, I haven't tried to write a comic novel. The uphill battle, when you're trying to write a number of different things, is you're accused of being overly ambitious or incoherent. Publishers like it when you write basically the same book. And sometimes readers do, too. They like your last book that's a courtroom drama but they don't like your next book that is a psychological novel. I've had people tell me: "You should always write political novels." "You should always write courtroom dramas." You should always write this, you should always write that. Well, I would kill myself if I felt I was writing to a specification. I honor those people who stick to one genre and one protagonist and do it well. Ross Macdonald, whom I learned from, did it. But this is not me.

William H. Coles
Many people express admiration for your dialogue. What are the essentials of dialogue for you? You mentioned trying to be clear and succinct in your prose in general.

Richard North Patterson
I haven't had to think about this as much as I've had to think about other aspects of writing because from the first I could write dialogue. I just could do it. I do tend to write about characters who are pretty smart, and it helps in writing dialogue because they're smart, frequently clever.

William H. Coles
And you don't have to rely on dialect.

Richard North Patterson
No. Dialogue is condensed speech. It is a distillation of how people actually talk. If you listen to people talk and try to diagram the sentences, they're distracted, there's "hmm" and "um," hemming and hawing, dangling clauses and all the rest. What you do is capture the essence of how people talk. Distill it. Compared to the way we generally speak, dialogue is sort of epigrammatic, and yet is recognizable speech. You don't actually think this is the way people talk. But coherence is important.

William H. Coles
Do you think about exposition and dialogue? I ask because I feel that exposition in dialogue sinks the opportunities for good dialogue. And do you revise a lot?

Richard North Patterson
I do try to develop exposition in dialogue. How people might actually learn from each other as opposed to some big concept. It's funny, I could have told you fifteen books ago how I do these things, but it's hard now because it's become second nature. I haven't written a line since Halloween of 2012, so it would be fun to try it. But I expect it would come back easily now.

William H. Coles
Obviously you have a sense of rhythm in dialogue, which seems to me an important aspect. Do you read your dialogue out loud in revision? Or do you try to get your own response to dialogue read by others?

Richard North Patterson
I rarely read aloud. But I can hear it as I write. There is this internal mechanism by which I hear what I am writing and whether it works or not. But I don't literally speak it aloud; it's a voice in my head.

William H. Coles
You've also said you outline a lot. I'd love to know the details of the outline and the process. It seems so important for fiction authors evolving plot and other aspects of their writing.

Richard North Patterson
Well, if I had a book going now, you would see on my desk seventy-five file folders divided into four sections. Those are the scenes or chapters from beginning to

the end of the book. In those are the key elements of what I believe should be in every scene or chapter, and the research notes keyed to that chapter. I didn't start out doing it that way, but as I began to do fiction that was more heavily researched and involved very complicated narratives on subjects that were not native to me but that I had learned about, I realized to control and distill the information and maintain the proper architecture of the book, I had to do it that way. So, every morning I'd get up and there would be a file folder sitting in front of me that represented the work for that day, and I would use that to write the scenes and chapters.

William H. Coles
And you outlined the scenes individually too?

Richard North Patterson
Yes. I might write well or less well that day. But I would never get up and wonder what I was going to do, because I already knew. In a way it demystified the process for me. I don't know any other writer who does it that extensively. I do leave myself room for surprise, and I'll change things around. But when you're writing about something as complicated as the Israeli-Palestinian problem in a very long novel based on a hundred or more interviews, and you have to find a way to make that material work as fiction, for me it requires a high degree of organization.

William H. Coles
If story is a series of interrelated scenes, outlining helps you interrelate the scenes?

Richard North Patterson
Absolutely. What is the relationship between scenes? I think the architecture of a novel is terribly important. Getting the architecture right is as important as the writing itself. I'll give you a for-instance. I generally don't criticize my fellow authors in print but I think Tom Wolfe can take it. He's a greatly talented writer and very successful, so if you ever use this, I doubt it will hurt his feelings . . . he'll probably simply recognize the truth. When I read *Bonfire of the Vanities*, which I love 80 percent of, the whole thing turned to Cliffs Notes in the last 20 percent. The novel became thin, the behavior of the characters became unbelievable, and you sensed the desperation of a cornered man who hadn't thought out his ending, trying to figure out a way to end this book. I read *A Man in Full*, the same thing, *I Am Charlotte Simmons*, the same thing. I later learned that my perception of his process was exactly right. He didn't know how he was going to end his novels—three months before publication, he'd still be trying to

figure it out. Well, here is a brilliantly talented writer with a great story going with all sorts of social realism and all sorts of atmosphere and he isn't doing the one thing that is necessary: take the story from beginning to end. Don't slight any part of the process!

William H. Coles
In that vein, do you outline motivations, emotional arcs, psychological movement for your characters?

Richard North Patterson
Even *Eden in Winter*, which is my novel coming out in mid-July this year, involved very intense interviews with psychiatrists about all sorts of aspects of characters, two principally, a man and a woman who have a very complicated, very fraught romantic attachment, part of it involving that she was formerly the lover of his, we assume, father. That's not only Freudian, it's Oedipal. I spent hours and hours talking to my psychiatrist friends about how this works and about how the characters' childhoods affected them, how they would react in this and that situation. Fabulously rewarding.

William H. Coles
That's what you mean by "drilling down"?

Richard North Patterson
I have scenes of psychotherapy in this book with pretty tough-minded dialogue between protagonist and psychotherapist. If that's been done in fiction, I haven't seen it. To me it was one of the rewarding aspects of the book, and one of the more successful.

William H. Coles
Fiction writers in general deal with show and tell, narrative development, and in-scene creation. You seem to have two goals in writing, an entertainment goal first. But you also have an "inform" goal. And to be able to inform in fiction requires a fair amount of narrative. Do you think about this? I would submit you've been successful at informing through narrative and entertaining through scene. How do you balance the two?

Richard North Patterson
Again, it's very hard for me to distill what I now do because it's second nature. Obviously, at some point in my career, I did think about these things quite explicitly. I just ceased to have to . . . you know . . . the horse knows the way. Let's discuss a Supreme Court nomination—how to get it through, or how to drop it.

A lot of explaining can be done in the normal course of depicting conversations between people who are trying to accomplish one thing or another. They talk about what they're up to and how to accomplish it and it comes across as what would actually happen as opposed to someone giving a speech about all this stuff. I mean, using dialogue between and among characters, as opposed to endless speech or interminable paragraphs just telling the reader something, is the better way to go. I wish I could explain it more clearly. I used to understand, and now I just do it. I don't know that I could teach fiction now. I probably could have fifteen years ago when I had to think about what I was doing. But now I just know what to do, I don't think about it.

William H. Coles
In the outline, do you pay attention strictly to a timeline? Particularly in placing flashbacks?

Richard North Patterson
Oh, yes. I use a lot of flashbacks.

William H. Coles
You do that naturally. You don't lay down a timeline with beginning to end and then situate the flashbacks?

Richard North Patterson
No. I just know where a flashback belongs. I think about it a lot. And I'll move things around.

William H. Coles
A flashback can stop story progress in many ways.

Richard North Patterson
It absolutely can. *No Safe Place*, a political novel of mine, intersperses chunks of current narrative with chunks of past-life childhood. I bring it forth to the present until they merge in a dramatic confluence. At that point you understand the whys and everything he's dealing with. So that actually works. You have to have a fair amount of confidence to do that, which I don't lack. But it worked wonderfully well.

William H. Coles
But you did outline this basically in the initial stages of the story?

Richard North Patterson
Absolutely. That was the plan. To write the novel with that form and that structure was always the plan.

William H. Coles
If I could impose on you to just go along with me for a while, I'd like to see how you'd develop a current political situation into a story. I'd like to see your thoughts about outlining it before you start writing. I'm thinking about Bowe Bergdahl, the soldier who was living imprisoned with the Taliban for five years and for whom Obama has traded five Taliban prisoners at Guantanamo for his freedom. It's an interesting story with a lot of deep societal questions, it seems to me. How would you approach it? From Bowe's point of view? Or would you go from the president's? Would you choose a third-person narrator and use multiple points of view? And what are the essentials that you would find interesting to bring out the societal issues?

Richard North Patterson
Well, in real life I'd think about it longer than the thirty seconds I've been given . . .

William H. Coles
I'm being a little unfair, certainly.

Richard North Patterson
Off the top, I'd start with Bergdahl being court marshaled, which dealt with whether he was derelict in his duties and the whole disappearance, and then go back in time as prisms for his account and the accounts of other people. The protagonist is in one way or another charged with defending him. And so you've got the protagonist's needs, goals, but you also have his or her mission, interviewing lots of people and coming to some sense of how and why it all happened. That would be a way of doing it. And probably effective. Who is this guy? What kind of soldier was he? Why did he disappear? What is our obligation to him, and how does it change depending on whether he was a deserter, gone walkabout, a good soldier . . . all of that? I can understand the resentment of people who felt lives were lost looking for him.

William H. Coles
His comrades.

Richard North Patterson
Yes. As an ironic aside, in *Eden in Winter* there is a section where the protagonist is ensnarled in his own family drama in Martha's Vineyard but has another life as a CIA special operative and has to go back to Afghanistan, and in that section his mission becomes an attempt to follow up a lead about Bergdahl's whereabouts. And then based on the assumption he might be in a particular village, to attempt to go in there and extract him if he is. I won't say more about it, but I've been interested to see the real Bergdorf surface. Because there were periodic efforts to find out where he was. I talked to a special ops guy about that very thing.

William H. Coles
How would you bring in the president's attitudes, and make it dramatic without assessing blame or making judgments? Was it a political move or a humanitarian move?

Richard North Patterson
I think what you do is have very complicated contentions and arguments within the inner circle of the White House, including the presidency, about everything. The ethical, moral aspects. I mean, he's talking to his political advisors; he's talking to military folks; he's talking to people about the consequences of letting five Talibans go. He's going to be aware that if this thing goes wrong in some way or another, it could be disastrous. You have the parents. I think you could make that all pretty interesting. I'm not sure I would have produced mom and dad in the Rose Garden, I will say that.

William H. Coles
That was not a good choice. We don't need time to get a perspective on that. In wrapping up, I'd like to have your view as to the future of story. I'm assuming we both agree that story is an essential aspect of human learning, transitioning from prehistoric man to Homer through the Middle Ages with troubadours to contemporary mass production of stories in TV and film. The importance of fiction in expressing important concepts about society and what it means to be human is shrinking. The fiction writer aspires to become a significant literary figure by writing meaningful stories, despite little chance of ever being read. What is happening to traditional publishing? How will the internet play out for future writers wanting to get their work out? Will fiction, particularly literary prose, gain prominence through the internet? And if so, how can we as authors take advantage of it?

Richard North Patterson
Well, I tend to be a pessimist and a skeptic, I will cop to that right away. It doesn't mean I'm right, it means I have a point of view. Off the top, I think gatekeepers are a good thing. I don't mean that every good novel gets published. Karl Marlantes wrote the Vietnam novel *Matterhorn* that nobody touched for thirty years, and finally some small press picked it up and *The Atlantic* picked it up and it's easily the best novel of the Vietnam War I've ever read. So that's a case where the gatekeepers failed, although once the book was in print, thank God, reviewers did it a service by expressing their admiration. The idea seems to be that the internet makes publishing more democratic; that you don't need a publisher; you can just put your memoir out about how mom killed your pet gerbil and ruined your life, and somebody is going to read that.

How do we know what is good? And given that a lot of crap is published anyhow by traditional publishing, think about all the stuff that is eliminated that is really awful. I tend to think the notion of the internet is a democratizing force for fiction generally means that there will be more wasted time unless ways are determined to indicate why a reader wants to read this book rather than six others. I read reviews. That's how I generally choose what to read unless it's recommended by a friend I thrust. And the review pool is shrinking, so there is a lot less than there was when I had my first best-seller twenty years ago and I had great reviews all over. That was a great help.

Second of all, I'm as prone to Kindling things as anyone else because I can take a Kindle on an airplane, Kindle when I work out on the treadmill. But Kindle is a disadvantage to writers because we make about a quarter on those of what we make on a hardcover sale. More and more fiction is Kindled, and that just makes it harder for writers to make a living. I think both of us were born in the most fortunate sweet spot in history. We were American in the postwar era when we were predominant, we had a rising economy, a rising middle class, and we had to take on some of the serious social deficits in the 1990s. That was when I hit my real success in the golden age of publishing. Publishers were paying writers a lot of money, there were a lot of review media, there was a lot of channels for publishing books. Those have shrunk. And publishers are threatened. They're telling writers to go to Twitter camp and do their own PR. But if you are tweeting, you're not writing, you're just putting out a lot of crap about the sandwich you ate that day.

I went to a dinner party with a friend of mine, who is a very distinguished novelist and with whom I share a common point of view about a lot of things. Somebody asked if we tweeted and emailed fans and my friend said, "For twenty-five bucks you get my book, you don't get a relationship with me." You can either be emailing somebody or tweeting somebody or you can be writing your fiction. What you ought to be doing is spending time with your family. I don't think it's the job of a fiction writer to become a carnival barker. I have answered every piece of fan mail I've ever gotten, except from the obviously insane. If a reader went to the trouble of writing me a letter and sending it to the publisher, they deserve an acknowledgment and a reaction.

William H. Coles
That's admirable.

Richard North Patterson
But I will not put my email out for public consumption so people can email me every random thought they ever have. I'd be spending all my life doing it. Life is short. Writing time is precious. So is time with friends and family. I do not want to spend time saying, "Look at me, look at me."

William H. Coles
We, I mean the people who run the website with me, handle this by hiring people to run Facebook and Twitter. And recently LinkedIn and Goodreads.

Richard North Patterson
Well, that is a necessary tool. I can say pretty confidently I've written my last book. Here is another thing about the internet and video games. Thirty-six years ago now, I took a course from a prominent Southern writer. Fifteen of us were selected from two hundred manuscripts. One of things he had us do was read the first thirty pagers of *Madame Bovary*, in which Flaubert describes the village brick by brick and the characters. The Southern writer said, "It's a wonderful piece of writing but for a modern audience, you're going to have to do that in about three paragraphs." His point was that the attention span and patience of the modern reader is very different from Flaubert's time. How much more so now that our kids are thinking in very short bursts and flitting from this to that on the internet. I don't think any of that argues well for the art of fiction as I understand it.

William H. Coles
The staying power and longevity of a writer's work is in question. The whole thing about flash fiction and getting twitterish in writing is a huge change. I'm not ready to make the compromise for brevity and slang over quality, and I hope there are many other authors who feel the same. I still love to read the opening

to *Anna Karenina,* for example. That's not condensed. I hope that will continue to be valued.

Richard North Patterson
War and Peace is possibly one of the greatest novels ever written. I gave it to my daughter and she loved it.

William H. Coles
Thank you so much for your participation and your contribution. It's been an enjoyable and informative conversation.

Michael Ray Interview

9 January, 2009
William H. Coles

Michael Ray was born in Washington, DC, and attended Mater Dei School, Georgetown Preparatory School, and Vanderbilt University. He has written for many magazines on music, film, and books. He started at *Zoetrope: All-Story* in 2002, where he is now the editor. In addition to his editorial duties, he writes scripts for films.

William H. Coles
What is a zoetrope?

Michael Ray
The zoetrope was a precursor to the motion picture camera, popular around the early twentieth century. It is a cylinder with slats cut in it, a light in the center, and pictures inside. You spin the cylinder, look in through the slats, and it gives a semblance of motion.

William H. Coles
In the same era, there were those stereoscopes, where you viewed a card with two side-by-side, slightly different pictures through a handheld magnifier. This gave the effect of a three-dimensional image, that was, of course, static. Was its static nature a metaphor maybe for prose, in contrast to the movement in the cinematic image, that was the reason the name "zoetrope" was chosen for the magazine?

Michael Ray
The magazine was founded by Francis Ford Coppola, who had previously founded a film company called American Zoetrope in the 1970s. He is a romantic for the classic arts and was drawn to the zoetrope as a precursor to film. The name *Zoetrope: All-Story* takes "Zoetrope" from the film company and "All-Story" as an homage to a magazine that was produced by Frank Munsey in the 1930s. I can show you a copy. In the 1930s there was great public support for the arts. You had these writers like Dorothy Parker, Ring Lardner, and F. Scott Fitzgerald, who could make a living selling stories. Coppola wanted this magazine to work in the same ways . . . to provide a forum for people telling

stories. He agreed with Alfred Hitchcock, who said the short story is the art form most akin to film because as a viewer you can consume it in one sitting. Novels are more often adapted to films, but it's a clumsy process of conflation, whereas with a story, the filmmaker can build on what's there. Coppola also felt that in other industries there is a lot of emphasis on R&D; he felt the basis of good film is good story, and he therefore had an obligation to provide a forum for storytellers.

William H. Coles
What are the elements of good story as perceived by you, someone who chooses them and publishes them?

Michael Ray
A story has two principal components. First, purpose. What is the story about? When I read stories, I'm thinking: What is this about? Is the idea interesting? The second component is the facility with which the writer achieves that purpose. I think the best stories allow a reader to look past the imposition of the page and immerse him- or herself in the world of the story.

William H. Coles
Is this characterization?

Michael Ray
Characterization and the internal logic of the story—the sense that things make sense, that the story is credible. That things operate by reason, and there are consequences for actions.

William H. Coles
Is narration important? Are there rules you look for? Some stories are all narrator, others rely on character for telling.

Michael Ray
We're open to any perspective in voice, and we want the magazine to feel diverse. There are no fixed rules. Magazines can be more ambitious in the narratives we publish because we're building an overarching brand. In contrast, mainstream book publishers base an entire marketing campaign on one writer. Magazines can take more chances, and we try to embrace that. We only publish thirty stories a year, and depending on the year, we receive between six and ten thousand submissions. We really want to feel strongly about everything we publish. The process is so subjective. If you put somebody else in my position here, the magazine would look totally different. We want a magazine in which

every story could be somebody's favorite. If I'm publishing six stories, I'd rather publish three stories that people love and three stories that people hate, rather than, you know, six stories people feel apathetic about.

William H. Coles
Which says you want quality stories that are memorable, with meaning, and characters that will impact readers.

Michael Ray
Yes. We want stories that are going for something. There are a lot of people writing short fiction, and we really want stories where, whether you like them or you don't like them, in the end you're glad you read them.

William H. Coles
Will short fiction survive in the way we've become used to over the past few decades, or will it change? Will it even exist?

Michael Ray
I think narratives will always survive. When you look at the evolution of forms, the novel was the great narrative form of the nineteenth century, film is the great narrative form of the twentieth century, and in the twenty-first century you would think it would be something else. Novels require the mediation of the intellect, whereas in film, images and sound predominate and you can connect more easily on an emotional level. Your immersion can be more total and immediate. In some sense, you're doing less work as a viewer of films than as a reader of books. If the forms of narrative are becoming more encompassing and multidimensional, I would think the next form would be narratives you can affect . . . which you can already see developing in role-playing games on the internet. In these games you play a character and direct the path of the narrative. That's all based on character, on an internal logic of this world, and maybe that's the narrative form that succeeds film. So, while the forms might change, narrative seems eternal. Even the oldest religious traditions are based in narrative. It's an elemental way of organizing ideas.

William H. Coles
Is it true that story is an essential need for humans, in the same way that we all need sleep and food?

Michael Ray
I think so.

William H. Coles
It's a way we communicate—how we enjoy life and enjoy the past. Story is important. As you've indicated, there are so many forms for delivery. I fear for fiction's survival as a significant form for storytelling. Nonfiction—memoir and creative nonfiction—is replacing fiction as a writer technique and in the stories chosen for publication. Yet fiction has special qualities for story presentation not available in other forms.

Michael Ray
I think it's often hard to make meaningful distinctions between fiction and nonfiction. One of my favorite writers of the twentieth century is Richard Yates. If you look at his books, it's hard to call them fiction. They're so based on his own life. And for writers, everything, at some point, is based on personal experience, or something they've heard—I mean, every writer I know walks around with a notebook. They hear something on the subway or hear someone's name and think that would be a great name for a character. A writer is always borrowing from the real world, which makes sense if the objective is to reflect the real world. It's hard for me to think of fiction wholly cloistered from nonfiction.

People ask: Is the short story dead? Well, people are reading fewer story collections. For me, even coming from a magazine that focuses on short stories, that specific question is less interesting than the evolution of narrative. I think things are going to change as we have different ways of telling stories, but people will still tell stories. Story starts at its base origin, say, as people sitting around a campfire, telling stories about their ancestors that have didactic purposes, entertainment purposes, or that just help people relate experiences and teach that world to the next generation. The ways to do that evolve. If you look at the role-playing games, their narratives become so abstracted and mutable that it's hard to think of them as stories in the same way you think of story in a more static form. Basically, the people who write these games set out characters, define the rules that govern a society, and describe how people interact. These are their ambitions. And that's how a story works. With a story, you decide the rules that are going to govern this society, and then you define two characters and put them in a room, and if you've done that initial definition well, the characters determine where you're going.

William H. Coles
Is there morality involved?

Michael Ray
You mean is there some sort of moral commentary?

William H. Coles
No, more in the sense of John Gardner's ideas of moral fiction.

Michael Ray
Well, I guess on a certain level. I mean, if this is realist fiction, you're borrowing your morals from the society that surrounds you. If you're writing science fiction or fantasy, what most likely distinguishes those forms are the rules that govern the characters who exist in that world. Some professional writers tell me the hardest thing with a lot of stories is simply starting—deciding that the base idea is worth writing about. Others just decide on a setting and two characters and start writing. They assume that since there are two characters, at some point there will be some sort of conflict.

William H. Coles
And that's how the drama evolves.

Michael Ray
Person A does this to person B; how does B react? Then you follow them along. That does not mean you end up with a story you can sell, but you end up with a story.

William H. Coles
To make a story great, doesn't the story have to have some idea of the morality? For consistency—to prevent moral wandering. In both the drama and the conflict.

Michael Ray
Yes, I think a story should be governed by a consistent set of rules from beginning to end—though I'm sure, as with every rule, there are exceptions. How many times have you read something where the rules are leading toward some resolution, and then the writer throws out some twist that seems completely ungrounded in what preceded it? That's never satisfying. You create characters, you define some consistent rules around them, and they act within those rules. The rules can be as simple as in order to live in this town—say, New York or San Francisco—you must make this amount of money, you have to have sufficient resources.

William H. Coles
Then you focus on consistency and how much the reader will believe?

Michael Ray
Yes.

William H. Coles
Does fictionalization exist? Is it a process writers should understand?

Michael Ray
What do you mean by fictionalization?

William H. Coles
It's a term that comes up frequently in writing courses. As I understand it, it means writing from experience and then "fictionalizing" that experience so that it becomes "fiction." Thinking about what's happened in your life that's important to you, people who are important to you, then describing with freedom from the reality. It's somewhat similar to what you've described, although creating two characters in a setting seems to be all imagination, and therefore fiction.

Michael Ray
Anything will be based on experience. Anything you imagine is based on experience.

William H. Coles
Charles D'Ambrosio has said to be careful when you're writing from experience because experience locks in the decisions you will make about your characters and blunts their potential as characters. As I think about it more, I agree that writing from experience can temper drama and cloud theme—and meaning potential, too.

Michael Ray
In terms of putting two characters in a room, the difference between writing memoir or a diary entry and writing a story is that with a story, you're not writing about yourself; you're writing about this character. It's a difficult thing to do and maybe that line between how you would react and how that character would react is ineffable, but I think you need to think about character as something wholly apart from yourself.

William H. Coles
And that can be the advantage of working through a narrator as you're writing a story? This separates the author from the story?

Michael Ray
It can. It comes down to your objectives in writing. Writing your own experience, if that is what's interesting to you, is fine. A totally acceptable ambition. But don't expect other people to be interested in it. One of our successful workshop teachers advises to take some experience that is meaningful to you and then set up some proxy for it. Because you can't really write about your mother. Choose a proxy for your mother, then you imbue that person with all these unique qualities. But again, I'm hesitant about identifying any fixed rules. Everybody solves problems differently. Successful writers have found ways that work for them. Try different ways. For many, the most direct way is to write first person based on your own experience. Just be careful that you don't lose objectivity.

William H. Coles
If someone wants to write a great story—an Anton Chekhov type of story that is going to live for generations—they have to start with, as you said, a good idea. The idea has to be more than something that pleased me, or something I laughed at, or someone I know who was successful at something. Instead, writers need to address what about this situation or event from my life will help me create a great story. Is that reasonable?

Michael Ray
Something I talk to writers about during the editorial process is reserving room in the story for the reader to participate in its understanding. As a writer, if you immerse yourself too much in the story, you risk standing between your story and your reader. The best stories stand outside their authorship, becoming interesting and powerful to people who don't know the author or care about the author. With the present educational system for writers—workshops, MFAs—stories can get too worked over. In that environment, writers can become disproportionately focused on one particular impact they intend for a story to have upon a reader. They work the story to have that impact; they workshop it; other people give them advice; and they work it over and over and over. These stories can be really polished but ultimately unsatisfying, as they lack any true sense of discovery. As a reader you can watch the story's various mechanisms working toward one end, and I think you then instinctively resist that end, or that feeling the writer is working so hard to create. And you know you can read the story again and its only potential is to affect you in exactly the same way. It's been so sharpened to a single point, and that's not the way life happens.

Think about great music. You can listen to something over and over and discover something new every time. Part of creating that as a writer is not working so hard to have one impact, not leading somebody to one specific understanding.

It's like putting blinders on somebody and trying to get them to see this one purpose, and in the process, you've blinded, or blunted, that person's capability to see all the other impacts the story might have. This is something I talk a lot about with writers. Especially if you're publishing in a magazine like ours, you can rely on a sophisticated readership—people who really want to engage in stories. And if you can write the whole story to the point that there is only one way of understanding it, you may need to strip back that exposition. The more that process of understanding can happen off the page, in the reader's head, the more the reader internalizes the story, imbuing it with emotions beyond anything you could fully describe.

William H. Coles
Do you see in your seminars and courses a tendency to revise the prose in order to get the effect when the real improvement needed lies in core desire of characters, motivations, plot structure, need for action in static situations?

Michael Ray
Absolutely. You need to work on those bigger, more fundamental things—on purpose—before you work on the way the purpose is achieved. In an ideal editorial process here, when we have sufficient time, I like to start with a writer by making a list of questions: Why does this character do this? Why does he say yes to this question rather than saying no? And then reminding the writer that even when I understand the reasons, that everything about the story is a decision, and that all the decisions should abide by some kind of logic, and characters should make sense, and in essence have the writer defend the character. You can only defend it if the base motivations and the character itself are credible and interesting. Once the characters are strong, the conflict is strong, the structure of the story is interesting, then you start to deal with the prose. Obviously the prose is the easiest thing to deal with first, and I think that's where people want to go first, thinking: if I replace this period with a semicolon, I'll change the pacing here and then that solves the problem. But your problem might be more fundamental.

William H. Coles
Or the need to make the prose clever—an oxymoron here, or alliteration. That rarely fixes the problem if you're trying to write great stories.

Michael Ray
All the prose needs to serve the story's purpose. The purpose should dictate the prose.

William H. Coles
We've covered a number of issues about the writing process. Isn't it of value for each writer to address each of these issues and come to their own attitudes and directions to incorporate into the writing process?

Michael Ray
The only time you need to think about other people in your writing is if you want other people to read your writing. That's when you consider: How do people read? How do people think about character? What are people looking for? These become important questions. Again, I think it is a totally respectful ambition to write and write and write just to improve to where you feel proud of your work with no intention of showing it to other people. In some ways that is the most direct path to a satisfying experience. But once you set publishing as your goal, then you're assigning the definition of success to somebody else, which can be frustrating. But if you do want others to read your work, you need to think about how people approach reading and what they are looking for.

William H. Coles
A lot of this is thinking before we write. Doesn't that make our writing more effective?

Michael Ray
Again, different people write different ways. George Saunders taught that he starts writing and keeps writing until he decides it's not interesting. But he's got decades of experience and tremendous talent.

William H. Coles
Is a reader able to pick up that attitude in a writer as opposed to a writer who thinks and plans ahead? Is a difference discernible to the reader?

Michael Ray
George thinks that every sentence should entertain. If a story doesn't work, he says (and I hope I'm remembering this correctly) that he works back through, sentence by sentence, until he finds one that isn't working, changes it, and then goes in a direction that does work. I've talked to other writers who think about a story incessantly and won't start writing until they know what the last sentence is going to be. They need that kind of certainty in order to start.

William H. Coles
If you consider a story as a series of interrelated scenes, and you're creating a scene, isn't that process more focused to story purpose when you know the

ending? The scene can't be a boxcar in a freight train of tanker cars. A scene needs to be a stateroom on a cruise ship churning toward an exciting destination.

Michael Ray
That assumes that your first draft is your final draft. If you're writing spontaneously and then working back through, the last scene might invalidate everything that came before. And then you rewrite to build to that last scene.

William H. Coles
Would it help to think of a story as a matrix? If a value in a matrix changes, every other value in that matrix is also affected. If you have story and ending, and the ending changes, then you need to go back and address if each story element is still working for the story purpose and for the ending. Not revise in isolation.

Michael Ray
In thinking about the ambitions for a story—and again he is one of my favorite writers—Charlie D'Ambrosio wrote a story I love called "Drummond and Son." It was in the *New Yorker* five or six years ago. It's about a father and a son, and the son has schizophrenia and the father fixes typewriters. Charlie said that when he started with it, his sole intent was to write a story in which a father could tell a son that he loved him and it wouldn't be sentimental. That's where he started.

William H. Coles
That's a great idea.

Michael Ray
It is. And then he worked toward that. And when it happens, it's really powerful.

William H. Coles
That's what can make a story great? The preordained plot idea?

Michael Ray
My purpose in bringing it up is that he set out with a specific objective and was never distracted from that purpose. And that is what the story builds toward. With him, it's an interesting idea. But put it in another writer's hands, it's a different idea. He was able to pull it off in a really powerful way. Stories have a gestalt; it's not just one thing. You can have a great concept and fail. But Charlie's immensely talented, and he succeeded.

William H. Coles
He has a great imagination. He creates wonderful scenes. It's a lesson for all of us struggling along to study someone with that degree of imagination.

Michael Ray
You mentioned those little prose tricks some writers are really fond of, like alliteration and excessive description. Charlie's work is beautiful on a prose level without any of those tricks. He's writing in plainspoken ways.

William H. Coles
Clarity is a gift. And imagery. I have a number of specific questions I'd like to ask before we end. First, what about a story submitted to *Zoetrope: All-Story* makes it suitable for adaptation to a screenplay? Isn't that what Coppola was looking for originally?

Michael Ray
I should clarify our relationship between story and screenplay. When Francis founded the magazine, the idea was to find stories that filmmakers would adapt into films. He was trying to collect these great stories. And over the years that has evolved simply to a focus on stories. So when we're publishing the magazine, we're not thinking: Would this story make a great screenplay? We're thinking: Is this a great short story? The things that make a story great are the things that make a narrative great, and the things that make a narrative great make a great film. In film there are specific endemic needs that don't apply to other forms of narrative. But at the base, it has to be a great story. The only thing in the magazine that relates to film in every issue is our Classic Reprint, which is a story that inspired a great film. That is, again, to underscore this relationship between different art forms—short story and film—and what really is important in narrative. Even in a magazine of short stories, what we are really focused on is narrative. And we understand that narrative can appear in many different forms.

William H. Coles
Narrative is a fuzzy concept for me. It can be a noun or an adjective, and then there's the verb form, "to narrate." When you say narrative is important to you, are you referring to one of those, or all of them?

Michael Ray
Again, a narrative that is important is something that has a purpose, something that is achieved with facility.

William H. Coles
So you mean a process rather than an end product?

Michael Ray
I guess it depends on where you set your bounds of a narrative. Like in modern role-playing games, those narratives play out continually. The story evolves over years and different players.

William H. Coles
You're talking about the "telling" of the story . . . related to process but not exclusively the "how to"?

Michael Ray
With the role-playing games, the narrative goes on for years; with the short story it's confined to, say, three to twelve thousand words.

William H. Coles
So you are applying the term "narrative" to everything in the storytelling process?

Michael Ray
Yes. And it's all storytelling. Think about it with your kids. The purpose of telling them stories is to teach them things, to organize morals, and to entertain them. It has the same purpose as a short story.

William H. Coles
The word has varied definitions. When we think of narration in a story we may think of a narrative passage, in contrast to dialogue, in-scene, internal reflection, or transition. It's a point of confusion for me when you use narrative to mean the way a story is delivered.

Michael Ray
Right. I'm thinking about the whole narrative arc. We focus on short story. There's a William Faulkner quote that all novelists are failed poets. He believed that ambitious writers start with poetry because it's the most direct and unrelenting form of narrative. Failing at poetry, they try short stories, and then they try novels. A short story is so compact that every sentence needs to serve some purpose.

William H. Coles
With clarity.

Michael Ray
Yes, with clarity. And maybe each sentence will not serve the same purpose, but each needs to be there for a purpose. Great short stories can be intense, sentence to sentence, because you can be in control of all components throughout. The novel needs ebb and flow, because if you take a short story's intensity to 350 pages, people are going to crack. What we do in the editorial process is strip back everything that isn't purposeful to get at the core, constantly asking if you can tell this in fewer words.

William H. Coles
What will be the effect of online publishing for print publishers and for writers trying to achieve recognition in the print medium?

Michael Ray
Online publishing creates more venues for writing. This is great. It allows more opportunities to reach an audience. But it also splinters the audience. People are now reading in all sorts of venues. In the writing community there is still a premium on publishing in print—I think because there are fewer venues for it. I was doing a talk at Stanford one Saturday, and I went into the auditorium and there were maybe a hundred people, and I was thinking gosh, this is great. People say no one reads short fiction anymore, but look at all the people here! Coming on a Saturday. But as we got to the Q&A it became clear that the people were not readers but writers who wanted to appear in our magazine and others like it. This was at the time when *The Atlantic* was no longer going to do a story in every issue, and Philip Gourevitch had just taken over the *Paris Review* and people thought he was going to do less fiction. And people were still decrying the loss of *Story* magazine. I asked them, if these are the venues for your work, how many of you actually subscribe to these magazines? Very few hands went up.

William H. Coles
How do you feel about that?

Michael Ray
As much as people talk about the decline of print and that there are not enough short-story magazines around and that no one is reading, the people who are most concerned are the writers. If you as a writer want print to survive, you should read it. Subscribe. We get more submissions than we have subscribers.

William H. Coles
Do you feel strongly enough about it that you would not publish someone who is not a subscriber?

Michael Ray
No, we want to publish the best work that we can, and any limit upon the pool of stories from which to select undermines that intention. People always feel that their one subscription is not going to make a difference, but it's like any other public art. If it's not supported and consumed, it's not going to last. I do understand that there is only so much time in a day, and you have a job, a family, and you want to write, then where does your reading work in? But if you want these forums to survive you have to support them.

William H. Coles
This leads to a delicate question. What is *Zoetrope*'s attitude toward contests, and what is your philosophy for the future? I ask because many print and online magazines are beginning to shift the burden of operating costs from subscribers and donors to those who submit their creative work necessary for the magazine. The cost can be significant. Hundreds of dollars a year. It seems unfair. How are you dealing with it?

Michael Ray
We don't charge for regular submissions. People need to understand the economies that govern literary magazines. I don't know of any literary magazines that support themselves on subscriptions and sales alone. And it's getting more difficult. We do host a contest. It's a part of keeping the magazine around. We've designed the contest to serve writers as best we can. We submit the winning and finalist stories to the top literary agencies for consideration. Every year a few of these emerging writers attract agents as a result. And we publish the winning story as a supplement to our spring issue.

William H. Coles
Are there rules to follow when you run a contest? Anonymity? Everything is read. Competent judges with consistent ideas about the contest.

Michael Ray
Yes. That is something we take very seriously. We do the same with stories submitted. When we accept contest stories, we log each one, then assign the story a number—the contact information is stored separately so that all reading is absolutely anonymous.

William H. Coles
Thanks for the clarification. The general feeling is a distrust of the number of these contests that now operate in literary publishing.

Michael Ray
I certainly can't defend the concept of contests. I can only speak to how we conduct ours. As much as writers decry the winnowing of print platforms for their work, if you want to appear in magazines, I'm not saying you should subscribe to *Zoetrope* but you should subscribe to or otherwise support some magazine. Otherwise, these publications won't last. This is a very, very challenging economy for magazines, particularly those that aren't product focused.

William H. Coles
Thank you for doing this interview, for taking the time, and for sharing your ideas and thoughts. It's been great. I learned a lot!

Michael Ray
Absolutely. I enjoyed the conversation.

Jim Shepard Interview

16-18 July, 2009
William H. Coles

Jim Shepard is the J. Leland Miller Professor of English at Williams College. He previously taught at the University of Michigan. He is the recipient of numerous grants and awards, including the John Simon Guggenheim Memorial Award. He attended Trinity College and did a postgraduate degree at Brown University.

William H. Coles
You obviously love stories expressed in prose. What is it about fiction that allows it to survive in a world where stories are increasingly delivered through TV, DVD, and film?

Jim Shephard
Well, if you mean, what are the uses of literature as opposed to those other forms, to build a story on the page is quite different from having it barraged at you in visual terms. There is something to be said for encountering language, negotiating language, and constructing for yourself in your imagination the narrative that in film is largely provided for you. You're much more of a passive receptor in film, although, God knows, you're also proposing and adjusting expectations as you go. You have to do interpretive work in movies, but not nearly as much. I do think there is something about stories in prose that is irreplaceable.

William H. Coles
Does the ability to enter with ease into a character's consciousness in prose contribute to the difference with film?

Jim Shephard
That's a huge part of it. David Shields has said how impatient he is with plot and overwhelmingly narrative-driven prose, and how much he loves fiction when it's discursive and ruminative. Certainly that's an aspect of fiction that film has the most trouble with. Film is helpless in the face of novels and short stories that are interior. Voice-over is a very poor substitute for a long interior monologue. An obvious reason for that is film is inherently dependent on what you can visualize. But when you're dealing with intricate, ruminative material,

it's a huge help to be able to go at your own pace . . . to be able to stop and think, "I'm not sure I follow that." Then go back, reconsider, think about a sentence for a minute. None of that's possible in film. We almost never stop movies to consider a little more fully what we just saw. We might watch it again, we might talk to our friends afterward, we might say, "What did you make of that scene?" But it's very rare that we stop the film and go, "Jeez, what did I just see?" But it's absolutely commonplace in reading.

William H. Coles
Does that mean the development of ironies and other rhetorical devices is easier in fiction than in film?

Jim Shephard
Possibly. Certainly, the idea of complicated conceptual notions. Not all teachers say you should watch movies, but all teachers say you should read books because that process of working things through intricately happens more with words on a page than with movies. In fact, even the most powerful, intricate, and complicated movies can be experienced, again, as a series of sensations. You can just decide you're not going to pay attention to the complexities of the movie.

William H. Coles
You're an excellent teacher. What about teaching creative writing gives you pleasure?

Jim Shephard
I love to work out ways of articulating what is going on. In writing fiction you're surprising yourself in some ways. A lot of fiction, for me, is stuff that I understand intuitively but haven't really worked out. Teaching is forcing myself to not say to people, "You know what I'm talking about." They say, "No, I don't know what you're talking about. You'll have to help me with that." That kind of disciplined thinking is useful.

William H. Coles
Based on your teaching experience, what qualities do great fiction writers have that cannot be taught?

Jim Shephard
I think it might have been Flannery O'Connor who said creative writing can't be taught, but it can be learned. Then the idea, also from Flannery O'Connor, that fiction writing is a gift: I can't give you that gift but if you do have that gift, I can help you develop it. I'm probably a good enough teacher that I could take

someone who has good, basic literary skills and help them, with enough work, create a good publishable novel. But that's a long way from making them a great writer. A great writer, it seems to me, has inherent ways of thinking, ways of engaging the world, that you would say, "Wow. You may have all sorts of other problems; you may not know how to shape a novel, you may not know how to make certain mechanical decisions, but clearly you are someone with enormous talent that you obviously came into the room with."

William H. Coles
When you analyze stories, or suggest how we as students analyze stories, you have a four-step process. You say you should read through the manuscript uninterrupted; then read through and make notations; then start a few pages from the end, go to the beginning, and read through again so you can see if there is story continuity, particularly with emotions; and then make a careful evaluation tracing the emotions of the characters. I assume you're looking for those emotions to be logical within the story framework.

Jim Shephard
Certainly, logical in the story.

William H. Coles
In class you rarely discuss the episodic scene progression of a story, or backstory, or plot tension, or even dramatic elements as they fit into that front story. Is it useful, when you're looking at ways to write stories, to think in terms of theme and meaning, scene structure that progresses the story, and then (and you teach this very well) working toward an understanding of the human condition that the reader (and character, and sometimes author) didn't recognize before?

Jim Shephard
A lot of stuff that might feel neglected, like dramatic elements, actually are dealt with all the time under the heading of the empirical elements that support the emotional and thematic claims being made. In other words, when we're tracking something like this series of emotional stakes for a character or this series of thematic ideas that the story seems to want to develop, we're noticing a pattern of dramatic elements that lead us to those ideas. In today's case, we were talking about a series of relationships to altruism that the narrator, the protagonist in the story, had. The way we go about that is to say, "Here are the events of the story that made us think about that in the first place."

William H. Coles
Ah, yes. I see.

Jim Shephard
So those elements that seem like more traditional subjects of a workshop are always being uncovered and deployed, but they're being uncovered and deployed to another purpose and that is: What is the story's overall agenda? What is the story's covert agenda? And if it's literary fiction, I would argue that those agendas are almost never purely narrative, or never purely structural, because that would suggest that we're all hunting for the perfect new mousetrap—a new narrative design or dramatic design that no one has ever come up with. As David Shields said today and Aimee Bender echoed, we're trying to find the most useful form—if you're thinking about dramatic and narrative elements—for the story at its core, emotional and thematic. Really, what I want to write about are these emotional and thematic issues embodied in this world.

William H. Coles
Can't you develop emotional and thematic themes through dramatic structure?

Jim Shephard
Yes. I'm not suggesting those are antithetical by any means. Even a writer who seems as uninterested in emotions and thematic as Ernest Hemingway in the superb story "Big Two-Hearted River" Nick doesn't have a lot of emotions . . . there aren't a lot of issues that keep coming up. In fact, you're confronted with what seems like nothing but a series of narrative events. Nick hikes to down to the river, he makes a campfire, he heats some beans, he burns the top of his mouth, he decides he's not going to fish one side of the river versus another part of the river. Even though we're in Nick's point of view, we seem to learn nothing about him emotionally. We only know he likes fishing, he likes camping. But all literature operates by having us assume that whatever it is we're learning is in some way a human agenda. In other words, all literary fiction seeks to answer the question: Why am I reading this? But that answer is only tangentially presented in the case of "Big Two-Hearted River." Hemingway thinks we should know about the world, and he's very good at showing us the world. But he would be quite dismayed if you said, "Well, that's really what this is all about." Every one of these narrative events, in fact, we're supposed to use to postulate about Nick's interior life. That becomes part of the story's subject—that when Nick gets into a rough place, being a guy, he goes down and camps and washes his mind free of things.

William H. Coles
Right.

Jim Shephard
We think we'll never know what's bothering Nick, but Hemingway tries to select exactly the right details so that the careful reader can say, "You know, I think this is about something he's trying to get away from." It's not a symbolic Easter egg hunt where you wonder, this stands for that. Instead, you figure, these are very quiet preoccupations that keep coming up. These are the sorts of things that make Nick uncomfortable. What do they have in common?

That's also something I do in teaching fiction, something you can train yourself as a writer to do with your own work. You can muse, "I thought I was writing a story about fishing, and I thought to myself, you know, I'm sorry, that's not enough, but I also went back and thought, what else is here?" Everyone has had friends and loved ones who have gone off on little rants, little tears, where they thought they were safely on one subject, but you've later realized they're telling you a lot more than you thought they were.

William H. Coles
One lecture this week was on obsession in fiction. The idea that the author can serve the story better if there is some obsession within the author that carries over as an energy force into the writing. That makes sense. However, it does rely on voice almost entirely, and it also seems to rely on the author becoming the voice of the story, becoming the narrator of the story. Is that erroneous thinking? I've come to believe that in some stories the writer needs to create as objective a narrator as possible—to step back in order to develop that story well.

Jim Shephard
I think a lot depends on how narrowly you read the nature of the obsession. Obviously, one kind of energy is the narrator who says, "I'm going to kill this guy and I'm not thinking about anything else," and you thinking, "Well, this guy's certainly obsessive." You can also imagine a narrator who sounds as if he has an enormous British stiff-upper-lip detachment about the world who is just going to describe to us what Westhampton looks like on a sunny day. He does it in what seems to be detached, omniscient, and careful prose, but we begin to register that this person is a lot more interested in Westhampton than we thought, given the details we're getting. There's a focus here that is a little more intense than we expected. That is a version of obsession I assume Steve Almond was talking about, where you decide on a certain intensity of connection, intensity of interest. The obvious first impression would be to make this guy a raving wild-eyed nut waving his arms because that's an easy way of getting attention. I've done that a lot. But another way is to start with people you've known who seem utterly rational, utterly reasonable, who keep coming

back to the same subject. That's the kind of obsessiveness that's fascinating, right? What you don't want, I think, is genuine diffidence.

If you imagine the opposite of obsession to be "I can sort of take this or leave it," a kind of intensity does start to drain out and we find ourselves saying, "Why are you telling me this again? You just think you're describing the city well?" We're wary because so many fictions don't succeed at getting to the heart of the matter. They don't seem to be exercising their writerly muscles. I was joking in class that you can describe a cloud very beautifully for however long, and we think . . .

William H. Coles
It's a cloud.

Jim Shephard
"What's a cloud," finally. The Anton Chekhov line about that is: "A bear in the woods is a bear; a bear in contact with a human being is a story." The idea: I don't care how well you can describe a bear unless that person describing it is my subject.

William H. Coles
Related to this is the whole idea of voice and intensity. Is there any advantage to thinking of character voice, narrator voice, and authorial voice as separate? So when you're writing on the page, anything that is coming through one of these three portals holds true to what the character, or the narrator, or author can reasonably know about the story and the world given the different times they may be speaking in (in story time), and the different times they have lived in reality and story time. I ask this because you often see in stories where there seem to be different sources for information from different times and different backgrounds, which risks confusing the reader, or losing their interest.

Jim Shephard
Some people have more of a capacity for fluidity in respect to point of view and distance between what seems to be the fiction's agenda and the speaker's agenda. I'm sufficiently wary of ever knowing an author that I resist narrator as author and think more in terms of narrator fiction, because even the authorial voice may change dramatically from work to work. So I tend to make the distinction that way. But having said that, a lot of us like fictions that are very clearly demarcated: this is clearly a narrator who is not speaking for the fiction, maybe he's slightly unreliable, maybe he's more limited, whatever, or this is clearly omniscient.

Really, though, starting halfway through the twentieth century, those categories began to get pretty fluid. There started to be all sorts of narration. The operative analogy would be that you get liftoff. You would be in a third-person narration, a close third person, say: Bill looked over at Jim. "What the hell is he on about right now," Bill thought. "And my underwear is riding up in the back and I'm uncomfortable." And you think, "Wow, we're really right with Bill." And the next paragraph is something like: he'd been like this ever since seventh grade when that kid dumped the ice cream on his head. And you're thinking, "That's not exactly Bill anymore." But we don't have that much trouble with a voice that lifts off like that depending on how dramatically the liftoffs work, what they are doing.

William H. Coles
And how related they are?

Jim Shephard
And how related they are. It's become a fluid set of categories. We don't think of them as portals anymore, but imagine them as something sliding along a scale. But having said that, there are number of readers out there who say, "No! Once I get a voice, I want that voice to stay in that register." And there are lots of books that accommodate them. My most recent novel, *Project X*, is close third person, a teenage boy, and there is nothing in the voice or anywhere near it that is not something he could have generated. You have all these options.

William H. Coles
As we're speaking about that, I'd like to ask about the unreliable narrator. What are the mechanisms in using the unreliable narrator to develop significant ironies, and other rhetorical-based resources, that contribute to the meaning of the fiction?

Jim Shephard
With the advent of postmodernism and the overthrow of some of the verities—and with modernism before that—there's been a sense that there are all sorts of people who are absolutely certain about stuff. They may not be totally objective, but it's their certainty and nobody else's certainty. And with that the usage of unreliable narrator has grown, I think. I propose that has everything to do with allowing these obsessive and passionate figures their point of view, and remembering that all sorts of fiction has all sorts of tools in the toolbox to allow us to step back slightly and go, "Well, he's clearly not telling the truth." What's fascinating about that is the continuum we were just talking about. Do we need to get out of point of view? How far out? Something like that is utterly

unaffected by the issue of unreliability. In other words, you would think, "If I'm going to do an unreliable narrator, there's going to have to be moments when I lift and I go—although Bill said this, he's full of maroon sod, he had no idea what he was talking about."

William H. Coles
So the reader has to know what's reliable and what's not reliable.

Jim Shephard
Right. And you think that would be the only way to do it, but as we were saying, it turns out you can stay very, very tightly into that sensibility and yet expose it all the time. As I was saying, one of the easiest ways of conceiving of that is remembering that when people make assertions, they often follow them up with their evidence, their empirical evidence, and you think, "That doesn't make any sense at all." Suddenly you realize, "You're not very reliable." Someone says, "Hey, I met that friend of yours who you said was such a nice guy. He wasn't a nice guy at all. I told him to pick up the check for thirteen people and he said, 'Why should I do that?'" And you're like, why *should* he do that? And suddenly you realize this guy is not so reliable, right? But we always assume reliability until proven otherwise. You don't open a novel that says, "My name is Bill, and I was born in Arizona," and have the reader go. "I bet that's not true."

William H. Coles
"I bet he was born in New Mexico."

Jim Shephard
Yeah. "I think Bill's lying to me." We assume Bill's telling the truth until we have incontrovertible evidence to the contrary.

William H. Coles
That holds true for the narrator more than the character.

Jim Shephard
Yes, even more so. Because that's very strange when the narrator lies. There are fictions that do that, that say, "Oh, reader, did I say this? Maybe I'm not telling the truth." That's very tricky, because a lot of readers, not just traditional readers, will go, "Well, now wait a minute. I'm not going to play anymore." You then suddenly realize just how dangerous that is for the illusions. The writers are usually working very, very hard to prevent you from dwelling too long on the truth or lack of it.

William H. Coles
And breaking the fictional dream, that sort of thing.

Jim Shephard
Right. As soon as the writer goes, "You thought she's a woman but she's really a man," the reader goes, "Why did I think that? He didn't do a very good woman in the first place." Then the whole thing starts to fall apart.

William H. Coles
Let's talk about the second person. It's a form that you've used at times. I'll just quote Rob Spillman, who in a recent interview said that he didn't like second person because as soon as the narrator says, "You're walking down the street," Rob thinks, "But I'm not walking down the street!" He calls it that confrontational character point of view. How is second person useful to you?

Jim Shephard
I haven't used it very much, for some of those reasons. It is by far the most aggressive point of view. There is a way in which it so foregrounds the gesture that first and third person do so easily, which is to get you as reader to identify. It's so aggressively insistent on that in a way that you immediately resist. If I say, "I was walking down the street," you immediately think, "I can imagine that." If I say, "He was walking down the street," you say, "Okay, I'm picturing that." But if I say, "You are walking down the street," you say, "No, I wasn't." You immediately start resisting.

It got popular for a little while. Jay McInerney's book *Bright Lights, Big City* created a kind of fad with it. That imperative aggressiveness—you are sitting down, you are having dinner, you are thinking you'll never be happy again—created a kind of you-are-in-the-moment, but you're also feeling like a kind of zombie, as if you've had agency taken away from you. You get up, you're going outside. You go, "I guess I'm going outside." The quality was useful for McInerney to render what it was like to be trapped inside the drug scene, the party scene, in New York. God knows the character was having the time of his life. The conceit of that book was that he was kind of trapped, he only wished he could get out and do X, Y, and Z. The second person was useful for that. I think it's an extremely limited form otherwise. I'm trying to remember when I've used it. I haven't used it very often.

William H. Coles
It's very rarely used in a whole novel.

Jim Shephard
It's very hard to pull off in a whole novel.

William H. Coles
You speak of an interesting concept. You call it the R of R, the rate of revelation. This seems related to pacing.

Jim Shephard
It's what constitutes pacing.

William H. Coles
Pacing of information. But it must also relate to point-of-view delivery. For example, in multiple points of view the author has to consider frequency and time of revelation thorough a specific point of view and the pacing as well.

Jim Shephard
I suppose, but I wanted to make clear that it was informational, or interior. People tend to think of pace as: Am I having enough things happen? Am I having them happen fast enough? That's how you increase pace. But remember it's information, not event. Obviously events can be information, and you can accelerate the pace. For example, the building has collapsed and Bill is trapped and Jim saves him and they both run out before the fire begins. But really what we're looking for is information. So, you also imagine a situation without anything happening. The pace picks up dramatically just because the information dump picks up dramatically. For example, Bill and Jim were sitting at the table, they were chatting, Bill was wearing white, Jim was wearing light green, the computer whirred, Bill was thinking, I'm an idiot, I'm a horrible person, I'm a pederast, I'm a this, I'm a that . . .

William H. Coles
I think of that all the time. [*smiling*]

Jim Shephard
As that list gets out, notice the pace is picking up. We're still sitting at a table. In fact, time has stopped, but the pace is accelerating because the reader thinks, "Holy God, he thinks he's this, he thinks he's that." This list has nothing to do with the event but has everything to do with what we're learning. We would never say, what a drag, all this complaining. We would think, "Whoa, I really felt I was learning something there." So it has to do with the rate at which complicated information is being downloaded.

William H. Coles
And the credibility and value of that information as it's being delivered.

Jim Shephard
Sure. Because the credibility is itself information. Unreliability is new information. I didn't know I couldn't trust Bill.

William H. Coles
Got it. I've noticed that in classes you seem to place stories into categories. In terms of our discussions, you may see a story as a romance, or a Gothic detective story. Then you explore those categories. As students revise, should they attempt identify the type of story they're writing and look to examples for what to do and not to do?

Jim Shephard
I would hate to think my first priority is to figure out what kind of box things go in. You'll notice, however, these categories are useful only if you imagine a near infinitude of categories. If you're thinking of Gothic detective, you're thinking of a massive number of categories. I'm not trying so much to say, "Okay, this is a Gothic detective story, and what are the rules of that, because a student has to follow those rules," as much as to say, the strategies being deployed here are strategies, which you should recognize from other forms you've seen.

William H. Coles
Can a student recognize a category to look to other examples?

Jim Shephard
I think so. What we're doing in culture is continually hybridizing stuff that's come before. If you have a priest character who says, "I was saying Mass the other day and this beautiful slinky blonde came up to me and I knew what she wanted, I knew she was trouble, but I couldn't resist taking her into the back and having her confess to me." And I say to you, "What does that sound like?" You go, "Hm, that sounds like hard-boiled detective fiction." That's a category. And what you need to know is that there are elements to that category that have associations that you're exploiting. But that doesn't mean you're writing hard-boiled detective fiction. What that means is that you are taking all these cultural strains within yourself and using them if and when you need them. I would fully expect to teach for years—and I teach a lot of workshops—and never have Gothic detective come up again. It's a particular, singular thing.

William H. Coles
This seems to revolve around withholding information. In genre fiction, you manipulate information to build tension.

Jim Shephard
Right.

William H. Coles
Yet in the broad category of literary fiction, you give all the information necessary for story progression up front, and then discover why it happened and what will occur.

Jim Shephard
There is some of that. Genre fiction is really not that interested in the complexities of the human being at the heart of the matter. I mean, it certainly wants to have persuasive characters populating the stories, but if you're writing standard science fiction it is about this one human being going, "Here's an amazing premise—imagine if all vegetables were robots in some way, how would that affect a human." But that's not what you the reader are essentially interested in, and the human beings are going to help you understand that as opposed to using that to help you understand the human beings.

William H. Coles
Would you speak on conflict, which seems so essential to fiction? Internal emotional conflict, conflict on the dramatic plot level, and conflict in the prose itself?

Jim Shephard
It seems pretty clear that conflict is what drives fiction. There is an emotional conflict, meaning, some kind of conflict where characters have an emotional stake, and that conflict is comprised of at least nearly equal forces in battle. Those are forces that need to be close to intractable.

William H. Coles
For each character?

Jim Shephard
Yes. Usually it's not the case where one character embodies one side of it and another the opposite. It's a little bit like the conflict I discuss where I love my father and I hate my father. And that gets embodied in conflictual relationship between me and my father. But notice the conflict is not breaking down to one

side a character is taking (I love father) or the other (I hate father). The conflict is embodied by putting the two people into motion.

What I mean by the intractability of it is we think in a situation like that, "Boy, how are you going to deal with that? I love my father and I hate my father. And I don't see one of those sides winning out anytime soon." As opposed to a conflict like: Billy was a thoughtful liberal boy who was wondering if he should join the Nazi party. And you're like, "That's an easy conflict to resolve." There are conflicts in unsuccessful stories where the story pretends it's a difficult conflict to negotiate and the reader doesn't find it difficult at all. Once there was a really sensitive boy who had a really neglectful mother and what do you think about that, reader? And the reader thinks the mother's in the wrong and the boy's in the right.

William H. Coles
It comes down to the credibility of that conflict for that moment?

Jim Shephard
You don't want to say "credibility," because the writer of that story would go, "What? You don't believe that that sensitive little boy would have that mean mother?" It's not an issue of credibility. I certainly believe it. It's an issue you're trying to present the reader with something that is intractably difficult to negotiate. Something that is worthy of our going, "Ah, what would I do about that?"

William H. Coles
In the story setting?

Jim Shephard
Right, in the story setting. And what you mean by embodying the conflict in drama is that we're expecting this not to be solely a meditation, but in fact these ideas to be pressured and set forward into motion in the world. I love my father or I hate my father is a conflict that could go on inside my head. Or you could say something like, "I love my father and I hate my father and we're going to put into dramatic form because my dad and I are going to take a trip across the country in a Volkswagen Bug." Now you have a dramatic form for the conflict. And that will actually help you find more dramatic forms. What happens when they see the first rest stop and Dad says, "I think we should go another hundred miles." And the son says, "Let's stop here." Whatever it is that they fight about, they're going to start fighting about it. And now you have a way of embodying the conflict.

William H. Coles
And as you go through revision, those are opportunities?

Jim Shephard
Those are opportunities. Sometimes you'll not make the most of those opportunities; sometimes you'll not notice you had an opportunity; and sometimes you try to protect the characters from this conflict because "I like my characters and I don't want any unpleasantness."

William H. Coles
You frequently speak of agency, which I perceive as the non-fatalistic possibilities that a character has to act and change. And you've indicated that intense rage tends to suppress the agency of a character.

Jim Shephard
Hm. I'm not sure that happens. There are a number of things that will suppress agency in a story. Rage—I can certainly imagine how rage can do that, but I wouldn't make that link inevitable, necessarily. I would say that a lot of stories suffer from the story's lack of understanding just how much agency these characters have. That often takes the form of characters who seem to be set on by the world. The world does all sorts of things to them and they just deal with it. That is often the way life actually works. Life does things to you, and you deal with it. But the deal-with-it part is where your agency comes in. And that's where the story resides. Right? So Bill gets the same hand dealt to him that Fred got, and Bill handles it very differently. That's the story, the basis for the story, the excuse for the story . . . what the world handed Bill. Bill got shingles and Fred got shingles—both on their wedding day. The way Bill dealt with it was very different. And if Bill dealt with it smoothly, and without any trouble, it's an anecdote. I got shingles on my wedding day. No problem.

William H. Coles
No story.

Jim Shephard
I got shingles on my wedding day and I left my bride at the altar without a note. Now you've got a problem. And notice the story is not about shingles. The story is about an inadequate response to shingles.

William H. Coles
Does erotic intensity decrease agency?

Jim Shephard
It certainly has the effect of making you *believe* that agency has been decreased. Someone in the throes of erotic intensity says, "I just couldn't control myself. Therefore, I'm not responsible." But all you need to know about the disingenuousness of that is to image your wife or your lover saying, "What are you getting at me for? I slept with your best friend. But I couldn't control myself." And you're like, "Why don't you give it a shot?" And there is also something about erotic intensity that is deeply pleasurable, so we tend to suspect that giving yourself over to that irrationality is not entirely irrational. This is not irrational; I'm going to go with this.

William H. Coles
What are the consequences of in-the-moment narration on emotional complexities?

Jim Shephard
You need to be highly self-aware if you're in the moment because you don't have any retrospective distance. The story needs to be expert enough in employing its other cues to complicate the limitations of the speaker in the moment. Somebody might expose his own limitations as a thinker by saying, "You know, my dad came in. He seemed perfectly fine with it. He was white-knuckled the whole time." With in-the-moment narration, you might say, "I'm going to be super intricate with my breakdown of something." And there are writers who can do that—Nicholson Baker, Henry James, Virginia Woolf. Or you might say, "I'm going to narrate what's going on in the moment, the way Ernest Hemingway is in the moment." But there are going to be other clues telling us. Again the example being, "Dad was fine, his knuckles were a little white and he was gritting his teeth, but he was fine." You go, "I don't think he was fine. I think there is something else going on."

William H. Coles
Are there gender-specific differences to the way writers structure stories and render stories?

Jim Shephard
There probably are. The same way you would be surprised to get hard-boiled detective fiction from a woman. But those are only tendencies. Not hard-and-fast rules.

William H. Coles
The reason I ask is because a significant majority of books are purchased by

women, and the percentage is much higher, I understand, for literary fiction. And the majority of agents and editors are women. What's your feeling about electronic publishing?

Jim Shephard
It's becoming a much bigger thing. I just sold a story to a purely electronic magazine called *Electric Literature*. I've done that with one other story that is in the new collection. I did that back then because I couldn't get anyone else to take it. Now it's becoming a more viable option. It is, for better and for worse, the future. But I also don't think it's going to replace my typewriter and hard copy.

William H. Coles
Do you get the same enjoyment reading a novel, say, on Kindle?

Jim Shephard
I won't read it. If that's what reading turns into, I'll probably stop reading. My understanding is that *Electronic Literature* offers you the option of hard copy if you want it. You can download it and print it out. If I'm reading other peoples' work, that's what I'm doing. I need hard copies. On the other hand, online publishing is such an obvious way of streamlining costs and delivering content that of course it's going to get bigger and bigger and bigger.

William H. Coles
And with shorter time from submission to publication. What are key films for writers to study to improve their fiction?

Jim Shephard
That's an interesting idea. I'm not sure I ever thought about movies that can help you write fiction.

William H. Coles
You use movie examples often in your classes.

Jim Shephard
I do. Although very specific examples. There is greater currency. I think far more people have seen *Chinatown* than have read Cormac McCarthy's *The Road*. Also seeing it is a way of making the example a little more vivid. That's why I use so many examples in class. It puts people into the scenario. At least it allows you to visualize on the page a little bit easier. Interpreting and decoding is so difficult sometimes. It's very easy to think you're only dealing with marks on the

page. With traditional fiction, you're supposed to be imagining a sort of reality, a dream.

William H. Coles
The writer is creating an illusion.

Jim Shephard
Yes, and with that illusion you're supposed to be thinking, "Wait." Like in your story "The Golden Flute." She stood there a minute, all by herself. If I'd been showing a movie of that, nobody in the room would have had any trouble understanding. A minute is a long time. But the readers flew right over it as if it said she stood there for a second. She didn't stand there for a second! That's why you need to be a close reader. But that's also why you need to understand why, when you're reading this stuff, you're making an image in your mind. If you make an image, it changes things.

William H. Coles
And that's the advantage of prose.
I regret our time is up. Many thanks. I've really enjoyed this..

Jim Shephard
Thank you.

Rob Spillman Interview

July 17, 2008
William H. Coles

Rob Spillman is the editor of *Tin House,* a literary magazine that has been honored in *Best American Stories, Best American Essays, Best American Poetry, O. Henry Prize Stories,* the *Pushcart Prize Anthology,* and numerous other anthologies. He is also the executive editor of Tin House Books. His writing has appeared in *Book Forum,* the *Boston Review, Connoisseur, Details, GQ, Nerve,* the *New York Times Book Review, Real Simple, Rolling Stone, Salon, Spin, Sports Illustrated, Vanity Fair, Vogue, Worth,* and other magazines, newspapers, essay collections, and online journals. He has worked for Random House, *Vanity Fair,* and the *New Yorker.*

William H. Coles
Let's begin with a general question. Is the literary story surviving? Is it healthy? Or is it in decline?

Rob Spillman
I think it's thriving. My anecdotal evidence is that I get two thousand submissions a month, which means twenty-four thousand per year, and there are a lot of very good literary magazines out there—*One Story, McSweeney's, Virginia Quarterly.* And if you look at *Best American Stories* or the Pushcart Prize or O'Henry Prize anthologies every year, there is really high-quality work. I've gone to festivals around the world from Saint Petersburg to Nairobi, and the rest of the world is certainly embracing the form. I see a lot of energy and vitality in foreign writers. A lot of second-generation American writers are embracing the form and doing a lot with it.

William H. Coles
Is it an American form?

Rob Spillman
I think the new generation of foreign-born or second-generation American writers—people like Junot Díaz, Edwidge Danticat, Yiyun Li, and Nathan Englander—are bringing in a different slant to the story, a new sense of urgency.

William H. Coles
On the sort of negative symptom side, I heard you say that five thousand would be a good sale on a collection for a publisher, and for a small publisher, two or three thousand might be what one could expect.

Rob Spillman
Per book.

William H. Coles
That means one in ninety thousand or one hundred thousand Americans might buy a collection of short stories. Are the economics solid enough to be confident that publishers will continue to publish, and readers will continue to read?

Rob Spillman
I think it's unrealistic to make a living as a short-story writer, just as it's unrealistic to make a living strictly as a poet. Even Robert Pinsky, the poet laureate, is a teacher and a lecturer, and I bet you he gets a lot more money from lectures and teaching than the sales from his early books. Look at the most successful short-story writers. For instance Lorrie Moore teaches, she came to our festival. It depends on what kind of writer you are, but teaching and lecturing is a part of the permanent scene. Not too many people are writers like Cormac McCarthy, locked away, just doing their thing.

William H. Coles
Is there any thrust in the United States to seek government funding to create an archive for unpublished short stories? To save it as an art form so it doesn't have to pass through a filter of publication before being archived?

Rob Spillman
I think the private sector is doing that much more so than government. Google Books is scanning, Project Gutenberg.

William H. Coles
But they're scanning published books. Is there another way to vet these books rather than just through publishing?

Rob Spillman
No. I think it's nonhierarchical and it's self-selecting. I think more and more literary magazines, including us, are putting up more and more material for free, and . . . it self-selects. The good stuff gets found. I'm a real firm believer that good work rises. One of my favorite publishing stories at Tin House is

from when I was judging a competition for the festival in Russia. They had a scholarship to go to this conference, and we received six hundred and fifty applications. I pulled out one story that I really liked from the six hundred and fifty and at the same time one of my readers pulled out a different story from the unsolicited pile in-house and put it in front of me and said, "You really should read this story." And I read that story and I loved that one too, and it turned out they were by the same person—a forty-one-year-old woman. She'd never published anywhere before and she'd just started sending out her stories, and through two different sources they rose up. Her name is Dylan Landis, and she is about to have her first collection of short stories out. But these two different stories rose up from two different stacks of work. They both jumped out.

William H. Coles
And the message is: get your writing to a level that it can rise.

Rob Spillman
Yes.

William H. Coles
What is the most common mistake writers make in failing to engage a reader in their stories? And on a related note, what mistakes do writers make the dissipate the energy and vitality in their stories?

Rob Spillman
I see over and over two common mistakes, especially with beginning writers. The first one is throat clearing at the beginning of a story, where you work your way in—which everybody does, everybody feels their way into the story. But a good writer will throw away the first four pages. My example is, someone walks across a beautiful campus and then sits down and insults you. No one cares about the walk across the campus; start with the insult. The other one is what I call Doogie Howser syndrome, which is from the television show about the teen doctor who at the very end of each episode always sat down at his computer and typed into his diary: "What I learned today is that friends are invaluable." Even good writers will do this. They will keep you engaged for twenty pages and then they will pull back and say, "What I learned today is that friends are invaluable." No, no, no, no. You've been showing us for twenty pages. You don't need to tell us. Those mistakes are both very fixable. The other thing—the main thing—is confidence. I don't care what genre, what voice, where the setting, I will go anywhere if it is confidently told. If you firmly take me . . . that's a hard thing, you know, to never apologize but jump in and tell your story.

William H. Coles
Confidence. More than competence?

Rob Spillman
Confidence can overcome incompetence sometimes. I would much rather be taken off a cliff with a story than read a boring work with all the ribbons and bows in place.

William H. Coles
And is that voice?

Rob Spillman
I think that's voice *and* confidence. Take me wherever you want to take me confidently.

William H. Coles
Memoir has been on top for at least a few years, and certainly has shoved literary fiction to the side somewhat. What would be your advice to writers? Should they be preparing to write memoir-like prose, or memoir, or should they just write what's in their hearts?

Rob Spillman
What's in their hearts. For some people the memoir form is perfect. It really is their way; they can't deal with things fictionally, so they take a nonfiction route. And that's fine. My feeling is that the material chooses itself. I know a lot of people who have bounced back and forth trying to write the same story, whether fiction or nonfiction, and one way then clearly clicks with them. You know they don't have the freedom they need with nonfiction, so they just do it fictional, or they don't feel like they're telling the truth in fiction, so they need to do it with nonfiction.

William H. Coles
When it does click, what are the pluses for fictionalization as a technique? What does fiction do for a story?

Rob Spillman
That nonfiction can't do?

William H. Coles
Yes.

Rob Spillman
Well, you are the master, you can take the seed of the situation. If your subject is based in reality, you can take the seed of the emotion but amplify it, you can alter the chronology, you can add brothers and sisters to make it even more dramatic. With memoir, you can play with the form, like Nick Flynn does with his memoir, but you really . . . the facts are the facts. You can't invent a brother or sister with your memoir.

William H. Coles
You can, but you'll get sued.

Rob Spillman
You can, but it's not right.

William H. Coles
Is there a difference between the stories you like and the ones you publish?

Rob Spillman
I publish what I like. It's a collaborative process with my editors, but I love my job because I get paid to read what I like, then I get to publish it.

William H. Coles
Writers shouldn't try to write for your tastes.

Rob Spillman
No. My advice for people who are starting to submit is to really do your homework. I tend to like very voice-driven fiction and nonfiction, but not everybody does. Do your homework and look at literary magazines. Start off with *Best American Stories*, the O. Henry Prize stories, and the Pushcart Prize anthology and see who publishes what kind of fiction. If you look at Pushcart and see five things and they are all coming out of *Tin House, One Story, Ploughshares,* or whatever, when you start submitting you can say in all honesty, "I just read the most recent issue of *Ploughshares* and I really enjoyed this or that story." It makes a difference.

William H. Coles
What do you look for in an author's structure and style?

Rob Spillman
Again, confidence. If you jump in, jump confidently. I have a pet peeve regarding the second person that I call the second-person accusatory: "You are walking down the street." I go, "No, I am not walking down the street." I hand those stories to another editor who likes them, and they will hand one back to me if it

really is good. Formally, I love to be surprised. Flashbacks are hard. Being in the scene is the most important thing. Tell it in scenes.

William H. Coles
When you recommend that authors read, do you recommend reading all the work of one author or selected works by many authors?

Rob Spillman
If you come across an author who particularly speaks to you, I think it's worth it to read a lot by that author because not that many writers will really speak to you. Toni Morrison talks about finding a writer who gives you permission to be yourself. You know, it's not necessarily like this is exactly me, but when the little voice in your head says if this single mother is getting up at four in the morning—this is what Toni Morrison did, she got up at four in the morning before she went to her job as an editor while she was writing her first couple of books—I mean if she can do it, by God, I'm going to give it a try. No whining.

I personally read by recommendation, so I tend to jump around. I depend on my friends telling me to read X or Y. I also think it's good exercise to find classic great stories, stories that you really respond to, and then sit and type them out. Copy them word for word. By typing them you feel the rhythms of how they do it, and also you notice how the best short stories have no wasted words. No excess. If you actually type it, you feel the rhythm. Also reading out loud, whether it's your own work or the story, you hear the music of the story. I think it's very important for writers to read their own work aloud before they send it out.

William H. Coles
Do you think people will start reading stories short and long on computer screens? What will be the impact on writers for the next couple of decades?

Rob Spillman
I read a lot on the computer. I get a lot of emailed submissions and I read a lot of international writers that I can only find through the internet, and I don't like to print things out to read them, generally. But I think with nonfiction there are more opportunities to embed stories in your work, whereas for fiction I think there is always going to be the sort of tactile pleasure of holding the object, and that's one of the things we did with *Tin House*. We wanted to make a nice tactile thing that you could carry around and keep. It is a one-on-one experience with your magazine or book. I think there is always going to be that pleasure.

William H. Coles
Are there favorite classics that you recommend to learn the craft?

Rob Spillman
You can't go wrong with looking at the masters of the form: Raymond Carver, John Cheever, Alice Munro, Denis Johnson, Lorrie Moore, George Saunders, Aimee Bender, Deborah Eisenberg, Joy Williams. There are some very strong writers working right now in the short-fiction genre.

William H. Coles
Do you recommend films that can help one improve story structure?

Rob Spillman
The films of Todd Haynes: *Safe*, *Velvet Goldmine*, and *I'm Not There*. Anything that gets you thinking outside the box, because we are so linearly trained. Or Quentin Tarantino's *Pulp Fiction*, where he starts the movie a third of the way through the story and then comes back and finishes. You can put the middle at the beginning. It's a good exercise. Start with the end, then the middle, and then the beginning. You know, give yourself these challenges to break yourself out of the box.

William H. Coles
What is your concept of voice? It seems difficult to define. How do writers develop it internally, so it becomes external?

Rob Spillman
Unfortunately, it's not simple and it's hard work. It's literally writing thousands and thousands of words and just keep writing and writing and hopefully things will start to click. Who wrote *L.A. Confidential*?

William H. Coles
James Ellroy.

Rob Spillman
There is a famous story about him when he turned in a novel. I think it was his third one, and it was seven hundred pages long, and his editor said, "This is brilliant, but it really has to be five hundred pages. I just can't publish seven hundred pages." So he and his agent looked at it, and the agent said, "You know, instead of cutting scenes, let's cut words." So they cut words from each sentence and made it much snappier. They didn't cut any scenes, they just compressed the

language, and as they were doing it they were realizing, this is so much sharper and better.

William H. Coles
And it strengthened voice too?

Rob Spillman
Yes. And the voice just popped. It became his voice.

William H. Coles
As an extension of voice, what are the common point-of-view errors you see? In classes, there seems to be a special struggle with first person.

Rob Spillman
I think one of the problems is being too interior. It's a common problem for beginning writers to go, "Where am I? Where am I in space and time?" You should always have a note to yourself—where am I in space and time? And also, I think, especially beginning writers if they are writing something about reality, something that is true to them, don't paint the scene as you're seeing it in your own head. I strongly advise everybody: if you're doing something based on reality, sketch the room, just a little architectural drawing, a box, and draw what's in the room and use Skittles as your characters and move them around in the box, and if one Skittle's facing west they are looking at some things, and the other Skittle is looking east what are they seeing? It takes you out of your head. Again, where am I in space and time? Because you want to keep the reader in your story at all times. And if the reader is going—wait, the sun just set, why are they talking about breakfast? Or if you forget a transition. Anything that takes you out of the moment threatens the authority and competence of the writer, which you never want to do. I want to forget there is a writer and look up from the story and go, oh, wow.

William H. Coles
You lose the reader at that point.

Rob Spillman
Yes. As an editor who is looking at these stories, I will say, "Well, this writer has no control, so why should I keep reading?" A couple of those incidents will take you out.

William H. Coles
Thank you very much for contributing to www.storyinliteraryfiction.com. It's been great.

Rob Spillman
My pleasure.

Kirby Wilkins Interview

15 September, 2012
William H. Coles

Kirby Wilkins was division chair for thirty-one years at Cabrillo College, where he taught creative writing. Previously he taught at the Foothill Writers' Conference (1991–2001) and at the Surprise Valley Writers' Conference. He studied with Wallace Stegner in the Stanford University Creative Writing Program. His novels include *King Season* (Arbor House, 1985), set in Alaska, and *Quantum Web* (Holt, 1990), and he has published a short-story collection titled *Vanishing* (Bookpeople, 1984).

William H. Coles
Let's start with your conceptualization of story. Story is so important to human culture and society, but even more fundamentally in that humans depend on story for communication to get ideas and thoughts across.

Kirby Wilkins
The importance of story is indisputable, obviously. Particularly oral stories that come down through cultures, like the stories of Odysseus, the Iliad, Beowulf.

William H. Coles
Gilgamesh.

Kirby Wilkins
Those stories were told to carry on tradition, for memory. They were retold in the community, in the family. That is the most important aspect of story. But that's not where we are now.

William H. Coles
For the prose fiction writer, what are the features of story as you see it that make it readable, memorable, entertaining?

Kirby Wilkins
For me, the development of story has always been organic. It's had to do with getting far enough into myself, into what I know about the world and what I feel about the world, to finally bring up a shape of some sort. And then the technique

comes in—you maybe heal after that. There are writers who I think are more akin to the oral story tradition who just tell story. When I read T. Coraghessan Boyle—I'm not wild about it because he's so facile—but he tells story. You easily imagine him telling those stories without revision, which I know he doesn't. I'm not the type who conceptualizes story. It's strictly something I do from within myself that's organic, and if I bring any technique to it, it's what happens next. Once I've got something I can give it more shape, help it, speed it up, give it some sort of ending. Endings are frequently a problem.

I also think that the stories in my particular case—early stories in the collection *Vanishing*—reflected my view of life, which I didn't realize until they all came together. It's a fairly bleak view, a kind of existential 1950s view in which there's not a lot of meaning and not a lot of love. There's an emptiness in the characters' lives. What emerges is a worldview I had at the time. Less so now. That came from the writing itself. I admire writers who are prolific and turn out stories like Joyce Carol Oates. I've never felt that I was in that class.

William H. Coles
A story begins, of course, and as you said, a story ends. Do you have some feeling as you write that the end is going to happen, or do you let the end sort of fall off the cliff?

Kirby Wilkins
The famous *New Yorker* stories didn't end, they dribbled out. I personally don't want to know the end when I start. I want to discover the end and let it be a bit of a surprise. The act of writing leads me to the point where it's got to end. Sometimes that happens naturally and sometimes I artificially say, "Wait a minute, I've got to get out of this somehow. What's going on here?" But in many cases—including every story in *Vanishing*—the story evolved and ended. In my own reading I tend to prefer a more organic story. One that's a little less predictable in terms of plot manipulation.

William H. Coles
Should a fictional story be entertaining?

Kirby Wilkins
Yes, it should. But we get into trouble there if we're competing with big entertainment, like films. You want people to read it and enjoy it and come away not just entertained, but, I hope, moved in some way. That would be nice. The stress on entertainment now is hazardous because you're up against overwhelming odds through other media, which I think has put some pressure on fiction to

be extremely snappy right out of the box. You need the catcher, you've got to sink the hook, and a lot of times that's kind of artificial, but maybe an economic necessity. But I've always found that kind of approach difficult. You want the reader to keep reading after page one, and there are many ways to do that.

William H. Coles
You have a distinct control over discussion of student manuscripts in class. Can you walk us through the very specific things you say at the beginning? You give a valuable list of things that shape the discussion:

Is there tension, and how soon do you feel it?
Is there movement?
How important is place, and if it is mentioned, is it important?
What are the motivations?
Do you know the characters?
What is the timeline? How is it compressed?
What stands out? Image? Dialogue?
Is there a theme? (Present in most serious fiction.)
Ask: what? why? how?

Kirby Wilkins
That evolves from the whole approach to the class and to dealing with student manuscripts. It does directly relate to my own experience in writing school in the 1950s, specifically at Stanford University. I didn't realize it fully until later, but it was quite a destructive experience to be in classes that were very pushy in terms of aiming toward publication, fame, and fortune. The effect at that point was to turn me completely off. But then there was Walter Van Tilburg Clark, who was a very supportive man. He is well known to anybody who lives in Reno, Nevada. *The Track of the Cat* is one of his books. Also *The Ox-Bow Incident. The City of Trembling Leaves.*

He was for a while sort of the great white hope. It looked like he was really coming as a writer, but right about the time I had him as a teacher, he quit writing. Nobody ever knew why. The people who loved him didn't know what was going on. He couldn't write, he was frozen. I was frozen up myself when I had the class with him. He was extremely sympathetic. I didn't do any great writing with him, but I had a man who understood about writing.

That shaped my whole philosophy, which is: a writing workshop of any kind has got to be completely supportive of the participants, but not pussyfoot around the issues. So it's a delicate balance. You want to look at manuscripts, you want to offer comments. You would like as many of those comments as possible to come from students themselves and not from you. There needs to be an attitude of respect toward the people in the class regardless of the quality of the manuscript. Many writing programs are ego-fests where it's important to put people down and be top dog and have the teacher's attention. I try to stay away from that and work with the students in the class, bring the students along, let them do the work as much as possible. To that extent I offer that list of questions you quoted above.

If you're reading in class, you're not reading as a reader anymore, you're now a writer reading as a writer. Then there are different things you're looking for, structural things, like, How does a piece begin? How soon is there tension? There should be tension immediately that provides entertainment value. Something's amiss. Not necessarily dramatic, not sinking the fishhook, but there's something not quite right.

William H. Coles
Something out of balance?

Kirby Wilkins
Yes. And that unravels and unfolds as you move into the story. A short story's quite different than a novel in that respect. A short story is, some people have said, more difficult to write than a novel. The novel allows you a little more sloppiness, a little more room, a little more space to kind of wander around in.

William H. Coles
Last night, when you were giving your lecture, you answered a question from a woman who gave some background on a story she was writing. Everybody admired how you asked her specific questions to help her find within herself ideas, thoughts . . . images too, I think. Does that come naturally? Can you give us some specifics about how you did that? It was so effective.

Kirby Wilkins
Thank you. That moment was nice for me too because of the way she responded. I have talked to her since, and it turns out there's even more to the story. But it goes back to this fundamental philosophy between Walter Clark and Wallace Stegner at Stanford and San Francisco State, in my experience in the early 1960s, and that is respect for the people, the students. Instead of answering questions with authority as the expert, I would much prefer to have that come through from the student. In this case it's about Socratic questions. The idea is to zero in on a couple of things, let her respond to those. In that case, they were

abstractions. She talked of the tall Indian man, and she's new in town, and so the immediate question was, How did you know he was Indian? And she cuts loose: "Oh, well, the Indians dress completely differently, they wear the hats, they wear these clothes." Then there was a pause, and I asked, "What did you say the problem was in your writing?" Everybody laughed because of course, there it was.

William H. Coles
She'd solved it on her own.

Kirby Wilkins
Then she said she walks across the street—and at that point I didn't know she's just gotten off a bus—she goes to a laundromat, which I thought was amazing, coming to a strange town and going to the laundromat. And she's also got two kids in tow. And so just pressing for those details from her, which she was quick enough to give, pleased everybody. It pleased me to find out information. She was doing what any writer has to do, which is go deeper into the material. And because it was all on a public stage, I suppose it made it more dramatic. All I did was push a little deeper and let it come from her. I didn't have to say anything.

William H. Coles
Here's one of those impossible metaphysical kinds of questions.

Kirby Wilkins
I love those.

William H. Coles
What is voice for a writer?

Kirby Wilkins
We heard a discussion of poetic voice, which I didn't entirely agree with. Fictional voice is, in my view, after all these years of teaching, the single most important aspect of writing. But you can't lay it on; you can't invent it. It has to do with your character, your angle of vision, the way you see the world, the way you project as a narrator, and the kind of language you use. There are famous voices you recognize immediately, for instance the Ernest Hemingway voice, which infected generations of people. Another voice you could probably recognize a mile off is William Faulkner. But I think voice is more fluid for most of us. An author could write a series of stories and people might not be sure they're written by the same person. So I'm not sure it's a steadfast voice. That's a voice that develops in a unique piece of fiction and it comes from the choices the

writer's making and the way the writer approaches the material. And of course the language the writer uses develops voice. It's not easy to define, but I think when all the elements come together in those first opening lines of a story, the effects are huge. It's best not to be self-conscious about it. Not "I think I'm going to have a tough voice here," but create a voice that drives the story.

When the reader picks it up and reads the first couple of paragraphs, they either put the story down or they keep going. And if they keep going, in my case mostly, it's the voice that's written on the page. No human voice behind it all—they're entering my head and resonating in some way that makes me want to keep moving.

William H. Coles
Is that the authorial voice? The persona of the writer?

Kirby Wilkins
The writer. And it's not even quite a persona because it's not a stand-in for the writer; it's the writer's language on the page. It's not as though you can back up as you might from a person, and figure out who the guy is behind the person. I hate to say it's a mysterious or mystical process, but there is no person like that. I mean, the writer wrote the words, wrote the story. There's the story that resonates in our mind with a kind of voice. That voice may in fact surprise the writer him- or herself. So I'm not sure it's a persona exactly. It's tempting to say that, but I'm not sure.

William H. Coles
When considering the voice of the author, is it different than that of the narrator? Or the character? Is there a distinctive voice for each?

Kirby Wilkins
What do you mean by the narrator? The person telling the story?

William H. Coles
Yes. In my conceptualization, an author creates a story, a narrator tells the story, and the character acts in the story. But there are all sorts of fluctuations. For example, in first person, sometimes the author is the narrator.

Kirby Wilkins
So, in first person, who is the narrator telling the story? That narrator's not the author?

William H. Coles
Well, it depends on who's writing, of course. I personally try to separate the author from the narrator so that the narrator's background and perceptions are imagined differently, and hopefully more effectively, than when the author is relying on their own worldview, which is necessarily limited. This allows more potential and flexibility in the way the overall voice of the piece goes forward. I'm wondering about your thinking about this, and how it plays out in your writing. Do you ever think about narrator-distinctive voice, character-distinctive voice? I've come to believe that in creating a character's voice, it helps the work to have the reader recognize that this is one unique character's dialogue. The author is creating a character's voice, and that character's voice can only be consistent if the environment and the experience of that character are specific and consistently maintained.

Contemporary literature, quite frankly, doesn't deal with this very often. To see it done well, you have to go back to the classics of the nineteenth and twentieth centuries: C. S. Forester, Jane Austen, the Brontës. Although the author is present in these works as their creator, the author is not *in* the work. There is no distinct authorial presence in the story world. Rather, they create the story and deliver it through a separate narrator related to the story world.

Kirby Wilkins
I'm still not totally clear about the separation you're suggesting between author and narrator, but I think I know what you mean. That is, in a third-person story where characters are thinking certain ways, and even in close third person where you're in somebody's mind throughout the entire story and seeing the world through their eyes—okay, that's the character's perception of the world. I, the author, have invented that character and his or her voice. But you're right, there's a distinction in that the voice of the story at that point and the way that character is seen and moves and thinks—it's not entirely me doing that. I'm assuming it's not a narrator, because the narrator's not telling the story. The narrator's sort of creating the story, allowing the story to happen. But is that me? That's an interesting question.

William H. Coles
I perceive an advantage for that narrator separation in the sense that every story is essentially written in the past, about something that has happened, even if you put the story in the present or future tense. Everything in the author's mind has happened, from a place with a different perception.

Kirby Wilkins
If you're writing a Civil War story (and I'm not talking about historical fiction, I'm just saying that's the setting for your fictional story), you've got a historical setting. Let's say you've put your narrator in 1940, and you've positioned your story as occurring in 1864. There is an advantage of writing through that narrator using all that narrator's perceptions, thoughts, attitudes, opinions from 1940. That narrator has a totally different perspective of the Civil War than the author's in 2012. It is a rich source of ironies. That's getting pretty tricky, because you're talking about a narrator who exists in 1940 as a person, as a character.

William H. Coles
Yes. But not always as an in-story character. Story narrators are often not characterized, or even identified. Instead, they remain a presence in the story, with a specific voice and worldview.

Kirby Wilkins
So, if we're reading now, in 2012, how do we know that it's a character from 1940 narrating the story?

William H. Coles
The reader doesn't need to be told that the character is speaking and thinking in 1940. But the reader needs to assume that for credibility and reliability in their perception and acceptance of the story. All this is subliminal in most cases.

Kirby Wilkins
You're going to have to have cues in a case like that. Otherwise, why not just tell the story of the Civil War right now? We'll get the research together and get it started and there's a character doing X and somebody else doing Y. I mean, that's writing a story about the Civil War. How would you and I create a novel with the patina of a voice from 1940? I can't get my mind around how we would do it.

William H. Coles
In the 1940s the thoughts and actions of the narrator, the character, or even the author are different. For example, the voice in 1940 will have an entirely different view of the race issue from that of 2012, or from the time of Thomas Jefferson, or any other time. It is timeline specific. The advantage, it would seem, is creating believable and accurate voices for characters and narrator that contribute to the storytelling. Accurate voices help distinguish characters, and help provide broader interpretation of story meaning and themes.

Kirby Wilkins
Well, no. To my way of thinking, it's almost an impossible thing to do because when the book is picked up in the bookstore, which it wouldn't be anymore because it would be online, but anyway it's on the Kindle, you're reading a book about the Civil War. I'm not seeing any way we're going to know that it's a 1940 narrative.

William H. Coles
Not a 1940 narrative. Simply a voice that supports the character's (and narrator's) position on the story timeline.

Kirby Wilkins
It's virtually impossible except in the postmodern mode where you can play all kinds of games and tricks. But in a conventional realistic novel, you don't want to break that narrative stance, the consistency.

William H. Coles
I understand.

Kirby Wilkins
Otherwise you're going to lose your reader.

William H. Coles
Not lose the reader as much as allow room for the reader to join the story narrative. Let me ask you about point of view and voice. Are they the same thing? And if not, how do they differ and how do you use them?

Kirby Wilkins
I don't think they're the same thing, but they're related. One of the deceptive things about first person is that it seems to be a clear point of view. We know where we are from where some guy's talking to us. In fact, that's a stance, it's an invented character, it's also a creation—as much a creation as a third person. But we buy into first person a little more easily. Third person gets trickier. The third-person voice you adopt can be some slangy voice, maybe New Orleans or whatever. You take a voice of a character who has a voice in the story. Outside the story, you the writer are creating that voice. First person, the banter of voice is not so clear because nobody's talking now. Now we've got a person on the page, moving around, doing things, who's being seen from a particular angle, either a so-called omniscient, way back, up close, stream of consciousness. Those choices, how close and intimate we become with the third-person character, are in my mind curious and have something to do with voice.

I know when I'm most comfortable with a close third-person voice because I'm almost in a stream of consciousness. I'm up so close that everything is really in that person's mind and it's a free-flowing association going on. That seems to be my natural, default mode. Other people, not at all. They have to be further back. The choices may have something to do with where the author sees the world.

William H. Coles
Are all first-person narrations unreliable?

Kirby Wilkins
We never know how reliable they are as long as we're stuck in the first person all the way through. I think the good ones—and I'm being very vague here—have to have some questions in the reader's mind around if this person is really right or not. I'm blanking on the title, but I'm thinking here of a book that just weighs two points of view, a man's point of view and a woman's point of view, about the same events in America. And of course they're wildly different—so much so that you expect it to be resolved in some way. I mean, they can't both be right, so something's going on here. Well, the author in that case does not help us out. He's deliberately not helping out in the first-person box. Just dropped us in and said good luck. One of these people must be unreliable, lying, but they're both very winning.

William H. Coles
Do you see writing novels and/or short stories as a structured procedure?

Kirby Wilkins
Yes.

William H. Coles
You called it "organic" earlier, but you also think are there times when structure can help? Structure seems to relate to drama in many ways. Structure also seems to relate to logic and continuity. And when you need logic and continuity to get across complex emotional changes, do you look to structure?

Kirby Wilkins
Definitely in revision, yes. It seems to me, at the point the questions you're raising apply, something's got to be moved around, and there's got to be motivation. You've jumped from point A to point B, but there's nothing in between. In issues of motivation, you get into the plot. Yes, at that point trying to work a finished product, those are the kinds of technical aspects that are internalized, but you certainly have to do them. And sometimes miraculously an occasional

writing will have the flow and the satisfactory plot resolution that doesn't need much tinkering.

William H. Coles
Do you use second person, either the "you" voice or "we" voice?

Kirby Wilkins
Not much. Maybe in a couple of stories. And I like to play with it in class as leads for material. It's a person, not actually a fictional voice. So I kind of like the intimacy of that. But in terms of using it in fiction . . .

William H. Coles
That seems to be a direct approach to the reader.

Kirby Wilkins
It is a direct approach. It's like you're having a little chat with the reader.

William H. Coles
"We're going down the street," or "You're going down the street and you walk into the café and you order a sandwich," or "We went to the fair and looked at the pigs." What do you see as advantages to the use of the second-person voice—the "we" voice or the "you" voice—in contemporary fiction?

Kirby Wilkins
It's a completely different voice that can get aggravating for the reader—having somebody addressing you as "you" all the time as if you're bosom buddies. Particularly if the person saying "you" is not a very nice person, it makes it even harder. "You go into the store." The reader thinks, "Really? Why?" Or: "You think she's ugly as sin, but you like the way swings her butt." The reader may think, "That's not what I would think. Why am I reading this?" How would you use "we" as a second person?

William H. Coles
I don't think I myself would. But people say things like: "We looked to the other people in the lifeboat, maybe twenty or thirty." Note how this implies that the reader, being part of the we, can't see or count. Or: "We went to church and we thought, 'God is here today.'" The reader thinks, "Really? I was with you doing that?"

Kirby Wilkins
Okay.

William H. Coles
We went to church, we lit a candle, we watched that candle melt, the flame yellow orange, and it brought an idea to us. And the reader asks, "That's not what I would remember. Why am I included?" Always the author confronting the reader, and demanding suspension of disbelief.

Kirby Wilkins
In what you're making up there, there is an implied other person besides the reader. There's somebody else going along.

William H. Coles
Yes. The author demands the reader join in if they are to continue reading. It's more than use of "we" as plural second-person descriptive. It's including the reader by addressing them as "you" plus someone else, often unclear.

Kirby Wilkins
Okay, I'm hearing it a bit now. I don't have a feeling about that one at all. The "you" voice is what I like to play with.

William H. Coles
What do you perceive as the changes in literary fiction in the last century, and do you perceive them as positive or negative?

Kirby Wilkins
I don't know. I think literary fiction as a concept is fairly recent. I'm not sure there was much literary fiction before. There was just "fiction." My father read Hemingway. People read John Dos Passos, John Steinbeck. I mean, those were good writers, not literary writers. They become literary writers as we look back, but at the time they were part of the culture and they wrote. I think literary fiction is partly an artifact of that distancing, and the writing schools reflect that in a way, proposing that a literary story is opposed to a popular story, with the latter, of course, having lower status. The literary story appeals more to people with education and a degree of sophistication, who are willing to give it the time. I'm not sure when that happened or why it happened, but I do think it's become more exaggerated. I mean, is Stephen King a literary writer?

William H. Coles
No. But a very good writer.

Kirby Wilkins
He's a popular writer. He's a genre writer. But will he persist on the shelves of

literature and with time be seen as literature? I don't think his characterizations are strong enough and his plots are too fatalistic. Raymond Carver, whom I like a lot, is certainly relegated to literary status. He might have had a little more outreach than other literary writers.

William H. Coles
Right.

Kirby Wilkins
Joyce Carol Oates?

William H. Coles
Literary. But with widely variable quality in her output.

Kirby Wilkins
Literary? Oates publishes like mad. I don't know how many novels she sells. But it's an odd distinction. I'm not sure when it crept in, but it seems to me a little artificial, and it's been accelerated by the 822 writing programs and people learning to write. Look what's become of literary fiction, which apparently means somewhat more serious or more demanding fiction than would appeal to the popular reader. It's aimed at a slightly different audience.

William H. Coles
Would you think that, being character-based, fiction could be assigned to literary fiction whereas plot-oriented fiction would be genre?

Kirby Wilkins
I'm sure that that's partly it. A good popular writer who is writing, publishing, and making a living from it is certainly using techniques that involve plot. A lot of it is the expectation of the audience.

William H. Coles
Fatalistic plot. The asteroid's coming toward Earth and we've got to figure out a way to save the planet.

Kirby Wilkins
Yes. And maybe what they call chick lit. That implies an audience. When people are writing chick lit, they have an audience, with expectations. I'm not sure what the age range for chick lit readers is. Whereas the literary writer almost *doesn't* have an audience unless they're picked up, get good reviews, *New York Times* reviews, climb the ladder of critical success, but still probably never going

to make it into the top ten in the *New York Times* but at least will have a solid reputation, enough sales that maybe they might bring out a paperback. That will help in getting into writing conferences and writing program faculties and the things that literary writers can do.

William H. Coles
How does memoir fit into this spectrum?

Kirby Wilkins
I have no idea. All I know is there's a lot more memoir being written. It may be almost a turn against literary fiction. Memoir seems to be real; as you open the book, at least it's got you hooked there. "I'm going to find out something real about the world." There's a call for it, and that seems to be about a need for voyeurism on the part of readers. A lot of writers now are wanting to expose themselves.

William H. Coles
Expose things that wouldn't have been exposed in the last century. Salacious detail.

Kirby Wilkins
A memoir's the last place you're going to get it about the person themselves. I mean, they will be telling all kinds of salacious detail about their friends, who was screwing whom and so forth. But inadvertently telling a lot about themselves, too. I have read almost no contemporary memoir. There's nothing wrong with it. A lot of my students are interested in it. But to my way of thinking, somewhat cynically, memoir is a form of fiction. Creative nonfiction. For some fiction writers it's hardly even necessary to conceal some of the things you used to have to conceal. So I'm not sure what's going on out there. Whatever it is, I suppose maybe I'll find out someday.

William H. Coles
I wanted to ask you about your experience with Wallace Stegner. You mentioned that it wasn't so positive.

Kirby Wilkins
As a teacher of literature, he's a Western author and a formulator of the Western movement, with a mystique. That 1950s Stanford writing school spun out of Iowa and it was, I guess, the first one on the West Coast. San Francisco State followed soon after. Stegner was quite ambitious. He was opening a new program, which was not that common then, and he wanted to succeed. He

was pushing. He wanted results, which is fine. In my own defense, I've had at least half a dozen friends who quit writing after they left the Stanford writing program. So something was amiss there. For me as an undergraduate, the graduate students were part of the problem. I'd written a couple stories that my undergraduate teachers liked, and then I got in with the big fellows. I shouldn't have been in there because I was just barely a developing writer, didn't know my ass from first base. So that's one problem. The other is that, in retrospect, there was insufficient respect for the student writers. I mean, if something's bad, it's bad, period. We're not talking about improving it necessarily; it's just a piece of shit. Well, it wasn't quite that bad, but it was in that kind of background. And when you're in a delicate state, not even sure what you're doing, it can be quite damaging. I knew good writers who were more confident than I was who went in the program and never wrote again afterward.

In the early days at Stanford there was too much push because Stegner wanted to get up equal with Iowa right away. That push worked for some people. I mean, the Stanford program is famous for the writers it has put out in the Stanford Fellowship Program. For me it became the definition of what not to do when I taught. Everything has been sort of anti-Stanford.

William H. Coles
It's ironic then that the present director of the Iowa workshop is a graduate of the Stanford program.

Kirby Wilkins
Doesn't surprise me at all. Mine is a very personal opinion. But I've run into enough roadkill that I feel confident.

William H. Coles
I understand. Do you have any recommended reads, contemporary or classic, for students?

Kirby Wilkins
I have such a lousy memory, I've got to go back and look up things I've read because I've forgotten them. But in terms of things that made a distinctive impact on my thinking, my writing, two or three come immediately to mind. In the 1950s it's Hemingway. For better or worse, because I think there's a downside to Hemingway. But if they haven't read the stories, the novels—and increasingly I think people haven't—they need to. And more recently for me, very important have been Raymond Carver's stories. Their bleakness appeals to me, that existential emptiness in the suburban world.

William H. Coles
And the minimalism.

Kirby Wilkins
And the minimalism. I think you could make a direct link between Carver and Hemingway. Another minimalist who is important for me is James Salter, particularly the novel *Light Years*. Extremely powerful. He went out of style in the early 1950s, nobody knew anything about him, and then he was rescued by North Point Press, which produced fine paperback work. They're really beautiful books, just gorgeous. You hate to think such a book as *Light Years* was ever lost. You want minimalism? Salter has so much white space you can't believe it. And he also has a nice way with erotic material, as in his book *A Sport and a Pastime*, which is entirely erotic. But *Light Years*, it's amazing. You can't believe what that man did.

William H. Coles
It's been a pleasure talking to you, and I certainly have learned a great deal. Thank you very much for talking to www.storyinliteraryfiction.com.

Kirby Wilkins
It's a pleasure talking to someone who knows so much about literature.

William H. Coles
Thank you. That's very kind.

Susan Yeagley and Kevin Nealon Interview

January 10, 2009
William H. Coles

Susan Yeagley was born in Nashville, graduated cum laude from USC's famed film school, and trained at the Groundlings in Los Angeles in comedy. She has worked in film and television in various distinguished roles, including as Jessica Wicks in *Parks and Recreation*, and she hosted World's Funniest Commercials in 2006 and 2007. She is married to Kevin Nealon.

Kevin Nealon was born in St. Louis, Missouri, and grew up in Connecticut. He excels at stand-up comedy, and has appeared on *Saturday Night Live* for nine seasons, creating such memorable characters as Mr. Subliminal, Franz of Hans and Franz, Mr. No Depth Perception, anchor of "Weekend Update." He played lead roles in *Weeds* and *Man with a Plan*. He is married to Susan Yeagley.

William H. Coles
First, let's talk about what humor is to you. How do you live with humor? How does humor relate to being human? Writers rarely think about humor and how it acts to shape lives, but it's so central to humanity.

Kevin Nealon
I think everybody has a funny bone as far as appreciating, laughing . . . some sense of humor. They may seem humorless as a person but . . .

Susan Yeagley
. . . there's always something that makes them laugh.

Kevin Nealon
I don't think the body is capable of surviving without having that release.

William H. Coles
Is humor then, a release of tension?

Kevin Nealon
It's a gift for humanity. It allows humanity to continue on, to get along with each other. It keeps people balanced.

William H. Coles
Is there a negative aspect to humor when it falls into ridicule? Buffoonery? When laughter comes at the expense of someone not conforming to the expected?

Kevin Nealon
There are a lot of different reasons why people laugh at things, whether it is buffoonery or intellectual comedy. I don't think anything is off-limits. Everybody has a different reason for laughing. And it is so subjective.

William H. Coles
Do they laugh because of surprise and an awareness of differences in what is expected versus what actually is?

Kevin Nealon
Sure. For me it's surprise sometimes. Other times it's not conforming to the way things should be. Or misdirection. Sometimes it's shock.

Susan Yeagley
It's seeing a church lady swear. It's watching someone who is very athletic fall down on the ice.

William H. Coles
Is it how we think about our construct of society? How a joke or new thought differs from your idea of society at the moment.

Susan Yeagley
Yes.

Kevin Nealon
The hardest I laugh comes from real humor. Kids are the funniest. I used to love watching *Candid Camera*, or the Bill Cosby show where he interviewed the kids—I think Art Linkletter did it before him—because kids are the most innocent and they say things that don't conform with the way the world is. That makes me laugh a lot. That's a good, honest laugh.

William H. Coles
Yesterday I boarded an airplane and the pilot and flight attendant were greeting

passengers. A mother came along with her three-year-old boy. The pilot said. "Hey, Tiger," as a greeting to the little boy. After a brief pause, the kid said, "I'm not a tiger." Everyone broke out laughing. It was funny. But why? The more I thought about it, I didn't know. It must relate to children and their innocence. Is that right?

Kevin Nealon
Yeah. With the limited knowledge that they have and trying to rationalize things using their sensibilities. We're so further advanced than they are . . . but we don't have the freeness of the way they think. I remember one time my little brother was about five or six, and he went to wash his hands and he came back about two seconds later. I said, "Did you wash your hands?" He said "Yeah." I said. "Did you use soap?" He said, "No." I said, "How do you expect to kill the germs?" He said, "I drown them."

William H. Coles
In a book you recently recommended, Steve Martin's *Born Standing Up*, there is a story about a comedian-magician Dave Steward, who had this opening joke. Steve Martin's words: "He walked from behind the counter and stood on the floor of the magic shop, announcing, 'And now, the glove into the dove trick!' He threw a white magician's glove into the air. It hit the floor and lay there. He stared at it and then went on to the next trick. It was the first time I had ever seen laughter created out of absence." I don't understand this. Is it humorous when people are unable to perform something we expect them to do? What is funny about some serious daredevil riding a motorcycle up a ramp and trying to jump over twenty-five school buses, barely clearing the ramp, and crashing? Yet that type of scenario can provoke a laugh.

Kevin Nealon
I think it's all a mindset. I was on *Saturday Night Live*, and we had athletes come on as guest hosts. They were hilarious because no one expected them to be funny. But they were used to hitting their marks because they were used to taking directions from their coaches so they knew where to be on stage, when to be there. When people go to watch something that is not supposed to be funny, they're very forgiving and it allows it to be funny. Michael Jordon was funny. Wayne Gretzky was funny singing Elvis in a Hawaiian luau situation. If that person was an actor or a comedian, that person wouldn't be funny doing it. It's like when people come to see comedy in a stand-up club—this goes back to talking about being imaginative—for your fiction writers, I think people come into a room and they sit down and they open up their imagination, they go on that ride of the comedian, let their imagination run wild with comedian.

Susan Yeagley
And they've also had a couple of drinks.

William H. Coles
That would help.

Kevin Nealon
The comedian is almost like a tour guide for their imagination.

William H. Coles
Are they there to be amused? What is the core feeling they desire? Do they just want to forget about the day?

Susan Yeagley
Escapism. Life is hard. After working nine to ten hours on the job, you go to a comedy club, let your shoulders drop, and get to laugh about your life, laugh about your relationships, and have someone get into it such that it's fresh and new. It's a release. It's escapism. When I go to a comedy club, I just want to go somewhere where my day hasn't taken me.

William H. Coles
So that's a relief. Escapism as a relief.

Kevin Nealon
There are a lot of different psychologies. When there's a group in a room dealing with one person, I think laughter is contagious. It's more funny with people than when you're alone. Somehow, the general laughter kind of lubricates your laughter. And a lot of times when people laugh and they're with other people, they'll look at the other person, and laugh, nod their heads . . . they're kind of lubricating one another with their laughter and it's more fun.

William H. Coles
Do we use humor to bond with people?

Susan Yeagley
Yes.

William H. Coles
Do we explore the boundaries of someone's humor and if it seems to fit our own, we begin to like that person?

Susan Yeagley
Yes.

Kevin Nealon
I think the big thing about comedy is people being able to relate to it. That's what makes a successful comedian. Someone like Jerry Seinfeld is talking about things that people can relate to—like a sock in the dryer–and it takes down a kind of barrier.

William H. Coles
That's true in your series *Weeds*, isn't it?

Kevin Nealon
Yes.

William H. Coles
Do you hurt when you're not funny?

Susan Yeagley
No.

William H. Coles
What do you feel?

Kevin Nealon
You mean when something's funny for you and it's not for others?

William H. Coles
No, no. When you're on stage, your desire is to please, your success depends upon people laughing at what you say. When it doesn't work, how do you feel about that? Why are you up there anyway? For admiration? And then what happens when you don't succeed? How do you feel?

Susan Yeagley
It's different with what Kevin does because he's doing live performances and I'm doing TV. If I'm not getting a laugh on a line that we did get a laugh on in rehearsals, we can always stop. That's the luxury of TV and film: we can stop, go back to the writers, and say, "Hey, can we punch this joke up?" Or, "Can we rewrite a couple pages here?" That's a luxury I have as a comedic actress. Now Kevin, on stage, is a one-shot deal. It's different.

Kevin Nealon
I've done it long enough that I know things that typically work, and if doesn't work for an audience, I'll know. People sometimes say: it's never the audience. But it *is* the audience sometimes.

William H. Coles
You mean these are plumbers who are not going to respond?

Susan Yeagley
Two hundred years old.

Kevin Nealon
I've done an act where I killed in one room but maybe, very rarely, people would sit there, maybe they're all tired, or they're drunk, or it's Friday and it's the second show and they're tired and drunk. I've seen people sleeping—they're that tired. They had the whole week working; who knows what is going on in their personal life? So, it can be the audience sometimes.

William H. Coles
It depends on how a person feels at the moment. If you hurt, or you're depressed, it's harder to be amused. And that's not your fault as the comedian, you don't feel like you've failed.

Kevin Nealon
But that's not to say you can't make that group laugh with something else. If you can kind of veer off your act, maybe take a different path that addresses why they are not laughing, that loosens them up. A lot of comics will say, "I'm bombing." The room goes crazy. They love it.

William H. Coles
There is another mystery that came to me as I was working on humor for writers, and that is the timing aspect. People say Johnny Carson had exquisite timing. I thought I knew what that meant but I really didn't. Is it presenting contrast at the right moment? What makes the right moment? What about the surroundings make the timing so important?

Susan Yeagley
It's music in my head. I can hear when to say something.

William H. Coles
Because you know what the response will be?

Susan Yeagley
It's a rhythm, like row, row, row your boat. The song. I can hear when the joke needs to be delivered. Or the tone of it. This sounds very vague, but I can hear what needs to be said next in a way that will be hopefully comedic . . . and well received.

Kevin Nealon
Subconsciously you know how people think, you know how long it takes for them to process something, you know the direction they are thinking, and then you lay in that misdirection.

William H. Coles
Ah. I'm starting to get it.
Kevin Nealon
But you have to lay that in there, the punch line or whatever, at that moment when you know they're processing something in a different way.

William H. Coles
So, the surprise processing has to be right for them because of their specific intellect and processing abilities?

Kevin Nealon
Yes. And I think if you've been doing it long enough, you can look at somebody and know where they're at. You know when to time it perfectly.

Susan Yeagley
Last night on stage Kevin was talking about Christmas and how his family had a cap on Christmas giving where you just buy fifty dollars' worth of gifts. The audience imagines a fifty-dollar Christmas gift, and then he lays this into it . . .

Kevin Nealon
I say, "We got this secret Santa works that doesn't allow more than fifty dollars on each person, so I got my father a Chrysler, and my mother a seat in the Illinois senate." And I got a big laugh.

William H. Coles
Neat. I like all this about the importance of imagination and spontaneity. Another mystery to me is the idea of dissecting humor. I was introduced to a famous humorist when I was in New Orleans, and I asked about humor. He said, "I don't talk about humor. You've either got it or you don't. And if you've got it, you can lose it if you start dissecting it." This was a real fear for him. To

me it seemed an extension of the common belief that if you have to explain a joke, the joke isn't funny anymore. The question is: if funny is a glob and you start making it into little globs . . .

Susan Yeagley
. . . picking at it . . .

William H. Coles
. . . the funny goes away. What is the essence of that? I don't understand.

Susan Yeagley
Honestly, in eight years of marriage it is not something that Kevin and I have ever talked about. We've never dissected humor. We'll run something by each other: "Do you think this is funny? Or this?" But in terms of going in with a microscope and looking at it, we rarely if ever do that.

Kevin Nealon
Just because if you have to explain something to somebody does not mean it's not funny. It's like the tree falls in the forest and hits the ground. By all standards it's a funny joke, but if that person doesn't get it, he doesn't get it. It doesn't mean the joke is not funny; it means it's not funny to that person.

William H. Coles
But if you explain a joke, it's no longer that joke anymore?

Susan Yeagley
Right.

Kevin Nealon
Although sometimes the explanation can be funny.

Susan Yeagley
It's kind of funny, if you're explaining it to someone.

William H. Coles
Or divulging your need to explain it.

Susan Yeagley
Right.

Kevin Nealon
It's like stand-up comedy. There's a lot of comics out there that I don't think are funny. But they're making a great living because a lot of people think they're funny. I personally don't get why they're funny, but they're funny to some people.

William H. Coles
Isn't that true of every performing art? Music, certainly.

Susan Yeagley
Whether they are commercially successful or not. We don't necessarily have to say we think they're funny, but the world has embraced them.

Kevin Nealon
They're making other people laugh . . . that they have no taste. [*laughing*]

Susan Yeagley
Or they have five houses based on the fact they sell tickets.

Kevin Nealon
Comedy is subjective. Nobody can say what is right or wrong. You cannot have a board that says this joke is not funny. What may not be funny for some may be funny to others.

William H. Coles
One key for me is that people who are funny at least have an interest in, if not an understanding of, human nature. Funny people know what it means to be human, and that's why it's so interesting to writers. Now I'd like to do an exercise regarding characterization in writing. We're not trying to make a character discover how to be funny. We're trying to identify what humor means to this character, whether they are conscious of it or not, and how they use it in trying to be human. Writers must think about character motivations and how humor relates. We can think of a character as composed of three major elements: a core desire, a formed morality, and a sense of humor. Using your skills as humorists, I'd like to let your imaginations and your humor evolve the character and story development. Help me make a person from real life a valuable fictional character. We'll not carry the real person's personality onto the page (that would be description, not creation), and we have free rein to change anything to achieve an effective personality for our story.

For the first test case, I've chosen Hillary Clinton. Let me explain why. It's a single image, really, that raises possibilities for me, an image that seems to be the crack in the armor of her public persona that might tell us more about who she really is. After Bill Clinton had sex in the Oval Office . . .

Susan Yeagley
He did? [*laughing*]

William H. Coles
You weren't there?

Susan Yeagley
[*shaking head no*]

William H. Coles
. . . denied it before the nation, was impeached at the first level, and Hilary seemed irate and humiliated. Yet there is one famous image of her walking hand in hand with Bill on one side and daughter Chelsea on the other. What made her do that? What were the complexities in her that made some people see her reaction differently—defiance, forgiveness, submission, political fodder?

Now, how can we make her an interesting character? What is her core desire? Motivations? Then we'll put that into a plot with an ending we know will work, consistent with our characterization. Then refine what we've learned about her, without in any way depending on her real self after we've discovered her soul. We are creating a new character, with a new name, new desires, that will work well in the conflict, action, and significant meaning we want in the story.

Hillary Clinton. She's a fascinating piece of US culture. What interests you about Hillary? Or does she interest you at all? Is she a flat personality?

Susan Yeagley
Oh, she's very interesting to me because on one hand, you've got this strong, independent powerhouse, and yet when her husband had the affair, or affairs, she transitioned into being very vulnerable, and there was a tenderness to her that we hadn't seen.

William H. Coles
Did you feel that was real, or for political gain?

Susan Yeagley
I don't think it was political gain. I think she was getting by every minute . . . probably at that time it was a struggle. I think it was very genuine. She was

holding on for dear life. I think she was a hurt, heartbroken wife. Yet, knowing she had a role as first lady . . .

William H. Coles
Did she love him?

Susan Yeagley
Oh, I'm sure. I'm sure they love each other.

Kevin Nealon
I think when you are in the spotlight like that you behave differently than you would if you were in the private sector. She knew everybody was watching her. And I personally think she is not only personally a strong woman, but also very determined . . . and aggressive, to become powerful.

Susan Yeagley
There is nothing wrong with that.

Kevin Nealon
But to the extent that she would stay with somebody like that for those political gains. I think that's a big part of it.

William H. Coles
That, in a sense, is opposite to what you were talking about, Susan. You saw her from a woman's point of view. That she was hurt and responding.

Susan Yeagley
I think she was mad as hell.

Kevin Nealon
I agree.

Susan Yeagley
She was angry, livid.

Kevin Nealon
Embarrassed.

Susan Yeagley
Horrified.

Kevin Nealon
Humiliated. And I think Bill Clinton . . . that's where there is a lot of comedy. If we could have been a fly on the wall in that house hearing the president get his . . .

William H. Coles
And his explanation?

Susan Yeagley
His explanation. Brilliant.

William H. Coles
So that might be the value of where a story might go.

Susan Yeagley
That's the single one-scene.

William H. Coles
So, what would be the conflict? What would she be trying to do with him? Would she be trying to get him to apologize? To change? Undo the sex?

Kevin Nealon
I think the first order of business is for her to rip him a new one. And he'd better just sit there and take it and listen. And not try to defend himself. And then I think she's got him in the palm of her hand.

William H. Coles
If we use that as the ending scene—say she comes into the Oval Office, for effect—how are we going to structure that ending scene? What is the conflict? What is the resolution, as we're writing? What are the lines?

Susan Yeagley
It's always details, details, details. Does she put down her LL Bean catalog and her Starbucks coffee? I mean, all the things we describe to make someone work.

William H. Coles
How do we hold together what she was in the beginning, which was a combination of being hurt, that she does love her husband, and that she's so politically driven. That's the essence of her we want in the ending. How do we hold onto that in the last scene?

The ART of CREATING STORY

Kevin Nealon
She's got to strike a deal with him at the end. She has to have a verbal deal, or a promise, to the extent that he will be supportive of her and her request for more power. I think to make it funny, to use your imagination, there have to be some really ludicrous demands that he can't say no to.

Susan Yeagley
Yes. She has to pull out a list of twenty things that she wants from him, and those . . .

William H. Coles
"Never unzip your fly in public."

Susan Yeagley
That list is what she has to give him. And he has to sit in a place, almost like a timeout where he can't move, and he has to hear the demands. It would be a funny scene.

Kevin Nealon
And also, he has to retain his powerful . . . ahhh . . .

Susan Yeagley
Aura.

Kevin Nealon
And he has to show that he still wears the pants in the family. That it's not her, although it is her. Somehow he has to do that.

William H. Coles
Could we start the story earlier? Before . . .

Susan Yeagley
Before Monica Lewinsky?

William H. Coles
Go back to an earlier affair, like Paula Jones.

Susan Yeagley
Or Gennifer Flowers.

William H. Coles
Yes, like that. Then carry it through with a series of events that build to the last scene. This would give momentum and more meaning as we got to the ending.

Kevin Nealon
It could even be that we find out later that Hillary was the original one who had the affair with Monika Lewinsky. Now she's super jealous. Now she's cheating on her with him.

William H. Coles
That brings in irony, humor.

Susan Yeagley
Or the ending scene could be Hillary driving Bill to a church and taking him down into the basement to visit his first sex-addition support group. Where he has to say, "My name's Bill, and I'm addicted to oral sex." Or whatever he would say. And she sits in with him and there are different political leaders in the sex addition class. That would be a scene that could be quite comedic.

Kevin Nealon
Again. It's all misdirection. It's how the shock value and surprise work.

William H. Coles
Now we can't carry Hillary and Bill into our story. Their background in a power setting is important, but we don't want to imply reality. We have to take the essence. We need to change names, and change some aspect of the character. Are there things that we can add to the character? You suggested many, including lesbianism. In addition, doesn't this have to be a story from two points of view? Doesn't there have to be a narrator as the source of the two characters' points of view, and maybe even carrying the meaning?

Susan Yeagley
Yes. Maybe there's something she does that drives him crazy—nothing would ever justify his actions, of course. But maybe she has an online gambling problem at night, and when he's wanting to get it on with her, she's doing Hollywood-Poker.com.

William H. Coles
That's a funny image.

Kevin Nealon
And he finds this out because he's gotten on the computer to go to porno.

Susan Yeagley
He sees the Bank of America account dwindling because she's got a funnel where they can just take deposits out of their account.

Kevin Nealon
Yeah, little subtle things like that. And maybe the reason she suspects he's had oral sex, even before it's come out, is because he's been wearing this beret.

Susan Yeagley
And he's been collecting berets . . .

William H. Coles
And not just to cover a bald spot.

Susan Yeagley
And he's actually invited the milliner to the White House to make hats.

William H. Coles
There seems a need for caution as we develop a comedic route. We begin to lose the significant meaning the literary writer is trying to express. We need to preserve her core value and understanding of the world. Do you see what I mean? As the character becomes more comedic, the character becomes less credible.

Susan Yeagley
They become more clownish.

William H. Coles
Yes. And yet the essence of humor is also what is needed. What we need to do is create and retain her core desires. Her political desire in conflict with her love for her husband.

Susan Yeagley
I think you keep the setting strong. We're in the White House. If you keep the codes of the White House, the codes of being first lady, the codes of being president, then that's in place, then you have a lot of leeway. I think if we were writing this scene for a sitcom, we'd have to be sure that set is spot-on Oval Office, or the Lincoln Bedroom.

William H. Coles
So this can't be the director of GM and his wife?

Susan Yeagley
It could be. But we'd have to have . . . setting is so important for whatever the characters are discussing.

William H. Coles
So it could work if we found as important a setting.

Susan Yeagley
Yes [*hesitantly*].

William H. Coles
In essence, this story could not make people remember Bill and Hillary. We can't have the reader believing you are describing them, even in a fiction way. So we have to move it to another power setting.

Susan Yeagley
Or you could move it to a sweet town in Georgia; you could move it to New York City. It could be some art dealers. But wherever it is, it has to be authentic and true to those peoples' lives.

Kevin Nealon
To get back to what you were asking about what she could do. She could have an enabler to allow him to pursue his addiction.

William H. Coles
And what would be her purpose in that?

Kevin Nealon
To get to the next step. To stay in the White House.

William H. Coles
To fulfill her political desires?

Kevin Nealon
Yes. It's like, how much will someone put up with to get what they want?

William H. Coles
Great stuff. I'd like to do one more: Sarah Palin. I've chosen her because you

comedians have taken her and created tremendously funny and important sketches. Tina Fey's interpretation has won many awards. What about this woman is funny? What about her personality would make her essence contribute to a great literary character? How could we create a story that would get across what we discover about her—and keep it credible? What are your thoughts about her as a good character? Is she too bland?

Kevin Nealon
I think she's an interesting character because she's a dichotomy of what we expect. Here she is, the governor of a very macho state—hunting, dogsledding—and is a woman with four kids.

Susan Yeagley
Five.

William H. Coles
She's got that photo where she is standing, I think, with her foot on the head of a dead moose.

Kevin Nealon
She's an ex-beauty-pageant contestant. Here she is coming out of that state . . .

William H. Coles
And she played the flute. Remember that?

Kevin Nealon
Yep. And a Republican, thrust into the spotlight.

William H. Coles
Intelligent, do you think?

Kevin Nealon
Intelligent enough to fool people. But most people can see through her with the winks, the cuteness.

William H. Coles
How about the pig joke? Soccer moms.

Kevin Nealon
The pig with lipstick.

William H. Coles
Yes.

Kevin Nealon
I don't think it was her joke, was it?

Susan Yeagley
She started it.

William H. Coles
I'm sure it wasn't hers originally. But that's the one she used in her acceptance speech.

Susan Yeagley
"What's the difference between a pit bull and a soccer mom. Lipstick."

William H. Coles
I thought it was a pig.

Kevin Nealon
But that was a phrase I think a lot of politicians had used. A pig and lipstick.

William H. Coles
Yes.

Kevin Nealon
And somehow it was used in relation to her.

William H. Coles
Was that an intelligent idea on her part?

Susan Yeagley
I always wince when politicians do comedy. I'm not going to be on the L.A. Lakers . . . try to play basketball. It's a little hard to watch when politicians do jokes. It's so forced. And someone wrote it for them. And the delivery is usually artless. And that's why the pig-lipstick joke . . . and everybody laughs in the room when politicians perform jokes, everyone laughs so robustly when it it's really not that funny, but they want to show they're supportive.

William H. Coles
Palin is incredibly focused and energetic. And she's successful. She comes from a

small town in Alaska, and she's a vice presidential candidate. I don't understand. She's not a good flautist, she's probably not a good hunter, she's certainly not a good comedian, she doesn't speak well, in that you don't get a sense of fathomless intelligence when you hear her speak. But she was able by pure willpower to get to this level. What about her allowed her to do this? To answer that would begin to make her an interesting character.

Susan Yeagley
I think it was ambition. I think ambition trumped all the other qualities that were not up to par.

William H. Coles
Ambition to do what?

Susan Yeagley
Ambition to be publicly recognized. Fame.

Kevin Nealon
Power.

William H. Coles
So those are the core desires?

Kevin Nealon
You know this whole story, this whole series of events, would be a perfect story to use your imagination with as a writer to create . . . who was that director? The guy with all those underdog movies from the 1930s and 1940s . . . *It's a Wonderful Life*.

Susan Yeagley
Frank Capra.

Kevin Nealon
Yes, you could take this story of Sarah Palin and use your imagination to turn it into a real underdog type of story. And make it great while in real life it was ludicrous.

William H. Coles
But not a Horatio Alger story. Not in a tragedy sense, but in a comedic sense about how she was able to go through this impossible scenario?

Kevin Nealon
Then you could use all kinds of imagination as far as her home life. Her husband . . .

Susan Yeagley
Her husband!

Kevin Nealon
Dogsledding and the kids.

William H. Coles
One of the serious events is her Down's syndrome child. I think she always handled that well. How would that motivate her?

Kevin Nealon
That's a perfect example of a writer using his imagination, taking a story and then building on it and creating a whole different story.

William H. Coles
What would you suggest might be some conflicts?

Susan Yeagley
Look at the marriage and we'd have to say—the woman, the husband, having to be the breadwinner . . .

Kevin Nealon
Having all those children.

Susan Yeagley
Having a teenage daughter pregnant. There's a conflict. She's preaching family values and abstinence and she's got a pregnant teenage daughter; there is a conflict there. I don't know if that's necessarily funny.

Kevin Nealon
Conflict is also being a small-town person in a big town like Washington.

William H. Coles
Perfect. Exactly. And she seems uncomfortable in Washington.

Susan Yeagley
And also, this kind of delicate-flower beauty-pageant woman skinning a caribou. There's something interesting about that.

William H. Coles
Tina Fey used that too when she did the bit about the beauty pageant with the wink. What about going to a conflict? Could the conflict be moving to Washington and the way she uses Washington?

Susan Yeagley
I see one interesting conflict here is that she is a very attractive woman who wants to be seen as attractive *and* smart, but underneath that, maybe she's just attractive. So maybe her whole fight is to be shown as a woman who is capable.

Kevin Nealon
Also, I think the conflict is being, by traditional standards, the mother who is the breadwinner and the power position, and the husband takes a second seat, and they have all these kids—and dealing with the public scrutiny.

William H. Coles
For a reader there could be great interest in that domestic conflict. It has gender; it has freshness of modern society with the position of the woman. And the husband's reaction. Again, this story might work out in two points of view. Or at least an overriding narrator involvement. The differences between a writer not having the luxury of visual images of film makes the point-of-view resources all the more important. The writer can use internal reflection and internal monologue to advantage, though. Wouldn't the advantage of internal monologue with the husband be great? He has to feel a little bit inferior on occasion.

Susan Yeagley
I'd also like to see him with his buddies on the Alaskan fishing boat. Two hundred miles out: that would be an interesting scene where the guys are cracking open a beer with the line overboard, and they're fishing, and he's sharing what his wife is doing.

William H. Coles
Could you imagine a point of view from the unmarried father of the daughter?

Susan Yeagley
Bristol Palin.

William H. Coles
Yes. Couldn't there be perception advantages? He sees the family very objectively, he's trying to get out of marrying this woman who is the daughter of a very famous person . . .

Susan Yeagley
And his mother just got arrested for drugs.

William H. Coles
Is that right?

Susan Yeagley
I think she was locked up for taking drugs.

William H. Coles
Maybe the story should go to him? To the children. Maybe go back and rethink the entire situation. His awakening, and realization of what he has to lose—he has a lifetime of things coming up—

Susan Yeagley
The seventeen-year-old?

William H. Coles
Yeah.

Susan Yeagley
That is interesting.

Kevin Nealon
That seems an unlikely but more interesting point of view.

Susan Yeagley
It could be her.

Kevin Nealon
This kid coming from a dysfunctional family. Getting involved in a family that is dysfunctional on a higher level. And being swept up in all that.

William H. Coles
I'm thinking this is something I want to work on.

Susan Yeagley
The seventeen-year-old boy.

William H. Coles
It's interesting that this energy didn't really occur as we were talking about Sarah Palin.

Susan Yeagley
Look at the choices he has on his plate. Whether or not to marry her. And if he does, what will that look like in front of him? And what if he doesn't marry? What does that look like in front of him? And also, he's privy to dialogue and conversations; he sees who these people really are. And we also don't know of this thing with his high school sweetheart, Bristol Palin. Was it a one-night stand in the back of a car? Or was he in love with her for three years? Or was he in love with another girl in high school and Bristol came along at the right time? We don't know where his heart is. What are his aspirations? Maybe he wants nothing to do with politics.

William H. Coles
Perfect.

Susan Yeagley
And maybe he's a liberal Democrat.

Kevin Nealon
It's like a modern-day version of the Beverly Hillbillies come to Washington. A dysfunctional family.

William H. Coles
That's an interesting thought.

Kevin Nealon
A fish out of water. A caribou out of water.

William H. Coles
One thing I'd like to give to writers: great literary fiction writing is not just description of someone the author knows or an event that moved the author in some way. I would hope that writers will turn back to Chekhov and the other great literary prose fiction storytellers. Those writers who develop characters who in turn move plot, all with the purpose of providing a meaning for the

story—a meaning that may not be easily identified but that the reader always has the sense that this is significant and new to him or her.

Your contribution today has been tremendous, to let us see imaginations and senses of humor in action to create a significant fictional story, stimulated by real people and scenarios, created, but not just described. You provide the options to achieve the power of an imagined story. I thank you for taking the time.

Susan Yeagley and Kevin Nealon
Thank you.

APPENDICES

Appendix A

BLOG POSTS

How do unsuccessful novel writers build houses? 491

Ferreting out MacGuffins in a literary fiction story 493

Lasting literary story characters mature and blossom like sturdy oaks. How do you do that? 495

What would you do if you had a chance to, right now, start your life again? 497

What do you do to make scenes come alive in literary fiction? 499

If you're a writer and no one reads your stuff, be sure to make your openings irresistible 501

Mastering the power of a literary fictional story 505

When is a fiction story a literary art form? 507

How writers "murder their darlings" (and stay out of prison) 509

Character-based plot: not easy but so effective 511

Want to write literary stories that last? 515

Errant simile and erosion of literary style 517

To be ... and when not to be ... in developing literary style 519

A prescription for creating great literary fiction 521

Rate and logic in revealing story information in literary fiction 523

Creating great scenes in literary fiction without excessive, ineffective, detail! 525

Mastering the power of literary story 527

How funny are you? 529

Fictional dream, literary style, and storytelling 531

- Keep readers involved when writing literary fiction stories 533
- What EM Forster taught us about flat and round characters and how to use it.. 535
- Are you a storyteller? 537
- Action and imagery.. 539
- When to use backstory in literary fiction.. 541
- Why select stories succeed best as literary fiction.................................... 543
- A fiction-writer changes style with image-words 545
- What to do for writer's block 547
- Improve storytelling by flexiblity in writing style...................................... 549
- Career planning for aspiring, literary-fiction-story writers 551
- A secret of great literary fiction stories as art.. 553
- Is it, or is it not, irony? 555
- Meaning in the literary fictional story... 557
- The quest for greatness in literary fiction and the failure of authorial self.. 559
- The seven fundamentals for writing fiction stories 563
- What do you do to make scenes come alive in literary fiction? 565

How do unsuccessful novel writers build houses?
January 9, 2017 by William H. Coles

You get a backhoe and dig a BIG hole. You back up a cement truck and pour three BIG mounds of cement. While cement hardens, you cut down two giant oaks, strip the leaves, and throw the trunks with limbs in the big hole on top of the cement. You pour, 100 gallons of glue, a quarter ton of bolts and nails, five porcelain toilets, and three bathtubs. You add 800 light bulbs of various sizes throughout the growing muddle. You mix three hundred gallons of paint in different, preferable incompatible (noncliché) colors, and splash the paint at random over all you've assembled. Let the mess simmer for five months during a horribly hot summer, if possible. Add 3800 roof tiles–no need to remove from the packaging. Voila! A house.

Structure–beginning, middle, and end.
Writers need structure, an overall outline that directs happenings, action, emotional arcs, and prioritizes ideas and timing of information transfer. Literary stories have images and movement that are delivered logically structured on a timeline. Author ideas and thoughts generated by chance and randomly applied to story, no matter the quality of idea or thought, are not as effective as imagined elements structured into coherent, logical web the supports story momentum.

Purpose.
Fiction writers need altruism and must: not write for fame and fortune, not write to be published to claim "author" at social gatherings, but write to engage, entertain, and enlighten readers by creating and telling a story well and building characters specific for story understanding and meaning.

Creativity and imagination.
Writers need to imagine and create, not remember and describe. Imagination for fiction does not come from sitting alone in a dark, sound proof, unheated room until memories emerge from author life experiences like sea creatures from a peat bog. In fiction, scenes are imagined that move the plot, build characters consistent with the timeline, and relate to purpose and theme of the story. Authors default to their own worldview and life experiences fail to reach advantages of imagined fiction available to the world beyond self.

Ferreting out MacGuffins in a literary fiction story
January 23, 2017 by William H. Coles

This down and out musician has broken up with his girl in New Orleans so he pockets his blues harmonica, drags his guitar behind him, and plods on the road to Yazoo City, Mississippi, to find a gig. He's miles away on a back road in a poverty-infested rural countryside when a girl about seven appears and offers him a wad of chewing gum she takes from her mouth with thumb and forefinger. He politely declines but to respond to her generosity, he plays a tune, Empty Bed Blues, on his harmonica. She's unimpressed. During a doze, the girl grabs his harmonica and runs off. He follows her into a ramshackle two-room paint-peeling-gray clapboard-house where her mother lies on her back on a bare mattress, both legs bent at the knees, her bloated abdomen contracting and showing a matted-hair football-shaped blob with each labor contraction. Damn, it's about to arrive. Our hero has never even seen or thought about how babies come out.

Wikipedia tells us: "In fiction a MACGUFFIN (sometimes McGuffin or maguffin) is a plot device in the form of some goal, desired object, or other motivator that the protagonist pursues, often with little or no narrative explanation. The specific nature of a MacGuffin is typically unimportant to the overall plot. The most common type of MacGuffin is a person, place, or thing (such as money or an object of value). Other more abstract types include victory, glory, survival, power, love, or some unexplained driving force."
"The MacGuffin technique is common in films, especially thrillers. Usually the MacGuffin is the central focus of the film in the first act, and thereafter declines in importance. It may reappear at the climax of the story but sometimes is actually forgotten . . ."

Okay. Thanks Wikipedia. In our story, the harmonica is a plot device, a MacGuffin. But fiction writers crave significance. So how does a plot device become a symbol? Let's look to Wiki again; now things get a little wonky: "SYMBOLS are the basis of all human understanding and serve as vehicles of conception for all human knowledge. Symbols facilitate understanding of the world in which we live, thus serving as the grounds upon which we make judgments. In this way, people use symbols . . . to make sense of the world around them . . ." Okay Wiki. Symbols impart meaning about people and the world. Let's explore more.

Two older couples are on tour in India, one married, the other in a relationship. The married woman wears an extravagant diamond necklace inappropriate on a tour through a poverty-stricken country, a symbol of an arrogant man's wealth and status and his domination of a submissive woman who detests wearing the necklace in public. The necklace is stolen and the woman dies from an illness contracted from the thieves. For the rest of the trip, the in-a-relationship couple grieve for their friend and the woman works tirelessly to relieve the suffering of the destitute poor. The man admires the decent nobility and gracious compassion of his partner and near the end of the tour he buys an inexpensive jade necklace to commit to the marriage the woman desires as the ultimate expression of his love and esteem. Two necklaces acting as different symbols both driving plot.
MacGuffins and symbols are both useful in literary fiction storytelling but rarely are they the purpose for the story; instead, they are discovered, defined, and refined in late stages of revision.

Lasting literary story characters mature and blossom like sturdy oaks. How do you do that?

February 6, 2017 by William H. Coles

Here's a *two-sentence story* to make a point about building characters when creating literary fiction.

> Harry flew a kite at the beach to entertain his invalid son. But the kite got away and Harry seethed with anger.

Didn't grab you, I would presume. Let me tell it again, this time with emphasis on characterization entwined in IN-SCENE action.

> A wind gust elevated the dragon kite and the string ran through Harry's hand fast enough to hurt.
> "Let me do it, Daddy," his son Raymond said as he limped to Harry's side. The boy held out his hand that trembled without stop from a congenital palsy. Could he hold the string? Fly the kite? He wanted to so badly.
> "Hold it tight," Harry said placing the string in the boy's hand. The kite dipped then suddenly soared, the string taut again. "I dropped it," the boy said crying. Harry reached out but the kite had ascended too far to reach the string.
> Harry cursed as the kite disappeared untethered, driven out to the sea by the off-shore wind.
> "I didn't mean to," the boy said, "Don't hit me."

In literary fiction, effective character development is essential and compliments plot movement.

Here's a snippet from another STORY that emphasizes characterization, "The Perennial Student." In essence, the narrative is more SHOWING than telling. If an assistant professor is to advance to full professor, he must successfully discipline a student who dominates his creative-writing class with crude offensive writing and comments. Here's an abridged excerpt that exemplifies techniques of in-scene "showing" and character-specific DIALOGUE.

Possum waited inside the entrance hall of the ivy-coated building that housed the Departments of English and Computer Science when Denise entered through the left side of the twelve-foot oak doors. How innocent she looked.

"Denise," he called, "over here." She squinted toward the sound of his voice.

"Will?" she said. All his other students respectfully called him Mr. Possum.

"Yes. Over here. Behind the statue. I need to talk to you."

He had practiced. Now was the moment he'd been dreading. He guided her to the quietest corner of the foyer. The hot summer air seemed to press them together.

"Look, Denise. You have really made a contribution to the class."

"Oh, thank you," she interrupted. "That's so cool."

"Writing is sensitive business," he started again.

"Only when you let it all hang out."

"It's not particularly an issue of hanging out."

"You got to tell it like it is. Tell the truth."

He tasted the first sourness of defeat. How could this mundane woman with her formidable convictions force him to feel so hopeless?

"I did not mean that we should not tell the truth. It is a question of adjusting to the sensitivity of the writer."

"I know sensitivity. You teach us real good." She smiled. "It's all about no pain, no gain."

Was she mocking him with her stare of excessive interest? He worried someone might overhear. My God, how she made him flounder. "Each creative composition is so personal it makes a writer vulnerable," he said.

She nodded in full agreement.

He decided to be direct. "I must ask you to be considerate of other class members in your comments."

She recoiled slightly, frowning. "Shutting me down?"

"No. Not 'shutting you down.' Just soften your comments."

"It's the men, isn't?" she asked.

Possum swallowed. "No. It's not just the men!" Discrimination? Was she thinking of filing a complaint? His tongue stuck to the dry roof of his mouth.

Of course great literary stories are created by mostly educated writers with talent and will to succeed, but even more important is applying learned techniques of story creation and imaginative telling that provide engagement, entertainment, and enlightenment for the reader.

What would you do if you had a chance to, right now, start your life again?

February 20, 2017 by William H. Coles

What have you achieved? Is it what you wanted? Are you satisfied? Here's the idea. On occasion, life forces new directions that demand a new "you." How would you make a better "you"? Take this example of a doctor at the top of his profession who loses all and changes who he is to survive. Literary fiction can show significant change by creating dramatic stories with theme and meaning. Here's an example of how. (Excerpt from the award-winning novel "McDowell.")

Hiram McDowell is an arrogant, proud doctor. He's ignored and stomped on a lot of innocent people, failed to value friendships, and failed in love and family, but he's listed in the top two hundred of America's most influential people. Then he's accused of a felonious death, goes to prison, escapes, and survives as a criminal fugitive. Here's a glimpse of his new life–a desolate wilderness country-scene in a Montana farm house where a family with a disabled child has taken him in. The experience changes who he will become.

>On a summer evening after dinner, Selena came out from her bedroom in an ankle-length white nightgown, barefoot, carrying a hand-blown glass bowl partially filled with water. She sat on a three-legged stool. Maud closed her book and laid it on the floor by the chair. "Pops," she called to the kitchen. Pops came out and sat in a chair at the table. Selena's freshly washed and dried long hair glowed with a youthful golden radiance. With slow deliberation, she dipped the fingers of her right hand in the water inside the transparent glass vessel on her lap and she began slowly circling the rim until a sound emerged, course and variable at first but with a quick adjustment, even and constant with a strange ethereal quality. She sang with a single tone in perfect pitch with the sound from the vessel, her voice was pure and full without vibrato. Then she progressed to intervals–a minor third, a sixth, a major seventh. She continued for fifteen minutes then unassumingly stood and went back to her room. No one spoke, struck by the beauty of the presentation. Maud sat with her head back, eyes closed. Pops remained at the table, his head in his hands.

The next morning Hiram saw Maud reading and drinking from her ever-present cup of coffee.

"That was beautiful singing . . . what Selena did last night," he said. "She's unique. I've never heard a voice like that. Her presentation was beautiful."

Maud said nothing.

"She should sing out in public. Make a recording to sell. It's really cheap to do."

"You'd see her doing night clubs. A celebrity?"

"No. But she could entertain a lot of people and make money doing it."

"She used to sing at the church before it closed."

"She has a spiritual quality that shouldn't be limited to a church."

"What do you think she wants?" Maud asked.

"I don't think she knows her potential," he said.

"To do what?"

"Produce and enjoy a valuable profession entertaining."

"And why would she do that?"

"To be successful."

"But what is this success? What do you think that means to her?"

Hiram tried to block his rising frustration at Maud's persistence in questioning the obvious. "I don't know. Admiration for her talent. Financial independence."

Maud got up bringing her coffee cup and sat down at the table where Hiram was working.

"You were pleased with what she did for you. She made you feel good."

"I was awestruck."

"She did it for you, you know. She likes you. And she wanted to give you something of value. Something without strings attached. Uniquely hers, too. She doesn't think in terms of success and money. Subtle meanings, competition, maneuvering mean nothing to her."

So what's happened? He's beginning to evolve from selfish to selfless, from taking to giving, from indifference to caring. As he makes a difference in the lives of others, he's rewarded with new satisfaction never before experienced.

This story is literary fiction–imagination, drama, in-scene delivery with strong characterization, themes and meanings, and a purpose for telling a story. Literary fiction enlightens readers with discoveries that may awaken self-awareness and human understanding.

What do you do to make scenes come alive in literary fiction?

March 6, 2017 by William H. Coles

Literary imagined scenes come alive with CONFLICT and ACTION in language, narration, story, and dialogue. It's not inherent for most writers striving to write literary fiction. To start, writers and storytellers are dependent on these basics: 1) literature is written works that have merit and lasting potential as an art form, and 2) fiction creates imagined events and characters. For success in inserting conflict and action, writers master vibrant in-scene writing—an important staple of effective story delivery—supporting concrete-imagery, credible dialogue, and action prose in narrative.

Here are examples of conflict and action in dialogue, narrative, and a descriptive scene using senses, thoughts and perceptions. These examples are not exclusive. With an active imagination, a myriad of ways can be created by an author to achieve action and conflict in creative fiction. The examples:

1) A family whose parents have just been buried are dividing the parents' possessions among them. Carrie, the youngest, is working in the tool shed. Martha, Henry, and Jessie argue over who gets items in the house—and no one wants the responsibility of bringing up Carrie.

Now, to make the scene alive, conflict is inserted, mainly in dialogue. Conflict results in action, the fuel for great fictional prose.

> "I am not taking on responsibility for a seventeen-year-old," Henry said, pausing mid-brushstroke and turning from the window frame he was painting to make the house sellable.
> "Quiet, she'll hear you," Martha said from the kitchen, throwing a cracked and chipped casserole dish into a metal trash can with a crash of splintering glass. She turned back to scrub glassware in the sink.
> Jessie went to the front door to look for Carrie. "She's carrying stuff out of the tool shed," she said.
> "Don't let her throw out any power tools," Henry said.
> "She's laying things out for us to see."

"She'll take the best."
"She doesn't want power tools!"
"Anything of value."
"Stop it. She's your sister."
"You think so much of her, you take care of her."
"I've only got a one-bedroom apartment," Jessie said, picking up a broom and sweeping with a flurry of useless strokes.

From the novella *Sister Carrie*

2) For conflict in a narrative passage, here's an excerpt from Conrad's *Heart of Darkness*.

" . . . I was circumventing Kurtz as though it had been a boyish game. I came upon him, and, if he had not heard me coming, I would have fallen over him too, but he got up in time. He rose, unsteady, long, pale, indistinct, like a vapor exhaled by the earth, and swayed slightly, misty and silent before me; while at my back the fires loomed between the trees, and the murmur of many voices issued from the forest. I had cut him off cleverly; but when actually confronting him I seemed to come to my senses, I saw the danger in its right proportion. It was by no means over yet."

3) Here is a remarkable scene from Faulkner's "Barn Burning" where "alive" is achieved without describing action per se, but with use of accurate, imaginative language and sensual perceptions.

The store in which the justice of the Peace's court was sitting smelled of cheese. The boy, crouched on his nail keg at the back of the crowded room, knew he smelled cheese, and more: from where he sat he could see the ranked shelves close-packed with the solid, squat, dynamic shapes of tin cans whose labels his stomach read, not from the lettering which meant nothing to his mind but from the scarlet devils and the silver curve of fish – this, the cheese which he knew he smelled and the hermetic meat which his intestines believed he smelled coming in intermittent gusts momentary and brief between the other constant one, the smell and sense just a little of fear because mostly of despair and grief, the old fierce pull of blood. He could not see the table where the Justice sat and before which his father and his father's enemy (our enemy he thought in that despair; ourn! mine and hisn both! He's my father!) stood, but he could hear them, the two of them that is, because his father had said no word yet: . . .

It's a complicated subject to grasp, much less master and incorporate, but essential for literary fiction storytelling.

If you're a writer and no one reads your stuff, be sure to make your openings irresistible

March 20, 2017 by William H. Coles

Look. I can't help it. I feel bad and often dislike those who don't heed me. But over time, as a writer, when I fail to engage a reader, I've come to believe I'm to blame, not others, and here's the logic.

We benefit when we learn to attract and hold the attention of another human being(s); it allows us to transmit ideas and feelings. In every facet of our lives—one-on-one, audience performance, letter-writing—or a novel, a telephone call, an email or a tweet—we need to discover how to immediately tweak a brain cell, pluck a heart string, or corral curiosity with one essential element—a good start. Writers especially have to grab readers' attention in the first few sentences. For examples:

>—My one unbreakable rule was never pick up a hitchhiker. And never at night. But at the far edge of the headlights this girl showed up in the breakdown lane near mile marker 381, kind of humped over as if she didn't even know I was bearing down on her ... not like a hooker who'd be standing straight with her hand waving shoulder-high and her head tilted like a come-on ... or some hidden robber's decoy girl waving with both arms like the ship was sinking. I slowed with no thought of stopping.
>
>"Inside the Matryoshka" by William H. Coles

>—It was the last daylight hour of a December afternoon more than twenty years ago—I was twenty-three, writing and publishing my first short stories, and like many a *Bildungsroman* hero before me, already contemplating my own massive *Bildungsroman*—when I arrived at his hideaway to meet the great man.
>
>"The Ghost Writer" by Philip Roth

This opening from *The New Yorker* doesn't work for many:

>"The Dungeon Master has detention. We wait at his house by the county road.

The Dungeon Master's little brother Marco puts out corn chips and orange soda."

"The Dungeon Master" by Sam Lypsite

It's unclear, and there is little promise of action, conflict, or engaging prose. Let's look at a few generally accepted GREAT FIRST LINES from literature:

"Call me Ishmael."—Herman Melville, Moby-Dick (1851)

"Lolita, light of my life, fire of my loins."—Vladimir Nabokov, "Lolita" (1955)

"If you really want to hear about it, the first thing you'll probably want to know is where I was born, and what my lousy childhood was like, and how my parents were occupied and all before they had me, and all that David Copperfield kind of crap, but I don't feel like going into it, if you want to know the truth."—J. D. Salinger, "The Catcher in the Rye" (1951)

"It was the day my grandmother exploded."—Iain M. Banks, "The Crow Road" (1992)

"When Dick Gibson was a little boy he was not Dick Gibson."—Stanley Elkin, "The Dick Gibson Show" (1971)

"It is a truth universally acknowledged, that a single man in possession of a good fortune, must be in want of a wife."—Jane Austen, "Pride and Prejudice" (1813)

"He—for there could be no doubt of his sex, though the fashion of the time did something to disguise it—was in the act of slicing at the head of a Moor which swung from the rafters."—Virginia Woolf, "Orlando" (1928)

HOW TO DO IT
Here are guidelines for starters, but, in truth, great beginning lines come from the unique imagination and are not copied from others. (Although gleaned from prose fiction, most guidelines apply to any means of communication.)

1) Engagement. Intellectually others must become involved in what you're saying.
2) Clarity. Openings must be understood.

3) Promise of enlightenment, or to agree or disagree, or to assist or resist. (e.g. We are three steps away from learning that life exists on Mars.)
4) Promise of learning something unique, new, and valuable, OR, something revealing, salacious, controversial, withheld, or buried.
5) Reversal of interest—surprise, incongruity, humor.

TAKE-HOME MESSAGE
Be prepared to use your imagination to create the great, engaging story-opening. Then make it sizzle.

Mastering the power of a literary fictional story
April 3, 2017 by William H. Coles

A writer's imagination in fiction opens the gates to creating great literary stories. To shape great literary stories, authors master skillful characterization and apply centuries-proved story structures that have matured from creative writers of the past—Tolstoy, Chekhov, Dostoevsky, Flaubert, Bronte(s), Sophocles, Hemingway, Faulkner, and so many others.

Most writers today want to realize their dreams of a writer's life style and acclaim; they write for admiration, fame, and fortune. Nothing wrong with that; it's a path to happy successful careers for many. But some authors want to create meaningful stories that might contribute to understanding the constantly-evolving humanity, stories that are read and reread and passed onto future generations. Homer, Austen, Conrad, Melville, Forster, Woolf, transmit the soul of their generations with lasting, penetrating impact, and for example, by uniquely portraying thoughts and emotions, nature of love, core human desires, sense of morality–all with drama, imagery, and action.

How can a writer today achieve memorable meritorious stories? Study the techniques of the storytellers of the past that are indelibly etched in the collective human consciousness. Discover elements of powerful lasting literary stories that work for you as an author and incorporate those elements into your writing and storytelling.

ELEMENTAL TRUTHS
Stories are about events and people. In great literature, story frequently reveals not only what happens but how humans live and how life changes them. There are no secret formulas but there are commonalities that generate power for stories to move and evolve with mankind into future generations. Here are elements for thought.

1) WRITE WITH PURPOSE. As you write, search what is in you that drives you to write your story. A purpose clarifies prose, scenes, characters, narration,

point of view and plot that become more focused and unified, especially in revision.

2) THEME AND MEANING. Theme is recurrent idea; meaning is significant ideas. What can a reader learn from reading that is new and significant?

3) CHANGE. Characters change as stories progress and so do readers after reading a great story. Change examples: enlightenment (discovery or experience a new way of thinking), a shift in morality, a reversal, coming of age, etc.

4) DRAMA. Show in-scene dramatic conflict and action when possible. Abstract and static descriptions of character and scene (telling) are necessary but often less effective in developing characterization.

5) UNIQUE AND FASCINATING CHARACTERS. Core desires, abilities, imagination, motivations, sense of morality, strong vivid worldview.

6) STRUCTURE. 1) Beginning, middle, end. 2) Carefully-considered timeline. 3) character-based plots. 4) Emotional arcs. 5) Logical and credible happenings sequenced for story unity.

When is a fiction story a literary art form?
April 17, 2017 by William H. Coles

Literature is written stories considered superior and of lasting merit—an art form. Fiction portrays imagined events and people. If you're a writer, you can't know what stories from today will be the literature of tomorrow, but you can write the best story possible using the techniques of past writers who've reached literary status: Austen, Flaubert, Chekhov, Homer, Tolstoy, Melville, Hawthorne, Woolf, Henry James, Babel, Twain, and the like. In the main, these authors have common, basic elements of story construction that may, for the contemporary writer, mature into meritorious longevity.

Who cares? "Fiction writers continue to evolve and their works may very well be literature without the 'contrived' constraints from the past," many might say. But in reality, literary fiction stories structured for artistic characterization, meaningful purpose, and enlightenment about the human condition, are infrequent, rarely published, and are increasingly difficult to access when they are available. Unfortunately, the "literary fiction" of today mostly masquerades as memoir, autobiography, "creative" writing, and the literature-of-self. How can literary fiction regain distinction? Here are important literary STORY ELEMENTS contemporary writers should assimilate if not master:

First, expert CHARACTERIZATION is the essential of a great literary fictional story; well-formed character traits reveal desires and motives that drive meaningful plots. Equally important is STRUCTURE with Aristotelian principles that allow transfer of ideas and images to enlighten readers, usually about the intricacies of human existence. DICTION must be clear and well-written to vitalize prose and story. Lyricism—when story-specific and character enhancing—can enrich story effects without diminishing essential importance of in-scene action and dramatic narration.

Most important? Great literary-fiction stories as art are IMAGINED and CREATED, not just remembered and described. True, memory stimulates imagination evoking reflections on life and living, but a self-important writer believing events and characters described from personal experience are equal to imagined and created stories usually fails to reach maximum potential as an artist.

And what is an ART form?
Art, in literature, is expressed by human creative skills and imagination that produce beauty and emotional power. Beautiful stories emerge by character uniqueness; a narrator's reliability and perception of the human condition; the creation of accurate story-related imagery and metaphor; reader engagement to sense story is happening rather than being told; and from writers concerned with their art, not their wealth or fame.

A confessional memoir and autobiography published as "fiction" for catharsis or forgiveness rarely reaches the threshold possible with imagined and created literary fiction. The literature-of-self is created mostly from the author's world view and experience. By contrast, great literary fiction evolves from 1) the author's study and understanding of the possible worldviews of other humans and characters, 2) experienced and observed compassionate understanding of humanity, and 3) as often as possible, enlightenment about metaphysical questions that plague us all–who are we? why are we here? what is justice? what is love?

How writers "murder their darlings" (and stay out of prison)
May 1, 2017 by William H. Coles

Creative-writing students are sometimes advised to "murder your darlings," usually in a glib, demeaning way by a teacher or critic. The concept has major importance for a successful writer and it's sad that the phrase has a cutesy-clever quality that causes it's value often to be discounted and ignored. Here are a few thoughts.

"Darlings" are felt by the proud writer to be clever, erudite, intellectually unique pieces of writing that to most readers may be excessive, illogical, overwritten, distracting, and often irritating. In essence, a "darling" is assumed to be acceptable, even great, by the author but not by most readers. It can be subtle and it occurs when the writer is unconsciously trying to impress the reader with his or her talent and aptitude rather than focusing on creating readable, enjoyable, and informative prose.

"Darlings" are not easy to find in one's work. The trick is, as an author, to predict in readers what they might consider as poor writing, and to delete or change. Of course, when authors write, they're not trying to create "darlings." To discover "darlings," writers must assume they might be present and be willing to look for them by: 1) avoiding baseless admiration for their creations and maintaining appropriate modesty for their talent, 2) revising their works with objectivity and with a knowledgeable critical appraisal of what they've written.

Here are some examples that represent categories of writing that a writer might use as a guide to "darling" hunting when revising his or her work.

1. NON SEQUITUR [Something that does not follow logically what comes before.]
>　—His faith is important to him and he believes passionately in the gospel and the resurrection of Jesus Christ, and you know, the whole concept of running up and down a court to throw a bloated ball through a metal ring would be, to him, a reprehensible opprobrious waste of energy.

2. OVERWRITING
—". . . we're huddled beneath a blue tarp next to the midden, sipping coffee and ingesting some terrestrial chemical elements in the form of cookies." [Smithsonian, March 2017, pg. 32]

3. HYPERBOLE [Exaggerated statements or claims.]
—The food was fantastic, chock full of bursting flavors with a scrumptious lingering aftertaste to please the gods.

4. CLICHÉ [Element of an artistic work which has become overused to the point of losing its original meaning or effect, even to the point of being trite or irritating.]
—That is not my cup of tea.
—Everyone's best interest.
—Two score and three years ago, I brought forth to this community, to this congregation, the glory that is God.

5. FLAWED METAPHOR [Metaphor: a thing symbolic or representative of something else so the comparison enhances interpretation and meaning.]
—That backhoe is a blooming iris. [No meaning. The items compared are too disparate.}
—She's as graceful as a turtle on its back. (Could be consider sarcastic, but not successful metaphoric comparison.)

6. ERRANT DIALOGUE [Example exaggerated for emphasis.]
—"Last night I dreamt I heard a thousand, screaming, lost souls trapped in the fiery depths of hell for eternity," the nurse said as she used tweezers to gently tease pus-embedded gauze from the charred skin on her patient's back.

7. PRETENTIOUS VOCABULARY
—reprehensible opprobrious waste of energy
—terrestrial chemical elements in the form of cookies
—mawkishly pseudo-intellectual quality

CONCLUSION
Potentially perceived bad writing, a highly variable judgment, can take many forms that writers need to identify; the above categories serve as common sources of error that can be used in revision as guidelines for objective analysis and recognition of unwanted missteps– "darlings."

Character-based plot: not easy but so effective
May 15, 2017 by William H. Coles

ADVANTAGE OF ACTION

Showing story and character in action-scenes with concrete imagery, supportive narration, and dynamic prose enriches display of character emotion, morality, desire, history, and worldview… all with pleasurable, enlightening, and lasting effects on readers. Of course, narrative telling is important–it can be more figurative, abstract, and metaphorical–but for intensity and impact, in-scene action is often the better choice to develop character with story.

The first example tells of a happening. There is no action or significant characterization:

> Harry flew a kite at the beach to entertain his invalid son but the kite got away, and Harry seethed with anger.

Here is the same event shows in-scene action that helps develop character:

> A wind gust elevated the dragon kite and the string ran through Harry's hand fast enough to hurt.
> "Let me do it, Daddy," his son Raymond said as he limped to Harry's side. The boy held out his hand that, when awake, trembled nonstop from a congenital palsy. Could he hold the string? Fly the kite? He wanted to so badly.
> "Hold tight," Harry urged placing the string in the boy's hand. The kite dipped then suddenly soared, the string taught again.
> The boy cried out. "I dropped it." Harry reached out but the kite had ascended too far to grab the trailing string.
> The untethered kite disappeared, driven out to the sea by a gusty off-shore wind.
> "I didn't mean too," the boy said, "Please don't hit me."

CHARACTER-BASED PLOT

Historically, great literary fictional characters reveal the complexities of being human through memorable, riveting, thought-provoking characterization that lasts in the collective human consciousness for generations.

A major element of creating a great character is CHARACTER-BASED PLOT where a character's thoughts, feelings, and actions are often integral to logical plot-progression rather than a character simply reacting to fatalistic or serendipitous plot events.

BASIC PLOT-CONCEPT EXAMPLES
A. **Character reacting** to plot events:

> *1) Fatalism.*
> Pablo spotted the meteorite as it plunged through the atmosphere and he unsuccessfully ran for his life.
>
> *2) Serendipity.*
> Homeless Willy was starved and he walked the streets for a handout when he came across a ham and cheese sandwich wrapped in cellophane lying on the sidewalk.

B. **Character-motivated** plot progression.

> Mary, fed up with her lying abusive husband, drove with her children to live with her mother in Canada and when she came to the mile-long narrows suspension-bridge her life-long fear of heights made her ignore a "road closed" sign and she detoured onto a wintery road in an attempt to reach the ferry. The car skidded on black ice plunging over a cliff killing all.

In essence, a meteorite kills the man (fatalistic), a hungry man finds food (serendipity), a mother's fears and distress kill her and her family (character-based).

CHARACTER-BASED PLOT EXAMPLE FROM CLASSIC LITERATURE
Gustave Flaubert has a scene in *Madame Bovary* that uses character-based plot development with both in-scene and narrator perspective to show character individuality and complexity. The basic plot is: Emma Bovary convinced her husband, Charles, she needed piano lessons as a ruse to meet her lover in town . . . and, after a few weeks, everyone thought her piano playing improved.

From *Madame Bovary*–part three, chapter four (text abbreviated).

> One evening when Charles was listening to her, she began the same piece four times over, each time with much vexation, while he, not noticing any difference, cried– "Bravo! Very good! You are wrong to stop. Go on!"

The ART of CREATING STORY

"Oh, no; it is execrable! My fingers are quite rusty."

The next day he begged her to play him something again. "Very well; to please you!"

And Charles confessed she had gone off a little. She played wrong notes and blundered; then, stopping short– "Ah! it is no use. I ought to take some lessons; but–" She bit her lips and added, "Twenty francs a lesson, that's too dear!"

"Yes, so it is–rather," said Charles, giggling stupidly. "But it seems to me that one might be able to do it for less; for there are artists of no reputation, and who are often better than the celebrities."

"Find them!" said Emma.

The next day when he came home he looked at her shyly.

"Madame Liegard assured me that her three young ladies who are at La Misericorde have lessons at fifty sous apiece!"

[Emma} shrugged her shoulders and did not open her piano again. But when she passed by it (if Bovary were there), she sighed– "Ah! my poor piano!" And when anyone came to see her, she did not fail to inform them she had given up music, and could not begin again now for important reasons. Then people commiserated her– "What a pity! she had so much talent!" They even spoke to Bovary about it. They put him to shame, and especially the chemist.

"You are wrong [. . .] my good friend [. . .] by inducing madame (Emma) to study; you [would be] economizing on the subsequent musical education of your child."

So Charles returned once more to this question of the piano. Emma replied bitterly that it would be better to sell it. This poor piano that had given her vanity so much satisfaction–to see it go was to Bovary like the indefinable suicide of a part of herself.

"If you liked," he said, "a lesson from time to time, that wouldn't after all be very ruinous."

"But lessons," she replied, "are only of use when followed up."

And thus it was she set about obtaining her husband's permission to go to town once a week to see her lover. At the end of a month she was even considered to have made considerable progress.

FUNDAMENTAL IDEA: The plot progresses revealing Emma's deceitful clever, selfish, unscrupulous behavior and Charles's doting, clueless, naive, yet caring nature, adds to the composition of unique, lasting, memorable literary characters.

Want to write literary stories that last?
June 5, 2017 by William H. Coles

Consider this.

Characterization vs. character development.
Stories about humans require characterization–gender, appearance, background, abilities. But in literary fictional stories, the characters also develop–they change their emotional and intellectual souls, as well as their desires and motivations, which are instrumental in plot progression (character-based plot).

Dramatization.
Drama is conflict that results in action and resolution and is essential for plot but also advances character. Opportunities for conflict prevail at many levels of telling a story—plot, scene, dialog, prose, imagery, etc. and character development is most effective in dramatized story action rather than passive narrator-telling. Note how clear plot conflicts contribute to greatness in these novels. *The Scarlet Letter.* When the husband sees Hester's shame, he asks a man in the crowd about her and is told the story of his wife's adultery. He angrily exclaims that the child's father, the partner in the adulterous act, should also be *punished and vows to find* the man. *Moby Dick.* … Ahab … announces he is *out for revenge* on the white whale which took one leg from the knee down and left him with a prosthesis fashioned from a whale's jawbone. (Both descriptions excerpted from Wikipedia.)

Universality.
Literary writers strive to bring readers into stories to immerse a reader in a fictional dream and create works that have a greater meaning to more people than expected when first written. Analysis of any work of fiction reveals one or more essential universal struggles–friendship, family, money, identity, spirituality, liberty, sex, death, and others–that put characters at risk of danger—mental, emotional, physical. These are the magma of story action and resultant resolution, and almost always associate with reader access and involvement in the story world.

Suspension of disbelief.
Literary stories are frequently more meaningful when readers believe in characters and events in a story world. Successful genre writers of Sci-Fi or fantasy (such as Ray Bradbury) please story readers able to suspend belief that story and characters either are real or could be real from worlds not yet proven to exist. These successful stories entertain and delight. Literary fiction is imagined people and events and is constructed so there is pervasive belief the story could be real in the reader's world. No need for suspension of disbelief. about the possible existence of a character. The advantage is fortifying meaning and theme in the literary story. Literary fiction has evolved over centuries at the least to enlighten new understanding–an epiphany, a new way of thinking or behaving, or an aroused emotional response–that expands knowledge of the human condition. Superman is a memorable creation but readers gain little knowledge about the complexities of human action and emotions from his stories. Captain Ahab, or Emma Bovary, are fictional characters who could be "real" without suspension of disbelief … and are intensely human.

Author and story.
Writers usually write memoirs about themselves; literary writers write about characters who are not the author and are created in environments imagined and created (often inspired by reality) for enhancement of story purpose. Contemporary writers tend to blur the two processes often muting the potential effects of both memoir and fiction and thwarting story purpose.

Disclaimer.
No one can know which contemporary written-works will be considered great literature in the future. It's essential that writers rely on doing their own thing, that includes making their stories unique and fascinating. But study of great fiction from the past suggests writers do better to think about literary story as a process of imagination rather than a transcription of reality, and most important, to learn that techniques and attitudes about fiction matured from past won't hurt the success of the "literature" of the future … whatever that might be.

Errant simile and erosion of literary style
June 19, 2017 by William H. Coles

Writing literary-fiction stories is two opposite yet creative desires competing with each other: (1) to develop strong stories with unique characters racing through a dramatic plot to provide engagement, entertainment and enlightenment, (2) to showcase the power of the written word in the glory of language and its imaginative use for reflection, enjoyment, and enlightenment. Here's the problem: the use of metaphoric simile is like hiring a bikini-clad beauty-queen to play point-guard for the NBA's Boston Celtics; it would draw attention of most fans but almost surely wouldn't be effective for team-winning. In essence, the trick of simile-use in fiction is a balance between two basic desires, to write exquisite admirable prose and to create entertaining effective stories seamlessly.

A SIMILE is a figure of speech that directly compares two things using connecting words such as like, as, so, than, or various verbs such as "resemble" and should be arresting visually be a subtle, hidden comparison that resonates and enhances understanding of the object of comparison without calling attention to it as a figure of speech. Successful similes in literature evoke clear resonating images that are unique, entertaining, simple, original. A memorable simile rises far above a functional description, must be within the purpose of the story, and worthy of the effort required for creation. In the main, successful similes are scattered in the prose: as stars in the sky, not a voluminous moon; as foot soldiers, not a mounted general; as members of the choir, not a garish soloist; as citizens in a beehive, not the queen bee.

Simile can achieve a rare impact when simile-comparison is appropriate to the subject and slightly understated. But when authorial vanity and self-admiration calls too much attention to the simile itself, the result is disruptive and disappointing.

And, as a suggestion for best results, the successful simile is nurtured in thoughtful revision rather than erupting from gut instinct.

See what you think of these EXAMPLES:

1. "O My Luve's like a red, red rose." (Robert Burns). MISS?
   Even in Burns' time, doomed to become a cliché comparison.

2. "Elderly American ladies leaning on their canes listed toward me like towers of Pisa." (*Lolita*. Vladimir Nabokov) MISS?
   Even out of context, it is not subtle and calls attention to the figure of speech itself.

3. "Past him, ten feet from his front wheels, flung the Seattle Express like a flying volcano." (*Arrowsmith*. Sinclair Lewis) MISS?
   The flying volcano does little to subtly enhance the image of a train.

4. "She entered with ungainly struggle like some huge awkward chicken, torn, squawking, out of its coop." (*The Adventure of the Three Gables*. Sir Arthur Conan Doyle) HIT? or MISS?
   In certain contexts, especially humorous, this could be a "hit" but almost always it is still a show-stopper in the narrative and then a "miss."

5. "Time has not stood still. It has washed over me, washed me away, as if I'm nothing more than a woman of sand, left by a careless child too near the water."— (*The Handmaid's Tale*. Margaret Atwood) HIT?
   Unarguably . . . resonantly effective.

6. ". . . and to follow her thought was like following a voice which speaks too quickly to be taken down by one's pencil . . ." (*To the Lighthouse*. Virginia Woolf) HIT?
   Subtle yet effective wordsmithing and by a master of fiction.

7. The dragonfly's transparent wings glistened in the sun like mica. (After Stanley Kunitz) HIT?
   Hidden similarity of brilliant image with unique color and intensity.

Would you agree with any of these assessments? Remember, for literary fiction, successful similes have clear elements: APPROPRIATE COMPARISON, SUBTLE, RESONANT, UNDERSTATED, ORIGINAL, INCANDESCENT, SIMPLE, CLEAR.

To be ... and when not to be ... in developing literary style
July 17, 2017 by William H. Coles

The delight of a reader of **literary fiction** is often affected by a writer's use of "to be" as an auxiliary verb. Authors need skill in recognizing what is best for their stories and the readers they want to engage. Intuition alone–without desire, hard-work experience, and talent–is rarely effective.

ACTIVE/PASSIVE voices (transitive verbs)
In active voice, action focuses on the doer of the action, while the passive voice focuses on the action itself.

Active voice requires two (or more) participants: the subject of the sentence doing the action, and a recipient of the action. Jake (subject) threw the ball (object of the action).

In **passive voice**, the object (recipient) of the action becomes the subject of the sentence. From above example: The ball (object of the action) was thrown by Jake (subject). The actor may not be stated but implied. Kennedy was shot (by Oswald). Active voice: Oswald shot Kennedy.

EXAMPLES
Active. *A great flood formed the river.* Flood (actor) the doer-subject, the river the recipient of the action.
Passive. *The river was formed (by a great flood).* River (subject) recipient of action. Flood, the doer.

Active: *The committee approved the new policy.*
Passive: *The policy was approved by the committee.*

PROGRESSIVE TENSE
Progressive tense shows an action still in progress and is formed with "to be" and the present participle. Example: The bus went fast. The bus was going fast [action in progress].

EXAMPLES
1) From classic literature.
> The day was going fast now. Only the tops of the Gabilan mountains flamed with the light of the sun that had gone from the valley. A water snake slipped along on the pool, its head held up like a little periscope. The reeds jerked slightly in the current. Far off toward the highway a man shouted something, and another man shouted back. The sycamore limbs rustled under a little wind that died immediately. [Steinbeck, John. *Of Mice and Men.*]

2) Rewritten in passive voice (not by Steinbeck).
> The day was going fast now. The tops of the mountains were flaming with sunlight that was leaving the valley. A water snake was slipping along on the pool, its head was up like a little periscope. The reeds were jerking slightly in the current. Far off toward the highway a man was shouting something, another man shouted back. The sycamore limbs were rustled under a little wind that died immediately.

GUIDANCE: The above example passages of active/passive have a different tone and quality of image transfer, brevity, and clarity. When you can say something in the active voice, don't use passive voice. Active voice is direct, straight and easily understood. There are, however, times when the passive voice, not the active, is used: 1) when the doer of the action is not known (My bracelet was stolen.), 2) when the doer of the action in known by all (Orange juice is sold here.), 3) or where action is more important than the doer (Healthcare is an inherent right for children.), 4) and others.

MESSAGE
There is no right or wrong in creating fiction, only success or lack thereof in engaging the desired reader.

The use of forms of "to be" in fiction changes style of presentation: action, emphasis, clarity, writer's thinking process, pacing, word count, and often significance.

Being aware of your passive/active writing can transform you, the writer, in life from an admiring fan sitting in an audience to a performer pleasing fans with great writing and storytelling.

A prescription for creating great literary fiction
July 31, 2017 by William H. Coles

Fiction writers imagine. And it's in the realm of the imagination that stories and characters are not stifled by the constraints of describing real people and real events. Fiction creates its own "reality" with purpose to create meaningful, engaging, unique stories.

BASICS
Literature is written work considered to have lasting artistic merit. Fiction is imagined events and people.

IDEA
Great literary stories that last for generations have hard-to-achieve imagined and created elements for characterization and plot development that will shape the thoughts, memory, and even actions of readers.

ELEMENTS
1) *Character-based* story. In essence, literature stories are about people. Great stories have characters who do more than just react to plot events. Instead, character's souls and personalities, sometimes innocence or refusal to learn and believe, cause plot reactions. Here's a simple example—Little Red Riding Hood.

Plot based. Red leaves her home to visit grandma. On the path through the woods a wolf discovers her destination. He runs ahead and when Red arrives, he devours her.

Character-based. Red is determined to go to grandma's house through the woods. Her mother is apprehensive and tells her not to dally, not to talk to strangers, and to run away from danger. Red puts her sore feet in a stream on the way and stops to pick bluebells. She meets a wolf and tells him of her excitement at visiting grandma. She thinks the wolf is her friend. The wolf leaves to be at grandma's when she arrives, pretends to be grandma, and devours Red.

In the second scenario, Red's disobeys her mother, fails to run from danger, and her innocence about danger and her lack of fear for the dangers in the world cause her death. A character-based lot.

Fictional characters who drive plots? Madame Bovary. Captain Ahab. Hester Prynne. Anna Karenina. Flem Snopes.

2) Character *enlightenment*. Fatalistic plot points and marionette-character development are avoided. Does the character's *understanding* about the world or human nature shift, does a character's *perception* of the world and other living things change; is there a change in morality, etc.

Coming of age does not guarantee significance if the character stumbles through life's transitions into adulthood. Something must happen that corresponds to the author's purpose in writing the literary story. Essentially, the character often leaves a shallow, hollow shell and moves into a thoughtful, rich existence brimming with thought and feeling. It doesn't have to be hurricane strength though; in fact subtlety can almost always heighten the effect of the character change on the reader. Great characters may also be presented with the opportunity to change but refuse, either willingly or unwillingly. But the failure to change must be due to the character's nature and can't be accidental.

3) *Significant* change of character. Being alive, time changes us all second by second. But for literature a change in character is best if profound as writer can make it without sentimentality or loss of credibility (that the character could be real). Events in the story are related to some character trait that often precipitates action that would not have occurred without recognition of "who I am and what I've done and whom I will become."

Significance is often morally related, but also can be self-recognition of prejudice, injustice, intolerance, frustration, etc.

Harry Potter has far different effect on readers than Holden Caulfield, and one might surmise that Caulfield is a product of who he is, and Harry Potter is a character reacting to plot circumstances. Some readers enjoy connecting with a character's heart-felt constitution and a feeling soul acting in an environment that could be real. Something for serious literary-fiction authors to think about in their creations.

Rate and logic in revealing story information in literary fiction

August 14, 2017 by William H. Coles

All writing conveys information and, in fiction stories, how and when information is revealed impacts the understanding of the story as well as shapes points of expectation and installs suspense and credibility. Little Red Riding Hood is essentially a story about predators of children, about how children must: obey their parents, know the dangers of world, and never speak to strangers. The story has many forms, all have persisted for more than a century because crucial dramatic information is revealed that delivers meaning with impact, an essential element in this story's longevity. Compare these two examples.

(1) Little red Riding Hood is determined to take a basket of goodies through the woods to grandma's house. (2) Her mother warns her of the danger, not to talk to strangers, and not to dilly-dally. (3) In the woods she meets a wolf and tells him about her journey. (4) The wolf runs ahead and devours Granny. (5) Red finally gets to Granny's; the wolf, now dressed in Granny's nightgown, eats her.

Okay. Basic essentials and the story is there: a desire, parental warning, telling stranger of grandmother, wolf eating grandma because Red disobeys and ignores truths, Red punished for her errant ways.

Now look at a different rate and positioning of information revelation.

(4) Little Red Riding Hood's grandmother was killed. (3) Red met a wolf in the woods on her journey to grandma's house and told him about grandma even though (2) Red's mother warned her of the danger of speaking to strangers *and* the dangers lurking in the woods. (5) So when Red finally gets to Granny's, the wolf, now dressed in Granny's nightgown, eats her. (4) The wolf had run ahead of Red to devour Granny.

A story is still there but not as effective. Information revelation is not prioritized and many ideas are followed by what seem to be non-sequiturs, a consequence in the second story of the story timeline disrupted by events being told that happen at different times in story time—Granny died and then we're told the wolf ran ahead of Red, for example. (Inattention to a timeline and rate of revelation of story information is a very common writer's error that often weakens the potential of a story's effect.)

MESSAGE

In creating effective stories, the author must be aware of ideas and how their logical positioning and delivery makes or breaks the story for readers. Compare these processes of (1) positioning scrabble tiles on a board to find winning combinations, or (2) sifting through jigsaw-puzzle pieces to join them for a complete, understandable, and meaningful image.

Creating great scenes in literary fiction without excessive, ineffective, detail!

October 16, 2017 by William H. Coles

In fiction storytelling, creating setting is tertiary to dramatic plot and characterization and needs to contribute to the story. Therefore, for best and succinct effects, setting should have momentum and evoke image. Compare these two descriptions: *The locomotive with colorful cars behind followed the track that snaked through the valley.* No momentum or concrete images–basically ineffective. Now: *The steam of the locomotive reddened the face of the engineer as he leaned out the window. The track curved many times ahead. He wondered, as the clouds gathered, if the printed banners with the czar's name flapping above the red, green and white decorations so carefully applied on the cars behind by the birthday celebrants, would be dampened, maybe even destroyed by rain. He gripped the waist-high metal lever jutting up through a slit in the locomotive cab's floor and shoved it forward. The locomotive strained ahead tilting to the left when it reached the first turn.* Both momentum and images utilized, although would need editing and condensation for most stories!

Here's another concept. Imagine the all-encompassing totality of your scene and prioritize spot images as selected pieces of a jigsaw puzzle that will stimulate the reader's imagination to create a personalized imagined scene that supports the story and characters. A few carefully selected "puzzle pieces" used as descriptive stimulus allows the reader to engage and participate in making the story their "own." Better quality "puzzle pieces" allow fewer words for the reader to feel the scene is complete and brevity prevails, improving readability. Here are ways to make good choices!

The image must be concrete (paper clip), not abstract (fastener). The word choice must be image-generating (cracked porcelain tea cup, or the blue and yellow Easter egg). Modifiers should usually not be judgmental: six-feet tall rather than huge, which is not only judgmental but abstract; ruddy cheeks is usually better than healthy cheeks, but only if it fits. Avoid clichés. Use specific and concrete nouns and adjectives–sparrow, not bird; sixteen-story skyscraper, not tall building. As you create, keep in mind, for best fiction and stories, long descriptive passages for setting are for past generations.

You may also find clever ways to use dialogue attribution by slipping in scenic elements when appropriate. (Look out! he yelled, slapping the pit bull with his walking stick and shoving the child toward her mother.) You can often incorporate image provoking detail in internal reflections. *(She thought his Mohawk haircut, two brass hoop-earrings in his left earlobe, and silver tongue-stub oppressively unattractive.)*

Mastering the power of literary story
October 30, 2017 by William H. Coles

A writer's imagination in fiction opens the gates to creating great literary stories. To shape great literary stories, authors master skillful characterization and apply centuries-proved story structure that has matured from creative writers of the past.

Most writers today dream of a writer's life style and acclaim; they write for admiration, fame and fortune. Nothing wrong with that; it brings successful careers for many. But some writers want to create stories that last into future generations and will provide understanding of the constantly-evolving meaning of being human. Literary fiction stories can uniquely portray thoughts and emotions, nature of love, core human desires, sense of morality, transmit the soul of their generations with *lasting* penetrating impact that visual storytelling modes (such as film, video) *often lack*.

How can a writer today achieve memorable meritorious stories about events and people as great literature? So many of the past great fiction writers—Tolstoy, Chekhov, Dostoevsky, Flaubert, Bronte(s), Sophocles, Hemingway, Faulkner, Homer, Austen, Conrad, Melville, Forster, Woolf, and so many others—reveal how humans live and how life changes them. There are no secret formulas but there are commonalities that generate power to move readers and propel stories to evolve with mankind into future generations.

Elemental Truths For Learning to Create Great Fiction

1) WRITE WITH PURPOSE. Does the writer want fame and fortune, or engage, entertain, and enlighten readers in significant and individual ways by imaginative and skillful story presentation.
2) THEME AND MEANING. Theme is recurrent ideas; meaning is significant ideas. Lasting stories contain both.
3) CHANGE. Characters change as stories progress and so do readers after reading a great story. Examples: enlightenment (discovery or experience a new way of thinking), a shift in morality, a reversal in thinking, a coming of age.

4) DRAMA. Drama is conflict, action, resolution and is useful in many levels of story writing, character development, plot, scene construction, and prose. Dramatization is the major skill for characterization, especially with skills in writing in-scene, dramatic conflict and action.

5) UNIQUE AND FASCINATING CHARACTERS.
—a) Major characters' CORE DESIRES, which they rarely know and keep secret.
—b) Logical and credible MOTIVATIONS.
—c) Sense of MORALITY dramatized.

6) STRUCTURE.
Almost all great stories are structured in the telling: beginning, middle, and end and paced story-related ideas and happenings only. In literary stories consider:
—a) Carefully considered TIMELINE for credibility and comprehension.
—b) CHARACTER-BASED PLOTS. Character desires and motivations, strengths and weaknesses help drive story plot (with less reliance on fatalism or serendipity).
—c) Emotional ARCS (e.g. angry–>loving).
—d) Logical and credible ideas and happenings SEQUENCED with transitions.

How funny are you?

November 13, 2017 by William H. Coles

How funny are you? Do you make people smile and laugh? Is anyone void of humor?

For fiction writers, these are not trivial questions. A literary writer builds and molds character to an imagined story. Since most characters need some aspect of humor, what is humor all about for a writer?

I interviewed two comedy professionals (husband and wife): *Kevin Nealon*, film actor, TV (Weeds, Man with a Plan), standup comedian, and in cast of Saturday Night Live (1986–1995, 174 episodes) and creator of memorable characters such as Hans, Mr. Subliminal, and Weekend Edition; *Susan Yeagley*, television actor and show host, film star (Mascots), comedy series, (Parks and Recreation, Rules of Engagement) who trained at USC film school and the Groundlings in LA.

I started with the question–can a human exist without a sense of humor? Humor is an elemental way humans release tensions–the body needs to have that sense of release–and humans use humor to connect with each other. Probably all humans have at least the potential for a sense of humor. It is obvious that humor varies relating to background, social perceptions, geographical location, culture, maturity, level of education, to name a few essentials.

It's probably no surprise that **surprise** is at the core of the instigation of the humor response. You can find it in a **misunderstanding**, or a **misdirection**: stimuli based on expressing something we never thought about before, often in a form of syntactical manipulation. And it's always based on the design to surprise.

Misunderstanding–This woman was in a dress shop and found a dress she liked. "Could I try on that dress in the window?" she said. The shop assistant looked up: "Sorry, Madame, you'll have to use the changing rooms like everyone else."

Misdirection–A CEO stands before his company's shareholders to honor an employee for twenty-five years of loyal service. Today we would like to thank Albert for his service to our company. Albert is someone who does not know the meaning of impossible task, who does not know the meaning of lunch break, who does not understand the meaning of the word no. So we have taken a collection and bought Albert a dictionary.

[Simple examples, neither a Yeagley or Nealon joke.]

And of course humor is **timing** too. Subconsciously, a comedian knows how people think, knows how long it takes for them to process something, knows the direction they are thinking, and then lays the punchline, or whatever, at that moment when you know recipient is processing something in a different way.

Fictional dream, literary style, and storytelling
November 27, 2017 by William H. Coles

Improve writing of fiction stories.

Literature (written works of superior, lasting quality as an "art form" and fiction (imagined story and characters) are specific concepts that vitalize a writer to engage, entertain, and enlighten readers and achieve acceptance and endearment of the writer as storyteller and master of written works.

Engagement of a reader is a beneficial authorial achievement; invariably readers enjoy and learn from stories they feel a part of. To improve the skill, writers must find and correct individual strengths and weaknesses compatible with their style. No golden rules exist; but essential creative ideas abound in the talented writer.

Quality in-scene narration can be essential for a writer to capture the reader and give space for the reader to participate in the conflicts, characterizations, enlightenments that the fiction story can provide. Space means creating, for example, through action, dialogue, resolutions, morality, discovery, a character that one reader might say, *wow! I love a story about a faulty hero* while another reader might simultaneously think about the same character, *an antihero is exactly what provides reality and credibility here*. Written story-works provide opportunities for readers to build their own unique, internalized interpretations of characters and story (created and directed by the author, of course) that satisfy and please by discovery.

John Gardner introduced the concept of the fictional dream, an idea that has been inspected, interpreted, dissected, revised, and often ignored for decades. Basically, a writer creates a dream for the reader that is like submerging into an oceanic fictional world where characters and story absorb the reader without forcing the reader to leave the dream and "break the surface" back into reality.

Writers often break a reader's fictional-dream with correctable errors such as: non-sequiturs, lack of logic or credibility, grammatical errors, inappropriate metaphor, misspellings, inaccurate word choice, faulty ideation, and—a most common correctable error—poor narrative choice or delivery. Story narrators provide crucial story information outside a character's knowledge or capabilities such as exposition, pre-scene setup, anecdote, commentary, back story. To maintain a reader in the fictive story-dream, narrator-information is discreetly infused in scènes and narrative passages without calling attention to narrator presence.

Examples.
The scene: an inexperienced pilot goes into a death spiral killing himself and his passenger.

> 1) She prayed when Harry gripped the Cessna's throttle so tight his knuckles turned white; the engine whining on the edge of a power stall, the wing dipping to pull us into a death spiral. Harry moaned, frozen in fear. Her eyes stared to the side window where views of the earth alternated with the clouds in terrifying disorientation. And then, in an instant and with inexplicable surprise, she felt nothing—her senses stripped.
> *Comment. 3rd person POV. In-context, reader concentration and story involvement maintained.*

> 2) She never wanted to take this flight. Heights terrified her. And she was sick from the erratic lurches they were experiencing. The engine whined as the nose of the Cessna rotated up. Harry had less than 35 hours of instrument training, a death spiral from loss of control could kill them. They were less than 3000 feet from the ground. The wing dipped, the plane plunged twisting toward the earth to impact a few seconds later, exploding, dark fuel-smoke whorling upward . . . the world turning silent.
> *Comment. A narrator describes action and exposition—the reader is an observer—blocking potential for a fictional dream.*

Caution.
Even though the concept of fictional dream is not well understood and is subject to different interpretations and acceptance, awareness of the fiction dream helps authors to engage, entertain, and enlighten a reader by mastering storytelling narrative techniques and writing competency.

Keep readers involved when writing literary fiction stories
December 11, 2017 by William H. Coles

If you write a literary story to engage, involve, and enlighten receptive readers, you should (1) as an author, know the story world well and create characters from their unique worldviews (2) create a narrator who is of the story world, not you the author, (the author creates the narrator with that narrator's unique worldview, experiences, and memory). Author as narrator is a habit that almost always constricts creativity and promotes narrative description from a fixed reality rather than creating with imagination in a literary fiction story.

Imagined and creative storytelling inspires mystery, suspense, pending discovery, moral perplexity, and surprise in the story world. And in every good story, something else is going to be discovered or happen. Don't create so nothing can happen. Don't let the ideation, dialogue, or imagery of your fiction descend to inaction. Involve the reader's mind with options and opportunities, obstacles to be conquered, solid stimulating imagery, and the unexpected. When you ignore opportunities to engage your readers, you commit your style to cliché and stereotypes. Here are examples of ways to keep readers involved.

EXAMPLE 1
"Lock that damn dog in the garage."
"Okay."
   Comment: *Response kills action and suspense.*
"Lock that damn dog in the garage," George said.
"He bites!"
   Comment: *Response inserts possible danger ... and adds suspense.*
"Lock that damn dog in the garage," George said.
"Mother would never allow that."
   Comment: *Response adds to characterization.*
Note: *sometimes no direct response adds suspense by allowing the reader to wonder.*

EXAMPLE 2
Claire led the police to the bathroom. Harold's torso was submerged, his head back on the edge of the tub.
"Where are the goddamn the winnings?" Claire screamed, gripping Harold's

arm near the shoulder.

"He's dead," the cop said.

She dropped to her knees and sobbed.

>Comment: *Don't kill off characters when they may supply mystery and suspense and keep plot moving. What if the author used—*

"He's breathing!" the cop said, awkwardly struggling to apply CPR.

She shook Harold again. "You creep. Where's the lock-box key?"

>Comment: *When character's die, character development stops, removing opportunity for suspense and mystery.*

EXAMPLE 3 You can infuse mystery and suspense in descriptive narrative.

He hit the tennis ball out.

>Comment: *The action is closed. But there is opportunity to keep the prose alive.*

He hit the ball with a soft touch and the ball arched over Jeremy's head, descending toward the backline.

EXAMPLE 4

He didn't believe in God. Or heaven.

>Comment. *Character's ideas are shut leaving no opening for change. Provide uncertainty.*

Could he ever believe in a God that would allow him to be falsely accused of a crime he did not commit, and be doomed to live without faith in devine justice? It would be hell. Could he bear it?

EXAMPLE 5 (Keep prose active and vibrant—with a sense of in the moment.)

Imageic language enhanced with motion and conflict maintains a reader's interest word by word. In writing, the reader's mind is active in creating and forming images. Basically, successful authors don't create still-life images, they paint action scenes that intrigue and engage the reader with images that live on the page.

—Static. Not effective. *There was a bird on a limb.*

—Improved with some action. *The flying bird settled on the limb.*

—A lot of energy with action and imagery. *The olive branch quivered when the claws of the sparrow grasped the sturdy twig.*

MESSAGE. Great literary fiction stories are living works of art. The reader is involved. Memoir, creative nonfiction, biography, character sketch, essay, will not, by nature, provide imagined work that engages a reader with the potential of a literary fiction story.

What EM Forster taught us about flat and round characters and how to use it

January 8, 2018 by William H. Coles

In *Aspects of the Novel* (1927), EM Forster wrote ideas, now cherished by many writers, about flat and round characters. Here are highlights of ideas expressed in the book.

Flat characters, in pure form, are constructed around a single idea or quality, are so consistent without change that they are easily recognized and remembered, may be summed up in a few words. not as great achievements as round characters, and are best when comic rather than tragic. Contrary to many contemporary thinkers, flat characters are very useful to authors; they "never need reintroducing, never run away, have not to be watched for development, and provide their own atmosphere—little luminous disks of a pre-arranged size, pushed hither and thither across the void or between the stars; most satisfactory." The complexity of the novel "often requires flat people as well as round, and the outcome of their collisions parallels life more accurately." "It is only round people who are fit to perform tragically for any length of time and can move us to any feelings" (except humor and appropriateness).

"All [of Austen's] characters are round, or capable of rotundity," are never caricatures, and are highly organized. A round character gives readers a slightly new pleasure each time they come into the story, as opposed to the merely repetitive-pleasure result of a flat character.

"The perfect novelist touches all his material directly, seems to pass the creative finger down every sentence and into every word. The test of a round character is whether it is capable of surprising in a convincing way. If it never surprises, it is flat. If it does not convince, it is a flat pretending to be round. It has the incalculability of life about it—life within the pages of a book." Rotundity achieves the novelist's task of acclimatization and harmonizes the human race with the fiction.

Authors immersed in telling their own process fail to achieve effective characterization. "It is [author] confidences about the individual people that do harm, and beckon the reader away from the people to an examination of the novelist's mind. The novelists "who betrays too much interest in their own method can never be more than interesting; [they have] given up the creation of character and summoned us to help analyze [their] own mind, and a heavy drop in the emotional thermometer results.

Forster shares good advice and admirable thinking, and here is what the contemporary novelist has to build characters: description, internal reflection; action; conflict and resolution; emotional arcs; vibrant, purposeful dialogue; motivations and desires; narration; point of view, and change. Great characterization is the gift of complexity and construction a fiction author taps to create great, lasting, memorable, and meaningful characters that populate the best of literary stories.

The attitude and skills for the writer of great literary-fiction stories are: *imagine and create, not just remember and describe.*

Are you a storyteller?
January 22, 2018 by William H. Coles

Every living human has a story to tell, and most believe they'll get around to it someday… and if they get around to it, they'll be blissfully successful even if totally unaware of what an effective story is and how difficult it is to do well.

Of course, stories can be how you want to think they are—memoirs, essay, non-fiction, history, character sketches, creative journalism, diary entries, or even letters, but the literary story (a written work that is considered lasting and of artistic merit) has proven to be the most long-lasting written form for the last few centuries. It's one thing to scribble away to get your story onto paper, even published, without attaining thresholds of excellence to please a reader—thresholds of engagement, entertainment, and enlightenment. If you love your characters and thrive on pride in the content of your story, you owe it to yourself to do the best you can to succeed by creating a story with potential to be read, assimilated, admired, and remembered. Consider this.

Great stories:
1. Provide character and pilot movement through time organized by the author, and not described as randomly-displaced, disjointed events from reality revealed with obscuration of origin and meaning.
2. Are infused with drama.
3. Emphasize characterization.
4. Create plots with architecture and credibility, theme and meaning.
5. Narrate to provide effective story information, images, and ideation.
6. Excite with excellent prose.
7. Require imagination and creativity rather than just remembering and describing.

Wait, you say. I want to tell my story . . . a story about me, my family, my experiences, my friends and acquaintances . . . a memoir that comes from the heart and doesn't need contrived structuring and superfluous overthinking. Well then, great, if that's how you feel, just do it do it and all the best. And if you're a good writer, your work may well be received and lauded. But for those storytellers dedicated to excellence in writing fiction as literature, great stories are created by diligent intellectual pursuit of knowledge about story construction and experience in writing effective, clear, logical prose. And most important, for excellence, fiction writers must have an unvarying desire to engage, entertain, and enlighten a reader. To write well and create a great literary fiction story is a path to lasting pride and satisfaction.

Action and imagery
February 5, 2018 by William H. Coles

Concepts for making your story writing better.
A story in fiction, to be admired and remembered, needs, among many, these essential elements—action, conflict, and active imaginative-words.

In-scene storytelling is often more effective to engage and involve readers than telling-narration. The first example tells of a happening in narrative; the second, for comparison, is written in scene.

Narrative
   Harry flew a kite at the beach to entertain his invalid son but the kite got away, and Harry seethed with anger.

Many writers would think that changing from past to present tense would provide immediacy of action. *Harry flies a kite at the beach to entertain his invalid son but the kite gets away, and Harry seethes with anger.* From a reader's pleasure-view, not much improvement. And, in fact, in-scene reader involvement can be well established in past tense (without inherent problems of present tense), and is usually preferable, at least here.

Compare in scene
Here is the same scene with the idea expressed using expanded, selected word choice; insertion of active (rather than passive) construction; and use of concrete imagery… all bolded to emphasize.

   A wind **gust elevated** the **dragon** kite and the string **ran through** Harry's hand fast enough to **hurt.**
   "Let me do it, Daddy," his son Raymond said as he **limped** to Harry's side. The boy held out his hand that, when awake, **trembled** from a congenital **palsy.** Could he hold the string? Fly the kite? He wanted to so badly.
   "Hold tight," Harry urged, placing the string in the boy's hand. The kite **dipped** then suddenly **soared**, the string **taught** again.

The boy cried out. "I **dropped** it." Harry reached out but the kite had **lofted** too far to grab the **trailing string.**

The kite **disappeared**, driven out to the **sea** by the force of the wind.

"I didn't mean too," the boy said, "Please don't **hit** me."

Note the **words**:

Active verbs: elevated, ran through (hand), hurt, limped, trembled, dipped, soared, dropped, lofted, disappeared, hit.
Concrete nouns: gust, palsy, string, sea.
Concrete modifiers: dragon, taught, trailing.

To improve as a fiction writer and storyteller:
1. ritualize use of a dictionary and Thesaurus to search for the right words;
2. develop in-scene writing techniques (to replace narrative telling); be concrete–not abstract; keep perspective close to the action; keep characters' sensations in their senses—sight, hearing, touching, tasting, smelling;
3. avoid passive constructions; and
4. rigorously seek the right balance for the story being told between narrative and in-scene telling

When to use backstory in literary fiction
February 19, 2018 by William H. Coles

In general, in fiction, **backstory** should only be employed to advance the front story. For excellence, the concept is almost always required in short stories but is also useful in the broader sweep of a novel.

Example 1. Scene: no backstory. Story momentum intact.
The curtain parted just far enough for Maria to step forward into the spotlight and then closed. She bowed to the audience applause and cupped one hand in the other in a gesture of formality. She nodded to the piano player who, after a pause, started playing to guide her to the always difficult major-seventh opening note of the aria. The first flush of the piano introductory chords expanded out over the audience. Maria listened for the cue to pinpoint her starting note, it was coming . . .oh, no! but the pianist skipped the refrain with her critical cue note she *must* have. Would he still recover, do it right? She glared, tried to make eye contact. He plodded on. The audience turned into a thousand hostile critics instead of an adoring group of friends she liked to imagine. He'd circumnavigated to return to the intro. He was seven bars from her entrance. It was coming!. God! She took a deep breath, searching her memory for some clue to her starting pitch that had now escaped her the strain an impending failure.

Example 2. Scene with backstory (italicized). Same story but momentum interrupted by backstory.
The curtain parted just far enough for Maria to step forward into the spotlight and then closed. She bowed to the audience applause and cupped one hand in the other in a gesture of formality. She nodded to the pianist who started the intro. *She had met with him briefly yesterday. A dull sullen young man, but attractive with dark brown eyes and an inerasable black shadow of a dark beard shaved hours ago. She had carefully explained how she needed the refrain in the intro before the aria. She could only start when she heard the fifth to orient her to the nonchordal tone the composer insisted on using. She thought he had understood. And they had practiced, in the short time available, all the passages religiously.* Now he'd forgotten the refrain. He finished the intro and

went directly to the aria. Panic rose in her. She could never hit the crucial major seventh so unique to this composer . . . but she had to go forward. She felt the audience's expectant stares, heard their breathing. When she sang the note, the pianist's head jerked toward her. He knew what he had done.

To build as a significant dramatic happening with impact, the scene needs momentum. Backstory stops the momentum as a result of authorial lack of purpose. Indeed, if information about the accompanist—attraction, dislike, lack of respect for his talent, etc.—is important to the story, it should be skillfully embedded outside this action-scene. As is, it represents an author intent on just writing—filling a space with written words–rather than dedication to structuring and creating a story for the purpose of engaging, entertaining, and enlightening a reader.

Why select stories succeed best as literary fiction
March 5, 2018 by William H. Coles

Great literary fiction storytelling as an art form is not for all readers, and its success is not measured solely on volume of commercial book sales but rather the number of readers moved or enlightened by characters and story, usually about what it means to be human. Many of the literary stories that have lasted into new generations of readers have important, common characteristics; here are the principles.

1. Characterization.

The fictional humans that populate successful literary fiction seem real to the reader, either in the context of the reader's world, or the story world created by the author. It is the creation of these "real "characters to be moved by as well as to move story events that assembles character-based story and plot in most successful literary fiction. As Virginia Woolf wrote, "*. . . they [characters] live and are complex by means of their effect upon many different people who serve to mirror them in the round. . .*" When considering "*. . . the permanent quality of literature . . . think away the surface animation, the likeness to life, and there remains . . . a deeper pleasure, an exquisite discrimination of human values.*

2. Author's role.

Woolf taught us: "*Always in imaginative literature, . . . characters speak for themselves and the author has no part . . .*" In effect, there is no "I" in most great literary fiction. Woolf, in *A Common Reader,* gives Emily Brontë as an example; "*. . . she was inspired by some more general conception. The impulse which urged her to create was not her own suffering or her own injuries. She looked out upon a world cleft into gigantic disorder and felt within her the power to unite it in a book. That gigantic ambition is to be felt throughout the novel [*Wuthering Heights*]—a struggle, half thwarted but of superb conviction, to say something through the mouths of her characters which is not merely 'I love' or 'I hate', but 'we, the whole human race' and 'you, the eternal powers . . .'*"

3. Narrative voices.

Contemporary stories depend on particular action to keep a story moving. In developing character, there is often a shift from "*. . . the actual body with all its associations and movements . . .*" to the general, [abstract], more poetic prose. Woolf suggests, for literary fiction, the need for a voice that combines action and poetics without interrupting the movement of the story whole, a voice *"similar to what the choruses of Greek drama supplied—the old men or women who take no active part in the drama, the undifferentiated voices who sing like birds in the pauses of the wind; who can comment, or sum up, or allow the poet to speak himself or supply, by contrast, another side to his conception. Always in imaginative literature, where characters speak for themselves and the author has no part, the need of that voice* [similar to a chorus] *is making itself felt*.

To some extent, memoir and creative nonfiction have invaded the realm of imaginative literary fiction melding memoir and biography with fiction as literature. The disappearance of classic-fiction stories is at least partially due to academics failing to educate writing students to the intricacies of the great, successful literary fiction of the past.

A fiction-writer changes style with image-words
April 2, 2018 by William H. Coles

What if the writer can, with words, create images in a reader's mind that primarily stimulate setting and character in a fiction story. It's a matter of choice, imagination, purpose, and style, and very individual. Using basic-story information of plot momentum, let's augment basic story action-information with setting and characterization with authorial style changes as examples.

They went to the birthday party of a man. Is it appropriate to develop setting and character in scene or narrative when the plot purpose is to simply move characters to a party? Will it inhibit or captivate a reader's interest? Consider these examples.

Examples of style change with use of imagery.

1) BASIC DETAIL with IMAGES embossing SETTING.

> The locomotive with colorful cars behind followed the track that snaked through the valley. The steam of the locomotive reddened the face of the engineer as he leaned out the window. He wondered, as the clouds gathered, if the printed banners with the czar's name flapping above the red, green and white decorations so carefully applied on the cars behind by the birthday celebrants, would be dampened, maybe even destroyed, by rain. He gripped the waist-high metal lever jutting up through a slit in the floor and shoved it forward. The locomotive strained ahead tilting to the left when it reached the first turn.

2) BASIC PLOT information but DIFFERENT IMAGES. A different fiction-prose style.

> The packed cable car left Fisherman's wharf with a bell clang and a screech of steel on steel. Most of my fellow students had some colorfully wrapped birthday gift to give to Mr. Faraday. I teetered on an outer step of the car holding a hand rail while being jostled between a muscular middle-aged man in a skin-tight cyclist suit and aerodynamically sleek helmet and a reeking,

unshaven, wrinkled old man in a torn, too-big, woolen overcoat. The cable car nosed down after we turned onto Powell and we shifted our weight to remain as close to upright as possible. Without warning, rain pelted my face, and I knew by the squishy feel of the rolled white-paper banner that I had painted with purple-ink birthday greetings was ruined.

3) The above image-detail may be too much and exaggerated for some stories, an unacceptable style. Here using same plot basic information, people going to a party, is the same story development WITHOUT IMAGERY that emphasizes characterization.

All the students were crowded into the bus. We silently resented the trip to our professor's pretentious and unwelcoming mansion for his birthday celebration to pronounce our fallacious– but demanded–admiration for him. When we arrived, dense rain fell us as we stepped from the bus and the celebration banner I had painted was ruined and I threw it under the bus, happy not to have to exude feigned respect.

Take Away.

With careful thought and considered judgement, images in a fiction-writer's story can delineate style, build characters, and stimulate setting visualization. But it may be easy to overdo in some styles to the detriment of story momentum and loss of reader engagement.

What to do for writer's block
April 26, 2018 by William H. Coles

All literary fiction writers have problems with productivity related to ability and individual writing strategies. Writer's block is a common term but it really doesn't define a specific problem or suggest a consistent or dependable way to solve and proceed. The symptoms can be devastating—staring at a blank screen or page jilted by inspiration with quashed creativity. Here are famous authors' solutions that might just squiggle your own path, for better or worse, to recovery.

>***Maya Angelou:** "Writing is like any art or sport. Practice makes perfect. Inspiration will only come if you push yourself to keep putting pen to paper." ***Neil Gaiman:** "Put it [your writing] aside for a few days, or longer, do other things, try not to think about it." ***Mark Twain:** "Outline, outline, outline!" In essence, break your "complex overwhelming tasks into small manageable tasks," and then start on the first one. ***Ernest Hemingway:** "… keep some inspiration in reserve. "Always stop while you are going good and don't think about it or worry about it until you start to write the next day." Let your subconscious work all the time. "But if you think about it … you will kill it and your brain will be tired before you start." ***Hilary Mantel:** "… clear your mind … because your mind is overwhelmed by … thoughts … that are crowding your brain. You need to create a space for your inspiration to fill."

You'll have to judge which and how many strategies might work for you, but here are some thoughts on creativity and desire that may help.

So resolving "writer's block" is more than just the need to plug in your nonfunctioning computer or routinely do hundreds of undisciplined "writing crunches" … or, for that matter, to stop thinking. Consider that inability to create may be a symptom of who you are as a writer and what level of accomplishment you've achieved. Are you writing for excellence in creating fiction story as an art form or are you writing to be published to convince others you are an author? And are you intensely dedicated to the life-long learning of writing literary fiction and storytelling, and analyzing (not copying) the great stories you admire that have lasted as art forms?

And think about the immediate. Are you objectively conscious of the daily effect your emotional and/or psychological states have on your productivity. If you can believe life's minicrises or drained physical or mental energy contribute to difficulty in generating innovative creativity, don't be hard on yourself by blaming your troubles on a lack of ability and determination but accept that the individual, day to day process and success of creative writing is always in flux and will be influenced by your emotional state. To weather the inevitable breakdowns that seem to affect all of us, you might try this type of thinking.

Actually, finding a solution to loss of creative productive fiction that is personally satisfying and artistically accepted takes years to develop, like what a professional classic pianist must go through to practice superb technic and perfect performance to create individuality in interpretation and sound, and learn from extensive analysis of other artists how to generate an admirable career. So, as authors, we might respond to the often inevitable expected downtime in our creativity by savoring our "writer's block" writing time to study these skills: writing of craft; developing clear effective prose; analyzing secrets of other writers; improving story structure and character-based dramatic plots, and always looking to other nonwriting personal-skills that require: concentration, mental and physical coordination, focus of attention on individual thinking and skill improvements, and that accumulatively produce synergistic success in reaching goals. It is true writers achieve success in what they do as well as recover from obstacles by delicate adjustments of who they are and with truthful self-awareness.

Improve storytelling by flexiblity in writing style
May 11, 2018 by William H. Coles

A few literary-fiction storytellers effortless adjust to setting changes, different narrator perspectives, and point of view shifts. Most writers must work to develop changes in writing style when story scene requires improvement for reader acceptance. Her are a few skills that might be considered.

I. SUCCINCTNESS

More elaborate prose.

> Helen wanted commitment—meaning us married and settled in her seventeen-room, early twentieth-century house in town with tennis court and three-car garage. She believed if we changed the furniture and decorated with art we chose together, we could be happy newlyweds. But every time I stepped into her house, memories of her ex-husband rustled around me in the walls like trapped rodents. He was a sixty-four-year-old famous, successful neurosurgeon who was cavorting around Florida with his twenty-four-year-old office receptionist, who Helen and I thought too overweight and shaggy to be attractive to anyone but a lecherous older man still in midlife crisis. In truth, I could never replace her ex in his former home even though Helen insisted she had erased him from her life. But I suspected she longed for the life they had created together, a life of almost constant in-home entertaining and guest-admiration, a life of uncramped comfort in her echo-filled interior permeated with shelved, walk-in closets, and eight-burner kitchen stove surrounded by acres of counter space. Although I never confronted her, I knew she wanted legitimacy for our relationship to recreate her previous high-society life.

Less elaborate prose.

> Helen believed we would be happy newlyweds living in her mansion. But for me, memories of her ex-husband, a sixty-four-year-old neurosurgeon cavorting in Florida with his twenty-four-year-old office receptionist, rustled in the house walls like trapped rodents. I could never replace her ex in his former home, even with her longing for legitimacy of our relationship to recreate her previous high-society privileged existence.

II. SYNTAX: OBJECT VS SUBJECT EMPHASIS

The Baker's Grand Bakeoff Prize was won by me. **(Passive-object emphasis)**
I won the Baker's Grand Bakeoff Prize. **(Active-subject emphasis)**

Use of passive tense or active tense can, at appropriate times, change the effect of prose on a reader.

III. STIMULATE IMAGES

The packed cable car left Fisherman's wharf with a bell clang and a screech of steel on steel. Most of my fellow students carried birthday gifts for Mr. Faraday and in my right hand I clutched I a rolled white-paper banner that I had painted with purple-ink greeting and blue and red stars The cable car nosed down after we turned onto Powell and we shifted our weight to remain as close to upright as possible; I teetered on an outer step of the car holding a hand rail while being jostled between a muscular middle-aged man in a skin-tight cyclist suit and aerodynamically sleek helmet and a reeking, unshaven, wrinkled old man in a torn, too-big, woolen overcoat. Without warning, rain pelted my face, and I knew by the squishy feel of the banner it was ruined.

Career planning for aspiring, literary-fiction-story writers
June 13, 2018 by William H. Coles

Plan #1
Want to be an author?
Just **do it** and enjoy.
That's enough for most of us! Writing is a pleasure and we don't have to be the best for all readers or achieve some impossible measure of success.

BUT–
If you want satisfaction for: a) being the best author of the best story you can write that might persist for generations, b) creating stories that speak to contemporary and future readers about the complexities of being human, then you may want to write a fiction story as an art form that engages, entertains, and enlightens, and consider these questions to focus your writing career, even with modest expectations.

Plan #2
1. Why are you writing:
–to be known as an "author" **or**
–to write creatively and please a targeted group of readers?
No writer, no matter how great or accomplished, pleases even a small fraction of all potential readers, so perspicacious writers know who they want to please then develop their strategy for success with purpose. An enduring truth is creating great stories as an art form is no guarantee for fame and fortune, or universal appeal, but can be durably and reliably satisfying.

2. Do you have **purpose** to your writing? Do you want to enlighten, stimulate thought, create emotion, entertain? Do you strive for your storytelling to be valuable for your readers rather than trying to impress them with the superiority of your intellect and creativity? *Create excellence in your own way but maintain modesty.*

3. Are you good enough to achieve your dream of becoming an author? To avoid crushing your enthusiasm, try testing works-in-progress by seeking critiques by readers and teachers who are sympathetic to your writing style. Submit for publication routinely but don't be surprised or depressed by multiple rejections that are the accepted norm regardless of an author's ability and, if considered selectively, can give insight to your level of achievement.

4. Should you take courses?
Creative writing workshops give mixed results; they depend inordinately on evaluations of your work by fellow student–novices, at times arrogant and condescending, who inflict imprudent opinion and detrimental criticism. The value and reputation of **MFA programs** declines with the proliferation of conferred degrees in creative writing from academic settings struggling to survive financially. Consider carefully. Almost invariably, mentorship and/or self-study will value your time and accentuate your career far better than MFA programs with deficient teaching and time-consuming, defective scholarship.

5. Is your **vocabulary** commensurate with your aspirations? Improvement in vocabulary is a necessary, lifetime endeavor for all writers. Do you have the time and the will for improvement?

TAKE AWAY
For maximum, lasting pride and self-satisfaction in telling fiction stories, discover who you are as a writer, learn to imagine and create, know what you want to achieve, and focus intently on improvement of craft and storytelling.

A secret of great literary fiction stories as art
June 29, 2018 by William H. Coles

We live by stories, descriptions of people and events, real or fictional, that inform or entertain. Stories are ubiquitous as air, essential as a heartbeat, and as varied in the telling as there are humans to tell.

The story as a fiction art-form in prose has evolved over the past few centuries, but recently has declined as literature, a regrettable fact emitting from failure of contemporary authors to strive for "art" in their "creative" writing. What is lost? Imagined fiction and literature as written works considered to have lasting artistic value. The loss of written story as an art form distresses few and those enriched by fiction-story as art increasingly must reach back to past authors. So what makes a literary story so unique?

Virginia Woolf, in A Common Reader, helps sort out the values of literature as art; in essence great literary fiction is about understanding humanity. Charlotte and Emily Brontë's books are Woolf's prime examples, classics of English literature. Charlotte, when she wrote about Jane Eyre, said the passion of "'I love', 'I hate', 'I suffer'", although more intense, was on a level of her own (Charlotte's passion). Having quoted this, Woolf proceeds to point out the difference to Emily's Wuthering Heights. In both books, settings carry emotion and "light up the meaning" of the books as powerful symbols of "vast and slumbering passions in human nature" that fulfill the needs of a reader better than words or actions "can convey." But it's humanity that dominates the telling, and it's where Woolf discovers differences between the two sisters that are revealing of the process of created fiction.

Woolf considers Emily the greater poet and points out the stature of her talent. "There is no 'I' in Wuthering Heights. The love is not [just] the love of men and women. The urge to create Wuthering Heights was not her [Emily's] own suffering or her own injuries. "She [Emily] looked out upon a world cleft into gigantic disorder and felt within her the power to unite it in a book. That gigantic ambition is to be felt throughout the novel—a struggle, half thwarted but of superb conviction, to say something through the mouths of her characters which is not merely 'I love', 'I hate,' but 'we, the whole human race', and 'you, the eternal powers …'"

Woolf is quick to point out "that it is not strange that it should be so; rather it is astonishing that she [Emily] can make us feel what she had it in her to say at all." It is the "suggestion of power underlying the apparitions of human nature and lifting them up into the presence of greatness that gives the book its huge stature among other novels." Emily "could tear up all we know about human beings and fill these unrecognizable transparencies with such a gust of life that they transcend reality." An artistry that many contemporary authors of novels seem incapable of achieving! Woolf continues: "For the self-centered and self-limited writers have a power denied the more catholic and broad-minded. Their impressions are close packed and strongly stamped between narrow walls. Nothing issues from their minds which has not been marked by their own impress. They learn little from other writers, and what they adopt they cannot assimilate. "…a stiff and decorous journalism", prose that is "awkward and unyielding." And it's not unreasonable to suggest to today's proliferating plethora of writers of fiction that such deft thoughts (of Woolf) are the necessary nourishment, now lacking, of every contemporary teacher of creative writing, most of whom sequester in academics, and their students.

So there it is. A major void in the skill of creating great fiction that has, and is, marring the future of established value of literature in the written word as art.

Is it, or is it not, irony?
November 7, 2018 by William H. Coles

As a figure of speech, irony adds meanings to situations, develops readers' interest, makes literature more intriguing, and commands use of imagination to comprehend meanings. Moreover, it brings life to both drama and literature.

Look to these well-known examples from Greek antiquity. Antony at Caesar's funeral:

> I come to bury Caesar, not to praise him.
> For Brutus is an honorable man;

The first irony of Antony's speech is that he is unequivocally there to praise Caesar. Antony is, in fact, lying. This is a calculated tactic to disarm a crowd firmly on the side of Brutus when Antony takes the pulpit.

> And second, Brutus is *not* an honorable man.

Here is another example where irony creates character far beyond simple narrative, the Greek drama Oedipus Rex (Sophocles):

> "Upon the murderer I invoke this curse – whether he is one man and all unknown,
> Or one of many – may he wear out his life in misery to miserable doom!"

The above lines are an example of verbal and dramatic irony. It was predicted that a man guilty of killing his father and marrying his own mother brought a curse on the city and its people. In the above-mentioned lines, Oedipus curses the man who is the cause of the curse but is ignorant that he is that man, and thus he is cursing himself. But the audience knows the truth–dramatic irony.

Typically, irony uses language:
(1) that signifies the opposite.
(2) in a situation that ends differently than anticipated.
(3) where there is a difference between appearance and reality.

Wayne C. Booth is a scholarly ironist. Here is an example from his book (1). In reading, consider these concepts: "ironic stroke, victimization, deliberate absurdity, circle of ironists, circle of inferences, intellectual dance."

> As my family recently walked toward the cathedral, highly visible before us, in Angers, a cement worker looked at us and said, at first without a smile "The Cathedral is that way" – pointing to it – "and the Palace of Justice is there" pointing to the sign on a building right before our eyes [that said]: "Palais de Justice." I knew that he intended an ironic stroke, though I could not at first be sure whether we were to be excluded as mere victims – stupid American tourists who would not recognize the deliberate absurdity of such obvious and uncalled-for directions. But we were clearly welcomed within the circle of ironists as I said, "Oh, yes, and the workers are here (pointing to them and the Americans are here (pointing to us). His laughter told me that he now knew that I knew that he knew that I . . . The circle of inferences were closed, and we knew each other in ways that only extended conversation could otherwise have revealed. Total strangers, we had just performed an intricate intellectual dance together, and we knew that we were somehow akin.

It may or may not be an irony that Booth's book on irony is often difficult to comprehend. But the joy he transmits of being an ironist of quality stimulates further study. And the effects of irony and metaphor to better transmit significant meaning in literature, and in life, truly seem to make the effort to become an ironist worthwhile.

Booth explores five handicaps to ironic success in understanding literature: Ignorance, Inability to Pay Attention, Prejudice, Lack of Practice, Emotional Inadequacy. A challenge! But if interested, his book is worth the read for further understanding.

1. *The Rhetoric of Irony.* Wayne C Booth. 1974 [ISBN 0-226-06553-7]

Meaning in the literary fictional story
November 19th, 2009 by William H. Coles

Meaning in fiction isa often conceived as an element of writing that may or may not be inserted into a story, like a plastic baby doll in a Mardi Gras king cake. But meaning, its presence or lack of, is ubiquitous in a literary story, like the taste of sugar in a meringue. Writers seem to disagree, or at least not seek uniformity, on what meaning actually is in a story. Some seem to believe meaning equates with morality; others seem to think that it is equated with significance and, as a result, subsequently means ponderous and difficult, perceived attributes that make them avoid meaning altogether. For some, meaning has an existential twist—the worth of life. In speaking of great literary stories, however, it is most helpful to agree that for meaning to be memorable and to last in the human consciousness, a great literary story has meaning embedded in a defined environment: a story that is character based, has a beginning, middle and end where something happens to the character who progresses through time, and at the end of the story, the character and the reader change to see life and humanity in new ways. In *Misery* (sometimes translated as Heartache), in a few pages Chekhov reveals change in a character that focuses and enlightens the reader about grief and humanity, aspects of love and grief they had not thought of for some time, if at all. It is an awakening for these readers. And it provides unique satisfaction.

Many beginning writers tend to assume that meaning imparts a thou-shalt-not-kill or do-not-commit-adultery message; but a simple, clear change in perception about how the world and humanity is viewed can be significant and transfer meaning that has impact. To achieve this, there is a change in the way the reader (and the character) perceives the world after reading (and, for the character, acting in) the story. This is, of course, the beautiful potential fiction gives to a writer, and that nonfiction can not achieve because of the restrictions of the necessity in describing what happened.

So this meaning, which can be associated with Joyce's epiphany although it probably needs broader thinking to be effective for a contemporary writer, is essential for a story to have impact, be remembered, and persist on to future generations of readers.

Useful meaning for writers occurs in a variety of complex ways. As scary as it may seem, metaphysical questions are essential in literary fiction where it is not sufficient for the reader to simply discover who killed whom, or if the crack in the dam will rupture and flood the village. In essence, the development of every fictional character directly or obliquely addresses difficult, unanswerable metaphysical questions such as: Who are we? Why are we here? What should I do? At the core, great literary stories deal with what it means to be human and the anguish of confronting omnipresent metaphysical questions. Where do I go when I die? Is there a God? Does God care about me? Why do I suffer? Readers learn from seeing how fictional characters struggle with their humanity, their lack of perfection, their doubts and fears. It is reasonable to conclude that any well-written literary story that is memorable will be significant in what it demonstrates through story action about enlightenment of the human condition. It often is not simply right/wrong morality, politics, or issues of conformity. Rather, it most frequently considers moments of grace, illuminating thoughts, or revelations of the significance of actions among humans. It always deals with human interaction on a concrete level in the story line with metaphysical abstractions permeating the prose. And it is always best expressed through dramatization.

Rarely is meaning determined in a story before the writing begins. The perceptive writer sees the meaning in every good story as a process of discovery from inside, not predetermined and inserted. And, for respect of the story, the writer then allows the discovered meaning to permeate and solidify within the prose, but avoids hammering the reader through overly forceful prose focused only on meaning.

Meaning often requires the complexities of fictional prose to transfer maximally effective meaning to the reader. When a reader is engaged, the reader feels rather than just contemplates. It is imaginative character development and plot construction that permits fiction to engage a reader in a story with meaning. Nonfiction, and fiction dependent on description of happenings without imagination, does not engage with the same potential of fiction for significant meaning.

The quest for greatness in literary fiction and the failure of authorial self
May 16th, 2012 by William H. Coles

In Brooklyn, in a rock-bottom economy, a sixty-one year old unmarried mother will be evicted from the apartment she has lived in for eighteen years. She is a college graduate but lost her job as a magazine writer more than a decade ago. For more than a year she has failed to find a single ad hoc writing assignment or editing job. Even a token payment on the more than $10,000 in back rent could delay action, so she appeals to friends and family: her 24-year-old daughter–an unsettled, unemployed, college dropout who takes family welfare money and disappears into a social strata the woman does not approve–refuses to assist; a life-long friend tries unsuccessfully to mortgage her house to help; the husband of her dead sister is amused by her predicament and refuses to help. Methodically, she applies to New York State, the county, and the city for relief assistance. The employees she deals with are presented stereotypically as either incompetent, uncaring, or vicious in their refusals.

In the end, the protagonist refuses a $9,000 dollar loan from the city–she expected an unencumbered grant–and she turns down employment as a receptionist that Social Services has arranged because she feels it is beneath her dignity and not commensurable to her educational achievements.

The writer has more than adequate skills. The entire 6800 word story is well paced. The prose is more than adequate and although the work is "fiction," the story is based on perceived personal injustices and frustrating experiences in life of the author that have left her angry from a vague but very real ingrained sense of being discriminated against and mistreated. The author was deeply involved in her plight and with her writing, fully expected a reader to be involved in her anger and her despair. Her writing purpose was to vent … to expose a perceived crass, cruel, social system and the greedy cruelty of a landlord. But she couldn't step back from the story to create a story with credible characters and reliable narrator that would promote valid sympathy and understanding. The secondary characterizations of welfare and social workers, family and friends, were skewed to stereotypical, single-minded, ogres. Motivations were also difficult to accept.

She wrote on the premise that living in an apartment for eighteen years entitled a tenant continued occupancy without paying rent. And finally, the author-protagonist refused to take work, or accept assistance, without sufficient reason. A story created without objectivity by an author writing for self and ignoring the needs of the reader that a well constructed and reasonably delivered fiction story could provide.

How does a writer lose his or her way? There are no rules. Judgment changes with the progression of society and the maturation of the writer. And even more daunting, there are thousands of decisions to make about appropriateness and effectiveness of story elements to create a story as an art form. A great literary author doesn't make many mistakes, allow even a few contradictions or inconsistencies, or think illogically.

How might this author have created a more acceptable story? Primarily through objective characterization, writing through a broader understanding of the desires, actions, and motivations of all involved, and letting the outrage emerge in the reader–rather than being told to the reader–so as to avoid unsubstantiated victimization.

All writers need to write from a broad view of the world. They need to incorporate points of view that allow consistently objective creation of characters so the story is accepted and achieves a reader-identified purpose. They need to avoid excessive use of authorial subjective voice and create stories through accurate and unique character voice and story worlds.

Great fiction is imagined, character based, dramatic storytelling in perfected prose that is remembered, reread, and imbedded in the literary consciousness of readers sufficiently to pass onto future generations. It is sad, but the few contemporary writers who might achieve greatness can fit in the back of a mini van.

The most common failure among writers is just inadequate ineffective prose–prose that is unclear, purposeless, arrhythmic, uselessly ungrammatical, and with non sequitur ideation. Without well-written prose, great fictional literary stories cannot be created . . . no exceptions.

Those writers who learn to write well, and creatively, often fail in storytelling, succumbing to many pitfalls–a result of insufficient learning and practice that results in failure to embrace:

1. *Structure.* Ignoring necessity of a definitive beginning, middle, and end, with full control of information release and prioritization of scenes and action and internal reflection.
2. *Emotional arcs.* Inability to maintain character thoughts and feelings in a logical progression that ends in change and enlightenment.
3. *Drama.* Insufficient skill to infuse conflict, action, and resolution at all levels of writing and storytelling.
4. *Purpose.* Writing without story purpose and ignoring meaning and theme, and a significant message.
5. *Characterization.* Failure to creatively construct characters with a connected series of actions, thoughts, and feelings.
6. *Reader satisfaction.* Failure to provide engagement, entertainment, and enlightenment for reader in story structure and delivery.

The rare writers who accomplish creative prose and effective storytelling are not guaranteed success for greatness. At this level, an author needs to be more than who they are: they need to understand the world and humanity and how they fit into it; they need to be able to write from their characters' worlds to create effective, entertaining, meaningful stories; they need to write with a definable and consistent moral cobweb in their fiction; they need to suppress arrogance, acting with humility in creating their stories. And authors must never write to achieve an imagined, famous image as a writer, or to fulfill the dream of financial riches from their work; with little doubt, writing is not a reasonable or practical way for most humans to attain fame and fortune.

Writers must understand humor . . . what about an individual molds his or her humor–or prevents a humor response–that produces pleasure and understanding in a reader. Finally, writers must seek to define what they feel is beauty in the broad context of their generation. Beauty is subjective and individual, but an author's matured understanding of why people and things are beautiful to specific characters enhances characterization and imagery specific to a story that promotes great stories. Where is beauty in art, music, literature, life, religion, nature, science? In essence, defining beauty helps crystallize understanding of human nature.

But most of all, authors need to develop understanding and supportive attitudes towards others, including their readers. And they need to write stories with a purpose–without limiting themselves to their own lives and attitudes–to convince readers of opinions or evoke emotions. They need to enlighten readers through exceptionally imagined and constructed characters, and strive for meaningful credible enlightenment. In essence, literary authors are challenged to reach beyond their own limitations, and write from a broader understanding of humanity and the world we live in.

The seven fundamentals for writing fiction stories
April 26th, 2016 by William H. Coles

There are many ways to think about the great writing of great fictional stories. Both readers and writers can benefit by learning seven elements and appreciating the interaction of these elements in an individual story. For the reader, appreciation of authorial skills can be more easily enjoyed and admired, and for writers, learning to determine their strengths and weakness in the creation of the different elements can be valuable to balance story for an effective presentation.

Prose
Characterization
Plot
Narration (POV)
Setting
Imagery
Meaning/purpose

Prose relates to diction, syntax, and voice. Lyric prose with intense poetic elements can be used to pleasing effects for a reader both as a secondary and prime element. Most readers prefer a distinct, often authoritative voice for narrator and characters.

Characterization is a key element for a literary story and is often most effective by in scene action predominating over discursive narrative telling. It's importance in story development in the great stories is unique and individual and requires talent and practice. Dialogue, narrative, internalization, flashback, diction, memory, voice are opportunities for character development in effective ways different, and at times superior, to characterization in film or in drama. Almost without exception, great stories.

Plot is all that happens in a story. For great stories plot is almost always structured with a beginning, middle, and end; frequently is character-based; depends for momentum on reversals and recognition, mystery and suspense; is primarily linear, and is interwoven with emotional, character, and story arcs. Great plots provide conflicts early, both in story and among characters.

Narration is storytelling. Characters act out in fiction stories, narrators tell story, and authors create story with imagination and uniqueness. *Point-of-view* choice is tailored to the needs of story. Each point of view has advantages and disadvantages and must conform to reasonable story-related credibility and reliability reliability, and adjust to requirements of suspension of disbelief. Authorial control of the narration through the narrator must be consistent in style, transparent (no authorial intrusion), carefully chosen for story understanding and purpose,, and meticulously crafted.

In writing fiction stories, *Point-of-view* choice is tailored to the needs of the story.

Setting orients the reader to time, place, and physical and psychic distance from story action, environment, and obstacles to plot progression. Most stories provide settings through subtle integration in other elements avoiding extensive description. Yet, some stories rely on the poetry of beautiful settings.
Fiction stories are *not* character sketches, memoir, biography, or journalism with untruths.

Imagery relies on imaginative prose with innovative yet absolutely accurate word choice within the boundaries set up by story development. Momentum in the writing with image-inducing prose should be pervasive to avoid loss of engagement of the reader.

Theme/purpose. Every story should engage a reader, entertain the reader, please the reader, and provide recognition or enlightenment (theme/meaning) so the readers will never see the world again exactly the way they did before the story was read. Fiction stories are *not* character sketches, memoir, biography, or journalism with untruths. And every story has to have more than an authorial catharsis describing authorial lives and events with description without imagination and discursive rumination of authorial thoughts and opinions. Fiction is art that emerges from imagination and is created with skill, structure, and revision.

Fiction is art that emerges from imagination and is created with skill, structure, and revision.

What do you do to make scenes come alive in literary fiction?

Monday, March 6th, 2017 by William H. Coles

Literary imagined scenes come alive with CONFLICT and ACTION in language, narration, story, and dialogue. It's not inherent for most writers striving to write literary fiction. To start, writers and storytellers are dependent on these basics: 1) literature is written works that have merit and lasting potential as an art form, and 2) fiction creates imagined events and characters. For success in inserting conflict and action, writers master vibrant in-scene writing–an important staple of effective story delivery–supporting concrete-imagery, credible dialogue, and action prose in narrative.

Here are examples of conflict and action in dialogue, narrative, and a descriptive scene using senses, thoughts and perceptions. These examples are not exclusive. With an active imagination, a myriad of ways can be created by an author to achieve action and conflict in creative fiction. The examples:

1) A family whose parents have just been buried are dividing the parents' possessions among them. Carrie, the youngest, is working in the tool shed. Martha, Henry, and Jessie argue over who gets items in the house–and no one wants the responsibility of bringing up Carrie.

Now, to make the scene alive, conflict is inserted, mainly in dialogue. Conflict results in action, the fuel for great fictional prose.

> "I am not taking on responsibility for a seventeen-year-old," Henry said, pausing mid-brushstroke and turning from the window frame he was painting to make the house sellable.
> "Quiet, she'll hear you," Martha said from the kitchen, throwing a cracked and chipped casserole dish into a metal trash can with a crash of splintering glass. She turned back to scrub glassware in the sink.
> Jessie went to the front door to look for Carrie. "She's carrying stuff out of the tool shed," she said.
> "Don't let her throw out any power tools," Henry said.
> "She's laying things out for us to see."

"She'll take the best."
"She doesn't want power tools!"
"Anything of value."
"Stop it. She's your sister."
"You think so much of her, you take care of her."
"I've only got a one-bedroom apartment," Jessie said, picking up a broom and sweeping with a flurry of useless strokes.

From the novella **Sister Carrie**

2) For conflict in a narrative passage, here's an excerpt from Conrad's *Heart of Darkness*.

" . . . I was circumventing Kurtz as though it had been a boyish game. I came upon him, and, if he had not heard me coming, I would have fallen over him too, but he got up in time. He rose, unsteady, long, pale, indistinct, like a vapor exhaled by the earth, and swayed slightly, misty and silent before me; while at my back the fires loomed between the trees, and the murmur of many voices issued from the forest. I had cut him off cleverly; but when actually confronting him I seemed to come to my senses, I saw the danger in its right proportion. It was by no means over yet."

3) Here is a remarkable scene from Faulkner's "Barn Burning" where "alive" is achieved without describing action per se, but with use of accurate, imaginative language and sensual perceptions.

The store in which the justice of the Peace's court was sitting smelled of cheese. The boy, crouched on his nail keg at the back of the crowded room, knew he smelled cheese, and more: from where he sat he could see the ranked shelves close-packed with the solid, squat, dynamic shapes of tin cans whose labels his stomach read, not from the lettering which meant nothing to his mind but from the scarlet devils and the silver curve of fish – this, the cheese which he knew he smelled and the hermetic meat which his intestines believed he smelled coming in intermittent gusts momentary and brief between the other constant one, the smell and sense just a little of fear because mostly of despair and grief, the old fierce pull of blood. He could not see the table where the Justice sat and before which his father and his father's enemy (our enemy he thought in that despair; ourn! mine and hisn both! He's my father!) stood, but he could hear them, the two of them that is, because his father had said no word yet: . . .

It's a complicated subject to grasp, much less master and incorporate, but essential for literary fiction storytelling.

Appendix B
SHORT STORIES

Examples of the principles and skills advanced in The Art of Creating Story.

The Gift 569
　A determined mother protects her deformed child from the destructive sympathies of family and society.

The Amish Girl 583
　A girl and boy in love challenge diverse cultural values.

Speaking of the Dead 601
　At a funeral to deliver a eulogy for a dead wife he despised, a college professor learns from a stranger the merit of forgiveness.

The Miracle of Madame Villard 613
　Miracles emerge in the chaos of the French revolution.

The Stonecutter 635
　Stonecutter's son falls hopelessly in love with a client.

Homunculus 645
　In the late 19th century, a circus dwarf falls in love with trapeze artists failing to value those who cherish her.

The Necklace 657
　Two couples on tour find new meaning in their lives after the theft of a precious necklace.

Suchin's Escape 669
　An abducted Chinese girl, trapped in the New Orleans sex trade, struggles for freedom from her captors.

Clouds 685
　A mother drives her handicapped son to be institutionalized.

The Gift

Illustration by Peter Healy

The Gift

In 1959, a week after her seventeenth birthday, Catherine missed her period in February, and then in March. By late April she was not sleeping well and most of her waking hours were spoiled by nausea and hating everything she ate. Her mother, Agnes, made an emergency appointment with Dr. Crowder.

"Stay here," Dr. Crowder said to Catherine before he left the exam room. The receptionist had brought Agnes into his private office, where she sat in the wing chair for consultations.

"She's pregnant," he said.

Agnes's face paled with the accusation. "She's a child," she said.

How often mothers would not let their children grow up. He gave her time to absorb the truth. "She's a young woman who is going to have a baby," he said.

Agnes wept, her hands to her face. Dr. Crowder handed her tissues from a desk drawer. After some moments, Agnes blew her nose and breathed deeply with a long exhale.

"Have you told her?" Agnes said.

"I've told only you. But she's not stupid."

"Can something be—you know—done?"

Dr. Crowder stared. He had been the family physician for more than thirty years. He had delivered Catherine. "You might find someone. But never ask me, Agnes." he said. "I do not approve."

Agnes flushed. Now she was ashamed. "It will ruin us," she explained.

Bullshit, thought the doctor. Birth is a miracle. Oh, yes, life was fragile, dangerous, and loaded with inexplicable injustices, but he still loved humanity. And he stayed in practice well beyond retirement to marvel as his patients juggled life's inflated minutiae in their own creative ways.

"I'll send her away," Agnes continued.

"Let her make the decision," Dr. Crowder said.

"No. I'll make up an excuse."

"Think about it. There would be gossip if she stayed. But if you and Harold were supportive and proud, the gossips would cease caring after a while. And life would go on."

"It's a sin," Agnes said.

"I doubt having a baby is a sin," Dr. Crowder said.

But Agnes could not trust the advice of an idealistic doctor who she thought was immune to reality, nor the judgment of her errant child who was too young and too stubborn to know what her slip-up would do to a prominent family.

At home, to her husband, Harold, who knew otherwise, Agnes dismissed Catherine's nausea as tummy upset and refused to discuss the baby with Catherine for hours. She blamed Catherine's problem on Harold's family, all of whom were pig-headed and arrogant.

After dinner, alone with Catherine in Catherine's room, she demanded to know the father of the child. She shouted the most likely possibility. But Catherine refused to answer. "So many you don't even know?" Agnes asked. Then Agnes sent Harold into the bedroom for a one-on-one (she hoped he would beat the crap out of Catherine). Agnes leaned with her ear against the bedroom door so she could hear every word. She was appalled: he felt lucky to have a grandchild. Birth was God's gift to each of us, and how lucky this baby was to have Catherine for a mother. Not one word of condemnation. It was typical of her husband to turn disaster into a conspiracy against all she had accomplished.

Agnes kept her plan simple. After the birth, far away, an immediate adoption was the only solution, and after the town no longer remembered or cared, Catherine could return to live out her penance.

Dry-eyed, Catherine lay on top of her bedcovers on her back, which was already the most comfortable position for her. Her father's visit had renewed her confidence. She was a good girl, a girl who made love to only one and with a sincere passion and respect that justified her action. Even with her first suspicions, she could not destroy her lover's future with burdens he could not yet handle. There was virtue in a love baby, far different from sluts who made love to anyone, and whores who got paid, a fact she had shouted to her mother when her mother had used the word.

In the days after the doctor's appointment, Catherine endured her mother's frequent side glances and wet hissing sounds, and turned away when her mother reminded her how evil premarital sex was. But soon her mother's unpredictable outbursts became so irrational that Catherine ignored her, and turned to prayer for her baby. Her mother then developed a distracting twitch under her right eye, loud speech, short sentences—and long, cold silences.

In due time Agnes found the priest, who was hesitant at first to help. Agnes made him admit he had arranged clandestine solutions to similar problems, saying she knew, at least secondhand, of a girl he had protected. He soon admitted compliance. He said infant victims of accidental pregnancies deserved a life away from the debauchery of their mothers, who must spend their lives seeking full-time repentance to receive grace. He would help.

Two weeks before school let out for the summer, Agnes took Catherine to the airport. She gave Catherine numbered instructions on a folded piece of notepaper tucked in a paper-bound English-French dictionary. Agnes cried briefly at the gate, but she felt only relief when the plane finally took off. She was profoundly afraid of flying, but she felt no apprehension about Catherine's trip, and although she had hated the pain and discomfort of her own pregnancy, she did not worry about Catherine's delivery in a foreign country. Whatever happened, good or bad, Catherine had brought it on herself. All was in the hands of God now. She could not be expected to do more, and she was confident that many parents would have done much less, and much less effectively.

The convent school looked like a fortress, with a high stone wall around the buildings that were set next to a wide, rapidly flowing river at the northern edge of the town in the south of France, where the trees were already full with spring and the air warm even at night. From the hill, visible from the school and anywhere in town, a thirteenth-century buttressed cathedral jutted two spires toward the heavens.

The Mother Superior was cool and distant but not mean or dismissive, and Catherine, after a few weeks, liked her authoritative efficiency. Catherine began school and attended mass daily, but understood almost nothing. To help, a novice taught her French in private sessions after atins and after the evening meal.

For weeks, Catherine's sickness came on her at unexpected times. But the Sister in the infirmary gave her medicines and arranged special foods from the kitchen, and soon Catherine felt fine.

Catherine's best friend was Sister Mary Margaret, an impish little nun who rarely thought of God outside of church, but who was eager to be involved with Catherine's delivery of God's gift. Sister Mary Margaret listened to Catherine's fear of dying when the baby came out. "It is impossible," Sister Mary Margaret said confidently in French, although she had never seen a birth. "What if God punishes me with a hairy monster?" Catherine asked hesitantly. "God does not always seem to care, but He is not mean," Sister Mary Margaret said. Then Catherine told her of her fear of being stoned by French peasants—she had seen that in a film, for other sins, with Boris Karloff. Sister Mary Margaret gave her lyrical bubbly laugh that Catherine loved and frowned as she tried to find the right words in English. "C'est fou," she said.

Agnes did not write to further emphasize her indignation at her daughter's sin. Catherine sent only rare postcards to her mother, but sent long letters about her new life to her father at the office. Catherine counted the days for her father's return letters about home that he faithfully wrote.

And Catherine wrote to her priest.

Dear Father O'Leary:

The Mother Superior speaks English okay and spoke of you at both my meetings with her. She smiles with her memories of when you met. She introduced me to the people who want to adopt. The woman put her hands under my blouse on my bare belly to feel her "petite poupée." I didn't like it but I try to be Christian.

Except for Sister Mary Margaret, one of the nuns, I still can talk to only a few here. The novices laugh when I use French words and they don't try to understand my English. But I take walks through the town with Sister and visit the cathedral daily that is half a mile from the school.

The women here sew beautiful clothes that they sell in Paris. They have taught me and I now make baby booties and soft nightgowns for my baby. I crochet lace for the sleeves and the hem, even though Mother Superior says new parents will be waiting to take him ... or her, away. She says it is best for all that way. As time grows close, I want to keep my baby, but I will not go back on my word.

I help the groundskeeper herd the goats that graze on the lawns of the school. He is a gentle man who sings lively songs in a high voice while he works. He makes goat cheese to give to the poor that tastes awful. But I pretend to like it to please him.

Yours in Christ,
Catti

When labor pains started regularly, Catherine went to the convent infirmary, where there were two iron beds with mattresses. Sister Teresa, the midwife, gave Catherine a draught after the delivery. Catherine slept. When she woke, Sister Mary Margaret sat on a chair next to the bed, her back six inches from the splat. The sheets were clean. Catherine accepted a glass of apple cider from her friend. Catherine's body hurt when she rose up to drink. She returned the glass and fell back, exhausted at the effort.

"Well?' Catherine asked Sister. "Did you see my baby?"

Sister was silent.

"Is it a girl?" Catherine asked.

"A little girl," Sister said in English.

Catherine found her friend's hesitancy unexpected, and she turned on the bed to see her friend better. Sister was sobbing.

"What's the matter, Maggie?"

Sister stood up and turned so Catherine could not see her face, then she hurried out the door.

"Please don't go," Catherine called. But Sister did not stop.

Catherine slept that afternoon. Sister Mary Maggie returned in the evening. Catherine was glad to see her.

"I want to see my baby," Catherine said again.

"The baby is gone already."

"So soon?"

"It was Mother Superior's plan."

"What's gotten into you? I thought you were my friend."

Sister Mary Margaret cried again.

"You're useless," Catherine said, immediately sorry when Sister turned her head away. "I want to talk to Mother Superior."

"It is not possible," Sister said.

Catherine threw her feet over the edge of the bed, wincing with pain. "I will go to her," she said.

"No! I will be punished. I was not supposed to tell you."

"Tell me what?"

Sister began crying again.

"What? Tell me, Maggie."

"The baby."

Catherine knew her friend too well to not fear the worst.

"Is the baby dead?" Catherine finally asked.

"Oh, no, not dead."

"What then?"

"She is—alive good."

"What is that? What is not right about a baby? Tell me!"

Sister did not speak but squeezed her eyes shut, helping Catherine stand and holding her arm as they went to Mother Superior. Twice Catherine had to sit on a bench to rest. Her friend could not speak for her sobs. "Run ahead. Tell Mother Superior I'm coming," Catherine said. Sister hesitated. "Go," Catherine said, disturbed by her friend's crying.

Catherine was surprised that Mother Superior hugged her for the first time ever, firmly and long. Mother Superior stepped back. "The family would not take her," she said.

Catherine looked to the floor away from Mother Superior. "Why?"

"The baby is not well. They were afraid."

"What is wrong?"

"I didn't see her. But she has no feet."

"That is ridiculous," Catherine said. "I must see her."

"I had the baby sent to a special hospital for children near Lyon. She will be given special care."

"And the parents?"

"They have refused to be involved."

"I must go," Catherine said.

"No. She will have the care she needs to grow—and serve Christ."

"I must see her. I will pay the way. Father has sent me more than I need."

"It is not the money."

"I will go. I do not need your blessing."

"You always have my blessings, child."

"I must go too," Sister Mary Margaret said, looking directly into the eyes of Mother Superior.

Catherine used her savings and she and Sister, with the now-silent gardener and cheese maker driving, took a wagon to the train station in the next town. With stops, the train took six and a half hours to the city. To save money for the return trip, Catherine and Maggie walked two miles from the station to the hospital.

At the hospital, Catherine looked down at the baby, covered in a nightgown. Catherine had already decided her name was Patricia, not Audrey, as the nun dressed in a black-and-white starched habit had told her. Patricia was in a little nightgown with buttons on the back. One arm in a sleeve waved. The other sleeve partially covered a short arm that ended in three finger stubs that jerked up and out. The nightgown hem lay flat. Catherine retracted the edge. The right leg ended in a smooth knob above where the knee should be. The other leg tapered to an end above where the ankle would be—with no foot. The corner of the baby's mouth tried to smile in a strong effort with unsure results, and the eyes wiggled and waved, sparkling as if sharing the irony of trying to make everything all work right.

"You have seen enough?" the nurse said. Her harsh accent was difficult to understand.

Catherine removed the little nightgown. She smiled at her child, and the child's roving eyes seem to fix on her, at least for a few seconds, until they wandered off, but they came back again. And how soft her skin was, her red hair so fine. Her eyes were faded of color, but inquisitive and sharp. Her lips continued to wiggle at times in an uncoordinated smile.

"She is mine," Catherine said.

"She must stay here with us," the nurse said firmly.

She put the nightgown back on her daughter. She touched the side of her cheek. The little arm waved. She touched the chest with her index finger. There was a little passage of gas with a squeeze of the face.

Searching for French words exasperated Catherine. "Tell her Maggie," she said to Sister Mary Margaret. "Tell her who I am. And get some milk and food for the trip."

Maggie explained in French. The nurse listened intently without response.

Catherine began to take off her sweater to use as a blanket, but the nurse, with a gentle hand on Catherine's arm, let Catherine know to keep her sweater—and then wrapped little Patricia in a hospital blanket. "It is for you," she said in broken English. When Catherine was holding Patricia against her breast, the Sister leaned over and kissed the back of Patricia's head. "Elle est miraculée," she said.

At the convent every nun and novice was immediately infected with motherly instincts for Patricia. Even the gardener and goat-herder, as the pater familias, made daily visits with milk and fresh-cut pansies. Sister cooked while Catherine fed Patricia, and she rocked Patricia when Catherine needed rest to regain her strength. And Catherine took Patricia to church, to market, to herd the goats. She sewed, after many trial designs, a special sling that supported Patricia. Patricia was comfortable when carried on Catherine's chest or back, and she could face in or out, and sleep when she wanted.

Catherine with Patricia became a common sight in town and the surrounding fields and wooded paths. Strangers to Catherine waved with pride and familiarity. Catherine loved Patricia's laugh as she jiggled her in the sling; loved her intense stares at new flowers they found in the gardens or in the wild; loved the "ooh" of watching a worm on a stone, or a hawk circling in the sky.

Patricia became adept at getting around the house, using her stumps all together to scurry like a tilted crab. But she was limited outside, and Catherine could see that Patricia would need some upright means of mobility.

Catherine visited veterans who lost limbs in the war, and talked to them about support. They used limbs usually provided by the army, premade, and not specially designed. But she learned unique problems for each disability, and studied the principles of various prosthetics. She found a furniture maker and explored different woods—ash and yew and oak—for strong support for Patricia's shorter leg. For the other leg she needed a sturdy foot. At first, a foot replica in walnut was tried, but eventually, a functional design looking like a miniature toboggan with laminated woods from saplings was found to be best. Catherine used her sewing skills to attach and brace the prosthetic legs with shoulder straps and snug waistbands. These were attached for stability to the wooden prosthetics by threading through multiple holes. And Patricia, with a laugh, toddled around for a while, tumbling often, and then adapted with the speed of the young until she could walk, albeit stiffly and with a tilt backward. This worked for almost a year. But it was not enough. In the leg without a knee, Catherine knew she needed a hinged prosthesis. She wrote Father O'Leary and received a quick response.

> Dear Catti,
>
> I was pleased to discover our own Dr. Crowder went to school with a world authority. Poor Dr. Crowder has had a stroke and cannot walk and he speaks so slowly we can barely understand him. But his mind is sharp and his wife now writes letters for him, and records drafts he dictates for his memoir. I am sure he would help in any way he can.
>
> God Bless,
> Father O'Leary

She received a reply from her letter to Dr. Crowder in two weeks.

> Dear Catherine,
>
> How nice to hear from you. You are one of my favorite patients. And I was also glad to hear your little Patricia is saying her first words. I imagine they're all in French, which is a beautiful language.
> I do know about artificial arms and legs. But you must come home to see the best. She will need to be refitted often as she grows, and you will have to travel to Boston. But it is a very good idea.
> I am a mess with this stroke. But I love my memories.
>
> Sincerely,
> Amory F. Crowder

When Catherine and Patricia left for home, more than a hundred people from the convent and town came to wish them well. Even Mother Superior cried and Sister Mary Margaret had to be pried away from her hugs of Catherine and Patricia.

Harold and Agnes were at the airport terminal gate when Patricia and Catherine arrived.
  Little Patricia took her first look at Grandma and howled.

"Is that any way to treat your grandmother," Agnes said curtly.

"It's not you, mother. The trip has her constipated."

Catherine picked up Patricia and snuggled her on her shoulder. Patricia's footless longer leg poked out below her dress.

"She doesn't look so bad," Agnes said.

"Let me show you, Mother." Patricia loved to be touched, and loved to be moved. She gurgled with pleasure. "Your grandchild."

"I didn't mean she wasn't perfect."

"Dis 'bon jour'," Catherine said to Patricia.

Agnes frowned at the French. Although she thought she knew what it meant, she was always suspicious that there was some meaning in foreign words that might be against her.

"Say hello," Catherine said, sensing her mother's feelings.

"Lo," Patricia said, and waved her arm at her grandmother, and she smiled. "Lo," she said again.

Agnes gasped at her impulse to reach out and hold her grandchild, and she took back her hands before she had extended them too far, slipping them in the pockets of her sweater.

"Take her," Catherine said.

"Oh, I'll scare her."

"I'll take her," Harold said stepping forward.

Agnes reached out quickly. "I'll do it, Harold, " she said.

As Agnes took Patricia, clutching her chest under the arms, Patricia smiled. "Pooh bear," she said with a little spittle.

Catherine handed Patricia a small brown bear with one button-eye missing, and Patricia held it out to her grandmother.

Agnes held her face rigid in resistance to revealing any pleasure. Catherine tensed. But Patricia could not contain her natural affection for people, and she grinned with a warm bubbly sound. Patricia held out her bear again to her grandmother, who smiled, taking the bear and giving it a big hug. Catherine relaxed as her mother jiggled Patricia from side to side, and thanked God for Patricia's magical gift of making others happy.

Agnes held Patricia in her lap on the ride home.

Patricia discovered Catherine's toys in a trunk and in dresser drawers in Catherine's room, which had not been used since Catherine left. Harold had bought a child's bed, but everything else was the same. Agnes found energy she had not had for years: she baked and swept, she arose early before the alarm, and she took daily photos of her family. Catherine got a job as a receptionist in the office of a doctor Dr. Crowder knew. And the newest advances in jointed prosthetics were fitted to Patricia in Boston; they were waiting the new limb any day.

Three times a week Catherine took Patricia to the YMCA pool and taught her to swim dressed in a one-piece red bathing suit Catherine had sewn herself from a design she had seen in a magazine. Patricia learned to swim quickly, smoothing out her first awkward movements, and Catherine was pleased to think it toned muscles in new ways that Patricia did not normally use and would prepare her for heavier, more complicated prosthetics.

One evening, after Patricia was asleep, Harold and Agnes sat with Catherine in the living room after dinner.

"I don't like you taking Patricia swimming," Agnes said. "People will stare."

Catherine had sensed her mother's disapproval weeks ago. "Why should she not go swimming?"

"It will make her feel different."

"She is different, mother."

"But you shouldn't make her feel bad."

"She has to learn to accept the stares and not feel bad."

"At least you could cover her. That skimpy bathing suit doesn't hide anything."

"That skimpy bathing suit is what most of the children wear."

"But they're different."

"She's not ashamed, mother. She's pretty and very smart. And she has every reason to be proud."

"I didn't mean that, Catherine. Don't twist my words. I just don't want her hurt by those who think her differences should not be exposed. That's all."

"They are curious, mother. People do stare. But for most it isn't mean and it doesn't last long. And Patricia can be seen for who she is."

"She'll never go out on her own if you keep it up."

"I want her to go out on her own able to handle anything that she might face."

"Be quiet, Agnes," Harold said.

"Don't talk to me like that, Harold. This is important."

"It's not your business. Stay out of it," he said.

"You're always against me. I am not pleased, Harold."

Harold folded his paper, running the dull edge between his forefinger and thumb until it was sharp and then placing it on the footstool. "Take her swimming," he said to Catherine. "Take her everywhere she wants to go."

"That's not what I meant and you know it," Agnes said.

"Be quiet," Harold said as he left the room.

Six weeks later, for Patricia's birthday, they had a party in the kitchen with a cake and candles, balloons and presents. Harold gave Patricia books. Catherine gave her a necklace with a garnet single-stone pendant. And Agnes went to the garage and carried in a small wheelchair with a leather seat support and shining chrome spokes on thick rubber-tired wheels.

"Look at that!" she said to Patricia.

Patricia smiled.

"Can you say thank you?" Catherine said.

"Thank you," Patricia said to her grandmother.

That night, after Catherine heard Harold finish reading one of Patricia's new stories, Pinocchio, to Patricia in bed and she had fallen asleep, Catherine approached her mother in the living room. "You must take the wheelchair back."

"Nonsense. I had it specially made," Agnes said.

"She doesn't need a wheelchair," Catherine said.

Harold came down from the upstairs and sat in his armchair.

"She can't keep up," Agnes said. "I almost lost her in the store."

"She does very well, mother. Just slow down a little."

"The new leg has been good," Harold said.

"She'll be going to school soon. She can't always be strapping on legs," Agnes said.

"She is not a victim, mother. Ignore what she can't do. Help her do what she can."

"How unloving that is, Catherine. How selfish," Agnes said. "You are making her life miserable. You've always been selfish. From the beginning."

Harold's jaws were clenched, and his hands balled into fists. "I will not allow this, Agnes. Take back the chair."

"Ridiculous."

"Take back the chair!"

"It's all right, Daddy."

"No, it's not all right." He stood.

"Don't you walk out on me," Agnes said.

He went into the kitchen. Catherine followed. He had the chair in his hands.

"What are you doing?"

"You're right. She is not a victim, Catherine. I don't want this around."

She had never seen her father this angry.

"I'm taking it to the office for now. Tomorrow, I'll be sure it's returned—or destroyed."

Agnes came into the kitchen as Harold left through the back door, taking the wheelchair to the car.

"Don't you dare—" Agnes began.

"Say one more word and I'll explode." He shut the door.

Two weeks later, Catherine went to her father's office at the bank during the lunch hour. She had brought sandwiches and sodas for both of them.

"We have to go back," Catherine said to her father.
"Because of Mother?"
"We both miss Maggie, and all the nuns."
"But it's your mother, isn't it?"
"I hope to find work. But could you help with our trips to Boston?"
"Of course," he said.
They ate in silence for a few moments.
"Your mother loves you both, you know."
Catherine thought for a moment. "She seems ashamed of Patricia sometimes. And she's always been ashamed of me. I don't think shame and love can mix."
It was some time before he responded. "After I married your mother, I discovered that what she wanted most was to love, but she never knew how," he said while stuffing his sandwich wrapper in a bag. "She didn't know what she was searching for. A true disability, I think."
"Do you still love her?" Catherine said.
"She gave me you—and Patricia."
They finished eating in silence and then arranged return to France within the week.

Patricia returned to the States fifteen years later when Catherine, who had established a clothing design business in France that gained worldwide attention, moved to New York to expand her designs to the American market. Patricia went to Stanford the same year. She wore knee-length dresses or pants when she wanted, her choice based on what was appropriate for the occasion. Harold died of a heart attack, and Catherine and Patricia returned home to visit Agnes on Thanksgiving and Christmas holidays. Pleasant times for all, except for Agnes's silences smoldering with unstated resentment about how life and her family had treated her unfairly—silences punctuated by biting remarks about how Catherine and Patricia's choice of apparel failed to meet her approval.

The Amish Girl

Illustration by Dilleen Marsh

The Amish Girl

Peter Pisano failed computer science and Russian literature at the state university, credits he needed to graduate, so he took courses at Hunchett College in Ohio in the summer of '06. He lived on campus but often took his meals in the only restaurant—the Whispering Maiden—in the small town of Raspier, which had two cross streets and no traffic lights and was juxtaposed with the campus entrance like the cap on an acorn. On many days, especially on weekends, the Amish set up a table or two on the grassy central island on the main street to display food and furniture they made for sale. Usually a buggy or a wagon was parked nearby, the horse tethered to a parking meter or a tree. One evening, Peter saw a lone girl sitting next to a table with baked goods. His meal had been more tasteless than usual, and he had eaten little. He wanted dessert.

The girl wore a gray, ankle-length wool dress and a white bonnet that covered her head, and that tied under her chin so that only wispy dark strands of hair showed above her brow. She looked down and away as he approached.

He studied the table. A hefty assortment: apple, cherry, and mincemeat pies; muffins; shoofly and whoopie pies; and cookies with raisins and oatmeal. On a small wooden display shelf were loaves of wheat bread, and tall, round chocolate cakes frosted in white.

"Do you sell a piece of the pie?" he asked. "Say, maybe the apple?"

She had still not looked at him and did not respond.

"Look," he said. "I live in the dorms and I have no place to keep a pie, so I can't buy the whole thing."

She looked at him briefly, her warm, intelligent eyes clear and bright as if carved from diamonds. Then she looked away.

He took that as a no. He went back to examining the baked goods for smaller items.

"This whoopie pie. It's small. What's the price?"

She stood gracefully, the folds of her dress straightening and covering her ankle boots with brass lace-holes and hard, steel-reinforced toes.

Her hand reached out, her fingers long, the nails short but trimmed with care. The perfection of the pale skin on the back of her hand was marred by a recent abrasion scab. She pointed to a slip of notebook paper with "whoopie pies, 29¢," on it.

More than reasonable. He picked up a small sample of whoopie pie, one of many that had been cut into half-inch irregular squares to entice customers. The chocolate taste was bitter and the crème inside, between the two exterior cake layers, was a lumpy, bland paste. He made a face in spite of himself. He decided to find a candy bar at the general store that was only a few hundred feet up the street.

"Another day," he said, walking away. The girl ran up to him, touching his arm and leading him back toward the table. He saw her eyes up close now. A deep, enigmatic ocean blue without the coldness he imagined in these people. With a stainless steel bread knife she cut a triangular piece of apple pie, placed it on a paper towel, and handed it to him, stepping back.

"How much do I owe you?" he asked.

She waved her hand dismissively as she shook her head no.

"I'd be happy to pay," he said.

She shook her head again.

"Thank you," he said. With his feet together, heels touching, he gave a little bow.

She smiled.

"Goodbye," he said.

She did not answer.

He ate the pie with his fingers as he strolled back to his room, down the wide, tree-lined gravel path that bisected the campus. His spirits lifted and he found he was uncharacteristically smiling at people he passed on the way.

In the morning on Saturday he tried to study in his room. The morning sun blazed well above the horizon. Lacy high clouds moved lazily across an azure sky. He decided to drive to Columbus, catch a movie, and hang out at a bar where he knew he could get served and meet people from the University—maybe a girl, although most of the women available in Columbus were bar girls who didn't excite him much anymore. He'd lately been eyeing college girls he might take home to his parents. He drove with the top down in his two-seat, deep-red, imported sports car.

The road snaked over hills and through fields and copses. For four miles he saw no traffic. He came over a small hill and braked, gearing down with loud swell-whines of the engine as he closed in on a farm wagon with two large wheels in the back and two smaller wheels in front. A man wearing a brimmed straw hat and coveralls, with a boy dressed the same next to him, loosely held the reins attached to a team of horses. In the back, with the tailgate down, two girls sat with their legs dangling. He pulled out to pass but visibility was blocked by another hill. With irritation, he tucked back in behind the wagon, staying in second gear and riding the clutch to meet its pace.

The older girl was the one who gave him the piece of pie. He eased the car a little closer. Her dress today, although still plain and frumpy, suggested a trim, feminine body. He could see glimpses of her ankles as she flexed and extended them in time to the wagon's movements. He imagined her in a short skirt, a dark blue maybe, showing her legs. Her blouse would be plain, glinting with the luster of opal buttons, and well tailored, the way he liked women's clothing, with a deep color, and open to show her neck and suggest the curve of her breasts.

The younger girl touched her arm and said something that made her laugh. Her head tilted slightly so that her lush hair obscured the lower part of her face. He pulled out to see if the way was clear. The man waved to him to pass. He downshifted to gain speed quickly. She waved before he lost sight of her.

No college girls were at the bar, but he met a high school grad who was working temporarily as a waitress until she could find a career in singing. She was watching a soap on the TV above the bar. She was fake blond, plump, and easy to giggle, an outgoing girl but with an air of desperation in her banter that wiped out the usual attraction he would have had for her. When she wanted to go to her place, he refused, saying he had to study. He felt bad; she looked ready to cry, but he could not imagine any enjoyment at being with her. He went to a movie before heading back to campus to sit in his room and stare blankly at his assignments.

On Monday he failed the midterm exam, missing the cutoff by two points. One question! He argued with his professor, who finally agreed to allow a make up. If he passed the make up, he could finish. If not, he was out. The repeat test would be Thursday afternoon in two weeks at five o'clock.

The next weekend he devoted to study at the library. The air was hot and stuffy, filled with musky smells of sandwich remnants and the lingering perspiration of students doomed to failure. From a third-floor window he saw the distinctive shape of an Amish buggy on the street in town. He tried, but it was impossible to read, and he decided to take a break.

She sat alone on a three-legged stool. She watched him approach, gazing not at his face, but at his chest, as if she'd discovered a shirt button that needed tidying up.

"Hello," he said.

She looked away.

"Do you speak?"

She turned on the stool so her back was partially toward him. He sidestepped so he was in front of her.

"Why not say something?" he said, looking down on her.

She turned back to her original position, her back almost completely to him. He did not move.

"This is ridiculous," he said. "You could say hello."

With her elbows on her knees, she put her head in her hands. "Please," she said. "Go away." Her voice trembled.

He laughed. "I knew you could talk." He sidestepped to be in front of her again.

"You selling much?"

She shook her head no.

"You must have sold something."

She shook her head no again, more emphatically.

"You look intelligent enough to speak," he said.

Her eyes turned hard with anger. "I'm not stupid," she said.

"Did I say stupid? I said you looked intelligent."

"I am not allowed to talk to strange boys."

"I'm not strange. What if I was married? Could you talk to me then?"

"That would be permitted."

"I'm married," he laughed. "And I have nine kids."

He expected she would smile, but she looked away, flustered and angry at his condescension.

"Was that your sister on the wagon?"

She did not move.

"You don't look like sisters."

"She is my cousin." She still did not look at him.

"You take care of her?"

"She does not need to be taken care of. She is a competent young lady."

She still would not meet his gaze. He sat down on the grass in front of her, his legs out, leaning back on his hands.

"Do you like sitting out here? No customers. No one to talk to."

She turned her head to stare at him.

"It is not for me to like or dislike. It is what I do."

"Do you go to school?"

She turned her head away again. "I am not to talk about myself."

"You ashamed?" he challenged.

Her head snapped back to look at him. "I am not proud."

He looked off into the distance as he spoke.

"I'm stuck in this know-nothing town with a roommate who won't talk to me, students gone for the summer, teachers who think I'm too distracted or dumb to pass. And I have to pass to graduate or my father will kill me. He's rich but never went to college. I'd be the only college graduate in my father's family for three generations. That's what he tells me."

She leaned slightly toward him, studying his face intently. "Did your mother go to school?" she asked.

He nodded. "She works in a pharmacy. She's pretty smart."

She looked away again.

"You people don't go to college, do you?" he asked.

"Of course."

"Women too?"

"Some."

"Do you want to go to college?"

She still looked away.

"You do, don't you?"

She was silent.

"I'll bet you read all the time."

She said nothing.

"You don't watch TV, do you? I heard that. You don't have electricity."

"We do have electricity."

"Do you have lights in your house?"

"We have power tools. My father has a milking machine."

She was sitting stiff and proper now, her hands on her knees that were together. Her chin was up, her head tilted back. He uncrossed his legs and looked away from her.

"Seems dull to me. Like you're missing a lot."

"That's not true," she said.

"How would you know? You never tried to live out in the world, have you?"

She looked down, staring straight at him now. "I don't like talking to you."

She stood and he watched her go to the wagon for boxes. She carefully wrapped each of the baked goods one by one, and packed them. When a box was full, she placed it in the wagon and returned to pack more.

He stood up before she was finished.

"How much is that pie?" he asked, pointing to an unwrapped pie.

"The mince?" she said. She picked up the pie. "One dollar and forty-two cents."

"I'll take it."

She covered it and placed it in a plastic bag. He handed her two dollars from his wallet.

She frowned. She handed back one dollar. "I don't have the change."

He held out the dollar to return it to her.

"It's worth two dollars," he said.

She shook her head.

"Take it," he insisted.

"It would not be right."

He shrugged and put the dollar back in his wallet.

"Nice talking to you," he said, and backed away.

Walking toward the dorm with his pie in its bag swinging at his side, he could still see the remarkable blue of her eyes, like gazing into a clear mountain stream that reflected a cloudless morning sky.

The next day he awoke before dawn and sat down to study. After two hours, he had read fewer than five pages. He looked through his pockets for change but found none. He shuffled through papers and books on his roommate's small table that served as a desk. He found scattered coins and carefully, with his finger, slid a quarter, a dime, a nickel, and two pennies off the edge of the desk into his open hand. He walked to town.

She looked exactly the same as before. Probably the same clothes, he imagined, washed and dried overnight as she slept alone, maybe on a pallet on the floor, or, at most, a cot for one in a room with her siblings and maybe her cousin.

There were three women today. He walked up to them.

"Hi," he said. The girl turned away.

"May I help you?" an older Amish woman said, walking toward him.

"I owe that girl money."

"I can take it."

"No. I came to pay my debt."

The woman hesitated and decided not to interfere. "Hannah!" she said.

The girl turned.

He reached into his left pocket and held out the five coins to her.

"I don't want that," she said.

"No," he said. "I owe you. Take it."

She hesitated and then held out her hand.

"Thanks," he said. Her hand touched his in the transfer of coins.

She shifted her weight awkwardly from her left leg to her right. She looked down at the dust at his feet.

"Did you like the pie?" she asked softly, still looking down.

He wasn't even sure where the pie was. Somewhere in the room, still in its bag, untouched. He hadn't even thought about it.

"Did you make it?"

She nodded.

He smiled. "It was great," he said.

But she turned abruptly to stare intensely at him—and coldly. She trusted only honesty, he saw that plainly.

"Could we talk?" he whispered so only she could hear.

She walked to the display table and said something to the woman who had first greeted him. The woman picked up a whoopie pie with a piece of waxed paper and approached him.

"Here," she said.

"I didn't buy a pie," he protested.

"No, it's yours."

He was about to say no again, but over the woman's shoulder he saw the girl staring at him impassively. It was her doing.

"Thank you, ma'am," he said, taking the pie, stepping aside, and then nodding to the girl.

He carried the whoopie pie palm up and walked back to campus. He took a bite. Heavenly. The pie was gone when he reached the dorm. He tried to study in his room but he wasn't in the mood and went to the gym to hang out.

Every day at his mealtime walk to and from the Whispering Maiden he looked to see if the Amish were there. Four times he saw someone, but never Hannah. No one in town knew the Amish well or where Hannah might live. Twice he drove the roads that wound through the local Amish countryside. Although he retraced the routes over and over, he saw no sign of Hannah, or very many women—only men with straw hats working the fields or tending cattle.

On a Wednesday he received a note from Mrs. Mangrove, who owned the Whispering Maiden. The envelope was sealed and had only "Peter" written in pencil on the front.

"Where did this come from?" he asked Mrs. Mangrove.

"Amish girl comes all secretive like and asks if I know you. She describes you, tall, dark hair, college student. I said of course I know you. Peter, I say. You eat here five or six times a week. Then she writes your name on the envelope and says soft, like a dove cooing, would I give this to you and you only. So here it is."

He put it in his pocket.

"Ain't you going to open it?" Mrs. Mangrove asked.

"It can wait," he said casually, going to his usual table in the corner where he could see the TV screen over the bar at the front of the room.

He waited until he was in his room. The note said she would be in Ambiance. The booth would be set up there on Saturday. Her father would leave in the morning about seven-thirty.

He slept poorly that night and the next day, Saturday, just after dawn, he drove to Ambiance to see Hannah. She was waiting, expecting, and smiled with pleasure at seeing him. She took his hand. He tried to hold her but she backed away. "Not here," she said. "I can't."

And with the impact of a meteor, his heart was aching as he had never known before.

"When can I see you? When can we talk? I want to talk," he said.

"It is so hard."

She sat down on the stool, glancing around for anyone near. But it was early. She patted a chair for him to sit. She wiped her eyes with her dress sleeve.

"I am to be married in the fall," she said.

His heart sank. Married! "So soon?" he blurted out.

"My dress is being made. Only a few know. It will be announced soon." She looked away. "He is a nice man. We will have a nice family together."

"But do you—love him?"

She turned her head back to him, glaring. "Don't ask that."

He searched for words. "But that's what marriage is about."

"What do you know about a woman's love?" she asked, irritated. "The scripture teaches us love is selfless, love is giving. Love is an open heart and mind."

He paused. "Love is how you feel," he finally said.

"Oh, how selfish that is." She looked down and held her face in her hands.

"I know how I feel," he said.

She cried again, her body trembling.

He saw a woman in Amish dress approaching from the north, walking down the path. "Someone's coming."

"Jumping Jehovah," she said, "It's mother." She wiped her face. "Go. Before she sees you."

"When will I see you?"

"Go," she said. "Hurry."

Two days passed. He didn't see her in town and waited for some sign. Finally, he received another note. She would be at a crafts fair in Cranton. Alone. Early in the morning. She prays he can come.

The tent with furniture displayed had its side flaps down and the front flap opened only partway. Her face showed her joy at seeing him. She had arranged two stools in the back. She reached out and took both his hands. He felt the warmth of her palms. They sat facing each other.

"I'm so glad you came," she said, withdrawing her hands. "I think about you."

He hesitated. He had never opened his heart to a woman. Never. He was afraid he would lose something, some essence of his strength, like Samson. Her stare spoke of her love for him, and he needed to speak. Finally he said, "You're very pretty." She held his hand. It was a touch of desire and caring, selfless, without guile. He wondered what it would be like to be with a girl like this—so unaware, so pure.

"I failed my test," he said. "I don't want to go home. My father will find out what's happened."

"Oh, no."

"There is no make up this time."

They sat silent for a minute. She looked at him. "Ely knows something is wrong in my heart."

He looked puzzled.

"He's my fiancé. I didn't say anything, of course. He said, 'You're avoiding me, Hannah. Have I done something to offend you?'"

They sat, silent; she did not look at him for more than a minute. "I'm going to take some time off before I have to go back home," he said. "I thought I'd go to the beach."

"Is it far?"

"Myrtle Beach. In South Carolina."

"It is good, Peter," she said. "To take time off. Do not feel guilt."

He hesitated, mulling over the other part of the idea. Finally, he said, "Would you come with me?"

She gasped and put her head in her hands. He could not tell what she was feeling. "I didn't mean anything—" he stammered.

She was crying.

"Really."

"Oh, no," she said, looking up. "Oh, no. You don't understand. I mean it is my prayer. Dear God. I feel so guilty thinking I must get away. To be me. In my heart I believe it is what God wants for me. But I cannot make Ely miserable. That's not God's will. And Mother is so against any of us doing anything away from home."

He was confused.

"It would be a sin," she said.

"It would be time off."

"What would we do? Where would we stay?"

"I'd get you a separate room. We'd be like friends on spring break. All the college kids do it."

"Mother wouldn't allow it."

"Couldn't you just leave her a note? Tell her you're all right and you'll be back soon."

"Father would be so angry."

"I could talk to him."

"Never. Never do that."

Her eyes moistened. She paused to contain her emotion. "You are never from my mind," she said softly. "I miss you when you are not in sight."

He was sure she spoke truth. He had never had any woman feel this way about him. It frightened him a little.

"I want to be with you," he said. "I can't just keep buying pies and seeing you at dawn."

She didn't respond for a moment, and again he was afraid he had offended her.

She reached out and took his hands again. "It would be so enjoyable. And it's not a sin. It's not, to go with friends to the beach."

He was pleased. He started to embrace her. She pushed him away. "No. Someone might come." She kissed him on the cheek.

They sat back down with an acceptable distance between them.

"Will you come?"

She sighed. "Oh, Peter. I'll try."

"When can we go?"

She didn't know. But she would find out and tell him.

The next day Mrs. Mangrove slipped him another note with a conspiratorial smile. "The Amish girl," she whispered unnecessarily. He opened the note as Mrs. Mangrove stared. Hannah would be ready at four in the morning on Friday. She gave a spot at a country crossroads where she could be concealed in bushes by an abandoned farm shed.

She was there when he arrived eight minutes early. She ran to the car and got in, carrying her belongings in a laundry sack. He ran the stop sign in his eagerness to get her away from her heritage. She was giddy, asking questions about Myrtle Beach, how long it would take. She didn't have anything to wear. She wanted to eat at a Burger King. She'd been to one before, she assured him. It was great.

"What did you tell your parents?" he asked.

"I wrote Mother a note. I told her I was going on a trip with a friend for a few days." She looked at him. "That was okay, wasn't it? I mean I didn't know how long we'd be gone or when you had to be back home."

"Fine," he said. "I can stay as long as you want. I don't want to go home yet."

She was silent for some time. "I'm so lucky. That you've come into my life."

He smiled at her. She'd taken off her hairnet and her hair cascaded, freshly washed, around the sides of her round face. Her full lips were a vibrant, deep red. Her eyes glittered with expectation.

"You're very pretty," he said.

She blushed, her cheeks and ears the shade of a ripe apple.

"I want to buy you some new clothes," he said.

"A dress?"

"If that's what you want. Two or three if you find what you like."

She glowed in the reflection of the early morning sun. He was fascinated by her.

Peter made it to I-40 and in a few hours found a shopping mall near Raleigh. She picked out frilly, little-girl dresses, nothing above the knee or open at the neck. But he smiled at her joy.

In twelve hours they were in Myrtle Beach. He found separate rooms on different levels at a motel on the beach. She ate a hamburger and a milkshake at Burger King. Then, in bare feet, they walked the beach. She let him hold her hand, so delicate, yet substantive and strong. After their stroll, he took her to her room and knelt with her by her bedside when she prayed for her family and for him. He wanted to kiss her, but he decided it was not the right time.

The next morning she was up long before he arrived at her door. She was sewing. She had rearranged the room, storing the lamps, the coffee maker, and the TV in the closet. At breakfast in the motel lobby, she told him of discovering how the shower worked, and how she usually bathed in a round copper tub with heated well water.

He bought her a bathing suit that she chose: loose fitting, one piece. When she modeled it for him, she felt comfortable only with a towel wrapped around her. But he still could detect small breasts, and a firm, cute butt. To him she was unique and beautiful. Now he held her hand and wanted to do so much more, to hold her in his arms, stroke her, sweep back the hair from her face and look into her eyes, but she seemed oblivious to the extent of his passion. She loved him, but she did not know his need to possess her, to culminate the expression of love he wanted to deliver to her.

The next day they went to movies, and the local formal gardens the following day. Then the amusement park. She was afraid of the roller coaster but did bumper cars—keeping her eyes shut—and gripped his arm with both hands. She liked the water rides. He won a teddy bear at a shooting gallery; it was only six inches tall, and she smiled and held it to her heart when he gave it to her. But at the end of each day she retreated alone into her room before dark to read her Bible. Once, after sunset, when he hesitated outside her closed door, he heard her quietly singing familiar hymns in a clear, pure voice. He wished she wanted to be together, and went to the beach to sit alone.

With her first—and also the last—time swimming, she was not comfortable in her bathing suit; "someone will see" she said, and she wore his blue sweatshirt with the long sleeves the entire time, in and out of the water. So they walked the beach the next few days fully clothed and sat in the sand side by side and talked.

She worried about Ely and what he was going through; she hoped her parents would forgive her; she loved her cousin, the one on the wagon, and she wondered if her cousin's feelings about her would change. He began to feel her sadness at being away, even though she gushed her gratitude for his bringing her many times a day. What captured his heart even more was her seeming inability to have an evil thought. She freely talked of her frustrations and dislikes, but she did not hate, or seek revenge, or feel jealousy. And when she told him earnestly about what she felt, the wind on the beach swirling her hair around her face, her eyes intently holding his, he wanted them never to part.

When he went to see her to start the fifth day she was crying. She missed her family. She wanted to go back.

Her distress pained him. "I'll pack," he said. "We can leave tomorrow before eight." They'd be home after dark but before midnight.

She nodded but did not say anything as he closed the door to her room.

As they traveled back to her home, he began to broach the future. Could he continue to see her? he asked. Of course, she said, but she could not say how.

When they were on I-77, he put the top up on the car at a rest stop so she could hear him speak while driving. For the next hundred miles he talked, she listened, her eyes moist, her breathing faster than normal. He told her she was the most beautiful human being he had ever known. That she was beautiful outside, but even more beautiful inside. That he was going back to learn his father's used car business, and he knew they were ready for each other at this moment in their lives. He wanted to be together. He wanted to spend his life with her. Together they could be more than they would ever be apart. He hoped she wanted the same. To be together.

He knew his sincerity, his inability to look at her more than a few times while he poured out his inner truths, had affected her. He was the man who could make her happy. She would learn no man could desire her with so much love. And surely she'd never seen such love among her family and friends. Ely probably had a genuine interest in her in a paternal way, but different—distracted, even. He knew his time with her had made her feel alive and special. His heart began to ache again with the need for her. He wished they were back at the beach, and they could lie on the bed full-length and she could lose herself in the touch of him.

She undid her seat belt so she could reach him over the gearshift console and she kissed him on the cheek close to his lips.

He looked for a place to pull off the interstate. He needed to feel her next to him.

She settled back down in the seat and fastened her seat belt again. "I have to get back. I've got to work things out," she said, undoubtedly sensing his want to stop, and fearing her loss of control for something she did not really understand.

"I'm afraid I'll never see you again!"

"You will," she said.

"I don't mean at the baked-goods stand."

"I have to plan. I have to talk to Mother. She's the only one who might convince Father. But I will work it out, Peter. I will."

He heard the determination of an adult in her voice for the first time. But his aching need for her was suddenly coated in a deep sadness.

"Can I talk to them?" he asked.

"Maybe later," she said. "I'll need to talk to them first. It will take time for them to understand."

"How much time?"

"I'm not sure."

Two hours later he let her out about a half-mile from her house. She did not want anyone to see him or the car. She wanted to tell them about her trip and her friend, and then tell them about her love.

He agreed because he felt her need for him was starting to move closer to his infinite need for her. And he loved her all the more; he knew she had changed for him. He knew, before he had come into her life, she would never have withheld the stark truth from her family. Now she was scheming to change them. Risking the honest comfort in her life.

He got out of the car and kissed her. She was crying.

"When can I see you?" he asked. "Tomorrow?"

"Come the day after tomorrow. Two o'clock. After midday meal. Father will be in the fields. I'll have my chores done. I want you to meet my mother first. She'll understand."

He spent most of the next day in the gym. Exercise lessened the pain of missing her. But in spite of complete exhaustion, he could not sleep well that night.

At two o'clock the next day, he stopped his car in front of the farm just to the side of the unpaved path that led from the road to the house. Near the barn, a man worked on a horse-drawn iron tilling machine. Cattle grazed in a pasture to the right, and on the left mature corn swayed in the brisk breeze. He waited, unsure what to do, hoping Hannah would see him, come to him. But there was no activity. He got out of the car, straightened his tie, and buttoned the second button on his dark-blue sports jacket.

He knocked on the solid wood door and waited. On the repeat knock the door opened. A man in coveralls stared at him without speaking.

"Is Hannah here?" Peter stammered.

The man glared for a few seconds.

"She told me to come," Peter offered.

The door slammed.

He knew she would be here. He hadn't misjudged her caring for him. He waited a few more seconds and knocked again.

The door opened quickly. Only a few inches. A small woman in a gray dress and a white bonnet looked up at him.

"I came to see Hannah," he said.

"That is not possible."

"She said to meet her."

"She is no longer living here."

Words failed him for a few seconds.

"I must see her."

"She is on her way to live with my husband's cousin."

"Where can I find her?"

"You can't. She is far away."

A new tall man with broad shoulders moved to stand behind the woman and looked down on Peter.

"Are you Ely?" Peter asked.

"It is of no consequence to you who I am."

"Go," the woman said. "You are not wanted." The door closed.

He went to the car and waited, sure that Hannah was close. The two windows at the front of the house had the blinds drawn. He watched, but no one looked out. By late afternoon two men walked toward the barn, looking over their shoulders at him for a few seconds, but without stopping.

He got out of the car, took off his coat and tie, and walked to the barn. They were feeding cattle lined up for milking. They did not acknowledge his presence.

"Where is Hannah?"

They continued working.

"You know where she is. I want to see her."

"She will not see you," the older man said.

"Let her tell me that. I want to know that is what she wants."

The older man dropped his pitchfork to come to him. The man was taller than Peter and when he stopped, they were almost face to face and only a few inches separated them; Peter stepped back.

"Hannah has sinned," the man said. "Against God and her family."

"She did not sin," Peter said loudly.

"God bless you, young man. For your caring. But she is gone."

"Tell me."

The younger man Peter was sure was Ely walked to stand beside the older man. "You will never find her," he said, his tone angry and bitter.

"Go," the older man said.

Over the next few months, Peter asked for news of Hannah in many Amish communities. People listened but either did not know or would not say. In the fall, one old woman, vending quilts near the Pennsylvania town of Cadmium, said, "You mean that Wisconsin girl?"

"Could it be Ohio?"

"You're right. It probably was Ohio, come to think of it. "That girl was sent to Belize. There was a heap of trouble."

Peter described Hannah. About five feet five. Unique close-set eyes the color of an early morning sky that turned deep-sea dark when frustrated. A quick, ready smile, a musical laugh. Auburn hair. A narrow waist and long, straight, shapely legs, thin like an adolescent girl younger than her seventeen years. And beautiful hands that would, when she got excited and the words tumbled out, spring and circle in the air like swallows in flight. "Is that the one?"

The woman shook her head. "Wouldn't know, really. Saw that little girl only once when she was a baby, and then only from afar."

Speaking of the Dead

Illustration by Betty Harper

Speaking of the Dead

After a six-hour drive north from Toronto, John Hampton arrived at the family home of his wife, Grace, and her daughter Candy, both dead six days. The house was dark. His sister-in-law, Ruth, greeted him in a nightgown and robe, and knee-length woolen socks. She led him toward an attic room. He hadn't seen her in more than four years.

"Henrietta's in the bedroom attached to yours. You'll have to share the loo. You know her, don't you? Candy's roommate?"

"I don't think so. I didn't see Candy often."

"Oh, you'd remember. Tall, slim girl. Round face. Crystal-blue eyes. Black hair cut in a pageboy. Unusual, so you can't forget."

"Is she nice?"

"You don't even have to talk to her if you don't want to. People call her Henri. I don't like her much. She's silent in a standoffish way. Definitely not shy. And I don't think she was happy about saying a few words in memory of Candy at the funeral when I asked her. I think she almost said no."

"An adventure in the attic," John said.

"She won't bother you."

"Especially if she doesn't talk."

"Roger will be coming to the vigil and the funeral," Ruth said. "I'm so sorry."

Roger was Grace's first husband, father to Candy, and a lawyer—general law—whom Grace had left during their first year of marriage, three months pregnant, for good schools and a life in the city.

Ruth went back to bed.

The attic air was frigid, fed through cracks under the eaves. Exhausted, John lay down on the single bed to await the slow coming of sleep, the corpses of Grace and Candy brought to Barrow and awaiting burial invading his thoughts. He felt the generations of dead that still occupied this austere, two-story, insulation-deficient frame farm house, as the living impatiently survived the bitter, long-winter cold to see the sun and its yearned-for relief in the spring.

At 2:24 AM, someone stood in the door that separated the two bedrooms. Henrietta! She wore a flannel nightgown with a hem that came to just above prominent knees. She stood motionless; her arms by her sides looking awkward, as if they were hastily attached as replacements.

"What are you doing?" he asked, throwing back the covers and sitting on the edge of the bed. "Are you all right?"

She began to walk slowly, her arms angled out purposelessly in front of her, her glazed eyes staring straight ahead. She was asleep. She turned toward the hall, quickly out of sight. He slipped on his untied shoes and followed her. Without holding onto anything, she started to descend the stairs that led to the garage: twenty narrow, steep steps to the first landing. He rushed to her, taking her elbow and gently leading her back to her room and bed. She did not wake, and he returned to bed. But two hours later a crash of glass and metal followed by a moan came from her room. She'd knocked over a lamp. John rushed to her, tried to help her, but she pushed him away.

"Where am I?" she asked with fear.

"In the attic at Ruth's. Candy's aunt. I'm John Hampton."

She understood and calmed a little. He guided her back to bed and pulled up a chair, determined to watch at least for a while until he was sure she was asleep again. But she remained awake, agitated at times.

"I'm worried," she said, "about the eulogy."

"You'll do fine."

"I'm not worried about performance. I speak well before others. It's what to say."

"What about Candy at school?"

"Students don't seem to know her as you would expect. And many didn't seem to care."

"There must be things about her past you could use."

"I didn't like her," she said. "There were times I stayed with a friend rather than go back to the room where she'd be."

"Think of adjectives."

"Self-centered, mean, lazy, directionless." She smiled with self-deprecation. "Selfish, and not too bright."

"We need to think about it a little more." He smiled.

"She used recreational drugs. I think to addiction. The papers didn't say, but I think that's what killed her."

"Grace died on the way to the hospital to see her before she died. A friend was driving."

"How can I find positives in that scenario?"

"Why do it, then?"

"I promised. Ruth really wanted testimonials the family could cherish. How could I turn her down? The family didn't feel competent to do it right. I didn't know it would be impossible."

"You didn't know her well enough. Ruth is the most understanding of the lot of them. Talk to her again."

"It's a matter of integrity, of my word."

"It's not a moral issue. You just can't find the right material."

"I'll think about it," Henri said.

He suggested they get some sleep.

Henrietta was waiting for breakfast in the living room with four family members when John descended from the attic the next morning. She stood when he introduced himself. She said nothing but nodded her head slightly, with servant-like civility so pronounced that he actually waited for any hint of a curtsy. She retreated to a sofa, picking up a magazine from a side table, never looking back. She seemed tired, and she gave no sign that she recalled her sleepwalking, or their conversation.

At the table, Henrietta sat next to Jason, Ruth's youngest son.

"Do you like your school?" she asked Jason.

"Not much."

"Where do you go?"

"Barrow High."

"You like it at Hursthaven?" John asked Henri.

"I don't," she said.

The sputtering of bacon grease crescendoed as Ruth added more rashers for new diners coming in from outside through the front door.

"I'm sorry about Candy," Henri said to Jason. "Were you close?"

"Naw," Jason said. He was large, about sixteen, and spoke slowly with a lisp.

"What will you miss most about her?" Henri asked. Jason continued eating. John doubted Jason even remembered the last time he saw Candy, who rarely came this far north, and when she did, she stayed with her father, Roger, and not the family.

"I'm giving a eulogy at the funeral. What do you think I should say?" Henri asked Jason.

John didn't wait to listen to the response. Henri was doing for Candy's eulogy what he needed to do for Grace. What in the name of God could he say that was good about a wife who had just spurned him? Ten days before her death, she had confessed to him a four-year affair with her boss at the university. She was moving out to live with her lover. John was shocked and angry and quickly despised her for her deceit, her dishonesty. His emotions frightened him in their magnitude, emotions that suppressed caring she was gone. He did not care in the least! He never spoke to her again, and moved to a hotel so he could dull the humiliation of her abandonment.

And Grace's family and friends might carry his words to their graves. The family did not approve of Grace's first divorce and her contact with family had been limited to letters to Ruth on the holidays.

When John tuned back into conversations at the table, he admired Henri's determined interviews with family members. Once, her blue eyes locked on his, glittering with a porcelain luster and incandescence in stark contrast to the statuesque immobility of her features, appropriate for the gravity of the moment. Her facial features had a unique incongruity that was magnetically attractive. And she was obviously smart.

"Was she your favorite cousin?" Henri asked a young man in coveralls. He shrugged.

Henri left the table to sit in the living room and read, legs crossed, her head bent in concentration.

"I'll go over the list for the vigil with you if you like," Ruth called to John as he stood after half-finishing servings of flapjacks buttered and flavored with maple syrup, and bacon and sausage.

"Thanks," he said with real gratitude. He would know few; he was married to Grace for twelve years but he met the family only twice, and had never visited here at the family home.

"There are pictures and memorabilia in the living room," Ruth said. "Upstairs in the guest bedroom, too. Take anything you fancy. She would have wanted you to have them."

After breakfast, hidden away in the sewing room where a horizontal rug loom dominated the center of the room, convenient to hide comfortably in an easy chair near the window, he reviewed, as chief librarian, two books for presentation at the Library Society meeting next week. But his mind skated without direction. He had to pretend grief, having not experienced it, and never let the family know that Grace and he were no longer soul mates, or even friends, when she died.

He went to bathe and dress for the visit to the funeral home where the vigil would be held, and to reluctantly pay the bill for Grace's interment. She had no entitlements as an adulterer in his mind. But he had no choice; Ruth and her siblings, with few financial resources, had convinced Roger of his commitment to Candy's burial, and after pointing out the mounting expenses for the vigil, presumed John's responsibility for Grace's burial. Their thoughts were just and he could not refuse.

On return from the funeral home, after dinner and before bed, John looked at pictures and mementos as Ruth had suggested. There were photos of Grace alone before marriage, and with Roger, her first husband, and Candy, their only child. And there were many photos of Grace with John, mostly on vacation to the Galapagos, Machu Picchu, the Outback, the Great Wall, the Lake District. On the mantel over the fireplace, photos of Grace's graduation, summa cum laude, and of her with her fellow psychology department faculty members at the university were displayed. Her lover was there, but he was not standing close to Grace. One five-by-seven showed Grace in a circle of children at Toronto Children's, where she methodically volunteered and donated. She was generous. But the memories irritated him, reminded him of her deception and his humiliation. He would never take mementos of Grace to haunt him, and he left them untouched for Ruth and the family.

The vigil was at the funeral home. Both caskets were displayed, exactly the same in color, so that it was impossible to know which was Grace's and which was Candy's unless you went up close and read the engraved brass plates on the ends. Grace's family and friends had, as tradition dictated, baked and cooked, peeled and chopped, sweetened and salted relentlessly to contain their grief.

The room was crowded, overheated, and loud, as family greeted friends and acquaintances, almost all of whom they had not seen for many winters. John saw Henrietta standing alone. She had on a plaid wool skirt with a thin black belt and a collared off-white blouse that buttoned down the front. She looked expensively au courant in a traditional way. John overheard her talking to Roger, Candy's father.

"Did you see her often?" Henrietta asked Roger.

"Once or twice a year. She came to visit. Always in summer," he said.

"Candy was so accomplished. What were you most proud of?"

Roger hesitated. He seemed lost for an answer. "I don't want to talk about it," he said.

Henrietta leaned toward him slightly. "I'm so sorry."

"You're not family."

"I didn't mean to pry."

"You're giving the eulogy tomorrow, aren't you?"

"Ruth asked me."

"I wasn't asked."

"Why?"

"This family doesn't like me. We've barely spoken for two decades," Roger said. "They took Grace's side. She left me when she was pregnant with Candy. Did you know that?"

Henri stayed silent.

"Without a thought of anyone but herself," he continued.

"Did you seek reconciliation?"

Roger's eyes were hard. "On my knees, for Christ's sake. And years later. I begged her not to marry him." He waved his hand toward John.

Henrietta expressed condolences and walked to join others. A few minutes later she approached John.

"How's it going?" John asked.

"It's going miserably. It's as if Candy touched no one's memory."

"What did Roger say? At least he seemed to have some caring for Candy."

"I didn't see it."

"You'll find something to work with."

"I'm having doubts."

John smiled and changed the subject. "Do you find vigils unsettling?" he asked.

"This is my first. It's more social than I expected."

"Lacking a certain gravitas of respect for those departed?"

She smiled. "I guess there is a caring. The industry of the preparation and consumption seems to block thinking about the reality of the day."

"Did you expect tears?"

"Maybe reflection in silence. A reverence in stance. A control of motion." She was mature to three times her age, as if she'd been too intellectually busy to have a childhood.

"You're religious, then?"

"In my own way," she said.

Ruth approached. "You two surviving under the eaves?" she asked.

"Is there anything I can do to help?" Henri asked.

Ruth replied that she could use some help with cleanup. "And again thank you both for saying a few words tomorrow," she said. "It must be hard, having been so close to Candy and Grace for so long. But it will mean so much to the family."

Henrietta's glance to John conveyed her growing lack of enthusiasm at being trapped by her impulsive acceptance to speak. "Is it time to start picking up empties?" she asked.

"You could start bringing in plates and glasses from the entrance hall. Put them in the kitchen."

Henri walked away.

A few minutes later John left to return to the farm to read in his secluded spot in the sewing room. He went to bed just before nine.

His room was especially dark this night, the light from the single dormer window almost extinguished by low-lying, dark, snow-impregnated clouds.

Chilling wind gusts swiped the side of the house, disturbing him with their crisply tactile, inhuman echoes.

Henri shook his shoulder to awaken him just before midnight. He sat up with his feet on the floor, pulling the covers over his lap. She'd pulled a chair up to within a few feet of him.

"You were sobbing and moaning," she said leaning slightly toward him, concern in her eyes. "Are you all right?"

He was unaware of what he dreamed while he slept. The cover of his pillow was wet, his throat tight when he tried to speak.

"Is it about your wife?"

"Definitely not!"

"Why do you say that? You loved her?"

"Married twelve years. Our marriage changed over that time."

Even in the dark shadows he could see concern in Henri's eyes, definitely not just curiosity.

He took deep breaths to relax his chest and his extremities. "In the early days, we traveled worldwide together. And we thought the same about a lot of things. We could talk late into the night—thinking together."

"It sounds idyllic."

"It wasn't perfect. She was busy with her teaching and lecturing, and we were often apart. And she worried about Candy, who lived a while with her former husband, then went to school in Ottawa, and almost never visited Grace."

"Candy rarely spoke of her mother while we were roommates," Henri said.

"It bothered Grace at first. Later, she didn't seem to care as much."

"Do you still love her?"

"Grace had an affair with her chair at the college for four years before she confessed. It hurt me."

"Were you able to forgive?"

"I don't know. It hasn't been long. But I think so, at times at least."

"But you didn't love her at the end?"

He closed his eyes. He was calmer now than when he awoke, although his soul ached with almost a burn to it. After a few minutes it eased. "No," he said.

"Was it the deception?" Henri asked.

John thought for a few seconds. "It was discovering she didn't love me—when I never doubted her love."

"Because she loved another didn't mean she didn't love you."

He hesitated. "No. It was gone. She didn't love me."

"Does that mean you can't grieve her death? The good times?"

"What's to grieve?"

"Will you be able to speak tomorrow?"

"Of course. I'll think of something. Mention her promotions. Her publications. Her charitable works."

"But you're angry."

"Anyone would be angry, their wife leaving them for another man."

A barn owl screeched behind the house, faintly.

"You loved her once."

"Yes. I did. But it faded, even before she left."

"It seems her need for change would never go away. Almost inevitable."

"I don't want anyone to know she wasn't living with me at the end. Her new lover was driving her to the hospital; they'd heard Candy was close to death. His blood alcohol was .15. Think about the folly. She'd be alive today if she'd been faithful, stayed to rediscover what we'd had."

"What will you say at the funeral? How can you avoid the circumstances? You don't love her the way you did when you married."

"Those early years were good," he said. He felt a rush of deep sadness never before experienced, a flood released after these eight days since the accident. He had an unbound urge to weep. He squeezed his eyes shut and set his jaw until his anguish eased enough so that he could speak.

"Is it always there or does it come in waves?" Henri asked.

He lay back down on the bed, turning his pillow wet side down. A minute passed and he seemed to regain control of his breathing.

"It just came on," he said, staring into the darkness that obscured the details of the ceiling.

"It's not easy to forgive," Henri said.

"I am the resurrection and the life," saith the Lord; "he that believeth in me, though he were dead, yet shall he live: and whosoever liveth and believeth in me shall never die." John 1:25–26

The one-room church had a single steeple and oak pews. The congregation shivered in coats and gloves, the cold unrelieved by the single electric heater in the back. At the front right, a minister spoke from a raised pulpit. Nine choir members sat in metal folding chairs to the left, an upright piano against the wall behind them. After the gathering, with the coffins placed end to end in front of the congregation and the greetings complete, Henri was introduced to speak. She ignored the podium, standing between the two coffins. With assuredness, she negotiated Candy's short, checkered life. She enhanced memories of the family she had so doggedly sought, which revealed the good in Candy's life that no one had ever seen before. Henri swerved away from Candy's lack of connection to others by naming the few people she'd had ties to, and making those tenuous ties seem to be remarkable accomplishments for

Candy. Throughout, her poignant gaze gave every mourner a sense of profundity in her words. She painted Candy's valiant struggle against life's fears that all humans face, the temptations, the needs. "Candy didn't evade life's inexplicable perils. She never shunned her responsibilities even when faced with injustice and impossible choices. Candy became a Joan of Arc for her own survival."

Her words were tasteful and truthful—though never addressing the negatives—and beautifully rendered. John wished he could have led a standing applause.

John followed. Henri's position between the coffins had been so effective that he likewise chose not to mount the pulpit and stood in front of the congregation, although with more distance from the caskets. He breathed slowly and deeply. He paced his beginning with silence, looking out over family and childhood friends of Grace, whom she had never really nurtured.

Anger surged as he thought of her treatment of him and others, anger that constricted his thinking to her betrayal. He lost control of his thoughts and feelings and fought to regain them. God, he couldn't let his aggrieved anger corrode his opportunity to make the family proud, give them the satisfaction of kindred respect. The effectiveness of his silent pause was waning. "We have gathered—" he began, and he searched for the forgiveness that had released his grief last night. And it was there. Grace was who she was and she could not help herself, always moving on and searching. She had loved him. And he forgave her.

He spoke from the depth of grief for the woman he had loved for years, not the woman who died eight days ago. He spoke of their intellectual compatibilities. He described discovering nature together, and how it would have never happened without Grace. He spoke about Grace's need to mold her thinking to address the hard metaphysical questions of life, how she searched for answers in science and social work. "'Why are we here? What is our purpose? How you answer forms the essence of who you are,' she'd say, always with kind advice and direction. And she would work hard for long hours rather than ask someone to do something for her."

Then, with intimate expression, John explained how humor surprised Grace, warming her to others. He could see every mind before him following his thoughts, see them appreciating the severity of the loss of Grace. Never did he let anger misdirect his thoughts from an ever-present pride of having Grace in their existence. He ended with his head down, exhausted from his effort, and absorbed the depth of the silence inside the church that told him of the emotions he had stirred.

He moved slowly to sit in the front row next to Henri. Out of view of others, she took his hand and squeezed it gently without looking at him. He felt a lasting peace and thanked God for strength to overcome his weaknesses.

After the service and goodbyes, John was standing at his car, packed and ready for the drive to Toronto. He saw Henri about to get into the passenger side of a white Honda across the parking lot. She stopped when she saw him and stood still looking at him, and he at her, for many seconds. His heart ached. She was going back to Ottawa with a friend of the family.

Her gaze mesmerized him. How lucky the man would be if Henri ever decided to marry.

She waved. She smiled. He lost sight of her as she got in the car. Faintly, he heard the door close.

The Honda carrying Henri turned onto the highway, disappearing in a couple of minutes into the spurned intensity of the persistent storm. John did not move. Snow layered his world, spotting the velvet collar of his Chesterfield. Cold penetrated his clothes as if spring might never arrive.

The Miracle of Madame Villard

Illustration by Peter Healy

The Miracle of Madame Villard

Paris, 1793

The hands of the faith healer probed the lump on Jean-Luc's mother's neck. Stone hard it was, and fixed like a burl on a log.

"She will need strained carrot and turnip broth fortified with smushed, dried eucalyptus root," the faith healer said to the father staring at her, rigid with concern.

The mother's eyes burned with owl-like intensity, brimming with much fear and little hope. The father's eyes were glazed and opaque, hiding the memories of his dear wife, Charlotte, mother of his two sons, core of the family, whose once-lovely hands were now callused from her work as a seamstress, her once-warm heart cold as winter with age.

The boy, Jean-Luc, was sixteen and man size. The faith healer had seen him grow clever, learning his father's ironmonger's trade quickly and creating strong, pleasing designs. How his eyes burned with love for his mother.

The faith healer stood and motioned to Jean-Luc and his father to step outside into the alley. The chilled night breeze swirled among the single-room dwellings as low clouds moved swiftly overhead to cover and uncover the bright half-moon in the black sky. To the east, the glow of fires from the riots near the Bastille outlined the rooftops of the city.

"She needs a miracle," the faith healer whispered. She had seen many sick with these throat lumps before. They were hard to feed and often choked to death. "The good Saint Marcouf. He is the saint of neck swellings," she said to the boy and his father.

"How do we pray?" the father asked.

"In the Cathedral near Dieppe," the faith healer said, unable to instruct in a man's contact with his Lord, "where the Saint cured a girl well after the time of Charlemagne. The bones of his hand lie in a glass case, on a velvet pillow the color of ruby. The faithful who have touched have been cured. I have heard it from two pilgrims. I have no doubt of the power of his healings."

"She cannot walk to the north coast," Jean-Luc said.

"There is a public coach still running once a week. It takes three days."

"We have no money for coach fare," Jean-Luc's father said. "No one buys my ironwork now with the revolution."

"Sell at the executions. The rich and poor attend. And vendors make a fortune."

"I can sell my candleholder lamps, Father," Jean-Luc said.

"And I will find work outside the shop," the father said. "I will ask my cousin for work."

Jean-Luc ran back inside and knelt next to his mother. "We will take you to the saint, Mother."

"Jules?" the mother asked.

"I'm Jean-Luc, Mama. Jules has been gone for a year. Remember?"

Jean-Luc's father went to find work the next morning. Jean-Luc fed his mother gruel with a spoon, then left for the Place de la Concorde, where an execution was scheduled. He carried one lamp and tied two to the sash of his tunic.

Already the crowds murmured with excitement. Vendor business was brisk. Workers placed benches for peripheral seating for the wealthy as spectators mingled near the guillotine to secure the best views.

Jean-Luc went near the northwest corner. An aristocratic girl his age paraded in a stately manner along the path, followed by two boys and a girl, all fashionably dressed. The girl's full-length, white silk dress floated around her and the points of pink slippers peeked out from under the hem with each step. How delicate she was. Her high cheekbones spoke of class and privilege. Her brown eyes brooded in the frame of her light, straw-colored hair. Her slender hands were as if fashioned from porcelain.

Jean-Luc approached with his candleholder lamp held out in front of him.

She was afraid. At first her heart stopped, but an instant later, it raced with fear and excitement. She stopped and held out an arm to stop her companions. This huge boy-peasant was capable of breaking her in half, but his confident, healthy smile erased her fear. His black hair danced with joyous curls. His warm, blue eyes seemed cut from a sun-soaked morning sky. Suddenly, she wanted to surrender. She stepped forward, away from her friends, so they would not see her confusion.

"What have we here?" She smiled tentatively at Jean-Luc, then glanced toward her friends before looking back at him. "You. The giant. What in the world are you holding?"

Jean-Luc stared into the chestnut brown of the girl's angelic eyes; he had almost forgotten his purpose and his arm had fallen limp to his side, his hand still holding the lamp. He held up the sample again.

"It is for tapers. Very useful. See how the flame is protected by the curve—"

"It's iron," she said. How his eyes sparkled like gems.

"But sturdy," said Jean-Luc.

"But not brass. And not hand-blown glass, either. Are you giving them away?"

"No. It is for sale. Reasonable, too. My mother is very sick."

"Let me touch it!"

He handed it to her. She took it both hands and held it up.

"Where would you use this?" the girl asked the friend to her right.

"In the stable," her friend giggled.

"Exactly," the girl said. She had angered as she realized the folly of her emotions. This boy had robbed her, against her will, of her required disdain for peasants. And he had flustered her thinking and tarnished the respect of her friends too. "And when do you light a taper among the wild beasts in a stable?" she asked.

"Never. Never a taper in a stable," the girl's friend replied. There was laughter among them all now.

"I made it for a lady's bedroom," Jean-Luc said. The girl's eyes—full of possession as she regained control of her superiority—were quick to engage Jean-Luc's.

"The flame holds steady when you walk from room to room," Jean-Luc said.

"An iron tool for a lady's bedroom," the girl said. "You will die even poorer than you are now."

She smiled to her entourage one by one, holding the lamp away from her as if it might soil her dress.

"It is very reasonable at two deniers," Jean-Luc said. "I'm sure you could find it useful. Give it to a friend."

"A friend! My God." She rolled both eyes to the heavens. "Francis. Give him a sous for the damn thing. He needs the charity."

Francis, so hopelessly in love with the girl even a slug couldn't fail to notice it, stepped up and put his fingers in his waistcoat pocket. He pull out a coin and held it so Jean-Luc could not reach it.

"Thank you, sir," Jean-Luc said. The girl, still carrying his lamp, had turned her back.

"You are a fool," Francis retorted. He pocketed the coin.

"My lamp. You owe me," Jean-Luc said.

"Nothing." Francis said. "It is worthless."

The girl threw the lamp under the wheels of a passing wagon, and she and Francis left with her friends. Jean-Luc retrieved his lamp. It was bent and needed much repair.

Jean-Luc circled the crowded Place without a sale. Late in the afternoon, he headed home past burning government buildings. Acrid smoke trickled into the air above the city and was quickly dissipated by the wind. Sporadic fights erupted throughout the district, and he took side streets to be safe from the violent bands of revolutionaries. The alley of his parents' house was already dark with early evening when he arrived.

The faith healer stood outside the door. Her arms were crossed, her gaze locked on him.

"Your father's been burned. They're bringing him home."

"What happened?"

"Revolutionaries went to the shop. Your father had just returned. They wanted weapons to kill. They found none. They set to burning and left him half-conscious inside."

"Will he be all right?"

"He will not last the night." She looked up the alley.

Two men carried his father on a plank, his arms and legs dangling. Jean-Luc ran to him and peered down into his face. "Father?" he whispered.

His father's eyes were closed, his face on the left side swollen purple and bleeding. His father said nothing.

The men left his father on his pallet in the house. The faith healer rubbed oils on parts of his charred skin and covered oozing flesh with scraps of gray cloth. Jean-Luc sat crossed-legged by his father's damaged body. His father opened his one good eye.

"Jean-Luc," he said. "Tomorrow. I found work with my distant cousin. The executioner at the Place de Grève. In the morning. You go. Remember. They call him Aiguisé."

"I will go, Father."

"Take care of your mother, son." He closed his eye. "She is a good woman."

Jean-Luc went to his mother, who sat on her stool in the corner facing the wall.

"Papa's dying," Jean-Luc said.

For many seconds she remained motionless and said nothing. "Something smells," she finally said. "Bring me a wet cloth."

Jean-Luc dipped a cloth in a pan of rainwater and brought it to his mother. She held it to her nose.

Jean-Luc sat by his father for the rest of the night. There was no motion when the soul left the body, and Jean-Luc did not know the moment his father died.

The next day, Jean-Luc arrived at the Place de Grève as he had promised. His father's cousin, the executioner called Aiguisé, wore black. He was bald, like many in the family. Aiguisé worked alone on a square platform passing a river whetstone over the guillotine blade that had been lowered three-quarters for the sharpening. He gave no sign that he recognized Jean-Luc.

"Get off!" Aiguisé said. "Stay in the crowd."

"I'm am Auguste Villard's son."

Aiguisé's head turned to stare. "You've grown! Where is your father?"

"He is dead from a fire."

"And you take his place?"

"My mother is very sick. She needs a miracle."

Aiguisé returned to his sharpening. "Your father should never have married a woman not from around here."

"She was very beautiful," Jean-Luc said.

"Mean, boy. Basque, she was. And mad-dog mean."

"She loves God."

"Stop your nonsense."

Aiguisé laid down his whetstone on the neck collar of the guillotine. He showed Jean-Luc the mop, the wooden pail with iron trim, the straw broom with the thick wooden handle, and the gunnysack: "Hold it wide open to catch the head. Then take it to the family, who must wait near the stairs," Aiguisé said.

Jean-Luc practiced holding the sack.

"Wider! And round, not like a slit."

The crowd had grown fifty gawkers deep in a few minutes. Aiguisé gave Jean-Luc the broom.

"My money?" Jean-Luc asked. With four executions planned in three days he would have enough for coach fare.

"When we finish," replied Aiguisé. "Half what was for your father. You are a child."

"I am family."

"Far removed," said Aiguisé. Near the guillotine Jean-Luc swept away leaves, twigs, acorns, ground dust, and the dirt that fell from Aiguisé's boots.

"Sweep the stairs," Aiguisé said, sharpening the blade again. His reputation for a clean cut brought rich purses from the accused.

Two men led a frail woman in a white linen dress. Countess Christine Roquefort. She walked in bitty steps, her ankles shackled, her dress hem dragging over the bloodstained platform planks. The men forced her to kneel in a corner opposite the guillotine. The crowd heckled. She stared defiantly.

A priest approached. From his hand she swatted a Bible that fell face down. The priest turned and left, and the crowd chanted for action. But Aiguisé was not ready, hammering a dowel into one of the triangular supports for more strength.

"Get her offering," Aiguisé said to Jean-Luc over the crowd noise. Jean-Luc propped the broom near the guillotine and walked across the platform to the woman. He went down on one knee. She stared at him with light-blue, wet eyes rimmed with red.

"Let me go," she said.

"God Bless. I take my father's place," he said.

"I married a man of title. Is that a crime?" she sobbed.

"It is God's will," Jean-Luc said echoing the litany of the cathedral.

"God's will is to save me." Her intense stare held fear and determination. "This is your destiny!"

"I am the sweeper," he said.

"You are more than that, boy. It is your judgment! Did you think of that?" The desperate woman glared to convince.

Jean-Luc shuddered with the chill she had given him. She pleaded again, but he could not respond. He rose, astonished at her words.

She reached into the slit in her dress over her bosom to pull out a velvet purse dyed indigo. It had a gold braided drawstring. She held it to her chest just below the neck.

"My God, boy. Help me," she said.

Jean-Luc did not move, speechless.

"Take the money for yourself. Let me go," she said.

Jean-Luc looked away as temptation gripped him. He had no doubt the purse held more money than he had ever seen, and more than enough to take his mother to the miracle.

"If you will not act," she said to Jean-Luc, her voice cracking with stress, "tell the murderer to be swift." She held out the purse.

Jean-Luc took the purse to Aiguisé.

"Barely enough," Aiguisé said. "She could afford more."

"She said to be swift."

"What is swift? They are fools. The blade always falls the same speed. I have no control. It is the sharpness that makes me special."

Aiguisé positioned Jean-Luc near the front of the guillotine, then anchored the woman in the neck collar, securing it with a metal bolt. "Why me?" the woman cried. "You devil!"

Aiguisé stood back to the side. He raised his arm, his other hand on the blade release. The crowd roared. The wind in the trees fragmented the sun's glare and the angled blade shimmered with an almost human excitement.

Aiguisé pulled. The plunge began. Jean-Luc gasped.

He grabbed the broom, stepped forward and shoved the handle between the plunging blade and the Countess's neck. The blade cracked the handle in two and rebounded, slightly slicing into the victim's neck only by an inch. She moaned. Her legs kicked back—her body thrashed. "Finish! Finish!" she yelled.

Aiguisé pummeled Jean-Luc's head twice with his axe handle and Jean-Luc fell to the planks. Aiguisé raised the guillotine blade high enough to clear the wound, and with one stroke of his axe completed the severing of the woman's head.

In the silence, the head lay on its right side. One eyelid twitched. Aiguisé clutched the hair and held up the Countess Roquefort for the crowd to see, shielding the ragged axe cut at the neck with his arm. The crowd cheered. As he struggled to put the head into the sack, the countess's nose hung up on the edge. "Merde," he said. Finally it slipped in.

Aiguisé moved quickly to Jean-Luc and delivered a powerful kick to his stomach. "I'll kill you," he said. He walked to the stairs to lower the sacked head to the family.

Jean-Luc bled from his nose and mouth and his stomach churned, but he crawled to the edge of the platform and fell over the edge before Aiguisé reached him. Hands from the crowd broke his fall and stood him up. "Run," a voice said. The crowd parted. Jean-Luc ran until he was home, Aiguisé's threats still ringing in his ears.

To escape Aiguisé, Jean-Luc left home within an hour and carried his mother on his back as he hurried on the road that led to Saint Marcouf's miracle. Hours later, when the moon set, he found hay bales in a field to keep them warm. The next morning he collected walnuts to eat, and then they were back on the north road again. The burning sun was unshielded by clouds, and soon Jean-Luc's tunic was damp. His mother rode with her arms around his neck, her legs held steady by his arms, her head nodding on the back of his shoulder as she dozed. He stopped often to let her rest.

By mid-afternoon they had crossed two rivers.

"I'm hungry," his mother said, her first words in many hours.

He made her comfortable by the side of the road and went over fields of sunflowers to find wild red raspberries tucked near the cracked and pitted stones of a segment of Roman wall. He filled his sash.

He returned to the road. His mother stood next to a short man who held the lead of a white goat harnessed to a two-wheeled cart. He spread the fingers of his free hand and combed through wild, curly gray hair to no effect. Jean-Luc ran to his mother and to give her the berries. But she ate goat cheese.

"Who are you?" Jean-Luc asked the man.

"Are you Jules?" the man, Emile, asked.

"I am Jean-Luc. And this is my mother, Madame Villard."

"Ah, this woman said Jules would pay for whatever I gave her."

"Jules is my brother. A revolutionary. He has been gone more than a year."

Jean-Luc looked to his mother, who gazed at him. She had a faint smile, and her eyes sparkled with conspiracy.

"We have no money," Jean-Luc said.

Emile poured milk he'd intended for Charlotte back into a pail.

"I must insist, my friend. This is my only income. It cannot be free."

Charlotte finished eating the cheese, and Jean-Luc moved to give her the berries.

"I do not lie, Mister. My father is dead. My mother is sick. See her neck lump? We are on our way to the cathedral near Dieppe for a saint miracle. Do you know the Saint Marcouf?"

Emile turned to Charlotte. "Eat no more," he said. But she had finished.

Jean-Luc looked into the man's cart. Lying in a box protected by a Persian carpet was a lute, the body pierced by two ragged-edged holes, the surface partially burned—strings missing, two pegs bent. In the midst of pots and pans and other containers lay a hurdy-gurdy with the crank twisted and useless.

"What do you do, boy?" Emile asked.

"I am an ironmonger. I learned from my father." He closed his eyes for a few seconds at the thought of his dead father.

"Do you make weapons for revolutionaries?"

"That is not God's will."

Charlotte ate berries. "Good," she said.

"You do not look like thieves," Emile said.

Jean-Luc pointed to the hurdy-gurdy. "If you are going our way, walk with us. At night, when we rest, I can fix the crank as compensation."

"You repair instruments?"

"That one is easy for me."

"Could you do the lute too? I must have a fine instrument to regain my career."

"I do not do woodwork. Only the iron."

"It is the finest of hurdy-gurdies. I saved it from my patron's drawing room before he was beheaded."

"It will be like new."

Emile thought for a moment. "I have no choice," he mumbled.

They walked. Jean-Luc still carried his mother on his back, Emile beside him reached barely to his shoulder height, dipping with each step from a leg injured by horse kick in his youth,. The goat and the cart followed behind.

"Put the woman in the cart. We'll make better time," Emile said after a few miles.

They put down the back gate of the cart. Jean-Luc's mother now faced where they had been; her legs hung down, she steadied herself gripping the sides, and she could lean back against Emile's collection of pots and pans.

The road entered a large forest where cool shadows refreshed the travelers. Emile broke out in song in a clear tenor voice. He used the rhythm of their steps as accompaniment. Birds in the forest broke their wary silence and sang full-throated.

"I am good, no?" Emile said.

"Sing more," Charlotte said.

That night Emile searched for a patch of pine needles in a copse of trees. He tied the goat near grass for grazing. He lit a fire and they ate cheese and drank wine from Emile's bottle. "Not too much," he said. "We'll need some for tomorrow."

Emile took his lute from the goat cart and sang. Charlotte rocked to the melodies. Jean-Luc repaired the hurdy-gurdy without tools and Emile saw immediate economic potential in the strong, sure hands of the boy. Emile needed money for costumes to establish himself as a court musician again.

The fire had died down to glowing ash when Jean-Luc stretched out near his mother. Sleep did not come, and he stared at the sky believing his father was waiting for them among the glittering stars.

The predawn chill brought shivers to Charlotte, and Jean-Luc carried her until after dawn to warm her. When the sun was well above the trees, Emile handed the goat lead to Jean-Luc and, without stopping, took a brass gong from his sack in the cart and picked up a dry stick. He showed Charlotte how to hit the gong. Then he picked up his lute and sang as he walked. Charlotte banged away with little sense of the rhythm.

"Great," said Emile. "Now we'll practice a little more."

And after many repeats, it did sound better.

Just before noon they came to a village. In the center near the well was the day market of three produce vendors and one hawker of firewood. Emile stopped his group, anchored the goat, and told Charlotte to stand up and hold her gong. He brought the hurdy-gurdy to the back of the goat cart and told Jean-Luc how to turn the handle and press two keys. Emile instructed him to play without letting up when he nodded, and to stop when he nodded again. He stepped from the cart, placed a tin cup at an arm's length from his feet, and clapped, holding his lute under his arm.

Five adults, three children, and two dogs turned to stare.

Emile nodded and the hurdy-gurdy droned. "Charlotte," he called.

Nothing.

"Hit the gong!"

Charlotte responded and gave some rhythm close to what they'd practiced.

Emile played the lute and sang. He swayed. His head bobbed. Then he nodded and stopped singing. The drone stopped.

Bang, bang, bang, went the gong.

"Charlotte."

Bang, bang, bang.

"Charlotte!"

Emile ran to her and took the stick from her hand. The audience stood stock still. He applauded as an example. No one responded. He picked up his cup and held it out. Every one of the crowd turned their backs, and the dogs sank back into the dust.

Emile came back to the cart.

"You've got to stop when I stop," he said to Charlotte.

"I thought she did well," said Jean-Luc.

"Well, she did fine. It was excellent. She just has to stop when I stop. We lose the effect if she doesn't."

"I'll stop," Charlotte said earnestly.

"Let's do it again," Jean-Luc said.

Emile put the cup down. Nodded and started. Same song. And they all stopped together. Emile bowed.

A girl of seven in a brown flax dress stepped over and dropped a single, thin, copper denier into the cup.

"Thank you little darling," Emile said.

When he returned to the cart, he looked warmly at Charlotte and Jean-Luc.

"That was better. We are professionals."

But his eyes said he knew their survival depended on Jean-Luc's repairs.

"We are many days from the saint," Jean-Luc said. His mother was smiling.

"Unhitch the goat," Emile said.

The next afternoon they came to a town near a crossroads with a square and a small church.

"This is ideal for a show," Emile said.

"We have no time for more shows," Jean-Luc said intently. "Already my mother is tiring earlier every day."

"We will need the money, boy. It will not take long."

Emile stood, with Charlotte and Jean-Luc behind, near a well. A crowd of seventeen people formed a semicircle two to three deep. A few listeners dropped coins in the cup. The group was more polished now. Charlotte obviously enjoyed herself, a distinct change from the beginning of her trip. She was also more attentive and lucid, and although the lump in her neck was bigger, she spoke more often, straining to be heard.

A slender girl stood at the crowd edge in an ankle-length brown dress of good quality, but streaked with stains and impregnated with dust. Her slippers were scuffed and worn, and the left one had a hole near the toe. Her long and curly blond hair partly hid her high cheekbones, deep-set blue eyes, and oval face. Her small but expressive mouth was set in a determined line, her thin lips chapped.

When the group stopped playing, she ran forward and scooped up the money cup. Emile reached for her. She dodged around him. "Get her," Emile yelled.

Jean-Luc laid down the hurdy-gurdy and ran. Within fifty yards, he grabbed her dress but she twisted away and ran faster. He tripped and fell. She held the cup with one hand, and with the other hand she picked up the coins and swallowed them one by one as she ran. The effort slowed her and Jean-Luc caught up. This time he tackled her around the waist and brought her to the ground; she kicked and pounded his chest with her hands. He grabbed her wrists and pinned her down, his face inches away from hers. He stared into her angry eyes. She spit at him but he did not let go of her arms.

Emile caught up.

"She swallowed our money," Jean-Luc said.

"Clever. But I have seen it many times in Paris."

"It is lost. We will have nothing to honor the saint."

"It does not vomit well." Emile thought for a few seconds. "But we will take her with us until it passes."

"I hate you," the girl said.

"You are a thief. You should be locked in prison and branded."

"Shall I let her up?" Jean-Luc asked.

"Careful. Hold her tight. We will tie her."

At the cart, Jean-Luc restrained her again as Emile tied her hands behind her back. With leather strips he strapped her arms to her chest, and then placed a spare goat collar with a rope around her neck.

"Lay her down. Sit on her legs," Emile said.

Emile reached into a sack for a bottle half filled with light, amber-colored oil. He steadied the girl's head with his knees, pinched her nose, and forced her mouth open with a stick.

"Pour it in," Emile said to Jean-Luc.

Jean-Luc, still straddling the girl, poured oil into her mouth. She wrenched her lips so the oil seeped out. On the next try, Emile covered her mouth with his hand and pinched her nostrils so she could not breathe. She swallowed.

"Damn. She wasted half of it." Emile said. "Do it again."

When all the oil was used, Jean-Luc lifted the girl to her feet.

"I hate you," she sputtered again.

As they prepared to travel, Charlotte walked to the girl and spoke kindly.

"What shall we call you?" she said.

The girl turned her head away.

They started moving. Emile led the goat. Jean-Luc led the girl on the leash; she kept the rope taut with resistance, even though it hurt her neck. Charlotte rode in the back of the cart, gazing left and right at the birds and trees. After more than an hour the girl slackened the rope between her and Jean-Luc.

"Is that pig your father?" she whispered.

Jean-Luc looked at her for a moment. "That is Emile."

"Is that your mother?" She looked to Charlotte.

"My father is dead," Jean-Luc said.

"How old are you?"

"I am older than you."

"You look young."

"I'm almost seventeen."

"I'm fifteen. Almost sixteen."

They walked for a while.

"Where is your family?" Jean-Luc asked.

"Dead. The carriage went over a cliff into the river. The revolutionaries."

Emile hummed to himself contentedly.

"He is your uncle?" the girl asked.

"I do not know him well," Jean-Luc said.

Emile laughed. "I am our leader."

Charlotte called from the back of the cart, her voice strained from the lump. "Tell us your name, child."

"Yes, ma'am. I'm called Sapphire."

"Sapphire is a gem," Charlotte said.

Sapphire shut her eyes for a moment. "My mama said that," she said. "That I was a gem."

Emile laughed, but not unkindly. "And now you are a thief."

"Only for food. I am hungry."

"That gives you no reason to eat our coins."

"Let the child be!" Charlotte said.

Jean-Luc looked briefly in surprise at his mother; how she had changed since Paris.

"You are too big for a boy," Sapphire whispered to Jean-Luc.

"And you talk too much," he replied.

The fire was embers. The food had been sparse this evening. Charlotte slept on a blanket on her side in fetal position. Emile lay on his back with his hands behind his head, his eyes closed but not asleep.

Jean-Luc slept soundly on his back near Sapphire, who faced away from him on her side. Her hands were tied behind her with the end line knotted around Jean-Luc's wrist. A second rope bound Sapphire's leg to Jean-Luc's ankle. Sapphire could not move without waking Jean-Luc.

It was well after midnight when Sapphire suddenly tried to sit up, falling back on her side. "I gotta go! I'm going to explode," she yelled.

Emile rose. Jean-Luc sat up. Charlotte moaned in her sleep.

Emile poked Charlotte. "Get up! Go with her!" He helped Jean-Luc untie Sapphire.

Charlotte led Sapphire among tree trunks away from view toward a stream.

They heard moans. From the dark Sapphire yelled. "I'm dirty."

"Finish, child. Get it all out," Charlotte said. "I'll wash your dress in the stream."

Jean-Luc and Emile took torches to the site. Charlotte tended Sapphire away from their view. Emile and Jean-Luc sorted out the coins and cleaned them in the stream water.

"I hate shit," Emile said.

The next morning at dawn, Emile, Jean-Luc, and Charlotte prepared for their journey to the saint. Sapphire stood apart in still-damp clothes, her hair tousled, exhausted from her ordeal and little sleep.

Jean-Luc looked sternly at her. "Do not follow. We must travel fast for my mother."

"I would never follow you," Sapphire said.

Charlotte smiled. "Go back to your kin."

"I have no kin."

"Find an orphanage," Emile said. "There are many near the sea."

"I do not want to be an orphan."

Emile laughed. "You cannot change what you are."

"She is not a thief," Jean-Luc said.

"That is not what I meant," Emile said. "Orphans are orphans."

"She is only a child," Charlotte said.

Emile led the goat cart forward. From the back, Charlotte watched as Sapphire stood still. After a quarter of a mile, Charlotte waved. Sapphire stood motionless. Charlotte waved again. This time Sapphire raised her hand head-high, and lowered it slowly. Sapphire had not moved when she vanished from Charlotte's sight.

On the road, Jean-Luc, Charlotte, and Emile passed recruits going toward Paris to join army regiments. They passed revolutionaries eager to attack aristocrats. They saw displaced families wandering with no place to receive them. Just before noon, Emile stopped a farmer's widow with her possessions in a horse-drawn wagon. He had seen tools—an anvil, sturdy tongs, bellows. He spoke to Jean-Luc. "See those tools? You can make repairs."

"We do not have time for repairs," Jean-Luc said.

"We are poor," Emile said. "An extra hour here and there. We will have money for your saint and my lute. We can start earlier in the morning to make up the time."

"You have given us no money," Jean-Luc said.

Emile paused. "I am the treasurer," he said.

Jean-Luc scoffed but saw the tools as useful. Emile bargained a good price. In the next village they sang and played; Jean-Luc spotted a wagon wheel in need of repair, then a broken bucket handle. Emile approached the owners and set prices.

Two days later, on market day in a midsize town, they set up before a lively crowd of twenty or more. Emile started a dance tune. Feet tapped. Hands clapped. The crowd grew as villagers came from all directions. As Emile grinned with their success, Sapphire emerged from a clump of trees at the edge of the square.

She skirted the crowd, staying far away from Jean-Luc, Charlotte, and Emile. She danced, her arms wide, her skirts rippling back and forth, the whites of her legs bright in the sun, her worn slippers stirring clouds of dust. Most of the crowd watched her, not the musicians, and began to sway to her rhythm. In one wild leap she stepped on her dress hem and ripped a fair hole, but she danced on.

The crowd cheered. She skipped and jumped, twirling in the now-tight space between the players and the crowd. Jean-Luc glanced at Emile. Emile's brow creased with concern. Sapphire kicked high. Charlotte banged away at her gong, fascinated by Sapphire, and let out a cry of delight. Emile gave Charlotte a stern look. Sapphire kicked again. Leapt. Kicked again. The crowd laughed with pleasure at her skill and enthusiasm.

Emile signaled the group to stop. Sapphire faced the crowd, feet together, and bowed. Then she ran among the spectators using her skirts held loose in her hands to form a pouch—as a collector. The crowd gave coins. "Bravo! Bravo!" Then she paused before a youth dressed as a country gentleman. He eyed her and dropped a shiny copper among her coins, more money than the musicians would earn in two or three performances. Sapphire held the shiny coin high so Jean-Luc, Charlotte, and especially Emile could see its color glinting in the sun.

"We can't allow that," Emile said.

Charlotte put down her gong and ran to Sapphire to hug her.

"It is our money," Emile said.

Jean-Luc turned to him. "That's true, but she did do the dance."

"We can't afford competition," Emile said.

Charlotte brought Sapphire back to the goat cart.

"I dance good?" Sapphire asked Jean-Luc.

Emile smiled. Jean-Luc put the hurdy-gurdy in the wagon.

"We are a singing group. We do not need dancing during our performance," Emile said.

Charlotte pointed to Sapphire's coins. "See how much money she collected?"

"On our talent," Emile said.

"She danced well," Jean-Luc said.

"Do you think she'd be a good addition to our troupe? Is that what you mean?" Emile countered with sarcasm.

Jean-Luc hesitated. "I did not mean that. Another traveler will slow us down."

Charlotte raised her hand. "A traveler will not slow us. Anyone can walk faster than a goat with a cart."

"But we cannot share what we earn, Mother," Jean-Luc said.

"That is very true," Emile said. "We have not made nearly enough money to buy even a secondhand lute."

Jean-Luc flushed with anger. "We need money for the saint."

"My point exactly." Emile touched his arm and said to Sapphire. "Give me the money, child."

Sapphire shook her head "no."

"I'll take it," Emile said.

Sapphire did not budge.

"It is hers," Charlotte said.

"It can't be all hers," Emile said. "We made the music."

"She pleased the crowd," Jean-Luc said.

Emile frowned and after a thoughtful silence he said, "All right! Keep it." He looked to Jean-Luc. "You think we ought to let her come along? Washed up, she might bring in more generous customers. The men will like her." He turned to Charlotte. "What do you think?"

"She won't eat much," Charlotte said.

"Then it's done," Emile said.

Sapphire did a little hop-step. Charlotte took her hand.

"We must reach the saint soon," Jean-Luc said, but no one was listening.

The next night the troupe made camp in a clearing of woods. A cooking fire burned with fresh logs. Emile mouthed the line of a new song and picked a melody on the few remaining strings of his lute. Charlotte and Jean-Luc rested. Sapphire, wrapped in a shawl, worked to repair the tear in her dress. She had tied the fabric into a crude knot to conceal the hole.

Charlotte stood, turning so she faced away from the others. She shamelessly pulled up her dress, exposing her loose-skinned, wrinkled buttocks. From her waist, she untied a string that held a small cloth sack. She let her skirts down and opened the sack, removing a piece of fine linen, folded over twice and four inches long. She knelt next to Sapphire and unfolded the linen. Five needles gleamed with reflections from the fire.

"They are beautiful," Sapphire said.

"Mama sewed for Marie Antoinette," Jean-Luc said.

Charlotte put on a modest face. "Not for her exactly!" she said proudly.

"Her court," Jean-Luc said.

"Lace on undergarments. And only for two."

"Still, you were famous."

"Pooh," Charlotte said. Still, she was pleased.

Charlotte tried to show Sapphire how to repair her dress, but her stiff fingers with swollen knuckles could not pick up a needle.

Emile turned to Charlotte. "I can help," he said. He went to the goat cart and returned with candle stubs in a pot that he placed on a few embers from the fire. The wax melted. He carried the pot to Charlotte, testing the wax temperature with his finger.

"Excellent for the rheumatism." he said. "Hold out your hand."

Emile guided Charlotte's hand, dipping her knuckles into the wax.

"Oouuuee," Charlotte said happily. She extended and flexed her fingers. She picked up a needle, and with improved facility stitched around the hole in Sapphire's dress to show her the technique.

Sapphire stared intently, and then took the needle and tried her skill.

The next morning, as Charlotte and Sapphire walked toward the men who were hitching the goat to the cart, Charlotte handed Sapphire the linen pouch that contained her needles. "You are very good at your sewing, Sapphire," she said.

"I will gladly carry these for you, Madame," she said, holding out the needles.

"No. They are yours to keep."

Sapphire looked away to hide her tears. She could not speak.

Late the next afternoon, they crested a hill. Jean-Luc pointed to the west. "The cathedral!" They hurried to the arched doors of the entrance, gazing at stone statues of the disciples. Inside, they took the stairs to the stone-lined crypt, descending into the dank and the cold one by one with Emile leading. Jean-Luc carried Charlotte in his arms. Her eyes were closed and she was breathing with difficulty. She had weakened over the last two days of travel.

The walls were scarred with scratches and marks of pilgrims' testimonials. A stack of broken crutches, bandages, splints, clothing, canes, and walking sticks rose almost to the ceiling.

A novice in a white frock on a three-legged stool guarded the low, arched door to the small room of the saint. Light flickered from candles on iron sconces around a case of glass and forged brass. In the case, bones of a human hand lay on a red velvet pillow trimmed with threads of gold. They stood before the youthful novice.

"Let us pass," said Jean-Luc. "We must touch the saint for a miracle."

"Two sous. Many give more," said the novice in a high, prepubescent voice.

"God does not sell miracles," said Sapphire.

The novice shrugged. "Many pray here. Where you can see the saint. It can be sufficient."

"But we are poor," Sapphire said.

"Find your miracle elsewhere," the novice said, shrugging with indifference.

"Give us our earnings, Emile," Sapphire said.

Emile hesitated.

"It is for Mother," she said emphatically. She counted their combined worth. "Nineteen denier."

"Any offering will please God," the novice said. "But bishop allows no exceptions." He sighed. "I will join you in your prayers."

"We must go in," Sapphire said. "She is dying."

The novice began the litany of a tired, brief prayer. Charlotte's raspy breathing filled the silent, tomb-stale air when he finished.

Emile reached into his coat. "I have the money for my lute."

Emile added coins to those Sapphire had in her hand.

Sapphire gave the exact amount to the novice. "May you rot in hell," she said.

"Bless," the novice replied.

Minutes later, in the cove of the Saint Marcouf, Jean-Luc held his mother up to the saint. The novice raised the case and held it to one side. Sapphire took Charlotte's hand.

"Be quick," the novice said.

Emile glared at him.

The hand of Charlotte touched a bone of the saint. Sapphire whispered a prayer. "Praise God," said Jean-Luc. The novice put the case back in place.

An hour later, Jean-Luc sat on a boulder, one of many that lined each side of the path to the cathedral, and held his mother. Emile and Sapphire stood before them. Charlotte opened her eyes and, with effort, reached out to take Sapphire's hand. "You are my child now," she said. When the soul passed from Charlotte, she shivered from foot to head as if the life was stripped from her like skin from a rabbit.

They buried Charlotte in a field within hours. Emile insisted on going to town to sell what he could for the trip back. "I'll meet you tomorrow at the shed where we spent the night," he said.

Sapphire and Jean-Luc found a place near a stream to rest for the night. In the morning, an early mist turned into a drizzle as they walked to where Charlotte was buried. Their steps were tired and listless. Jean-Luc and Sapphire prayed at the unmarked grave until noon.

"There was no miracle," Sapphire said.

"She was close to God," he said, "near the end." He smiled at her. "And she liked you."

Sapphire cried. "I have no one."

"Emile and I will take care of you. Mother would have wanted that."

"Is that what you want?" she asked.

He shrugged, his cheeks and ears tinged with blush.

Then they walked the two miles to the shed without speaking. The door was open.

"I do not smell the goat," Jean-Luc said.

"It is like Emile not to come. He must not be here," Sapphire said.

"He will come. He said so."

Sapphire walked into the shed. Jean-Luc had to bend almost half over to follow.

In the center of the dirt floor were the tools for metalwork, carefully stacked, and the gong Charlotte had played.

"He's been here," said Jean-Luc.

"Why has he left all this?" Sapphire said.

"I think it is for us."

"But why?" She paused. Someone was approaching.

A frail boy of six came through the door with a leather purse in his right hand.

"Who are you?" Jean-Luc asked.

The boy hesitated. "The man with the stick-out hair said I give you this or he make me disappear." The boy held out the purse.

Sapphire opened the purse. "More than fifty denier," she said. "From the treasury."

Jean-Luc began to pack the tools in a sack. He looked at the boy. "What did the man say?"

"He said tell you my father gone ..." The boy struggled to get it right. " ... my little sister born dead and my mother died too."

The boy shifted his weight nervously from one foot to the other.

Sapphire looked at Jean-Luc. "He's an orphan!"

The boy shook his head from side to side. "I don't want to be an orphan," he said.

Sapphire took the boy's hand. "He can be our family, can't he?" she said to Jean-Luc.

Jean-Luc laughed warmly.

The Stonecutter

Illustration by Peter Healy

The Stonecutter

I was fifteen, never yet in love, and yearning to leave home when a red two-seated convertible drove up to our gate. The driver's door opened, and a girl of twenty-two with a perfectly shaped, light-skinned body emerged in a see-through dress that showed almost everything. I imagined the rest.

My father, a tall, imposing figure of a black man with bulging muscles from carving statues and grave markers for the dearly departed, tried not to look. He felt strange around women, I assumed because my mother had left when I was two. He never talked about her or much of anything, and we lived alone on a twelve-acre plot of half-swamp property where I suffered his long silences, broken only by the sharp blows of a hammer driving a metal chisel into stone.

Well, this girl was a treat for both of us. She closed the door and looked to our been-here-forever, two-room shack raised two feet off the ground by concrete blocks, with only a screen door on the front and all the windows up to catch a breeze. My father worked on, but slipped a glance when he knew she wasn't looking.

She walked through the opening in the iron fence that stood on the front line of the property. That gate had never kept anything in or out. My great-grandfather had installed it in the time of Calvin Coolidge to let people know he had made some cash farming, and my father was too proud to recycle it. Neither the shack nor the fence impressed the girl.

"You lost?" I asked, walking up to her, smelling the freshness of soap and perfume seeping through the humid air.

"I'm looking for—" she turned as if she might go back to the car to find the name.

"Ephraim Picard. Graveyard Stones and Statues?" I said.

"Yes. But I expected—" she paused, looking at me with soft, deep-water eyes that made me want her so bad I thought I might explode.

"A sign that say the business here?" I said.

"A professional building. Displays of the work."

"Papa don't do things up 'head of time.'"

"I know that. I just expected examples."

"I show you something in the barn might satisfy you some," I said, and waved for her to follow. We headed for our barn, not very big and without doors on the front or back so birds flew through without landing. A rusted, out-of-gas forklift half-blocked the door, and I put out my hand for her, which she took, and helped her wobble in her spike-heeled shoes over the two prongs of the fork into the barn.

"Quite the gentleman," she laughed.

Inside on the dirt floor sat blocks of stone and marble randomly stacked, mostly by me. I led her to one corner that was in shadows, but with enough light to see the only sample I could think of showing her. I pulled a tarp off a marble sculpture of a woman's head propped up on two stacked wooden crates.

"Why has it got all those lines through it?" she asked.

"It got smashed," I said. Her hands lightly touched the surface, like a blind person trying to remember someone.

"What happened?"

"Nothing," I said quickly. But Papa had made it and destroyed it.

"Can I see the rest of it?"

I pointed to a rusted tub filled with marble chips, most smaller than an egg from being smashed with a hammer.

"Takes time—gluing it back together."

She stood back, walking from side to side to see the whole head.

"Does he always do Negroes?"

"Not always."

"Well, she must be beautiful in person," she said.

"She is," I said, but I didn't really know. I had only been two.

"You Ephraim?"

"I'm Willie."

"Well, I'd like to talk to Mr. Picard, then."

I led her out of the barn, helping her again over the forklift, but she said nothing about my manners this time.

We approached my father, carving a marble angel. She stared. It wasn't a typical graveyard cupid-looking angel made by Italians and chubby with fat as if it couldn't fly. That wasn't Father's way. This angel had a small body with huge, muscular wings stretched out on each side. It looked like a hawk in a dive, the smooth-topped head cranked back as if catching the full force of the wind, the legs bent back at the knees. My father didn't put clothes on his angels, and I wondered what this woman thought about male private parts hanging down.

"You needing something?" Father didn't stop working.

"My father—well, my stepfather—was killed in Statesville, Georgia. At a rally. Maybe you heard of him. Reverend Al Jackson?"

"That was your daddy?" I said.

My father and I had seen the Reverend once, in a church we rarely attended upriver about a mile. He was campaigning for senator or governor—I don't remember. People yelled and cheered. He had a fat stomach and bulgy eyes, and his solid-black capped-toe shoes were polished so they reflected the sun like the mirror surface of a still pond.

She spoke past me to my father. "His will said he wanted a graveyard statue done by you. He made special arrangements with a cemetery near New Orleans that takes Negroes."

"Takes time," my father said.

"He got special permission from the committee because of who he was, and he wanted it to be bigger than real. Will you do it?"

It wasn't his busiest time, and I thought he'd be eager. But then again, he wasn't a man to jump at anything fast. I, of course, wanted to see this girl as much as I could. With time, I knew I could get her to like me. I was full-grown for fifteen and packed with muscle from lifting those blocks for my father.

She waited for an answer. My father had an infuriating habit of not talking when the silences between him and others clearly demanded some words.

"He do it," I said.

"Will you?" she said to my father.

"Bigger than life takes time," he said again, in his deep voice husky from not talking often enough.

"It's in the will I should oversee the progress."

"Why you?" I asked.

"A prerequisite for my inheritance." She added, "Every day that I come, you'll have to sign and date my book. For the judge."

"I do the writing," I said proudly, "He don't write." Father had worked cane; then he was cleanup boy for a white tomb maker near Lafayette for a while. He learned to carve by watching. I guess he never even thought about school; he'd worked steady and hard his entire life.

"When will you start?" she asked my father. "I need to know when to come back. To keep the terms of the will."

"Pick the stone tomorrow," Father finally said, still working.

"Not today?"

"You need to bring all his pictures," he said to her.

She sighed and walked back to her car. I ran to catch up with her.

"You miss him?" I asked. "Your stepdaddy?"

"I hated his guts," she said, with so much anger I stopped short. I couldn't think of questions to keep her hanging around, and she got in her car and drove off.

The next day I stayed home from school, eager to be with her, and she brought photos and newspaper cutouts of the Reverend for my father to work from. The sky was heavy with gray clouds and a thin gentle rain came down.

Father led her to the barn; I followed. He waved his hand at the blocks available. She went straight to a slab of marble veined with copper-colored lines the shade of her skin, but my father shook his head and pointed to a huge block of granite.

"I'm supposed to supervise," she said loudly. "I like this one."

"You ain't doing the carving," he said. "That marble ain't big enough."

She walked away fast to let him know she wasn't pleased. Father went back to the angel. She sat on a gravestone already finished and inscribed for a Baton Rouge preacher. I sat down beside her.

"Don't know how to call you, seeing as I'll be the one to do the signing," I said.

"My name is Annatilda Jones. AnnaTee."

"AnnaTee," I said. "He'll make it real good."

"The marble's more elegant," she said sharply.

She didn't know the granite gave power. "You can see the man come out of the big block," I said. "It's cool."

She held her head in her hands. "I can't believe he made me do this," she said.

"The Reverend must have trusted you something hard," I said.

"He was cruel. Arrogant. Thought only of himself," she shot back. "That's why he made me do it."

"What happened to your real daddy?"

"He left my mother early. She was Reverend Al's third wife."

"Me too," I said.

"He's not your real daddy?"

I told her fast it was my mother who had left. And when she asked, I told her how I had never seen her or heard from her.

"You miss your mother?"

"Don't miss her," I said.

The rain came thicker and we moved under the overhang to the barn, away from where Father still worked.

"Why does he work outside?" she asked, her voice soft and friendly for the first time.

"For the light. We ain't got electric out here in the country." Of course, in the seventies, electricity was available everywhere in Louisiana. But my father didn't see a need for it.

"I hope all his statues of people don't come out looking as angry as that angel."

"Naw," I said, "Don't worry." My father was famous for his carving.

Even after a few weeks, AnnaTee didn't gain any interest as to what the Reverend was going to be in stone, but I was like a frog waiting on a fly watching my father finding the man with his hammer and chisel. It is still a mystery to me how he knew what to chip off and what to leave on.

One day, AnnaTee and I were talking. She was sitting on a rough stone block, leaning back with her hands behind her, her head slightly back. I had my back against the barn wall with my feet out.

"You got a boyfriend?" I asked.

When she stared at me, I couldn't tell what she was thinking and my heart dropped like a stone. I'd screwed up. Then she grinned.

"Why are you asking?"

"Just wondering."

"You wouldn't have a crush?" she said with a little laugh.

"I ain't got no crush," I said, but my heart pounded and ached at the same time. I went into the house and sat on the floor next to my bed. I picked notes on a rusty dobro my uncle had given me, but I couldn't make music. I refused to go out, even when I knew it was time for her to leave.

I waited every day before going to school to see if AnnaTee would show. I missed her some days when she came late, but not very many. The more time I spent with her, the more curious I became about why she hated the Reverend so much. At the time, I saw hating the Reverend the same as hating God. And I worried about what God's thoughts were about me. The more I spent time around AnnaTee, my shame about my father's ignorance and poverty seemed to keep growing.

"You go to college?" I asked.

"Morehouse."

"What you doing now?"

"Don't know what I'll do. But I was travel secretary for the big man."

"The Reverend?"

"He wasn't reverend. He was base. The whole world was blinded by his smooth tongue." Her anger surprised me again.

"He did good for the ordinary folk. I read it in the paper at school," I said. I had stayed after school to learn about the Reverend. I saw pictures of him with the president, the secretary of state. In one photo, he had his arm around Martin Luther King Jr.

"He was a crook. He spent the money for the poor."

"I can't believe it," I said. The Reverend was a great man! He had died for all of us. He didn't give a damn about bad people hating him, trying to hunt him down like wild boar.

"His bodyguards cost a quarter of a million dollars a year! He flew in a private jet that my mother can't sell for a half of what he paid."

"He must have been good to you sometimes."

"Of course he was good to me sometimes. Of course."

"Then I don't see why you hate him so much."

She glared at me. "You wouldn't know what it means to a woman. He put moves on me! Twice. Even with my mother in the same house thinking he was God's disciple!"

She was shaking, and I felt bad for causing it. I searched for a word to soothe her, but I was lost.

"Maybe he didn't mean it," I said.

"Of course he meant it!" She hung her head and closed her eyes, and I just watched her for many minutes. Then she looked at me, her forehead ridged with lines of determination.

"You don't know about your mother, do you?"

I shook my head.

"Come with me," she said. She was breathing hard and walked with long strides like she was on a freedom march. She led me straight to Father.

"What happened to the boy's mother?" she said. Father kept working. "I know you know. Tell him."

The sound of the hammer striking the metal quickened a little.

"She left you, didn't she? She left you."

"Shut your mouth," my father said, moving the chisel to a new sight, starting to strike again even faster.

"You destroyed all this boy had left. Her statue."

"Ain't your doing," he said, his voice seething.

"It's not much to give!" she said. "Ease this boy's longing with the truth."

My father dropped the chisel and raised his hand. I lunged at him, grabbing his arm. He shoved me to the ground. I moaned from a pain in my leg.

"Ha!" AnnaTee said, backing away. "Is that what you did? Is that why she left you?"

My father picked up the chisel and went back to working. He was trembling.

"Come," I said, grabbing AnnaTee's arm. I moved her toward her car.

"You'll lose him," she called to my father. "You could at least tell him it wasn't his fault!"

"Don't say no more," I whispered.

She broke away and ran back to my father. "You're evil," she yelled.

My father threw his tools to the ground within inches of her feet, his tight fists at chest high.

"Loosen up. Let the good times roll." AnnaTee laughed.

My father glared. "She loved another," he said.

"Oh! That's so sad. Boo hoo," she said.

"Maybe. Maybe not," he said. Slowly he opened his hands and lowered them to his sides. He headed toward the house.

She hissed. "I hate men," she said as I walked with her back to her car.

Soon after, AnnaTee stopped coming. She told us she had argued to the court that she would come on and off for three months and that was enough. The judge had agreed. It took Father another two months to finish the Reverend, and when the statue was washed and treated, my father said for me to call and tell AnnaTee when he'd have it installed.

I walked toward the state route, then turned up the levee road to go to Aaron's Shell and Grocery store, where there was a pay phone nailed to an outside pole. I dialed AnnaTee's number and knew her voice when she answered; I'd been cursed to remember it in my lonely times often enough.

"This is Willie."

"Who?"

"Stonecutter's son," I said speaking too loudly. "He's setting it up Tuesday. Doing the unveiling on Wednesday."

"I'll see if I can make it," she said.

Then I called my father's cousin Arno in Morgan City, who hauled trash in a truck big enough to lay the Reverend down for the trip to New Orleans, and who owned the unbroken pulleys and intact chains to get him upright again. I skipped school and rode in the truck the eighty miles to New Orleans between Father and Cousin Arno, and helped them bolt the Reverend—after dark—in his final resting place above the tomb, which was no easy task since he was more than eight feet high and weighed more than half a ton.

I stayed the night with Cousin Arno's sister-in-law, who lived in the Treme, and I got to walk the streets of the French Quarter.

The next day, Father, Cousin Arno, and I went to the cemetery about an hour past sunrise. AnnaTee was there waiting! After a few moments, her mother came, and then friends of the Reverend, and even two crews from TV stations in New Orleans.

The Reverend was covered by six sewn-together bedsheets that were held tight at the base by a rope. A minister of God climbed up on the tomb, with my father's help, to speak about the Reverend, and to God. I went to AnnaTee, who stood off from the crowd a little.

"Hi." It was not what I wanted to say. I wanted to tell her how much I'd missed her, how I wished daily she'd come to see the Reverend—and me. She stared at the fluttering sheets. A breeze gusted, and the sheets flapped.

"You want to see him?" I asked.

"I dread it," she said. I was inches from her, and I could sense how tense she was.

My father walked over to her.

"I brought my checkbook," she said.

"The Reverend Jackson pay me last year he visited. Told me about you."

"He paid you for his statue?" She sounded as if she thought my father was lying. It was all news to me.

"Enough for Willie's college."

"Bought his own monument!" she said mostly to herself, shaking her head.

The minister had finished his words to the crowd, and Cousin Arno cut the fasteners and the sheets fell. AnnaTee's face didn't change one bit. It was like her features were in stone.

From a distance, I looked up to the Reverend, standing straight as a tree, his arms crossed over his chest and resting on his stomach. He was in a suit and tie; his feet, in fancy tassel shoes, were set together, and were small like his hands. The pale stone made him ghostlike, and at first look he seemed angry, mostly in the way he stood. But as you studied the lines in his face and his granite eyes that looked down, the anger faded: he showed fear as plain as if he'd been alive and ready to speak. He'd been alone in the world.

AnnaTee felt something too. As if the Reverend himself was talking to her mind. She cried.

I'd had little experience with women, and I turned to Father, standing behind us. For the first time I could remember, my father's face softened and his mouth turned up a little, not much at all, but a lot for him, and like a bolt of lightning from a gray sky, I was proud of him. Proud of his work. Proud what he'd done for the Reverend, who was, as promised, bigger than life. And for AnnaTee, who had her inheritance. I smiled back.

"What you think?" I asked AnnaTee.

She didn't try to speak for a minute or so. "It's so big. I think that's what hit me."

"I think he was a great man," I said.

"It's not what I expected to feel," she said. Her face softened with a little less hate than before.

Then she hugged me, long enough for me to hug her back. "You're sweet, Willie," she said. "You'll do just great in college."

Being sweet wasn't at all what I wanted to hear, but I formed an immediate plan. I would stay with my father on the property until I finished school. I would grow up and be educated. AnnaTee would learn to love me.

But the truth still hurts, even after these many years. Papa died when I was in college, and the letters I wrote to AnnaTee came back unopened. I never saw her again.

Homunculus

Illustration by Peter Healy

Homunculus

Didi sits on a three-legged stool on the stage in a sideshow tent. It's the third show of the night. She listens to the barker, Captain Withers, as he gathers a new crowd outside. "Didi, the Dynamic Dwarf! The doll of the midway!"

Onstage, Didi is hidden behind the wooden facade of a miniature house with a hinged door, two fake windows, and an angled roofline bent on each side of the peak. The tent air is hot and stuffy, and sweat trickles from her armpit down her side. She wonders if it is due to nerves or the weather.

"This tiny morsel—born of ancient royal heritage—is the reincarnation of Cleopatra, an Egyptian goddess. The smallest woman in the world. Thirty-two inches low. You will see every detail of God's amazing work right here, tonight, gentlemen, and for two nights only."

Didi's real name—Gloria Pinkham—is rarely used, a smudged memory from the real world. After eight years with the circus, she barely remembers the shape of her mama's house on a side street in Lewiston, Maine. She carries a scratched daguerreotype of her mother sitting in a chair; her father, stiff as a cigar-store Indian, stands by her side with a hat in his hand. The war killed him when Didi was four; he faded away in some Georgia prison. He left her no memories.

Captain Withers yells until he fills the first four rows of the twelve benches with customers. Didi doesn't care how many; she gets food, shelter, and a few dollars every month if there are two, ten, or twenty. These farmers and farmers' boys are like fish in a pond—different sizes and hard to tell apart. They've never been more than twenty miles from their mothers or wives, and they clump together like curdled cream to gawk at something from away. She sees in their gaze how they undress her, their curious glares often speckled with desire. She loves to be wanted and she wants to be loved. But she hates pity; when she sees it in a sucker's eyes she looks away and pretends it's not there.

Captain Withers signals those inside when he yells, "You're lucky, my friends, the show is just starting," and blows his whistle. Didi opens the hinged door in the house facade and steps out onto a stage that dances with the shadows of four flickering torches. Wisps of smoke cloud the air. Growls, shrieks, and cries pulse from the midway and dampen the scattered applause. The eighteen-by-twelve-foot stage with collapsible support beams rises three feet above the ground. The front is slightly lower than the back, and there is barely enough room for the miniature dogcart in front of the dollhouse facade. To make Didi look smaller, the cart has oversize wheels and a single seat on a small frame. Didi mounts the single step, and sits on the seat and waves. She wants them to enjoy her. She watches the faces of the men and boys with the same intensity as they watch her. Men mystify her. Didi wants a husband to pamper, children to correct, a house to come home to even if it is just during the winter when the circus doesn't travel. She dreams of Lazlo the Hungarian trapeze artist.

Rudy, the Daring Dwarf, handles Terry the Terrier, who is harnessed in front of the cart. With a leash, Rudy leads the dog through a tight figure-eight journey around the stage. Then Didi steps down. Rudy picks up a half-size banjo from behind the house facade and strums. Didi sings a song, "Wandering in the Garden of My Mother's Withered Roses." When Rudy signals with his hand, Terry wags his tail. Didi unhooks her gown and it falls away; Rudy dashes to collect it. Terry barks. Didi wears a see-through costume, over white undergarments, that resembles a nightgown and glitters with sequined trim. Her breasts swell in the golden silk of the fabric. Didi pulls up the hem, shows her baby-like ankle, part of her stubby leg. She climbs back into her dogcart carriage, holding her nightgown so that much of her backside is exposed. Seated, she crosses her legs so her dress rides up her thighs and Rudy comes over and kisses her on the cheek. Off they go. Off the stage. Behind the facade. The act takes less than five minutes.

As Rudy and Didi leave the stage, Billy Batton, the full-size sideshow buffoon, walks up and down the rows of spectators whispering, "You want to see Didi's thing? Her woman stuff? Over there." Billy collects additional money and points to the tent flap where gentlemen go, one at a time, into a booth the size of a one-hole outhouse. In the dark, a two-inch diameter hole glows weakly from candlelight on the other side. It's on the back wall, about four feet above the ground, and easy to find.

With one eye pressed to the hole, a customer sees Didi's feminine parts. They are perched on a table covered with purple-red velvet drapes mounded to suggest that Didi is lying on her back with her knees raised and her legs spread apart. The edge of the drape can't quite cover a little piece of gold cloth with sequins—the same cut of cloth as Didi's gown. Between the two leg mounds is a slit the size of the spine of a small hymnal that reveals moist flesh poorly illuminated by two candles in glass hurricane shades on a side table. These are really the private parts of a freshly killed lamb.

In the dressing tent, Didi is folding up her white dress to place it in the trunk with her golden gown when Captain Withers grabs her by the arm. "Tell Rudy one more show."

"We ain't finished?"

"You talk too much for a runt."

Didi wishes Captain Withers would drop dead. She hates his voice. She hates his yellow teeth and his breath that stinks like the floor of a chicken coop. And she hates what he makes up about her. About her savage beginnings. About how all the dwarves crave her. And she's thirty-four inches, not thirty-two. One time in Indiana, when Didi tried to run away to marry a barber's son, Captain Withers whipped her.

Rudy stamps his feet when she tells him about the show. It's something a full-grown man wouldn't do, and she feels embarrassed for Rudy—and for herself. "It's not fair," he says.

"Of course it's not fair. It's not fair being some shrunk-up freak either."

After the last show, Rudy helps Didi fold her costumes. He walks her back to the wagon where six of the thirteen circus dwarves sleep. Rudy touches Didi's bare arm and tries to hold her hand, but she takes it away.

"Let's get out," he says. "You and me."

Didi laughs. He is a funny little man, always dreaming the impossible. His only skills are making Terry the Terrier do its tricks and making people smile with his curious thoughts. And he wants to hold her in the night, he says, forever, and keep her warm when the drafts sneak through the boards of the wagon.

Rudy stops her near the utility wagon. He grabs her shoulders and turns her small body toward him. His wide face is round with teeth that are too big and lips too small to hide them. His eyes are wide apart and give him a dull-witted look, although Didi knows he is very smart. He writes letters for her, and reads the ones that come from her mother.

"I'm going. With or without you."

"Poof," says Didi.

"I mean it."

"Where would you go?"

"I'll figure it out."

"And you'll starve. You'll be eaten by wolves."

"You'll see," says Rudy. Didi hears a resolve in his voice. Would he really leave without her? She has assumed that he will always be there for her, always leading her wagon. But she says nothing, and they turn to climb the small, closely spaced steps into the wagon where four dwarves play cards and a fifth is playing "Oh! Susanna" on a harmonica, a sweet and lively tune that makes Didi happy and sad at the same time. "It rained all day the day I left, the weather it was dry / Susanna, don't you cry."

That night Captain Withers dies. He does not drop dead exactly, but he is found on his cot in his wagon, twisted at the waist, his legs in a grotesque pose of writhing. Most of the circus people think it was some sort of fit. He lost all control of his bowels and bladder and snot hangs out his nose. With her low vantage point, Didi gets a direct peek at dead Captain Withers's open eyes. He looks afraid. She whimpers to impress the other circus people who are near, but she wants to laugh and clap at the same time.

"He did the best he could," says Rudy.

"You're crazy," says Didi. A crew from the animal wagons takes Captain Withers out near the river and buries him and his soiled nightclothes in a damp, shallow grave. Some sideshow people watch. Didi doesn't go, but Rudy tells her about it, and she worries that the hasty grave is too shallow to bury the mean spirit of Captain Withers. She dreads his image in nightmares, and fears wicked spirit visitations from his black soul. She asks Rudy about the grave.

"Graves don't matter. I'll take care of you," he says. But Didi wants Lazlo the trapeze artist, not Rudy. And she doesn't want the ghost of Captain Withers to haunt her.

The next morning the new barker, Colonel Phister, who is part owner, starts to make changes. "To not go broke," he says, "not to belly up." He does not like Didi's act. "Never have," he says. He wants an act that will make the farmers and their boys come back the same night to see it, as he puts it, "again." Pay more money. At first Didi is excited; she dreams of a better position on the midway, with new costumes. But Colonel Phister wants to double-bill her. "We'll make more money with the giant," he says.

"Gargantuan does his own act," Didi complains.

"He's a dud. There ain't no surprise. No one pays to see a giant in a tent when you can't miss seeing him outside on the midway. We got to do something original."

Colonel Phister thinks Gargu the Giant should be the one to unloose Didi's dress. Fumble a little. Build some tension.

"What about the dog?" Rudy asks.

"No dog. Just play that goddamn banjo. And change that stupid song. Get one of them nigger tunes."

Gargu the Giant is slow to think. "Why you want to change the act?" he asks, looking down on Didi, Rudy, and Colonel Phister. Didi thinks that if she's got to share billing, she'd rather it be in the big tent with Lazlo.

"I could work with Lazlo and the trapeze family."

"That's stupid. Ain't no runts in the big tent."

"We work with the clowns," Rudy replies.

"That's different," says Colonel Phister.

"Can't we wait for winter quarters?" says Didi. "Take some time to work things out?"

But Colonel Phister sees economic potential. "Now," he responds. They change the act on the road. Didi has new billing: "GARGU the GIANT and DIDI the DYNAMIC DWARF with Rudy the Daring Dwarf playing BANJO."

They decide to have Didi enter on the dogcart after all, and do away with the dollhouse facade, which needs painting anyway. When Gargu the Giant tries to pick up Didi, he grips her waist so hard she cries out. She refuses to let him touch her. So they get an eight-rung little ladder that they prop against Gargu's chest. Rudy holds the base of the ladder steady. Didi climbs up, and when she is almost to the top, Gargu kisses her and puts her on his shoulder. Rudy takes the ladder away. It is from there, holding onto Gargu's hair on the back of his head for support, that Didi sings her new song, "Oh, Susanna."

"The sun so hot I froze to death / Susanna, don't you cry."

Colonel Phister wants Didi to show her body. He gives her a shorter see-through gown and has Gargu hold her up and look up under her dress. "Make 'em want to pay to see," Colonel Phister says. To dismount from Gargu's shoulder, Colonel Phister thinks Didi needs to have a whiz-bang ending. "Jump."

"I'll kill myself," Didi protests.

"We'll borrow a trampoline from the Wondrous Polenskys."

"You can't make her jump. It's too dangerous. She's the star," says Rudy to Colonel Phister.

"She ain't no star. She's a runt on the midway."

Because the Polensky trampolines are too big for the stage, Colonel Phister has the carpenter build a circular wooden frame with a diameter the size of two barrelheads and stretch a canvas over the top. Didi jumps to fall on her back and spring up so she lands on her feet on the stage. She can't get the timing right, and she bounces crooked and lands in a heap.

"That's great," laughs Colonel Phister. But it hurts to fall wrong and Didi practices every day to get it right. She jumps off the water wagon onto the new special dwarf trampoline to practice landing on soft grass. Then she climbs back up an iron ladder bolted to the side of the wagon and jumps again. And again. Until she can land standing up almost every time.

Rudy is a pest. He finds flowers in the fields or next to the rivers, and brings them to Didi to celebrate the new act. In the mess tent, he offers part of his apple pan dowdy to Didi. He says he loves her. She smiles at his passion, but thinks he is short and ugly. She is ashamed of him; he is a joke of a man no one could love. And she resents his advances because he could never be Lazlo the Hungarian trapeze artist.

Lazlo wears white tights trimmed with sequins. Although he is barely five feet tall, he has wide shoulders and strong arms that hang down, each bent like a tightly strung bow. On each arm, a bicep bulges big as a potato. His black hair is cut short, and his small ears are low on his skull. His eyes are dark and close together. He is clean-shaven except for a thin mustache, and he has a big smile and good teeth that are only a little uneven in spacing. He flies through the air and the crowds hush so that Didi fears they might hear her heart racing. Every unmarried girl likes him. A lot of marrieds too. Many give themselves to him hoping he will marry them. Didi knows that Khatooma the Cat Woman and Rhonda, who is second billing for the Flying Rolands' horse riding act, both had to get their babies stopped. Lazlo's babies.

Didi is sure that Lazlo could love her if he knew her. Big people have loved little people. She's heard of long, happy lives together. And Lazlo isn't that big. He just needs to get to know her. And isn't she pretty? Doesn't she have long hair that flows to her waist? He could comb it for her. She could sew his costumes. They could have a house somewhere with china plates.

She has a plan. She hopes to talk to Lazlo alone, as if by accident. She will meet him after a show when he is going back to his family's wagon. She is smaller than a wagon wheel so that she can fit under many wagons without bending. She waits hidden in the shadow of the tent-pole wagon every evening for a time when Lazlo might walk by alone on his way from the main tent. For two nights, he is with someone. Then the third night he is alone, and she pops out and acts as if she is walking the other way.

"Hi, Lazlo. You did real good tonight."

"You think so?" Lazlo says. And he smiles. "You're mighty cute down there on the edge of center circle," he says. When she goes back to the wagon where the dwarves sleep, she smiles to herself and hums her new tune, "Oh, Susanna."

Each night, Didi goes back under the wagon to wait for accidental time with Lazlo. When Didi and Lazlo are alone, she tells him how accomplished he is, and she makes him laugh with stories about little Rudy and Rudy's silly ways.

In the tent where Madame Fortuna does her seances to talk with the dead, Didi climbs into the red velvet upholstered chair used for soul seekers. Madame Fortuna is Didi's big friend, and Didi talks to her often about Lazlo, about making a family.

"I love him," Didi says.

"Ah, vat eeze luf?" Schenectady-born Madame says in her European accent that Didi wishes she could learn. Didi practices alone, away from the others, dreaming she might have a real speaking part in the act someday. Lazlo has an accent.

"I want to be his wife."

Madame Fortuna takes off her turban and shakes out her thin hair. It is black, streaked with gray. Hidden in a wash of French perfume, Didi smells a mixture of sweat, mold, and dead shellfish.

Didi tells her about her meetings with Lazlo.

"You've got to make him want you," Madame Fortuna says.

Didi thinks for a moment. "He likes me. I know it."

"He's got to crave your body. Wake up in the night hot for your wares."

"You mean down there?" Didi nods to her private parts.

"Do you know a man can fit?"

"I've heard."

Madame Fortuna unties the sash that holds her robe. Her large breasts hang loose, ballooning her undershirt. "I mean did you make love to a big man? Did it work?"

Didi doesn't speak. She does not want to say she has never made love to any man. Big or small.

"Being with a man hurts me, Didi. And I ain't small by a long shot."

Didi squirms in her chair. She believes that when you love someone it can never hurt.

Madame clears her throat. "I'd forget it."

"I can do it," Didi blurts out.

"Look, honey, don't get mad. It just ain't possible."

"I'm a real girl. It ain't just lamb parts."

"Well, he's had every girl who would let him. He'd be glad to add you. With women, he's like Bill Cody shooting buffalo."

"I know he's not like that."

"He's an uncaring bastard, Didi. The worst kind of man."

"I could make him want me," Didi mumbles.

Madame Fortuna has not said what Didi wanted to hear. Now Didi thinks Madame is too old to know of these things about love, although she has been helpful before. Does she have a man? No. Besides, her tea leaves are tobacco, and she smells bad.

Didi is so angry with Madame Fortuna, she goes directly to Lazlo. She finds him practicing on a bar propped between wagons. Didi says she needs to talk to him.

"Of course." He smiles.

"Alone," says Didi.

Later that night, she meets him behind the laundry wagon. She is there early and he comes late. He slides down on the grass beside her and sits with his ankles crossed and his knees apart.

Didi tells him about the new act. She talks about Captain Withers dying before she says, "Do you think I'm pretty?"

"Exquisite," Lazlo says, and smiles down into her eyes.

"Could you love me, Lazlo?"

"I love you. Naturally." His accent seems thicker now.

"Really love me. Like a wife?"

"Ah. That is the question?"

"Of course it's the question, you oaf. It's what's important to me."

"You're a very pretty woman."

"But I'm too small." Didi pouts.

"No, you are very attractive. Desirable."

Didi takes his hand, feels the calluses on his palm, rough like cured leather and harder than amber. "Make love to me, Lazlo."

"Here?"

"No. We'll go over near the edge of the woods."

Lazlo squats to look into Didi's face. "You mean it?"

Didi nods. She looks up into his eyes. He still grins, but she is sure he is not making fun of her. He seems interested. Curious, maybe. She wonders—wasn't this what she wanted? She reaches out to put her finger on his lips. She feels the scratch of his waxed mustache.

"It is not possible?" Lazlo asks.

"Of course it is. I've known lots of small people who love big people."

"We must be quick."

"Of course."

"Be sure no one knows."

"Absolutely."

"I'll get a blanket," Lazlo says.

"Yes. Hurry," she says.

As Didi waits, Lazlo finds a washed blanket on a line strung between two wagons. It is dark among the wagons, and he touches the blanket's lower edge to see if it is dry. He yanks it off the line. Together they walk. Didi hurries to keep up. He reaches down and grabs her by her shoulders. Lifts her.

"Put me down."

Lazlo laughs. He walks a little faster. Didi twists out of his grip, sputtering, and when she is free she has to trot to keep up.

Lazlo finds a dark spot and throws the blanket onto a grassless patch of dirt under a tree. There is a late quarter-moon and a faint glow from the cooking fires of the circus. She sees the mussed blanket. From each corner she works to the center and smooths it as best she can.

Lazlo has taken off his pants. Didi looks away, embarrassed and afraid, and sees the low branch of a tree move. It could not be the wind.

"Lie down," she says.

"No. You." He still has on a tight shirt. He has kicked off his slippers.

She fears his weight. Her bones are easy to break. "I can't." When he bends slightly, she thinks it is to find his pants to leave, and she is surprised that she feels relief. But Lazlo moves his pants off the blanket and lies down on his back. His member looks different—still hard, but pointing to his chin and pulsating a little. Didi smiles because it looks silly.

She takes off her dress, but keeps her shoes on. She presses her palms together to keep from shaking. She pulls her undershirt over her head and stands next to Lazlo, who is looking at the stars with his hands locked behind his head. She straightens her back so her breasts jut out a little more, and she moves a few steps toward him.

Lazlo reaches up and touches her left breast, scratching her nipple with his rough skin. Didi senses his disappointment as he pulls away his hand. Did he expect more?

She reaches over to take his organ in her right hand. Her stubby fingers can't get around it so she uses both hands. It is warm, but not as hot as she expected. And she can feel the surge of Lazlo's heart pumping the blood into his organ. "Damn it. Be careful," he says.

"What happened?"

"It's tender sometimes," he says. "Ain't you had it before?"

Didi wonders why she feels dread instead of excitement. She tries to touch Lazlo carefully, standing next to him, barely needing to bend. She strokes his member with the tip of her finger.

"You jump on," he says.

"Do you love me?" Didi asks. But he doesn't answer.

She strokes him a few more times and he moans. He breathes hard. He tries to grab her breasts, but he can't get a hold of the little mounds. He grips her arm, draws her closer to him. His member is still between her palms, and it squirts like a cannon—three times, she thinks, but maybe four. She is so surprised she squeezes. He swats her hands away.

"I didn't—"

"Shit," says Lazlo.

She wipes her hands on her hip, then picks up her nightshirt and cleans off each finger of her left hand.

Didi tries to take his hand, but he jumps to his feet, puts on his pants, pulls the blanket from under her so fast she tumbles down, hurting her shoulder.

"Lazlo," she says softly, but he is too far away to hear. "Lazlo."

She stays on the ground, rolls onto her back in the same position Lazlo waited for her. She rubs the sore shoulder until the pain is dull. She looks to the sky and the stars. Follows the outlines of the Big Dipper and Orion's belt. Some stars twinkle in pairs, like eyes watching. In a few minutes, she is cold, and she rises to put on her clothes. Then she lies back down, still chilled, but not wanting to return to the cluster of wagons and tents. She watches the sky change, the moon covered by swirling clouds. She waits to go back until the sky is black and the fires among the wagons die to embers. From the woods, she walks slowly, her arms stretched out in front for protection, but she still trips on an unseen tree root. As she approaches the circus tents and wagons, the light is better, and she moves without stumbling. The sounds of the circus are muted, and she hears only the snorts of sleep and the restless pacing of animals in their cages. She opens the door and enters the dwarves' wagon. From the way they breathe, she knows they only pretend to be asleep. In the frail light coming through the open door, she sees the twisted blankets near the door where Rudy sleeps. He is not there. His satchel is gone. The nail where Terry the Terrier's leash hangs is empty. She feels the urgency in the way every dwarf is holding his or her breath, trying to be silent. She closes the door and gropes her way to her spot on the floor. When she lies on her pallet and closes her eyes, she hears a train whistle, a discharge of steam, and the stutter of steel wheels on iron rails, and she does not know if it is real or imagined.

She sits up. "Where is Rudy?"

"He's gone. We don't know," someone says.

"We can get someone to fill in for the act," whispers another.

"It's not the act," Didi cries, surprised at her anger. She lies back down, facing the bleak silence of harried dwarves, and the dark. Her shoulder throbs, and the pain seems to march into her chest, toward her heart.

The Necklace

Illustration by Peter Healy

The Necklace

On our first night in New Delhi, Helen and I ate dinner in our hotel with our new acquaintances, Betsy and Anwar, from Birmingham, Alabama, where Anwar practiced orthopedic surgery and she kept house.

"You two married?" Betsy asked Helen and me.

"We live together," Helen said. She didn't want to explain that we lived together most of the time in my cramped condominium facing Lake Ontario, but that she still had her house from her divorce, where she spent time during the week.

"Well, I declare," mooned Betsy. "An arrangement."

"A little more than that," Helen said, bristling.

With canny insight, Betsy had cut open the conflict between Helen and me—conflict we had not planned to share with strangers on an Asian tour.

Helen wanted commitment—meaning us married and settled in her seventeen-room, early-twentieth-century house in town with tennis court and three-car garage. She believed that if we changed the furniture and decorated with art we chose together, we could be happy newlyweds. But every time I stepped into her house, memories of her ex-husband rustled around me in the walls like trapped rodents. He was a sixty-four-year-old famous and successful neurosurgeon who was cavorting around Florida with his twenty-four-year-old office receptionist, who Helen and I thought too overweight and shaggy to be attractive to anyone but a lecherous older man still in a midlife crisis. I was convinced I could never replace her ex in his former home even though Helen insisted she had erased him from her life, which I thought was probably true. But I suspected she longed for the life they had created together, a life of almost constant in-home entertaining and guests' admiration for the uncramped comfort of her echo-filled interior, shelved walk-in closets, and eight-burner stove surrounded by acres of counter space. Although I never confronted her, I knew she wanted legitimacy for our relationship and to re-create her previous high-society life.

Despite our lack-of-a-forever-marriage commitment, Helen and I were intimate good buddies, and we leveled our friendship canoe pretty well by stroking carefully in unison on opposite sides. She was an eager traveler—we loved tours—and she rarely complained as she followed routes on maps with her clear-polished fingernail and tirelessly read guidebooks where she marked pages with dog-ears and pieces torn from in-flight airline magazines.

In Delhi, on the next night at dinner at the hotel, we learned that Betsy and Anwar had been married for sixteen years. Helen gave me a raised eyebrow. When we were alone in our room, she expressed her usual suspicions about how happy couples really were in their marriages. She pointed out blaring incongruities about Betsy and Anwar. Even on tour, Anwar was our best-dressed traveler and wore beige Italian silk suits, dark blue or maroon Egyptian cotton shirts, no-pattern ties of magenta or gold, and narrow hand-cut shoes with pointy European toes that looked painful. "That is one uptight dude," said Helen. In contrast, Betsy wore plain cotton dresses printed with flowers and insects, or swirl patterns in pastels, and serviceable cross-trainer running shoes. "A real homebody," she added. And both Helen and I had been puzzled by Betsy's one consistent ostentation: a necklace of seven diamonds graduated in size on each side of a central more-than-one-carat stone, all mounted in platinum.

"Zircons," I said to Helen, who was an expert from frequent expensive purchases from Tiffany jewelers in New York.

"The real McCoy," she said.

"Who'd wear a real necklace on a tour?" I asked.

"Only the socially insecure," she said.

"Why take the risk?"

"Beyond comprehension."

So the very next evening at dinner I asked Betsy about the necklace.

"Aren't you afraid you might lose it?"

"All the time," Betsy said. "I love it so much. Anwar gave it to me."

"I hope it's insured?" I said. Helen threw me her you're-out-of-line look.

"Of course, but it could never be replaced," said Betsy.

"Women shouldn't have possessions that are not used," Anwar said emphatically.

Helen frowned. She hated sexism and inflexible pronouncements. But despite her many ingrained opinions, she was socially adept and completely capable of hiding her real thoughts. She tilted her head slightly as if in agreement with Anwar. But after dinner, when we were alone at the bar, Helen turned irritable. "I'm sick of that goddamn necklace."

"You've got prettier ones," I said.

"It's just not appropriate," she said.

"Low-class?" I asked.

"Nouveau riche," she said. "Ridiculous."

That night, I fantasized out loud to Helen about Betsy shielding her necklace with her washcloth in the shower as she lathered up, clutching it with both hands while Anwar made love on top of her, refusing to remove the prized possession when she went for a mammogram. Helen said my imagination was out of control.

For three days we toured, shopped, and ate spicy food. On the fourth day in India we waited for our special tour to the Red Fort. Helen and I were drained of energy from jet lag and often sleepless from uncomfortable foreign beds. The group felt the exhaustion, too. Anwar's laugh, a measured breathy monotone, cut among the tour group as he busied himself reloading film into his camera. Betsy felt the group's irritation with Anwar's pithy apercus; she glared intently at guidebooks without reading or speaking, her lips pursed, refusing to look at Anwar. Finally the bus arrived that, an hour later, delivered us to the Red Fort.

The hot, humid air clutched our skins as we stepped down one by one from the bus interior and beggars swarmed around us, desperately reaching out.

"It's so sad," Helen said, looking at one emaciated woman with a toothless smile and vacuous eyes.

Most of our group stayed within a few feet of each other as we walked—except Betsy, her diamonds sparkling, lagging behind to give a few coins to a child, and Anwar, who stayed in front next to the guide, a place he preferred so he could ask questions.

"I'm not sure I'll ever love India," Helen whispered to me. "There's too great a difference between the haves and the have-nots." I squeezed her hand.

We trudged on behind the guide and Anwar until Betsy's yell stopped us all. A thin woman with sores out on her arms and leathery skin with a yellow hue clutched Betsy's knees. Betsy struggled, her arms flailing, but she went down, the woman on top of her. Betsy struggled to get up, pushing the woman away. A shoeless man knocked Betsy forward facedown to the ground. He yanked the necklace from her neck before she could get her hands free. The two thieves disappeared into the crowd that opened and closed to swallow them. I ran to Betsy. Others followed. She sat on the ground, whimpering.

"Are you all right?" someone asked. Betsy sobbed.

Helen found a tissue in her bag and dabbed at bleeding, dirt-encrusted scrapes on Betsy's arms and knees .

"Get the police," Anwar yelled at the guide. Within minutes uniformed officials wrote notes for reports. Our group fidgeted, openly afraid of the crowd, and demanded our return to the hotel.

Anwar stiffened. He thought he saw the thief. A grinning old man with something sparkling on his neck stood maybe fifty feet away from us.

Anwar bolted away from where Betsy still lay.

"That's not him," I yelled. "It's metallic."

Anwar ignored me. The old man's eyes widened as his mouth dropped open.

Once in full stride, Anwar was as quick as a leopard. "Thief," Anwar screamed, his face flushed. He closed the gap and threw the man to the ground, kicking him in the ribs with his pointed shoes. Once, twice. The man howled, pushed up on his knees, lunged to his feet and ran for his life, his malnourished and arthritic frame swaying to the right in a grotesque limp.

Anwar surged after him but the natives closed in a protective clump around the man, who disappeared.

"It probably wasn't my necklace," Betsy said, still in tears, when Anwar returned to the bus.

"Oh, shut up," Anwar said.

"I just meant—he didn't look the same."

"Betsy, it's the principle. A thief is a thief."

Anwar's teeth gleamed in a sudden smile as his eyes swept over each of our stares. His face softened. Helen shivered at his transparent goodwill. He hugged Betsy briefly. "That's my little pumpkin. Sorry, honey. It's all so unfair," he said. But I could see—and Helen was looking too—how he could not hide his anger-induced trembling.

All but a few refused the tour of the Red Fort, eager and thankful to get back to the comfort of the hotel. Helen and I felt hopelessness for Betsy and, with the window drapes tightly closed, tried to rest in our room. Later we retreated to the hotel shop to look at faux-ivory carvings and Hindu masks.

At dinner that night, only Anwar joined Helen and me at our table.

"Betsy's not feeling well," he said.

"I'm so sorry about Betsy's necklace," Helen said, looking to me for support. I looked appropriately sad, but it was damned hard to be sincere. Earlier, alone with our analyses, Helen and I agreed. Betsy had asked for trouble. We were not unsympathetic, but the necklace had been a stupid idea.

"These beggars are animals. Barely human," Anwar said. Helen tensed and was about to say something contrary but I touched her leg with my hand under the table.

After dinner Helen and I settled on the two-person sofa in our room. Helen shook her head. "I had a little trouble with the animal bit. These are desperate human beings."

Helen read out loud the details of our trip to the Taj Mahal. My eyelids were heavy and I fought to keep my head from nodding. A noise, like a scratching, was outside our room. Helen stopped. I jerked fully awake. Faint rapid raps came from our door, too timid for maids. I moved when Helen threw me a demanding glance. I opened the door cautiously. Betsy wore a white T-shirt and capri pants, her hair in disarray.

"Sit on the sofa," Helen said to Betsy. "I'm so sorry. That necklace was beautiful on you."

Tears rolled down Betsy's face again. "Oh, it's not the loss," Betsy sniffled. "I never really liked wearing it. It's that Anwar blames me!"

"You?"

"For not keeping up with the group. It wouldn't have happened if I had been careful."

"You weren't that far back," I said.

"He's crazy sometimes. He thinks I'm a silly woman too stupid to do anything right. You don't know how small I feel around him."

Helen shot me another of our private glances that Betsy could not see.

"You can find another necklace," I said. "Helen could help when we get back."

"We can never replace the necklace of his dead mother. That's why he insisted I wear it all the time. To remind him."

Helen gave me a so-there nod. Anwar's fault, she was saying. I gave her an exasperated glance.

"Can I sleep here tonight?" Betsy whispered. "You could close the bedroom door for privacy."

"Of course you're welcome," Helen said.

"You don't want to be in your own bed?" I asked.

"I'm afraid," Betsy said. "Anwar is a stubborn man. His feelings get buried inside."

"I don't understand," Helen said.

"He hit me. He didn't mean to. It just came out." Betsy said. "The first time ever."

"Are you hurt?"

"It wasn't hard." But even though the light was low, I thought I saw a faint purple of a beginning bruise near her temple.

Helen helped Betsy settle, then came to bed. "Call out if you need me," Helen said. Helen quietly closed the bedroom door and we whispered for an hour about Betsy and Anwar. "It's as if he possesses her," Helen said angrily. "Like marriage is bondage."

"She's really kind," I said. "And she's not stupid."

"Not at all. She's the real jewel. If he only knew," Helen said before her eyes closed and her head snuggled onto my shoulder. "He had the chance to do her right," she whispered, "but he failed."

"I don't understand."

"To forgive her. At least not blame her. There's not a drop of evil in her."

I agreed.

The next morning Betsy looked exhausted but was cheery to a fault. She did not mention Anwar or the necklace. She refused to take a shower in our bathroom, and went back to their room determined to greet the room-service maids who brought morning tea.

"It's as if Anwar loved that necklace more than her," Helen said after Betsy left.

This was our free day before the Taj Mahal excursion. I had decided we would visit the museum of historical artifacts.

"You go," Helen said. "I'm going to ask Betsy to go shopping. She'll need me."

"I'll ask Anwar if he wants to go to the museum," I said. Anwar had plans to join another doctor on a tour to visit a hospital to claim the trip as a tax deduction. But on reflection, he decided to go with me. "I can go to the hospital earlier," he said.

At the museum, Anwar and I learned more of Asian culture in the endless halls of glass-enclosed objects—decaying authentication of past generations' existence. But I missed Helen. I liked sharing thoughts with her.

When we were walking down a hall between display rooms, I said to Anwar, "If you have photos of the necklace, I'm sure Helen has the connections to replicate it exactly."

"Jesus, John. It's the sentimental value. It was passed down in my family for generations."

"Betsy is strung out about the loss."

"I told her, John. Over and over. Stay close to me. She didn't listen."

"It might not have made any difference. She was only a few feet away from us."

"It was her responsibility. She failed. I can't forgive that."

We split up when we reached the end of the hall, and I did not see him until we met at the exit to find transportation back to the hotel.

Helen and I did not sleep well, but the next day we joined the tour for the Taj Mahal with Betsy and Anwar and most of our group. The road to Agra stretched through fields with dung, garbage dumps with human scavengers, and polluted rivers too thick to flow. Human adults and children stood roadside and stared at the passing traffic, an entire population seemingly abandoned by humanity. Then we saw the Taj Mahal, an ostentatious jewel glimmering in the refuse-packed, ravaged landscape.

We toured the Taj with the group. Anwar assertively maintained a distance from Betsy, who stayed close to Helen. Helen and I separated from the group upon leaving the Taj to sit on benches and discover the symmetrical elegance of the architecture. Light from reflecting pools threw shadows on Helen's face, and my gaze stayed fixed on her beauty, marred only by her painful thoughts of the ubiquitous poor.

"We have so much," she said. "And we never value what we have. The gods are angry."

"You think the theft was divine vengeance?" I asked with more incredulity than I wanted.

"The money that necklace would bring could feed a family of ten for years. We have responsibilities to our fellow humans," she said.

That seemed a little too much, but I got her point. "Wearing a necklace isn't a sin," I said to relieve her guilt.

"When it's worth thousands," she said, "who knows what's a sin?" Helen's faith held a creator with more than a touch of retribution, and she held complex beliefs in cause and effect. I slid closer to her on the bench and touched her hand. She cared so much it became a burden at times, but how could I comfort her with careless council?

We returned with the group to the bus. Fifteen to twenty beggars surged toward us. "I don't think I can take much more of this," I said. Helen elbowed me, pointing to a gaunt woman wrapped in a torn sari who held out a naked male child in her arms. The woman begged with unrecognizable words.

"What does that mean?" I said to Anwar.

"She just wants money," he said. "The kid is for sympathy."

The woman held up the child.

"It's dead!" Helen sobbed and clutched me as if she might slip into an abyss.

The corpse was skin and bone, head back, legs bent, and already in the rigor of death. "It's okay, Helen, get on the bus," I said over the clamor of our fellow travelers.

"They pass that body around for days," Anwar said authoritatively, as if that might ease our outrage.

Helen grabbed our touring bag that held our stuff and her wallet. She broke away from my protective grasp, ran toward the beggars. They froze, unsure. Then, seeing no danger, they moved around in a swarm.

Helen dug in the bag. From her wallet she took all her currency: Indian, American, and a few other foreign bills and coins. She was dropping money into any close hand. Beggars dissolved into frenzy. She placed a ten-dollar American bill on the chest of the dead child now on the ground. A hand from the crowd scooped it up before Helen stood up.

Helen ran out of money but she gave them tissues, candy bars, peanut butter and cheese crackers, anything that was in the bag. The crowd grew to more than fifty with mystical rapidity. Helen seemed not to care. When she finally turned her dazed eyes to me, I saw her confusion, her pain. I waded into the crowd to retrieve her. I worried for her health and safety.

"It's not enough," she said.

"It's a start," I said.

It took a few minutes for everyone on tour to calm down and find a seat on the bus, and we began the trip back. We found seats together four rows back from Betsy and Anwar. "They have nothing," Helen said, still gasping. Our fellow travelers said little and seemed divided in opinion about Helen, between admiration and suspicions of insanity.

The return was silent except for the drone of the bus's diesel engine, whining with braking and acceleration. Helen sat rigidly staring ahead. Before we reached our hotel, the guide announced the scheduled stop at one last gift shop. "Half an hour," he announced.

Helen was spent, her mood sour, unwilling to look at one more expensive souvenir. "I can't," she said. She was selfless with worry in a way I had never noticed before. She seemed about to cry. "I can't do it."

"I'll take a look," I said, wanting to buy a gift to surprise her. She stayed on the bus with a few of the other weary travelers.

Inside the shop I looked into glass jewelry cases and at rows of shelves of carved Hindu gods with strange clothing and in awkward positions. A sparkle of reflection from a dark necklace of polished jade, vibrant with the living colors of a new-growth leaf and the plume of an exotic bird, caught my eye. I flagged a saleswoman. The necklace wasn't expensive, and I paid cash. I refused to have it gift wrapped, liking the red velvet draw sack it came in, and put it in my pocket.

That night Helen dressed for a cultural show of music and drama with Betsy and mostly other women in the tour group. Anwar and I had decided on a leisurely dinner and early retirement.

"You run today?" I asked.

He nodded.

"Dangerous?"

"Who knows? Lots of evil-looking characters but most either too malnourished or close to death to be able to do you any harm."

"I bought a necklace yesterday for Helen." I reached in my pocket to show him. "I'm going to surprise her." I thought it might give him some ideas for Betsy.

"Jade?" he asked, as if weighing the differences between jade and diamond with disdain.

"Good value," I said and showed him the price.

"My mother's necklace had been in the family for three generations. My grandfather was a Syrian diplomat. He bought it in London. My mother could only wear it when she traveled with my father, but she was very proud."

"Betsy loved it. You could see it in her eyes," I said.

But Anwar's eyes turned opaque and then he looked away. I pocketed my necklace for Helen, dejected that Anwar had no interest and had turned sullen. He said little for the next few minutes and we returned to our rooms to read.

I was reading in bed with the nightstand light on when Helen returned in tears.

"Betsy's sick. I thought she'd die," she said. "We were in the theater. She had a terrible headache. When I touched her she was burning with fever. She vomited. She fainted as I was getting her to the bus."

"Where is she?"

"The hospital. I went with her. Anwar came. He went crazy. Accused the doctor of not using the right medicines. He told me to leave." Helen's eyes squeezed shut with the thought of Anwar's exclusion.

"What was wrong?"

"Infection, I think. They didn't know exactly."

I held her. "We've got to go. They'll need us." I dressed quickly.

The hospital elevator glided two floors up, the doors parting smoothly. The door to Betsy's room was open. "Be careful," Anwar said to an ambulance crew as they lifted Betsy's writhing body roughly onto a gurney. "Don't drop her," he said.

Anwar saw us. "Fucking blockheads," he said to us.

"What's happened?" I asked as he held an IV bottle in transfer.

"Meningitis maybe." He didn't look at me, collecting a syringe with a needle and empty vial and putting them in a bag that he tucked under the gurney mattress.

"Will she be okay?" Helen asked.

He glared at us, as if we didn't exist. "How could I know that, Helen?" Anwar said with disdain. "Look at her. Why don't you tell me?"

Helen gasped, unable to respond.

"What can we do?" I asked.

The attendants tucked sheets around Betsy. Anwar hung the bottle on the end of a metal support pole at the corner of the gurney. Betsy's open eyes showed no recognition that we were there and were now searching without pause.

"There's nothing to do, John," Anwar said. "This hospital isn't worth a shit. I've hired a private jet to get us to Tokyo. If I can keep her stabilized, I'm taking her home." Now his voice held fear and concern.

Anwar and Betsy were on their way out the door. At the elevator, Anwar turned as Helen and I caught up.

"Can we make any calls? Send anything?" I asked.

"Just enjoy your trip," he said.

"Please let us know how she is?" Helen pleaded.

"When do you think I'll have time to call you?" he said. "You have a good time."

"We'll be worried," Helen said.

"I can't help that," Anwar said. Helen winced. "She might never come back," he said. "Even if she lives, she'll never be the same."

Helen cried silently, hurt by Anwar's rebukes. Anwar had reached under the covers to hold Betsy's almost lifeless hand. Just before the elevator doors opened, he cried silently.

In the elevator, on the gurney, Betsy now lay still, her eyes closed, her head turned. The attendants positioned necessary equipment under the gurney. Betsy's skin was drained of blood to the shade of alabaster. She retched once, her arms and legs jerking then her body relaxed as she went unconscious again. The doors closed and they were gone.

Helen paced in our room.

"If she lives," Helen said to me about Betsy, "maybe Anwar will finally appreciate her wonderful qualities."

"He seemed to really care," I said. "I'd never seen that in him before."

"I hope so. But too late. I hope Betsy knows he cared."

"I think he loves her—in his own way."

"I hope he gets the chance to tell her."

Finally, I got her to sit on the sofa and she held me tightly.

My last image of Betsy surfaced; she'd never be the same. I didn't think she'd live. But I said nothing to Helen. Still, she read my thoughts.

"She's a goofy good person," Helen sobbed, "loyal, devoted, caring. God, I hope she makes it."

The next evening after dinner, a faxed message waited in our inbox at reception. Betsy died in a Tokyo hospital. I searched Anwar's handwritten note for meaning, but the words—starting with "Dear friends,"—were cold and distant.

Helen read the message sitting on a lobby bench as I stood beside her. She carried deep concern for Betsy's soul. A moment of fear pierced me; I never wanted Helen to ever doubt that I loved her. I reached in my pocket and placed my gift necklace around her neck. Fixed the clasp. With the back of my hand, I touched the damp skin on the side of her face, smoothed a wayward strand of hair. I'd never seen her more beautiful.

"Am I possessed?" she asked with a dubious smile.

"Never possessed," I said. "Valued forever."

"I'll sell the house," she said with a wistful smile.

"We'll live wherever you choose," I said. I bent over and kissed her lightly on the ear. "I love you," I whispered.

Suchin's Escape

Illustration by Peter Healy

Suchin's Escape

Antoine lit a cigarette with the lighter from the dash of the twenty-seven-year-old 1976 Lincoln Continental and leaned forward with both forearms on the steering wheel. Harry beat out a rhythm on the dash with both hands—BOOM chee CHEE di di BOOM—and sang a song of lost love. Antoine liked the tune, liked the way his cousin could make it flow.

Antoine watched the green two-story frame house across from where they were parked on a side street in Gretna. The image of the thin child Suchin, the eleven-year-old Chinese girl, materialized in the dark, narrow alley between the houses, the blurred outline of a man blocking the alley behind her. She was naked except for a pair of patent-leather Mary Janes. She stopped before stepping into the glint of the morning sun and slid a lace-trimmed white dress over her head, pushing her arms out the sleeve holes. She smoothed the fabric in front with both hands and the hem fell to her ankles.

"She's done," Antoine said. Harry stopped his rhythm and got out of the car. He met the girl still in the shadows, grabbed her arm, and brought her quickly to the car, her moving feet barely touching the ground. Harry opened the back door and shoved her into the backseat.

"Don't push me," Suchin said, kicking out, her shoe heel glancing off Harry's arm.

The girl made money and this guy in the shadows was one of her many repeats. But Antoine didn't trust her. Something about the way her eyes held his, hard and cold in their darkness, and the way she never flinched if he had to cuff her.

"Tape her," he said. "I got a bad feeling."

"We ain't going that far," Harry said.

See! Even Harry was ornery now, started about the time this girl arrived in a shipment of twelve. Strange, too, because the kid was all girl—not anything womanly—like a twig in a forest of leafy branches.

"That Paradise Motel near the airport," Antoine said.

"Tape hurt," said Suchin.

That proved it. Pure trouble—the way she'd just butt in like she belonged.

"Ride with her, then," he said to Harry.

Harry shoved Suchin over to one side of the backseat to make room. He slammed the back door as Antoine cranked the motor.

"But don't put them locks down," Harry said.

Harry was a goddamn two-year-old trapped in the body of King Kong sometimes. Antoine undid the childproof locks on the back doors.

"Don't like the door locked," Harry said, feeling foolish even as the fear of being closed in grabbed him.

The Lincoln Continental rolled down the expressway. Antoine kept in the right lane, five miles an hour below the speed limit. Harry's big head blocked half his view out the rearview mirror. He checked the side mirrors for cops. He was clean but Harry had a prior for assault with a parole violation.

The kid wasn't in the mirror. He glanced back over his right shoulder. Nothing. She was either lying down or she'd slipped over next to the door. He reached for a rumpled cigarette pack wedged between the windshield and the dash, squeezed out the end of the last cigarette, extracted it with tight lips, and lit up.

The silence from the back seat mounted.

Then tap … tap … tap … tap. The kid was beating her shoe against the doorframe, grooving on the beat like a pro, the pulse asking for more. Sure enough, Harry's big hands clapped soft but firm with emphasis on the late off beats. Tap tap CLAP tap CLAP tap CLAP CLAP.

Without thinking Antoine beat his thumb against the steering wheel. He tucked the Lincoln in behind a bakery truck.

Harry started singing, his voice filling up the car, and the kid making ooou-ooous like a real backup.

"It's down" tap tap

"In Pascagoula" tap tap

"Where the women" tap tap

"Do the hoola" tap tap

"And the men" tap tap

"They the ones" tap tap.

"They the ones, whoooo—-oooooooooooo"

"Wicky … wicky … whacky—whacky—woo."

For a few bars Harry and Suchin clapped and tapped almost perfectly in their shared drive. Then they shifted in unison to a slower groove, four to the bar. Harry's voice fell off a minor third.

"Ohhhh, ohhhh," he wailed.

"Ouuuuu, ouuuuu" the kid chimed in.

"It's my woman, …ohhh, yeah,"

"That cheating woman," …

"ouuu, ouuu,"

"It's my woman, ohhh, yeah,"

"That done me wrong." Harry finished.

"Soooo wrong," the kid added. "Ouuuuu …"

Harry chuckled.

Then, smooth as a river running, the two of them were back working on and off the beat, setting up for another verse.

Goddamn her. She could work Harry like a dog jumping through hoops.

"Tolls," he said.

Harry shoved Suchin down in the footwell to hide her as Antoine held bills out to the collector. "Be quiet," he said. The engine strained when the Lincoln started up the bridge incline over the Mississippi. Two minutes later the car slowed in traffic. Suchin stiffened, her teeth clenched.

She yanked the door handle, shoved the door open, and rolled out headfirst, flipping on her back. In seconds she was up running toward the guardrail, the river, so much bigger than the stream that ran near her village in China. Horns blared. Fast cars moved in the opposite direction. Harry yelled behind her. How close was he? A sports car hit her, throwing her up on the hood, screeching to a stop. The girders above her weaved like dragons' tails.

Harry grabbed her before she slid off to the pavement, held her so close his hot breath smothered her face.

Her leg began to throb, she could barely see out one eye, but her heart squeezed fast and strong. "Shouldn't a done that," Harry whispered to her. "Antoine going to kill you."

The sports car guy came running up, screaming about his innocence. With one arm still holding Suchin, Harry picked him up and threw him against the side of the car so hard his head flew back on the roll bar with a crunch. Harry grunted satisfaction as the guy slumped half-conscious.

Suchin moaned when Harry put her in the car.

"Stay with her," Antoine said. He blew the horn, waved at people. He had to get moving before any cops came. He'd have to switch the plates again, find something in the Marriott parking garage from Ohio or Indiana this time. In a couple of minutes they were at the exit ramp. He was out of cigarettes.

The kid trembled, her head in Harry's hands, her shoulders on his thigh, her legs out on the seat.

"She breathing?" Antoine asked into the backseat.

"Blood coming out her mouth." A trickle of dark red mixed with spit-foam dripped on Harry's thigh. "Her leg getting big," he said.

Antoine caught a red light. He looked back. The girl's chest moved with quick in and outs. Her dress was torn. Her upper leg a sick purple. No one would pay for sex with a bleeding, moaning kid. He hated to stiff the guy on Airline Highway but he headed for Claiborne to get on the I-10.

"She bad," Harry said, "She real bad."

Suchin heard Harry's words as if the volume had been turned to maximum on a set of headphones. She did not think about dying and she wondered if she could run with her leg hurting.

She coughed.

"What was that?" Antoine said.

Harry saw a bloody tooth on the seat. "She bad," he repeated.

Well, shit. Antoine was going as fast as he could without putting them behind bars.

"Her eye look crooked," Harry said like he blamed Antoine.

It was Harry's fault she got out. No locks! Harry had jumped at the click of a deadbolt sliding home since he was in Angola for two years five months. Like he caught a phobia and now we can't lock the back doors.

Antoine wasn't being unreasonable. Okay. He didn't like kids. But he wasn't a monster. And he never let a guy down. Or a kid, for that matter. He was taking her to the doc, for Christ sake. How many guys would do that? "How many?" he said out loud.

"What you say?" Harry said.

But he didn't explain. Harry was slow to understand sometimes. And too soft to keep rules.

Antoine pulled into a mall and parked. Harry followed him, carrying the kid through the door between a liquor store and a Goodwill clothing outlet, marked in faded yellow letters:

OFFICE HOURS 10–2
   M, W, Th

The doc sat alone at a desk in a single room. Harry laid Suchin on a bare examining table with metal stirrups on one end.

"That's repulsive," the doc said, swiveling back and forth in his chair, his short-sleeved tan shirt with yellow brushlike swirl patterns unbuttoned halfway down the slope of his hairy chest. He was a hundred pounds overweight.

"Hit by a car."

"Take her to Charity."

"She's illegal."

"I don't do trauma."

Suchin's leg spasmed for a few seconds.

"The big man pays you damn good," Antoine said. "Too much."

"Not for this." The doc belched; Antoine was close enough to whiff the scent of decayed oranges and cheap booze—like the man's insides needed to be flushed down a toilet.

The doc stood up. He took a wooden tongue blade from his shirt pocket. He lifted the kid's dress fabric with the blade, careful not to touch anything bloody. Still with the tongue blade, he pushed up a swollen eyelid and stared at a pupil.

"She'll live."

"Aren't you going to X-ray or something?"

"Do you see an X-ray machine?"

"She could die."

"She isn't going to die!" he said.

The doc picked up a wallet off his desk and left through a back door that went straight to a service alley. "Office is closed," he said as he slammed the door shut.

Antoine pointed for Harry to get the kid.

"Where we going?"

"Auntie's," Antoine said. "She'll do something."

Suchin felt the big arms cradling her again, her mind clear. Her stomach churned. Her tongue probed the sore little craters where her teeth were gone. Her leg ached but she thought she could walk if she had to. With her non-blurred eye she searched from habit for locks on the doors. Then, when the sunlight glared on her, she squeezed her good eye closed and went limp to let Harry think her mind had shut down her body for a while.

The Lincoln got to Auntie's in Plaquemine Parish just before five, a rooster tail of almost-white dust pluming up behind that monster car. Auntie went downstairs out of the farmhouse, stood there waiting as they drove up, her arms crossed. She was heavy, big boned, and barren, her blood Indian, Creole, and black, and every corpuscle heavy with this love-hate feeling for kids. It was a mystery why she took care of them at all after being in the trade for thirty years.

"You whack this one?" Auntie said to Antoine as Harry worked at getting Suchin out of the car so she didn't hurt.

"Watch your mouth," Antoine said.

Auntie's hands probed Suchin's thigh while she was still in Harry's arms. Suchin cried out. She pushed on Suchin's belly. Suchin moaned. She looked under Suchin's swollen eyelid. Suchin's eye was seeing well now and she locked on Auntie's gaze. Auntie frowned and turned away.

"Put her to the right of the door in the bedroom," Auntie said to Harry, and pulled Antoine's shirt to move him a few feet so no one could hear.

"Cash up front," she said.

"She's big money. Next to top in the convention trade. She good for it. We ain't got cash."

"Out of where?" Auntie asked.

"Mere Bull. In Kenner."

"Tell Mere Bull she to bring that cash down here personal."

"You got my word," Antoine said sincerely.

"Ain't that a lot of slippery shit?"

Suchin lay on her back on a cot with no mattress. The only window had a yellow shade pulled down and the dim light from the filtered sun wasn't strong enough to define the floral details on the scruffy wallpaper. Two bunk beds were stacked as a unit against the opposite wall. On the lower bunk a lump of a girl bulged under a sheet, the ends of her straight long hair—shiny as a black lacquered piano—hanging over the edge. The upper bunk didn't have a mattress.

Harry was gone, but his words stayed with Suchin. "Give it up," he said, his breath tickling her ear. "The beat don't work good." He didn't touch her.

Suchin dozed to the sounds of flies chasing each other around the room. She woke just before all the light faded. The girl under the sheet hadn't moved. Suchin could hear Auntie bumping around somewhere down below, on the first floor.

Suchin ached all over, but less now. Her leg throbbed but when she stood and pressed down, the pain eased.

"Who you?" she called to the lump on the bed.

She waited a minute. "You living?"

She hobbled over slowly and peeled back the sheet. She sucked in a rush of air.

"You beautiful," she said, suddenly aware of trying to use her very best English. The girl had the delicately sculpted features of a porcelain doll and her eyes were wide open, the whites showing all around irises so brown they seemed almost as black as the pupil. She stared straight through Suchin, deep into some other galaxy.

"My name's Suchin. From China. Six months. Came on a ship."

The girl didn't change.

"You sleep like that?" Suchin asked. "Your eyes open?"

She thought the girl's eyes focused a little, her lips parted slightly.

"You like it here?"

The girl closed her eyes slowly, breathing faster, and turned away. She wasn't a druggie, Suchin thought. Her eyes were too hard for that.

Auntie's mountainous form filled the open door behind Suchin. Auntie came into the room, light from the hall making a faint halo behind her.

"She talk to you?" Auntie asked.

Suchin didn't move, keeping her back to Auntie.

"Well, don't you be bothering her," Auntie said. "She's having some time to herself until she talks again."

Suchin stayed stone still, not knowing how to feel about Auntie. But she wasn't afraid.

Auntie gave Suchin a bowl of red beans and rice with a plastic spoon stuck in it and pulled up a chair next to the girl to begin feeding her soup from a Campbell's can. "Mushroom only thing she'll eat. Don't like tomato," she said, mostly to herself.

When she finished Auntie turned to take Suchin's empty bowl. "You moving better than I thought. You scamming Auntie?"

Suchin stayed quiet.

"Well, you pick up that chamber potty and empty it in the bathroom down the hall before I lock up again. Wash it out good too."

For hours after Auntie closed the door and turned the key in the lock, Suchin lay on her cot, but no sleep came. She wondered where that girl's eyes were looking, what they saw. She wondered if she was thinking about the men. How men treated girls. She wondered if the girl thought too that if you did right, maybe someday a man take you away and be good to you. All the girls had heard of that happening—a nice man. But they never knew anyone it happened to, only knew by the storytelling that skipped from girl to girl like a flu bug.

It was still half dark when Suchin woke. The lump girl was sitting on the floor cross-legged, her hands on her stomach, and she was rocking slow—front, back, front.

Suchin eased off the bed and stretched, watching the girl. Suchin's leg and chest hurt less.

Two glasses of water and a saucer with two oven-cooked rolls sat on the floor inside the locked door. Suchin drank and ate a roll. "You want this?" she said, tempted to eat the second roll. But the girl said nothing and Suchin left the water and the roll close enough for her to reach.

Suchin's leg didn't bend easily, and she lay down on her side on the floor, her legs straight out to one side, her head propped up on her hand with her arm bent at the elbow.

The black-haired girl rocked. Forward. Back. Forward.

"My mother's dead. Father dead, too," Suchin said, staring under the bed as if to find some hidden non-person in the dark recess.

Back, forward, back, the girl went on, her eyes never blinking.

"Yours too? Your parents?"

Forward, back, forward, about as fast as a pendulum on a giant clock.

"It's okay. I know you're like the rest of us. Sometime you need to get away."

The girl still rocking.

The door unlocked and Auntie came in. "In the name of God, leave that child alone. You too healthy and she too sick for you to keep bothering her." She yanked Suchin up to sitting, then grabbed the girl's shoulder to stop her rocking and held a glass of water to the girl's mouth. The girl swallowed a few times.

"Now for you," she said, grabbing Suchin. "I'll take you to the bathroom to wash that dried blood off. Then I'll sew up that dress and give it a good wash."

That night after Auntie put them both in bed, Auntie came back in with a flashlight because the light socket for the screw-in bulb in the ceiling was empty. She sat in a chair next to the girl's bed, her back to Suchin. She opened a book with a torn red cover. Suchin was lying on her cot, looking at the ceiling.

"'It was Toto,'" Auntie read in a low, singsongy voice.

"Who was Toto?" Suchin asked.

"Shut your face," Auntie said shining the light straight into Suchin's eyes. "This is Helen's story."

Suchin turned away but not far enough so she couldn't hear.

"You don't need storytelling," Auntie said to Suchin before turning her flashlight back to the book again to read.

"'It was Toto that made Dorothy laugh, and saved her from growing as gray as her other surroundings.'" Auntie paused. "'Toto was not gray; he was a little black dog, with long silky hair and small black eyes that twinkled merrily on either side of his funny, wee nose. Toto played all day long, and Dorothy played with him, and loved him dearly.'"

"Who's Dorothy?" Suchin couldn't keep from asking.

"She's an orphan. Now hold your tongue." But the meanness was not in her voice.

Auntie continued loud enough that Suchin could hear. "Today, however, they were not playing. Uncle Henry sat upon the doorstep..."

Suchin wondered what Uncle Henry would do to Dorothy, then listened all about Kansas and Oz, a world that, as Auntie continued reading, Suchin imagined might be the real America.

The lightning bolt lit up the room bright as day just after two AM. Suchin sat straight up and in the after-flash, the room seemed pitch black; even the thin strip of pale yellow under the door from the hall overhead bulb was wiped out. Suchin stood up, limped to the window, and raised the shade. The sky swirled with gray clouds. Sheets of rain streaked across the yard and lightning pulsed the pewter sky.

The girl was sitting too, her eyes fixed on Suchin.

"It's okay," Suchin said, recovering quickly. She had survived too many nights in the open hut of her grandmother—or more recently the lean-to she shared with her uncle for a while—with storms raging around her to worry. She sat next to the girl.

"We got to get away," Suchin said. "You understand?"

The girl stared at her with eyes black in the darkness. She turned her head and her black hair flowed around her face.

"Now!"

"No," the girl said. Her voice was deep and raspy.

"We can do it."

"No!" She shoved Suchin away, took a deep breath, and screamed.

"What are you doing?"

"You go!" the girl said.

"You too."

"I can't," she said. "I don't think right sometimes."

The girl's eyes had shifted from terror to fierce determination. She screamed again, getting off the bed. She took the chair that Auntie had been reading in and smashed the window twice so all the glass was gone.

The key in the lock turned and Auntie rumbled in. The girl, after a quick glance of clear-bolt sanity thrown at Suchin, headed for the window, throwing herself half out, but not far enough to fall.

Auntie lunged across and grabbed the girl by the legs. "You crazy!" she said. "It's a long way down."

The door was open. Suchin slipped out, felt her way down the stairs, out the front door, across the porch. She could see orange groves outlined against the sky. Rain swept across her face until she reached the protection of the first line of trees. She stumbled on, running as fast as her sore leg would allow. It would be many minutes before Auntie could follow. She heard Helen still screaming, demanding Auntie's attention. Even hurting, Suchin knew she could keep her distance from someone as big and slow as Auntie. In minutes she reached the river and headed downstream, looking for something that would float. Soon the rain stopped, the wind died, and an almost full moon threw glints on the surface of the water.

Antoine and Harry arrived the next morning to take Suchin back. Auntie didn't offer them anything to drink.

"Last I saw of her she was headed for the grove, toward the river. It was a hell of a storm."

"We got to take her away," said Harry.

"Jesus," said Antoine. "Did you go after her?"

"I don't go looking for runaways."

"Mere Bull transferred her to Houston," Antoine said. "They got tight discipline down there. And she's a moneymaker."

"That girl full of Tabasco."

"There's only one road out. That's where she'll be."

"She don't know the road or the river."

"You think she's hiding?"

"Maybe. But she's smart as they come. Might be long gone by now."

Antoine signaled Harry to move to the car. "Road's the only way out."

"Where's my money?" Auntie asked.

"I ain't paying for letting the kid get away," Antoine said.

Antoine was out the door, following Harry to the car.

Auntie grabbed her shotgun from behind the kitchen door, stepped back outside.

"Cocksucker," Auntie yelled. She was waving the shotgun, holding it with one hand in the middle. "You ever show up here again, I'll blow your head off."

There was a white girl standing in the doorway behind Auntie. Even from a distance she was ghostly beautiful, with her white skin and long black hair glistening like black silk. One of the nut cases Auntie was famous for bringing back into the world for service. Antoine slammed the door and drove off.

"That Auntie's one weird bitch," he said to Harry. "Probably let the kid go."

Antoine and Harry used up a tank of gas cruising the only long road that led out of the parish, but they didn't see the girl.

"You think she all right?" Harry asked.

"She's got to be alive or we're gator meat," Antoine said. "She's worth a lot of money."

Antoine had to poke Harry to keep him awake, keep him looking. You big dumb gorilla, he thought. But Harry was good kin. Shit. They'd drawn women's tits on the bathroom walls at school together. They'd buddied up with whores. Harry had saved his life too, once on a B&E when the owner tried to kill him with a shotgun, and once in a knife fight in the Ninth Ward.

At night they slept in the car in a truck stop parking lot, then headed south in the early morning. They changed their approach, asking in the towns for anyone who'd seen a pretty, barefoot Chinese girl about four feet high wearing a ripped-up white dress.

It was just after eleven o'clock they cornered Suchin in the storeroom of a convenience store just north of Venice. The woman owner had let a Chinese girl sleep there for a few hours after her daughter found her down near the river and brought her home.

Suchin awoke, startled by an outside noise. The windowless room was black until the door opened and light from the store's fluorescent overhead bulbs outlined Antoine's silhouette coming toward her. Framed in the door behind him was the bulk of Harry. Antoine gripped her arm, with the force she knew and dreaded, and pulled her upright. In seconds, he'd dragged her into the store toward the high counter where the woman owner stood watching. Suchin looked around. Through the glass door on the front she could see two gas pumps with a red pickup truck parked in front. The tailgate was down and long lengths of lumber stuck out a few feet, a red flag hanging limply on the end of the longest board. A door to the restroom opened. She watched a man come out, go through the door toward the pickup. Harry went into the restroom.

Antoine let her go and turned to buy a lighter and cigarettes. She slipped down the aisle between the motor oil and the potato chips, out the door. She grabbed the lumber on the back of the truck and pulled herself up as the truck accelerated and lurched without a stop onto the road. She was in the truck and lying face down, the truck bed vibrating under her as it went through gears to reach cruising speed. She stayed low. Within two minutes, looking back, she saw the Lincoln, the headlights flashing. It gained on the truck, the horn blaring. The pickup slowed. Antoine pulled up to the side of the truck. He was yelling for the pickup to pull over. The pickup stopped. Antoine parked the Lincoln in front of the truck, off the road. Suchin slipped down from the truck bed and limped up a drive toward a house, but Antoine and Harry reached her before she could hide.

Harry was breathing hard.

"What a way to make a living," Antoine said as he and Harry took Suchin back toward the Lincoln.

The pickup truck driver was explaining that he didn't know she was there.

"I'm cool," Antoine said.

"Why are you chasing her?"

"Wise up, man. Forget you ever saw her."

While Harry held Suchin, Antoine emptied the trunk of the Lincoln—a bag of golf clubs, a Styrofoam cooler, fishing rods, a small outboard motor, and a five-gallon can of gasoline. He put them in the back seat. Then with two-inch tape he bound Suchin's arms to her chest with around-the-body passes from shoulders to waist. It was hard for Suchin to take a deep breath.

"I could keep her up front," Harry said.

Antoine lifted Suchin's dress and made seven passes of tape around her thighs. "I ain't taking any chances. We got a long way to go." He made seven more passes of tape around her ankles. She was still standing when he picked her up and put her in the trunk. "Damn if she can get out of that."

Harry held the trunk lid open when Antoine tried to close it.

Antoine wanted to belt Harry, but he held back. They needed to be moving. "Be sure it's locked," Antoine said and went to the front.

Harry turned Suchin on her back, took a loose tire iron out from under her and put it next to the back of the seat where it wouldn't hurt and shut the lid. In minutes they were on their way to Houston, back through New Orleans because that was the only way out of the delta.

Antoine smoked continuously as he drove. Harry slept with his head against the door until they reached Port Sulfur. Suchin had cried out a few times, but there were no sounds from the trunk now.

"Maybe she don't need to go to Houston," Harry said.

"And maybe Mere Bull and the big man will just be happy that all that money to get the kid bought in China on top of the cash to ship her and slip her in will never be returned."

"Houston not a good place."

"Maybe they send her back when she gets broken in," Antoine said.

"She got the beat."

"They're kids, for Christ's sake. You got to learn not to care, Harry. They ain't like regular people."

They stayed quiet, passing through Algiers, then New Orleans, then up on the I-10. Soon they were near the airport.

Suchin was yelling.

"See if you can tell what she wants," Antoine said.

Harry leaned over the seat and pushed the motor and gas can aside. "She needs to pee."

"Shit. Tell her we ain't stopping till we get to Houston."

Harry told her loud so she could hear through the backseat.

"I got to go bad!" she yelled. Antoine heard that.

Harry came back in the front seat. "We got to let her pee."

"Okay. Okay!" Antoine pulled onto the breakdown lane where it was dark. He popped the trunk lid. "Go get her."

Antoine opened the front and rear doors on the right side. "Bring her in between the doors. No one will see."

Harry set her down on her feet between the doors and had to hold her upright; she was too tightly taped to bend.

"I can't sit," she said.

"Do it standing up then."

"I can't."

"We got to cut the tape," Harry said.

"We ain't cutting the tape. I've only got a couple feet left."

"Let it go," Antoine said to Suchin and hit her lightly on the head. Harry still held her, afraid she'd fall over.

"I can't." But in a few seconds her dress went dark, and then a puddle formed in the dust.

"I'm wet."

"That's so terrible," Antoine whined.

"We should have cut the tape," Harry said.

"Put her in the back. I ain't touching her."

"We got something to wipe her off?"

"Some paper towels under the seat."

They were back on the road. Harry rested against the door but didn't sleep. Antoine turned on the radio.

"What if she calls out or something?" Harry said.

"Won't make any difference."

"We won't hear!"

"Okay, I'll turn it down!" Antoine turned the music down a little.

Harry reached forward and turned it off.

"Hey, asshole, I'm not going all the way to Houston without music," Antoine said.

Traffic was light. Antoine drafted behind an eighteen-wheeler in the slow lane to avoid attention.

Suchin called out about half an hour later. "I can't breathe!"

"Did you hear that?"

"She must be breathing. She's yelling, for Christ's sake."

"We got to check."

"We don't have to check. I'm not stopping until we need gas."

"There might be no air back there."

"There's enough."

Harry stared straight ahead for a few minutes. "She ain't said nothing," he said.

"We got an hour, Harry. An hour before we need gas!"

Harry growled as he turned to shove Antoine on the shoulder, shoving him up against the driver's-side door. "We got to check."

Antoine looked at Harry in surprise. "Jesus, Harry. Don't ever do that again. I'd have to whack you." He kept driving.

Harry was breathing fast, his eyes wide with anger. He drew back and threw a right fist at the side of Antoine's head. Antoine blacked out for a few seconds, his hands slipping off the wheel, the cruise control holding steady. The Lincoln left the road. Antoine came alert in seconds, realized the danger, turned the wheel, jammed on the brakes; the car swerved to the left and the right, then hit a low bridge abutment head-on. Harry moaned.

The engine hissed but had stopped running, pushed back against the firewall by the impact. The dashboard was crumpled, the steering wheel inches from Antoine's chest, the front window cracked and mostly gone. Night air floated into the car, damp and oppressive, mixing with the stinging smell of gasoline from the tipped gas can in the back seat.

"Can you move?" Antoine asked Harry. Harry worked to open the door.

"Get out!" Antoine said. Antoine's door was crushed and he slid out Harry's side.

He could not let the kid be found, or any evidence remain in the car. "Run," he said. He reached in his pocket, lit a lighter, and threw it in the back seat. There was a burst of flame. He pushed Harry. "Run. It'll blow."

"The key," Harry said. "The kid."

"Leave her!" Antoine said. But the keys were to many locks and could be evidence, and they were in his hand. He slipped them in his pocket. "It's going to blow."

Antoine started running.

Harry went to the trunk, pulling up on the lid. Nothing budged. He kicked, once, twice, three times. Fire flared in the open doors. Finally the trunk lid rose. Harry grabbed Suchin, her skin pale, her eyes shut.

Antoine was thirty yards away. The explosion, loud enough to hurt the ears, shot flames above the trees into the night sky. Metal and glass propelled with bullet speed. Harry didn't stop running, Suchin cradled in his arms. The clothes on his back burst into flame. His right carotid artery had been severed by a piece of glass that still glinted on the side of his neck, but he stumbled on, finally falling forward. Suchin hit the ground face first. Harry fell just behind her.

Antoine reached Harry in seconds and stomped out the few burning cloth fragments that remained. Then he rolled his cousin over. He was breathing.

Harry coughed on his own blood. His eyes opened. "She okay?" he asked.

Antoine swore. The flames threw flickering shadows on his face and pinpoint, wiggling reflections glowed on his eyes.

Antoine turned Suchin over. She'd been dead a while, he could tell from the bloodless facial wounds.

"Antoine," Harry gasped, "She okay?"

"She'll make it."

"You take care of her."

"Sure, man."

Despite the burning glow on his skin from the fire, Antoine shivered. He crossed himself.

Harry stopped breathing. The fire died in his eyes, the spirit shimmered out of him.

God bless you, you big dumb gorilla. The danger is in the caring—not the cops, or the FBI, or the syndicate. You cared too much. Like you ever listened.

Antoine knelt down and closed Harry's eyelids. He picked up the kid and tossed her into the flames of the Lincoln's burning trunk. Then, as cars stopped and people were closing in from many directions, he blended into the dark to zigzag a course that would take him away from the city for a while.

Clouds

Illustration by Peter Healy

Clouds

"Put your glasses on," Margaret said to her son. He touched his neck, wet with sweat, and wiped his hand on his T-shirt. The back window was down a few inches for ventilation and gave a steady, breathy growl at highway speeds.

"The glasses, Ben."

He picked up the thick lenses from the seat and, with a couple of missed tries, pulled the temple straps down over his head.

"We'll play a game, Ben," she said. "You want to play a game?"

"Play game," he said. She passed an eighteen-wheeler, leaving plenty of room, and tucked back into the slow lane. It was midmorning, and wavy lines of invisible heat from the road were already distorting the view. Ben rocked back and forth; she let him go on for a while.

"Can you see the clouds?" she asked. There was a line of cars slowed in the fast lane, and bumper to bumper. She kept a good distance to let them sort it out. Ben stopped rocking and was shaking his head from side to side.

"Look up," she said. "In the sky. Clouds are in the sky, Ben. Next to where God lives."

"God live," he said. He strained against the seat belt to lean forward and look up through the windshield.

"Can you see them?"

"See them," he said.

"Well, we'll find one and we'll name it. Tell what it is. There are all sorts of things up in the sky."

"I do good," he said.

"Of course you will."

"I do good," he said again.

"Find one up there. Keep looking. Tell me what it is."

He put his hand on the glass.

"You can't touch them, Ben. They're far away."

He took his hand down. "Far," he said.

"What does it look like, Ben? Does it remind you of something?"

Ben stared. Finally he said: "Weekie."

She didn't respond for a long moment. He was looking at her, grinning.

"She's gone, Ben."

"Gone," he said. He continued to look. "Story?" he said to the cloud.

"She's gone, Ben. She's in heaven with the angels. She won't be here to tell you stories anymore."

"I love you," he said to the cloud. Sorrow altered his usual smile and his eyes were moist.

"It's okay," she said, talking to herself as she often did these days. What if he did believe Weekie was a cloud? There was no harm.

He slept a while. So as not to wake him, she passed the rest stop where they would have exercised. A truck horn blast woke him. She said, "Look, Ben. More clouds."

In less than an hour she drove into the closest city to their small town. She found her ex-husband sitting in the park near the museum, where he usually was in the mornings on the rare days she had to find him. She parked at the curb on a yellow line and honked a few times. He folded his blanket into a long rectangle and wrapped it around his neck. He stuffed gloves and two long scarves into a laundry bag, then put on a woolen ski cap that he pulled down over his ears. She couldn't tell if he was sober. She hadn't seen any bottles near him as he packed up. He came to the car, opened the back door, and climbed in.

"It's Daddy, Ben."

"Daddy," Ben said.

She made no effort to greet her husband. Her intense aversion had turned to dispassionate distaste a couple of years ago. Even from the front seat she could smell the sweet, acrid breath of bad booze and indigestion.

"Hey, my little man," he said.

"Lil' man," Ben said without looking around, and he started rocking backward and forward.

She pulled to the side of a street and took a city map from a folder in the side door pocket. She studied the map on the steering wheel.

"He's no better," her ex-husband said. "He seems worse."

"Weekie died," she said, following a street on the map with her finger. "There's no one." She looked up in time to see her ex-husband shrug in the rearview mirror. She pulled back into traffic.

"You got the money?" he asked.

She didn't answer.

"All three hundred?"

"Three," Ben said.

"I ain't doing this if you ain't got it all," her ex-husband said.

Ben looked up, but they were in the city now and it wasn't easy to find clouds.

"You got it all?"

She paused at a stop sign, looking up the street for the office building.

The lawyer was not in today. But the receptionist was a notary.

"Won't a lawyer need to sign?" Margaret asked. The receptionist looked at the papers. "He's already signed," she said. She looked up. "I'll need identification."

She knew her ex-husband wanted the money first, but the presence of the receptionist kept him quiet. She handed over his expired driver's license—she kept for him so he wouldn't lose it—and the receptionist studied the picture intently for a few seconds and then looked at him. "Sign here," she said. Her ex-husband wrote his name. Then she let go of Ben's hand and signed below her ex-husband's scrawl.

Outside, he grabbed her arm.

"Don't touch me," she said. She backed away and reached into her purse. She gave him the money and waited as he counted.

"I'll drop you at the bus station," she said.

He seemed more subdued now that he had the money. She thought he was probably on his way to the Carolina coast for a while before he headed South for the winter. But she could never be sure.

She let him out at the bus station. He said nothing as he left. She turned off the motor. She took Ben's suitcase from the trunk and opened it on the backseat. She got a clean shirt and changed it for the already-damp one he had on. She left the suitcase on the backseat. As she slid in the front, she checked her folder again. She had the signed papers with her now, thank God, and the health records from the doctors and the hospital. She strapped Ben back into his seat. She drove, following the route signs out of the city, where she rarely came for business or pleasure. In twenty-five minutes she was back on the freeway.

"Look again for clouds, Ben. See what you can see."

Ben stared and after a while he said, "See."

"That's good, Ben."

"I did good."

"Yes."

She paused before she said, "Always look for clouds, Ben, and think about me coming to visit."

"Whizit," he said.

"'Visit' means come to see you. Come to be with you." But she knew she could rarely get off work to make this long drive.

She drove well under the speed limit for another two hours. The signs marking the distance to Gowanda were now spaced every few miles. Ben had been looking out the side window; for the last few miles his attention had still been on the sky.

"Cloud," Ben said excitedly.

She glanced up. "It looks like a cow."

"Mommie!" he said.

She laughed. "Mommie doesn't look like a cow," she said. But she was deeply touched.

She patted the side of his head with the palm of her hand while keeping her eyes on the road. She put her hand back on the wheel.

She wished she could feel better about his new accomplishment. But he'd forget her soon enough, and she'd be lost in the sky with Weekie. Her heart ached so that she frowned and took her eyes off the road for an instant to look at him. When she looked back to the road, she could just make out the sign for Gowanda—thirty-four miles.

She tried not to think of the relief she hoped would come when he had caregivers. But an unformed dream of future normalcy had invaded her heart and mind, and it brought on the ever-present pain of guilt.

She pulled into a rest stop and took him into a stall in the ladies' restroom. After he finished, she bought him goldfish crackers from a vending machine and opened the bag for him when they were back in the car.

He finished the goldfish, and she gave him a Mars bar with the wrapper off. He ate it slowly but took big bites. She wiped stray chocolate off his hands and mouth with a tissue from a box she kept under the seat behind her feet.

"What is it, Ben?"

He pointed to the sky. He turned. "Mommie." He grinned.

She followed the signs. The road was two lanes now. She wanted to stop the car and take him in her arms, envelop him with a hug he'd never forget. But it would only confuse him, scare him. She saw the three-story institute, its main building with a clock tower and a wing on each side, like open arms, the grounds not well tended. She pulled up a long drive that curved to the front entrance. She could see paint peeling on the windowsills, and the brick walls pocked with holes from lost mortar and crumbled bricks. A door to the side of the main double door had two pieces of white typing paper tacked side by side at eye level and "Reception" written in black marker.

"I did good?" Ben asked as she unbuckled his seat belt.

"Yes, Ben. You did real good."

Short Stories by William H. Coles

The Activist, The Amish Girl, The Bear, Big Gene, Captain Withers's Wife, The Cart Boy, Clouds, Crossing Over, Curse of a Lonely Heart, Dilemma, Dr. Greiner's Day in Court, Facing Grace with Gloria, Father Ryan, Gatemouth Willie Brown on Guitar, The Gift, The Golden Flute, Grief, Homunculus, The Indelible Myth, Inside the Matryoshka, Lost Papers, The Miracle of Madame Villard, The Necklace, Nemesis, On the Road to Yazoo City, The Perennial Student, Reddog, Sister Carrie, Speaking of the Dead, The Stonecutter, Suchin's Escape, The Thirteen Nudes of Ernest Goings, The War of the Flies, The Wreck of the Amtrak's Silver Service

Other Books by William H. Coles

Guardian of Deceit
The Surgeon's Wife
The Spirit of Want
Sister Carrie
McDowell
Facing Grace with Gloria and Other Stories
The Necklace and Other Stories
Story in Literary Fiction: A Manual for Writers
Literary Fiction as an Art Form: A Text for Writers
The Short Fiction of William H. Coles 2001-2011
The Illustrated Fiction of William H. Coles 2000-2012
Creating Literary Stories: A Fiction Writer's Guide
The Short Fiction of William H. Coles: 2000-2016
The Illustrated Short Fiction of William H. Coles: 2000-2016

www.ingramcontent.com/pod-product-compliance
Lightning Source LLC
Chambersburg PA
CBHW060416010526
44118CB00017B/2243